Educational Media and Technology Yearbook

EDUCATIONAL MEDIA AND TECHNOLOGY YEARBOOK

Robert Maribe Branch and Mary Ann Fitzgerald, Editors

2001 VOLUME 26

Published in Cooperation with the
ERIC® Clearinghouse on Information & Technology
and the
Association for Educational Communications
and Technology

2001
Libraries Unlimited, Inc. • Englewood, Colorado

LIBRARIES UNLIMITED, INC.
P.O. Box 6633
Englewood, CO 80155-6633
1-800-237-6124
www.lu.com

Suggested Cataloging:

Educational media and technology yearbook, 2001 volume 26 /
    Robert Maribe Branch and Mary Ann Fitzgerald, editors--
Englewood, Colo.: Libraries Unlimited, 2001.
    p. cm.
    Includes bibliographical references and index.
    ISBN 1-56308-876-2
    ISSN 8755-2094
    Published in cooperation with the ERIC® Clearinghouse on Information
& Technology and the Association for Educational Communications and
Technology.
    1. Educational technology--yearbooks.   2. Instructional materials
centers--yearbooks.   I. ERIC Clearinghouse on Information & Technology.
II. Association for Educational Communications and Technology.
III. Branch, Robert Maribe.   IV. Mary Ann Fitzgerald.
LB 1028.3.E372   2001   370.778

Contents

Part Three
ORGANIZATIONS AND ASSOCIATIONS
IN NORTH AMERICA

Part Four
GRADUATE PROGRAMS

Part Five
MEDIAGRAPHY
Print and Nonprint Resources

Preface

The purpose of the 26th volume of the *Educational Media and Technology Yearbook* is to focus on the meaningful integration of technology. This volume of the *Yearbook* provides information to help media and technology professionals practice their craft in a changing and expanding field. This volume continues to be based on the following assumptions:

- Technology represents tools that act as extensions of the educator.

- Media serve as delivery systems for educational communications.

- Technology is *not* restricted to machines and hardware, but includes techniques and procedures derived from scientific research about ways to promote change in human performance.

- The fundamental tenet is that educational media and technology should be used to

    achieve authentic learning objectives,

    situate learning tasks,

    negotiate the complexities of guided learning,

    facilitate the construction of knowledge,

    support skill acquisition, and

    manage diversity.

The *Educational Media and Technology Yearbook* has become a standard reference in many libraries and professional collections. The intent of this *2001 Yearbook* edition is that readers become more informed about the purposes, activities, programs of study, and accomplishments of the organizations and associations dedicated to the advancement of educational communications and technology. This volume of the *Yearbook* contains sections devoted to Trends and Issues, School and Library Media, Organizations and Associations in North America, Graduate Programs, and a Mediagraphy of print and nonprint resources. The topics herein allow this volume to remain consistent with most standard references in which the contents contain elements that readers expect to find in each new edition.

You are invited to submit manuscripts to the *Educational Media and Technology Yearbook* editorial office for consideration for publication. Only manuscripts submitted electronically, such as e-mail attachments or via file transfer, will be reviewed, unless by prior arrangement.

Robert Maribe Branch

rbranch@coe.uga.edu

Contributors to
Educational Media and Technology Yearbook 2001

Mary Alice Anderson
Media Specialist
Winona Middle School
166 West Broadway
Winona, MN 55987

Kay Bishop
Associate Professor
School of Library and Information Science
CIS 1040
4202 East Fowler Avenue
Tampa, FL 33620-7800

Oratile Maribe Branch
Acorps
Performance Consultants
118 Robins Nest
Athens, GA 30606

Robert Maribe Branch, Ed.D.
Associate Professor
The University of Georgia
Department of Instructional Technology
604 Aderhold Hall
Athens, GA 30602

Andrew Brovey
Department of Curriculum and
    Instructional Technology
Valdosta State University
Valdosta, GA 31698-0101

Christina Dunn
Director, Collections and Technical Services
National Center for Education Statistics
U.S. Department of Education
555 New Jersey Avenue, NW
Room 422g
Washington, DC 20208-5651

Mary Ann Fitzgerald, Ph.D.
Assistant Professor
The University of Georgia
Department of Instructional Technology
604 Aderhold Hall
Athens, GA 30602

Melissa R. Gibson
University of Kentucky
320 McCabe Student
Mitchell, SD 57301

Phillip Harris, Ph.D.
Executive Director
Association for Educational Communi-
    cations and Technology
1800 N. Stockton Drive, Suite 2
Bloomington, IN 47404

Diane Kester
Department of Broadcasting, Librarian-
    ship, and Educational Technology
East Carolina University
113 Joyner East
Greenville, NC 27858

Lavine Kowlas
Research Assistant
University of Durban-Westville
Private Bag 54001
Durban, South Africa

Joan Mazur
335 Dickey Hall
University of Kentucky
Lexington, KY 40506

Michael Molenda, Ph.D.
Professor
Indiana University
Instructional Systems Technology
Education 2234
Bloomington, IN 47405

Kyle L. Peck, Ph.D.
Professor
Instructional Systems Program
Pennsylvania State University
University Park, PA 16802

Brooke Price
1704 Ironwood Road
Marietta, GA 30067

Catherine Price
Department of Curriculum and
    Instructional Technology
Valdosta State University
Valdosta, GA 31698-0101

Arthur Recesso
Department of Curriculum and
    Instructional Technology
Valdosta State University
Valdosta, GA 31698-0101

Greg Sherman, Ph.D.
Assistant Professor
Virginia Polytechnic Institute and
    State University
Instructional Technology
220 War Memorial Hall
Blacksburg, VA 24060

Reshma Sookrajh, Ph.D.
Researcher
University of Durban-Westville
Private Bag 54001
Durban, South Africa

William Sugar
Department of Broadcasting, Librarian-
    ship, and Educational Technology
East Carolina University
113 Joyner East
Greenville, NC 27858

Carmel Vaccare
Director of Emerging Technologies
Institute for Teaching Through Tech-
    nology and Innovative Practices
P.O. Box 794
606 Broad Street
South Boston, VA 24592

Jinx Watson
School of Information Sciences
University of Tennessee
804 Volunteer Boulevard
Knoxville, TN 37996

Ellen Wiley
Department of Curriculum and
    Instructional Technology
Valdosta State University
Valdosta, GA 31698-0101

Jane Zahner
Department of Curriculum and
    Instructional Technology
Valdosta State University
Valdosta, GA 31698-0101

Part One
Trends and Issues

Introduction

New technological applications are usually preceded by trends. Resources dedicated to media development are usually proportionate to the importance attached to the prevailing issues. Although trends do not necessarily predict the future, there is logic in tracing the trends of educational media and technology to determine indicators for the future of the field. Soothsaying notwithstanding, this section assesses the status of instructional technology in the United States as we end the 20th century and identifies the trends that appear to be taking shape as we begin the 21st century. Mike Molenda and Michael Sullivan scan the domains in which instructional technology is employed, particularly corporate training and formal education, kindergarten through university, and reveal a diverse and complex picture.

This section features an extension of a project begun in 1998 by Professor Mike Molenda at Indiana University, and continued in 2000, to document the status of instructional technology in the United States. The most apparent trend is that status regarding instructional technology may vary among the three broad sectors in which it is employed: K–12 education, higher education, and corporate training. Molenda and Harris explain in this volume of the *Yearbook* that the processes of adoption or resistance seem to be driven by underlying socioeconomic forces. The dominant driver of change continues to be the "technological imperative," or the impulse to seek technological solutions to problems as new technologies evolve. The current "imperative" seems to be digitization: converting analog forms of storage and transmission to digital form.

Vaccare and Sherman introduce the 4S model for selecting instructional technologies. The 4S model uses the criteria "Simple, Stable, Scalable, and Sustainable" as a filter. A fifth S is added to facilitate the selection process by recognizing the social aspects inherent in any use of technologies for instruction. A social dimension that uses culture and interaction as the primary consideration in the deployment of any instructional technology within the context of the 4S model is explained in further detail in their chapter.

Kyle Peck cites Thoreau, who said, "Our inventions are wont to be pretty toys, which distract our attention from serious things. They are but improved means to an unimproved end." Peck helps us understand that many of the current uses of technology are "guilty as charged," but many are not. We can't sit back and let critics examine only the weak applications that result in more expensive "business as usual," then talk about the value of modern technologies in schools. We also can't be casual observers as naïve reporters describe the powerful applications of learning technologies using methods incapable of revealing the progress students are making that can't be measured on "fill in the blank" or "fill in the bubble" tests. Peck presents a chapter that charges us to create a body of research using authentic tasks that are carefully assessed in terms of the difficult challenges students can meet.

Sookrajh and Kowlas interpret the modernizing impulse of electronic technology for education as liberating in the way in which it creates opportunities to forge research communities. An online, multicultural database is presented as a technology as well as a disciplinary socially embedded research process. Their chapter, "The Online Database as an Empowering Research Tool," represents an important development in the way in which research on multicultural education is being conceptualized, represented, materialized, and accessed in South Africa.

Robert Maribe Branch

Issues and Trends in
Instructional Technology

Michael Molenda
Indiana University

Phillip Harris
*Association for Educational
Communications and Technology*

This is an extension of a project begun in 1998 (Molenda, Russell, and Smaldino 1998) and continued in 2000 (Molenda and Sullivan 2000) to document the status of instructional technology (IT) in the United States. Having observed developments over several years, we are able to venture some conjectures about trends that seem to be taking shape. What is most apparent is that status and trends regarding IT vary among the three broad sectors in which they are employed: K–12 education, higher education, and corporate training. Some generalizations are possible, but only within sectors.

As a framework for our observations we chose several broad issues that cut across sectors and have been of perennial interest in the literature of the IT field: rate of adoption of different forms of technology for delivery of instruction, institutional constraints on acceptance of IT, and challenges to existing paradigms.

In addition, the processes of adoption or resistance seem to be driven by underlying socioeconomic forces. The dominant driver of change continues to be the "technological imperative": the impulse to seek technological solutions to problems as new technologies evolve. The current "imperative" seems to be digitization, converting analog forms of storage and transmission to digital form.

A second driver of change, especially in the United States, is the privatization of functions—such as elementary, secondary, and higher education—that previously were viewed mainly as public responsibilities. Privatization, in turn, seems to be driven by other underlying forces. One is a "libertarian" proclivity, once a minor political force but now embraced with some enthusiasm across the spectrum of political parties and interest groups. Even K–12 education, once viewed as a vehicle for community welfare, is now increasingly viewed as a private benefit, hence worthy of private rather than public financial support.

A third driver is *corporatization,* a term that has many meanings but is used here to refer to the tendency of nonprofit organizations, such as universities, to operate more and more like businesses. In an era of shrinking government support, nonprofits are compelled both to operate with more businesslike efficiency and to find ways to support themselves within the marketplace. As a consequence, faculty governance and faculty autonomy in arranging instruction are increasingly eroded.

A fourth underlying driver of change in IT is the growing societal demand for continuing education. As information technology permeates the workplace, more and more employees need continual upgrading of their skills. Further, technological change causes alteration in (sometimes elimination of) the jobs themselves, precipitating additional types of job retraining needs. Some of these continuing education needs are met in the workplace through corporate training. Programs leading to certification or degrees are more likely supplied by post-secondary institutions. Public schools are expected to provide entry-level skills in reading, math, computer literacy, and social abilities. Overall, this adds up to an exceptional challenge—and opportunity—for providers of education and training.

CORPORATE TRAINING AND DEVELOPMENT

Issue 1: Use of Technology-Based Media for Delivery of Instruction

Low-Tech Formats

Face-to-face classroom instruction is still the most universally applied format of training, being used in 90 percent of companies (Industry Report 1999, 54). In terms of the percentage of time spent in training, classroom instruction stands at about 75 percent overall, a small increase over 1998. Print materials—manuals and workbooks—are next in popularity, being used at 74 percent of companies, holding about steady over the past three years (Industry Report 1999, 54).

Traditional Audiovisual Media

Videotapes are used at 69 percent of companies, a significant decrease from a high of 92 percent in 1995 but only a slight drop over the past three years. Use of audiocassettes, too, has been declining, from 50 percent in 1995 to 36 percent in 1999. The use of slides and overhead transparencies has not been tracked consistently over the years, but these media formats seem to be receding slowly as they are replaced by computer-based display media. The use of games and simulations (non-computer-based) has declined markedly, from 63 to 23 percent since the mid-1990s, but has held steady for the past three years (Industry Report 1999, 54).

Computer-Based Media

What has been replacing the traditional delivery systems is instruction that is delivered via computer. In the early 1990s, this meant delivery via floppy disk or local network (LAN); more recently, this means delivery via CD-ROM or Internet/intranet. Taken together, these computer-mediated delivery systems account for about 14 percent of all time spent in training, surprisingly, a small dip from the estimate of 19 percent given the preceding year (Industry Report 1999, 54). This leveling off in the growth of computer-based media may indicate that corporations are still experimenting to find the proper fit of technological delivery within their toolkits (McMurrer, Van Buren, and Woodwell 2000, 15). Another interpretation is that survey respondents are drawing a distinction between lessons that are strictly computer-delivered and those in which there is a live instructor who interacts with learners online. The latter is clearly a large and growing segment as Web delivery gradually replaces delivery via diskette.

Meanwhile, the projections for online learning growth continue to be bullish. *Fortune* predicts that the proportion of corporate training offered online will grow to 50 percent by 2003 (Bylinsky 2000). As one example of this direction, in 2000 IBM claimed that it saved $200 million by moving 20 percent of its training online (Higher Education Technology News 2000).

Outsourcing Through Portals

More and more, those seeking online courses from sources outside their company are doing so through portals, websites designed to offer one-stop entry to a variety of Web services and resources. An entire class of "vertical portals," or "vortals," has grown up to cater to the corporate training market. Some of the leading examples are edupoint.com, trainingnet.com, knowledgeplanet.com, and click2learn.com. Each serves as a gateway to hundreds or even thousands of online courses. In addition, they offer such services as testing, company-based tracking, and secure discussion areas (Armstrong 2000).

Issue 3: Challenges to Existing Instructional Technology Paradigms

Instructional System Design (ISD) Questioned

The popularity of "Constructivism" in academia has led to widespread discussion about the adequacy of systems approach models for designing instruction. Willis and Wright (2000) propose a model for constructivist instructional design. Their R2D2 model explicitly rejects many of the assumptions on which the older ISD models were based. Parallel to this movement in the corporate world, dissatisfaction with the ISD model has grown for reasons more connected with efficiency and effectiveness. This dissatisfaction culminated in a lead article in *Training* magazine (Gordon and Zemke 2000) in which experts were quoted who charge that the ISD approach is too slow and clumsy for the fast-changing digital environment, fails to focus on what is most important, and tends to produce uninspired solutions. They do not propose a superior alternative approach, but a dialog may develop around this issue.

Performance Improvement and Knowledge Management

Molenda and Sullivan (2000) pointed out the shift in focus from training to performance improvement. They argue that whereas it used to be acceptable to measure the value of the training department in terms of the number of courses offered or the number of employees trained, now it is increasingly expected that the human resources department (HRD) will demonstrate how its activities actually affect employee performance, and hence profits. This expectation from top management dovetails with practitioners' growing acceptance of the notion that instruction is just one among many types of interventions that affect employee performance. Within the framework of performance improvement, the design of instruction takes place alongside the design of other interventions, such as electronic performance support systems and incentive systems, and all these are implemented together through a process of change management.

Another paradigm shift facing HRD is that of knowledge management. The knowledge and skills possessed by employees is increasingly characterized as "intellectual capital." As such, it is seen as one of the most valuable assets of an organization. The creation and management of these assets, or knowledge management (KM), is becoming viewed as the primary source of competitive advantage within a growing number of industries, ranging from auto manufacturing to consulting services (Van Buren and King 2000). However, it has proven difficult to establish concrete procedures for managing knowledge. In 1999 industry leaders, acting through the American Society for Training and Development (ASTD), decided to focus on the development of methods for *measuring* intellectual, or knowledge, assets (Bassie and Lewis 1999, 3). The idea is that it will continue to be difficult to manage an entity that we are not able to measure in the first place.

Object-Oriented Design

This approach to instructional design revolves around the dissection of content into small chunks, or "knowledge objects," that can be recombined to create instructional or informational products. This approach is key to the automation of instructional design and hence to greater efficiency in the process. M. David Merrill (1998) has developed a well-elaborated theory for object-oriented design. Several successful commercial applications have grown out of this work, especially at LeadingWay and Mindware. Other consulting firms, such as NETg and IBT Technologies, use variations of this technology. Cisco Systems creates "reusable learning objects" by combining several "reusable information objects" with an overview, summary, and assessment. Firms such as these have demonstrated success in providing major clients with instructional and KM systems that can be developed rapidly and at lower cost than their competitors.

In a related development, there is an international effort to establish open specifications for the technical building blocks of online learning. The effort is led by the IMS Global Learning Consortium, Inc., which has produced the IMS Meta-data Specification. Meta-data are the labels that are put on information objects, enabling these objects to be stored and retrieved efficiently as building blocks. The IMS specification, in turn, has been incorporated into the Sharable Courseware Object Reference Model (SCORM), developed by the Advanced Distributed Learning (ADL) Co-Laboratory. As standards such as these are promulgated, the producers of online learning programs can expect dramatic breakthroughs in productivity. This pertains not only to the corporate sector but also to the K–12 and higher education sectors, wherever instruction is being produced in digital form.

An exceptional synthesis and interpretation of these paradigm shifts is provided in H. Wayne Hodgins's futures paper, commissioned by the National Governors' Association and ASTD, concluding that, "Technology will largely obviate the need for formal, classroom type, event based learning to produce know-what and know how" (2000, 5).

HIGHER EDUCATION

Issue 1: Use of Technology-Based Media for Delivery of Instruction

The beginning of the 21st century may well go down in the history of instructional technology as the time when information technology passed from marginal to mainstream status in higher education. By early 2000, for the first time, it was noted that the Internet was used routinely on a daily basis by a majority of students, faculty, and staff at colleges and universities of all types. This does not mean, however, that The Revolution has come. Most colleges use technology to extend and improve their course offerings, not to replace programs. Most distance education courses supplement ongoing residential programs.

Classroom Media

A 1999 survey (Campus Computing Project 1999) indicates modest increases in Internet-related uses in college courses, compared with the previous year. Just over one-half of all college courses (53 percent) use e-mail, an increase of 9 percent in one year. Just over one-third (39 percent) require students to explore Internet resources, an increase of 6 percent. Just over one-fourth (28 percent) offer class materials and resources such as World Wide Web pages, an increase of 50 percent. This indicates that change is taking place gradually, with computer-based media still playing a supplementary role in classroom instruction.

Distance Education

The most visible trend in technology in higher education continues to be the virtual "land rush" mentality surrounding distance education (DE). This is particularly true among the larger public universities. Although only one-third of all post-secondary institutions currently offer DE courses, the figure rises to 78 percent of all four-year public universities and 87 percent of all large universities (U.S. Department of Education 1999). The total number of courses offered has more than doubled in the past five years, as have the number of accredited degree programs, to about one-third of all public universities (Market Data Retrieval 1999). Interestingly, the number of institutions offering DE *degree programs* has not grown substantially in the past couple of years. The expansion in degree programs appears to be among institutions that were already offering DE. These institutions have substantially increased the number of DE courses, enrollments, and degree programs that they offer (U.S. Department of Education 1999).

Regarding delivery of DE courses, approximately one-half of all institutions use two-way interactive TV and/or one-way broadcast of prerecorded programs. The popularity of these delivery systems has not changed in the past five years. What has changed is the popularity of Internet-based courses; such courses are now offered at 60 percent of all colleges, compared with 22 percent five years ago (U.S. Department of Education 1999). So, virtually all the growth in DE offerings has been fueled by the burgeoning of Internet and World Wide Web offerings.

DE Course Management. The rapid growth in Internet-based DE courses has created a market for supportive software. In addition to a half-dozen major brands of commercial course management software (such as Blackboard and WebCT), several universities have developed competing systems (such as Prometheus at George Washington University and Oncourse at Indiana University). Beyond this, vendors also offer complete turnkey systems for offering online courses; eCollege.com, Eduprise.com, Pensare, Inc., and click2learn.com are among the major players.

DE Competition. Because geographic boundaries are irrelevant to online learning, higher education institutions are being driven to think in terms of capturing a share of the national—or even global—market. It is not clear yet, however, what a successful business model might be for "dual-mode" institutions—those that offer both traditional residential programs and distance programs (Carnevale 2000). Distance-only universities such as the Open University and Jones International University, which was accredited to offer degrees in 1999, have demonstrated a successful model for that type of institution. But the jury is out on how traditional universities can make the transition. Western Governors University, a degree-granting e-university offering courses drawn from many consortium members, enrolls only some 200 degree seekers and is not yet accredited. On the other hand, the Electronic Campus of the Southern Regional Education Board (SREB) enrolls more than 20,000 students in over 100 already accredited degree programs, essentially serving as a portal to those seeking degrees from one of the cooperating dual-mode universities. State-wide "virtual universities" following this model have been created in California, Ohio, Oklahoma, Kansas, Kentucky, Tennessee, and South Dakota.

A third path is being explored by some large, "brand-name" universities; University of Maryland and Columbia University have formed for-profit subsidiaries to offer online degree programs. The idea is to attempt to exploit their "intellectual capital" without diluting the brand-name value of the residential university.

This competition is driven not only by universities among themselves, but also by for-profit course providers. The market for online learning is expected to be huge, so major investors, such as Michael Milken's Knowledge Universe and Paul Allen's click2learn.com, are jumping into the fray by offering courses to adult learners, including both college students and corporate trainees. The newest business model, referred to as eduCommerce, has for-profit course providers teaming with corporate sponsors to offer free courses with the expectation that learners will develop loyalty to the sponsor's brand and buy their products. Providers such as Hungry Minds.com and notHarvard.com, only a year or two into operation, already claim tens of millions of subscribers.

Issue 2: Constraints on Acceptance and Use of Technology

Faculty Acceptance

Faculty adoption of computer-based media for classroom use continues at a steady pace, with the gradual expansion of use of e-mail and Web pages. For most users, however, this is still a marginal activity. That is, the technology is adopted to the extent that usage is consistent with conventional roles. Faculty continue to do what they do, but the tools make the job marginally more efficient or effective.

Involvement in DE may be pushing the venture into technology. About 10 percent of all faculty who are members of the National Education Association (NEA)—concentrated in public universities other than research universities—are now teaching DE courses. Typically, these are the same people who are also teaching traditional courses, and they teach DE courses as part of their normal teaching load without extra compensation (National Education Association 2000). They do express some trepidation that they may be harmed financially by this arrangement, but they persist, motivated, it appears, by the opportunity to reach students who would otherwise not take a course (National Education Association 2000, 35–36).

Technical Infrastructure and Support

Higher education institutions are having a struggle building and maintaining adequate computer infrastructure and then providing user support to staff. In EDUCAUSE's survey of institutional representatives, when asked which issues were most important for their campus's strategic success, the two leading issues were "funding information technology" and "faculty development, support, and training" (Roche 2000). The same two issues emerged as the top concerns among chief information technology officers in another survey (Campus Computing Project 1999), and the importance of these issues has increased consistently over the past three years. The pressure can be expected to continue as demand for services expands and as universities face major network upgrades to take advantage of the capabilities of Internet 2.

Recruiting and holding qualified information technology staff members is also a major headache. When asked which issues they were spending most of their time addressing, the number one issue was "information technology staffing" (Roche 2000). This headache, also, is expected to get worse as the shortage of information technology specialists continues to grow.

Issue 3: Challenges to Existing Paradigms

Changing Faculty Roles

As enrollments increase (especially of working adults) and government financial support declines, demands for greater productivity are becoming louder than ever. Higher education institutions are searching for ways to get more output for less input. This quest is stated bluntly in an EDUCAUSE report: "Along with the focus on accountability comes pressure to adopt the business model, with greater emphasis on the bottom line" (Twigg and Oblinger 1996). Of course, because personnel costs make up about 80 percent of college budgets, controlling costs means reducing the labor-intensive nature of the conventional teaching-learning process. This means substituting capital for labor, technology for teachers, which in turn means a change in work processes. At this point, faculty resistance can be expected to rise and, indeed, to evolve from passive to active form.

Advance signals of faculty resistance to qualitative role changes have come in the form of political action. During 2000, all the major faculty collective bargaining agencies—the NEA, the AFT, and AAUP—passed resolutions demanding faculty control over courses, compensation for development and teaching of DE courses, and retention of intellectual property rights for online materials. The latter issue, intellectual property rights, is increasingly visible. As "digital content" is created, "intellectual capital" is created, and ownership becomes an important question. Universities are beginning to stake out explicit claims, at least on courses that are developed with university resources.

K–12 EDUCATION

The beginning of the 21st century marked a major watershed in the history of instructional technology. The big story is that as the 1990s ended, virtually all U.S. public schools had attained access to computers and Internet, and a *majority* of all teachers reported using computer-based technology for instructional purposes. However, it could not be said that most schools would be classed as "technology-intensive," as defined by Anderson and Ronnkvist (1999, 9). By their criteria, only 22 percent of elementary, 29 percent of middle, and 31 percent of high schools are technology intensive.

Instructional technology is also enjoying unprecedented prominence in the public spotlight. An example is the appointment of the Web-based Education Commission by the U.S. Congress and White House in 1999 with the mission of making recommendations for federal policies about the role of the Web in education. Through the testimony of expert witnesses the Commission has created an impressive knowledge base about trends, issues, and visions for the future (Barab 2000; Dede 2000; Ellis 2000; Fenwick 2000; Ladd 2000; Richards 2000; Rukeyser 2000).

Issue 1: Use of Technology-Based Media for Delivery of Instruction

Traditional Audiovisual Media

Owing to the shift in popular attention to computer-based media, there has been little research in recent years to track school use of the more "mature" technologies. Reports from regional media center directors (D. Whitmarsh, personal communication, July 26, 2000; L. Maclin, personal communication, July 25, 2000; L. Ritt, personal communication, July 28, 2000) indicate that circulation of film and video programs is holding steady after a decline from the high point in the late 1970s. In a survey of media specialists in Virginia, the vast majority reported that at least three-fourths of the teachers in their schools use some type of video in their classes (Center for Community Research 1999, 2). One factor that has helped sustain usage is that many teachers now can search for and order these materials through online ordering systems.

In a small-scale 1999 survey, a national sample of school technology coordinators reported that about three-quarters of all classrooms have VCRs and that two-thirds have access to cable or satellite TV. However, only about one-third of all teachers use cable or satellite systems on a regular basis. The survey also found that about one-half of all classrooms are equipped with whiteboards, replacing chalkboards, and that four of five classrooms are equipped with overhead projectors. The respondents estimated that about one-third of all teachers use the overhead projector daily (Misanchuk, Pyke, and Tuzun 1999, 3).

A limiting factor is that new teachers graduating from teacher education programs are receiving less exposure to audiovisual media utilization. Where courses in "technology use" are required, the content emphasis has shifted strongly to computer technology. A survey of video-using teachers revealed that only 5 percent attributed their utilization skills to college courses; the great majority were self-taught (Center for Community Research 1999, 4).

Computer-Based Media

In the late 1990s there was a near obsession in the K–12 education community with achieving "wired" status. The federal government supports this access financially through the Universal Service program for schools and libraries, more commonly known as the E-Rate. It is a federal initiative authorized by Congress as part of the Telecommunications Act of 1996 that provides discounts on telecommunications and Internet technologies to elementary and secondary schools and public libraries. The discounts themselves range between 20 and 90 percent, depending on the level of need among the students at a particular school. Provided with over $2 billion per year, tens of thousands of schools have been able to achieve Internet access.

Consequently, more than 90 percent of schools now have some level of access to the Internet (Becker 1999, 2; Market Data Retrieval 1999), up from 32 percent before the initiation of E-Rate in 1996. Fully 51 percent of instructional rooms in public schools are connected (U.S. Department of Education 1999). Another requisite besides network connection is an adequate number of computers. As of 1999, more than 90 percent of schools had some computers in classrooms, up from 73 percent in 1998. On the average, there was one computer for every 6 students (Market Data Retrieval 1999).

Teacher Computer Use. Teachers who say they use computers or Internet "a lot" report that they use them for the following purposes: to create instructional materials (39 percent), to keep classroom records (34 percent), to communicate with colleagues (23 percent), to gather information for planning lessons (16 percent), to prepare classroom presentations (8 percent), and to access model lesson plans (6 percent) (Rowand 2000).

Student Computer Use. The surveys of Becker and his colleagues (Becker, Ravitz, and Wong 1999) provide the most detailed and trustworthy data on how teachers direct their students to use computers. They report that earlier in the 1990s, "students in elementary schools, and into middle school grades, primarily used computers to do skill-related drills and to play 'edutainment' games. . . . In students' secondary school experience, computers became a subject in itself"(p. 47). But by 1998 those patterns were beginning to change:

> It is still true that at the high school level a majority of intensive experiences with computers that students have are in courses outside the academic core–most often in computer classes and business education classes. It is also still true that the majorities of teachers across grades 4 to 12 either do not use computers at all with their students or do so only occasionally; the "typical" teacher provides students with fewer than ten opportunities to use computers during a school year. Nevertheless, we have found that those academic subject-matter teachers who do have their students use computers frequently, do so in ways that are different from the "traditional" focus on computer-basal drills and learning games and computer "literacy" (p. 47).

However, across the academic subjects at both elementary and secondary levels, the most common objectives that teachers have for their students' use of computers no longer are "practicing skills just taught" or "learning computer skills." Instead, the objectives most often named have to do with students gaining access to information and improving their writing. Moreover, the kinds of software that teachers report using most often with their students–word processing programs, CD-ROM reference materials, and World Wide Web browser software–confirm that what students do most often on school computers involves searching for information and ideas through electronic media and expressing themselves in writing; not practicing math and grammar drills, playing games, or learning computer skills as isolated skills.

Apart from Web browsers and word processing programs, most of the other specific software titles that teachers report to be most valuable for their students–such as Hyperstudio, Sketchpad, and Photoshop–are evidence that at least some teachers are having students use computers as productivity tools in complex projects that may involve higher-order thinking, designing a product, and explaining their ideas and constructions to an external audience (Becker, Ravitz, and Wong 1999, 48). Some interpret this shift as a move toward integration of technology in a more constructivist vein.

What students actually *do* when they use the Internet and World Wide Web has been unclear until recently. In a first-of-its-kind study of actual student Internet usage in America's classrooms, a sampling was done on actual school Internet traffic (N2H2 2000). It was found that although brand-name portal sites such as Yahoo! and AltaVista generate the highest page-views, as a category they drop to sixth out of seven when measured by average per-page viewing time. The Top 300 most visited websites by school users fall into seven categories, in this order: portals and search, instructional and reference and computing, music and entertainment, commerce and e-services, news and sport, business and finance, and communities. However, when average time spent per page is used as the metric, instructional and reference and computing (60 seconds per page) comes first, with news and sports second, and business and finance third (N2H2, 4). As an example, Yahoo is ranked number 1 in terms of page views, but falls to below number 200 when ranked by average per-page viewing time. So, students do appear to be spending much of their online time viewing substantive material, or, in Internet terms, content-rich sites are "stickiest."

Issue 2: Constraints on Acceptance and Use of Technology

Staff Development

The issue of teacher preparation is certainly related to both the extent of student access and the quality of usage of the Internet. One might assume that the tremendous growth in access to the Internet had been accompanied by a corresponding effort in staff development to prepare teachers for a major movement in instructional practice. In fact, only three of ten teachers reported attending any form of professional development on this topic during the previous 12 months (Becker 1999, 17).

Preservice Preparation

On the whole, public school teachers who have access to computers or Internet at school do not express a high level of confidence in their ability to use computers: Only 33 percent feel "well" or "very well" prepared. However, newer teachers do seem to be better prepared. Teachers with three or fewer years of teaching experience were more likely to feel well prepared than teachers with twenty or more years of experience (31 percent versus 19 percent) (Rowand 2000, 74). New national standards for technology skills for teachers, promulgated by the International Society for Technology in Education (ISTE) in 2000, are expected to have an influence on preservice teacher preparation in the future.

Technology Support

Survey data gathered by Becker and his colleagues show that teacher use of technology is highly correlated with level of support at the building level (Ronnkvist, Dexter, and Anderson 2000). Support entails a wide range of services: facilities, presence of a support staff, personal help and guidance, professional development, and professional incentives. Although 87 percent of schools have someone serving in the role of technology coordinator, only 19 percent of these people reported working full-time in that capacity. Whether teachers are at schools with full-time or part-time technology coordinators, they receive little assistance integrating technology into their curriculum. Full-time coordinators spent roughly two hours per week on this task, and part-time coordinators spent even less time (Ronnkvist, Dexter, and Anderson 2000, 5). Overall, "less than half (41 percent) of the teachers believed that both technical and instructional support were available to them at least some of the times they needed it. For about 10 percent of the teachers, technical help was not available at all; and twice that number (20 percent) indicated they had no instructional help available to them" (Ronnkvist, Dexter, and Anderson 2000, 13). Given the high correlation found between technology support and technology use, this shortcoming may be viewed as a major constraint.

Outdated Hardware

Among those teachers who use software for instruction, 47 percent say there are software titles they would like to use but cannot because their school computers are not powerful enough (Education Week 2000). This is not surprising because it is clear that schools are struggling with the challenge of acquiring and maintaining a hardware base. Some of this is attributable to the "one-time purchase" mentality. In fact, initial purchase costs represent only about one-quarter of the "total cost of ownership" (TCO), and districts are ill prepared for the long-term costs involved with maintaining and replacing computer equipment (Fitzgerald 1999).

Curricular Match

Approximately half of all teachers who use computers say that it is somewhat or very difficult to find software or Internet sites that fit their specific classroom needs. Likewise, 59 percent give the software in their classrooms a C or lower when it comes to matching with state and district tests (Education Week 2000). As the grade level increases, teachers have a harder time finding software that meets their classroom needs.

Issue 3: Core Versus Supplementary Use of Technology

We seem to be re-experiencing with computers our past history with film, radio, and television. Despite the claimed potentiality of the new media to revolutionize classroom practice, we find instead a pattern of "niche markets" and supplementary use. In the most recent *Education Week* survey, it was found that only 17 percent of teachers who use software specifically designed for K–12 subjects say the software is a "primary resource related to classroom instruction" (Education Week 2000). Similarly, only 9 percent of teachers who use websites for instruction say they are a "primary resources," and 88 percent use them as a "supplementary resource" (Education Week 2000).

Saul Rockman, a leading school technology consultant, echoes statements made in earlier generations about radio and television: "The truth is that if one removed computer technology from the classrooms of this nation's schools, the results would neither raise nor lower student achievement test scores, SATs, or any of the bottom-line criteria that business, civic, and government leaders consider to be the outcomes of education" (Salpeter 1998).

Issue 4: Challenges to Existing Paradigms

Home Schooling

The dominant paradigm for schooling in the United States for almost 200 years has been going to a public (or, to a lesser extent, a private) school. But home schooling has emerged as an increasingly popular alternative. In less than 10 years, the number of home-schooled students in the United States has more than tripled to 1.7 million, as parents seek more personalized curricula for their children and grow increasingly concerned about the safety of public schools. However, many parents feel unqualified to teach certain subjects, especially to older students. The World Wide Web is helping to fill the instructional gap. Some home-schooled students use online courses, such as The Learning Odyssey, as a supplement to their regular studies; others actually enroll in an online school such as the Christa Mcauliffe Academy, the Laurel Spring School, or Child U. This seems to be yet another case where the burgeoning of technology is driving social change.

CONCLUSIONS

The rapid emergence of new technological developments, the convergence of previously distinguishable media–such as video and computer text–into digital format, and accompanying changes in the affected businesses make it increasingly difficult to be sure what the issues are and what entities to try to measure. For example, up to now it seemed important to count the number of schools having computers or Internet connections. But as we approach universal access in the United States, these numbers lose meaning.

The spotlight is shifting toward patterns of *use* and the consequences of those patterns of use: Precisely how are teachers employing computer-based media in the instructional process? What effect is this use having on student performance, on the role of the teacher and professor, on compensation practices, on intellectual property rights, on power relationships? These effects are much more difficult to observe and measure.

What is becoming clear is that we are experiencing deja vu regarding instructors' responses to today's new media, comparable to the patterns of previous media, such as film, radio, and television. The new medium emerges with great fanfare. Public pressure builds to employ it in education. Schools and colleges acquire the hardware needed to enter the game. Software lags behind. Instructor adoption lags even farther behind, eventually growing to substantial proportions before plateauing, but never reaching the levels predicted by the cheerleaders.

So we know that hardware penetration is a necessary, but not sufficient, condition for productive use of technology in instruction. The key stakeholders decide how quickly and to what extent new technologies are adopted. We know that different stakeholders move at different rates in the various public and private sectors. Their decisions depend greatly on their perceptions of the personal advantage offered by the new technology as well as their organizations' demands on them to find ways of making their practice more productive.

These organizational dynamics, explained in greater detail in Molenda and Sullivan (2000), go far toward explaining the variations in rate and extent of use of technology in different sectors.

REFERENCES

Anderson, R. E., and Ronnkvist, A. *The presence of computers in American schools*. Irvine, CA: Center for Research on Information Technology and Organizations, University of California, and University of Minnesota, June 1999.

Armstrong, J. (2000, June). The biggest, baddest learning portals. *Training*, 61–63.

Barab, S. (2000). *Written testimony for the Web-based Education Commission. Web-based Education Commission*. [Online]. Available: http://www.hpcnet.org/cgi-bin/global/a_bus_card.cgi?store_SiteID=155038. (Accessed February 22, 2001).

Bassie, L., and Lewis, E., eds. (1999). *The ASTD trends watch*. Alexandria, VA: American Society for Training & Development.

Becker, H. J. *Internet use by teachers: Conditions of professional use and teacher-directed student use*. Irvine, CA: Center for Research on Information Technology and Organizations, University of California, and University of Minnesota, 1999.

Becker, H. J., Ravitz, J. L., and Wong, Y. T. (1999). *Teacher and teacher-directed student use of computers and software*. Irvine, CA: Center for Research on Information Technology and Organizations, University of California, and University of Minnesota.

Bylinsky, G. (2000, June 26). Hot new technologies for American factories. Part 2. *Fortune* 142, 1. [Online]. Available: http://www.fortune.com/fortune/imt/2000/06/26/elearning2.html. (Accessed February 22, 2001).

The Campus Computing Project. (1999, October). *The 1999 National Survey of Information Technology in Higher Education: The Continuing Challenge of Instructional Integration and User Support*. [Online]. Available: http://www.campuscomputing.net. (Accessed February 22, 2001).

Carnevale, D. (2000, May 19). Two models for collaboration in distance education. *Chronicle of Higher Education*.

The Center for Community Research. (1999). *Virginia Public Television Instructional Television Survey–1999*. Salem, VA: The Center for Community Research, Roanoke College.

CEO Forum on Education and Technology. (2000). *The power of digital learning: Integrating digital content, year three*. Washington, DC: CEO Forum on Education and Technology.

Dede, C. (2000). *Testimony: Implications of emerging information technologies for education policies*. Web-based Education Commission. [Online]. Available: http://www.hpcnet.org/cgi-bin/global/a_bus_card.cgi?store_SiteID=155038. (Accessed February 22, 2001).

Education Week (2000). *Technology Counts '99 Survey Highlights*. [Online]. Available: http://www.edweek.org/sreports/tc99/articles/survey.htm. (Accessed February 22, 2001).

Ellis, E. A. (2000). *Testimony Presented on Behalf of the McGraw-Hill Companies*. Web-based Education Commission. [Online]. http://www.hpcnet.org/cgi-bin/global/a_bus_card.cgi?store_SiteID=155038. (Accessed February 22, 2001).

Evans, S. (2000, May 15). Net-based training goes the distance. *Washington Post*, F20.

Fenwick, J. (2000). *Testimony*. Web-based Education Commission. [Online]. Available: http://www
.hpcnet.org/cgi-bin/global/a_bus_card.cgi?store_SiteID=155038. (Accessed February 22, 2001).

Fitzgerald, S. (1999, September). Technology's real costs. Electronic school website: http://www
.electronic-school.com/199909/0999sbot.html. (Accessed February 22, 2001).

Gordon, J., and Zemke, R. (2000, April). The attack on ISD. *Training*, 42–53.

Higher Education Technology News. (2000, May 30). E-learning threatens the existence of the nation's
business schools. *Higher Education Technology News* 2:11, 82.

Hodgins, W. (2000). *Into the future: A vision paper*. Alexandria, VA. Commission on Technology and
Adult Learning, a joint project of the American Society for Training & Development and
National Governors' Association.

Industry report 1999. (1999, October). *Training*, 37–40, 53–54, 73–80.

Ladd, C. (2000). *Testimony of the Public Broadcasting Service (PBS)*. Web-based Education Commission.
[Online]. Available: http://www.hpcnet.org/cgi-bin/global/a_bus_card.cgi?store_SiteID=155038.
(Accessed February 22, 2001).

Market Data Retrieval (MDR). (1999). 1999 Higher Ed Technology Survey Findings. *DataPoints*
(newsletter). Shelton, CT: MDR.

McMurrer, D. P., Van Buren, M. E., and Woodwell, W. H. (2000). *The 2000 state of the industry report*.
Alexandria, VA: American Society for Training & Development.

Merrill, M. D. (1998, March–April). Knowledge analysis for effective instruction. *CBT Solutions*,
1–11.

Misanchuk, Melanie, Pyke, J. Garvey, and Hakan Tuzun. (1999, Spring). Trends and issues in educational media and technology in K–12 public schools in the United States. *Instructional Media*
24, 3–5.

Molenda, M., Russell, J., and Smaldino, S. (1998). Trends in media and technology in education and
training. In R. M. Branch and M. A. Fitzgerald (eds.), *Educational media and technology yearbook 1998: Volume 23*. Englewood, CO: Libraries Unlimited.

Molenda, M., and Sullivan, M. (2000). Issues and trends in instructional technology. In R. M. Branch
and M. A. Fitzgerald (eds.), *Educational media and technology yearbook 2000: Volume 25*.
Englewood, CO: Libraries Unlimited.

National Education Association (NEA). (2000). *A survey of traditional and distance learning higher
education members*. Washington, DC: National Education Association.

N2H2. (2000). *K–12 Internet Use: N2H2 Winter Quarter Learnings Report*. [Online]. Available: http://www
.n2h2.com/edwhite/. (Accessed February 22, 2001).

Richards, J. (2000). *Testimony*. Web-based Education Commission. [Online]. Available: http://www
.hpcnet.org/cgi-bin/global/a_bus_card.cgi?store_SiteID=155038. (Accessed February 22, 2001).

Roche, J. (2000) *Checking the Radar: Survey Identifies Key IT Issues*. EDUCAUSE. [Online]. Available:
http://www.educause. edu/issues/survey2000/report.html. (Accessed February 22, 2001).

Ronnkvist, A., Dexter, S. L., and Anderson, R. E. *Technology support: Its depth, breadth and impact in
America's schools*. Irvine, CA: Center for Research on information Technology and Organizations, University of California, and University of Minnesota, 2000.

Rowand, C. (2000, Summer). Teacher use of computers and the Internet in public schools. *Education
Statistics Quarterly*, 72–75.

Rukeyser, W. L. (2000). *Testimony*. Web-based Education Commission. [Online]. Available: http://www.
hpcnet.org/cgi-bin/global/a_bus_card.cgi?store_SiteID=155038. (Accessed February 22, 2001).

Salpeter, J. (1998, May). Interview with Saul Rockman. *Technology & Learning*. [Online]. Available:
http://www.techlearning.com/content/reviews/articles/rockman.html. (Accessed February 22, 2001).

Twigg, C. A., and Oblinger, D. G. (1996). The virtual university. EDUCAUSE Website, www.educause
.edu/nlii/VU.html. (Accessed February 22, 2001).

U.S. Department of Education. National Center for Education Statistics. (1999). *Distance education at postsecondary education institutions: 1997–98*. NCES 2000-013. Written by Laurie Lewis, Kyle Snow, Elizabeth Farris, and Douglas Levin. Project Officer: Bernie Greene. Washington, DC: U.S. Department of Education, National Center for Education Statistics.

Van Buren, M. E., and King, S. B. (2000). *The 2000 ASTD international comparisons report*. Alexandria, VA: American Society for Training & Development.

Willis, J., and Wright, K. E. (2000, March–April). A general set of procedures for constructivist instructional design: the new R2D2 model. *Educational Technology*, 5–20.

A Pragmatic Model for Instructional Technology Selection

Carmel Vaccare
Institute for Teaching Through Technology and Innovative Practices

Greg Sherman
Virginia Tech University

ABSTRACT

The 4S model uses the criteria "Simple, Stable, Scalable, and Sustainable" as a filter for selecting instructional technologies. A fifth S is added to undergird the selection process by recognizing the social aspects inherent in any use of technologies for instruction. A social constructivist view of learning can coexist with a behaviorist view in the 4S filtering process. This article considers a social dimension that uses culture and interaction as the primary consideration in the deployment of any instructional technology within the context of the 4S model.

INTRODUCTION: THE 4S MODEL

A number of models for selecting the most appropriate instructional media for a given instructional need have been developed and refined over the past 20 years. A good example of such a model is Reiser and Gagné's "Media Selection Flowchart" (1983). Within this flowchart, instructional designers and developers make decisions about potential "candidate" media. Decisions are based on such issues as the need for a live instructor, the readability level of the learners, and the types of skills being facilitated by the instruction. These models assume a designer's desire to select the best medium for a given population with specific instructional needs. Unfortunately, the selection of a technology (primarily electronic media) for use in education has traditionally been based on what is available as opposed to what is appropriate (Gagné 1987). At an institutional level, the first line of decision-making often resides with the technology support people. They are responsible for integrating and maintaining new technology in the institution. Their primary responsibilities are to ensure reliability and security, and they are not necessarily interested in instructional efficacy. Education needs a system to create a dialogue between the technical realities and the pedagogical necessities. This article presents a new model for aiding not only technology decision makers but also faculty, instructional designers, and technical support personnel. The model represents a process for selecting which types of technologies should be made available to instructional developers within their institutions. This model also aids developers in determining the most appropriate available technologies for their particular instructional needs. The model easily extends across departments and disciplines to empower and enable anyone in the decision-making process. Generally speaking, when solving an instructional problem one can only see what is at hand. Instructional developers tend to find new instructional delivery tools by happenstance or through the referral of others in anticipation of a potential use. At any given point in time there are media development and delivery tools that are readily available through a prior institutional or departmental acquisition. Rarely is the time available to search for a possibly better tool, even if the instructional developer is aware that such an alternative already exists. A new tool means training, without a guarantee that it will deliver in the best possible manner. Fortunately or unfortunately, Web-based technologies today present a much larger range of available media options for instructional developers.

The proposed model of instructional delivery mode and method selection has two functional parts. The first part is the selection process predicated on a "4S" classification process. (Is the technology *S*imple, *S*table, *S*calable, and *S*ustainable?) This phase of the 4S model constitutes an initial filter for the selection process. Technologies chosen through this process become part of an instructional toolkit. The second part of the model focuses on the choice of particular tools based on the criteria of time, place, and degree of interactivity criteria. Models such as the Southwest Research Institute's "Automated Media Selection Model" (1996–1999) are based on similar criteria, with added selection criteria of cost and other resource issues.

4S CLASSIFICATION PROCESS

Whether a technology is classified as Simple depends on factors such as learning curve, ease of use, ease of access, availability of support, and system demands. The learning curve for a given tool applies not only to the lesson developer but also to the user. A tool that creates content easily but is difficult to navigate because of a poor interface can lead to user frustration and cognitive dissonance. We can spend more time learning to utilize a tool than simply choosing and using alternate means of delivery. Fifty years of instructional design research paints a compelling picture with respect to the lack of significant difference in the mode of delivery to learning (see Clark 1994). The availability of support for the developing and delivery of content can also lead to frustration. If development or delivery is halted for want of information on the use of a tool, then a cognitive barrier is raised and the academic content is hidden from the user. All technologies are like semi-permeable membranes, through which some things pass while some things are blocked. For example, a computer chat environment may possess a number of meritorious features with respect to a particular learning environment, but the act of "chatting" is, in fact, limited by the user's ability to type as well as decode the symbols behind the graphic user interface. Simple technologies should be transparent so as not to create an extraneous barrier between the material and the developer or to the learner. Unless a technology is simple, it is unlikely that an average faculty member will take the time to learn, develop, deliver, or otherwise use the technology. A lack of simplicity can translate into a barrier for the learner. Simplicity depends on the technology directly.

A Stable classification depends on a technology's functional reliability. Stability is also dependent on whether the parameters under which the technology operates must be specified, that is, are plug-ins necessary for a particular Web browser? The less stable the technology, the greater the chance that it will interfere with learning, the more likely frustration will exist, and the less likely a faculty member will rely on it for course delivery.

If material is only available in one place at one time, stability is an easier issue to deal with. It is easier to control or compensate for variation in equipment and delivery. When a student is at home, the settings on the monitor, Internet access speed, whether the student has sufficient hardware or software, and so forth, become salient points for design and support. Stability in a distributed environment relies on technical design and support. When technologies are not collocated, maintenance and support considerations must be part of the instructional design process. Stability depends on the technology and the technical infrastructure of an institution.

The ideal Scalable technologies can, for example, be used by one or many without hardware or software limitations. The more Scalable the technology, the more environments it is available in and the easier it is to upgrade or customize to meet the needs of the user. Scalable technology can adapt to meet increased or changing demands of the users. Can the technology in question be used in different places, at different times? Is it based on proprietary software or hardware that limits its functionality? Is the technology based on existing and/or emerging standards that will promote a long "shelf life?" Faculty who must often re-purpose course content for different venues, or in response to changes in technology, will be less likely to update material. A technology that depends on a single company can either be a solid investment or a confined vault. An example of a single company's product aiding scalability is Microsoft Word™. It has been reported that Microsoft Word has captured over 90 percent of the word processing market share. Word files are saved in a format that is readable by most word processors. It has become a de facto standard. RealNetwork's "Real-Video" is another standard format. It delivers audio and video content across the Internet with minimal bandwidth demands for such data, but it can also simultaneously deliver a higher quality stream at greater bandwidths. A limitation is that it depends on a proprietary server to scale for increasing the number of concurrent users. There is always a cost, a trade off, associated with making a decision to use any product. If the content is in a format that is no longer supported, how hard is it to convert? This is an issue that runs deep into the heart of archiving digital libraries. In the end, Scalability is tied to the particular technology's inherent strengths and weaknesses as well as its place in the broader marketplace.

Whether a technology is Sustainable depends on the institution more than on the technology itself. Are there physical and fiscal resources that will be dedicated to maintaining and supporting the technology for its foreseeable life expectancy? If there is no explicit commitment of support, the technology becomes an expensive doorstop. It becomes a wedge against new efforts when it is used as an example of a waste of resources and just another failed attempt to deliver on technological promise.

Resources aren't the only factors influencing sustainability. Is there a cultural acceptance of the particular technology? An institution that commits to a particular technology should take into account the prevailing culture and the true costs of change. An example of ignoring the prevailing culture would be an institution with a strong history of small and personal classes that embarks on a rapid deployment of technologies associated with distance education. Not that sustainability wouldn't or couldn't be successful, but it adds dimensions that must be addressed on a non-technical level.

How flexible is the technology, and can it be adapted for changing environments? This has to do with the technology itself, and like scalability, it is related to the marketplace and the manufacturer's commitment. With the rapid changes in technologies, an institution must commit to bearing costs, both real and imagined, for adapting and converting past efforts. Good faith in an institution's reasonable efforts to sustain one's present and future efforts is critical to morale and for undertaking future projects. Students ultimately suffer from a lack of institutional commitment.

The boundaries between Simple, Stable, Scalable, and Sustainable classifications overlap and are not meant to be rigid. To summarize:

- Simplicity directly depends on the user-friendly aspects of a technology.

- Stability depends on the technology and its relationship to the technical infrastructure of an institution.

- Scalability is tied to the technology and its place in the broader marketplace.

- Sustainability largely depends on the institution more than on the technology itself.

There are no perfect technologies or designs. By framing decisions concerning technologies as Simple, Stable, Scalable, and Sustainable, the inherent compromises are defined and made manageable. Inordinate compromises are avoided before time and resources are squandered.

CHOOSING TOOLS

The process for using the 4S model can be summed up in the following steps:

1. Determine available technologies/tools through the 4S filter.

2. Choose an educational goal or learning objective.

3. Determine time and place dependency.

4. Decide on degree of interaction necessary.

5. Map appropriate tools for instructional events.

Note that there isn't always a technology to fill the need. In these cases resources, time, and/or money should be assessed for research and training. If the costs are too high or appropriate technologies are unavailable, one must be willing to forgo the technology rather than make an ill-advised compromise.

Figure 1 presents a pre-existing model for determining delivery mode, time, and place relationships, and is adapted for re-purposing course content and identifying appropriate technologies.

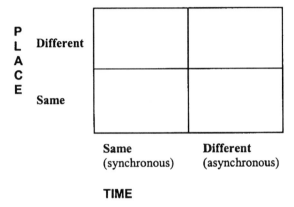

Figure 1. Time and Place Quadrants. *Source:* **Coldeway 1986.**

The lower left quadrant for same time and same place is assumed to be the most valuable venue because of the logistics and expense of arranging for all participants to be collocated. The traditional class is a lecture in which students and the teacher gather in the same room at the same time. The quadrant above it could be seen as a video broadcast or a class delivered via videoconferencing, at the same time in different locations. If material is necessary for background information, a logical concern is whether time (not necessarily order) is relevant to the material. Can a lecture be delivered asynchronously by videotape, text, Internet, and so forth rather than using a traditional lecture format of students and teacher concurrently in the same physical space? The time factor is also determined by whether an immediate response or a discussion is required. This is in contrast to when a delay, or an asynchronous interaction, is desired to promote reflection.

After dividing the instructional events by time, dependency on physical location can be determined. Is there a laboratory or piece of equipment that is necessary for content or access? Must the student be collocated with other students to participate in an instructional event? The previous questions need not be either/or decisions; several time/place quadrants can be appropriate venues for delivery and participation.

If the instructional event is dependent on specialized equipment such as computer, language, or biology lab equipment, the question of whether the students must be there at the same time or merely need access can shift quadrants of time as well as resources to manage the location. Another example would be the necessity for a high degree of network bandwidth, which may or may not be under the institution's control. This mapping of content and events allows one to choose technologies that can cover several quadrants for effective and efficient instruction. A presentation may be delivered in a traditional classroom setting while being recorded for future review over the Internet with addition hyperlinks for a more in-depth exposition. Some examples are shown in their respective quadrants in Figure 2.

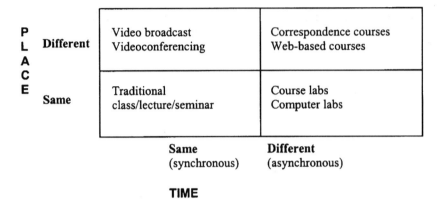

Figure 2. Time and Place Quadrants with Examples.

Up to this point in the presentation of a model for selecting instructional technologies, only factors related to the technology and its implementation have been considered. Specific needs of the learners have been overlooked. In the design, development, and implementation of learning environments, a very important determining factor in the use of technology is the degree of interactivity. Eric Brown (1998) pointed out that where technology or bandwidth are concerned, a linear scale ranging from no interactivity to a high degree of collaboration also is a scale of complexity and cost (see Figure 3). The infrastructure and costs of videoconferencing may appear inexpensive, but the infrastructure and support are hidden and substantial. Brown's scale can be modified and overlaid with cognitive involvement or the level of external interaction. "Interaction" in the sense of people and technology represents the degree to which user (learner) input affects message presentation (Sherman 1999). The scale in Figure 3 assumes that internal sources and individual contexts are self-contained with limited interaction, as in reading a book or reviewing videotape alone. This does not negate the social constructivist view; it merely reflects a lack of active discourse or involvement beyond a personal "zone" (Vygotsky 1978).

Internal sources	External sources
Individual contexts	Stimuli
Self-contained	Other people

Figure 3. Brown Scale Modified by Sherman for the Degree of Interaction.

Interactivity results in feedback, which alters the direction or scope of the presentation. Interactivity can range from none to conversation with other individuals or with a system that generates responses based on user input. The interactivity present in a "traditional" didactic presentation is limited to the opportunities that the students have to communicate with the instructor. Likewise, the amount and type of interactivity present in a computer-supported distance learning environment is defined by the manner in which the learners can and do communicate with the technology (hardware, software, and possibly people). For interaction to occur with or through the technology, learner inputs must initiate some type of response. This response may be "social" in nature, with an actual person responding verbally to learner input (or the perception of a real person responding to input). The social nature of the input-feedback experience can be determined by the conversational nature of verbal responses as well as temporal proximity—that is, how immediately the "person" on the other end of the technology responds to learner input.

In addition to real or perceived social interactivity, distance learning technologies can also provide a variety of instructional feedback mediated by the technology itself. For example, when a learner responds to a question within a piece of software (or website), the system itself can respond in a number of different ways to the learner's input, depending on the complexity of the technology and the software programming. The following list describes the different types of feedback possible in an instructional question-feedback situation (Hannafin and Peck 1988):

- *Knowledge of response.* Learners are informed that they have submitted a correct or incorrect response. This type of feedback mechanism is often used in situations where the leaner must respond until a correct answer is submitted.

- *Knowledge of correct response.* Learners are informed about what the correct response is.

- *Corrective feedback.* Learners submitting an incorrect response to a practice item are informed of the correct answer and offered information about the nature of their error.

- *Elaborative feedback.* Whether they respond correctly or not, learners are informed of the correct response and are presented with additional information/examples related to the correct response.

- *Advisement feedback.* Learners are informed about the consequences of specific responses or patterns of responses, and may receive recommendations about future choices.

The individual brings internal knowledge and contexts to a non-interactive instructional event. As multiple forms of interaction are introduced, the options for discussion and interpretation increase. In current computer-based instruction (CBI), the interaction and feedback are limited to predetermined, programmed interactions and feedback. Whether a machine can progress into a Socratic method remains to be determined (Vaccare 1996).

When the capacity for interactions with other people is introduced, the possibilities and directions for context and movement in the Zone of Proximal Development are greatly enhanced (Vygotsky 1978).

When deciding which technologies will be most appropriate for organizations wishing to implement distance learning environments, it is important to consider not only the more traditional 4S factors (*S*imple, *S*table, *S*calable, and *S*ustainable), but also the fifth "S": social interaction considerations. As described, social interactions can be cultivated by and through technology to facilitate real or perceived interpersonal interactions as well as interactions between user input and the messages "built into" the technology via software programming. Figure 4 illustrates a modification of the Time/Place Quadrant (see Figure 1) combined with the scale for the Degree of Interaction (see Figure 3). Once time and place dependency is combined with the level of interactivity for the instructional event, one can select the appropriate tools derived from the 4S process.

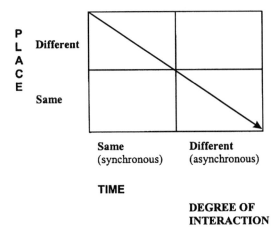

Figure 4. Integration of Time, Place, and Degree of Interaction.

The modified quadrant has a three-dimensional area that can be used to map instructional events in a more realistic manner than is possible using the quadrant alone. An approach to mapping a tool to this quadrant can be to identify

- when instructional events must occur at the same time or when the material/activity is less time constrained;
- if the activity is dependent on (a) specific location(s);
- if more than one person must be involved; and
- the degree of interactivity or collaboration required.

The tool selection process and the mapping of technologies to instructional goals can occur independently of one another. But neither occurs in a vacuum. Pedagogy is a necessary and sufficient factor for determining when technologies may be warranted or appropriate. If using technology makes pedagogical sense, then a review of the available tools is initiated. But the choices of tools that are available rarely depend on pedagogy alone.

REFERENCES

Brown, Eric. (1998). Personal communications.

Clark, R. (1994). Media will never influence learning. *Educational Technology Research and Development*, 42:2, 21–29.

Coldeway, D. O. (1986). Learner characteristics and success. In I. Mugridge and D. Kaufman (eds.), Distance Education in Canada. London: Croom Helm.

Gagné, Robert M., ed. (1987). *Instructional technology: Foundations*. Hillsdale, NJ: Lawrence Erlbaum.

Hannafin, M., and Peck, K. (1988). *The design, development, and evaluation of instructional software*. New York, London: Macmillan.

Reiser, R., and Gagné, R. (1983). *Selecting media for instruction*. Englewood Cliffs, NJ: Educational Technologies Publications.

Sherman, G. P. (1999). *Egocentric versus exocentric map perspectives within educational virtual reality environments*. Proceedings of the annual convention of the Association for Educational Communication and Technology, Houston, TX.

Southwest Research Institute. (1996–1999). Automated Media Selection Model: Beta 1.01.

Vaccare, Carmel. (1996). From the Turing Test to the teachable moment. Unpublished paper prepared for the Department of Instructional Technology, Virginia Tech.

Vygotsky, L. S. (1978). Cole, M., John-Steiner, V., Scribner, S., and Souberman, E., eds. *Mind in society The development of higher psychological processes*. Cambridge, MA: Harvard University Press.

Our Biggest Challenge
Proving the Power of Technologies in Educational Settings

Kyle L. Peck
Professor of Education, Instructional Systems Program
The Pennsylvania State University

I have witnessed the significant power of learning technologies, and yet I fear for their future in American schools. My first experiences with computers in the classroom were in the late 1970s, when I brought the first two microcomputers into Leadville, Colorado, a small, beautiful mountain town at 10,000 feet in the Rocky Mountains. As the result of my first attempt at grant writing, I was able to purchase two Radio Shack TRS-80 micros and put them in the hands of sixth- and seventh-grade students. I saw the students who took control of them change in important ways, and my beliefs about learning and education began to change with them. Despite the incredible difference in the power of those computers and the ones in today's classrooms, the lessons I learned more than 20 years ago are the same lessons increasing numbers of teachers are learning today. The most important lesson, by far, is that when students have meaningful access to computers and are expected to take control of them and put them to work to solve real problems, students:

- engage in higher-order thinking;

- will spend countless hours engaged in important cognitive challenges; and

- will amaze their parents and teachers with what they can accomplish.

DON'T SHOOT THE MESSENGER!

Although I am a vocal advocate for learning technologies, and I know that the readers of this *Yearbook* are as well, I feel that it is my responsibility to bring you bad news. I fear we are about to learn another important lesson about these powerful technologies in schools: If we do not provide ample evidence of the power of these technologies, soon, and in forms and locations that the public will respect, a backlash against the use (and cost) of these technologies will abruptly end the progress we have seen in the past decade, making these powerful learning technologies available only to the privileged.

Twenty years ago Seymour Papert (1980) described microcomputer technologies as "infinitely plastic," pointing out that they are incredibly versatile and can change roles from moment to moment or classroom to classroom. In one session they might be providing computer-based instruction, in the next supporting student work with online databases, and in the next serving as an incubator for creativity and higher-order skills as students run small businesses and/or develop multimedia productions. This amazing versatility is a double edged sword, however, because few people outside schools understand the diverse roles computer technologies can and do play, and few of those who do understand can resist comparing the computer's potential contributions in a misguided search for the "best" or the "right" way to use computers in schools. Because the cost of technologies is becoming an increasingly large percentage of the school's budget, and because taxpayers' resistance to what they perceive as "the high cost of education" is growing, we must be prepared to justify the important uses of technologies in our schools. Unfortunately, we are not.

LEARNING TECHNOLOGIES ARE EXPENSIVE, BUT SCHOOLS ARE PAYING

Spending on learning technologies has been increasing by leaps and bounds. It is estimated that American schools will spend close to $9 billion on computers and related technologies in the 2000–2001 school year (White 1997a), and annual increases have been approximately 20 percent over the past five years (White 1997b). Taxpayers are becoming increasingly "cranky" about supporting what they might call this "alleged investment," and the growth in the overall number of computers available for student use is starting to decrease as a greater percentage of each year's technology money is devoted to replacing and/or upgrading outdated technologies rather than adding to the total number of computers available.

THERE ARE MANY ADVOCATES, BUT FEW OFFER EVIDENCE

Advocates of learning technologies remain vocal about the potential they see, but, perhaps blinded by their own advocacy, they rarely provide compelling evidence. For example, the California Education Technology Task Force (1996), in its report, *Connect, Compute, and Compete,* stated:

> Our purpose in this report is not to build the case regarding the virtues of computers in the classroom. We're convinced. . . . We don't presume that technology is the only issue worthy of attention when it comes to public instruction. Many factors influence education policies: among them class size, teacher salaries, hours of classroom instruction, and adequate facilities. . . . Our research has led us to the conclusion that, more than any other single measure, computers and network technologies, properly implemented, will bolster California's continuing efforts to right what's wrong with our public schools.

Although the authors of the report were convinced of the value of technology, many consumers of the report were not, and the percentage of people who are not convinced seems to be growing. Almost everywhere you look there are articles describing interesting technology-related educational projects, but few offer any serious data-based evaluation describing the benefits of the project. The little formal research that does exist is often based on very short treatments with convenient, under-motivated populations.

THE RESEARCH BASE IS INADEQUATE, GIVEN THE POTENTIAL AND COST

Edward Miller, former editor of the *Harvard Education Letter*, offers this description of the research on technologies in education: "Most knowledgeable people agree that most of the research isn't valid. It's so flawed it shouldn't even be called research. Essentially, it's just worthless" (in Oppenheimer 1997). Miller contends that when the seriously flawed studies are removed from the analysis, what remains is inconclusive.

In the absence of a solid research base, some people interpret the minimal existing body of research negatively, jumping to unwarranted conclusions. Perhaps they forget that there are many factors in the educational equation, and that the use of technology is but one. For example, Samuel Sava, executive director of the National Association of Elementary School Principals, indicates that 37 percent of students in the United States use computers in at least some math lessons—nearly triple the international average. Yet this increased use seemed to make no difference to math results. In sum, if computers make a difference, it has yet to show up in achievement (in Bronner 1997). Like many others, he looks for an influence of one variable, technology, without controlling for other variables (like parental support, hours of instruction, and many other factors present in international comparisons). If we don't provide studies that answer important questions well, people will "fill in the gaps," jumping to invalid conclusions.

Dinty Moore, in *The Emperor's Virtual Clothes* (p. xv), offers the following perspective, which might just as well describe the debate about technologies in schools:

> When it comes to the Information Superhighway, this much is clear: one side's overstatement rapidly drowns out the other side's hyperbole, and that hyperbole is itself instantaneously suffocated under a smothering layer of gross media exaggeration. No one really knows, in other words. They are all just guessing.

A BACKLASH AGAINST TECHNOLOGIES IN SCHOOLS HAS BEGUN

Doug Johnson (1998), media supervisor for the Mankato Public Schools, was among the first to call for crucial research and to recognize that a backlash against technology use in schools was underway:

> Why then is it difficult, if not impossible, to find definitive studies that show the positive impact technology has had on learning? And why is it vital that we in education begin to find ways to assess that impact? . . . A backlash against technology in the popular press has begun.

New York Times author Eric Bronner (1997) also witnessed this turning of popular opinion, stating: "Given the price and the lack of data on the benefits, the conviction that computers are fundamentally altering the modern era, and that therefore children ought to be involved with them at the earliest possible age, is facing an intellectual backlash." When they stop and think about it, most people recognize that even today's potentially powerful technologies are merely tools and that these tools can be used well or badly, and for good purposes or for debatable purposes. Sherry Turkle, a professor at MIT, represents a growing number of bright, hopeful educators who are increasingly cautious about the ways in which technologies are employed. Turkle states: "The possibilities of using this thing poorly so outweigh the chance of using it well, it makes people like us, who are fundamentally optimistic about computers, very reticent" (in Oppenheimer 1997). Author Michael Schrage (Educom Review Staff, 1998) is another voice calling for us to think again about how we use these new tools. He points out how little we actually know about the use of technologies in schools and questions the direction in which many are headed:

> I think that there is an extraordinary amount of experimentation going on in educational technology and in bringing technology to education. Unfortunately there is as much unhealthy experimentation as there is healthy experimentation. My personal experience is that the overwhelming majority of people who want to bring technology and the Internet and interactivity to the schools believe that they are inherently doing a good thing, that they are doing God's work for education, K-12 or beyond. And I think that's a hypothesis to be tested, not a proven fact. I think there are ideologues and idealists in the worst meaning of the phrase and I am afraid it is that bias—the bias that better technology or more technology is an inevitably good thing rather than something to be self-critical and self-skeptical about—that is provoking a backlash against technology in education.

Steve Jobs, founder and former CEO of Apple Computer and long-time advocate of computers in schools, has increasing doubts about technology's ability to help change school and about misguided beliefs that "the use of technology in school" is inherently good. In an interview with *Wired* magazine (Wolf 1996), he asserts that,

> What's wrong with education cannot be fixed with technology. No amount of technology will make a dent. . . . You're not going to solve the problems by putting all knowledge onto CD-ROMs. We can put a Web site in every school— none of this is bad. It's bad only if it lulls us into thinking we're doing something to solve the problem with education. Lincoln did not have a Web site at the log cabin where his parents home-schooled him, and he turned out pretty interesting. Historical precedent shows that we can turn out amazing human beings without technology. Precedent also shows that we can turn out very uninteresting human beings with technology.

In some *classrooms*, also, the backlash has begun. High school English teacher Marilyn Darch says, "Computers are like lollipops that rot your teeth. The kids love them. But once they get hooked, they get bored without all the whoopie stuff. It makes reading a book seem tedious. Books don't have sound effects, and their brains have to do all the work" (in Stoll 1995, 140).

People outside the educational system, like Clifford Stoll (1995), are starting to say things like, "Wait a second. They spent seven million dollars so their students can watch television in school. I'm wondering how many teachers they could hire and how many books they could buy for seven million dollars. What's wrong with this picture?" (p. 117).

But before we pass judgment, we should ask, "What IS 'technology in schools'?" It is a series of very different experiences, employed by very different teachers. For some students it is an amazing, higher-order challenge, whereas for others it seems to be a mindless set of trivial tasks.

For Clifford Stoll, the use of computers in school was obviously an inferior experience. He reports: "We loved them because we didn't have to think for an hour, teachers loved them because they didn't have to teach, and parents loved them because it showed their schools were high-tech. But no learning happened" (in Oppenheimer 1997). But for students at the Centre Learning Community Charter School in State College, Pennsylvania, things couldn't be more different. For them, computer technologies are crucial "mindtools" that allow them to accomplish things they couldn't possibly do otherwise (see http://clccharter.org to understand what these students do with technologies). Their technologies change how they spend their school time *and* their discretionary time, and who they are as thinkers and people— for the better! These two contrasting examples support Alan Lesgold's proposition that the computer is "an amplifier," capable of enhancing both powerful and "thoughtless" practices (in Oppenheimer 1997). We need to work hard to determine which uses are powerful and which are not, through formal, "action research."

WE MUST DEMONSTRATE TECHNOLOGIES' CONTRIBUTIONS TO HIGHER-ORDER OUTCOMES, THROUGH LEGITIMATE RESEARCH

Todd Oppenheimer (1997), a critic of technologies in schools, says, "To be fair, educators on both sides of the computer debate acknowledge that today's tests of students achievement are shockingly crude. They're especially weak in measuring intangibles such as enthusiasm and self-motivation, which do seem evident in Apple's classrooms and other computer-rich schools." But what would an effective assessment of the power of technologies look like?

The Northwest Regional Educational Laboratory (1997) describes its criteria for an effective assessment system, pointing out that such a system would be composed of *several* methods:

> The assessment exercises or tasks should be valid and appropriate representa-
> tions of the standards students are expected to achieve. A sound assessment
> system provides information about a full range of knowledge and abilities
> considered valuable and important for students to learn, and therefore requires
> a variety of assessment methods. Multiple choice tests, the type of assessment
> most commonly used at present, are inadequate to measure many of the most
> important educational outcomes, and do not allow for diversity in learning
> styles or cultural differences. More appropriate tools include portfolios, open
> ended questions, extended reading and writing experiences which include
> rough drafts and revisions, individual and group projects, and exhibitions.

H. K. Suen and J. Parkes (1996) describe a promising approach to assessment known as "Complex Authentic Performance Assessment," which seems to meet the Northwest Regional Educational Laboratory's criteria:

> The typical authentic performance assessment involves the assignment of
> problem-solving projects for which students are given an extended period of
> time to work. There is no single correct answer and there may be many different
> ways of solving the same problem. Students will need to apply knowledge
> across domains and use various available resources. The student is evaluated
> on both the product and the process of the task. That is, the student is evaluated
> on both the outcome of the performance and on how the student arrived at that
> outcome. Typically, the student is required to keep a journal describing his/her
> approach to the problem, getting resources, and solving the problem. . . . An
> authentic performance task may be assigned to a team of students as a team
> project rather than to an individual. Through such team projects, we can assess
> product, process, attitude, and team work.

This approach, and perhaps *only* this approach, will provide the kind of data we need about the real contributions technologies are making to the development of students' cognitive and interpersonal abilities. Yes, it's expensive, but isn't the value of knowing how technologies are contributing, which might have the power to stopping a potentially crippling backlash in its tracks, worth the investment?

One project at Kent State University appears to demonstrate that its leaders understand the type of investigation that will be capable of providing the evidence that is desperately needed. Dale Cook, a summit professor for learning technology and project director at Ohio State University, states: "Ohio is spending three quarters of a billion dollars on technology in classrooms, but no one knows the impact (of technology) on K-12 learning. We're doing things that will get us better answers. Schools can then make better decisions on what technology they need and how to use it." The project is watching students carefully as they use technologies and is producing qualitative research on how these technologies are effecting student development. We need more of that. Lots more.

CONCLUSION

Henry David Thoreau (1960) said in the nineteenth century that, "Our inventions are wont to be pretty toys, which distract our attention from serious things. They are but improved means to an unimproved end." Many of the current uses of technology are "guilty as charged," but many are not. We can't sit back and let critics examine only the weak applications that result in more expensive "business as usual," then talk about the value of modern technologies in schools. We can't be casual observers as naïve reporters describe the powerful applications of learning technologies using methods incapable of revealing the progress students are making that can't be measured on "fill in the blank" or "fill in the bubble" tests. We need to create a body of research using authentic tasks, assessed carefully, in terms of the difficult challenges students can meet, and we need to compare the ability of traditionally taught students and students who have spent years learning while in control of technologies to accomplish these tasks. Then, and only then, will we be able to gauge the power of learning technologies.

Remember, too, that, as innovative educator Chris Held once told me, "Technology can be the Trojan Horse through which change enters the school." Judah L. Schwartz, professor of education at Harvard University, and creator of *The Geometric Supposer* (a revolutionary "turning point" in educational software development), has expressed the hope that the introduction of computers will produce a rethinking of the structure and content of the curriculum (in Bronner 1997).

According to B. O. Taylor and P. Bullard (1995), " 'What gets measured gets done' is a simple maxim in school life. And what gets done fills the school day. Therefore, what states set as curricular criteria and standards for assessment, in large measure, determines what and how teachers teach" (p. 72). They also remind us: "If what gets measured gets done, then it makes sense that what gets measured should be an important focus during any change process. What gets measured establishes the criteria and standards for what really counts" (p. 74). By using modern tools to focus assessment on higher-order learning, we can improve the probability that students will develop higher-order skills, and we can demonstrate the power of learning technologies, earning public support and the ability to make powerful technologies available to *all* students.

REFERENCES

Bronner, E. (1997, November 30). The nation: High-tech teaching is losing its gloss. *New York Times*, p. B2.

California Education Technology Task Force. (1996). *Connect, Compute, and Compete: The Report of the California Education Technology Task Force.* [Online]. Available: http://165.74.253 .64/ftpbranch/retdiv/ccc_task/ccc.htm. (Accessed February 22, 2001).

Cook, Dale, personal communication, Ohio State University, 2000.

Educom Review Staff. (1998). Technology, silver bullets and big lies: Musings on the Information Age with author Michael Schrage. *Educom Review* 33:1. [Online]. Available: http://www.educause .edu/pub/er/review/reviewArticles/33132.html. (Accessed February 22, 2001).

Johnson, D. (1998). The less simple answer to evaluating technology's impact. *School Administrator* 55:4. [Online]. Available: http://www.aasa.org/publications/sa/1998_04/Johnson.htm. (Accessed February 22, 2001).

Moore, D. W. (1995). *The emperor's virtual clothes: The naked truth about Internet culture.* Chapel Hill, NC: Algonquin Books.

Northwest Regional Educational Laboratory. (1997). *Educate America: A Call for Equity in School Reform* (Student Assessment and Testing Section). [Online]. Available: http://www.nwrel.org /cnorse/booklets/educate/11.html. (Accessed February 22, 2001).

Oppenheimer, T. (1997). The computer delusion. *Atlantic Monthly* 280:1. [Online]. Available: http://www .theatlantic.com/issues/97jul/computer.htm. (Accessed February 22, 2001).

Papert, S. (1980). *Mindstorms: Children, computers, and powerful ideas.* New York: Basic Books.

Stoll, C. (1995). *Silicon snake oil: Second thoughts on the information highway.* New York: Doubleday.

Suen, H. K., and Parkes, J. (1996). Challenges and opportunities for student assessment in distance education. *The Distance Education Online Symposium* 6:7. [Online]. Available: http://www.music .ecu.edu/DistEd/EVALUATION.html. (Accessed February 22, 2001).

Taylor, B. O., and Bullard, P. (1995). *The revolution revisited: Effective schools and systemic reform.* Bloomington, IN: Phi Delta Kappa Educational Foundation.

Thoreau, H. D. (1960). *Walden or, life in the woods and on the duty of civil disobedience.* New York: New American Library of World Literature.

White, K. A. (1997a, July 9). School technology captures public's fascination, state dollars. *Education Week.* [Online]. Available: http://www.edweek.com/ew/1997/40tech.h16. (Accessed February 22, 2001).

White, K. A. (1997b, September 3). School technology spending on the rise, survey predicts. *Education Week.* [Online]. Available: http://www.edweek.com/ew/1997/01tech.h17. (Accessed February 22, 2001).

Wolf, G. (1996). Steve Jobs: The next insanely great thing. *Wired* 4:1. [Online]. Available: http://www.wired.com/wired/archive/4.02/jobs.html. (Accessed February 22, 2001).

The Online Database as an Empowering Research Tool

Reshma Sookrajh and Lavine Kowlas
University of Durban-Westville

ABSTRACT

In this article, the modernizing impulse of electronic technology for education is interpreted as liberating in the way in which it creates opportunities to forge research communities. The online multicultural database is presented as a technology as well as a disciplinary, socially embedded research process. This represents an important development in the way in which research on multicultural education is being conceptualized, represented, materialized, and accessed in South Africa. In so doing, this development recognizes the significance of connecting the subject of multicultural education with broader considerations of social justice by locating it within a transformative research unit

Transformative research begins with a recognition of changes in the South African National Education Department for higher education and policy implications for globalization. Thereafter, a description of the multicultural database is presented with a view to locating the multicultural database within a social relations context.

INTRODUCTION

The Internet, and more recently the World Wide Web (WWW), not only have had an impact on commerce and industry, but there are strong indications that it is in the process of changing the way that tertiary education is delivered (Appelborne 1999). C. J. Pilgrim and M. J. Greek (1998, 189) argue that it has the potential to significantly change the face of higher education. Some of the ways in which this is happening are profiled in the following research:

- There is a need to increase access to effective instructional materials in a variety of ways (Kinzie et al. 1996, 59; Oakman 1997, 33–34.)

- Technology support course instruction.

- Technology is redefining the methods we employ in teaching, research, and in communications between teachers and students (Pather, Petkova, and Erwin 1998,2; Pather and Erwin 1999).

- There is a need for higher education to reconceptualize the way teaching and research are being done (Barnard 1997, 30).

- Obtaining education in the early 2000s will be shaped inter alia, by combining computer and communication technologies (Blissmer 1996; Koutoumanos et al.1999, 2079).

- The introduction of computer-mediated communities and computer networks in the traditional educational process of universities has enormous potential.

- The integration of information and communication technologies is inevitable, and the future of education in the Information Society depends on its successful incorporation (Camacho 1998, 266).

- There is a growing trend to use WWW technologies in education (Koutoumanos et al. 1999, 2079; Rosenblum and Healy 1996; Casey 1998, 51)
- The WWW leads to student-centered learning and enhances the teaching and learning process (Mayes 1994; Wells and Anderson 1997, 96). However, a nationwide policy on educational technology needs to be formulated as part of the broad transformation goals for South Africa.

TECHNOLOGY AND EDUCATION POLICY

At a national level, the need for the implementation of new technologies in South Africa became evident after examining the broad transformation goals for higher education outlined in the *Green Paper on Higher Education Transformation* (South Africa (Republic) Department of Education 1996) and the *Education White Paper 3: A Programme for the Transformation of Higher Education* (General Notice, Ministry of Education 1997): "[T]he higher education systems must be transformed to redress past inequalities, to serve a new social order, to meet pressing national needs and to respond to **new realities and opportunities**."

To give effect to this aspect of policy (outlined in the *White Paper*), the National Department of Education is actively engaged in promoting technology-enhanced learning in South Africa. This plan supports the use of emerging technologies in the provision of course materials to learners "made up of predominately of the wide range of information and communications technologies: from the printed book and other printed materials to television and radio to multimedia computers and the Internet" (General Notice, Ministry of Education, 1997).

The national government's vision to transform the higher education system in South Africa is entrenched in the *Education White Paper 3* (General Notice, Ministry of Education 1997). Section 2.63 states more specifically that to meet the challenges of providing such an education system, the Ministry of Education "is committed to help harness the new teaching and learning technologies, especially through its technology enhanced learning initiative (TELI)."

It is evident that one of the pillars on which the transformation of the higher education system in South Africa is based is the provision of a resource-based learning system that promotes student-centered learning using new teaching and learning technologies. Clearly, the aim of the National Ministry was to bring higher education in line with world trends.

HISTORY OF CEREP

Formerly known as the Marco Education Policy Unit (MEPU), the Centre for Educational Research and Educational Policy (CEREP) forms part of the vibrant network of Education Policy Units (EPU) in South Africa, which were originally established by the broad democratic movement to develop progressive educational policies under and against apartheid. Through our programs CEREP is committed to developing capacity among those communities who are most disadvantaged as a consequence of education under apartheid, building democracy by nurturing a critical, open, and vibrant dialog with emerging educational policies and challenging racism, sexism, and classicism throughout the educational system.

CEREP is also engaged in research capacity building by attaching novice researchers, analysts, or evaluators to work with senior colleagues; appointing black and mainly women staff as part of a program that enables and empowers disadvantaged South Africans to conduct research; and providing training through workshops, seminars, and field assignments. CEREP provides systematic training to academic staff, post-graduate students, staff in non-governmental organizations, and officials in national and provincial government departments. At present CEREP has a burgeoning group of post-graduate students (honors in Education, 60; coursework for master's degree, 140; and an ever-increasing number of doctoral students, currently 40).

CEREP tries to illuminate inequalities in education by conducting research on the conditions inside South African classrooms, examining the degree to which policy addresses inequalities in schools, and evaluating the differing impact of policy in different contexts. It is with these issues in mind that the organizing principles for the design of the multicultural database was undertaken.

ORGANIZING PRINCIPLES OF THE DATABASE

The critical framework that was developed to design the multicultural database emerged largely from a legacy of apartheid-style segregated *multiracial education,* which evolved into a system where increasingly the school was understood as a site of cultural (but also gender, religious, and class) diversity. As a consequence, competing conceptions of culture and their corresponding challenges for multicultural curriculum in schools had come to the fore in South Africa (Moore 1994). Education for cultural diversity in South Africa presents itself as a complex arena of policy and practice (Muller 1993; Jansen and Shepherd 1996; Chisholm 1997; Suransky-Dekker 1998; Zafar 1998). Given South Africa's past, it should come as no surprise that the transition from white supremacist rule to multi-racial democracy has yielded a set of pertinent challenges for the field of education. Recent developments, such as the racial tensions between South African youth of Indian and African origins in schools in Pietermaritzburg, Phoenix (outside Durban) or in Vryburg (between South African youth of white Afrikaner and black African origins) confirm that there is a great need and much scope for innovative multicultural and anti-racist educational initia-tives. Indeed, the recent and influential research report of the South African Human Rights Commission confirms the ongoing and unresolved racial tensions in South African schools. Violent clashes at a Pretoria-West school protested a national conference on racism con-vened by the South African Human Rights Commission.

The conceptual framework of this proposed research project originated in the exten-sive post-1970s literature in the so-called developed world (Sleeter 1996; Banks and McGee-Banks 1995; Grant and Tate 1995; Fotiadis 1995; Gourd 1996, 1997; Hernandez 1997) as well as in developing countries (Freire 1997; Jansen 1998; Soudien 1996, 1998), where different emphases developed with respect to research on multicultural education. These research programs led to differing orientations, approaches, and descriptors, such as *anti-racist education, multicultural education,* and *education for diversity,* and to contested concepts such as *identity, race, ethnicity, difference,* and *diversity.*

With these concepts in mind, the dedicated database of multicultural education was designed within the tradition of what could be called *critical studies of multicultural educa-tion.* This means, first of all, that the database does not privilege any one identity construct but focuses broadly on how education policy and practice deals with *difference* (racial, religious, language differences, gender, etc.). Second, the database is interested in understanding which different identities assumed prominence in different countries at a particular historical juncture. For example, *race* may be the primary feature of public contestation in South Africa in the late 1990s, whereas *religion* or *language* may be the key features of such public discourses in schools. Third, how these concepts of difference are understood in each country is explained not in terms of the exoticism of culture or the celebration of tradition, but in relation to issues of power, politics, and privilege.

In terms of South African comparative research, the few examples that can be found tend to place heavy emphasis on American multicultural experiences and only make passing reference to the South African context in terms of what can be learned from the former (Muller 1994; Woodbridge 1994, 1996). In a literature search of over 400 journal articles and books written since 1990 on multicultural and anti-racist education, no comparative research was found systematically comparing a European context to the South African context. This database aimed to fill a gap in the research in this field by building on the few studies that hint at a broader research program examining multicultural education in South Africa and other countries.

The broad framework allowed investigation of issues such as race, gender, class, religion, spatiality (urban/rural), and culture. It also avoided the reduction of "multiculturalism" into a narrow treatment of culture as exotic or indigenous practices dislocated from issues of power, authority, and privilege. Moreover, this broader view allowed for critical dialog given the different ways in which matters of difference emerge, coalesce, and diverge in different social contexts.

A review of the existing software at the unit suggested a lack of global perspective. Manuel Castells (in Alexander 2000, 1) evoked the possibility that South Africa "like its ravaged neighbours" could fall into "the abyss of social exclusion" of the global economy. He further argued that "the real problem for South Africa is how to avoid being pushed aside itself from the harsh competition in the new global economy once its economy is open." Although South Africa, according to Castells (in Alexander 2000, 3) has a more of a chance relative to the rest of the continent to escape marginalization and to enter "the charmed circle of those countries that are technologically and economically salonfahig," it is a risky option.

The firm endeavor to compete in the global marketplace permeates most socioeconomic initiatives undertaken by the South African state. Education policy documents are replete with references to molding learners and institutions into global competitors. The committee appointed to review Curriculum 2005, in analyzing the values and purposes of the curriculum, mentions a dual challenge confronting curriculum designers. The first is the "post-apartheid" challenge, which is to ensure a requisite knowledge, values, and skills base that will, in turn, "provide the conditions for greater social justice, equity and development" (Report of the Review Committee on Curriculum Review 2005 2000, 38). The second is the need to align the curriculum to the "global competitiveness challenge." Arguing for an ontological and epistemological status of the database broadens the distribution of and access to information, reducing the burden of work on those researchers who adopt its rigors and accepts its benefits.

In having a social justice research agenda, the multicultural database assists in epistemologically reconstructing identities in a post apartheid context. Such a database could be used to address the political and social context within which materials are identified and selected. If we were to make claims about the new technical database, we needed to be clear about the different ways in which technologies affect specific groups and reconfigure social relations. The online database becomes empowering because it is treated as more than just a means for selecting, organizing, and collecting bibliographic data: It is a technology that is seen as a social relation by designing it within a social context. C. A. Bowers (1988) refers to the two incompatible cultural myths by those encouraging greater use if computers that "each innovation in computer technology is a further manifestation of social progress, and that technology is inherently neutral." In defense of the multicultural database, the neutrality of the information becomes evident by the way in which it is designed. This meant moving away from individual selectivity to what J. Pickles (1995, ix) refers to as "putative openness of new electronic information media and the rhetoric of 'voice', 'openness' and 'information'." There is no danger of computers eliminating the tacit heuristic forms of knowledge that are at the core of human experiences. There is very little chance of students becoming aware that the data suggest an interpretation of experiences limited by conceptual categories and perspectives of the individual who collects the data. There is very little possibility for the researcher to "detract from serious academic inquiry" (Quinlan 1997, 16) that may "rob" the student of search time (El-Tigi and Branch 1997, 25).

Gathering and selecting multicultural education material is done in a systematic way and is guided by organizing theoretical principles. The multicultural database is a tool and an approach to education information within contemporary social transformation and what passes for democracy. Thus, beyond technical change, the multicultural education database signifies new possibilities for information transfer that attracts a community of users, enabling new capabilities for research action. It fosters new "space" or opportunities for individual and collective research identities by shaping new imagined communities. It further links formerly separate peoples to give rise to a new notion of community that transcend parochial conceptions of people, language, race, gender, and pedagogy, which emerges as a real possibility through the intimate anonymity of electronic communication. The thrust to develop and diffuse institutional, academic, and professional foundations also implies or signals the wider participation by researchers in society. Thus the danger of technology amplifying selected aspects of human experiences while reducing the significance of others (Biraimah 1993, 283) is clearly reduced.

The multicultural database brings together the promise and possibility of collected/sifted information. It creates the stimulus to discover new ways in which researchers can overcome the problem of "distance" and enhance their abilities to exercise control over the knowledge of research into the different aspects of multicultural education. Concerns of integrity are minimal because reduced redundancy increases the likelihood of data integrity.

Online databases have many applications and are able to store bibliographic data that can be provided as an online catalog with searching and ordering capabilities. A database is an orderly collection of information:

> Knowledge that is explicit and can be reduced to discrete bits of data can be stored on a massive scale, manipulated in complex ways that do not distort the sense of accuracy, and recovered in a tireless and efficient manner. These amplification characteristics have been expressed by computer-education experts by the use of such terms as storage, database, and programming (Bowers 1988, 33).

The data are categorized into logical groups that are physically represented by tables, each of which holds a particular category of data. Each category of data is fragmented into separate tables so as to manipulate and locate data more efficiently. Fields are linked to coordinate data from more than one field during a query. The multicultural database has various fields of data (see Figure 1 and Table 1) such as books, tapes, journal articles, policy documents, theses and dissertations, conference papers, newspaper articles, and a current register of all people working in the field of multicultural education (see Table 1). Each field contains bibliographic details and location of materials. The database allows individuals to search information based on keywords or concepts. The fields are further categorized into microfocus areas within the topic of multicultural education, such as language, gender, higher education, race and culture, and science (see Table 2). Relevant data needs to be captured regularly so as to keep abreast of current developments in the field. The database now has 2,000 items captured and stored in the various fields (see Table 2). A catalog has been created so as to view references in a non-computerized form.

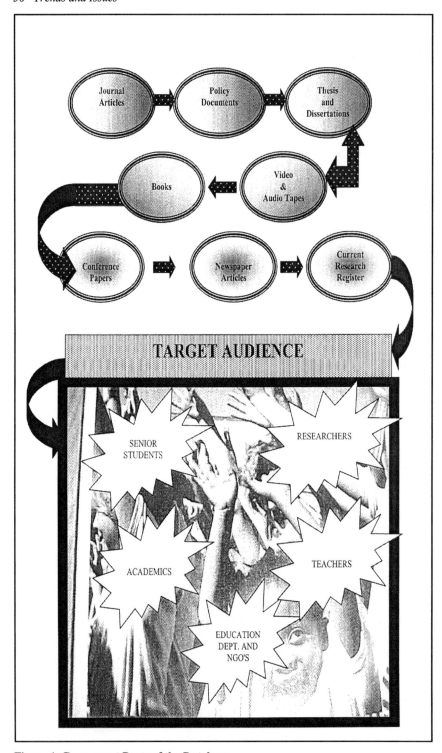

Figure 1. Component Parts of the Database.

DESCRIPTION OF THE DATABASE

As the data in Figure 1 and Tables 1 and 2 indicate, of the 2,000 items on multicultural education, a significant percentage (60.5) is the capture of items from journal articles. The possible reason for this is the availability of and easy access to journal articles. It is also cheaper to retrieve the hard copies of journal items, in comparison to the purchase of books (10 percent), many of which are published outside South Africa.

Table 1: Database Categories

Categories	Percentage
Books	10
Journal articles	60.5
Policy documents	5
Thesis and dissertations	5
Audio/visual tapes	0.5
Conference papers	1
Newspaper articles	10
Register of multicultural interest group	8

Table 2: Themes of Multicultural Education

Themes	Percentage
South African section	25
Race and culture	50
Gender	5
Language	10
Multicultural education and higher education	5
Science technology and multicultural education	5

THE SOUTH AFRICAN SECTION

The South African dedication to multicultural education on the database has revealed that there has been a steady amount of writing on diversity, in several categories:

- Research on open schools
- Desegregation in Colored and Indian schools
- Racial integration of public schools
- Theoretical and political issues in multicultural education

- Challenges to teachers in integrated schools
- Research describing problems of racial integration in schools
- Education, politics, and the law after apartheid
- Examining multicultural curriculum for transformation
- Identifying race as a category of analysis

Perhaps the most significant input on the database has been the report on racial integration and desegregation in South African public schools, commissioned by the Human Science Research Council.

In Table 3, a profile of items covered by the South African media on multicultural education clearly indicates the pervasive incidences of racial conflict and tension during the period 1995–2000. Schools and tertiary institutions continue to be characterized as sites of racial intolerance and discriminatory practices. It is clear that the media privileges "race" as a category of analysis, and in doing so sublimates other categories of oppression such as gender, language, special needs, ethnicity, religion, and class.

In most of these news items, it is argued that post-apartheid administrative, political, and policy bungling are major causes of school racial violence, in the absence of sustained transformative agendas.

Table 3: Media Items on Multicultural Education

1995	1996	1997	1998	1999	2000
Schools undergo racial revision	Admission procedures to marginalize black students	Student segregation/ polarization	Gender equality	Success stories of achieving schools, racial/ general	Language policy concerns
Integration accelerated	Language testing for admission	Notions of standards	Teacher redeployment	Crisis at tertiary institutes	Inadequate facilities
Religious intolerance	Racism in schools	Government cutbacks			Review of Curriculum 2005
Racial clashes	Violent racial clashes	Teacher redeployment to rural schools			Racial clashes at schools
Race-related gang riots	Violent racial clashes in tertiary institutes	Racial clashes/ tensions			National racism conference
Language policy	Staff/student racism	Curriculum 2005 concerns			Gender concerns
Student/staff racism		Implementation			
		High fees marginalize Blacks			
Tertiary institutes racial violence		AIDS and race concerns			

RACE AND CULTURE

The database items on race and culture refer generally to the real challenge in racism and how racism works side by side with assertion of different cultural identities. This is done within a social critical education context. In these items, the notion of racism is constructed by different societies in different ways; it is historically specific and not necessarily directed against the same group of people at all times and in all places. The different media items understand culture not only as entrenching differences but as failing to explore the effect that power imbalances and issues such as class or material living conditions have on people. Within this theme, a sizable corpus explore the relationship between science technology and anti-racist education.

SCIENCE AND MULTICULTURAL EDUCATION

In this category, issues of gender, race, pedagogy, culture, and language feature prominently. It also covers articles on approaches by teachers to implement global and indigenous science curriculum systems that focus on the learner's experience as integral to learning. Items regarding cultural and linguistic bias of science education in teaching and learning are also located within the theory of scientific knowledge as socially constructed.

LANGUAGE

Largely, the writings on language present language as a cultural dynamic of human society and its social impact within multilingual settings. Items dealing with indigenous language rights and transmission of culture are located within the democratic language planning theme. At a micro level of inquiry, explorations of meaning in the multilingual classroom also feature within a discourse analysis context.

GENDER

Of the many items on gender, practical suggestions are made to address issues of gender equity and change in gender composition of whole school reform. Science and gender bias are repeated issues. Of special note is an increasing number of items on gender and inequality in higher education.

HIGHER EDUCATION AND MULTICULTURAL EDUCATION

Within this theme, it would appear that items on anti-racist curriculum in higher education feature prominently. Gender and language disparities among Blacks and minority groups in higher education are also tabulated. There are also selected items on preservice teacher preparation and experiences and attitudes of preservice teachers for culturally diverse sites.

CONCLUSION

In analyzing the database, it can be said that the database privileges "race and culture" as critical areas of research in multicultural education. This is also true for the South African section of the database. This is not surprising given the history of colonialism followed by apartheid and the strongly racialized distribution of power. Race is presented in items that view it as a social construct, "the use of which was part of the process of domination and oppression under apartheid, and its deconstruction is implicit in the notion of a non-racial society" (Smith 1999,161).

Heim (1992, 59) has argued that "cyberspace is more than a breakthrough in electronic media or in computer interface design. With its virtual environments and simulated worlds, "cyberspace is a . . . tool for examining our very sense of reality." In an attempt to endorse the independent character of the multicultural database, an examination of the nature and its uses for researchers was undertaken. It is evident that the multicultural database provides access to more and better information by identifying, collating, and homogenizing issues, which allows for critical research in multicultural education.

REFERENCES

Alexander, N. (2000). Manuel Castells and the New South Africa. Unpublished monograph.

Appelborne, P. (1999). Education.Com. *The New York Times, Education Life Supplement* 148, 26–29, 36–37.

Banks, J. A., and McGee-Banks, C., eds. (1995). *Handbook of multicultural education.* New York: Macmillan.

Barnard, J. (1997). The World Wide Web and higher education: The promise of virtual universities and online libraries. *Educational Technology* 37:3, 30–34.

Biraimah, K. (1993). The non-neutrality of educational computer software. *Computers and Education* 20:4, 283–290.

Blissmer, R. H. (1996). *Introducing computers—Concepts, systems and applications.* New York: John Wiley & Sons.

Bowers, C. A. (1988). *The cultural dimensions of educational computing: Understanding the non-neutrality of technology.* New York: Teachers College Press.

Camacho, M. L. A. S. M. (1998). Virtual reality, a tool for a new educational paradigm. *Educational Media International* 35:4, 266–271.

Casey, D. (1998). Learning "from" or "through" the Web: Models of Web-based education. *SIGSCE Bulletin* 30:3, 51–54.

Chisholm, L. (1997). The restructuring of South African education and training in comparative context. In P. Kallaway, G. Kruss, A. Fataar,. and G. Donn, eds., *Education under apartheid.* Cape Town, South Africa: UCT Press.

El-Tigi, M., and Branch, R. M. (1997). Designing for interaction, learner control and feedback during Web-based learning. *Educational Technology* 37:5, 23–29.

Fotiadis, K. (1995). Multiculturalism in education: An Australian perspective. *Multicultural Teaching* 13:2, 35–37.

Freire, P. (1997). *Pedagogy of the oppressed* (rev. 20th anniv. ed.). New York: Continuum Press.

General Notice, Ministry of Education. (1997). *Education White Paper 3: A Programme for the Transformation of Higher Education.* No. 1196. [Online]. Available: http://www.polity.org.za /govdocs/white_papers/educwp3.html. (Accessed February 22, 2001).

Gourd, K. (1996, April 10). *What does a teacher know? Equity pedagogy from a liberatory perspective.* Paper presented at the AGM of the American Educational Association, New York.

Gourd, K. (1997, March 28). *Tensions between discipline-based content instruction and teaching for social justice.* Paper presented at the AGM of the American Educational Association, Chicago.

Grant, C. A., and Tate, W. F. (1995). Multicultural education through the lens of multicultural education research literature. In J. A. Banks and C. McGee-Banks (eds.), *Handbook of multicultural education.* New York: Macmillan.

Heim, M. (1992). The erotic ontology of cyberspace. In M. Benedikt (ed.), *Cyberspace: First steps.* Cambridge, MA: MIT Press.

Hernandez, H. (1997). *Teaching in multilingual classrooms: A teacher's guide to context, process, and content.* London: Merrill Prentice Hall.

Jansen, J. (1995). Our teachers see children, not colour: The politics of diversity in South African schools. In M. Cross, Z. Mkwanzai, and G. Kline (eds.), *Unity, diversity, and reconciliation: Debate on the politics of curriculum in South Africa*. Cape Town, South Africa: SAPES Trust; and London: Trentham Books.

Jansen, J. (1998). Critical theory and the school curriculum. In P. Higgs (ed.), *Metatheory in educational theory and practice*. London: Heinemann.

Jansen, J., and Shepherd, N. (1996, Spring). Multicultural education: Research trends in South African education. *RreFF Review*.

Kinzie, M. B., Larsen, V. A., Burch, J. B., and Baker, S. M. (1996). Frog dissection via the World Wide Web. *Educational Technology and Development* 44:2, 56–59.

Koutoumanos, A., Retalis, S., Sgouropoulou, C., Skordalakis, E., and Tsamasfyros, G. (1999). Requirements specification of a Web-based educational system in higher education. In K. Despotis and C. Zopounidis (eds.), *Proceedings of the 5th International Conference of the Decisions Science Institute* (Athens, Greece).

Mayes, T. (1994). *Hypermedia and CognitiveTools*. [Online]. Available: http://www.icbl.hw.ac.uk/ctl/mayes/paper9.html. (Accessed December 12, 1997).

Moore, B. (1994). Multicultural education in South Africa : Some theoretical perspectives. *Perspectives in Education* 15:2, 239–262.

Muller, J. (1993). Difference, identity, and community: American perspectives on the curriculum. In N. Taylor, ed., *Inventing knowledge: Contests in curriculum construction*. Cape Town, South Africa: Maskew Miller Longman.

Oakman, L. (1997). *The computer triangle*. New York: John Wiley & Sons.

Pather, S., and Erwin, C. J. (1999). *Usage of Web-based technologies for course delivery at technikons and universities in KZN*. Proceedings of the 4th KZN Research Conference in Computer Science, Information Systems & Software Engineering, ML Sultan Technikon, Durban.

Pather, S., Petkova, O., and Erwin, G. I. (1998). *An investigation of the Internet usage at technikons and universities in Kwa Zulu Natal*. Proceedings of the 28th Conference of the South African Computing Lecturers' Association, University of Stellenbosch, Stellenbosch.

Pickles, J., ed. (1995). *Ground truth. The social implications of geographic information systems*. New York, London: Guilford Press.

Pilgrim, C. J., and Greek, M. J. (1998). The Swinebume On-Line Educational Project. *SIGSCE Bulletin* 30:3, 189–192.

Quinlan, L. A. (1997). Creating a classroom kaleidoscope with the World Wide Web. *Educational Technology* 37:3, 15–22.

Report of the Review Committee on Curriculum 2005. (2000, May 31). A. *South African curriculum for the twenty-first century*. Pretoria, South Africa: Ministry of Education, Department of Tertiary Education.

Sleeter, C. E. (1996). *Multicultural education as social activism*. Albany, NY: State University of New York Press.

Smith, D. (1999). Social justice and the ethics of development in post-apartheid South Africa. *Ethics, Place and Environment* 2:2, 157–177.

Soudien, C. (1996). Race, culture and curriculum development in the USA. *Curriculum Studies* 4:1, 43–65.

Soudien, C. (1998). "We know why we're here": The experience of African children in a "coloured" school in Cape Town, South Africa. *Race, Ethnicity and Education* 1:1, 7–29.

South Africa (Republic) Department of Education. (1996). *Green Paper on Higher Education Transformation*. [Online]. Available: http://www.polity.org.za/govdocs/green_papers/hegreenp.html. (Accessed February 22, 2001).

Suransky-Dekker, A. C. (1998). Portraits of Black schooling in South Africa. *Qualitative Studies in Education*.

Wells, J. G., and Anderson, D. K. (1997). Learners in a telecommunications course: Adoption, diffusion, and stages of concern. *Journal of Research on Computing in Education* 30:1, 83–105.

Woodbridge, N. B. (1994). Towards a teacher-training model for multicultural education: Evaluating a California course utilising the "PEDAGOGICS" structure. *South African Journal of Education* 14:2, 65–68.

Woodbridge, N. B. (1996). Utilising the "CHROMATICS" structure to understand Afrocultural expression and its implications for schooling: An American perspective. *South African Journal of Education* 6:2, 99–103.

Zafar, S. (1998). *School-based initiatives to address racial and cultural diversity in newly integrating public schools*. EPU Research Report, Education Policy Unit, University of Natal.

Part Two
School Library Media Section

Introduction

Anyone who paid attention to the world of school library media in the year 2000 noticed several prominent national trends and themes. Across the United States, school systems reported vacancies in media centers and difficulties in hiring new media specialists. *US News and World Report* published an article marking this shortage (Lord 2000), describing the flight of media specialists to the business world, where salaries were higher and information skills in demand. Likewise, severe shortages appeared among faculty of colleges teaching school library media students. These shortages reflect the overall aging of the librarian population: 45 percent of librarians are expected to reach retirement age between 1990 and 2010 (St. Lifer 2000). Thus, due to a wave of retirements in the coming years and decreases in numbers of new people entering the profession, the shortage in media specialists will continue and likely worsen. A shortfall of 25,000 is projected for 2005 (Lord 2000). One fear verbalized by many is that this predicted shortfall may lead to feelings among school administrators and policymakers that school librarians are expendable, given the difficulty of hiring them.

What can be done about this looming shortage? One suggestion offered at the Treasure Mountain conference in Birmingham, Alabama, in late 1999 was distance learning. Available in many configurations, distance learning is a technical wave currently sweeping through all educational venues, a trend that shows no sign of peaking yet. Distance learning has been suggested as one way to provide education to greater numbers of people, simultaneously alleviating travel and scheduling factors. Perhaps distance learning will figure in the struggle to prepare more media specialists. Virtual degree programs preparing media specialists are appearing in many parts of the United States and the world.

A related technology issue is the use of the Internet in K–12 education. Although the nation's schools are becoming increasingly wired due to local, state, and federal initiatives, controversy roils over how the Internet is to be used in classrooms. One major issue amounts to the old one of censorship: How much freedom will be given to children in their searches of the Internet for information, given its "bad neighborhoods" of pornography, hate sites, and misinformation? In 2000, debates raged over whether libraries should install filtering software. In extreme cases, librarians were accused of wanting children to see obscene material. On a pedagogical level, teachers discussed ways that the Internet could support curriculum as the use of telecommunications spread to more and more classrooms.

In addition to these issues, media specialists continued to struggle with roles. *Information Power* (AASL/AECT, 1998) prescribed four roles for media specialists: instructional partner, teacher, information specialist, and program administrator. Growing levels of technology in schools without adequate levels of support continued to vie for already busy media specialists' time. Also, teachers need training in how to use this technology, a clear priority for staff development, placing yet another demand on the media specialist's time. The phenomenal popularity of reading management software like *Accelerated Reader* (Advantage Learning Systems, 1999) exacerbated this problem, with some media specialists reporting that they spend most of their time circulating books and shelving them according to reading level.

How can media specialists possibly accomplish all the tasks set forth for them by *Information Power*?

Certainly, the chapters in this section cannot solve these complex issues. However, perhaps they can lend some insight into them. Christina Dunn's article, "Assessment of the Role of School Libraries in Support of Educational Reform," describes a large-scale statistical survey of conditions in schools across the United States, revealing staffing, resource, and service issues. The chapter by Sugar and Kester, "Adding Networking Skills to One's 'Tool Box'," another survey, reveals the need for sophisticated technological training among media specialists. Mary Alice Anderson's chapter, "The Media Specialist and Staff Development," further highlights the need for inservice training and suggests practical strategies for conducting it.

The next cluster of chapters addresses the struggle to implement *Information Power* roles. Kay Bishop's "Library Power and Student Learning" compares several implementations of the DeWitt Wallace-Reader's Digest initiative, targeted at improving library service through emphasis on the roles recommended by *Information Power*. Melissa Gibson's chapter, "It's Funner Now!" explores a combination of the information specialist and teacher roles as she describes her construction of a tool to help fifth graders conduct research projects. Jinx Watson's chapter, "Snapshots of a Teen Internet User," also addresses the information specialist role through exploring in depth a young man's Internet use. This chapter also deals, to a degree, with the concern about what teens do when left to explore the Internet on their own.

Finally, the Recesso et al. chapter, "From Bricks and Mortar to Clicks and Modems: The Redesign of a Graduate Program," addresses the media specialist shortage issue. It tells of one institution's efforts to start a virtual education specialist degree program in instructional technology. This piece may help other programs that are considering mounting similar efforts to ameliorate the media specialist shortage.

Altogether, the chapters in this section present a glimpse of issues in school library media practice in 2000 and some thoughts on how to deal with some of them in the years to come.

Mary Ann Fitzgerald

REFERENCES

Advantage Learning Systems. (1999). *The Accelerated Reader*, version 4.0.

American Association of School Librarians and Association for Educational Technology. (1998). *Information power*. Chicago: American Library Association.

Lord, M. (2000, June 6). Where have all the librarians gone? They've gone to dot coms, one by one. *US News and World Report*.

St. Lifer, E. (2000). The boomer brain drain: The last of a generation? *Library Journal* 125:8, 38–42.

Assessment of the Role of School and Public Libraries in Support of Educational Reform

Christina Dunn
Director, Collections and Technical Services
National Center for Education Statistics

Although school libraries have always viewed themselves as an essential part of the education establishment, their capacity for having an impact on education, and especially current educational reform efforts, is almost unknown. Since the National Education Goals were established in 1990, the library community has shown increased interest in demonstrating how school libraries support the goals in particular and educational reform in general.

Research into how school libraries are responding to the Goals 2000 initiatives has the potential to shape the future role of libraries as education and information providers. Regardless of the current level and type of participation, it behooves policymakers and the library and education communities to know more about the role of school libraries in supporting education to plan for and direct resources and to inform practice.

In fiscal year (FY) 1994, the U.S. Department of Education began an assessment of the role of school and public libraries in educational reform. Westat, Inc., in cooperation with the American Library Association, conducted the $1.3 million study funded under the Secretary's Fund for Innovation in Education. The following report is taken from *Assessment of the Role of School and Public Libraries in Support of Educational Reform,* a document prepared by Joan Michie and Bradford Chaney of Westat, Inc. for the U.S. Department of Education in 1999.

PURPOSE OF THE ASSESSMENT

Although education has been considered the primary purpose of school libraries, public libraries also have viewed education as an important part of their mission. Since the publication of *A Nation at Risk,* a report by the National Commission on Excellence in Education (1983), which warned of problems in the American educational system, the library community has wanted to be part of the reform efforts that were a response to the report.

Libraries must operate in the context of changes within educational systems and the greater society. Among the educational reforms that have occurred since *A Nation at Risk* was published are the development of the National Education Goals and curriculum standards for each of the content areas. Societal changes include advances in technology and the accompanying information explosion. As a result of these changes, school and public libraries find themselves in the position of reexamining their resources, staff skills, programs, and services.

The purpose of the Assessment of the Role of School and Public Libraries in Support of Educational Reform was to find out how school and public libraries were performing as education providers and how well they were responding to the country's urgent demands for school improvement. It was intended to inform researchers, policymakers, and practitioners about six key issues:

- To what extent are school and public libraries contributing to education reform, and to what extent can they contribute?

- What programs and services are school and public libraries providing to meet the needs of preschool and elementary and secondary (K–12) education providers?

- How well do these services and programs meet the needs of preschool and K–12 education providers?

- Do school and public libraries have the capacity—human and information resources, technology, and facilities—to respond adequately to identified needs and to support systemic reform?

- What new technologies are promoting student opportunity to learn by improving services and resources in school and public libraries?

- What can we learn from successful school and public library programs and services designed to support preschool and K–12 education? Can these programs serve as models for the improvement of all school and public libraries? What are the barriers to effective services and programs?

The assessment included a literature review; two national surveys; 10 case studies involving both school and public libraries; and four commissioned papers on selected topics—implications of school reform approaches for school library media services; school and public library relationships; preschool education through public libraries; and independent reading and school achievement. The national school library survey is the focus of this report. Highlights include staffing, the use of libraries by students and teachers, the amount and adequacy of materials and resources, programs and services, availability of technology, access to the Internet, education reform, and cooperation between school and public libraries. Although this report highlights the results of the survey of public and private school libraries, the results of that part of the public library survey having to do with cooperation with schools also has been included. It would not be possible to discuss school and public library cooperation without presenting both points of view.

THE NATIONAL SURVEY

Two national surveys were conducted in 1997. One was sent to public library outlets, and the other went to library media centers in both public and private schools. The sample size for each survey was approximately 1,000 and was representative of the specific library community. The sample of public schools was selected from the U.S. Department of Education's National Center for Education Statistics (NCES) Common Core of Data Public School Universe File; the sample of private schools from the NCES Private School Survey Universe File; and the sample of public libraries from the most recent NCES Public Library Universe System File. Response rates on the surveys were 86.5 percent, private schools; 90.6 percent, public schools; and 93.1 percent, public libraries, with an overall response rate of 90.1 percent. All response rates exceeded the NCES requirement. All specific statements of comparison made in this report have been tested for statistical significance through t-tests and are significant at the 95 percent confidence level or better.

On the public and private school surveys, data were collected from individual school library media centers (LMCs) rather than school systems. Survey findings for school library media centers are shown for all school libraries and by the following characteristics:

Public

Educational level—elementary, secondary

Size of school—less than 300, 300 to 499, 500 to 749, 750 or more

Free lunch—less than 20 percent, 20 to 49 percent, 50 percent or more

Region—Northeast, Southeast, Central, West

Private

Educational level—elementary, secondary; combined

Size of school—less than 150, 150 to 299, 300 to 499, 500 or more

Religious affiliation—Catholic, other religious, nonsectarian

Schools with School Library Media Centers

In 1996–1997, 98 percent of public schools and 78 percent of private schools had school library media centers. In spring 1997, a total of 44.8 million public school students and 4.3 million private school students attended schools with library media centers. The total number of schools with LMCs was 75,460 public schools and 16,569 private schools.

Student Use

Students made an average of 598 visits to the school library in public schools and 257 visits in private schools during a typical week in 1997. For both public and private schools, the number of visits was proportional to the school enrollment, with an average of one student visit for each student enrolled. However, this statistic does not imply that all students visited the library every week: Students who visited the library more than once in a typical week were counted once for each visit.

Almost three-fourths (70 percent) of all public school LMCs reported that they used flexible scheduling, although it was often used in combination with regular scheduling. Half of all libraries (50 percent) said that all classes were regularly scheduled, and 21 percent said that some but not all classes were regularly scheduled. Most secondary school LMCs (95 percent) used flexible scheduling, as did 60 percent of elementary school libraries. Regularly scheduling all classes primarily occurred at the elementary level, where it was used by two-thirds (66 percent) of the school libraries, compared to only one-eighth (12 percent) of secondary school libraries.

Staffing

School library media centers had a total of 249,338 staff at public schools and 68,991 staff at private. Most of the LMC staff worked part time, accounting for about 65 percent (160,901) in public schools and 87 percent (59,772) in private schools. The full-time staff at public schools were most typically state-certified library media specialists (56 percent); 11 percent were professional staff who were not certified as library media specialists and 33 percent were other paid employees (see Figure 1). The part-time staff were most typically volunteers (69 percent), although 12 percent were professional staff (either certified or not) and 18 percent were other paid employees. Private schools typically do not face the type of certification requirements found in public schools. Thus, only 29 percent of full-time library staff at private schools were certified as library media specialists.

Overall, 78 percent of public schools had a state-certified library media specialist, with an average of 0.7 state-certified librarians per school. If all staff are included, public school libraries had an average of 0.9 professional staff (including non-certified professional staff), 0.6 other paid employees, and 0.7 adult volunteers. On average, there were 648 enrolled students per professional librarian and 397 per paid staff. School enrollments appear to be a good indicator of the workload of school librarians, because the ratios of weekly patronage of the library to the number of staff were roughly the same as the ratios of enrollment to the number of staff (653 in weekly patronage per professional librarian, and 400 in weekly patronage per paid staff).

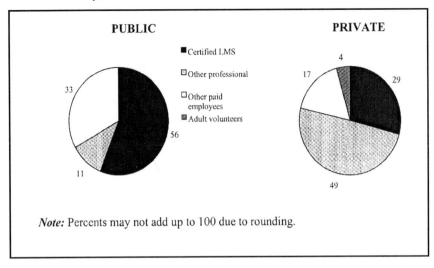

Figure 1. Staffing at School Library Media Centers (LMCs) by School Type and Type of Staff.

An estimated 11 percent of public schools with LMCs had neither a full-time nor a part-time librarian, an absence more frequent at the elementary than at the secondary level (15 percent versus 3 percent). However, such schools typically did have an aide at the library, with only 1 percent of all schools with a library media center having neither a librarian nor an aide. Private schools followed a different pattern. About one-third had no librarian (32 percent), and one-fifth (22 percent) had neither a librarian nor an aide.

Among public schools, 22 percent lacked a full- or part-time library media specialist who was state certified, and 39 percent lacked a full-time, state-certified library media specialist. Because the smallest public schools were the most likely to lack a full-time, state-certified library media specialist (73 percent versus 15 to 42 percent for larger schools), the percentage of students in schools without a full-time, state-certified library media specialist was lower than the percentage of schools without one (27 percent versus 39 percent).

School LMCs in the Southeast were more fully staffed than were those in other parts of the country. Only 2 percent in the Southeast did not have a librarian, compared to 10 to 19 percent for other regions. Only 5 percent of the school libraries in the Southeast did not have a full- or part-time, state-certified library media specialist, compared to 20 to 35 percent for other regions, and only 9 percent did not have a full-time, state-certified specialist, compared to 37 to 51 percent for other regions.

Collections

Public school library media centers had a total of 679 million items in their holdings in 1997, primarily consisting of 622 million books. These holdings constituted an average of 15.5 books and 17.7 items per student. The ratio of books and holdings to average weekly patronage was roughly the same (15.4 and 17.5, respectively). Libraries at the larger schools on average had more books per school (13,219 in schools with 750 or more students versus 5,424 in schools with fewer than 300 students), but fewer books per student (11.4 versus 27.6).

The school LMCs were asked about the adequacy of their holdings in supporting seven instructional areas: reading/English, mathematics, science, social studies, foreign languages, arts, and health and safety. For the first four of these areas, they were asked about the overall collection, print materials, video and other audiovisual (AV) materials, and computer software; for the last three, they were asked about the overall collection only.

The results varied greatly by subject area. Reading/English was the best area, with about one-fourth of public school libraries (24 percent) saying the overall collection was excellent and 57 percent saying it was adequate (see Figure 2). For social studies, 19 percent of the public school libraries said the holdings were excellent, and an additional 54 percent said they were adequate. Results for science were about the same as for social studies. In the other four subject areas, no more than 11 percent described the overall collection as excellent, although for three of the four areas, a majority did describe it as either adequate or excellent. Foreign languages showed a somewhat different pattern, with 23 percent of public school libraries reporting that materials in foreign languages were neither available nor needed; this primarily occurred at elementary rather than secondary schools (31 percent versus 6 percent).

For those four subject areas where data are available, public school libraries considered their print materials to be at a similar level of adequacy as their overall collection. However, they were frequently dissatisfied with their video/AV materials and computer software. Depending on the subject area, between 49 and 58 percent said their computer software was either inadequate or not available but needed, and between 38 and 52 percent said their video and other audiovisual materials were either inadequate or not available but needed.

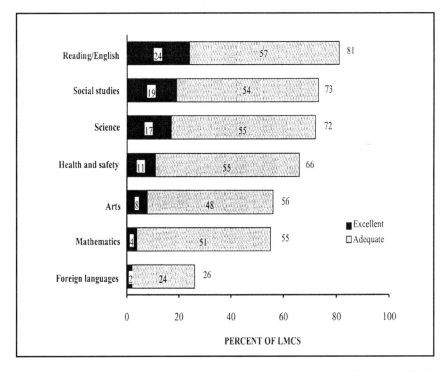

Figure 2. Percent of Public School Library Media Centers (LMCs) Reporting Their Overall Collection Holdings Were Excellent or Adequate, by Instructional Area.

School library media centers also were asked about the adequacy of their resources in five other areas. Approximately two-thirds of the LMCs at public schools said that their resources were either adequate or excellent with regard to picture books/easy readers (66 percent), high interest-low vocabulary (63 percent), and multicultural education (62 percent) (see Figure 3). By contrast, only 29 percent described their parenting materials as adequate or excellent, and only 19 percent described English as a second language as excellent or adequate. Generally, in each area about one-third or more felt that their resources were inadequate (30 to 45 percent, except for picture books/easy readers at 15 percent). One exception to the general pattern was resources for English as a second language, where approximately half of the library media centers (47 percent) said the category was not applicable.

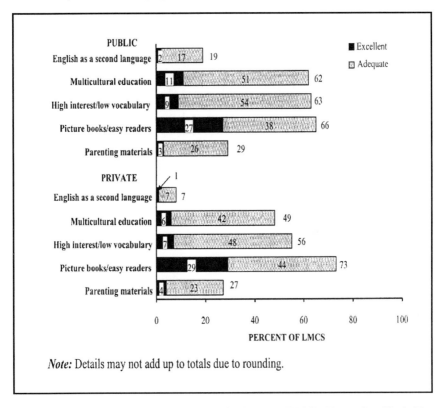

Figure 3. Percent of School Library Media Centers (LMCs) Reporting Their Resources Were Excellent or Adequate in Meeting the School's Needs, by Subject Area.

Except for picture books/easy readers, LMCs at private schools differed from those at public schools by more often saying that the category was not applicable. For example, 82 percent said that English as a second language was not applicable (compared with 47 percent for public schools), and 44 percent said that parenting materials were not applicable (compared with 27 percent).

Equipment/Technology

Overall, 78 percent of public school library media centers had a telephone in 1997. Other types of communications equipment were less common; 20 percent had a fax machine and 8 percent a TTY or other equipment for persons with disabilities.

Stand-alone computers in school libraries were more common than telephones, both in public schools (88 percent versus 78 percent) and in private schools (71 percent versus 51 percent). Some of the ways in which computers were set up and used include providing periodical indexes, encyclopedias, or other references on CD-ROM (77 percent); an automatic circulation system (61 percent); a computer with a shared line (51 percent); a computer with a dedicated line (48 percent); networked automated catalogs (41 percent); stand-alone automated catalogs (23 percent); and online database searching (23 percent).

School LMCs also often had various kinds of television equipment and services. At public schools, 92 percent had one or more VCRs, 72 percent had cable television, and 50 percent had a video laser disk player. Less common were closed circuit television (29 percent), a satellite dish (27 percent), and a television studio (8 percent).

School LMCs often can obtain computer access to the catalogs of other libraries, either through the Internet or through other networks. At public schools, 28 percent of library media centers could access the catalogs of a college or university library, 26 percent could access a public library, 20 percent could access other school library media centers, and 15 percent could access a community college library.

Access to and Use of the Internet

At public schools, the factors that most often constituted a major or moderate barrier to library media centers' access to the Internet were an insufficient amount of funds allocated for technology (72 percent), staff time (67 percent), telephone lines (58 percent), telecommunications equipment (57 percent), computers (56 percent), and training (49 percent) (see Figure 4).

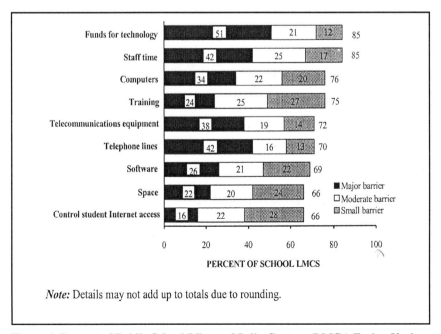

Note: Details may not add up to totals due to rounding.

Figure 4. Percent of Public School Library Media Centers (LMCs) Facing Various Barriers to Maximizing Internet Access.

Programs and Services

The services that library media centers at public schools said they provided frequently were reference assistance to students (93 percent) and reference assistance to teachers (73 percent) (see Figure 5). No other service was provided frequently by more than 40 percent of the libraries.

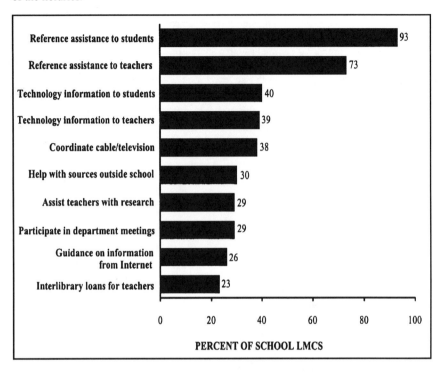

Figure 5. Services Provided Most Frequently by Public School Library Media Centers (LMCs).

Some tasks by their nature may be conducted regularly but not frequently. For example, even if working with teachers on textbook selection is an important role, it may be episodic rather than frequent. From this perspective, it is also useful to find out which services were sometimes provided as a way of establishing the range of activities in which library media centers are involved. Almost all traditional services were provided by LMCs at least sometimes for most public schools: reference assistance; interlibrary loan; assisting teachers with research projects for students; working on curriculum issues and serving on curriculum development teams; participating in grade-level or department/term meetings; coordinating in-school production of materials; and providing information about technology, including coordinating training about technology integration. The only instances where a majority of libraries reported never providing a service were serving on site-based management teams (65 percent), coordinating textbook selection (73 percent), and coordinating distance learning staff (73 percent). In addition, there were three activities in which close to half (i.e., 40 percent or more) of LMCs were never involved: coordinating video production (42 percent), coordinating access to the Internet (47 percent), and providing guidance on evaluating information from the Internet (46 percent).

In general, library media centers at private schools were less likely to provide each service than were public schools. For example, the two most frequently provided services were the same at private schools as at public schools, but the percentage providing those services was lower (78 percent versus 93 percent with regard to reference assistance to students, and 41 percent versus 73 percent with regard to reference assistance to teachers).

The relatively low level of public school libraries' involvement in site-based management teams was due, in part, to the fact that not all schools had site-based management. Among those public schools with site-based management, slightly over half (56 percent) of the LMCs had staff serving on the site-based management teams.

The services provided by school library media centers often varied depending on the subject area involved (see Table 1). In general, public school LMCs were most often involved in working with teachers in reading/English, social studies, and science, and they were least involved in foreign languages and mathematics. For example, about half (54 percent) of the public school library media centers reported working frequently with teachers in selecting and evaluating library media resources in reading/English, 43 percent in social studies, 36 percent in science, and 12 to 22 percent in other subject areas (see Table 1). Of the four listed services, the most commonly provided service was working with teachers in selecting and evaluating library media resources (12 to 54 percent), whereas it was less common for library media centers to work with teachers in curriculum development (3 to 17 percent), collaboratively teach curriculum units with classroom teachers (2 to 21 percent), or collaboratively evaluate curriculum units with classroom teachers (1 to 8 percent).

Table 1: Percent of Public School Library Media Centers That Frequently Provided Various Services to Classroom Teachers in 1996–1997, by Subject Area

Subject	Works with teachers in selecting and evaluating library media resources	Works with teachers on curriculum development	Collaboratively teaches curriculum units with classroom teachers	Collaboratively evaluates curriculum units with classroom teachers
Reading/English	54	17	21	8
Mathematics	15	4	3	2
Science	36	9	9	3
Social studies	43	13	14	5
Foreign language	12	3	2	1
Arts	19	5	4	2
Health and safety	22	6	4	2

Close to two-thirds (63 percent) of public schools with LMCs had an information skills curriculum. Most typically, the way in which those schools provided the instruction was by always integrating the instruction into other curriculum areas (61 percent); 11 percent always provided the instruction through an information skills course, and 28 percent used a combination of both means. The curriculum was generally developed by either the district (47 percent) or the school (36 percent) rather than by the state (17 percent). At private schools, the curriculum was primarily developed at the school (87 percent).

School library media centers were asked about eight other types of services, with the focus on how much those services were used (see Figure 6). Two services stood out as being available at a majority of public school libraries: services for children with disabilities (80 percent) and extended hours before or after school (59 percent). These services also received the greatest use, with 12 to 14 percent of public school LMCs indicating heavy usage and 28 to 40 percent indicating moderate usage (compared with 4 to 31 percent indicating heavy or moderate usage in the other areas). Additionally, tutoring was offered at about half of the public school libraries (47 percent), with 9 percent indicating heavy usage and 22 percent indicating moderate usage.

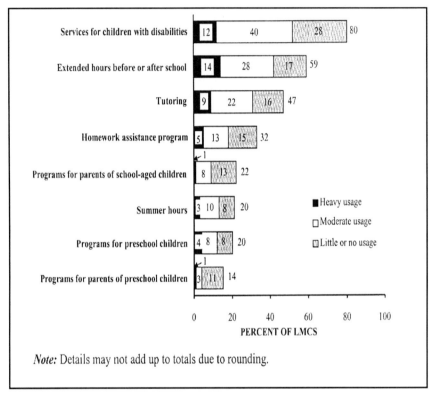

Note: Details may not add up to totals due to rounding.

Figure 6. Percent of Public School Library Media Centers (LMCs) Providing Various Services, and the Rate of Usage of Those Services.

Needs

School libraries may conduct formal needs assessments or perform other types of evaluations of the materials and services they provide. Overall, 38 percent of public school libraries and 42 percent of private school libraries said they had conducted a needs assessment in the previous two years. Some other common ways in which public school LMCs had evaluated their materials over the previous two years were informal evaluations involving only school staff (73 percent), a written survey of school staff (37 percent), an evaluation conducted by a district evaluator (23 percent), and an evaluation involving students or parents (21 percent). Counting these other types of evaluations, 79 percent of public school library media centers had conducted at least one type of evaluation in the previous two years, and 76 percent of those made changes based on the evaluations.

Of those public schools that had conducted needs assessment, the most common needs were for more computer equipment (92 percent), more materials (90 percent), rewiring the LMC (67 percent), more staff training (60 percent), and more library staff (56 percent) (see Figure 7). With respect to the first two of these needs, a large majority of schools reported having made changes (71 percent for more materials and 70 percent for more computer equipment). In the remaining areas, fewer than half of the schools had made changes. However, in four other areas (rewiring the LMC, adding a telephone line, flexible scheduling, and more staff training), more than half of the schools that identified needs in one of those areas also made changes in the same area.

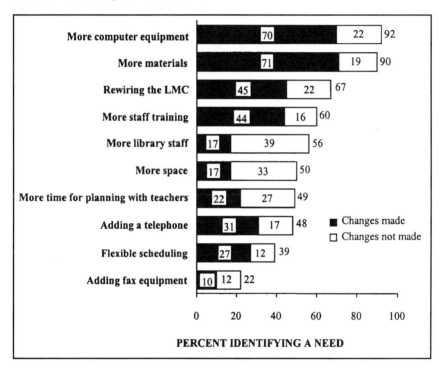

Figure 7. Percent of Public School Library Media Centers (LMCs) Identifying Various Needs through a Needs Assessment, and the Percent That Made Changes.

Between 29 and 87 percent of public school library media centers reported that each of 12 internal factors presented at least a small barrier to providing services and resources to students (see Figure 8). The barriers that were most often reported were insufficient time for planning with teachers (87 percent), outdated materials (85 percent), insufficient materials (84 percent), insufficient computer equipment (84 percent), and insufficient library staff (81 percent). In fact, three of these factors were described as *major* barriers by about one-third of the public school LMCs: insufficient library staff (36 percent), insufficient computer equipment (35 percent), and insufficient time for planning with teachers (34 percent).

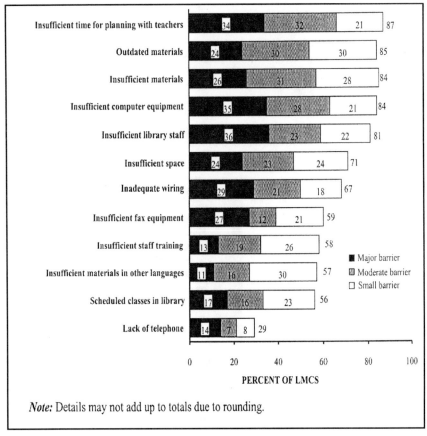

Figure 8. Percent of Public School Library Media Centers (LMCs) Reporting That Various Factors Were Barriers to Providing Services and Resources, and the Degree of the Barriers.

Involvement in Educational Reform Efforts

One of the papers commissioned for this study explores the implications of selected school reforms for library media services (Hartzell 1999). It focuses on 29 reforms that speak to the governance, curriculum, organization, and instructional practices at the building level. The reform ideas discussed have been divided into three clusters: (1) reforms that fundamentally restructure school governance, such as school-based management, school choice, and home schooling; (2) reforms targeting how schools deal with specific groups of students, such as at-risk students, high school students, and those in special education; and (3) a collection of 16 reforms that share only the goal of improving student achievement. Hartzell concludes that "many current school improvement proposals imply a need for more effective integration of library media services into curriculum and instruction, and even into administrative functions" (p. 50). However, he goes on to describe the formidable challenges faced by school library media specialists in working to achieve that integration.

Library media centers were asked about their involvement in programs designed to address eight of the National Education Goals. For each of five of the goals, roughly half of the public school LMCs were involved: teacher education and professional development (56 percent); safe, disciplined, and alcohol- and drug-free schools (55 percent); student achievement and citizenship (52 percent); parental participation (51 percent); and mathematics and science (45 percent). The three remaining goals (ready to learn, school completion, and adult literacy and lifelong learning) were each supported by approximately one-fourth of the libraries.

School library media centers had some involvement in programs or services designed to address new national or state standards in various curriculum areas. As with other library services, the degree of involvement varied by subject area. Public school libraries were most often involved in addressing standards in English (45 percent), social studies (44 percent), science (43 percent), and history (40 percent). However, even the areas least often addressed had the involvement of one-fifth or more of the libraries (24 percent for civics and 21 percent for physical education).

Overall, 76 percent of library media centers at public schools had materials to support professional development. Teachers often could obtain such materials through other libraries as well: 77 percent of the public school libraries said the materials were available through a local college or university library, 71 percent through a local public library, 66 percent through another library in the school system, and 44 percent through a library operated on a regional basis for several school districts. (The last category is low in part because 35 percent of school library media centers said there was no such regional library in their area. Only 3 to 16 percent of libraries said one of the other three types of libraries was not available in the local area.)

Libraries had a number of other resources for teachers. At public schools, 80 percent had subscriptions to professional journals, with a mean of eight journals per school at those schools with subscriptions. Also, 58 percent had *Information Power: Guidelines for School Library Media Programs;* 56 percent had materials on local school reforms, 51 percent on Goals 2000, and 45 percent on other state reforms (see Figure 9). Only 33 percent had the National Council of Teachers of Mathematics (NCTM) standards, which were the earliest set of standards produced under the current wave of reform, but 66 percent of the LMCs had materials on curriculum standards other than NCTM's standards.

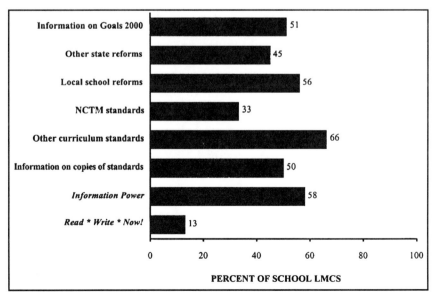

Figure 9. Percent of Public School Library Media Centers (LMCs) with Various Materials Relating to School Reform.

COOPERATION BETWEEN SCHOOLS
AND PUBLIC LIBRARIES

One of the papers commissioned for this study explored the range of successful cooperative relationships between school and public libraries and the factors that must be taken into account in establishing these relationships (Fitzgibbons 1999). It provides a historical perspective on these cooperative endeavors and discusses the unique and complementary roles and goals of school and public libraries. Fitzgibbons reviewed several specific cooperative efforts, including networks, resource-sharing arrangements, and combined school-public libraries as well as general efforts to cooperate and collaborate. She found that the factors leading to success in these activities included "a shared vision and common goals; a process of formal planning that involves the establishment of joint policies and procedures; commitment on the part of administrators, decisionmakers, staff, and the general public; active communication and interaction; and adequate funding and staffing that allows innovation and risktaking" (p. 1).

With cooperation between schools and public libraries a continuing interest in the library community, both the school and public library surveys contained questions about cooperative activities. Because the issue of cooperation needs to be considered from both points of view, responses are first described from the perspective of the respondents, school library media centers and public library outlets; then a comparison of the responses is provided.

Perspective: School Library Media Centers

Three-fifths (60 percent) of library media centers at public schools had participated in some type of cooperative activity with a local public library during the 12 months preceding the survey. On average, those LMCs that did participate in some type of cooperative activity said they had cooperated with 2.3 public libraries, for a total of 104,009 public libraries. The most likely types of participation were borrowing materials for teachers (48 percent of all library media centers at public schools), borrowing materials for the school library (43 percent), informing the public library of curriculum or homework needs (40 percent), coordinating about student research projects (36 percent), coordinating class visits to the public library (33 percent), and public librarians providing information about using the public library (32 percent) (see Figure 10). School libraries most typically reported that their participation in these activities was either rare or occasional (between 29 and 36 percent), and 2 to 12 percent said their participation was frequent.

At public schools, 21 percent of the library media centers worked with the public library in planning for a summer reading program conducted for school-aged children. Such participation was more common at elementary schools than at secondary schools (25 percent versus 11 percent).

For some public schools, interaction with the local public library may be facilitated because the school library media center is located in the same building as the local public library. This occurred at 4 percent of the public school library media centers. Only 3 percent of public school library media centers reported not having a local public library in their area. Most public school LMCs had several kinds of libraries in their area, including another library in the school system (89 percent), a local college or university library (84 percent), and a library operated on a regional basis for several school districts (65 percent).

Besides the local public libraries, another potential resource is the library at a local college or university. Among library media centers at public schools, 77 had such a library that provided access to resources for teachers, and 49 percent had one that provided access for students.

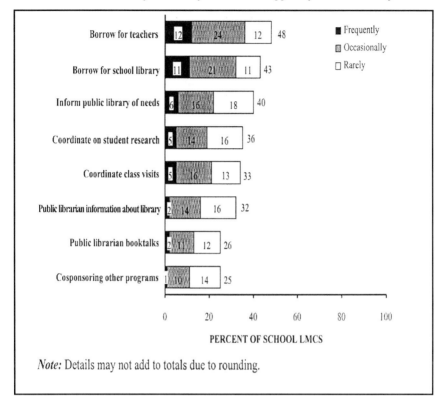

Figure 10. Public School Library Media Centers' (LMCs) Most Common Cooperative Activities with Local Public Libraries, and the Frequency of Those Activities.

Barriers to Cooperation with Public Libraries

The library media centers also were asked about the degree to which each of seven different factors was a barrier to the interaction between their school and the public library. The greatest barriers were the schedule of the school LMC staff and an insufficient number of school LMC staff, with 61–62 percent of library media centers citing each factor as either a major or a moderate barrier (see Figure 11). The only factor not listed as providing at least a small barrier by a majority of school libraries was distance (52 percent), although even this factor was a major barrier for 10 percent of the school libraries and a moderate barrier for 12 percent.

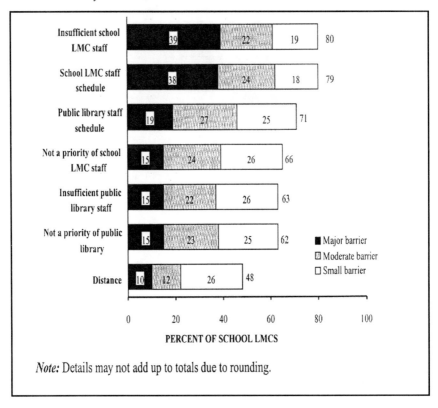

Figure 11. Percent of Public School Library Media Centers (LMCs) Indicating Various Factors Were Barriers to the Interaction between Their School and the Public Library, and the Degree of the Barriers.

Perspective: Public Libraries

Altogether, 86 percent of all public library outlets had participated in some kind of cooperative activity with a local public or private school during the 12 months preceding the survey. For central or main libraries, 97 percent were engaged in such cooperative activities. The most common cooperative activities, in which more than three-fourths of all public library outlets participated, were lending materials to classroom teachers and hosting class visits from the schools to the library (81 percent each) and introducing the public library summer reading program at schools (76 percent) (see Figure 12). Cooperative activities in which more than half of the public library outlets had participated were having the schools inform them of curriculum or upcoming homework needs (68 percent), visiting schools to promote or provide general information about using the public library (63 percent), and coordinating with schools regarding student research projects, including science fair projects (60 percent).

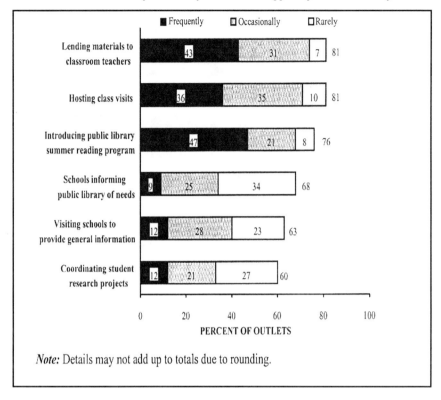

Figure 12. Public Library Outlets' Most Common Cooperative Activities with School Library Media Centers (LMCs), and the Frequency of Those Activities.

Approximately half of the outlets had *never* been involved in visiting schools to give booktalks (50 percent) or lending materials to the school library (51 percent) (see Figure 13). Other cooperative activities in which more than half of the outlets had *never* participated were conducting regular collaborative planning sessions (80 percent); providing information literacy training for teachers or students (76 percent); sharing equipment (75 percent); participating in automation projects such as shared online resources, searches, or catalogs (75 percent); participating in or providing joint inservice training for school and public librarians (75 percent); and cosponsoring programs regarding parental involvement (68 percent).

For public library outlets involved in cooperative activities with schools, the mean number of public schools in their service area was 6.7, and the mean number with which they cooperated was 4.9. The mean number of private schools located in a public library outlet's service area was 2.1, and the mean number of private schools with which the outlets cooperated was 1.3.

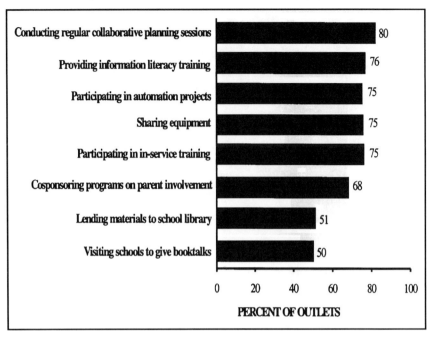

Figure 13. Percent of Public Library Outlets That Have Never Engaged in Various Cooperative Activities with School Library Media Centers (LMCs).

In conducting cooperative activities with schools, public library outlet staff reported that they interacted with teachers or counselors (83 percent of the outlets), school library media specialists (73 percent), and school administrators (67 percent). Staff of central or main libraries were more apt to interact with school staff than were the staff of branches or single location libraries.

In some cases, cooperation may be facilitated by the fact that a public library outlet and a school were located in the same building. Estimates indicated that 3 percent of public library outlets were located in a school building in 1997.

Public library outlets were asked about the adequacy of their resources in various school subject areas. For most of the more traditional subject areas such as history, geography, science, and reading/English, at least two-thirds of the outlets considered their resources to be adequate or excellent (see Figure 14). Foreign languages was an area in which only about one-third (37 percent) considered their resources to be adequate or excellent.

One way in which public libraries help school students is by providing various homework assistance programs. More than half of all outlets (58 percent) provide reserve collections for class assignments, and almost half (47 percent) provide telephone assistance for homework assignments. Reference packets in specific subjects are provided by 22 percent of all public library outlets. Less common services are homework centers (17 percent of all outlets) and homework hotlines (2 percent).

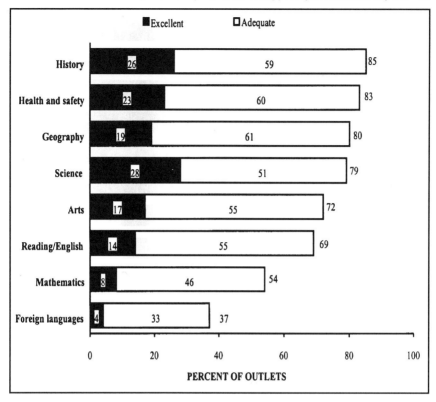

Figure 14. Percent of Public Library Outlets Reporting That They Were Adequately or Excellently Equipped to Provide Resources to Schools.

Public libraries can assist schools by participating in educational reform efforts. Public library outlets were asked if they had been involved in any programs designed specifically to address the eight National Education Goals during the five years prior to the survey. The goal with which the greatest number of outlets had been involved was adult literacy and lifelong learning (41 percent). The goal with which the fewest outlets had been involved was teacher education and professional development (9 percent).

Outlets were asked about the availability of various materials related to school reform. Approximately half of the outlets had the U.S. Department of Education's *Read * Write * Now!* literacy materials (53 percent). Fewer than 40 percent of the outlets had any of the other reform-related materials such as information on Goals 2000 (38 percent) or local school reform efforts (38 percent).

In spring 1997, 24 percent of all public library outlets reported that they coordinated or supported the U.S. Department of Education's *Read * Write * Now!* literacy program. Outlets with this program coordinated it with public schools (33 percent), private schools (12 percent), and other community learning partners (33 percent).

Barriers to Cooperation with Schools

Public libraries were asked about the barriers to the interaction between public library outlets and schools. Barriers indicated by about two-thirds of the outlets were that interaction was not a priority of the school LMC and insufficient public library staff (67 percent each), and almost half of the outlets considered these to be major or moderate barriers (see Figure 15). Additional barriers for more than half of the outlets were the schedule of public library staff (61 percent), schedule of the school LMC (59 percent), and insufficient school LMC staff (56 percent), and approximately one-third of the outlets considered these to be major or moderate barriers.

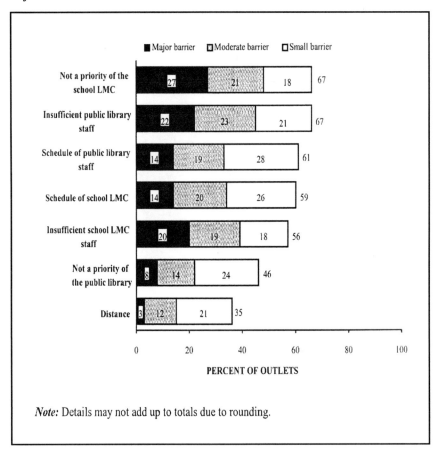

Figure 15. Percent of Public Library Outlets Indicating Various Factors Were Barriers to the Interaction between Their Outlet and the Schools, and the Degree of the Barriers.

Comparison of Perspectives

Public library outlets were more apt to participate in cooperative activities than were public school library media centers. In the 12 months preceding the surveys, 86 percent of the public library outlets had engaged in a cooperative activity with a school, whereas only 60 percent of the public school LMCs had participated in a cooperative activity with a public library. The most common cooperative activities were quite similar for the two types of libraries. However, the percentage of public library outlets reporting these activities and the frequency of occurrence was greater for the public library outlets. A possible reason for this difference is that public libraries may be supporting a number of school activities beyond those specifically associated with the school library media center.

Both the school and the public library surveys listed seven factors that might be barriers to cooperation. For five of the factors, a greater percentage of public school LMCs considered them to be barriers than did public library outlets. The most common factors identified by public school LMCs were their schedules and insufficient LMC staff. Similarly, insufficient public library staff and staff schedules were among the most common barriers identified by the public library outlets.

USING THE STUDY

The findings reported above can assist local, state, and federal policymakers as they identify those aspects of school library services and programs that promote opportunities to learn; develop standards and performance requirements for school libraries; identify research and demonstration needs related to school library programs, services, and resources; and assist parental involvement in education. Moreover, the findings should be useful to the library and education professions as they continue their efforts to inform practice. If school libraries are to realize their potential in helping communities address the National Education Goals, they must be able to discuss with authority and conviction how they are performing and are able to perform within the education system.

REFERENCES

Fitzgibbons, Shirley A. (1999). School and public library relationships: Essential ingredients in implementing educational reforms and improving student learning. Unpublished paper prepared for the U.S. Department of Education/Westat Project Assessment of the Role of School and Public Libraries in Support of Educational Reform.

Hartzell, Gary N. (1999). The implications of selected school reform and approaches for school library media services. Unpublished paper prepared for the U.S. Department of Education/Westat Project Assessment of the Role of School and Public Libraries in Support of Educational Reform.

National Commission on Excellence in Education. (1983). *A Nation at Risk.* [Online]. Available: http://www .ed.gov/pubs/NatAtRisk/. (Accessed February 19, 2001).

Adding Networking Skills to One's "Tool Box"
Proposed Instructional Interventions for the School Librarian and Technologist

William Sugar, Ph.D.
East Carolina University

Diane Kester, Ph.D.
East Carolina University

Twentieth-first century school media specialists and technology coordinators face an almost dizzying array of new technological terms. This is particularly true with computer networking terminology and local area networks. Not only are these individuals expected to recite the definitions of these terms, but they also must demonstrate the ability to be conversant with others and apply these concepts to solving practical problems. For example, consider the following terms: "star-bus topology," "routers," "hubs," "switches," and "unshielded twisted pair category 5 cable." Now, consider the following hypothetical request that Ms. Elizabeth Gibbons, an imaginary school media specialist, could have received from her principal.

> Ms. Gibbons . . . there is something wrong with our local area network. It appears that our star-bus topology is not connecting to our routers. Please check the connections to our unshielded twisted pair category 5 cable. I forgot. Do we have hubs or switches?

As you may imagine, Ms. Gibbons or any other school media specialist must have the capability to immediately understand these terms and then conceive of and propose potential solutions to this particular network problem. This hypothetical request illustrates the current demands and potential new knowledge bases that 21st-century school media specialists and technology coordinators must obtain.

PURPOSE OF STUDY

We examined the current status of computer networking in public schools and how the role of school media specialist is being affected. Essentially, we conducted a needs assessment of school "network coordinators." With these documented needs, we proposed instructional interventions to remedy these discovered "gaps." We also sought to identify the evolution of networking within the public schools and create a current "snapshot" of networking needs in public schools. We trace the origins of networks in schools to the mid-1980s. In its Network Planning Paper, the Library of Congress noted that, "local area networks are just beginning to appear in libraries because administrative data processing and bibliographic control create demands for local interconnections among micros and shared resources" (Miller 1985, 57).

The first edition of *Information Power: Guidelines for School Library Media Programs* (AASL 1988) described one of the challenges facing the school library media specialists as being is "to participate in networks that enhance access to resources located outside the school" (p. 12). A number of more recent articles (e.g., Jacobson 1997; Norman 1996; Pezzulo 1993; Schuyler 1996) in the school library media literature show a gradual increase in the importance of local area networks within a school setting. With this increased interest in local area networks, we sought to investigate the evolution of local area networks over 15 years and ascertain whether these networks are becoming prevalent in schools at the beginning of the 21st century.

METHOD

We sent a survey to 102 middle and high schools in eastern North Carolina's Clinical Schools Network (see Appendix A for the survey). A majority of these school systems are in rural counties. These surveys were addressed to media coordinators of the respective schools. Percentages of each answer were tabulated. Table 1 displays the responses. Answers from open-ended questions were categorized according to corresponding topic (see Table 1). We also conducted follow-up semi-structured interviews with three randomly selected media/network coordinators (see Appendix B for these follow-up questions).

RESULTS

We received 51 completed surveys, or a 50 percent return rate. Forty-five (89 percent) of our respondents were media coordinators/specialists, 4 percent were technology coordinators, and 2 percent were technology education instructors. Thirty-seven (73 percent) of our respondents said that they did not receive any professional training in networking. Conversely, 27 percent of respondents said that they did receive professional training. A majority of these respondents said that they received county inservice training whereas only two respondents received networking training from a particular company (i.e., Cisco and Apple).

Table 1: Survey Responses

Question	Result
What is or will be your networking operating system (you can select more than one if you have more than one network)?	Novell—86% Windows NT—12% Novell and Windows NT—6% Don't know—8 %
Who does or who will manage your school's computer network (you can select more than one job title)?	Media specialists—38% Technology coordinators—43% Network administrators—39% County representatives—14% Instructors—16% 41% of respondents share this responsibility
Who implements or who will implement the policies affecting the school's computer network (you can select more than one job title)?	Media coordinators—53% Technology coordinators—41% Network administrators—39% County—22% Instructors—8% Principals—9% 51% of respondents share this responsibility
Do you have or will you have a daily and weekly maintenance schedule of your school's computer network?	Yes—35% No—24% Don't know—41%

Table 1 continues on page 68.

What do you wish you had learned in your master's program (e.g., MLS, Instructional Technology) about networking?	Issues included: • Maintenance/troubleshooting • Independently work on network without county technicians • Everything . . . • Basic network operating systems operations • Desire to take class/inservice courses • Basic network configuration
Briefly list typical and/or atypical problems that you encounter with your school's computer network.	Problems included: • Hardware • Internet connection • Backups • Network operating systems operations • Software • Students • Human-related • Training

PERCEIVED INSTRUCTIONAL NEEDS

Our respondents commented on their perceived instructional needs with regards to networking. These comments were answers to the question: "What do you wish you had learned in your master's program (e.g., MLS, Instructional Technology) about networking?" (See survey in Appendix A.)

One category of response was a broad, ubiquitous answer: "Everything!" One respondent replied, "I received my Masters in 1980, so none of this was in existence at the school level" or another respondent remarked, "anything . . . we learned basically nothing about networking." Other comments refer to basic networking operations, maintenance tasks, and troubleshooting tips. One respondent wrote, "how it [network operating system] works, how to add programs, assigning user rights, installing printers, drive mappings, installing software, etc., etc." Another respondent indicated a common issue, troubleshooting a computer network. This respondent wrote, "troubleshooting, setting up printers, general instructions for administering network installing programs to network."

Another instructional need that was prominent in our survey results was the issue of independence. Some of our respondents indicated the need of being able to have enough knowledge of computer networks, basic maintenance tasks, and troubleshooting tips so that they would not have to depend entirely on their school district's network technician. These individuals realize that they will encounter daily problems and tasks with a network. They do not want to continually contact and rely on a county technician. One respondent noted: "Network technicians may take months before they can come for repairs." This technician would be responsible for servicing several schools in the school district. One respondent commented, "I would have liked to know enough to not have to depend on a technician or support person" and another concurred, "I would like to know enough about it [computer networks] to solve simple problems that may occur."

PERCEIVED NETWORK PROBLEMS

In an effort to determine the current "gaps" and problems affecting these network coordinators, we asked our respondents to "briefly list typical and/or atypical problems that you encounter with your school's computer network" (question 10). Some of these perceived problems were typical and could be expected from an average local area network. Respondents indicated that they sometimes had a "slow" Internet connection. They had problems with their printers, client workstations, cables, etc., and their "computers on network 'freeze' on a regular basis." They had software compatibility problems where they had Windows software interacting with a Novell network operating system. Our respondents also voiced concerns about typical network operating system issues, such as, "correcting/adding/deleting user accounts."

Other observed problems are what we call human-related. These problems do not directly involve actual network hardware or software, but rather people interacting with a particular local area network. This interaction also presents potential network problems. One respondent commented: "Most of our problems are of the human variety with so many hands on the equipment." Another respondent remarked that the media center has "to deal with teachers wanting you to fix it right now." Another culprit of these human-related problems is the typical student. Students "change settings, forget passwords, etc." One respondent is wary of "student hackers that know how to disable Internet."

DISCUSSION

One apparent result of our study is the consensus that computer networking is indeed becoming prevalent in 21st-century schools. The ability to share data, files and applications via a computer network is or will be available in a typical public school. Because of the continual maintenance and number of daily problems, there needs to be at least one person in charge of this network on site at the school. It should be noted that even though we foresee that each school will eventually manage its own network, individual schools are currently in different stages of networking. For example, in a randomly selected group of schools for our follow-up interviews, each school was in a different stage. One school had established Windows NT and Novell networks. Another school was replacing its old token ring network with an Ethernet network with a Novell operating system. The third school had just initiated its new Novell network.

In addition to the incorporation of network technologies into the school media center, a school media specialist must be able to manage the daily networking operations for the school's local area network. This does not mean that this individual must exclusively administer, manage, and troubleshoot, but the media specialist must have a working knowledge and awareness of common maintenance and troubleshooting network strategies. That is, a media coordinator and/or technology facilitator of a particular school must at least be knowledgeable about networking with the district's networking technicians. It is interesting to note that 41 percent of our respondents share the responsibility of managing their respective networks, and 51 percent of our respondents share the responsibility of setting policies of the network (see Table 1). We advocate that the task of network management not be exclusively one individual's duty but rather be shared among appropriate school personnel (e.g., media specialist, interested teachers, assistant principal, county technician, etc.).

Coupled with the need to be an active, knowledgeable network administrator, there definitely is a need for additional instruction and hands-on training on networking. Each of the network administrators who participated in the follow-up interviews expressed the need for additional instruction. One media specialist needed more networking operating system training and a basic understanding of network terminology (e.g., OSI model, router, physical topologies). One of the follow-up study respondents had no actual networking experience or knowledge. Our survey respondents also expressed the need for additional instruction. One of the respondents remarked, "I wish I could take a class on this now. A hand's on class."

Another respondent commented: "Librarians should be given continuous staff development in this area. So often we have to wait on others when we could fix small problems ourselves." In addition to the need for continuing education for school media specialists, a few respondents commented that teachers and appropriate staff members need to be effective network workstation users, and teachers need to attend a staff development workshop on how to effectively use the network.

PROPOSED INSTRUCTIONAL INTERVENTIONS

Based on the results of the survey and follow-up interviews, we offer potential instructional and non-instructional interventions to remedy the current gap in school media specialists' knowledge regarding computer networks.

One category of instructional interventions would focus on addressing school media specialists' understanding of basic networking terminology and typical network operating system tasks. The network "problems" expressed in the survey and follow-up interviews appear to be basic and could be remedied with a basic networking course and professional workshops. These basic network concepts could include physical and logical topologies, OSI model, etc. Basic network operating systems tasks could include adding and deleting users, assigning user rights, monitoring the network, etc. These concepts and tasks could be taught in graduate programs or via a continuing education program.

A necessary yet simple intervention could focus on troubleshooting tactics and computer network "rules of thumb." It is inevitable that there will be problems with a computer network. A network administrator must perform daily maintenance functions as well as troubleshoot network problems. Although specific troubleshooting tactics are difficult to teach, it would be possible to discuss troubleshooting heuristics. For example, one heuristic, or "rule of thumb," could be that when there is a network problem, first check the physical connections. Proposed inservice workshops could address these troubleshooting heuristics.

Another intervention could be the acquisition, adoption, and promotion of groupware (e.g., Lotus Notes) and other collaborative computing applications within the school environment. Teachers now can take advantage of a school network and improve their jobs by sharing files, having access to templates for form letters and common school office reports. According to one of our respondents, his school's network is currently being "under utilized." His network has more than 250 workstations with a Novell server, but the network is still not being used effectively. He sees the network as a glorified connection to the Internet and other wide area networks. To fully utilize a school's network, the integration of common files and applications should be available via this network, as well as applications and tools that promote collaboration among faculty, administrators, and staff. Groupware applications can promote and manage this collaboration. These applications would be a "conduit" for effective technology integration into the classroom. Groupware applications and other network tools could be used in a way that promotes technology integration into the classroom and as a way to manage school activities (e.g., grade reporting, discipline, and record keeping).

PROPOSED NON-INSTRUCTIONAL INTERVENTIONS

Interventions besides instructional ones focus on improving the school environment, so that a computer network can be effective. Administrators (e.g., principals, assistant principals, and superintendents) should have a working knowledge of networking, its terminology, and its benefits. With this understanding, administrators could promote an environment that facilitates effective networking and have a direct influence on networking decisions. Each of the respondents in our follow-up interviews described varying degrees of support from the administration regarding their networks. Promoting effective communications between network administrators and the school administration will remove any obstacles with regard to their computer networks.

In addition to a better working relationship with school administrators, there needs to be an improved alliance between network administrators and district network technicians. Besides this improved relationship, school districts should consider adding more resources to their networking budgets. One respondent suggested that "schools need to spend more money on networking repair and maintenance. Each school needs a technician." Although it may be currently unfeasible to have one network technician per school, the relationship between network administrator and county technician should be strengthened to develop an effective, collaborative networking team. School districts are beginning to realize the importance of having a technology facilitator position for each school. In fact, one state is considering adding this new position.

Other non-instructional interventions present apparent and simple solutions. Some of the respondents in our survey and follow-up interviews indicated that they did not have an established maintenance schedule and security policies. One of the respondents in our follow-up interview noted that user access to the current network has been restrictive; teachers found it difficult to log on to the school's network. These deficiencies could be easily solved by initiating a maintenance schedule and adopting effective security and user access policies. These simple interventions are aimed at providing an effective networking environment and do not require drastic changes in the existing school environment.

CONCLUSION

We are confident that computer network skills should be added to the school media specialists' and technology coordinators' "tool box." Twentieth-first-century media specialists and coordinators must augment their professional skills and become network "experts." This expertise will enable them to manage and troubleshoot their networks on a daily basis. Our instructional and non-instructional interventions will help facilitate this transition and give school media specialists the ability to add this additional set of skills to their "juggling" act. As a result of this study, it is our intention to document that networking is an essential skill for school media specialists and technology coordinators. We hope that a networking community is established within our regional school districts and also within other school districts. Computer networks should continue to be a current topic for the preparation of school media specialists and technology coordinators.

REFERENCES

American Association of School Librarians. (1988). *Information power: Guidelines for school library media programs*. Chicago: American Library Association.

Jacobson, S. (1997). What's new in intranets? *Electronic Learning* 16:16, 12.

Miller, R. F. (1985, May 6-8). The impact of technology on library networks and related organizations. In *Key issues in the networking field today*. Proceedings of the Library of Congress Network Advisory Committee Meeting, Washington, DC. Network Planning Paper No. 12. Washington, DC: Library of Congress.

Norman, H. (1996). *Local area networks for the small library: A how-to-do-it manual for school and public librarians*. (2nd ed.). New York: Neal-Schuman.

Pezzulo, J. (1993, February). Networking and the impact on school library media programs and services. *Computers in Libraries* 13, 46–47.

Schuyler, M. (1996, April). LAN's, WAN's, CD-ROM's and networking. *Computers in Libraries* 16, 40–43.

Note: North Carolina recently proposed a new position, technology facilitator, for each public school. See http://tps.dpi.state.nc.us/scd/techpositions/technology_facilitator.html for a description of this position.

APPENDIX A—LOCAL AREA NETWORK SURVEY

Please answer the following questions and return your completed survey in the enclosed envelope. It should take less than 10 minutes of your time. Please return it as soon as you can, preferably before the holiday break. Thank you for your participation! Please contact Dr. William Sugar (see contact information below) if you have any questions.

Name _____

School _____

Position _____

1. Do you have a computer network in the school identified above?

    __ Yes __ No

    If you answered "yes" in question 1, please go to question 3.

2. Is your school planning to have a computer network in the future?

    __ Yes __ No

    If you answered "no" in question 2, please go to question 9.

3. What is or will be your networking operating system (you can select more than one if you have more than one network)?

    __ Novell __ Windows NT __ Linux __ Other. Please list. __ Don't know

4. Who manages or will manage your school's computer network (you can select more than one job title)?

    __ Myself __ Librarian __ Technology coordinator __ Network administrator __ Other

    Please list job title _____

5. Who implements or will implement the policies affecting the school's computer network (you can select more than one job title)?

    __ Myself __ Librarian __ Technology coordinator __ Network administrator __ Other

    Please list job title _____

6. Did you receive any training to manage a computer network?

    __ Yes __ No

    If so, by whom? _____

7. Do you have or will you have a daily and weekly maintenance schedule of your school's computer network?

    __ Yes __ No __ Don't know

8. If you answered "yes" in question 7, check off the following items that you have a maintenance schedule for. If you answered "no" in question 7, check off the following items that you would like to implement in a maintenance schedule.

    __ Backups __ Users' accounts __ Users' files

    __ Network files __ Security policies

    __ Other. Please list.

    _____

    _____

9. What do you wish you had learned in your master's program (e.g., MLS, Instructional Technology) about networking?

    _____

    _____

    _____

    _____

10. Briefly list typical and/or atypical problems that you encounter with your school's computer network.

    _____

    _____

    _____

    _____

11. We are interested in following up this survey to obtain "Stories" about networking. We are interested in hearing stories about network troubleshooting strategies, any instructional advice for novices who are unfamiliar with networking, etc. If you have a story to share, please indicate your interest below. We will contact you to hear your story.

    __ Yes __ No

12.   Do you have any other information that you wish to add?

_____

_____

_____

If you want to see the results of this survey, please indicate your interest below. We will send the results to you.

___ Yes ___ No

Thank you again.

William Sugar
Assistant Professor
Department of Broadcasting,
   Librarianship & Educational
   Technology
East Carolina University
113 Joyner East
Greenville, NC 27858
252.328.1546/sugarw@eastnet.ecu.edu

Diane Kester
Associate Professor and Chair
Department of Broadcasting,
   Librarianship &
   Educational Technology
East Carolina University
113 Joyner East
Greenville, NC 27858

APPENDIX B—NETWORKING FOLLOW-UP QUESTIONS

Describe how many networking activities take place in a typical day.

_____

_____

Describe your particular setup:

    Types of computers (i.e., PC, Macintosh)
    Type of network (i.e., peer-to-peer, client/server)
    Type of server (e.g., mail, file, print)
    Network equipment (e.g., hubs, media, NICs)
    Instructional needs of clients
    Maintenance schedule
    Troubleshooting strategies
    Physical topology
    Network protocols (e.g., TCP/IP, Ethernet)
    Network operating system(s)

What types of problems do you encounter with networking?

Can you categorize them?

How much networking knowledge did you have prior to this position as "network administrator?"

What do you need to know now as a "network administrator?"

What types of networking topics would you want to have be covered in a network in-service workshop?

What types of support from the principal, superintendent, and county are you receiving regarding networking?

What types of support from the principal, superintendent, and county do you need with regard to networking?

Rate your comfort level with regard to networking.

The Media Specialist
and Staff Development

Mary Alice Anderson
Media Specialist
Winona Middle School
Winona, Minnesota

Staff development: Everyone talks about it, few schools provide enough of it, and not all states mandate it. A 1998 report noted that of 6,000 teachers and principals surveyed, only half had formal training in it (National Science Foundation/OERI 1998).

This article explains how media specialists can play an active role in providing staff development that helps teachers use information technology and other technologies to teach in a changing learning environment, integrating technology as a seamless tool in the curriculum. Key research about staff development is examined, the changing role of the media specialist is addressed, and examples of successful staff development in practice are shared.

A media specialist is a person who manages a building- or district-level school media/ technology program. Staff development is a process of improving teaching and learning; technology-related staff development helps teachers move from the application stage of technology use to the integration stage while improving the teaching and learning environment.

THE RESEARCH

The literature consistently points to better use of technology in education. Improved access, improved technology, and training are cited as reasons. For example, Henry Jay Becker (1994) noted several positive changes, including improved used of technology, more incorporation of constructivist practices, and a better understanding of how students learn. There is a correlation between attendance at staff development workshops and improved technology use. However, the majority of teachers are not yet using technology to its fullest potential to make meaningful changes in teaching and learning. The Milken Exchange on Educational Technology reported progress in the use of technology in education and the level of integration, but use of technology to dramatically change the learning environment is limited (Solmon 1998). Teachers receive an average of 12.8 hours of technology training that typically involves applications, computer use, the Internet, and integration. Integration training averages only 5.1 hours per teacher.

Key reasons for limited staff development are shortages of time and money and a perceived lack of need. *Professional Development: A Link to Better Learning* (CEO Forum, 1999) argues for long-term technology-related professional development throughout a teacher's career.

THE CHANGING ROLE OF THE
SCHOOL MEDIA SPECIALIST

By choice and demand the role of the school media specialist is evolving. Media specialists are expanding their service and resource provider roles to be more directly involved in student learning. Media programs are full-service programs, interacting with the entire school and community, providing access to information beyond the physical realm of the media center. Often media specialists are described as "change agents" and are encouraged to provide educational leadership. Most literature about media specialists and staff development addresses training for the media specialists; there is less written about the role of the media specialist as a provider of staff development.

In 1985 Marilyn Miller argued that media specialists working as change agents must carefully prioritize their program objectives and resource utilization (Miller and Spanjer 1985). Watkins and Craft (1988) describe scenarios in which the media specialist delivers staff development, teaming with the principal to provide support for teachers. In *Power Teaching*, Vandergrift (1994) addresses staff development as an expansion of the familiar teacher role, suggesting that coaching and mentoring may be the best way to reach teachers. She also encourages media specialists to move beyond the one-on-one model of providing formal staff development.

Information Power (AASL/AECT 1998), the recommended national guidelines for school media programs, addresses the staff development role for the first time in the 1998 revision. *Information Power* states that programs must offer ongoing staff development activities that "provide a venue for teachers, students, administrators, staff members, and others to learn from one another . . . the library media program models the active pursuit of up-to-date-and accurate knowledge that characterizes the modern learning community" (AASL/AECT 1998, 110–111).

Many teachers are eager to learn, and administrators appreciate media specialists who take the initiative to assist. Unfortunately, many media specialists are overwhelmed taking care of urgent technical needs and do not have the time or take the time to provide staff development. One Minnesota media specialist notes, "Because last year was my first year in the district and my first year as a media specialist, I didn't do a huge amount of staff development, but I am working on more" (B. Berg, personal communication, January 2000).

THE TIME IS NOW

The time is right for media specialists to be instructional leaders by proactively providing staff development on a larger and more formal scale. Staff development must be based on research about best practices. It must be effective, relevant, and practical. Media specialists need to be comfortable teaching other adults and apply principles of adult learning as they design and provide instruction. They can apply their information skills to acquire the necessary research base, share it in their educational settings, and work with educational leaders to plan and implement staff development programs in their buildings and districts. Principals want to see media specialists working with teachers to integrate technology into the curriculum process. They value and understand the importance of staff development and want media specialists to take a leadership role. The combination of a media specialist and principal working as a team to help teachers can be a key catalyst to the successful implementation and integration of technology throughout the building.

Most media specialists do not have the time or opportunity to reach all of the students in their schools; however, they can work with all of the teachers. Teachers are the doorkeepers to providing technology-rich learning experiences. By choosing to work with teachers and being involved in staff development, media specialists will promote effective use of resources and have a positive impact on student success.

Many media specialists are involved in the part of staff development that involves information technology. Sue Ludwigson, a middle school media specialist in Wisconsin, says: "Most often I have been asked to do a session on information technology. I have done sessions on our computer network, the Internet, cable TV, integration of media skills in the curriculum, to name a few." Sue is most proud "of just being asked to do staff development sessions. It shows the teachers' interest in the resources of the library media center program and that they value the department" (personal communication, January 2000).

Other media specialists spearhead the vision and leadership for all the technology training throughout the district. By expanding staff development to the whole realm of technology, the media specialist will increase the visibility and improve the perception of the media program. One example is the Code 77 project in Mankato, Minnesota. Under the leadership of district media director Doug Johnson, the district developed teacher competency rubrics in the early 1990s (Johnson 1992). As teachers received classroom technology they were asked to complete a minimum of 30 hours of staff development and develop plans for using the technology. The rubrics have evolved as technology and teacher needs have changed. Reflecting on progress, Johnson has noted that staff development must focus on improving the efficiency and effectiveness of teachers' work habits, rather than on the technology itself. If teachers cannot immediately grasp the practicality of a skill, the inservice is wasted (Johnson 1998).

GRASSROOTS EFFORT IN WINONA

Our grassroots efforts in Winona Middle School grew from a personal passion for staff development, a "just do it" attitude, and the belief that "someone has to do it." Our solid, ongoing staff development efforts help ensure that a school receives a good return on the investment made in technology. Winona Middle School is widely known for its ongoing staff development efforts. Staff development is officially part of the Winona Middle School media/technology program. Organizing and coordinating both building- and district-level staff development is a welcome addition to my job description. Administrative support is there because media specialist/principal conversations about technology occur frequently. Training needs are in the forefront. We are able to move forward efficiently with few bureaucratic roadblocks.

Training began when we installed our first computer lab in 1986. Technology-related staff development has been continuous since then. It evolved from building-level classes to ongoing, districtwide initiatives. From the beginning we offered after-school, summer, and day-time classes. A weeklong series of summer classes was added in 1993 when a second lab was added. The 20-hour series emphasized skills and curriculum integration. We designed staff development curriculum materials for the English and social studies teachers, who were especially expected to integrate technology into their instruction. These teachers received a letter from the principal asking them to attend the 20 hours of classes. This model letter from the principal continues to be used to encourage attendance.

Our biggest continuous effort is a series of after-school classes. The classes are relatively easy to coordinate and inexpensive to offer. Instructor salaries and printing are the only costs. We typically offer 40 to 50 classes each school year. Teachers are the target audience, but classes are open to all district employees, including substitutes and parent volunteers. Such participation is welcome because it helps build support. We try to be practical, striving for immediate success and classroom application.

Another local model is Celebrating Success with Technology (CST), our successful and widely recognized summer technology academy. CST began as a series of 12 classes for middle school staff in 1994, grew to 25 classes in 1995, and expanded to 45 to 50 classes in following years. CST is sponsored and paid for by the district; there are no fees for district employees or school volunteers. Educators from neighboring districts are invited to attend for a small fee. That income is used to pay instructor salaries for future classes.

District media specialists are intensely involved in organizing and teaching CST sessions. Winona Middle School media program staff handle the logistics. Classroom teachers, administrators, and technicians provide instruction. A diversity of instructors helps promote empowerment and ownership. Instruction provided by people who are not perceived as technically skilled helps foster ownership and empowerment and an "I can do it" attitude. For example, an elementary physical education teacher teaches one popular and successful class showing teachers how to use technology to create lesson plans. Community members such as personnel from a local cable company also provide training, strengthening the school-community ties.

FROM APPLICATION TO INTEGRATION

Staff development is evolving to reflect the growth in staff expertise and an increased need to emphasize curriculum integration. Statewide graduation standards and district curriculum realignment are having an impact on the need to use technology. Teachers often say they can do this or that, but do not know how to tie it together. Media specialists can be the bridge when they use their unique skills and perspective to provide the support teachers need to plan and implement integration. Many classes, especially those that meet for longer periods of time, have a specific curriculum focus such as integrating technology in the math and science curriculum or using online databases for persuasive writing research. Some classes focus only on the technology processes needed to complete graduation standards. A few hours of focused and committed time with a small group provide immediate and lasting benefits. The focus must be on student achievement. Hands-on experiences, group interaction, and opportunities for immediate classroom application are crucial. A media specialist must be careful to foster and encourage integration, rather than do the teacher's work.

FOCUS ON INFORMATION LITERACY

Media specialists should take the lead to embed information literacy in staff development, modeling effective information literacy principles as they teach. Media specialists bring a unique perspective to staff development. As stated in *Information Power*, acting as a technologist (rather than as a technician) and a collaborator with teachers, the library media specialist plays a critical role in designing student experiences that focus on authentic learning, information literacy, and curricular mastery—not simply on manipulating machinery. For example, June Gross, a media specialist in Minneapolis, offered a session titled "Making Good Lessons Better." Increasing availability of information technology and the "information anywhere, anytime" environment make it imperative that media specialists lead the way to help teachers as well as students acquire essential information literacy skills. Our experience is that classes billed as information literacy classes do not appeal to many teachers; it is more effective to embed information literacy in other classes. Real information literacy and an appreciation of what is needed to help students become truly information literate comes after teachers acquire familiarity with applications and roadblocks inherent to integration. Question/answer sessions and small group discussions are often more beneficial than hands-on activities.

COLLABORATION AND CURRICULUM DEVELOPMENT

The instructional and collaborative roles of the media specialist are promoted as a way to improve student learning. A few minutes spent up front is key to smooth lesson implementation. According to Donham (1998), collaboration is essential to library media programs because in the end it is required to integrate learning resources into the curriculum for the benefit of student learning. Informal staff development often evolves during collaborative experiences and should never be discounted as a valid type of staff development.

The 1994 and 1999 Colorado studies describing the impact of media programs on student achievement document the positive impact media specialist/teacher collaboration has on student achievement (Lance 1994, 1999) An example of collaborative involvement is the case of a South Dakota media specialist who was paid to work 90 hours throughout the summer with small groups of teachers, who also received a stipend. Teachers scheduled time to work with her on curriculum planning and to learn how to use resources pertinent to their needs.

I have worked extensively with teachers developing curriculum for graduation standards and new units or courses. Invariably these curriculum development times become fun "teachable-moments" as teachers learn to use the technologies they are asking students to use. These sessions meet immediate needs and are invaluable.

Exemplary technology using teachers tends to work in environments of collegial support (Becker 1994). Our own experiences suggest that learning from other staff is highly effective. Media specialists can both provide that support and arrange opportunities for other staff members to provide peer support. Many teachers at Winona Middle School have attributed their successes to the helpfulness of their peers. Support helps many people to surmount the hurdle of uncertainty. We "reward our champions" by making sure teachers who help others receive additional encouragement and incentives to continue. For example, they may be among the first to receive an upgraded classroom computer or have opportunities for more advanced training.

BE A ROLE MODEL FOR NEW TEACHERS

Media specialists can be role models for new staff. A new teacher's first real experience using technology in an instructional setting is likely to occur on the job. New teachers are often technically skilled but lack integration skills and may not be familiar with information technology specific to your school. They often welcome assistance in developing instructionally sound teaching and learning activities. A simple step such as asking a new teacher how things are is a small but positive start. In our district we conduct media/technology orientation for all new staff. Hands-on staff development for new building staff is scheduled for later in the fall, after they have had time to determine their curricular needs. This past fall new teachers worked a half-day in the media center with technology of their choice, focusing on upcoming instructional units.

Student teachers also welcome assistance provided by media specialists and are pleased to find the resources they have learned about and another experienced teacher who will help them. Successful student teacher/media specialist partnerships can do double duty as a role model for the student teacher's supervising teacher.

Preservice students often welcome the role-modeling of a media specialist. As an adjunct instructor at Winona State University, I am in the fortunate position to work with undergraduate students. Most universities welcome guest speakers, and media specialists who want to reach out should be able to find a willing audience.

Our district conducted a districtwide assessment of staff skills. The assessment showed a clear correlation between attendance at classes, skills, and the level of curriculum integration. Buildings with the lowest overall responses to how much technology is integrated into the curriculum are those with the lowest attendance at optional staff development sessions. For example, only 13 percent of the staff at one school reported that they integrate technology into student learning; teachers from that school rarely attend staff development classes. Conversely, a middle school staff reports a high degree of integration, and the school consistently has the highest percentage of its teachers attending classes. Our findings correspond with formal studies such as *Teaching, Learning and Computing* (National Science Foundation/OERI, 1998), which points out that attendance at classes does have a positive impact on the level of usage and integration.

Interviews with media specialists and administrators in our district revealed the same information as the staff self-assessment survey. Despite successful efforts and notable progress, there is still room for improvement.

When building-level media specialists do not actively promote or provide staff development in their own buildings, integration lags. Lance (1999) notes that, "when LMS exhibits leadership she or he is also more likely to . . . provide in-service training to teachers."

ADMINISTRATIVE SUPPORT

Principals who use technology are role models for their staffs. Principals appreciate media specialists who are experts and can help them out when help is needed. When administrators look good using technology, the media/technology program looks good. Administrators who have positive experiences using technology encourage teachers, who in turn encourage their students. Everyone wins.

Wise principals know that technology means more than wires and hardware, but may not have the skills to use technology or the knowledge needed to make wise decisions about integrating technology into the curriculum. Principals need many of the same skills as their teachers. Most likely they did not learn in a technology-rich environment and have had little or limited technology training in administrative classes. They also want to know how instructional technology can promote change within a school and how to help teachers integrate technology into their curriculum.

Media specialists can help their administrators acquire skills needed to use technology effectively and the knowledge to understand the importance of technology for student learning. When administrators are not involved, skilled, or supportive, there are even more gaps in the level of skill and integration. Too often administrators give only lip service to staff development. Principals must have an expectation that all teachers achieve a basic level of technology literacy and use technology in their teaching. It is not enough for the principal just to talk about training or promote it at a faculty meeting. A deadly mistake is giving in to those who refuse or cannot. Building leadership is critical to integration and programmatic change. It is imperative that administrators understand that staff development must be continuous and evolving and part of other district initiatives.

MOVING FORWARD

The continuing challenge is for media specialists to be even more involved in the big picture and districtwide initiatives. With technology and education continuing to change, there will always be a need for staff development. Technology must be increasingly integrated into other staff development initiatives just as it is integrated into curriculum. Media specialists need to continually acquire and upgrade their own understanding of both technology and curriculum. It is necessary to recognize and understand the slow nature of change in educational institutions, celebrate successes, and measure progress over time. At the same time, improved student learning and improved skills for all staff are not an option. All teachers must acquire the necessary skills, and media specialists must provide leadership. Staff development is the most important part of our many-faceted job.

REFERENCES

American Association of School Librarians & Association for Educational Communications and Technology. (1998). *Information power.* Chicago: American Library Association.

Becker, H. J. (1994). How exemplary computer-using teachers differ from other teachers: Implications for realizing the potential of computers in schools. *Journal of Research on Computing in Education* 26:3, 291–321.

CEO Forum. (1999). *Professional Development: A Link to Better Learning*. [Online]. Available: http://www.ceoforum.org/reports.cfm?RID=2. (Accessed February 22, 2001).

Donham, J. (1998). *Enhancing teaching and learning: A leadership guide for school library media specialists*. New York: Neal-Schuman.

Johnson, D. (1998). *The indispensable teacher's guide to computer skills*. Columbus, OH: Linworth.

Johnson, D. (1992). *CODE 77: An Action Research Report*. [Online]. Available: http://www.doug-johnson.com/dougwri/action.html. (Accessed February 22, 2001).

Lance, K. C. (1999). *Proof of the power*. [Online]. Available: http://www.lrs.org/pdf/Fastfacts/164proof.pdf. (Accessed February 22, 2001).

Lance, K. C. (1994). The impact of school library media centers on academic achievement. *School Library Media Quarterly* 22:3, 167–170, 172.

Miller, R., and Spanjer, A. (1985). The library media specialist as change maker: Implications from research. In S. L. Aaron and P. R. Scales, eds., *School library media annual*. Littleton, CO: Libraries Unlimited.

National Science Foundation & the Office of Educational Research and Improvement. (1998). *Teaching, Learning and Computing: 1998*. [Online]. Available: http://www.crito.uci.edu/TLC. (Accessed February 22, 2001).

Solmon, L. C. (1998). *Progress of Technology in the Schools: Report on 21 States*. [Online]. Available: http://www.mff.org/edtech/publication.taf?page=110. (Accessed February 22, 2001).

Vandergrift, K. E. (1994). *Power teaching: A primary role of the school library media specialist*. Chicago: American Library Association.

Watkins, J. F., and Craft, A. H. (1988). Library media specialists in a staff development role. *School Library Media Quarterly* 16:2, 110–114.

FURTHER READING

Anderson, M. A. (1998). Expectations: Building partnerships with principals. *Multimedia Schools* 5:5, 26, 28.

Anderson, M. A. (1998). Ongoing staff development: Sideways, bubbly, and chaotic. *Multimedia Schools* 5:1, 16–19.

Anderson, M. A. (1998). Internet staff development: A continuum. *Book Report* 17:3, 38–41.

Anderson, M. A. (1995). Changing roles, changing programs. *Book Report* 14:2, 17–18.

Haycock, K., ed. (1999). *Foundations for effective school library media programs*. Englewood, CO: Libraries Unlimited.

Veccia, S. (1997). DirectConnect: DISCovering excellence in school libraries. *Multimedia Schools* 4:3. [Online]. Available: http://www.infotoday.com/MMSchools/may97/dconn597.htm. (Accessed February 22, 2001).

Winona Public Schools. (1997–1999). *Technology Analysis Questionnaire*. [Online]. Available: http://wms.luminet.net/wmstechnology/assessment/staff_tech_assessment.html. (Accessed February 22, 2001).

Library Power and Student Learning

Kay Bishop
School of Library and Information Science
University of South Florida

INTRODUCTION

In 1988, the DeWitt Wallace-Reader's Digest Fund initiated Library Power, a $40 million national project to improve school library media services in elementary and middle school media centers. The initiative began in the New York City School System, eventually spreading to 19 communities and approximately 700 schools over a 10-year period. It was the largest nongovernmental school library program since the Knapp School Library Project in 1962.

The initiative was based on the recommendations contained in *Information Power: Guidelines for School Library Media Programs*, a 1988 publication of the American Association of School Libraries (AASL) and the Association for Educational Communications and Technology (AECT). These recommendations included: (1) creation of a national vision and new expectations for public elementary and middle school library programs; (2) creation of exemplary models of school library media programs that are integral to the educational process; (3) the strengthening of the roles of the school media specialist as a teacher, information specialist, and educational consultant; (4) collaboration among school media specialists, teachers, and administrators to improve the learning process; (5) demonstration of the contributions that school library media programs make to school reform; and (6) the creation of partnerships in the community to improve and support school library media programs.

The Library Power initiative concentrated its efforts in six areas: collection development, the operation of school library media centers on flexible scheduling, providing appropriate facilities, collaborative planning and instruction, staffing with full-time professional library media specialists, and providing ongoing professional development.

EVALUATION

Evaluation of the Library Power initiative was accomplished using a variety of techniques, including data from annual surveys of school library media specialists, postprogram surveys from principals and a sampling of teachers, collection maps and collaboration logs, and observations and interviews from case studies in 28 schools. Dianne McAfee Hopkins and Doug Zweizig of the School of Library and Information Science at the University of Wisconsin-Madison directed the evaluation of the Library Power initiative, including the training of the case study researchers.

THEMATIC CASE STUDIES: STUDENT LEARNING

Three case studies were assigned specifically to assess the impact of Library Power on student learning. One case study examined student learning in a middle school setting, and two case studies were conducted in elementary schools. All three case evaluators were university professors with experience as school library media specialists and qualitative researchers. A fourth school media university professor with extensive background in qualitative research oversaw the thematic case studies and provided direction and guide-lines to the case evaluators.

Methodology

The information for the case studies that focused on student learning was obtained through both quantitative and qualitative research methods. The school library media specialists at each school completed extensive questionnaires that asked for both numerical and qualita-tive information dealing with staffing, collaboration, facilities and equipment, scheduling, inservice training, collections, library and information skills, and student learning. Case evaluators were also provided with documentation gathered by local consultants who made visits to the schools during the two years of each study. The case evaluators spent three weeks (two the first year and one the second) at the schools. They gathered data through observa-tions, interviews, focus groups, conversations, content analysis of written materials produced by the school media specialists, teachers and students, and in one case, analysis of a video-cassette of student classroom presentations.

The frame of reference for the assessment of the student learning process in the three schools included the criteria for judging successful student learning as defined by Newmann, Secada, and Wehlage (1995): disciplined inquiry (including use of prior knowledge, in-depth understanding, and expression of conclusions through complex communication), construc-tion of knowledge, and value beyond the school assignment. In addition, the six-stage model of the information search process that has been identified in Kuhlthau's (1987) research was referred to while investigating the research processes of the students. The use of the inquiry approach was emphasized in the analysis of student learning.

The researchers addressed questions such as: (1) Are students having different learn-ing experiences as a result of Library Power? (2) Are students engaging in more high-quality, independent research? (3) Are students approaching topics/subjects in new ways? (4) Are students acquiring in-depth understanding of topics? and (5) Are students performing new tasks that are associated with active or constructivist learning?

Student Learning in the Three Schools

The impact of Library Power was studied in three schools in three separate locations.

School A

The middle school involved in the thematic case study was going through numerous changes as a result of construction of two new middle schools that drew on the student and teacher population. During the first year of the study (1996–1997), the school that had been built in 1963 for 650 students had an enrollment of 1,098 students in grades 7, 8, and 9. The building was suffering from much overcrowding. It was situated in a middle class neighbor-hood, and the ethnic background of the students was primarily Caucasian. The school had a fairly large special education program, with students with disabilities mainstreamed into regular classes during part of the day and special classes for gifted students in English, math, science, and social studies.

An active Library Power committee, made up of the media specialist, teachers, and administrators, directed the activities of Library Power in the school. A dynamic school media specialist, along with a media secretary and an audiovisual para-educator, functioned as a "family" and created a welcoming environment in the school media center. The media staff was well respected by both the teachers and administrators.

Library Power funds at School A had been used to enlarge and renovate the media center, to substantially update and add to the collection, to provide professional develop-ment for the media specialist and the teachers (particularly in the creation of collaborative thematic units), and for special projects such as author visits. Although Library Power funds were not specifically directed to technology, the provision of Library Power funds for the print collection made it possible for the school to move forward significantly in the area of technology. During the first year of the case evaluation several computer workstations and programs were added. In the second year the media computers were networked to the classrooms, Internet access was provided, and a security system and automated circulation and card catalog system were added. These rapid technology changes produced new and exciting learning opportunities in the media center. However, at times the media center staff faced frustrating problems because all the kinks had not been worked out of the technology implementation.

The heaviest users of the media center and its resources in School A were the seventh and eighth grades, which were divided into the traditional middle school teams. The case evaluator observed students conducting independent research, interviewed students (individually and in focus groups) about special class projects in which they were involved, and analyzed the written work and other creative products of the students. Abundant authentic learning experiences were observed.

One of the goals in the mission of School A's District Library Power Project was to "impact the instructional program for students by strengthening the teaching/learning process through staff development, curriculum integration and information literacy." School A's faculty members were involved in several collaborative planning and interdisciplinary teaming experiences by attending Library Power workshops in after-school hours. Along with the media specialist and administrators, the teachers developed ideas for units that they used in their classrooms. One faculty member made the following comment about such workshops: "One of the most helpful things that Library Power has done is to provide time to teachers to work on units. This takes much teacher time, and in addition to the time provided by Library Power the teachers have given much of their time."

Students readily expressed their opinions regarding the relevance of learning and the creation of products in the interdisciplinary units:

> **A seventh-grade boy:** It made it easier to understand when both classes did it. In English when we read *The Reluctant God*, we would come across a vocabulary word that we had learned in social studies and then you remember, "Oh yeah, I remember that word from social studies."

> **An eighth-grade girl:** It's more creative (to do projects). When you choose your own project and share them, there are so many different opinions and views . . . you can compare your views to what other people thought.

One of the characteristics of authentic learning is using what is learned to achieve a goal beyond the classroom. There were several instances of such learning at School A. One of the projects that most clearly exemplified this type of learning was a unit entitled "Booking It: Bridging the Generation Gap," in which the students were matched with residents of a retirement home. The students interviewed the residents and wrote biographies about them. They then invited the residents to the school media center, where they were served refreshments, introduced to the technology in the media center, and presented with their life stories. The English teacher involved with the project noted that she received more teacher and parent comments on that project than on any other project in which she had ever been involved. Student comments demonstrated learning that had value beyond the classroom:

> "I have more respect for older people now because they opened up to us and told us about themselves."

"It's better to go out and use your knowledge and go do something, rather than just sit in a classroom and learn about it."

One of the most successful programs funded by Library Power in School A were author visits. Four authors visited during the two-year evaluation of student learning at School A. The most enthusiastic responses relating to student learning at the school came from both teachers and students responding to the author visits:

> **An eighth-grade English teacher:** The Ben Mikaelsen visit made a great impact on students. I spent three weeks preparing for his visit with my classes. That's a long time to take out of an English class, but it was worth every minute. It all came together for the kids and they really bought his powerful message. Many of the students read more of his books as a direct influence of his visit.

> **A seventh-grade student:** I had never heard of two-voice poems, and I really like them. Now I sometimes find myself doing them at home when I am bored. I liked having him (Paul Fleischman) because he explained about why he did it. He wanted to be a musician or a composer and he puts all the sounds together. I had never thought about the sounds of my writing, but it is really a big factor.

The author visits provided learning experiences that helped the students begin to develop in-depth understanding of various issues, including the difficulties of growing up as a member of an ethnic minority, an appreciation of differences among people, the importance of being good role models, writing as a career, and the thought and process involved in writing poetry.

Several factors during the second year of the case study evaluation affected the programs funded by Library Power at School A. When the two new middle schools were built, several of the teachers that the media staff referred to as "the movers and shakers" left School A to join the faculties of the new schools. Some made decisions to go as a "whole team." The media specialist commented: "The big library users and big supporters of Library Power have moved on." The loss of several of the teachers had also "decimated" School A's Library Power committee, according to the school media specialist who then had to recruit new committee members.

The principal, who had been very supportive of Library Power and the media center program, had a heart attack during the second year and did not return to his administrative post at School A. All the social studies classes, which had been major users of the media center, adopted new textbooks during the year and, as noted by the media specialist, "They (the social studies teachers) are not using the media center as much. The materials are so new to them, they need time to soak it all up, and then I think they'll start expanding their curriculum again." The drop in enrollment from 1,098 to 820 students also affected the media center usage and materials circulation. Additionally, administrators and faculty members expressed concern about the proposed legislative cuts in education made by the state. There was fear that the cuts would result in the cutting back of media specialists, as had happened in other states. Although many positive results had come about from the Library Power funds at School A, there were some concerns about the future.

School B

The case evaluation of School B took place during the school's fourth year of participation in the Library Power Project. The case study researcher spent two weeks in the elementary school in 1997.

The school was situated in a comfortable middle class suburb of a large city. Ninety-two percent of the 551 students enrolled were Caucasian, and only 5 percent of the students entered the school without prior experience in a preschool or daycare setting. The use of 20 para-educators in addition to the regular full-time staff resulted in a low adult-to-student ratio. The school also enjoyed assistance from many parent volunteers.

In addition to Library Power, School B was involved in the Literacy League, an initiative supported by the district Public Education Business Coalition. Literacy League predated Library Power by six years and served as the model upon which the district's Library Power proposal was developed, with the focus on on-site professional development. The Literacy League provided teachers with professional development in the area of strategies for teaching reading and writing in a whole language environment. The two projects shared many common characteristics, particularly in collaborative teaching and staff development.

Collaboration between the school library media specialist and the teachers characterized the vision for Library Power at School B. Library Power staff developers in the school district worked as catalysts to facilitate the collaboration. Another key player in the provision of inservice time for teachers and the school media specialist was the principal, who was supportive of the Library Power initiative.

No structural changes were made to the media center in School B; however, some Library Power funds were used for refurbishing, including painting and adding shelving and counters for computer stations. A curriculum map had been created, and collection purchases in the media center reflected topics on the map. For example, several titles were purchased to support units on the Civil War, colonial America, and various wildlife topics. Technology was an emerging resource in the school, with four workstations to access the electronic catalog purchased with district-supported funds during the Library Power grant and four Macintosh workstations with several CD-ROM resources.

Flexible scheduling, a mandate of the Library Power initiative, was firmly established at School B. Classes came to the media center based on need, with students visiting the library in a free-flowing manner. The flexible scheduling and access resulted in a high use of the media center throughout the day.

Inquiry was taught directly in the school. The school district had a research model that was somewhat similar to Kuhlthau's (1987) information-seeking model. Units of study typically began with background building and inquiry, with the younger students creating "I wonder's" about the new topic of study and the older students generating research questions. In one instance the media specialist and a second-grade teacher taught a lesson on the praying mantis. The media specialist and teacher began with questions of their own:

Media Specialist: One thing that intrigued me was, "How did the praying mantis get its name?"

Teacher: I was wondering what it eats.

The students then added their questions:

Where does it live?

Does it live alone or with other praying mantises?

Does it use camouflage?

Is it dangerous or harmful?

The researcher noted that one outcome of the student-generated inquiry was the excitement about learning that the students exhibited.

During the two weeks that the researcher observed in School B, inquiry-based activities were seen at every grade level. The teachers and the media specialist were working on a scope and sequence for research skills so there would not be redundancy from year to year.

Assessment of student progress was also a topic of discussion, and teachers were beginning to experiment with conferencing and the use of rubrics. The plans for future development suggested a commitment to maintaining the inquiry-based learning model that had come into place during the Library Power initiative.

The principal's commitment to hiring new staff members who were able to effectively describe how to incorporate research into their teaching and the enthusiasm of the teachers and students for the inquiry-based learning indicated that the institutionalization of the benefits of the Library Power funding at School B had potential for survival beyond the life of the funding itself.

School C

In School C, an elementary school located in a large urban area, there was a strong emphasis on respect for self and others. The students were respectful to teachers and other adults, who enforced rules firmly. Teachers generously praised the students for their efforts and frequently used terms of endearment and physical touch when communicating with the students.

All 425 students in the school were African American and came primarily from the local area, which was a blue-collar community made up mostly of the working poor. Many of the students came from single-parent family homes, and more than 90 percent of the students qualified for free or reduced breakfast and lunch. Some of the students wore the school uniform of navy pants and pale yellow tops, but most of the students wore casual clothes.

The school, consisting of 21 classes of kindergarten through fifth grade, was overcrowded, but generally the classrooms were attractively decorated and pleasant in appearance. A newly renovated media center had opened two years before the school's involvement in Library Power.

The school media specialist was the only media staff member and had served the school for over 14 years. Most of the other 22 professionals and 11 paraprofessionals also had five or more years of experience at the school. The principal, however, joined the faculty just before the initiation of Library Power at School C.

The school media specialist and teachers had participated in a summer institute and developed a school vision for the media program at School C:

> Students at our school will possess a knowledge base that will enable them to be problem solvers and thinkers in this technological age. They will have the necessary skills to access information power. The library media center will be structured to afford all students the opportunity to work independently, in small groups or as entire classes on projects and research. Students will be able to come to the library media center any time during the school day. Collaborative planning between teachers, media specialist and principal is essential to providing well planned, formulated thematic units with the library media center being the "hub" of these student/teacher/media specialist learning activities.

The principal saw collaboration as the major thrust of Library Power. She supported the involvement of the media specialist with the teachers in the planning of instruction. In-service training in collaborative planning was provided through the Library Power funding. Projects involving parents in the school and the community were also made possible through Library Power. Most teachers interviewed by the researcher mentioned the improvement of the collection and involvement of parents as positive outcomes of Library Power. A second-grade teacher commented:

The children are moving more to the library, finding more information on their own, sharing information, making mini-reports. I love the flexible scheduling. We're researching every day. The collection is better. . . . Children are excited about the new materials.

Research using the school media center resources occurred at all grade levels in School B. The research projects were generally developed from classroom work and text-books used in the curriculum. Although some of the teachers at School C were beginning to use the media center to develop resource-based learning projects characterized by construction of knowledge, disciplined inquiry, and value beyond the school, most of the teachers did not use the media center in that way.

The researcher noted that some of the other innovations being implemented at School C had potential to support the resource-based approach to teaching and learning. The instructional liaison specialist who assisted teachers in implementing instructional programs at the school noted that the emphasis of one of the innovation programs was to "take the [text]books away and give more real life learning." School C had a number of special programs and initiatives in addition to Library Power. One program, Project First, was intended to prepare teachers for the integration of technology into their teaching. Other programs were related to reading and writing, developmentally appropriate instruction for kindergarten and first-grade students, and individualized reading intervention using tutors and mentors.

At School C, Library Power provided support for the school library media program by providing a better environment for learning through library refurbishment, providing more and better materials for learning, and providing opportunities for teachers and the media specialist to learn more about collaborative planning and working with the community. The impact on student learning, however, was limited by factors related to the readiness of those involved in the education system to embrace the philosophy of teaching and learning that underpins the Library Power initiative. Other limiting factors included the views of the teachers and media specialist about the nature of the children they teach, the nature of learning itself, and the purpose of teaching.

Major Findings in the Case Studies

There were many commonalities in the findings in the three case studies that focused on student learning. However, in each school there were individual factors that strongly affected student learning.

School A—Facilities and Collection Development

In School A the renovation of the school media center had a significant impact on student learning. Library Power funds were used to remove a spiral staircase which, in turn, opened up a large wall and floor space that was made into an area to house magazines, newspapers, high-interest low-level books on audiotapes, a large picture-poster file, and a comfortable reading area. An additional renovation was the removal of a wall, which opened up a class-room area that was then called "Media West." The addition of Media West increased the seating capacity of the media center from 60 to 89. "The renovation funds have enabled us to create two classroom spaces, thus serving more students each period," noted the media specialist. Improving the lighting in the media center was also part of the renovation plan. Faculty members and students frequently mentioned the changes in the renovation of the library media center:

A special education teacher: It was very hard to do research in here before. The library was not very user friendly. It was crowded, and tall shelves blocked the light from the windows. Sue had the shelves cut down, letting in the window light, and she took out the metal stairs, which weren't used by students anyway.

An eighth-grade student: It is amazing how different this media center looks. I was in here many times—even before I was a student since my brother and sister went to school here. This whole room (pointing to Media West) wasn't even here. The big, long circulation desk wasn't here. And it was dark. I love to come in here now. I come whenever I can.

One of the strongest impacts on student learning in School A was the purchase of resources obtained through the collection development portion of the Library Power grant. The provision of the resources did not in itself guarantee the presence of authentic learning at School A, but the new items certainly made such learning more likely to occur because many relevant resources had been lacking before the initiation of Library Power.

A major portion of the Library Power funds at School A was used for collection development, including the purchase of audiobooks, posters, study prints, kits, and laser disks. The reference collection, nonfiction books, and professional collections were targeted for major improvement. Titles in all areas were added to increase the multicultural perspectives. Serious deficiencies had existed in all these areas, and all teachers had submitted wish lists, with department consultants making the actual requests.

Staff and students were very aware of the availability of the resources and the differences these resources made to authentic learning:

A seventh-grade science teacher: In our plate tectonics project I wanted to make it possible for the students to use self-discovery. The study prints and laser disks from the media center were used by the students to make class presentations. Using the magazines on the electronic computer they were able to get to the most recent materials. Resources for science have greatly increased and made a real difference in learning. We are able to do much more research, and the kids feel more successful because they can now find the resources that they need. Before all these resources were available many of the teachers did not use the media center much with their classes.

In School A the renovations in the school library media center and the upgrading of the collection were major factors that contributed to authentic student learning. Without these changes, which were provided by the Library Power funds, the amount and quality of student research and use of resource-based learning would have been severely limited.

School B—Professional Development and Collaboration

One of the most significant Library Power contributions at School B was the development of inservices that were devoted to collaboration. Teachers and the school media specialists participated in summer institutes and learning labs throughout the school year. Two staff developers at the district level conducted these learning opportunities for all Library Power schools in the district. In the learning labs the teachers and media specialists observed in schools where inquiry-based learning occurred. The staff developers explained what was going on and conducted some debriefing with the participants. The researcher in School B stated:

Probably one of the most impressive things that I saw when I was there, was the on-site work that the two staff developers did. They would come in and actually co-teach with the library media specialist and the teacher, modeling how to engage children in inquiry. They would do it side by side so there would some-times be a team of three people working with a class. They helped develop and hone the skills that it takes to really support inquiry-based learning. This was a new way of teaching people throughout this school.

The researcher also observed the bonding of the library media specialist and the teacher as they became a team. This inservice continued throughout the entire time that the school received Library Power funding. It was an important key in collaboration and pro-fessional development in School B. This investment in staff development resulted in the adoption of inquiry-based learning and constructivism, which were important dimensions of the vision to teach students to be inquiring learners.

School C—Administrative Support

A very important aspect of School C was the leadership of the principal. Her support contributed strongly to the institutionalization of Library Power changes. The principal was the key figure in integrating the goals and strategies of Library Power into the instructional practices of the school. Her strong leadership made the changes seamless with the goals and objectives of the school. The principal carefully monitored what was happening in each classroom. She checked what was displayed in the halls and shared performance data with the entire staff. In her view, some collaboration was going on in the school but more was needed. She saw in the media center the potential for more openness and flexibility with students.

When results from statewide achievement tests arrived the principal and the media specialist looked at the library-based data. She asked questions such as: "How often were the students using the library?" and "Were teachers using the library?" She then used the data to show how increased use of the library by the students and increased collaboration with the librarian made a real difference in student learning. For example, in a third-grade class where the teacher and media specialist worked closely together, there was a 95 percent success rate on one portion of the achievement test. In contrast, the success rate of the children on the same portion of the achievement test was 19 percent in another third-grade class where collaboration had not occurred. Using the data in a clear, concentrated way with the staff, the principal always promoted the idea: "We look at how the children are performing and their being successful or not being successful. We then use that to shape our institutional practice."

Findings in this case study indicated that the administrative support in School C was one of the most important factors in strengthening student learning and the institutionaliza-tion of Library Power changes.

CONCLUSIONS AND IMPLICATIONS

The Library Power initiative was built on the recommendations of *Information Power: Guidelines for School Libraries*, which was the 1988 collaborative effort of AASL and AECT; thus, the validity of the components of the initiative was strengthened. District-level personnel were hired to direct the projects in each of the 19 sites, and matching funds from local districts or educational foundations were required, consequently increasing the responsibilities of each selected site. The assessment and the evaluation of Library Power were carefully planned and monitored by the School of Library and Information Science at Madison, Wisconsin. All case study evaluators for district sites and individual schools were trained in Madison, and ongoing consultation was available. Additionally, case study evaluators were selected for their successful experience with qualitative research. All these factors contributed to the success of the Library Power initiative and the research findings.

The Library Power Project has helped many students to become independent learners who are able to use disciplined inquiry processes. The students have flexible access to renovated school media centers filled with upgraded collections to use in their research and discovery, and they are able to acquire in-depth understanding of topics in which they are interested. Students' motivation for learning reaches beyond their classroom assignments and the walls of their schools.

The impact of Library Power reaches beyond the 19 sites and the 700 schools involved in the initiative. The findings from the research can be used in schools throughout the country and the world as they strive to improve student learning.

REFERENCES

Kuhlthau, C. C. (1987). An emerging theory of library instruction. *School Library Media Quarterly* 16:1, 23–28.

Newmann, F. M., Secada, W. G., and Wehlage, G. G. (1995). *A guide to authentic instruction and assessment: Vision, standards and scoring.* Madison, WI: Wisconsin Center for Education Research.

FURTHER READING

Zweizig, D. L., D. M. Hopkins, N. L. Webb, and G. Wehlage. (1999). *Lessons from Library Power: Enriching teaching and learning.* Englewood, CO: Libraries Unlimited.

"It's Funner Now!" Where Online Guidance Stops and Mentoring Starts
Fifth Graders' Perceptions of Doing Research with the *Research Buddy*

Melissa R. Gibson
University of Kentucky

Joan Mazur
University of Kentucky

The purpose of this chapter is to outline and discuss a dissertation study conducted to solve a daily-occurring problem in my school media center: Students do not exhibit elements of information literacy. Furthermore, I do not have adequate time to teach them. The focus of the research was to discover what a group of fifth graders thought about using a website called the *Research Buddy,* designed to help them do a research project. Findings from this qualitative study center on the comparison of student perceptions with observed student behavior.

RESEARCH PROBLEM

Increasingly, information literacy has become a priority in education. Standards and guidelines are in place (American Association of School Librarians & Association for Educational Communications and Technology 1998; Transformations 1993) to help ensure that our children "know how to obtain and use information properly" (American Library Association 1998). Research suggests that instruction by school library media specialists in this area is successful when libraries are flexibly scheduled, allowing for large blocks of time for students to work (Shannon 1996; Tallman and van Deusen 1995), and when librarians collaborate with classroom teachers (American Association of School Librarians & Association for Educational Communications and Technology 1998; Shannon 1996). In addition, library skills instruction has been shown to be more effective when taught as a process combined with classroom content (Dreher, Davis, Waynant, and Clewell 1997; Oliver and Oliver 1997; Todd 1995). However, in many libraries, including the one where I work, there is no opportunity for flexible scheduling or collaboration.

Therefore, it is important to discover if there are other means to teach information literacy in the form of tools and resources available to support children's learning of information problem solving (research). Virtually no research is available directly addressing fifth graders' perceptions of information problem solving using online assistance. However, there is literature concerning online information seeking (Edmonds, Moore, and Balcom 1990; Marchionini and Teague 1987; Neuman 1994; Sandlian 1995), general information seeking (Eisenberg and Berkowitz 1996; Kuhlthau 1988; Macrorie 1988; Marchionini 1995; Stripling and Pitts 1988; Wells and Chang-Wells 1992), hypertext (Nielsen 1993; Rouet, Levonen, Dillon, and Spiro 1996), and how learning occurs (Bransford, Sherwood, Vye, and Rieser 1986; Brooks and Brooks 1993; Brown, Collins, and Duguid 1989; Ertmer and Newby 1993; Hannafin et al. 1996; Jonassen 1996, 1997; Perkins 1992). The literature culminated in the development of the conceptual framework of the dissertation (see Figure 1).

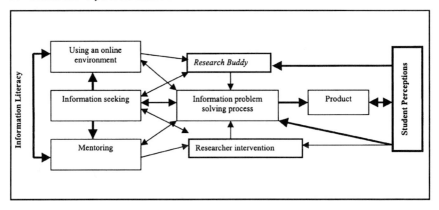

Figure 1: Conceptual Framework.

Fifth-grade elementary children are an under-represented group in information problem-solving research. To address gaps in the literature and knowledge base, children in this study were observed and questioned as they conducted individual research projects using a Web-based research assistance program (*Research Buddy*) in the spring of 1999.

DESIGN AND METHOD OF THE QUALITATIVE STUDY

Site and Research Buddy Program

At the research site, a neighborhood elementary school in an urban southeastern city, there was no flexible scheduling in the library, nor was there teacher-librarian collaboration for teaching research units. The media specialist taught 24 classes per week at Cabin Creek (a pseudonym), leaving few large blocks of time for student research in the schedule. These problems led to the creation of the *Research Buddy* (see Figure 2), a website devoted to guiding intermediate students through a research process called the *Big6® Information Problem Solving Process* (Eisenberg and Berkowitz, 1996). The *Research Buddy* was linked to the home page of the school library and accessible at any time on the Internet. Through its use, a student could learn a process for doing research and find tips for gathering, organizing, evaluating, and reflecting on information.

I conducted a formative evaluation of the *Research Buddy* in the spring of 1998. The study focused on the use of the *Research Buddy* by fifth-grade students. At that time, based on the formative results, I revised the website. Additionally, the formative data revealed that without more structure and computer experience, students would not voluntarily use it. The *Research Buddy* site contains over 100 pages, detailing the *Big6 Information Problem Solving Process*, including strategies and graphic organizers for completing this process. Most pages include a navigation bar containing links to a program map, glossary, index, help, *Big6* page, and journal writing instructions.

The *Big6* is a process for solving information problems that includes these six steps: Task Definition, Information-Seeking Strategies, Location and Access, Use of Information, Synthesis, and Evaluation. Although *Big6* is a systematic process, it is not necessarily used in a lock-step, linear manner. This characteristic makes it an appropriate choice for the non-linear medium of hypertext, which does not require students to do things in exactly the same way, appeals to students' differing learning styles, and offers choices of activities.

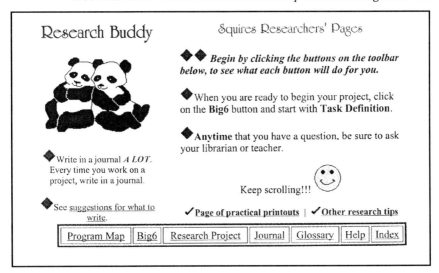

Figure 2. The *Research Buddy* Home Page (http://www.squires.fayette.k12.ky.us/library /research/research.htm).

Student Participants

Research subjects included 12 fifth-grade girls and one boy who constituted the Research Club. The students worked after school and during recess times on their projects. This diverse group included Kunam, an Indian-born girl; Nania, an African-American girl; Nebula and Orphica, two Caucasian girls who worked together on one project; T-Bone, the lone male; and the other students (JC, Maya, Lollipop, Pooh, Kristen, Sable, and Tigger). (The students in the study chose their own pseudonyms.) Within the group there was a mix of high, medium, and low reading levels (see Table 1). Nearly all students were also busy with other after-school school activities, including singers, Student Technology Leadership Program (STLP), basketball, soccer, and the gifted and talented program.

Data Sources and Collection Procedures

Data collected included questionnaires, interviews, informal observations, field notes, student journals, e-mail, log files, progress charts, and student projects (see Appendix). I analyzed data to study both how students used the *Research Buddy* and how they perceived it. I chose these particular types of data to best illustrate perceptions as well as to triangulate results for more credibility. In the text, I identify the data source by student pseudonym, type of data, and date; for example, _Kunamjn3/4 means Kunam's journal on March 4. Also, "ob" stands for observation, "int" for interview, and "fn" for field notes.

The students and I completed the study in two stages covering three months. For the first two months, students completed lessons allowing them to practice using the computers and to learn some library skills. During the last month, students actually worked with the *Research Buddy* to complete a research project of their choice. Students worked in the library, computer lab, their homes, and other classrooms. Nine students completed a project, although only five of them used the *Research Buddy*. Most students presented their completed projects as web pages; Nania completed a report. Being able to create a website appeared to generate much of the enthusiasm for the project.

Table 1: Student Demographics

Student	Reading Level*	Number of Interviews	Often in Library?	Project Completed	Study Score
Kunam	9.6	5	Yes	Yes	35
Nebula/Orphica	9.1/8.6	5/6	Towards end	Yes	26
Nania	4.2	4	Yes	Yes	18
JC	3.6	3	Yes	Yes	21
Maya	4.2	2	No	Yes	13
T-Bone	7.3	6	In beginning	Yes	13
Kristen	6.5	4	No	No	13
Pooh/Lollipop	7.2/4/3	2/2	No	Yes	13
Tigger	3.9	1	No	Yes	9
Sable	7.3	2	No	No	4

*This reading level is read as ninth grade, sixth month.

FOCUS QUESTIONS FOR STUDY

The study focused on students' perceptions of doing research with the *Research Buddy's* assistance and of the *Research Buddy* itself. Focus questions were: How do students perceive and use the *Research Buddy* for information problem-solving skills? Did they learn new skills? Does online guidance occur? What human mentoring will be required?

FINDINGS AND DISCUSSION

To examine the students' perceptions as opposed to what they actually did, I present an account for each of the students who used the *Research Buddy* the most to complete a project: Nania, Kunam, JC, Nebula, and Orphica. As students voiced their perceptions of the research process and the *Research Buddy*, I compared the perceptions with what they actually did. Following the discussion of each student case, I offer more conclusions.

Nania—"She Chose Me!"

Nania had less computer experience than the other Research Club members did because she did not participate in the first two months of lessons. After some deliberation, Nania decided to do her project about grizzly bears, and wrote a report. She covered the front of her neatly organized purple folder with yellow paper inscribed with the title "Grizzly Bears," and there were pictures of bears with computer-generated butterflies around the border. Nania's only original words in the entire folder were on the first page. "The report about Grizzly bears and about there habitat and other things about them sit back and enjoy, learn and listen. Have fun!"

When Nania described her research process to me before beginning her project, she said, "What I do is first I have to find out what I'm researching on." She was happy to get to choose her own topic and find information about it: "I never get to pick what I want to learn." In her journal, she combined entries about Task Definition and Information-Seeking Strategies, writing:

> Today I found what I'm doing my project on. I also learned what to do. What I'm doing my project on is Grizly Bears. . . . I'm going to see what ther habitat, what they eat, how they sleep, why they hybernat, and other important things about them, how they take care of their cubs. I need to use books, Computer, incyclaidia, My Brain things I already know, and maybe Enternet. . . . The 2 I think is the best is books, and Computer.. because they have alote of information.

For Information-Seeking Strategies, Nania said that the *Research Buddy* "helped me a lot," especially learning about the Internet and finding information. "I wouldn't know a lot of things. . . . I'd probably be lost." During the last interview she said, "I would probably have no clue what to do," and said she would have been asking me a lot more questions. In her first journal entry she wrote, "It helped me with my project. I understand what to do I thank the *Research Buddy*."

Most of the time, as Nania progressed through her project, she was adept at organizing her responsibilities for the day. She wrote, "Today I need to look up some more things on the computer about GB [grizzly bears]. Here is a list: Picture, how they take care babies, daily life, What they like to eat, and look through the information I have." About the *Research Buddy,* she said, "It guided me through the steps of putting the . . . report together." Nania's log files (see Appendix for an example of log files) indicated that she had read the Use of Information pages, but explored no extra hypertext links. "And I'd get the information, sometimes I'd print it out, get pictures and information. . . . I'd gather it all up. I'd keep it in a folder so I wouldn't lose it." She did not mention anything about reading for information, taking notes, or citing sources. Her use of technology during the project induced a change in her perception of doing research, as she did not mention using the computer for printouts before the project began. Evidently, her use of technology made her forget her earlier statement about writing out a "sloppy copy" and revising it. Nania told me she had been writing down information, "jotting down notes," and that she would next "probably look over my information and start writing down some information." However, I never saw her do that nor could tell from looking at her project that she had written notes. Although she had checked out books about bears, she included no material from books. She wrote in her journal only during her use of the *Research Buddy.*

Nania indicated on her final perception questionnaire (see Appendix) that she would use computer help screens. This was her one indicated change from her initial questionnaire in asking for help, as she noted that she would still ask a librarian and would talk to others about her projects. In an interview, she said, "[A teacher or librarian could help with] what kind of book to look up for the thing." The first time Nania read the *Research Buddy*, she asked my opinion about using fairy tales or animals for a topic. I told her, "It can be about anything you want, because I want you to be interested in it." Then she asked, "How can I find a book about grizzly bears?" and I directed her back to the *Research Buddy*.

Nania's perceptions about the *Research Buddy* instruction on organization of information matched her actual use, until she got to Use of Information. Nania's work showed only reproduction of information, with no higher-order thinking that involved synthesizing and evaluating what she had found. Once she started to find her information and learned to print it out, there was no evidence that she returned to read the parts of the *Research Buddy* about synthesis and evaluation.

Kunam—"This Is the Boring Part."

Kunam chose India for her topic, creating a sophisticated website. Her home page, *Welcome to Kunam's web page!* had links to three places of interest in India, where she was born. She completed more of the project requirements (see progress chart, Appendix) than any other student, and wrote faithfully 22 times in her journal.

Kunam noted that she had a clear focus before coming to the library. However, in her first interview, she did not mention anything similar to Task Definition. Kunam actually used the *Research Buddy* well for Task Definition and Information-Seeking Strategies. She wrote the questions for her topic and made a list of sources she would need. Kunam did not like the writing she had to do for Location and Access. In her journal she wrote, "Today I read about Location & Access. I thought it was fun, but I didn't like writing. The *Research Buddy* helped me by telling me what to do with the list I made last time." She wrote her source information in a chart, as the *Research Buddy* suggested. Later Kunam told me that she probably would have left this step out if she had not used the *Research Buddy*. "I wouldn't think about that very much, I would just find it . . . just keep finding it in other sources." She believed she did not need to think about where she would go for information. However, during this exercise she named some sources that she had not named as possibilities for information in her beginning interview. In her last interview, Kunam included Task Definition in her description about the research process. "First I would figure out what I wanted to find." The online assistance helped Kunam sharpen her focus.

Kunam thought that the Use of Information part of the *Research Buddy* was short and the same as the Location and Access part. "It didn't help me very much," she wrote. Her log files indicated that she read the three main pages about Use of Information and the initial pages of Location and Access. There was a wealth of information contained in both sections that she missed by not exploring any extra hypertext links. On her perception questionnaire, she had checked that she would not use computer help screens. Perhaps the *Research Buddy* felt like a computer help screen to her. Kunam printed out the graphic organizer page for keeping down information and asked me, "Do we have to do this, this is too hard."

When Kunam described at the beginning of the study how she would extract information, she said, "I write down all the important stuff, not the whole sentences, but little phrases to help me remember stuff from it. . . . I don't copy it I just write little notes." Later, she said that she would "do something with it where I could just take it somewhere, like I could print it or copy it, and take notes." The extensive use of technology during her project added terms to her vocabulary like, "print it or copy it." During her work she saved and printed out many pages, and worked diligently highlighting and rewriting her information. Kunam did not enjoy doing the "boring stuff," which was reading to highlight her information and type it into the web page. She wrote, "Today I found the information that I needed in my information. I didn't have much time today. I didn't have fun. This has gotten even more boring." Kunam was the only student who voluntarily did a bibliography and used the *Research Buddy* to learn how to do it. She was also the only student to complete her journal and timeline as requested.

Kunam's overall impression of the *Research Buddy* was unenthusiastic. She said, "Most of it that I read just told me about some of the steps to do, it didn't told me what to do, it just told me about it. But sometimes it told me what to do, but it didn't help me DO it that much." She thought it could have been more explicit and showed more examples about how to do procedures, especially web page authoring. Although she stated several times that the *Research Buddy* told her what to do, and helped her with the steps to do a project, Kunam said she would not use it again. "I read it already," she flatly stated.

Kunam was always concerned with time, which may have affected a protracted use of the *Research Buddy*. She would come into the library to work and then it would suddenly be time to stop. I believe that Kunam would have turned in a good project even without the *Research Buddy*. However, I thought that she used the *Research Buddy* effectively for the first five *Big6* steps. She wrote out questions for her topic, considered different sources, photocopied and highlighted information, wrote a bibliography, and wrote in her journal. I do not think Kunam would have done all of those steps without the prompting of the *Research Buddy*. In her final journal entry, Kunam wrote, "I like doing this research project a lot, especially since I'm doing a web page. I like doing web pages because you get to make links and everybody gets to see it when you are done. The part I didn't like was typing. The rest of it was fun. I had fun finding my information, too. I had a lot of fun."

JC—"I Can DO It!"

With T-Bone's assistance, JC created a web page using a dark, tiled photograph of two lions, with questions and answers written in bold white text. She listed six questions requiring factual answers, and these answers were included in parentheses directly after each question. A humorous line on her project stated, "What happens when a lion's tail points like a flag at you? RUN." She included no hypertext links on her page, and wrote several of her facts incorrectly.

JC, with the lowest reading level of the group (see Table 1), read the *Research Buddy*, and read it, and read it "so I can get it in my brain." Part of JC's problem was her reading level, but part of it was her party instinct. If there were other students around, she generally would talk or play. Once I went to check on JC while she was working in another classroom, and the teacher was sharing candy and conversation with her and Lollipop!

In the initial interview, JC stated that she depended on the teacher to give her a topic. "First, like, if it was my teacher or you, I would ask for my information." Her concepts about Task Definition did not change over the course of the study, although she used the *Research Buddy* and wrote some seed questions of her own about her topic. I felt that with mentoring, JC would be able to frame some good questions. JC wanted to know, "What baby cubs do once they're grown . . . and what the male lion's job is and what food do they eat, things like that." However, she answered none of those questions on her web page! In JC's last interview, she described doing a research project, with no elaboration on Task Definition. "Number one I would go to the library. See, because that's where books and things for information." In this project, JC did not learn the value of Task Definition.

One day JC was having a terrible time with her project, moaning, "I'm dumb, I'm dumb." I encouraged her to find her help from the *Research Buddy*, as I did not want to become her *Research Buddy* myself. She re-read it, but still asked, "What do I do next?" At the end of the study, JC stated, "[I] read it, but sometimes I'd get confused, but I just gotta read it over and over until it's clear in my mind." Finally, JC explained her problem. "I'm the type of person whose . . . needs explaining . . . it sounds like someone smart, like Nebula, she could understand it because she's very good at understanding things. I just need to understand it. Put it in student words. Kids. Just like grownups." It was too hard for her to read and comprehend.

According to her journal entries, JC used the *Research Buddy* for Information-Seeking Strategies and for her journal. She showed me her list of questions from the Task Definition section, and she had written a list of sources that she would use. JC had read Use of Information in the *Research Buddy*, which may have helped her take notes from a video about lions. JC had said that she was going to read steps five and six in the *Research Buddy*, and her log files indicated that she read the Synthesis section and one page only of the Evaluation section. She did not produce rubrics to evaluate her project.

JC wanted very much to help me by participating in this project, writing on March 26: "I like doing this project just to help Mrs. Gibson." However, she just could not use the *Research Buddy* effectively, because she had neither the necessary reading ability nor self-discipline. Her log files indicated less than one minute per page, although she accessed them more than once on different days. I had to admire her determination. She had checked on her perception questionnaire both times that when work is hard she would give up or only study the easy parts. However, JC kept going on this project. She kept trying to read and understand the *Research Buddy*, and she finished her project when students that were more capable did not. She said, "If I can keep confidence in me, I can DO it. If I say, 'JC, you can do this,' I can DO It."

Nebula and Orphica—"It's Funner Now!"

Two excellent students at Cabin Creek, Nebula and Orphica, worked together to complete a website about Lucille Ball. They learned quickly to compose a default page with links to an introduction and six other pages. Each page included a picture and information about the comedienne.

At the beginning of the project, Nebula wrote in her journal, "I thought that it would be a lot of reading, but it was actually kind of neat." Orphica stated, "I thought it was easy to understand and it has given me a good format in which to start my project. I feel that this program can really help you start your project." Nothing throughout the project seemed to dim their initial view of the *Research Buddy*. They continued to use most of the *Research Buddy*'s suggestions for their work. Especially impressive were Task Definition strategies, which simultaneously helped them outline questions to ask and gave them the ability to organize their information easily. " 'Cause we'll be able to know what, like if we have two questions that aren't answered we just look for those two things and we'll have everything." During their last interview (NO5/3), the girls had learned to spend more time on Task Definition. Orphica stated, "First, I would, figure out which would be the best topic to do and how much information I could probably get on it."

Some links in the *Research Buddy* they chose not to follow. "But we didn't think they would help us." They praised the data chart but did not use it. "I think that the chart for your questions really helps you organize, " said Orphica, but Nebula said, "We didn't use the data chart, because it was kind of confusing, and then because we're just writing out on plain paper." Orphica added, "The boxes are a little small to write. I wrote a whole summary down about Desi Arnaz and that would never fit in the box."

The girls used the journal questions, and they panicked when they read about bibliographies in the *Research Buddy* because they had not been citing their sources. They learned a valuable lesson, as Nebula later said: "We would save it and then we would print it. And write on there where we got it. So we would remember . . . for our bibliography." They decided to do a web page because of the suggestions in the Synthesis section. "Or we wouldn't have had the idea of doing a website. We wouldn't even think of that," Nebula said. Log files indicated that the girls never read the Evaluation part, but they articulated in interviews about how they would evaluate. "Accuracy, and appearance, and amount of information," said Nebula.

Part of their excitement with the project stemmed from the fact that they were getting to do a web page. Additionally, they thought web pages helped them to stay organized. Orphica said, "This is like a report, but it's kind of fun. . . . I think it's much easier. I'm going to start doing my reports just with a topic and then write it." Nebula added, "If you have something extra that you want to add you can put a hyperlink, and a whole other article about it [laughs]." Overall, they felt that the *Research Buddy* helped them to finish more quickly by getting organized and staying organized:

Nebula: It was hard work, but fun. I thought research like was boring, and,

Orphica: It's funner now.

Nebula: A little funner now.

Researcher: Okay, why is it a little funner now?

Nebula: Because we know how, and we know how to organize it, and so, we're not all messed up and we get it done quicker, easier.

It was exciting to see them working together, keeping each other on task and talking about their ideas. Most of the help the girls requested during their project was for web-building techniques. They were so involved in downloading pictures and making new links that they saved files everywhere, in the classrooms and the library. Nebula used her computer disk most of the time to save files, but sometimes she would inadvertently save them on the computer she used at the time. Other times, she would lose the disk, frantically call her mother at home, and have to save files on the hard drive. Even on the last day of the project, they were scurrying around, looking for misplaced files.

CONCLUSIONS

In view of the data gathered, it appeared that students used the *Research Buddy* mostly for Task Definition, Information-Seeking Strategies, and Location and Access, less for Use of Information and Synthesis, and not at all for Evaluation. The students who used the *Research Buddy* the most wrote seed questions about their topics and were able to use those questions to keep themselves organized and on task during the rest of the process. They consciously thought about sources they were going to use, possibly getting some new ideas from the *Research Buddy*. Students did not do a lot of extra clicking to explore hyper-text links in the *Research Buddy*, and there was not much use of the navigation bar. There-fore, I doubted that the students used much of what was written in each step, as they would only click what looked useful to them at the time. Nebula said, "There were like two [links] that we didn't, but we didn't think they would help us."

Eight of the students perceived the *Research Buddy* as a helper to them, mostly because it "guided me through the steps of putting the report together." Two of those eight hedged on how helpful it was. JC, who had the lowest reading level of the group, had difficulty with the language: "I'm the type of person can't understand much." Kunam, possibly the brightest and definitely the most serious of the group, said, "Sort of. It just told me the order that I had to do everything in, but it didn't tell me what I had to do." At the time, she was looking for specific help on authoring web pages, information that was not included as a procedure or as instruction in the *Research Buddy*. Two students who finished their projects without using the *Research Buddy* did not think it was a guide, and T-Bone, who read it, "really didn't need it at all" for his project (a tour of the school). Thus, most of the students who actually used the *Research Buddy* felt that it helped guide them through at least the first few steps of the research process.

As a guide, the *Research Buddy* was somewhat useful for some children by providing them with a procedure for their research, in lieu of participating in a community of inquirers. Such a community involves using procedures and purposes that are negotiated as learners interact with one another (Levstik and Smith 1996). The conceptual characteristics of infor-mation problem solving include hierarchical structure of knowledge with relatively simple concepts, but the iterative nature of information problem solving, the reflection necessary, and the sheer number of concepts and processes create an ill-structured domain. According to the contextual analysis framework (Jacobson and Spiro 1994), the type of instruction prescribed depends on the stage of the learners and the conceptual characteristics of the knowledge domain. Students may have seen the *Research Buddy* as a guide because each page included a small amount of instruction and then had a "next" button to click. For the students who did not see the *Research Buddy* as useful, it may be that this finding agrees with Park (1991). Park notes that the student might not have sufficient knowledge about the content, the metacognitive ability, or the appropriate cognitive strategies to be successful in the learning process. The Research Club students, with two months of practice on computer systems, were still in an early stage of learning. Some of the students evidently were not motivated to use it at all, such as T-Bone, Lollipop, Tigger, and Pooh.

However, students who followed the structured progress chart (see Appendix), which prompted them to use the *Research Buddy*, learned new skills. Kunam's concern with her chart led her to ask about bibliographies. Those who kept up with their journal questions were working on metacognitive activities, which may have aided in their success. When students journal, they analyze their problem-solving processes and learn about themselves as learners (Bransford, Sherwood, Vye, and Reiser 1986). The journal serves as a tool for formulating thoughts and developing constructs (Kuhlthau 1995).

Nania strongly felt that she had learned new skills and how to do the journal with the *Research Buddy*, but upon elaboration mentioned that she learned content about grizzly bears and how to save information on her disk. Because of her inexperience in computer use, she may have confused the *Research Buddy* pages with other Internet pages. Kunam did not think she had learned new skills, even though bibliographies were new to her. She remonstrated, "But I probably won't be able to remember all of it." JC did not think she had learned new skills, but mentioned that she had used some of the *Research Buddy* strategies in her other classes. However, she could not tell me what those strategies were, indicating that she probably did not use any. Kristen thought that she had learned more about Task Definition, but was unable to articulate exactly what. T-Bone did not think he had learned new skills. However, Orphica and Nebula credited the *Research Buddy* for the fact that they could organize information better, compare information, and use Task Definition to help them "think before you start doing everything."

One would think that the tendency to use the *Research Buddy* again would depend upon the perceived value of it. With so few of the students able to articulate what they had learned or feeling that they did not need it, I was surprised that nearly all the students said they would use it again. Students felt that the *Research Buddy* would help them either with social studies or science projects, with classwork to "see how to do it," or "because in middle school especially you have to do a lot of reports." T-Bone, who said he would not have used it for this project unless he had to, even said that he would probably use it, "because in middle school there will probably be some things that I forgot in fifth grade, and the *Research Buddy* would probably tell me." Maya said that she might use it "doing research in class or something, if I need to find some information at home." Kunam, who possibly learned the most from the *Research Buddy*, would not use it again.

What! You Mean We Have to Read?

Few of the students remembered using (or even seeing!) the navigation bar at the end of each *Big6* section. This was another indication that students did not completely read all pages of each section. Most log files indicated only one minute or less spent reading each page. T-Bone did use the index button on the navigation bar to find out about bibliographies after I asked him to write one. Orphica and Nebula used the index button to find the data chart again, and Nebula used the program map button once. JC remembered using the journal button one time.

I asked Nebula and Orphica if they thought the *Research Buddy* was too hard. Both of these good readers replied in the negative, and Nebula continued, "People might not want to do it, but it's not too hard." Although the Research Club students had two months to learn to use the hypertext-based programs at school, they were not yet quite hypertext-literate learners. Jonassen (1993) defines hypertext-literate learners as those who have developed a useful set of strategies for navigating and integrating information from hypertext.

Kunam hoped that it was "optional to read the pages in the *Research Buddy*," as she did not like to read long pages of information. "Especially when they have big words in them that I have trouble understanding." She was not alone in her dislike for reading, as Pooh and T-Bone complained about having to read. Pooh said in her journal, "I think it is too long to read so I printed out some pages to take home and study. I will try as much as I can to get it all read." Kunam, Nebula, and Orphica later happily noted that certain sections were short. Kunam wrote, "It wasn't long, so I didn't get bored."

Nebula and Orphica devised a cooperative system of reading the *Research Buddy*. When they were working together, they would take turns reading the paragraphs aloud. T-Bone said, "I think it's fun and boring because, I think it's fun when there's something I haven't learned already, but I just think it's pretty boring when I'm reading something that I already know." In a later journal entry, Kunam also mentioned, "I didn't like writing." Burdick (1998) states that when students say they do not like to read or write, it means that they do not have the desire to do so. These activities require additional time, vigilance, and effort, and unless the outcomes are attractive, students will not be motivated to self-regulate (Zimmerman and Schunk 1989). Perhaps the collaborative reading of Orphica and Nebula made reading the online assistance more attractive, as they did not complain about reading or writing.

From the beginning, none of the students felt they needed help with the writing process. Teachers at Cabin Creek Elementary stress writing, perhaps causing the students to feel confident about their writing abilities. Yet the only indications of synthesis were in Kunam's, Nebula's, and Orphica's projects. Finally, without using evaluation strategies, the students had no additional criteria to guide them. If the students had used the Evaluation step, they may have thought it helpful, since they appreciated the Task Definition strategies that helped them stay on task.

Kunam, Nebula, Orphica, JC, and Maya, who returned a later survey (see Appendix), were positive about the *Research Buddy*'s ability to help them do research. Those who returned the survey marked the majority of their answers in the "Agree" or "Strongly Agree" columns. They thought that the *Research Buddy* was fun to use and that it helped them to ask questions about their topics, think of places and sources to find information, organize their information, make a bibliography, think about their projects with the questions for journal writing, and learn new skills.

Research Was Information Seeking, Not Inquiry

Students believed that research meant finding information about a topic. They did not include the writing process or evaluation. The students' use of online assistance confirmed this assertion, as they used the *Research Buddy* mostly for the first three steps of the *Big6*: Task Definition, Information-Seeking Strategies, and Location and Access. The students' impoverished idea of research only begins to address the information literacy standards, touching on the first of accessing information. As Moore (1995) found, to correct such a limited view of research, a teaching link is needed between library skills and study skills to foster a more sophisticated view of information use.

Mentoring: The Little Guys Need Us

Kuhlthau (1995) found in her research that a student's understanding of the process of research through guided self-awareness substantially increased his or her confidence and competence in learning from information. Dreher, Davis, Waynant, and Clewell (1997) found that fourth-grade students who learned a research strategy during a project demonstrated improvement to search independently for information and apply what they had learned to a new problem. In this study, the *Research Buddy* alone did not provide enough impetus for a fifth-grade student to successfully work through and complete an information problem-solving project. Such a program, like a cognitive tool (Jonassen and Reeves 1996), relies on learners to supply the planning, decision making, and self-regulation necessary to promote reflection, discussion, and collaborative problem solving. The *Research Buddy* could only instruct and suggest, not motivate or self-regulate. For motivation and self-regulation, the students needed more from the environment in the way of mentoring from a real live human being.

In this study, I learned that we teachers would do well to spend more time helping students learn to work through Task Definition. Kuhlthau (1987) states that assignments need to be restructured with particular attention given to the earliest stages of the research process, as well as to guidance through the completion of a search. With easy access, it was also clear to me that, although not very effective used in isolation, the *Research Buddy* could become an avenue to promote collaboration between the classroom and library in the absence of a flexibly scheduled library. Alone, the *Research Buddy* did not meet all the needs that children had during their work. However, by encouraging its use, teachers and librarians could have common goals and could plan to be responsible for assessing different parts of work from the *Research Buddy* that the children complete. It was clear that for the Research Club students, mentoring was necessary to help them through a research process, and there had to be a point where online guidance stopped and mentoring started. At different times, they were frustrated, they were uninterested, they needed to know next steps, they were burned out, they were bored, they were frantic, and they needed a mentor.

Computers and Internet Are the Way to Go—Maybe?

As found in other studies (Breivik and Senn 1998; Burdick 1998; Dalrymple 1991), students in this study believed that computer information was the best, fastest, and easiest. Kristen wrote in her journal, "I chose computers, people, books. I picked those three sorces because they are easy to work with and have a lot of information for me." Nania thought she would find most of her useful information on the Internet, saying, "It has a lot of information." All of the students cited the Internet as one of the first places they would go to find information, and it was frequently the first choice. Kunam wrote, "The Internet has everything in it." However, students did not devise efficient searches, nor could they evaluate the quality of the information they found. In all data, students mentioned books 130 times versus the computer or Internet 168 times. However, from my observation of their actual process, five students used books a total of five times. It was a struggle to get them to use print materials, and I was usually directly involved when they did.

This corroborates Howe (1998) and Small and Ferreira (1994), who believe that children do not effectively or efficiently use electronic sources without instruction. The few preliminary Internet lessons the Research Club students completed did not cover evaluating information. The seduction of technology may increase information aliteracy (the ability to locate, evaluate, and use information without the desire to do so) because it allows children to get information and use it without even reading it, much less understanding it (Burdick 1998).

Other issues also arise from the findings in this study. Are we ready for computer information? Many students' problems in the study focused on the technical roadblocks. At times I felt like I was running a computer help desk, because the students in other classrooms would call about a technical problem for me to troubleshoot. Computers would freeze or crash, students would save information on the hard drives instead of the floppy disks, the printer would not print, URLs did not go where they were supposed to, and files got lost. This problem alone was probably the determining factor in Pooh's poor use of the *Research Buddy*. It seemed like every time she would stay to work, her assigned computer would not work, the lab was closed, other teachers would be using their computers, or the Internet would be down. She would sigh, grin, and say, "Well, I'll look at it from home."

The implications of children's romance with computers is that librarians will have to (1) provide more and more mentoring and instruction on the use of online information and (2) continue to emphasize the use of print resources that are not available online. In either case, it is important for children to be able to extract and evaluate the information they find in both types of resources (Moore 1995; Stripling 1995). Librarians are strategically placed to be able to help students learn how to work with all kinds of information, if they have adequate time. The *Research Buddy*, although not a cure, could provide valuable assistance if used in conjunction with support from classroom teachers and strategic mentoring.

REFERENCES

American Association of School Librarians & Association for Educational Communications and Technology. (1998). *Information power: Building partnerships for learning.* Chicago: American Library Association.

American Library Association. (1998, July). National information literacy standards announced. *ALA Cognotes*, 8.

Bransford, J. D., Sherwood, R., Vye, N., and Rieser, J. (1986). Teaching thinking and problem solving: Research foundations. *American Psychologist* 41:10, 1078–1089.

Breivik, P. S., and Senn, J. A. (1998). *Information literacy: Educating children for the 21st century.* Washington, DC: NEA Professional Library.

Brooks, J. G., and Brooks, M. G. (1993). *In search of understanding: The case for constructivist classrooms.* Alexandria, VA: Association for Supervision and Curriculum Development.

Brown, J. S., Collins, A., and Duguid, P. (1989). Situated cognition and the culture of learning. *Educational Researcher* 18:1, 32–42.

Burdick, T. (1998). Pleasure in information seeking: Reducing information aliteracy. *Emergency Librarian* 25:3, 13–17.

Dalrymple, P. W. (1991). Redesigning access: What we must do to help information seekers succeed in the electronic environment. In J. Varlejs (ed.), *Information literacy: Learning how to learn.* Jefferson, NC: McFarland & Co.

Dreher, M. J., Davis, K. A., Waynant, P., and Clewell, S. F. (1997, December 3–6). *Fourth-grade researchers: Helping children develop strategies for finding and using information.* Paper presented at the Annual Meeting of the National Reading Conference, Scottsdale, Arizona.

Edmonds, L., Moore, P., and Balcom, K. (1990). The effectiveness of an online catalog. *School Library Journal* 10, 28–32.

Eisenberg, M., and Berkowitz, B. (1996). *Information problem-solving: The Big Six skills approach to library & information skills instruction.* Norwood, NJ: Ablex.

Ertmer, P. A., and Newby, T. J. (1993). Behaviorism, cognitivism, constructivism: Comparing critical features from a design perspective. *Performance Improvement Quarterly* 6:4, 50–72.

Hannafin, M. J., Hannafin, K. M., Hooper, S. R., Rieber, L. P., and Kini, A. S. (1996). Research on and research with emerging technologies. In D. Jonassen (ed.), *Handbook of research for educational communications and technology.* New York: Simon & Schuster.

Howe, E. B. (1998). Integrating information technology into and across the curriculum: A short course for secondary students. *Knowledge Quest: Journal of the American Association of School Librarians* 26:2, 32–40.

Jacobson, M. J., and Spiro, R. J. (1994). A framework for the contextual analysis of technology-based learning environments. *Journal of Computing in Higher Education* 5:2, 3–32.

Jonassen, D. (1996). *Computers in the classroom: Mindtools for critical thinking.* Englewood Cliffs, NJ: Merrill.

Jonassen, D. (1993). Effects of semantically structured hypertext knowledge bases on users' knowledge structures. In C. McKnight, A. Dillon, and J. Richardson (eds.), *Hypertext: A psychological perspective.* Chichester, England: Horwood.

Jonassen, D. H. (1997). Instructional design models for well-structured and ill-structured problem-solving learning outcomes. *Educational Technology, Research & Development* 45:1, 65–94.

Jonassen, D. H., and Reeves, T. C. (1996). Learning with technology: Using computers as cognitive tools. In D. H. Jonassen (ed.), *Handbook of research for educational communications and technology.* New York: Simon & Schuster/Macmillan.

Kuhlthau, C. C. (1995). The process of learning from information. *School Libraries Worldwide* 1:1, 1–12.

Kuhlthau, C. C. (1988). A process approach to library skills instruction. In F. B. McDonald, ed., *The emerging school library media program.* Englewood, CO: Libraries Unlimited.

Kuhlthau, C. C. (1987). An emerging theory of library instruction. *School Library Media Quarterly* 16:1, 23–28.

Levstik, L. S., and Smith, D. B. (1996). "I've never done this before"; Building a community of historical inquiry in a third-grade classroom. *Advances in Research on Teaching* 6, 85–114.

Macrorie, K. (1988). *The I-search paper.* Portsmouth, NH: Boynton/Cook Heinemann.

Marchionini, G. (1995). *Information seeking in electronic environments.* New York: Cambridge University Press.

Marchionini, G., and Teague, J. (1987). Elementary students' use of electronic information services: An exploratory study. *Journal of Research on Computing in Education* 20:2, 139–155.

Moore, P. (1995). Information problem solving: A wider view of library skills. *Contemporary Educational Psychology* 20:1, 1–31.

Neuman, D. (1994). Designing databases as tools for higher-level learning: Insights from instructional systems design. *Educational Technology, Research and Development* 41:4, 25–46.

Nielsen, J. (1993). *Hypertext and hypermedia.* Boston: Kluwer Academic Press.

Oliver, R., and Oliver, H. (1997). Using context to promote learning from information-seeking tasks. *Journal of the American Society for Information Science* 48:6, 519–526.

Park, O. (1991). Hypermedia: Functional features and research issues. *Educational Technology* 31:8, 24–31.

Perkins, D. N. (1992). *Smart schools: Better thinking and learning for every child.* New York: The Free Press.

Rouet, J.-F., Levonen, J. J., Dillon, A., and Spiro, R. J. (1996). *Hypertext and cognition.* Mahwah, NJ: Lawrence Erlbaum Associates.

Sandlian, P. (1995). Rethinking the rules. *School Library Journal* 41:7, 22–25.

Shannon, D. M. (1996). Tracking the transition to a flexible access library program in two library power elementary schools. *School Library Media Quarterly* 24:3, 155–163.

Small, R. V., and Ferreira, S. M. (1994). Information location and use, motivation, and learning patterns when using print or multimedia information resources. *Journal of Educational Multimedia and Hypermedia* 3:3/4, 251–273.

Stripling, B. K. (1995). Learning-centered libraries: Implications from research. *School Library Media Quarterly* 23:3, 163–170.

Stripling, B. K., and Pitts, J. M. (1988). *Brainstorms and blueprints: Teaching library research as a thinking process.* Englewood, CO: Libraries Unlimited.

Tallman, J. I., and van Deusen, J. D. (1995). Is flexible scheduling always the answer? Some surprising results from a national study. In B. J. Morris (ed.), *School library media annual.* Englewood, CO: Libraries Unlimited.

Todd, R. J. (1995). Integrated information skills instruction: Does it make a difference? *School Library Media Quarterly* 23:2, 133–138.

Transformations: Kentucky's curriculum framework. Vol. 1. (1993). Frankfort, KY: Kentucky Department of Education.

Wells, G., and Chang-Wells, G. L. (1992). *Constructing knowledge together: Classrooms as centers of inquiry and literacy.* Portsmouth, NH: Heinemann.

Zimmerman, B. J., and Schunk, D. H., eds. (1989). *Self-regulated learning and academic achievement: Theory, research, and practice.* New York: Springer-Verlag.

APPENDIX: DATA COLLECTION INSTRUMENTS PERCEPTION QUESTIONNAIRE—THE INFORMATION SEARCH PROCESS/SELF-REGULATORY SKILLS

Put a check mark in the column that is most like you.

	Yes	No	Sometimes
Mentoring			
1. I ask the librarian for help with my research project.			
2. I find it helpful to talk to others about my topic.			
3. I talk to people who know about my topic.			
4. I use the help screens on the computer resources.			
Information-Seeking Skills			
5. I have a clear focus for my topic before using the library			
6. My thoughts about my topic change as I explore information			
7. I like to find everything I will need first and then read it.			
8. The library has the information I need.			
9. All the sources of information I need are listed in the OPAC.			
10. I make several trips to the library to research a topic.			
11. The information I need is in unexpected places in the library.			
12. I am successful in using the library			
13. I need materials other than books.			
14. A search is completed when I no longer find new information.			
15. A search is completed when I find enough information.			
Using Information Skills			
16. When reading, I try to connect the things I am reading about with what I already know.			
17. I take detailed notes from every source of information I look at.			
18. I make an outline before I write my paper.			
19. When I take notes from my reading, I write down the page numbers where I found the information.			
20. I use the table of contents to help me find information.			
21. I use the index to help me find information.			
22. I use the glossary to find meanings of words I don't know.			

	Yes	No	Sometimes
Critical Thinking			
23. I become more interested in a topic as I gather information			
24. When studying, I copy my notes over to help me remember material.			
25. When I study, I put important ideas into my own words.			
26. I use what I have learned from old homework assignments and the textbook to do new assignments.			
27. I ask myself questions to make sure I know the material I have been studying.			
28. When I'm reading, I stop once in a while and go over what I have read.			
29. I study or work where I will not be interrupted.			
30. I turn off the radio and TV so I can concentrate on what I am doing.			
31. It is hard for me to decide what the main ideas are in what I read.			
32. I check over my work to make sure I did it right.			
33. When I am studying a topic, I try to make everything fit together.			
Persistence/Motivation			
34. When work is hard, I either give up or study only the easy parts.			
35. Even when study materials are dull and uninteresting, I keep working until I finish.			
36. I work hard to get a good grade even when I don't like a class.			

Interview Questions

Beginning Interview

RESEARCH PROCESS

1. Take me step-by-step through the way you would do a research project.

2. How do you know what kind of information to look for when you start a project?

3. Where do you think you might find useful information for a project?

4. How would you find sources like books, encyclopedias, magazines, and computer resources?

COMPUTER EXPOSURE

1. Do you have a computer at home that you get to use? Tell me how you use it.

2. Once you find a good page of information in a book or on the computer, what do you do next? (If you are writing a report or making a presentation.)

MENTORING

1. What do you think a mentor is or does?

2. What are some problems you have had before in finding information? (Perhaps in a research project that you have done before.)

3. What kind of help did you have to ask for?

4. What kind of help do you need when you are working on a project?

Week 1 Interview

CRITICAL THINKING

1. Bring me up to date on your project. How is it going? What are you doing now?

2. Did you have any problems today with your project? How did you solve them?

3. How do you know if the information you found is any good?

4. How do you know when you have enough information?

5. Tell me about some times when you ask yourself questions. When do you do that?

6. When you get finished with your work, what sort of things do you think about it?

7. How would writing down information help you to think about it better?

Week 2–4 Interview

PRESENTING INFORMATION SKILLS

1. Bring me up to date on your project. How is it going? What are you doing now?

2. Did you have any problems today with your project? How did you solve them?

3. When you have finished finding all your information for your project, then what do you do next?

4. How are some ways that you could present the information you learn?

5. Why did you choose to work on this project, and how do you feel about it?

Example of Log Files

Nebula & Orphica, April 12, 1999

www.cabincreek.centerville.k12.ky.us/	Cabincreek_center-ville_k12_ky.htm	04/12/99	14:38:22
www.cabincreek.centerville.k12.ky.us/library/library.htm	Library.htm	04/12/99	14:41:54
www.cabincreek.centerville.k12.ky.us/library/research/research.htm	Research.htm	04/12/99	14:42:30
www.cabincreek.centerville.k12.ky.us/library/research/researc2.htm	Researc2.htm	04/12/99	14:42:36
www.cabincreek.centerville.k12.ky.us/library/research/big6.htm	big6.htm	04/12/99	14:42:42
www.cabincreek.centerville.k12.ky.us/library/research/big6~2.htm	big6~2.htm	04/12/99	14:42:44
www.cabincreek.centerville.k12.ky.us/library/research/redchek2.gif	Redchek2.gif	04/12/99	14:42:45
www.cabincreek.centerville.k12.ky.us/library/research/useof.htm	useof.htm	04/12/99	14:42:50
www.cabincreek.centerville.k12.ky.us/library/research/useof2.htm	useof2.htm	04/12/99	14:43:19
www.cabincreek.centerville.k12.ky.us/library/research/datachrt.htm	Datachrt.htm	04/12/99	14:59:38
www.cabincreek.centerville.k12.ky.us/library/research/read7.htm	read7.htm	04/12/99	15:10:42
www.cabincreek.centerville.k12.ky.us/library/research/read6.htm	read6.htm	04/12/99	15:10:43
www.cabincreek.centerville.k12.ky.us/library/research/read5.htm	read5.htm	04/12/99	15:10:55
www.cabincreek.centerville.k12.ky.us/library/research/read4.htm	read4.htm	04/12/99	15:10:56
www.cabincreek.centerville.k12.ky.us/library/research/read3.htm	read3.htm	04/12/99	15:11:00
www.cabincreek.centerville.k12.ky.us/library/research/read2.htm	read2.htm	04/12/99	15:11:02
www.cabincreek.centerville.k12.ky.us/library/research/reading.htm	Reading.htm	04/12/99	15:11:07

Research Agenda Checklist

Student number	1	2	3	4	5	6	7	8	9	10	11	12	13
Gatekeeping letters (3)	X	X	X	X	X	X	X	X	X	X	X	X	X
Consent and assent letters	X	X	X	X	X	X	X	X	X	X	X	X	X
Beginning questionnaire	X	X	X	X	X	X	X	X	X	X	X	X	X
First interview	X	X	X	X	X	X	X	X	X	X	X	X	X
Encarta lesson/learning time		5	4	3	1	0	3	1	0	1	4	1	1
World Wide Web lesson/learning time	6	6	7	3	2	0	2	4	3	5	8	4	4
OPAC lesson/learning time	3	4	2	1	1	0	1	1	0	0	4	1	0
SIRS Discoverer lesson/learning time	0	4	4	4	4	0	5	2	2	0	4	4	0
Location lesson/learning time	1	1	0	1	1	0	0	1	1	0	0	1	1
$Big6^{®}$ lesson/learning time	1	1	1	0	1	1	1	1	0	1	1	1	0
Journal & Timeline lesson/learning time	0	1	1	0	1	1	1	1	0	1	1	1	0
E-mail lesson/learning time	0	2	2	1	0	0	4	0	0	0	1	1	0
Web-page lesson/learning time	4	3	3	1	0	0	0	2	0	0	4	0	0
Internet Drivers License	X	X	X	X		X	X	X	X	X	X	X	
Interview 2–5	3	4	5	0	0	3	1	5	1	2	4	1	1
Saw research questions	X	X	X							X	X		
Meeting for presentation rubrics	0	0	0	0	0	0	0	0	0	0	0	0	0
Student journal perceptions		X	X						X	X		X	
Final project presentation/assessment	X	X	X		X	X	X	X	X	X	X	X	X
Ending questionnaire	X	X	X		X	X	X	X	X	X	X	X	X

Reading Buddy Progress Chart

Each time you finish one of the assignments, see Mrs. Gibson for a star to put on it. Each star is worth one Book Fair Buck.

Name	♥
Assent letter	
Beginning survey	
First interview	
World Wide Web lesson/learning time (up to 8)	
SIRS Discoverer lesson/learning time (up to 4)	
Encarta lesson/learning time (up to 4)	
OPAC lesson/learning time (up to 4)	
Location lesson/learning time	
Web-page lesson/learning time (optional)	
Big6® lesson/learning time	
I got my Internet Drivers License	
Journal & Timeline lesson/learning time	
I used the *Research Buddy,* wrote about it in my journal, and copied the browser history file to my disk(up to 8).	
I found at least 4 sources of information for a bibliography and showed them to Mrs. Gibson.	
Weekly interview 1	
Weekly interview 2	
Weekly interview 3	
Weekly interview 4	
I showed Mrs. Gibson how I organized my information.	
I showed Mrs. Gibson how I plan to present the information and met with her to decide on my presentation rubrics.	
I evaluated my project with the presentation rubrics that I had created earlier with Mrs. Gibson.	
I finished my timeline all on one page.	
I presented my research at the pizza/presentation party.	
I created a web page about my research (optional).	
I wrote a final summary in my journal about what I thought about using the *Research Buddy* to do research in the library.	
Additional library work visits (worth one star for each quality 30-minute time)	

Student Evaluation Survey

Name _____

Mark an "X" next to the number that best fits your answer. Please be totally honest about each answer, and think hard before you decide. Be especially careful about the last four, because the words are almost the same, but they mean very different things. Thank you so much for taking the time to do this.

5 = strongly agree

4 = agree

3 = neither agree nor disagree

2 = disagree

1 = strongly disagree

Questions	5	4	3	2	1
1. The *Research Buddy* helped me choose my topic.			2	1	2
2. The *Research Buddy* helped me ask questions about my topic.	2	1	1	1	
3. The *Research Buddy* helped me think of places and sources to find information.		3	2		
4. The *Research Buddy* helped me to find the information in the places (library, home, etc.).	1	1		2	1
5. The *Research Buddy* helped me to find the information in the sources (books, computers, etc.).		1	1	3	
6. The *Research Buddy* helped me to get the most important information out of what I found.		2	2	1	
7. The *Research Buddy* helped me to organize my information.	2	2		1	
8. The *Research Buddy* helped me to make a bibliography.	1	1	2		1
9. The *Research Buddy* helped me decide what to do for my project (report, web page, poster, etc.).		1	2	1	1
10. The *Research Buddy* helped me to evaluate my project.		2	3		
11. The *Research Buddy* helped me think about my project with the questions for my journal writing.	1	3	1		
12. The *Research Buddy* was fun to use.	1	3	1		
13. I learned new information about my topic because of this project.	3	2			
14. I learned new information about my topic because of the *Research Buddy.*			2	3	
15. I learned new skills about doing research because of this project.	1	3	1		
16. I learned new skills about doing research because of the *Research Buddy.*	2	2	1		

Snapshots of a Teen Internet User
One Way to Learn About Information Literacy

Jinx Watson
University of Tennessee

Those who develop or change school policy rarely solicit the insight of those it most directly affects: teachers and students. As a result, while continuing to invest in technology software, hardware and training, schools often neglect to assess students' perceptions and experience. Understanding students' use may assist teachers and school media specialists as they consider programs of information literacy. Too often, schools rely on prescriptive curricula that ignore students' real experience. We need to understand better how students relate to the new technologies, for both school and recreation. For purposes of this study, I have framed a phenomenological question, "What does it mean when a student says he uses the Internet?"

BACKGROUND

Since 1996, I have interviewed a small group of students whose school life has been influenced by the new technologies. In 1993, this group began to benefit from the state's "twenty-first century classrooms" (Tenn. Code Ann. 12-5-204). By eighth grade, in their third consecutive year of classroom technology funding, many of these students had begun to articulate the differences they perceived in reading both electronic and print modes (Watson 1998). They showed an understanding of the nuances of pace in both seeking specific information and browsing for pleasure. From their comments, I heard confidence in their use and pride in a level of personal expertise (Watson 1998). Their comments also confirmed others' research (Bilal 1998; Fidel et al. 1999) regarding motivation and satisfaction in using the Web. Two and one-half years after my first discussion with them—as they entered their junior year in high school—I interviewed several of the original group. Specifically, I wanted to examine whether the expressed confidence represented a generic adolescent developmental stage or whether the students continued to feel self-assurance from some level of real expertise in using the Internet. Their comments offered a major insight: The students revealed ease with the Internet for purposes of communicating with friends and with chat rooms for information on hobbies and interests, but showed reluctance in using online information for school and research purposes (Watson 1999). One student observed that the Internet is "too disorganized, and it's more self-aggrandizing junk out there than anything else" (Watson, 197). However, such an assessment did not appear during the students' discussion of searching the Internet for personal or familiar topics where "you have to take what you know and apply it to what you read" (p. 196). These student users knew intuitively how to apply "skills for electronic information evaluation" (Fitzgerald 1997) when they held prior knowledge. They preferred Internet communication capabilities and browsing for pleasure more than for school use because they felt inadequate in judging relevance of site information on little-known subjects.

One student's ease and straightforwardness invited me to consider framing a research focus on him, a single voice. I wrote previously (Watson 1999) that Mike (alias) has created what phenomenologists (Gadamer 1975; Pollio, Henley, and Thompson 1997) call "a stance" regarding his relationship with his computer and its capabilities. Mike's interviews each "revealed a distinct stance of use, comfort level, trust and understanding between (this) individual user and the Internet" (Watson 1999, 192). Pollio, Henley, and Thompson (1997) write that *stance* refers to the situated perspective or intention of a person within an experience (p. 8). Karolides (1997) describes stance as "orientation" to a subject. To learn from Mike's orientation to technology, we need to appreciate his perceptions of use. For example, as an eighth grader, Mike suggested that because technology use was in its infancy, seeking assistance to search electronically might be sanctioned, whereas requesting help in other school areas appeared inappropriate. Other students' comments confirmed his insight, which I labeled, "questions of openness and vulnerability in novice users" (Watson 1998, 1028). At the same time, in the first two interviews, Mike expressed self-assurance in sharing his own expertise in technology with peers and teachers (p. 1028). For purposes of the current study, I continue to probe Mike's stance towards the Internet. What sense does Mike make regarding his use of the Internet, and what has informed what he knows?

RELEVANT LITERATURE

Dervin (1992) suggests that "sense-making has been used to study the needs, images and satisfaction of users and potential users of information/communication systems . . . in short, what users want from systems, what they get and what they think of them" (p. 61). Kuhlthau (1993) reminds us that we must attend to the "interactive thoughts, actions and feelings in the process of [knowledge] construction" (pp. 8–9). By examining the narrative texts of Mike's reflection, perception, and "thinking aloud" (Ingwersen 1992, 99), we begin to perceive his levels of skill and mindset about searching the Internet. The voice of one teen offers a highly individualistic, and perhaps an idiosyncratic, look at how one might employ the Internet for seeking information and for pleasure. Such a study does not represent a general population. However, we may draw general inferences from such an inquiry, and the study can generate additional questions for educators as they think about teens and their Internet use. For both researchers and practitioners who contemplate information users' perceptions of their experiences, a close study of one subject may offer enough rich description to illuminate the complexities and problems we all ponder in searching electronically, despite differences in setting. Lawrence-Lightfoot and Davis (1997) remind us that, "A persistent irony—recognized and celebrated by novelists, poets, playwrights—is that as one moves closer to the unique characteristics of a person or a place, one discovers the universal" (p. 14).

In approaching the everyday world of one student and his relationship with the Internet, we deal concretely, rather than theoretically or abstractly, with issues of use. School practitioners will recognize the depth and complexity of one individual's experiences and be reminded that they are surrounded by hundreds of such snapshots in their daily work. The careful study of one student may also generate questions for teachers who create assignments or offer instruction in information literacy. Such a study may illuminate both the formal and incidental learning as well as the evolving affective stance, which influence student users of the Internet. By taking an in-depth look at one stance towards the Internet, we may add to the developing body of research on young people's information-seeking behavior.

METHODOLOGY

How might we go about the complex and elusive research task of revealing an individual's stance toward the Internet? To probe Mike's perspective, I structured follow-up questions to the previous interviews, such as, "What kind of time do you spend on the Internet these days? How active is your participation in the chat rooms that so involved you a year ago?"

The intent of such questions was not to be intrusive or to measure some standard, but rather to begin to understand one single student's developing relationship with the Internet.

For the third interview, Mike sat at a computer with Internet connectivity in his high school media center, and searched for information on his own interests and for one question that I had prescribed. He talked through his moves and commented on success or frustration in finding information. I tape-recorded his comments throughout his searching as well as during the interview session. I made notes from my observation of his movements, use of mouse and keyboard, time spent on reading screen displays, as well as other visible evidence of searching. His comments and my observation notes serve as data for a protocol analysis of his online use during one hour. To add to my understanding of Mike's stance, I re-read the interviews from the eighth grade (11/96) and summer prior to junior year (6/99). The three texts, which span three and one-half years, include interviews and talking out loud during searching. The data serve to represent Mike's evolving perspective on using the Internet.

After reading and re-reading the data to gain insight, I addressed the issue of trust-worthiness of the research (Guba 1981) by asking two school media specialists to read and comment on Mike's interview texts and subsequent drafts of my paper. A third specialist read a draft of my paper. Analogous to methods used in assessing writing samples holistically, I noted that we each identified similar themes worthy of analysis: evidence of developmental change in motivation for using the Internet and evidence of little growth in discussing and employing efficient search strategies. For purposes of this paper, I have focused on the first theme—developmentally influenced searching—and selected a key text from each interview to analyze.

Analyzing by Reading and Writing Text

The data sources for this phenomenological research rely on the texts of Mike's interviews. The qualitative analysis relies on reading the texts. When we read the texts or narrative of another, we employ a triple hermeneutic (Giddens 1976). The first is the conception of reality constructed by the student and the second is a reconstruction of that meaning into new frames of reference by the researcher (Richardson 1994). Ultimately, the reader of the research offers a third hermeneutic reading of the student's comments and the researcher's text. In probing the essence of each text, one engages in a process to examine and to involve oneself in what the subject is saying. Such involvement tries to make sense of the experience as the student perceives it, not by externally imposing standards to test a hypothesis.

In this analysis I employ three readings (Watson and Wilcox 2000). I gain an impression of the selected text first, with a "quick" reading. Within this impressionistic reading, I sense key themes and points worthy of closer reading. In the second round, I perform a "close" or hermeneutic reading that does not attempt to reproduce the phenomenon or experience but rather attempts to gain understanding and to offer interpretations. The third reading, "insights," connects my interpretations of the selected text to what we know of students or of searching in general. In this section, others' relevant research creates a context and extends the meaning found in an individual's close reading.

DISCUSSION

In the tradition of phenomenology, wherein such research may raise more questions than it answers, I shape the findings as questions for the reader to consider. Clues from the interview texts suggest that as Mike moves out of adolescence and into young adulthood, he searches the Internet primarily for information—school purposes and life decisions—and less for reasons of recreation or communication. I name this finding a question of *developmentally influenced searching.*

In the following selections, I read the text to seek Mike's intent and stance in searching online. In each of the three readings, the subject's words are represented in italics. My analysis of the text appears in plain type.

Story One

A Quick Reading

11/96. I wasn't exactly sure of addresses to use, so I would make up something to use. So I would make up some keywords and one of them that was not what I expected was one that I got into this morning. . . . I'm sure you know one of the issues on the Internet was too much violence on the Internet and stuff like that. So I was wanting to look into that so I typed in violence.com and it was not about violence particularly, ha ha. (Was it sexual violence?) *Yeah, I assume. I cut it off before it got on there. You know how it loads slowly from the top down? Well it got down there and there were four women with like leather tops on so I just backed it up real quick . . .*

A Close Reading

I wasn't exactly sure of addresses to use, so I would make up something to use. So I would make up some keywords . . .

Mike expresses confidence in solving the problem of how to begin the search. Rather than be stopped by lack of specific information, he enters a trial and error mode. He has some general knowledge about how the address window works and uses the vocabulary, "keyword." This word suggests some formal teaching, either by a school media specialist or a help button on the search engine.

and one of them that was not what I expected was one that I got into this morning . . .

Here, Mike shows either ignorance or innocence. Not *expecting* particular results might suggest he anticipates a perfect match between query and result, out of ignorance of the magnitude of information and thus, the need for framing more specific queries. On the other hand, he reveals innocence in believing that the specific information or image he seeks from such a general topic should be disclosed immediately, as he imagines it.

I'm sure you know one of the issues on the Internet was too much violence on the Internet and stuff like that. So I was wanting to look into that so I typed in violence.com and it was not about violence particularly, ha ha.

Adolescent bravado takes on many forms, but one that might be assumed in this passage lies in Mike's collegial reference, *I'm sure you know,* that, despite our age and role differences, we share similar issues and knowledge. His phrase, *look into that* suggests a kind of research, a personal and professional investigation worthy of both his and my interests. The format of his search query suggests his stated notion of using a keyword followed by a period and the abbreviation for commercial site. His language suggests some experience, some learning about site names. Nevertheless, he does not mention employing a specific search engine or directory, nor does he craft a thoughtful, focused query.

Mike's laughter at the end of this declaration may mask his feelings of guilt or transgression. The school's policy for students accessing inappropriate sites is swift suspension from school. The laughter sounds almost conspiratorial, either to make me an accomplice or to impress me with his "adult" insight.

(Was it sexual violence?)

Yeah, I assume. I cut it off before it got on there. You know how it loads slowly from the top down? Well it got down there and there were four women with like leather tops on so I just backed it up real quick . . .

Slowing down his humorous stance, but continuing to presume my knowledge—*you know*—Mike becomes serious here and lays out the steps to exit the site, letting me know that he has not examined the full page. "Backed it up" describes his strategy for exiting the compromising page.

Insights

As an eighth grader with three years of 21st-century classroom experience and a home computer with Internet connectivity, Mike has had some experience with searching. His overriding tone suggests familiarity, bordering on bravado, with using the Internet. He has learned about using a "keyword" but does not mention framing search questions for particular search engines or directories. His reference to the issue of violence on the Internet suggests either his awareness of the school policy regarding inappropriate sites or knowledge of society's debate regarding children's use of the Internet. As a thirteen year old, the selection and revelation of the search topic of violence reveals his developmental age and gender with the intention to shock or surprise (Lefrancois 1999).

Nevertheless, Mike's self-selected topic suggests a mode of browsing rather than an analytical search. Marchionini (1995) suggests that such an informal and interactive mode offers information about the search process itself, as well as content information. In his work on children's retrieval using an OPAC, Solomon (1993) writes that "retrieval intentions are important . . . (including) children's need to explore . . . even when they were lacking such a basic skill as reading" (p. 253). Mike self-censored his information seeking because of the unexpected or inappropriate content, but he gains insight into one consequence of casual browsing.

Story Two

A Quick Reading

6/99 . . . this is not a sexist remark at all, I'm just saying in this situation . . . a wife had gone in (a chat room) *and her husband was a knife collector. She didn't know what to look for. She didn't know what was good. And you know, she could talk to me and ask me questions about things I knew and then I've found several knife collectors on there that we can just swap information. You know, I have this, what do you have, where do you find yours? What's it worth? Others, there's an astounding number of different catalogs and magazines out there and if you find the right one, you find a knife for 75% off what you'd find in a store . . .* (and in the soccer chat room) *you're looking for colleges there in that situation. And I, uh, you know . . . there's no age group in these. So I can talk to people who are at University of Florida, University of, you know, UCLA, Indiana, North Carolina, Virginia, the big soccer schools. And get feedback from them about how they got there, what they like and don't like about their soccer program, etc.*

A Close Reading

> *. . . this is not a sexist remark at all, I'm just saying in this situation . . . a wife had gone in* (a chat room) *and her husband was a knife collector. She didn't know what to look for. She didn't know what was good. And you know, she could talk to me and ask me questions about things I knew*

Mike pardons the example by letting me know he's politically correct. His preferred chat rooms (knife collecting, hiking/hunting, and soccer) typically invite males and therefore, the non-collector—in this case, a woman—appears as an anomaly. Because she was not knowledgeable, Mike seizes the opportunity to share what he knows about the subject.

> *and then I've found several knife collectors on there that we can just swap information. You know, I have this, what do you have, where do you find yours? What's it worth?*

Mike's tone suggests very businesslike and matter-of-fact information exchanges. He mentions no real personal news, just hot tips about shared interests and valuable possessions. Because of his self-declared expertise, Mike can assess the information he receives for his purposes.

> *Others, there's an astounding number of different catalogs and magazines out there and if you find the right one, you find a knife for 75% off what you'd find in a store*

The reference to *others* suggests additional websites and reasons other than chat rooms for logging onto the Internet. The hyperbolic reference offers a tone of knowledgeable authority or possible justification for visiting commercial sites.

> (and in the soccer chat room) *you're looking for colleges there in that situation. And I, uh, you know . . . there's no age group in these. So I can talk to people who are at University of Florida, University of, you know, UCLA, Indiana, North Carolina, Virginia, the big soccer schools. And get feedback from them about how they got there, what they like and don't like about their soccer program, etc.*

Mike switches topics, perhaps because his example of knife collecting, buying, and selling has revealed interests too bourgeois or less noble, or perhaps as a rising junior, Mike must consider college. He defends his soccer chat room use by suggesting it offers one way to explore colleges. He makes no reference to news of scores, awards, or schedules of games. His tone suggests that one taps into such chat rooms to gather information for making life decisions. And because of the anonymity of the Internet, he does not have to reveal his age to his correspondents, nor be denied because of his age. He may appear in whatever guise he might choose: scholar, star athlete, father, or himself. Does he remember or care that his correspondent might don a mask, or change his age, as well, to chat?

Insights

Erik Erikson's landmark work (1963) portrays the adolescent period as one in which children begin to make sense of their own roles in society's technology and economy. Young people wrestle with feelings of inadequacy and inferiority as well as expertise and confidence as they try out roles, mimic others' behaviors, and make their way into the wider society. Universally, one's identity evolves from involving oneself "doing things beside and with others" (p. 260). Personal interests offer a natural motive for logging onto special interest chat rooms. The danger lies, of course, in whether or not a young person would experience negotiating those interests only in virtual terms, rather than in real life. Because Mike has not begun to work outside of school, nor does he own a car, he finds himself with hours of free time to browse and search the Internet at home. He can try out his thinking with adults in cyberspace; he can learn ways of negotiating his special interests and searching through informal and self-motivated means. Borgman, Hirsh, and Walter (1995) agree: "Children have a natural tendency to explore . . . (and be viewed) as active problem solvers, with an evolving information need that may be searched iteratively" (p. 665). Mike's special interests invite him to explore and seek information via chat rooms and websites. Such personal exploration offers him motivational and informal ways to discover new ways to navigate the Web.

Issues of discovery or prescriptive learning surface as pedagogical debate. Nevertheless, research in psychology regarding the retention of new knowledge suggests that initial learning is powerful (Tennessee Instructional Model 1984). Teaching first-time learners the tools and skills to search efficiently and effectively can offer an important foundation in information literacy. Thus, educators must assist novice researchers by capitalizing on the motivation of self-selected topics as well as structuring the learning about search strategies and tools.

Story Three

A Quick Reading

> 2/00: *I'm fairly structured, as far, as you know, I don't, whatever you want to call it, surf the Web or whatever. If I need something, then I'll get on, and I'll look for that something, but I don't usually just browse through everything. . . . Biggest thing is like I'm too busy more than anything. I don't spend a lot of time at all on the Internet and the Web because, you know, I work a lot a week, I have soccer every day of the week. . . . If there's something I need, then I'll get on and do it, and if not, I don't really fool with it. . Now I will admit that I use it for this personal thing. I would hardly call it research. . . . I've done searches . . . to find like a particular game, and you can read reviews or you can get suggestions or hints and stuff like that.*

A Close Reading

> *I'm fairly structured, as far, as you know, I don't, whatever you want to call it, surf the Web or whatever. If I need something, then I'll get on, and I'll look for that something, but I don't usually just browse through everything. . . .*

Mike's direct and assured tone in discussing his habits on the Internet suggest purpose and focus in his searching. No longer willing or able to spend time browsing, he shows disdain of the term, *surf*, and perhaps even of the activity. *Need*, rather than pleasure, now drives his logging onto the Internet. By using the term *structured*, he implies an analytic, purposeful approach.

> *Biggest thing is like I'm too busy more than anything. I don't spend a lot of time at all on the Internet and the Web because, you know, I work a lot a week, I have soccer every day of the week. . . . If there's something I need, then I'll get on and do it, and if not, I don't really fool with it.*

As a second semester junior in high school, Mike's work and soccer responsibility compete for his free time outside of school. Perhaps he is less isolated than in previous school years; his work and team sport suggest more sociability on real terms rather than the virtual sociability of electronic chat rooms. Such current obligations may appear more serious to him than using the Internet. Not *fooling* with it suggests that his former use of the Internet might be perceived as whimsy, recreation, even silly.

> *Now I will admit that I use it for this personal thing. I would hardly call it research. . . . I've done searches . . . to find like a particular game, and you can read reviews or you can get suggestions or hints and stuff like that*

Mike's confession reveals a mixed tone: He still does use the Internet for whimsy, but to maintain the profile of an adult, he adds that he reads the *reviews, gets suggestions*. He downplays his recreational use. Problematic in naturalistic research, interviews and surveys may reveal perceptions and aspiration, but to appreciate how much real time he searches for reviews and new games as compared to playing the games must be revealed in other, more quantifiable ways.

Insights

True to the developmental changes of his age, Mike's life changes from adolescence to young adult, with more responsibilities and commitments outside his own personal interests. Once an active member of three electronic chat rooms (Watson 1999), Mike, a student who helped teachers by backing up disks and repairing hardware (Watson 1998), now perceives that he logs on far fewer hours than ever in his life.

Surfing, browsing, and spending time on the Internet do not appeal to him in the way they might have during his earlier years. The notion of discovering either sites or strategies to search has little appeal. Mike calls himself *structured*, suggesting that focused, efficient searching appeals to him. Future research will determine to what extent Mike searches efficiently and effectively.

CONCLUSION

In sum, a question of developmentally influenced searching may inspire practitioners to tap into at least two of the developmental issues of young adolescents: their need to show and practice expertise in their personal pursuits and their necessity to communicate and socialize with each other. By inviting students to browse and surf in areas of their personal interests, as sanctioned school activities, educators may guide them in the "Nine Information Literacy Standards for Student Learning" described in *Information Power* (American Association of School Librarians & Association for Educational Communications and Technology 1998). Motivated to research personal, perhaps idiosyncratic topics of interest, students may be taught the protocols of search tools' capabilities and assessment in collegial settings. As a result, students may become more "authentic researchers" (Gordon 1999) of topics they might previously have only pursued outside of the classroom.

Gordon suggests that:

> Research in constructivist learning and information-seeking theory points to the need for the practitioner to create learning tasks that relate to the real world and offer opportunities for critical thinking, problem solving and meaningful learning . . . Concepts of relevance and information needs, as they emerge from constructivist-based research, suggest that learning tasks must offer diverse

opportunities for learning and interpreting information and data . . . a monolithic research assignment . . . is not adequate to accommodate the highly personalized model of learning and information searching that cognitive psychology presents. (1999, 6)

Thus, students' early adolescence may offer educators one of the prime periods for teaching the new tools and skills of information literacy. Over three and one-half years, Mike moved from active experimental use through a recreational stage to an "as need" basis, where he accesses the Internet for assignments or for consumer information. His change in usage reflects his new time constraints within the recognizable developmental stage of young adulthood. Tapping into Mike's self-proclaimed interests of soccer, knife collecting, and hiking/hunting (Watson 1999) as topics for sanctioned, authentic research in the classroom might offer rich opportunities for educators to direct Mike's information literacy skills. Novice searches require continuing motivation; without it, users often terminate searches (Nahl and Tenopir 1996). By the time students reach their junior year, working after school, driving cars, and becoming more social, they may find less time to develop personal areas of expertise and be less motivated to search for self-determined topics. Second, school programs might appropriately exploit young people's declaration that seeking help in searching is perceived as an approved activity in spite of the standard taboos for admitting need or failure (Watson 1998). Hirsh (1998) found that: "In some cases, students indicated that their friends helped them find information . . . [which students perceived as finding] on accident" (p. 66). Students expand their information literacy repertoire by trading search tips and learning new strategies, moving them from novice to more expert searchers. And, as students enter the adult world, they begin to take on more guarded behavior, perceiving peer assistance as a sign of weakness. The intermediate and middle school grades offer a powerful, developmentally appropriate period in which to teach initial skills of information seeking and assessment because of personal interest and collegial openness. Delaying the teaching of initial research skills and information literacy until high school may, by default, become more prescriptive rather than dynamic and motivational.

Readers of Mike's snapshots may relate to his described experiences with Internet searching and ask, "What do I make of these comments and questions for my own situation?" Mike's comments may offer new clues for teachers, school media specialists, and curriculum developers. They may raise questions about formal teaching and incidental learning of research skills and search strategies. But above all, a single portrait brings us back to ourselves as new learners, information seekers. Educators who are reminded of the complexity of a single human experience may create more informed school policy and design curricula that take the learner into greater consideration.

REFERENCES

American Association of School Librarians & Association for Educational Communications and Technology. (1998). *Information power: Building partnerships for learning*. Chicago: American Library Association.

Bilal, D. (1998). Children's search processes in using World Wide Web search engines: An exploratory study. In *Proceedings, information access in the global information economy, sixty-first ASIS annual meeting, Pittsburgh*. Medford, NJ: Information Today.

Borgman, C., Hirsh, S., and Walter, V. (1995). Children's searching behavior on browsing and keyword online catalogs: The science library catalog project. *Journal of the American Society for Information Science* 46:9, 663–684.

Dervin, B. (1992). From the mind's eye of the user: The sense-making qualitative-quantitative methodology. In J. Glazier and R. Powell (eds.), *Qualitative research in information management*. Englewood, CO: Libraries Unlimited.

Erikson, E. (1963). *Childhood and society*. New York: W. W. Norton.

Fidel, R., Davies, R., Douglass, M., Holder, J., Hopkins, C., Kushner, E., Miyagishima, B., and Toney, C. (1999). A visit to the information mall: Web searching behavior of high school students. *Journal of the American Society for Information Science* 50:1, 24–37.

Fitzgerald, M. A. (1997). Misinformation on the Internet: Applying evaluation skills to online information. *Emergency Librarian* 24:3, 9–14.

Gadamer, H. (1975). *Truth and method.* (G. Barden and J. Cumming, eds. and trans.). New York: The Seabury Press.

Giddens, A. (1976). *New rules of socio-logical method.* London: Hutchinson.

Gordon, C. (1999). Students as authentic researchers: A new prescription for the high school research assignment. *School Library Media Research* 2, 1–21. [Online]. Available: www.ala.org/aasl /SLMR/vol2/authentic.html. (Accessed February 22, 2001).

Guba, E. G. (1981). Criteria for assessing the trustworthiness of naturalistic inquiries. *Educational Communication and Technology Journal* 29, 75–91.

Hirsh, S. (1998, October 24–29). Relevance determinations in children's use of electronic resources: A case study. In *Proceedings, information access in the global information economy, sixty-first ASIS annual meeting, Pittsburgh.* Medford, NJ: Information Today.

Ingwersen, P. (1992). *Information retrieval interaction.* London: Taylor Graham.

Karolides, N. (1997). Challenging old habits of mind: Revisiting reader's stance. *The New Advocate* 10:2, 161–169.

Kuhlthau, C. (1993). *Seeking meaning: A process approach to library and information services.* Norwood, NJ: Ablex Publishing.

Lawrence-Lightfoot, S., and Davis, J. H. (1997). *The art and science of portraiture.* San Francisco, CA: Jossey Bass.

Lefrancois, G. (1999). *The lifespan.* (6th ed.). Belmont, CA: Wadsworth Publishing.

Marchionini, G. (1995). *Information seeking in electronic environments.* New York: Cambridge University Press.

Nahl, D., and Tenopir, C. (1996). Affective and cognitive searching behaviors of novice end-users of a full-text database. *Journal of American Society of Information Science* 47, 276–286.

Pollio, H., Henley, T., and Thompson, C. (1997). *The phenomenology of everyday life.* New York: Cambridge University Press.

Richardson, V. (1994). Conducting research on practice. *Educational Researcher* 23:5, 5–10.

Solomon, P. (1993). Children's information retrieval behavior: A case analysis of an OPAC. *Journal of American Society of Information Science* 44, 245–264.

Tennessee Instructional Model. (1984). *Module on retention.* Nashville, TN: The Tennessee State Department of Education.

Watson, J. S. (1999, November 10–14). Students and the World Wide Web: Issues of confidence and competence. In *Proceedings: Unleash the power! Third international forum on research in school librarianship, IASL, Birmingham, ALA.* Seattle: International Association of School Librarianship.

Watson, J. S. (1998). "If you don't have it, you can't find it:" A close look at students' perceptions of using technology. *Journal of the American Society for Information Science* 49, 1024–1036.

Watson, J. S., and Wilcox, S. (2000). Reading for understanding: Methods of reflecting on practice. *The Journal of Reflective Practice* 1:1.

ACKNOWLEDGMENTS

Thanks to Sue Diehl, Tena Litherland, and Scot Smith, school media specialists, for reading the interviews and conferring with me. Thanks to "Mike."

From Bricks and Mortar to Clicks and Modems
The Redesign of a Graduate Program

Arthur Recesso
Jane Zahner
Andrew Brovey
Ellen Wiley
Catherine Price
Valdosta State University

Is it difficult to design graduate programs in instructional technology or educational media? Given the broad and rapidly changing nature of the field, we would say yes. Is it difficult to quickly redesign an entire graduate program to be delivered online? Certainly, in any field. Is it necessary to rely on online course vendors to develop such programs? The answer is a qualified no, given an understanding of the considerable challenges and requirements of the task. This article discusses the process of redesign and, more important, the competencies of personnel and the quality of teamwork and leadership it takes to get this difficult job done.

During the 2000 summer semester, Valdosta State University's Department of Curriculum and Instructional Technology launched a completely online Education Specialist (Ed.S.) in Instructional Technology Program. The Ed.S. is a post-master's terminal degree intended for practitioners seeking advanced certification in their fields. In this article we describe the department's venture into creating its own online graduate degree program without the assistance of private vendors. The discussion is divided into broad topics: the new program design process, student recruitment, technologies used to build and support the program, and the resulting current program. Each topic is subdivided to include an overview, a description of the tasks involved, the challenges faced, and the outcomes in terms of expectations as compared to what really happened. Our intent is to offer an inside look at the in-house development of an online program. The faculty's combined orientation and expertise in instructional systems design as well as technological application, plus the even more important orientation toward shared decision making, collaborative design, formative evaluation, and group rewards, made the development of the program possible.

NEW PROGRAM DESIGN

Instructional technology is a fast-changing field, even when it comes to accreditation requirements and program standards. Putting together a new online program would have required careful alignment with the requirements and standards in any case, but with an upcoming National Council for Accreditation of Teacher Education (NCATE) visit, we were especially tasked to rebuild the Ed.S. program for Y2K and beyond.

The Ed.S. program had a history of changes based on shifting conditions in the instructional technology workplace and the evolving philosophy of the instructional technology program. There have been three iterations of the Ed.S. program designed during the past five years. The first, designed for implementation in 1997, focused on two populations, those students with the goal of becoming leaders in school media programs and those with the goal of becoming leaders in school- or system-level technology programs. In the first iteration there was overlap between the two program options in professional courses taught by other departments (educational psychology and the first research course), but great distinctions between the instructional technology courses intended for media specialists and other courses. The research sequence leading to a field-based project/thesis was taught within the department, with the exception of the first educational research course.

Almost before this first Ed.S. program got off the ground, university systemwide semester conversion required that the program (along with our M.Ed. in Instructional Technology program) be re-examined and a new framework developed. At this point the reality of the multiple roles of the school media specialist, the necessity for teamwork among technology professionals, and the commonality of the needs for technology and interpersonal skills in our two populations indicated that a more integrated program was needed. This second iteration was more streamlined and general, preparing students to become leaders and researchers in school- or system-level technology programs. This view included media specialists, recognizing them as technology leaders in their schools. The idea was that students with varying career goals could work together in a course called, for example, "Database/Internet Applications," and construct experiences and knowledge that would allow them to achieve their goals within the context of the course. The research sequence from the first iteration was maintained, and an additional elective was added to allow for more student individualization of the program.

With this evolutionary history, as well as lots of recent practice in program redesign, the process of creating the framework, objectives, new courses, and syllabi for the Ed.S. online was a somewhat familiar challenge. The first thing we did was to explore and re-examine the College of Education Conceptual Framework Principles, institutional accreditation requirements, and professional standards upon which we base our programs.

Conceptual frameworks guide professional education programs by defining the philosophy, rationale, and research base that support the essential instructional components of degree programs. The conceptual framework provides coherence in student outcomes, course activities, assessments, and internship or practicum experiences. Advanced degrees designed for practicing teachers utilize the following principles, adapted from those developed by the National Board for Professional Teaching Standards.

1. Graduates are committed to their roles as helping professionals.

2. Graduates are capable of excellence in their professional practice.

3. Graduates think about their practice, use research, and contribute to the knowledge base.

4. Graduates are members of learning communities.

Looking at our conceptual framework in relation to the Ed.S. in Instructional Technology provided the first of many examples of the differences within the target audience for our program. Although some of the students would fit in the practicing teachers classification (media specialists included), others (e.g., adult educators, industry trainers) would not. Upon examination of the framework, we found that there was no conflict between the previous four principles and our own concept of what the Ed.S. program should be and whom it should serve.

Our institution is accredited by the Southern Association of Colleges and Schools (SACS). Because the new Ed.S. was to be an entire program delivered online, it was necessary to file for what SACS calls "Substantive Change Procedure C: The Initiation of Off Campus Programs, Branch Campuses, and Other Distance Learning Activities." This document included

- descriptions of the nature of the change, including an assessment of need;

- the relationship of the off-campus programs or distance learning activities to institutional purpose and mission;

- the location where the instruction is offered, including group sites and geographical areas of individual access;
- means used by the institution to monitor and ensure the quality of the overall academic program(s) offered at the off-campus site or through distance learning activities;
- an explanation of how outside materials would be chosen or adapted;
- information about the faculty;
- learning resources;
- support services;
- the institution's organizational structure; and
- financial resources.

Constructing this document was a difficult exercise because our institution was new to online programs and did not have any division designated for dealing with organizational support issues. However, the institution did have experience in other off-campus and distance learning delivery modes. Within the department, nearly all of the faculty had designed and delivered at least one course that was wholly or substantially online. This combination of experiences made the "invention" of methods and support systems a rich, workable, and reasonable model for future online program development. It would be a good exercise for any group contemplating developing an online program to work through a local process approximating the Substantive Change Procedure; it will bring up issues and needs about which you may not have thought.

Our College of Education is accredited by NCATE, and with a review approaching in 2000, our program had to conform with their standards. The instructional technology program met guidelines of the Georgia Professional Standards Commission (GPSC), which sets standards for graduates to earn licensure and/or certification from the state of Georgia. NCATE standards had for some time stipulated that institutions should consider, in the design of both basic teacher education and advanced professional preparation programs, guidelines developed by appropriate professional associations. Instructional technology, unlike most of the programs housed in the College of Education, is much broader than those that focus strictly on teacher education. This difference created a challenge in deciding which standards would provide the framework for the new Ed.S. program. Three likely NCATE partners were ISTE (International Society for Technology in Education), AECT (Association for Educational Communications and Technology) and ALA/AASL (American Library Association/American Association of School Librarians).

An initial determination that had to be made in relation to standards was at what level the program would be classified. The Ed.S. is an "in-between" program, post-masters but not at the doctoral level. This determination came into play when deciding which of a particular organization's standards were appropriate for the program. For example, AECT, in requesting feedback on the Third Draft of Revised Accreditation Guides (1999), asked, "How would you distinguish initial from advanced programs?" To solve this problem we studied the objectives and assessments listed within competency matrices. It was clear to us that although all of our students would not be prepared by having completed a program at the level designated as initial, we did expect that they would be able to perform at the advanced level by the end of the program. Thus we focused on the advanced performance indicators, and looked to the ISTE, AECT, and ALA/AASL standards for advanced programs.

ISTE describes a Program for Advanced Preparation of Teachers of Educational Computing and Technology Leadership. The preparation materials state that standards apply to programs designed to prepare candidates to serve as educational computing and technology coordinators or specialists. Although few of our students were actually planning to be computing teachers, we were interested in these standards because of our program's identified mission of preparing technology leaders. In Georgia there is a category of leadership certificates that are issued in fields that prepare an individual to administer or supervise a school system, school, or school program. Unfortunately, Georgia does not recognize technology leadership as an "L" (leadership) certification field as yet. Ultimately we decided that ISTE standards were not the best fit for the Ed.S. program in our state, but found many well-described performance-based indicators that were eventually useful in development of course objectives and assessments.

As noted above, AECT has NCATE-approved standards for initial and advanced programs. Our Master's Program in Instructional Technology is based on the entry-level AECT standards within the framework of the five domains of instructional technology: design, development, utilization, management, and evaluation. This familiar and flexible framework, applied at the advanced level, seemed an appropriate choice for a basis for the Ed.S. program.

Additional professional standards were considered to provide the basis for this program. The most clearly defined target audience for the Ed.S. program is school library media specialists. The American Association of School Librarians (AASL) and its parent organization, the American Library Association (ALA), seemed appropriate beacons of guidance for programs of this type. In Georgia, media specialists' initial training (master's) comes through our program (instructional technology—library media) or other similar programs in the state. Media specialists are certified instructional service personnel in Georgia, with certification at the master's level (S-5) and specialist level (S-6). Service certificates (identified by the letter "S") are issued in fields that prepare an individual to provide support services to students, school personnel, and school operations. Although service personnel do not need to hold a teaching certificate in another field, most do, and move into the media specialist positions after a number of years in the classroom. Thus, to meet the accreditation requirements for programs training media specialists, certainly NCATE/AECT is appropriate, and meeting the Georgia Professional Standards Commission standards is required. However, in examining the well-developed standards for ALA/AASL we discovered that there were no advanced standards for media specialists; that is, the master's level was considered the terminal degree. Because the M.Ed. in Instructional Technology-Library Media was based in part on the ALA/AASL (along with AECT) standards, it seemed that media specialists coming into the Ed.S. would have already met those standards. Thus we chose to leave ALA/AASL out of the Ed.S. in Instructional Technology foundation in fact, but not in spirit.

Having reviewed and decided on the standards for the revision of the Ed.S. Program in Instructional Technology, it was time to develop objectives, assessments, and courses. The differences in the standards from those of the previous iteration of the Ed.S. in IT indicated that the program would not strongly resemble the previous program. We also knew that by requiring that all courses be online, we would not be able to include out-of-department courses in educational psychology, communications, and research that were included before. Although we did attempt partnerships with other departments, they were not able to commit the time and resources necessary to build quality online courses in the time period allowed. So the program evolved as an in-house project with all department faculty responsible for working together to build the program, each faculty member responsible for designing, developing, and delivering at least one course.

We began by working in a group of all involved faculty. We first proposed a series of "placeholder" courses with names like "theory," "tools," "consumer," "leadership," and "research." We then went through the AECT performance indicators matrix and filled in two columns describing courses/experiences and assessment. Some indicators fell into one course, many into multiple courses, and others were integrated into all. We did round-robin examinations of the indicators, looking for gaps or excessive overlap. We brainstormed course titles and descriptions. At this point we tried to focus on the objectives, the assessments, and how the program would fit together, without concentrating on the online delivery method. Four brand new courses were conceived and seven courses were targeted for redesign for online delivery. Once these were set, each faculty member developed a syllabus for his or her course. It was required that each syllabus be fully developed, with conceptual framework principles, objectives derived from AECT performance indicators, supporting course activities, and full descriptions of assessment activities. Again, we conducted round-robin examinations of the syllabi to check for gaps and overlap.

Assessment within the program and evaluation of the program were included in the initial planning. Some sample outcomes and assessments, written to be included in the university bulletin, are described below.

Selected Educational Outcomes

1. Students will model and promote ethical, legal, and equitable use of instructional technology.

2. Students will conduct, support, and apply research concerning technological applications in instructional environments.

3. Students will assume an influential leadership role in designing, developing, utilizing, managing, and evaluating instructional technology.

Assessments

1. Students demonstrate their ability to model and promote ethical, legal, and equitable use of instructional technology through documentation of course projects and multiple forms of faculty-student and peer computer-mediated communication.

2. Students are assessed on their research knowledge and skills by the faculty members on the thesis committee, who rate the written journal-ready thesis and the electronic presentation of results.

3. Students demonstrate their leadership skills through documentation of major field-based projects that include curriculum implementation, technology planning, and change management.

Program evaluation elements include the following:

- The IT Program Coordinator conducts a review of the program annually.

- The Department's Advisory Committee (faculty, current students, former students, and practitioners) is involved in an annual review of the program.

- NCATE (National Council for Accreditation of Teacher Education) and GPSC (Georgia Professional Standards Commission) review the program every five years.

- Regular and frequent assessments acquire student input for formative evaluation.

- Institutional course/instructor evaluations delivered online collect data similar to those for traditional courses.

- Special formats of instruments (student evaluations of instruction, exit surveys, and periodic assessments conducted by the IT coordinator) are created for the Web-based nature of the program.

STUDENT RECRUITMENT

Recruiting new students from a variety of backgrounds was a goal of our program. In addition to our traditional audience of M.Ed. in instructional technology graduates, we wanted to broaden the program to include teachers, training professionals, and individuals seeking initial certification as media specialists. We chose to market our new program through an information session, in print, online, and through document transfer.

Tasks Involved

Development of a program brochure was the first plan of attack for recruiting students for the new program. The brochure was developed and produced in house. The brochure was developed using Microsoft *Word*™ by a faculty member with prior experience in graphic design and production. Color copies of the brochure were printed using in-house resources. In the brochure we presented an overview of the program, admission requirements, the program of study, and a list of faculty credentials.

The brochure was first distributed at an information session scheduled during a state-wide media conference. Attendance for the information session exceeded our expectations and number of brochures. Four faculty members presented an overview of the program that included descriptions of proposed courses and the departmental philosophy behind the program to an audience primarily of K–12 educators. Questions were taken from the audience after the overview of the program. A signup sheet was used to gather names, e-mail addresses, addresses, and requests for additional information. After the conference this list was used to generate a database of possible students for the program. Brochures were printed and distributed to those who did not receive a copy in the information session.

An online version of the brochure was launched after the announcement of the program at the conference. Links to the site were located on the department, graduate school, and Ed.S. program websites. A file copy of the brochure was provided to the administrative assistant for attachment to information requests received via e-mail. A file copy was also supplied to the graduate school for printing and distribution.

In keeping with the online format of the program, we chose to post the program information with Internet-based free Web services and listservs. These services provided a broader distribution of program information. The response was overwhelming.

Based on inquires generated by the brochure, information session, and website, it was soon clear that a certification option designed to accommodate individuals seeking initial certification as media specialists was needed. This option includes satisfaction of required coursework in addition to the standard Ed.S. program. Information on the additional requirements was communicated via a flyer and through the website.

The program coordinator has communicated with potential applicants through e-mail and telephone conversations. Potential applicants have also generated interest in the program through sharing information about the program with their colleagues.

Challenges

Marketing a new program is always a challenge. However, our service area of 41 rural counties has contributed to the marketability of an online program. The challenge of keeping information sources current when developing a new program was addressed through the in-house brochure and website development. For example, a requirement listed in the college catalog stated that applicants must have three years of teaching experience. Given our goal of reaching beyond public education, this statement was modified to include "relevant professional experience" and added to our brochure and website. We were able to make necessary changes "on the fly" to correct potential recruiting problems before they began.

Expectations and Reality

We had expected enough initial interest in the program to enable us to start a cohort of 20. In response to the level of interest, we started three cohorts of 16 to 20 students during the first year. Although we had expected to expand beyond our typical service area, we did not expect this expansion to occur during the first cohort. However, applicants for the first cohort extended to include other areas of our state and beyond.

TECHNOLOGY

The decision to move an entire degree program online required significant technology-related resources. This section describes the computer-based tools, technical support, and faculty expertise and experience on which this initiative was based. We also describe the technology access and skills expected of students entering the program and briefly address institutional impacts.

The faculty of the Curriculum and Instructional Technology Department had all used e-mail and electronic document exchange in other courses. To varying degrees, they also had developed and successfully implemented Web-supported and Web-based courses at the graduate level of study, including courses such as "Distance Education" and "Using Networked Systems for Teaching and Learning." Most had previous experience in using the Georgia Statewide Academic and Medical System (GSAMS), a sophisticated, two-way videoconferencing system. Department faculty also possessed skills in designing, developing, utilizing, managing, and evaluating instruction. Most had attended one or more faculty development sessions on online instruction, including workshops on *WebCT*, a set of Web-based course development and delivery tools. All department faculty had also recently been awarded summer stipends for online course development, although not specifically designated for the Ed.S. program. Given the combination of these elements, department faculty possessed the expertise, resources, and motivation to create and deliver a quality program of advanced graduate study to students at a distance.

Tasks and Technical Resources

The hardware, software, telecommunications, and support staff required to deliver the online courses were, for the most part, well established on the Valdosta State University (VSU) campus. The campus network connection already provided sufficient bandwidth to deliver Internet access and certain multimedia elements, with faculty connecting from either a PC or Macintosh computer in their office via a 10/100 Ethernet network. Courses would be delivered using the Internet and the existing, year-old, campus *WebCT* version 2.0 course development and delivery system. *WebCT* is the standard online course development tool for higher education statewide and for VSU, and is used by over 1,100 institutions in 51 countries for online course development and delivery (for information about *WebCT*, see http://208.31.12.64/).

Staff from the VSU Office of Information Technology and College of Education provided general technical support for faculty. Department faculty, in turn, offered basic instruction in *WebCT* and ongoing support to students. Students could also contact the VSU technical assistance help desk for support.

Resources for developing the program were very limited. No additional facilities were required, nor were additional personnel hired. However, the burgeoning popularity of this degree program, a looming need for faculty to serve on dissertation committees, and other department initiatives soon demanded staffing consideration. Only minor budget adjustments were made. The cost for program startup was absorbed through internal reallocation of resources, primarily faculty and staff time. The faculty member coordinating program startup received release time from two courses. Other reallocation included limited reassigned time for faculty to develop and teach courses and some restructuring of technical support staff time. Working together, the department chairperson and faculty managed to rearrange workloads to accommodate the initiative. Faculty were released from one course during the semester prior to delivery to develop their online course. Based on our experiences, release time from at least one course for two semesters prior to delivery would be recommended. Other resources included telecommunications, computers, servers, software, and online development tools that were already available.

Students had access to online catalogs of holdings in VSU's Odum Library and the Georgia University System, as well as private, academic, public, and other libraries throughout the state of Georgia. We were particularly fortunate to have GALILEO (GeorgiA LIbrary LEarning Online), which provides Internet access to dozens of informational databases and full-text journal articles for educational institutions throughout Georgia. In addition, students could request articles and books through the campus library or their local library. Document delivery, currently extended to off-campus students, was provided through Odum Library. Faculty and students also had access to large collections of articles freely available on the Internet. Articles, required readings, and other content information were referenced through the *WebCT* online learning system. Initial student training in *WebCT* and online course access was done as part of a day-long session onsite in the department's Instructional Technology Laboratory.

Challenges

To make the Ed.S. degree available to a wider and more diverse audience, incoming students were not required to have a degree or advanced skills in using computers and related technologies. All students, however, did need basic computer and Internet access skills. The resulting class cohort had a wide variety of computer skills and experience. For this reason, approximately one-half of the initial onsite meeting with students was devoted to skill building, particularly within the *WebCT* environment. Because *WebCT* would be the primary delivery and communications vehicle for all program courses, we believed students' skills would gradually improve as they progressed through the program. We also deliberately chose student cohorts from the same geographic area, and, in fact, several of these students knew one another or had shared classes in the past. In this way, all students had a near-peer source of solace and support.

Students were responsible for arranging their own Internet access. Although many could access online course materials from relatively speedy network connections at school or work, we recognized that most adult students preferred access from home. Thus, course delivery and communication had to be effectively handled over dial-up POTS (plain old telephone service) connections. We chose 28.8 KBPS as the lowest common denominator and thus needed to test all course elements and technologies at that benchmark. This meant, for example, that compressed audio, video, and single-frame images were possible, but quality live video streaming was not. Still, we believed that the current range of multimedia tools available would effectively support program delivery, including freeware such as *RealProducer, RealPlayer, Yahoo Messenger,* and *Adobe Acrobat Reader.* The Microsoft *Office*™ suite, including the *FrontPage*™ web page authoring tool, was already available to faculty, and this suite offered relatively simple conversion to the HTML format. Faculty copies of *Adobe Acrobat* were purchased to convert a variety of files to PDF format, the most popular universal file format for the WWW. Faculty also explored and implemented alternative methods of communication, including inserting audio annotations in reviews of student work and using desktop videoconferencing tools such as Microsoft *NetMeeting*™ and *CUSeeMe.*

Expectations and Reality

The week before our first Ed.S. course began, the university installed an upgraded version (2.0) of the *WebCT* software. Fortunately, one faculty member had recently attended a *WebCT* trainers' workshop at the University of Georgia featuring the new version. Following the upgrade notice, three other department faculty attended a six-hour campus seminar introducing the new version. Unfortunately, the instructor for the first Ed.S. course could not attend due to other obligations. Although the new version was much improved, it required new login procedures and included many tweaks in operation, as well as a few new bugs (which we have since come to refer to colloquially as undocumented features). Although this upgrade affected many department classes, the Ed.S. cohort was the first student group to use the software. Naturally, this upgrade resulted in several glitches during initial training and in the first few weeks of the online course. In fact, in one case, the entire course site needed to be reconstructed.

During the pilot course the midterm exam was administered through the online system. The assessment component of *WebCT* is very user friendly in creating and providing exams. The professor designed the questions, input them to the system, then set the date, time, and time limit for the three-hour exam in short order. The system could even be set to allow one student access the night before all other students to accommodate an out-of-town trip. The trouble began as a few bugs were found in the assessment area after the exam took place. Final answers were not e-mailed to the instructor as requested in the system configuration. The time limit was set by the system to three minutes, rather than three hours as set by the instructor. Also, all paragraph answers were truncated. Fortunately, no data were lost and all of these issues were overcome. But it should be noted that the professor experienced exceptional technical assistance from campus personnel. Overall there were few glitches with *WebCT* or other technology used during the first semester, and all problems were resolved.

At present, the instructor addresses nearly all requests for technical support. We have since added a course link to *WebCT* student user guides from other institutions (see http://208.31.12.64/get/user_guide.html) and plan to make greater use of online help resources throughout the program. We also hope to reduce the time devoted to ongoing support through better initial preparation, that is, more time devoted to student skill building during the first session.

The approach to support classes through using a wide variety of technologies was a cautious one. All of the courses are heavily dependent on the *WebCT* system, and some rely on Microsoft *FrontPage*, but each of these programs has been proven stable and effective with other classes in previous semesters. During the pilot test, we experimented with some hardware and software that we had never used and that was quite new to the market. These technologies were a tremendous addition to the course, but these were ancillary to the core components that had to work for the program to be successful.

During the semester we used *Yahoo Messenger* to communicate via voice conferencing. Students established a free account (see http://yahoo.com) and were able to transmit live audio/voice through their computers. This was exciting and added a new dimension to the course to the extent that we decided to "meet" online twice a week in the evening just to talk about issues related to the class. At the time we only encountered one problem. There was no *Yahoo Messenger* program available to students with a Macintosh computer. Since that time, a Macintosh version has become available and is being used by our students. All students, even those with 28.8 modems, are able to converse clearly and easily.

We also experimented with video connectivity and experienced limited success. A student from Arizona and the instructor were able to connect using Microsoft *NetMeeting*, but the campus did not have current software or equipment available for multipoint connections enabling multiple people to meet online using video. The test with *NetMeeting* worked reasonably well; some choppy video and good audio were experienced. We were able to have a coherent conversation and discovered this to be a viable solution for future synchronous learning when technology improves.

Throughout the semester we tested video and audio streaming with varied success. Video and audio files were created successfully using Real Networks *Real Producer*. We created audio e-mail files and placed full video with audio files online. Students accessed the audio e-mail files using their existing e-mail program. The instructor was able to provide feedback much more easily, and with higher quality, as compared to regular e-mail. Students reacted positively to "hearing" what the instructor meant, rather than trying to read and decipher e-mail feedback. The audio and video capabilities of the Real Networks products also enhanced the instructor's ability to explain and present the details of required course projects and develop a student study guide for the exam. Online video and audio were accessible through web pages by using *Real Player*.

Technology was a critical element in the effective development and delivery of the program. It proved not to be a significant barrier to success, mainly due to our experience with *WebCT* and Microsoft *FrontPage*. We recognize that an advantage is the accessibility our department has to the technologies. Powerful Pentium III class computers were available in our offices and our computer lab, and we had capable technical people on staff at the university and in the College of Education. Institutions and departments without these capacities may reconsider attempting online program development.

PROGRAM DESCRIPTION

The entire Ed.S. program planning and design took three semesters. Faculty members worked collaboratively to select the conceptual framework, establish the goals, and set objectives of the program. Using the framework, faculty individually developed each of the courses.

The initial program design required each student to be accepted into a cohort that would progress in lock-step through the program. Students would take two courses online each semester and complete the program in five semesters. The culminating project was a journal-ready thesis giving the student fundamental experience in research and the publication process. We had planned for one cohort, but as we will discuss later, demand for the program changed our thinking about student numbers and the rigid cohort system.

Tasks Involved

After completing the design of the program our first task was to set a schedule for all of the classes. We determined a progression of courses guiding the students from essential theories to application to applied research. The program requires that two elective courses be taken. We had to ensure that these elective courses would be available to the student. Immediately, four existing courses were redesigned to be delivered online.

A program website had to be created as a place for prospective students to access information about the program. We designed a site (see http://teach.valdosta.edu/edsonline/edsonline .html) to provide complete information about the program. Information about the courses and faculty is being added continuously. Most recently we added short video clips as an introduction to some of the faculty. From this page students are able to access course lists, schedules, descriptions, online registration, and links to other university resources.

Typically a professor could provide an orientation and familiarization with technology during the initial meetings of a traditional program. This is not so for a completely online program. Fortunately, members of the department realized this fact before we started. An orientation session was required of all students, with the exception of one student from Arizona. He was the only student from outside the state of Georgia admitted to the pilot test. The orientation proved to be invaluable. We were able to introduce the program, have the students practice with the technology, and most important, get to know each other a little. We took advantage of this time to take pictures and video the session. By the second week of class we had pictures, locations, e-mail information, and other data online so that classmates could put names with faces and have some sense of collegiality. Again, these are elements inherently part of a traditional class that had to be "thought of" and then designed and implemented in an online course. The students reacted positively to these actions and noted that these steps added a human dimension to the class.

The on-campus orientation, held just before the semester began, had three primary goals: introduce students to the Ed.S. degree program, discuss initial course content, and provide foundational skills in using the *WebCT* system. Many of the students had to drive long distances, some three hours one way, and all held full-time jobs. Given these considerations, we planned a single, five-hour, introductory Saturday session including lunch onsite. We found this time to be sufficient in settling anxiety about participating in a new program and using the online technology. Due to the fact that students from long distances participate in the program, we intend to develop an online version of the orientation. Time for practice and individual tutoring on the technology has led to reductions in technical anxiety and ensuing requests for technical support. This arrangement also allows for increased socialization and better bonding within the cohort and between cohort and faculty.

Presently, the first four courses of the online Ed.S. program and four electives have been fully developed. The pilot has now become the first course of the program and is offered in conjunction with one other course, depending on which semester the student starts the program in. Students have been advised about their program plan via e-mail and online chat. Only two students of the forty-eight in the program have chosen to travel to campus for direct consultation. All students are currently in the lock-step cohort format.

Challenges

The greatest challenge was bringing a "human factor" to the online course. The degree to which we were able to accomplish personalization took all of our combined knowledge using online discussion lists and the chat room in *WebCT*, some experimentation and ultimately success with *Yahoo Messenger*, and the application of the Real Networks products. Placing the students' pictures, relevant personal information, and class video online was of value to everyone involved.

We have been fortunate to have support from the university, College of Education, and graduate school in offering the online program. The university does host other online programs, but they were developed using a private vendor. Had we gone the financially costly route of using a private vendor instead of the low-cost, in-house method, understandably we may not have experienced such ease of approval for the program. The greatest challenge has been finding the resources to reallocate faculty release time for development of the program and courses. Planning, developing, and managing an online course and online program requires considerably more time on the part of the faculty.

Expectations and Reality

Our initial design of the program intended for each cohort of students to take all courses online in lock-step for five semesters. Demand for the program has caused us to rethink this process and consider a more flexible schedule for students who cannot complete the courses in a specific order. Instead of the anticipated single cohort, we started with three cohorts, and are in the process of discussing the acceptance of more students.

In retrospect, more time should have been allocated to develop the first course. Two semesters' development time would be optimal for creating a new course to be delivered online. In our case the program framework took two semesters to create, leaving one semester to create the first course as a pilot for the program.

The pilot class was successful in many ways and is highly recommended for any program taking the plunge into complete online delivery. Everyone may not have the opportunity to formatively evaluate all courses, but one pilot provides enough feedback and experience to positively affect future courses and their instructors. A key element was letting the students know ahead of time what was going to be a critical element of the class, for example using *WebCT*, and what was being "piloted," for example *Yahoo Messenger* and Microsoft *Net-Meeting*. This helps to decrease anxiety and make the element of practicing with new technology a groundbreaking and fun event.

Our expectation was to have more technology, especially video, enabling synchronous learning by the end of the semester. Due to hardware and technical limitations we were not able to achieve this goal, but we have gained valuable knowledge about how this technology would be integrated into the classes and may result in more effective use once higher-quality hardware, software, and bandwidth become available.

We also acknowledge that student ISP and modem limitations affect our ability to apply these technologies. In rural South Georgia there is very limited access to broadband technologies (e.g., DSL, cable Internet, and satellite) throughout the region. Most students had access to a 56K modem and Internet connection, but there were a few who only had 28.8K Internet access through their provider. The first cohort as the pilot group had no access faster than 56K. The second and third cohorts consist of students from Northern Georgia and metro areas where broadband services are available. But our online program must continue to meet the needs of students accessing at the slowest speeds.

Our third cohort began in the fall of 2000. The trials of the spring semester have not discouraged us, or our students, but in fact have invigorated discussions and ideas about how to design and provide improved online courses and programs. At a minimum this process has helped us to better define the needs of our students as learners and our needs as teachers. We are confident that as the technology advances, our program and online courses will improve. Most important, by designing the program in-house we have ownership in what we provide to the students.

Complete information about Valdosta State University's Education Specialist in Instructional Technology Program is available at http://teach.valdosta.edu/edsonline/edsonline .html. Program Coordinator: Dr. Arthur Recesso, Asst. Professor, Department of Curriculum and Instructional Technology, amrecess@valdosta.edu.

Part Three
Organizations and Associations in North America

Introduction

Part Three includes annotated entries for associations and organizations headquartered in the United States and Canada whose interests are in some manner significant to the fields of instructional technology and educational media. For the most part, these organizations are associations of professionals in the field or agencies that offer services to the educational media community. Entries are separated into sections for the United States and Canada. The U.S. section begins with a classified list designed to facilitate location of organizations by their specialized interests or services. The Canadian section is small enough not to need such a list.

Information for this part was obtained by direct communication with each organization in 2000. Several organizations (marked by an asterisk) did not provide updated information, and their entries contain information from the 2000 edition. Several new organizations are listed as well. Readers are encouraged to contact the editors with names of unlisted media-related organizations for investigation and possible inclusion in the 2002 edition.

Figures quoted as dues refer to annual amounts unless stated otherwise.

Oratile Maribe Branch

Section Editor

United States

CLASSIFIED LIST

Adult and Continuing Education
(ALA Round Table) Continuing Library Education Network and Exchange (CLENERT)
Association for Continuing Higher Education (ACHE)
Association for Educational Communications and Technology (AECT)
ERIC Clearinghouse on Adult, Career, and Vocational Education (CE)
National Education Telecommunications Organization & Education Satellite Company (NETO/EDSAT)
National University Continuing Education Association (NUCEA)
Network for Continuing Medical Education (NCME)
PBS Adult Learning Service (ALS)
University Continuing Education Association (UCEA)

Children- and Youth-Related Organizations
Adjunct ERIC Clearinghouse for Child Care (ADJ/CC)
American Montessori Society
Association for Childhood Education International (ACEI)
Association for Library Service to Children (ALSC)
(CEC) Technology and Media Division (TAM)
Children's Television International, Inc.
Close Up Foundation
Computer Learning Foundation
Council for Exceptional Children (CEC)
ERIC Clearinghouse on Disabilities and Gifted Education (EC)
ERIC Clearinghouse on Elementary and Early Childhood Education (PS)
National Association for the Education of Young Children (NAEYC)
National PTA
Young Adult Library Services Association (YALSA)

Communication
Association for Educational Communications and Technology (AECT)
ERIC Clearinghouse on Information & Technology (IR)
ERIC Clearinghouse on Languages and Linguistics (FL)
ERIC Clearinghouse on Reading, English, and Communication Skills (CS)

Health Science Communications Association (HeSCA)
International Association of Business Communicators (IABC)
Lister Hill National Center for Biomedical Communications of the National Library of Medicine
National Communication Association (NCA)
National Council of the Churches of Christ

Computers
(AECT) Division of Interactive Systems and Computers (DISC)
Association for Computers and the Humanities (ACH)
Association for the Advancement of Computing in Education (AACE)
Computer Learning Foundation
Computer-Using Educators, Inc. (CUE)
International Society for Technology in Education (ISTE)
Online Computer Library Center (OCLC)
Society for Computer Simulation (SCS)

Copyright
Association of American Publishers (AAP)
Association of College and Research Libraries (ACRL)
Copyright Clearance Center (CCC)
Hollywood Film Archive
International Copyright Information Center (INCINC)
Library of Congress

Distance Education
Community College Satellite Network (CCSN)
Instructional Telecommunications Council (ITC)
International Society for Technology in Education (ISTE)
International Telecommunications Satellite Organization (INTELSAT)
National Education Telecommunications Organization & EDSAT Institute (NETO/EDSAT)

Education—General
American Society of Educators (ASE)
Association for Childhood Education International (ACEI)

Association for Experiential Education (AEE)
Council for Basic Education
Education Development Center, Inc.
ERIC Clearinghouse for Science, Mathematics,
and Environmental Education (SE)
ERIC Clearinghouse for Social Studies/Social
Science Education (ERIC/ChESS)
ERIC Clearinghouse on Counseling and Student
Services (CG)
ERIC Clearinghouse on Disabilities and Gifted
Education (EC)
ERIC Clearinghouse on Educational Management
(EA)
ERIC Clearinghouse on Elementary and Early
Childhood Education (PS)
ERIC Clearinghouse on Rural Education and
Small Schools (RC)
ERIC Clearinghouse on Teaching and Teacher
Education (SP)
ERIC Clearinghouse on Urban Education (UD)
Institute for Development of Educational Activi-
ties, Inc. (|I|D|E|A|)
Minorities in Media (MIM)
National Association of State Textbook Admin-
istrators (NASTA)
National Clearinghouse for Bilingual Education
National Council for Accreditation of Teacher
Education (NCATE)
National School Boards Association (NSBA)
Institute for the Transfer of Technology
to Education (ITTE)

Education—Higher

American Association of Community Colleges
(AACC)
American Association of State Colleges and
Universities
Association for Continuing Higher Education
(ACHE)
Association for Library and Information Science
Education (ALISE)
Community College Association for Instruction
and Technology (CCAIT)
Consortium of College and University Media
Centers (CCUMC)
ERIC Clearinghouse for Community Colleges (JC)
ERIC Clearinghouse on Higher Education (HE)
Northwest College and University Council for the
Management of Educational Technology
PBS Adult Learning Service
University Continuing Education Association
(UCEA)

Equipment

Association for Childhood Education Interna-
tional (ACEI)
Educational Products Information Exchange
(EPIE Institute)

ERIC Clearinghouse on Assessment and
Evaluation (TM)
ITA
Library and Information Technology Associa-
tion (LITA)
National School Supply and Equipment Asso-
ciation (NSSEA)
Society of Cable Telecommunications Engineers
(SCTE)

ERIC

ACCESS ERIC
Adjunct ERIC Clearinghouse for Art Education
(ADJ/AR)
Adjunct ERIC Clearinghouse for ESL Literacy
Education (ADJ/LE)
Adjunct ERIC Clearinghouse for United
States-Japan Studies (ADJ/JS)
Adjunct ERIC Clearinghouse on Clinical Schools
(ADJ/CL)
Adjunct ERIC Clearinghouse on Consumer
Education (ADJ/CN)
ERIC (Educational Resources Information Center)
ERIC Clearinghouse on Adult, Career, and
Vocational Education (CE)
ERIC Clearinghouse on Assessment and
Evaluation (TM)
ERIC Clearinghouse for Community Colleges
(JC)
ERIC Clearinghouse on Counseling and Student
Services (CG)
ERIC Clearinghouse on Educational Management
(EA)
ERIC Clearinghouse on Elementary and Early
Childhood Education (PS)
ERIC Clearinghouse on Disabilities and Gifted
Education (EC)
ERIC Clearinghouse on Higher Education (HE)
ERIC Clearinghouse on Information & Tech-
nology (IR)
ERIC Clearinghouse on Languages and Lin-
guistics (FL)
ERIC Clearinghouse on Reading, English, and
Communication Skills (CS)
ERIC Clearinghouse on Rural Education and
Small Schools (RC)
ERIC Clearinghouse for Science, Mathematics,
and Environmental Education (SE)
ERIC Clearinghouse for Social Studies/Social
Science Education (SO)
ERIC Clearinghouse on Teaching and Teacher
Education (SP)
ERIC Clearinghouse on Urban Education (UD)
ERIC Document Reproduction Service (EDRS)
ERIC Processing and Reference Facility

Film and Video

Academy of Motion Picture Arts and Sciences
(AMPAS)

(AECT) Division of Telecommunications (DOT)
(AECT) Industrial Training and Education Division
 (ITED)
Agency for Instructional Technology (AIT)
American Society of Cinematographers
Anthropology Film Center (AFC)
Association for Educational Communications
 and Technology (AECT)
Association of Independent Video and Filmmakers/
 Foundation for Independent Video and
 Film (AIVF/FIVF)
Cable in the Classroom
Central Educational Network (CEN)
Children's Television International, Inc.
Close Up Foundation
Community College Satellite Network
Council on International Non-theatrical Events
 (CINE)
Film Advisory Board
Film Arts Foundation (FAF)
Film/Video Arts, Inc.
Great Plains National ITV Library (GPN)
Hollywood Film Archive
International Teleconferencing Association (ITCA)
International Television Association (ITVA)
ITA
National Aeronautics and Space Administration
 (NASA)
National Alliance for Media Arts and Culture
 (NAMAC)
National Association of Broadcasters (NAB)
National Education Telecommunications Or-
 ganization & Education Satellite Company
 (NETO/EDSAT)
National Endowment for the Humanities (NEH)
National Film Board of Canada (NFBC)
National Film Information Service (offered by
 AMPAS)
National Information Center for Educational
 Media (NICEM)
National ITFS Association (NIA/ITFS)
National Telemedia Council, Inc. (NTC)
The New York Festivals
Pacific Film Archive (PFA)
PBS Adult Learning Service (ALS)
PBS VIDEO
Public Broadcasting Service (PBS)
Society of Cable Telecommunications Engineers
 (SCTE)

Games, Toys, Play, Simulation, Puppetry
Puppeteers of America, Inc. (POA)
Society for Computer Simulation (SCS)
USA Toy Library Association (USA-TLA)

Health-Related Organizations
Health Science Communications Association
 (HeSCA)

Lister Hill National Center for Biomedical
 Communications
Medical Library Association (MLA)
National Association for Visually Handicapped
 (NAVH)
Network for Continuing Medical Education
 (NCME)

Information Science
Association for Library and Information Science
 Education (ALISE)
ERIC Clearinghouse on Information and Tech-
 nology (IR)
Freedom of Information Center
International Information Management Congress
 (IMC)
Library and Information Technology Association
 (LITA)
Lister Hill National Center for Biomedical
 Communications
National Commission on Libraries and Infor-
 mation Science (NCLIS)

Innovation
Institute for Development of Educational
 Activities, Inc. (|I|D|E|A|)
Institute for the Future (IFTF)
World Future Society (WFS)

**Instructional Technology, Design, and
 Development**
(AECT) Division of Educational Media
 Management (DEMM)
(AECT) Division of Instructional Development
 (DID)
Agency for Instructional Technology (AIT)
Association for Educational Communications
 and Technology (AECT)
Community College Association for Instruction
 and Technology (CCAIT)
ERIC Clearinghouse on Information & Tech-
 nology (IR)
International Society for Performance and
 Instruction (ISPI)
Professors of Instructional Design and Tech-
 nology (PIDT)
Society for Applied Learning Technology (SALT)

International Education
Adjunct ERIC Clearinghouse for US-Japan
 Studies (ADJ/JS)
(AECT) International Division (INTL)
East-West Center
International Association for Learning Labora-
 tories, Inc. (IALL)
International Visual Literacy Association, Inc.
 (IVLA)

National Clearinghouse for Bilingual Education
(NCBE)

Language
ERIC Clearinghouse on Languages and Linguistics
(FL)
ERIC Clearinghouse on Reading, English, and
Communication (CS)
International Association for Learning Laboratories,
Inc. (IALL)
National Clearinghouse for Bilingual Education
(NCBE)

Libraries—Academic, Research
American Library Association (ALA)
Association of College and Research Libraries (ACRL)
ERIC Clearinghouse on Information & Technology
(IR)

Libraries—Public
American Library Association (ALA)
Association for Library Service to Children (ALSC)
ERIC Clearinghouse on Information & Technology
(IR)
Library Administration and Management Asso-
ciation (LAMA)
Library and Information Technology Association
(LITA)
Public Library Association (PLA)
Young Adult Library Services Association (YALSA)

Libraries and Media Centers—School
(AECT) Division of School Media Specialists
(DSMS)
(ALA Round Table) Continuing Library Educa-
tion Network and Exchange (CLENERT)
American Association of School Librarians (AASL)
American Library Association (ALA)
American Library Trustee Association (ALTA)
Association for Educational Communications
and Technology (AECT)
Association for Library Collections and Technical
Services (ALCTS)
Association for Library Service to Children (ALSC)
Catholic Library Association (CLA)
Consortium of College and University Media
Centers
ERIC Clearinghouse on Information &
Technology (IR)
International Association of School Librarianship
(IASL)
Library of Congress
National Alliance for Media Arts and Culture
(NAMAC)
National Association of Regional Media Centers
(NARMC)
National Commission on Libraries and Informa-
tion Science (NCLIS)

National Council of Teachers of English (NCTE),
Commission on Media
On-Line Audiovisual Catalogers (OLAC)
Southeastern Regional Media Leadership
Council (SRMLC)

Libraries—Special
American Library Association (ALA)
Association for Library Service to Children
(ALSC)
Association of Specialized and Cooperative
Library Agencies (ASCLA)
ERIC Clearinghouse on Information & Tech-
nology (IR)
Medical Library Association (MLA)
Special Libraries Association
Theater Library Association
USA Toy Library Association (USA-TLA)

Media Production
(AECT) Media Design and Production Division
(MDPD)
American Society of Cinematographers (ASC)
Association for Educational Communications
and Technology (AECT)
Association of Independent Video and Filmmakers/
Foundation for Independent Video and
Film (AIVF/FIVF)
Film Arts Foundation (FAF)
International Graphics Arts Education Associa-
tion (IGAEA)

Museums and Archives
(AECT) Archives
Association of Systematics Collections
George Eastman House
Hollywood Film Archive
Library of Congress
Museum Computer Network (MCN)
Museum of Modern Art
National Gallery of Art (NGA)
National Public Broadcasting Archives (NPBA)
Pacific Film Archive (PFA)
Smithsonian Institution

Photography
Electronic Camera Repair, C&C Associates
George Eastman House
International Center of Photography (ICP)
National Press Photographers Association, Inc.
(NPPA)
Photographic Society of America (PSA)
Society for Photographic Education (SPE)
Society of Photo Technologists (SPT)

Publishing
Graphic Arts Technical Foundation (GATF)

International Graphics Arts Education Association (IGAEA)
Magazine Publishers of America (MPA)
National Association of State Textbook Administrators (NASTA)

Radio
(AECT) Division of Telecommunications (DOT)
American Women in Radio and Television (AWRT)
Corporation for Public Broadcasting (CPB)
National Endowment for the Humanities (NEH)
National Federation of Community Broadcasters (NFCB)
National Public Broadcasting Archives (NPBA)
National Religious Broadcasters (NRB)
Western Public Radio (WPR)

Religious Education
Catholic Library Association (CLA)
National Council of the Churches of Christ in the USA
National Religious Broadcasters (NRB)

Research
(AECT) Research and Theory Division (RTD)
American Educational Research Association (AERA)
Appalachia Educational Laboratory, Inc. (AEL)
ECT Foundation
Education Development Center, Inc.
ERIC Clearinghouses
HOPE Reports
Mid-continent Regional Educational Laboratory (McREL)
National Center for Improving Science Education
National Education Knowledge Industry Association (NEKIA)
National Endowment for the Humanities (NEH)
National Science Foundation (NSF)
The NETWORK
North Central Regional Educational Laboratory (NCREL)
Northwest Regional Educational Laboratory (NWREL)
Pacific Regional Educational Laboratory (PREL)
Research for Better Schools, Inc. (RBS)
SouthEastern Regional Vision for Education (SERVE)
Southwest Educational Development Laboratory (SEDL)
WestEd

Special Education
American Foundation for the Blind (AFB)
Association for Experiential Education (AEE)
Association of Specialized and Cooperative Library Agencies (ASCLA)
Council for Exceptional Children (CEC)

ERIC Clearinghouse on Adult, Career, and Vocational Education (CE)
ERIC Clearinghouse on Disabilities and Gifted Education (EC)
National Association for Visually Handicapped (NAVH)
National Center to Improve Practice (NCIP)
Recording for the Blind and Dyslexic (RFB&D)

Telecommunications
(AECT) Division of Telecommunications (DOT)
Association for the Advancement of Computing in Education (AACE)
Association of Independent Video and Filmmakers/ Foundation for Independent Video and Film (AIVF/FIVF)
Community College Satellite Network (CCSN)
ERIC Clearinghouse on Information & Technology (IR)
Instructional Telecommunications Council (ITC)
International Telecommunications Satellite Organization (INTELSAT)
International Teleconferencing Association (ITCA)
Library and Information Technology Association (LITA)
National Education Telecommunications Organization & Education Satellite Company (NETO/EDSAT)
Research for Better Schools, Inc. (RBS)
Teachers and Writers Collaborative (T&W)

Television
American Women in Radio and Television (AWRT)
Central Educational Network (CEN)
Children's Television International, Inc. (CTI)
Corporation for Public Broadcasting (CPB)
International Television Association (ITVA)
National Cable Television Institute (NCTI)
National Federation of Community Broadcasters (NFCB)
Society of Cable Telecommunications Engineers (SCTE)

Training
(AECT) Industrial Training and Education Division (ITED)
American Management Association (AMA)
American Society for Training and Development (ASTD)
Association for Educational Communications and Technology (AECT)
ERIC Clearinghouse on Adult, Career, and Vocational Education (CE)
Federal Educational Technology Association (FETA)
International Society for Performance Improvement (ISPI)

ALPHABETICAL LIST

All dues are annual fees, unless stated otherwise.

*Academy of Motion Picture Arts and Sciences (AMPAS). 8949 Wilshire Blvd., Beverly Hills, CA 90211-1972. (310)247-3000. Fax (310)859-9351. Website http://www.oscars .org. Bruce Davis, Exec. Dir. An honorary organization composed of outstanding individuals in all phases of motion pictures. Seeks to advance the arts and sciences of motion picture technology and artistry. Presents annual film awards; offers artist-in-residence programs; operates reference library and National Film Information Service. *Membership:* 6,000. *Publications: Annual Index to Motion Picture Credits; Academy Players Directory.*

*Agency for Instructional Technology (AIT). Box A, Bloomington, IN 47402-0120. (812)339-2203. Fax (812)333-4218. E-mail ait@ait.net. Website http://www.ait.net. Michael F. Sullivan, Exec. Dir. AIT is a nonprofit educational organization established in 1962 to develop, acquire, and distribute quality technology-based resources, providing leadership to the educational technology policy community. AIT fulfills this mission by being the largest single provider of instructional television programs and is a major player in the development of curriculum products. AIT has established a national model for contextual learning materials. AIT's strength lies in sound instructional design, early and continual involvement of classroom practitioners, formative evaluation, and creative production of video. Web services videodisc, software, and print resources. AIT products have won many national and international awards, including the only Emmy and Peabody awards given to classroom television programs. Since 1970, 37 major curriculum packages have been developed by AIT through a process it pioneered. U.S. state and Canadian provincial agencies have cooperatively funded and widely used these learning resources. Funding for other product development comes from state, provincial, and local departments of education, federal and private institutions, corporations and private sponsors, and AIT's own resources. Currently, AIT offers 130 learning resource products, containing nearly 2,500 separate titles. Programming addresses pre-kindergarten through adult learners covering traditional curricular areas plus career development, early childhood, guidance, mental health, staff development, and vocational education. AIT programs account for 40 percent of the National Instructional Satellite Service (NISS) schedule, which is broadcast to K–12 classrooms across the country. AIT learning resources are used on six continents and teach nearly 34 million students in North America each year via electronic distribution and audio visual use. *Publications: TECHNOS: Quarterly for Education & Technology,* a forum for the discussion of ideas about the use of technology in education with a focus on reform ($28/yr, 4 issues). AIT is also the home of TECHNOS Press, publisher of *Final Exam* by Gerald W. Bracey. The Website offers an online catalog, compete with program descriptions, ordering information, and direct links to AIT Customer Service.

*American Association of Community Colleges (AACC). One Dupont Cir. NW, Suite 410, Washington, DC 20036-1176. (202)728-0200, ext. 216. Fax (202)833-2467. Website http://www.aacc.nche.edu. David Pierce, Pres. AACC serves the nation's 1,100 community, technical, and junior colleges through advocacy, professional development, publications, and national networking. The annual convention draws more than 2,500 middle and top-level administrators of two-year colleges. Twenty-four councils and eight commissions address priority areas for community colleges. AACC also operates the Community College Satellite Network, providing teleconferences and other programming and services to colleges. *Membership:* 1,113 institutions, 16 international, 5 foundations, 15 corporations, 157 individuals, and 70 educational associates. *Dues:* vary by category. *Meetings:* Workforce Development Institute (WDI), Jan 27-30, 1999, San Diego. *Publications: Community College Journal* (bi-mo.); *Community College Times* (bi-weekly newspaper); *College Times;* Community College Press (books and monographs).

American Association of School Librarians (AASL). 50 E. Huron St., Chicago, IL 60611. (312)280-4386. (800)545-2433, ext. 4386. Fax (312)664-7459. E-mail aasl@ala.org. Website http://www.ala.org/aasl. Julie A. Walker, Exec. Dir. A division of the American Library Association, AASL is interested in the general improvement and extension of school library media services for children and youth. Activities and projects of the association are divided among 30 committees and 3 sections. *Membership:* 7,820. *Dues:* Membership in ALA (1st yr., $50; 2nd yr., $75; 3rd and subsequent yrs., $100) plus $40. Inactive, student, retired, unemployed, and reduced-salary memberships are available. *Meetings:* National conference every two years; next national conference to be held in 2001. *Publication: School Library Media* (electronic research journal, http://www.ala.organization/aasl/SLMR/).

American Association of State Colleges and Universities (AASCU). One Dupont Cir. NW, Suite 700, Washington, DC 20036-1192. (202)293-7070. Fax (202)296-5819. James B. Appleberry, Pres. *Membership* is open to regionally accredited institutions of higher education (and those in the process of securing accreditation) that offer programs leading to the degree of Bachelor, Master, or Doctor, and that are wholly or partially state-supported and state-controlled. Organized and operated exclusively for educational, scientific, and literary purposes, its particular purposes are to improve higher education within its member institutions through cooperative planning, studies, and research on common educational problems and the development of a more unified program of action among its members; and to provide other needed and worthwhile educational services to the colleges and universities it may represent. *Membership:* 393 institutions (university), 28 systems, and 10 associates. *Dues:* based on current student enrollment at institution. *Publications: MEMO: To the President; The Center Associate; Office of Federal Program Reports; Office of Federal Program Deadlines.* (Catalogs of books and other publications available upon request.)

American Educational Research Association (AERA). 1230 17th St. NW, Washington, DC 20036. (202)223-9485. Fax (202)775-1824. E-mail aera@gmu.edu. Website http://www.asu .edu/aera. William J. Russell, Exec. Dir. AERA is an international professional organization with the primary goal of advancing educational research and its practical application. Its members include educators and administrators; directors of research, testing, or evaluation in federal, state, and local agencies; counselors; evaluators; graduate students; and behavioral scientists. The broad range of disciplines represented includes education, psychology, statistics, sociology, history, economics, philosophy, anthropology, and political science. AERA has over 120 Special Interest Groups including Advanced Technologies for Learning, Computer Applications in Education, Electronic Networking, Information Technology and Library Resources, Instructional Technology, and Text, Technology and Learning Strategies. *Membership:* 23,000. *Dues:* vary by category, ranging from $20 for students to $45 for voting. *Meetings:* 1999 Annual Meeting, April 19-23, Montreal. *Publications: Educational Researcher; American Educational Research Journal; Journal of Educational Statistics; Educational Evaluation and Policy Analysis; Review of Research in Education; Review of Educational Research.*

American Foundation for the Blind (AFB). 11 Penn Plaza, Suite 300, New York, NY 10001. (212)502-7600, (800)AFB-LINE (232-5463). Fax (212)502-7777. E-mail afbinfo@afb.org. Website http://www.afb.org. Carl R. Augusto, Pres.; Liz Greco, Vice Pres. of Communications. AFB is a leading national resource for people who are blind or visually impaired, the organizations that serve them, and the general public. A nonprofit organization founded in 1921 and recognized as Helen Keller's cause in the United States, AFB's mission is to enable people who are blind or visually impaired to achieve equality of access and opportunity that will ensure freedom of choice in their lives. AFB is headquartered in New York City with offices in Atlanta, Chicago, Dallas, and San Francisco. A governmental relations office in AFB is headquartered in New York City with offices in Atlanta, Chicago, Dallas, San Francisco, and Washington, DC. *Publications: AFB News* (free); *Journal of Visual Impairment & Blindness; AFB Press Catalog of Publications* (free).

American Library Association (ALA). 50 E. Huron St., Chicago, IL 60611. (312)944-6780. Fax (312)440-9374. Website http://www.ala.org. William R. Gordon, Exec. Dir. The ALA is the oldest and largest national library association. Its 58,000 members represent all types of libraries: state, public, school, and academic, as well as special libraries serving persons in government, commerce, the armed services, hospitals, prisons, and other institutions. The ALA is the chief advocate of achievement and maintenance of high-quality library information services through protection of the right to read, educating librarians, improving services, and making information widely accessible. See separate entries for the following affiliated and subordinate organizations: American Association of School Librarians, American Library Trustee Association, Association for Library Collections and Technical Services, Association for Library Service to Children, Association of College and Research Libraries, Association of Specialized and Cooperative Library Agencies, Library Administration and Management Association, Library and Information Technology Association, Public Library Association, Reference and User Services Association, Young Adult Library Services Association, and Continuing Library Education Network and Exchange Round Table. *Membership:* 58,000. *Dues:* Basic dues $50 first year, $100 renewing members. *Meetings:* 1999: Midwinter Meeting Jan 14-19, San Antonio, 2000. Annual Conference, Jun 24-Jul 1, New Orleans, DC. *Publications: American Libraries; Booklist; Choice; Book Links.*

American Library Trustee Association (ALTA). 50 E. Huron St., Chicago, IL 60611. (312)280-2161. Fax (312)280-3257. Website http://www.ala.org. Susan Roman, Exec. Dir. A division of the American Library Association, ALTA is interested in the development of effective library service for people in all types of communities and libraries. Members, as policymakers, are concerned with organizational patterns of service, the development of competent personnel, the provision of adequate financing, the passage of suitable legislation, and the encouragement of citizen support for libraries. *Membership:* 1,710. *Dues:* $50 plus membership in ALA. *Meetings:* Held in conjunction with ALA. *Publications: Trustee Voice* (q. newsletter); professional monographs and pamphlets.

American Management Association International (AMA). 1601 Broadway, New York, NY 10019-7420. (212)586-8100. Fax (212)903-8168. E-mail cust_serv@amanet.org. Website http://www.amanet.org. Barbara M. Barrett, Pres. and CEO. Founded in 1923, AMA provides educational forums worldwide where members and their colleagues learn superior, practical business skills and explore best practices of world-class organizations through interaction with each other and expert faculty practitioners. AMA's publishing program provides tools individuals use to extend learning beyond the classroom in a process of lifelong professional growth and development through education. AMA operates management centers and offices in Atlanta, Boston (Watertown), Chicago, Hamilton (NY), Kansas City (Leawood), New York, San Francisco, Saranac Lake (NY), and Washington, DC, and through AMA/International, in Brussels, Tokyo, Shanghai, Islamabad, and Buenos Aires. In addition, it has affiliated centers in Toronto, Mexico City, Sao Paulo, Taipei, Istanbul, Singapore, Jakarta, and Dubai. AMA offers conferences, seminars, and membership briefings where there is an interchange of information, ideas, and experience in a wide variety of management topics. Through its publication division, AMACOM, AMA publishes approximately 70 business-related books per year, as well as numerous surveys and management briefings. Other services offered by AMA include *FYI Video; Extension Institute* (self-study programs in both print and audio formats); *AMA Interactive Series* (self-paced learning on CD-ROM); *Operation Enterprise* (young adult program); *AMA On-Site* (videoconferences); the *Information Resource Center* (for AMA members only), a management information and library service; and six bookstores. *Membership:* over 75,000. *Dues:* corporate, $595-1645; growing company, $525-1845; indiv., $165 plus $40 per additional newsletter. *Publications* (periodicals): *Management Review* (membership); *Compensation & Benefits Review; Organizational Dynamics; HR Focus; President; Getting Results . . . ; and The Take-Charge Assistant.*

American Montessori Society (AMS). 281 Park Ave. S, New York, NY 10010. (212)358-1250. Fax (212)358-1256. Website http://www.amshq.org. Michael N. Eanes, Natl. Dir. Dedicated to promoting better education for all children through teaching strategies consistent with the Montessori system. Membership is composed of schools in the private and public sectors employing this method, as well as individuals. It serves as a resource center and clearinghouse for information and data on Montessori affiliates, trains teachers in different parts of the country, and conducts a consultation service and accreditation program for school members. *Dues:* teachers, schoolheads, $40; parents, $30; institutions, from $215 and up. *Meetings:* three regional and one national educational conference per year and four professional development symposia under the auspices of the AMS Teachers' Section. 39th Annual Conference, Apr 21-25, 1999, Cincinnati. *Publications: AMS Montessori LIFE* (q); *Schoolheads* (newsletter); *Montessori in Contemporary American Culture; Authentic American Montessori School; The Montessori School Management Guide;* AMS position papers.

American Society for Training and Development (ASTD). 1640 King St., Box 1443, Alexandria, VA 22313. (703)683-8100. Fax (703)683-8103. E-mail csc@astd.org. Website http://www.astd.org. Curtis E. Plott, Pres. and CEO. Founded in 1944, ASTD is the world's premiere professional association in the field of workplace learning and performance. ASTD's membership includes more than 70,000 people in organizations from every level of the field of workplace performance in more than 100 countries. Its leadership and members work in more than 15,000 multinational corporations, small and medium-sized businesses, government agencies, colleges, and universities. ASTD is the leading resource on workplace learning and performance issues, providing information, research, analysis, and practical information derived from its own research, the knowledge and experience of its members, its conferences and publications, and the coalitions and partnerships it has built through research and policy work. *Membership:* 70,000 National and Chapter members. *Dues:* $150. *Meetings:* International Conferences, May 22-27, 1999, Atlanta; May 20-25, 2000, Dallas. Technical Training Conferences, Sep 14-17, 1999, Minneapolis; Sep 19-22, 2000, Indianapolis. *Publications: Training & Development Magazine; Technical Training Magazine; Info-Line; The American Mosaic: An In-depth Report of Diversity on the Future of Diversity at Work; ASTD Directory of Academic Programs in T&D/HRD; Training and Development Handbook; Technical & Skills Training Handbook. Quarterly publications: Performance in Practice; National Report on Human Resources; Washington Policy Report.* ASTD also has recognized professional forums, most of which produce newsletters.

*American Society of Cinematographers (ASC). 1782 N. Orange Dr., Hollywood, CA 90028. (213)969-4333. Fax (213)876-4973. Fax (213)882-6391. Victor Kemper, Pres. ASC is an educational, cultural, and professional organization. *Membership:* 336. Membership is by invitation to those who are actively engaged as directors of photography and have demonstrated outstanding ability. Classifications are Active, Active Retired, Associates, and Honorary. *Meetings:* Book Bazaar (Open House); Awards Open House; Annual ASC Awards. *Publications: American Cinematographer Video Manual; Light on Her Face;* and *American Cinematographers Magazine.*

American Society of Educators (ASE). *Media & Methods Magazine.* 1429 Walnut St., Philadelphia, PA 19102. (215)563-6005. Fax (215)587-9706. E-mail michelesok@aol.com. Website http://www.media-methods.com. Michele Sokolof, Publisher & Editorial Dir. ASE services the information needs of K–12 teachers, librarians, media specialists, curriculum directors, and administrators in evaluating the practical applications of today's multimedia and technology resources for teaching and learning purposes. ASE's delivers timely information on technology integration in K–12 schools, classrooms, and labs through their bi-monthly yearly subscription: cost, $33.50.

American Women in Radio and Television (AWRT). 1650 Tyson Blvd., Suite 200, McLean, VA 22102-3915. (703)506-3290. Fax (703)506-3266. Jacci Duncan, Exec. Dir. Organization of professionals in the electronic media, including owners, managers, administrators, and those in creative positions in broadcasting, satellite, cable, advertising, and public relations. AWRT's objectives are to work worldwide to improve the quality of radio and television; to promote the entry, development, and advancement of women in the electronic media and allied fields; to serve as a medium of communication and idea exchange; and to become involved in community concerns. Organized in 1951. *Membership:* 40 chapters. Student memberships available. *Dues:* $125. *Publications: News and Views; Resource Directory; Careers in the Electronic Media; Sexual Harassment;* Mentoring Brochure (pamphlet).

Anthropology Film Center (AFC). 1626 Upper Canyon Rd., Santa Fe, NM 87501-6138. (505)983-4127. E-mail ziacine@ix.netcom.com, anthrofilm@nets.com, or anthrofilm @archaeologist.com. Website http://www.nets.com/anthrofilm. Carroll Williams, Dir. Offers the Ethnographic/Documentary Film Program, a 30-week full-time course in 16mm film in CD and DVD production and theory. Summer workshops are offered as well. AFC also provides consultation, research facilities, and a specialized library.

Appalachia Educational Laboratory, Inc. (AEL). P.O. Box 1348, Charleston, WV 25325. (304)347-0400, (800)624-9120. Fax (304)347-0487. E-mail aelinfo@ael.org. Website http://www.ael.org. Terry L. Eidell, Exec. Dir. One of 10 Office of Educational Research and Improvement (OERI) regional educational laboratories designed to help educators and policymakers solve educational problems in their schools. Using the best available information and the experience and expertise of education professionals, AEL seeks to identify solutions to education problems, tests new approaches, furnishes research results, and provides training to teachers and administrators. AEL serves Kentucky, Tennessee, Virginia, and West Virginia.

Association for Childhood Education International (ACEI). 17904 Georgia Ave., Suite 215, Olney, MD 20832. (301)570-2111. Fax (301)570-2212. E-mail ACEIHQ@aol.com. Website http://www.udel.edu/bateman/acei. Anne W. Bauer, Ed. and Dir. of *Publications*. ACEI publications reflect careful research, broad-based views, and consideration of a wide range of issues affecting children from infancy through early adolescence. Many are media-related in nature. The journal (*Childhood Education*) is essential for teachers, teachers-in-training, teacher educators, day care workers, administrators, and parents. Articles focus on child development and emphasize practical application. Regular departments include book reviews (child and adult); film reviews, pamphlets, software, research, and classroom idea-sparkers. Six issues are published yearly, including a theme issue devoted to critical concerns. *Membership:* 12,000. *Dues:* $45, professional; $26, student; $23, retired; $80, institutional. *Meeting:* 1999 Annual International Conference and Exhibition, Apr 7-11, San Antonio; 2000, Baltimore. *Publications: Childhood Education* (official journal) with *ACEI Exchange* (insert newsletter); *Journal of Research in Childhood Education;* professional division newsletters (*Focus on Infants and Toddlers, Focus on Pre-K and K, Focus on Elementary,* and *Focus on Middle School); Celebrating Family Literacy Through Intergenerational Programming; Selecting Educational Equipment for School and Home; Developmental Continuity Across Preschool and Primary Grades; Implications for Teachers; Developmentally Appropriate Middle Level Schools; Common Bonds: Antibias Teaching in a Diverse Society; Childhood 1892-1992; Infants and Toddlers with Special Needs and Their Families* (position paper); and pamphlets.

Association for Computers and the Humanities. c/o Elli Mylonas, Exec. Secretary, Box 1885-C15, Brown University, Providence, RI 02912. E-mail ach@stg.brown.edu. Website http://www.ach.org. The Association for Computers and the Humanities is a forum for humanists who incorporate computing into their teaching and research. *Membership:* 300.

Dues: $75. *Meetings:* Annual meetings held with the Association for Literary and Linguistic Computing. *Publication: Journal for Computers and the Humanities.*

Association for Continuing Higher Education (ACHE). Continuing Education, Trident Technical College, P.O. Box 118067, CE-P, Charleston, SC 29423-8067. (803)574-6658. Fax (803)574-6470. E-mail zpbarrineavi@trident.tec.sc.us. Website http://www.charleston .net/organization/ACHE/. Wayne Whelan, Exec. Vice Pres. ACHE is an institution-based organization of colleges, universities, and individuals dedicated to the promotion of life-long learning and excellence in continuing higher education. ACHE encourages professional networks, research, and exchange of information for its members and advocates continuing higher education as a means of enhancing and improving society. *Membership:* 1,622 individuals in 674 institutions. *Dues:* $60, professional; $240, institutional. *Meetings:* 1999 Annual Meeting, Nov 7-9, Cincinnati. 2000 Oct 14-17, Myrtle Beach, SC. *Publications: Journal of Continuing Higher Education* (3/yr.); *Five Minutes with ACHE* (newsletter, 10/yr.); *Proceedings* (annual).

Association for Educational Communications and Technology (AECT). 1025 Vermont Ave. NW, Suite 820, Washington, DC 20005. (202)347-7834. Fax (202)347-7839. Stanley Zenor, Exec. Dir. AECT is an international professional association concerned with the improvement of learning and instruction through media and technology. It serves as a central clearinghouse and communications center for its members, who include instructional technologists, library media specialists, religious educators, government media personnel, school administrators and specialists, and training media producers. AECT members also work in the armed forces, public libraries, museums, and other information agencies of many different kinds, including those related to the emerging fields of computer technology. Affiliated organizations include the Association for Media and Technology in Education in Canada (AMTEC), Community College Association for Instructional and Technology (CCAIT), Consortium of College and University Media Centers (CCUMC), Federal Educational Technology Association (FETA), Health Sciences Special Interest Group (HESIG), International Association for Learning Laboratories (IALL), International Visual Literacy Association (IVLA), Minorities in Media (MIM), National Association of Regional Media Centers (NARMC), New England Educational Media Association (NEEMA), and the Southeastern Regional Media Leadership Council (SRMLC). Each of these affiliated organizations has its own listing in the *Yearbook.* Two additional organizations, the AECT Archives and the ECT Foundation, are also related to the Association for Educational Communications and Technology and have independent listings. Divisions are listed below. *Membership:* 4,500. *Meetings:* 1999 Annual Convention and InCITE Exposition, Feb 10-14, Houston. *Publications: TechTrends* (6/yr., free with membership; $36 nonmembers); *Report to Members* (6/yr., newsletter); *Educational Technology Research and Development* (q., $40 members; $55 nonmembers); various division publications; several books; videotapes.

Association for Educational Communications and Technology (AECT) Divisions:

(AECT) Division of Educational Media Management (DEMM). 1025 Vermont Ave. NW, Suite 820, Washington, DC 20005-3516. (202)347-7834. Fax (202)347-7839. E-mail aect@aect.org. Website http://www.aect.org/Divisions/aectdiv.html and http://teams .lacoe.edu/demm/demm.html. Nancy McFarlin, Pres. E-mail mcfarlin@ksu.edu. As leaders in the field of educational media, members of DEMM are actively involved in the design, production, and instructional applications of new and emerging multimedia technologies. DEMM members are proactive media managers who provide solutions, share information on common problems, and support the development of model media programs. *Membership:* 438. *Dues:* One division membership included in the basic AECT membership; additional division memberships $10. *Meetings:* DEMM meets in conjunction with the annual AECT National Convention. *Publication: DEMM Perspective* (newsletter, q.).

(AECT) Division of Instructional Development (DID). 1025 Vermont Ave. NW, Suite 820, Washington, DC 20005. (202)347-7834. Rodney Earle, Pres. E-mail rodney-earle@byu.edu. DID is composed of individuals from business, government, and academic settings concerned with the systematic design of instruction and the development of solutions to performance problems. Members' interests include the study, evaluation, and refinement of design processes; the creation of new models of instructional development; the invention and improvement of techniques for managing the development of instruction; the development and application of professional ID competencies; the promotion of academic programs for preparation of ID professionals; and the dissemination of research and development work in ID. *Membership:* 726. *Dues:* One division membership included in the basic AECT membership; additional division memberships $10. *Meetings:* held in conjunction with the annual AECT Convention. *Publications: DID Newsletter*; occasional papers.

(AECT) Division of Interactive Systems and Computers (DISC). 1025 Vermont Ave. NW, Suite 820, Washington, DC 20005. (202)347-7834. E-mail garya@sprynet.com. Website http://www.aect.org/Divisions/disc.html. Gary Addison, Pres. Concerned with the generation, access, organization, storage, and delivery of all forms of information used in the processes of education and training. DISC promotes the networking of its members to facilitate sharing of expertise and interests. *Membership:* 686. *Dues:* One division membership included in the basic AECT membership; additional division memberships $10. *Meetings:* held in conjunction with the annual AECT Convention. *Publication:* Newsletter; listserv at DISC-L@vm.cc.purdue.edu (to subscribe, send the message "subscribe DISC-L firstname lastname").

(AECT) Division of Learning and Performance Environments (DLPE). 1025 Vermont Ave. NW, Suite 820, Washington, DC 20005. (202)347-7834. Website http://dlpe.base.org. Renee Eggers, Pres. E-mail eggersre@emporia.edu. Supports human learning and performance through the use of computer-based technology; design, development, evaluation, assessment, and implementation of learning environments and performance systems for adults. *Dues:* One division membership included in the basic AECT membership; additional division memberships $10. *Meetings:* held in conjunction with the annual AECT Convention.

(AECT) Division of School Media and Technology (DSMT). 1025 Vermont Ave. NW, Suite 820, Washington, DC 20005. (202)347-7834. E-mail freibergs@po.atlantic .county.lib.nj.us. Sherry Freiberg, Pres. DSMS strives to improve instruction and promotes excellence in student learning in the K–12 setting by developing, implementing, and evaluating media programs and by planning and integrating technology in the classroom. *Membership:* 902. *Dues:* One division membership included in the basic AECT membership; additional division memberships $10. *Meetings:* held in conjunction with the annual AECT Convention. *Publication:* Newsletter.

(AECT) Division of Telecommunications (DOT). 1025 Vermont Ave. NW, Suite 820, Washington, DC 20005. (202)347-7834. Steve Mitchell, Pres. E-mail mitchell@wneo.org. DOT represents those members with an interest in a broad range of telecommunications as a means of addressing the educational needs of students, the educational community, and the general public. *Membership:* 607. *Dues:* one division membership included in the basic AECT membership; additional division memberships $10. *Meetings:* held in conjunction with annual AECT Convention. *Publication:* Newsletter.

(AECT) Industrial Training and Education Division (ITED). 1025 Vermont Ave. NW, Suite 820, Washington, DC 20005. (202)347-7834. Rob Pearson, Pres. E-mail rpearson@passport.ca. ITED is involved with designing, planning, evaluating, and managing training and performance programs, and promoting appropriate uses of educational techniques and media. *Membership:* 273. *Dues:* one division membership included in the basic AECT membership; additional division memberships $10. *Meetings:* held in conjunction with annual AECT Convention. *Publication: ITED Newsletter.* Back issues of the *Newsletter* are indexed in the ERIC database (ED 409 883).

(AECT) International Division (INTL). 1025 Vermont Ave. NW, Suite 820, Washington, DC 20005. (202)347-7834. Badrul Khan, Pres. E-mail khanb@gwis2 .circ.gwu.edu. INTL encourages practice and research in educational communication and distance education for social and economic development across national and cultural lines, promotes international exchange and sharing of information, and enhances relationships among international leaders. *Membership:* 295. *Dues:* one division membership included in the basic AECT membership; additional division memberships $10. *Meetings:* held in conjunction with the annual AECT Convention. *Publication:* Newsletter.

(AECT) Media Design and Production Division (MDPD). 1025 Vermont Ave. NW, Suite 820, Washington, DC 20005. (202)347-7834. Chuck Stoddard, Pres. E-mail chuck@cc.usu.edu. MDPD provides an international network that focuses on enhancing the quality and effectiveness of mediated communication, in all media formats, in educational, governmental, hospital, and corporate settings through the interaction of instructional designers, trainers, researchers, and evaluators with media designers and production team specialists who utilize state-of-the-art production skills. *Membership:* 318. *Dues:* one division membership included in the basic AECT membership; additional division memberships $10. *Meetings:* held in conjunction with annual AECT Convention. *Publication:* Newsletter.

(AECT) Research and Theory Division (RTD). 1025 Vermont Ave. NW, Suite 820, Washington, DC 20005. (202)347-7834. Deborah Lowther, Pres. E-mail lowther.deborah@coe,memphis.edu. Seeks to improve the design, execution, utilization, and evaluation of educational technology research; to improve the qualifications and effectiveness of personnel engaged in educational technology research; to advise the educational practitioner as to the use of the research results; to improve research design, techniques, evaluation, and dissemination; to promote both applied and theoretical research on the systematic use of educational technology in the improvement of instruction; and to encourage the use of multiple research paradigms in examining issues related to technology in education. *Membership:* 452. *Dues:* one division membership included in the basic AECT membership; additional division memberships $10. *Meetings:* held in conjunction with annual AECT Convention. *Publication:* Newsletter.

(AECT) Systemic Change in Education Division (CHANGE). 1025 Vermont Ave. NW, Suite 820, Washington, DC 20005. (202)347-7834. Mary Herring Pres. E-mail mch002@alph.morningside.edu. CHANGE advocates fundamental changes in educational settings to improve the quality of education and to enable technology to achieve its potential. *Dues:* one division membership included in the basic AECT membership; additional division memberships $10. *Meetings:* held in conjunction with the annual AECT Convention. *Publication:* Newsletter.

AECT Archives. University of Maryland, Hornbake Library, College Park, MD 20742. E-mail tc65@umail.umd.edu. Website http://www.library.umd.edu/UMCP/NPBA/npba.html. Thomas Connors, Archivist, National Public Broadcasting Archives. (301)405-9255. Fax (301)314-2634. A collection of media, manuscripts, and related materials representing important developments in visual and audiovisual education and in instructional technology. The collection is housed as part of the National Public Broadcasting Archives. Maintained by the University of Maryland in cooperation with AECT. Open to researchers and scholars.

Association for Experiential Education (AEE). 2305 Canyon Blvd., Suite 100, Boulder, CO 80302-5651. (303)440-8844 ext. 10. Fax (303)440-9581. Website http://www.aee.org. Sharon Heinlen, Exec. Dir. AEE is a nonprofit, international, professional organization with roots in adventure education, committed to the development, practice, and evaluation of experiential learning in all settings. AEE's vision is to be a leading international organization for the development and application of experiential education principles and methodologies with the intent to create a just and compassionate world by transforming education and promoting positive social change. *Membership:* more than 2,500 members in over 30 countries including individuals and organizations with affiliations in education, recreation, outdoor adventure programming, mental health, youth service, physical education, management development training, corrections, programming for people with disabilities, and environmental education. *Dues:* $55-$95, indiv. (depending on annual income); $110-$125, family; $200-$500, organizations and corporations. *Meetings:* Annual AEE International Conference, fall. Regional Conferences held in the Northwest, Heartland, Southeast, Mid-South, Mid-Atlantic, Northeast, West, and Rocky Mountains. *Publications: Jobs Clearinghouse* (m.); *The Journal of Experiential Education* (3/yr.); *Experience and the Curriculum; Adventure Education; Adventure Therapy; Therapeutic Applications of Adventure Programming; Manual of Accreditation Standards for Adventure Programs; The Theory of Experiential Education, Third Edition; Experiential Learning in Schools and Higher Education; Ethical Issues in Experiential Education, Second Edition; The K.E.Y. (Keep Exploring Yourself) Group: An Experiential Personal Growth Group Manual; Book of Metaphors, Volume II; Women's Voices in Experiential Education;* bibliographies, directories of programs, and membership directory. *New publications since last year: Exploring the Boundaries of Adventure Therapy; A Guide to Women's Studies in the Outdoors; Administrative Practices of Accredited Adventure Programs; Fundamentals of Experience-Based Training; Wild Adventures: A Guidebook of Activities for Building Connections with Others and the Earth; Truth Zone: An Experimental Approach to Organizational Development.*

Association for Library and Information Science Education (ALISE). Sharon J. Rogers, Exec. Dir. P.O. Box 7640, Arlington, VA 22207. (703)522-1899. Fax (703)243-4551. E-mail sroger7@ibm.net. Website http://www.alise.org. Seeks to advance education for library and information science and produces annual *Library and Information Science Education Statistical Report.* Open to professional schools offering graduate programs in library and information science; personal memberships open to educators employed in such institutions; other memberships available to interested individuals. *Membership:* 500 individuals, 73 institutions. *Dues:* institutional, sliding scale, $325-600; $200 associate; $125 international; personal, $90 full-time; $50 part-time, $40 student, $50 retired. *Meetings:* 1999, Jan 26-29, Philadelphia; 2000, Jan 11-14, San Antonio; 2001, Jan 9-12, Washington, DC. *Publications: Journal of Education for Library and Information Science; ALISE Directory and Handbook; Library and Information Science Education Statistical Report.*

Association for Library Collections &Technical Services (ALCTS). 50 E. Huron St., Chicago, IL 60611. (312)944-6780. Fax (312)280-5033. E-mail alcts@ala.org. Karen Muller, Exec. Dir; Sheila S. Intner, Pres., July 1998-July 1999. A division of the American Library Association, ALCTS is dedicated to acquisition, identification, cataloging, classification, and preservation of library materials; the development and coordination of the country's library resources; and aspects of selection and evaluation involved in acquiring and developing library materials and resources. Sections include Acquisitions, Cataloging and Classification, Collection Management and Development, Preservation and Reformatting, and Serials. *Membership:* 4,984. *Dues:* $45 plus membership in ALA. *Meetings:* 2000, Chicago, Jul 6-12; 2001, San Francisco, Jun 14-20; 2002, Atlanta, June 13-19; ALA Midwinter Meeting; 2000, San Antonio, Jan 14-19; 2001, Washington, Jan 12-17; 2002, New Orleans, Jan 18-23 *Publications: Library Resources & Technical Services* (q.); *ALCTS Newsletter* (6/yr.); *ALCTS Network News (AN2)*, electronic newsletter issued irregularly.

Association for Library Service to Children (ALSC). 50 E. Huron St., Chicago, IL 60611. (312)280-2163. Fax (312)944-7671. Website http://www.ala.org/a/sc. E-mail alsc@ala.org. Susan Roman, Exec. Dir. A division of the American Library Association, ALSC is interested in the improvement and extension of library services for children in all types of libraries, evaluation and selection of book and nonbook library materials, and improvement of techniques of library services for children from preschool through the eighth grade or junior high school age. Committee membership open to ALSC members. *Membership:* 3,600. *Dues:* $45 plus membership in ALA. *Meetings:* annual conference and midwinter meeting with ALA National Institutes, next is October 2000 in Baltimore. *Publications: Journal of Youth Services in Libraries* (q.); *ALSC Newsletter* (q.).

Association for the Advancement of Computing in Education (AACE). P.O. Box 2966, Charlottesville, VA 22902. (804)973-3987. Fax (804)978-7449. E-mail aace@virginia.edu. Website http://www.aace.org. Gary Marks, Exec. Dir.; April Ballard, contact person. AACE is an international, educational, and professional organization dedicated to the advancement of learning and teaching at all levels with information technology. AACE publishes major journals, books, and CD-ROMs on the subject and organizes major conferences. AACE's membership includes researchers, developers, and practitioners in schools, colleges, and universities; administrators, policy decision-makers, trainers, adult educators, and other specialists in education, industry, and the government with an interest in advancing knowledge and learning with information technology in education. *Membership:* 6,500. *Dues:* basic membership of $75 includes one journal subscription and *Educational Technology Review* subscription. *Meetings:* SITE '99 and M/SET 99, Feb 28-Mar 4, San Antonio. Ed-Media/ Ed-Telecom 99, June, New Orleans. Web Net 99, Nov, Hawaii. SITE 2000, March, Phoenix. *Publications: Educational Technology Review (ED-TECH Review)* (2 or 3 times yearly); *Journal of Computers in Mathematics and Science Teaching (JCMST); Journal of Computing in Childhood Education (JCCE); Journal of Educational Multimedia and Hypermedia (JEMH); Journal of Interactive Learning Research (JILR)* (formerly *Journal of Artificial Intelligence in Education); Journal of Technology and Teacher Education (JTATE); International Journal of Educational Telecommunications (IJET).* A catalog of books and CD-ROMs is available upon request, or by visiting http://www.aace.organize/conf/pubs.

Association of American Publishers (AAP). 1718 Connecticut Avenue, N.W., Washington, DC 20009. (202)232-3335. Fax (202)745-0694. Website http://www.publishers.org. Patricia S. Schroeder, Pres. and CEO (DC); Judith Platt, Dir. of Communications/Public Affairs (jplatt@publishers.org). The Association of American Publishers is the national trade association of the U.S. book publishing industry. AAP was created in 1970 through the merger of the American Book Publishers Council, a trade publishing group, and the American Textbook Publishers Institute, a group of educational publishers. AAP's approximately 200 members include most of the major commercial book publishers in the United States, as well as smaller and nonprofit publishers, university presses, and scholarly societies. AAP members publish hardcover and paperback books in every field and a range of educational materials for the elementary, secondary, postsecondary, and professional markets. Members of the Association also produce computer software and electronic products and services, such as online databases and CD-ROMs. AAP's primary concerns are the protection of intellectual property rights in all media, the defense of free expression and freedom to publish at home and abroad, the management of new technologies, development of education markets and funding for instructional materials, and the development of national and global markets for its members products.

Association of College and Research Libraries (ACRL). 50 E. Huron St., Chicago, IL 60611-2795. (312)280-3248. Fax (312)280-2520. E-mail ajenkins@ala.org. Website http://www .ala.org/acrl.html. Althea H. Jenkins, Exec. Dir. An affiliate of the American Library Association, ACRL provides leadership for development, promotion, and improvement of academic and research library resources and services to facilitate learning, research, and the scholarly communications process. It provides access to library standards for colleges, universities, and two-year institutions, and publishes statistics on academic libraries. Committees include Academic or Research Librarian of the Year Award, Appointments, Hugh C. Atkinson Memorial Award, Budget and Finance, Colleagues, Committee on the Status of Academic Librarians, Constitution and Bylaws, Copyright, Council of Liaisons, Doctoral Dissertation Fellowship, Government Relations, Intellectual Freedom, International Relations, Samuel Lazerow Fellowship, Media Resources, *Membership*, Nominations, Orientation, Professional Development, Professional Enhancement, Publications, Racial and Ethnic Diversity, Research, K. G. Saur Award for the Best C&RL Article, Standards and Accreditation, Statistics. The association administers 15 different awards in three categories: Achievement and Distinguished Service Awards, Research Awards/Grants, and *Publications. Membership:* over 10,000. *Dues:* $35 (in addition to ALA membership). *Meetings:* 1999 ACRL National Conference, Apr 8-12, Detroit. *Publications: College & Research Libraries* (6/yr.); *College & Research Libraries News* (11/yr.); *Rare Books and Manuscripts Librarianship* (semi-annual); *CHOICE Magazine: Current Review for Academic Libraries* (11/yr.). *CLIP Notes* (current issues are nos. 16, 17, 20-26). Recent titles include: *Displays and Exhibits in College Libraries; Restructuring Academic Libraries; Documenting Cultural Diversity in the Resurgent American South; Choice Reviews in Women's Studies;* and *Proceedings of the 7th ACRL National Conference.* A free list of materials is available. ACRL also sponsors an open discussion listserv, ACRL-FRM@ALA.ORG.

*Association of Independent Video and Filmmakers/Foundation for Independent Video and Film (AIVF/FIVF). 304 Hudson St., 6th Floor, New York, NY 10013. (212)807-1400. Fax (212)463-8519. E-mail info@aivf.org. Website http://www.aivf.org. Elizabeth Peters, Exec., Dir. Michelle Coe, Program & Information Services Dir. AIVF is the national trade association for independent video and filmmakers, representing their needs and goals to industry, government, and the public. Programs include screenings and seminars, insurance for members and groups, and information and referral services. Recent activities include seminars in filmmaking technology, a screening series with mid-career artists, and or monthly forum with industry professionals. AIVF also has advocated public funding of the arts, public access to new telecommunications systems, and monitoring censorship issues. *Dues:* $45, indiv.; $75, library; $100, nonprofit organization; $150, business/industry; $25, student. *Publications: The Independent Film and Video Monthly; The AIVF Guide to International Film and Video Festivals; The AIVF Guide to Film and Video Distributors; The Next Step: Distributing Independent Films and Videos;* the AIVF Self Distribution Toolkit & the AIVF Film & Video Exhibitors Guide.

Association of Specialized and Cooperative Library Agencies (ASCLA). 50 E. Huron St., Chicago, IL 60611. (800)545-2433, ext. 4398. Fax (312)944-8085. E-mail ascla@ala.org. Website http://www.ala.org/ascla. Cathleen Bourdon, Exec. Dir. An affiliate of the American Library Association, ASCLA represents state library agencies, multitype library cooperatives, independent libraries and libraries serving special clienteles to promote the development of coordinated library services with equal access to information and material for all persons. The activities and programs of the association are carried out by 21 committees, 4 sections, and various discussion groups. *Membership:* 1,300. *Dues:* (in addition to ALA membership) $40, personal; $50, organization; $500, state library agency. *Meetings:* 1999 Conference, Jun 24-Jul 1, New Orleans. 2000, Jul 6-13, Chicago. *Publications: Interface* (q.); *The Americans with Disabilities Act: Its Impact on Libraries; Deafness: An Annotated Bibliography and Guide to Basic Materials; Library Standards for Adult Correctional Institutions 1992.* Write for free checklist of materials.

Association of Systematics Collections (ASC). 1725 K St. NW, Suite 601, Washington, DC 20006. (202)835-9050. E-mail asc@ascoll.org. Website http://www.ascoll.org. Fosters the care, management, and improvement of biological collections and promotes their utilization. Institutional members include free-standing museums, botanical gardens, college and university museums, and public institutions, including state biological surveys and agricultural research centers. ASC also represents affiliate societies, keeps members informed about funding and legislative issues, and provides technical consulting about collection care and taxonomy. *Membership:* 79 institutions, 25 societies, 1,200 newsletter subscribers. *Dues:* depend on the size of collections. *Publications: ASC Newsletter* (for members and nonmember subscribers, bi-mo.); *Guidelines for Institutional Policies and Planning in Natural History Collections*; *Access to Genetic Resources*; *Collections of Frozen Tissues*; *Guidelines for Institutional Database Policies.*

Cable in the Classroom. 1900 N. Beauregard St., Suite 108, Alexandria, VA 22311. (703)845-1400. Fax (703)845-1409. E-mail cicofc@aol.com. Website http://www.ciconline .org. Megan Hookey, Managing Dir. Cable in the Classroom is the cable industry's $420 million public service initiative to enrich education. It provides free cable connections to more than 77,000 public and private K–12 schools, reaching more than 82% of all U.S. students with commercial-free, quality educational programming. It also provides curriculum-related support materials for its programming and conducts Teacher Training and Media Literacy workshops throughout the country. *Membership:* Cable in the Classroom is a consortium of more than 8,500 local cable companies and 38 national cable programming networks. *Meetings:* Cable in the Classroom exhibits at 15 major education conferences each year. *Publications: Delivering the Future: Cable and Education Partnerships for the Information Age* (Dr. Bobbi Kamil); *Cable in the Classroom Magazine* (mo.); *Taking Charge of Your TV: A Guide to Critical Viewing for Parents and Children* (booklet, available on request).

Catholic Library Association (CLA). 100 North Street, Suite 224, Pittsfield, MA 01201-5109. (413)443-2CLA. Fax (413)442-2CLA. Jean R. Bostley, SSJ, Exec. Dir. Provides educational programs, services, and publications for Catholic libraries and librarians. *Membership:* approx. 1,000. *Dues:* $45, indiv.; special rates for students and retirees. *Meetings: Meetings* are held in conjunction with the National Catholic Educational Association: 2001, Apr 17-20, Milwaukee; 2002, Apr 2-5, Atlantic City; 2003, Apr 22-25, St. Louis. *Publications: Catholic Library World* (q.); *Catholic Periodical and Literature Index* (q. with annual cumulations).

C&C Associates. 11112 S. Spotted Rd., Cheney, WA 99004. (888)662-7678 or (509)624-9621. Fax (509)323-4811 or (509)624-5320. E-mail cc@iea.com. C&C Associates has the only Electronic Camera Repair Home Study course in the world. It has more than two centuries' experience with educating camera repair technicians. The only college certified camera repair instructor in the world teaches the 18-lesson course. C&C also publishes repair guides for cameras and also writes technical repair guides for several manufactures.

Central Educational Network (CEN). 1400 E. Touhy, Suite 260, Des Plaines, IL 60018-3305. (847)390-8700. Fax (847)390-9435. E-mail ceninfo@mcs.net. James A. Fellows, Pres. The Central Educational Network is a not-for-profit, public television membership organization dedicated to leading, supporting, and serving the needs and interests of community, university, and state organizations that are educating and enriching their citizens through public telecommunications services. CEN is associated with the American Telecommunications Group. ATG includes the American Center for Children and Media [Making Children's Television and Media Experiences Better], The Benton Academy for Public Telecommunications [Continuing Professional Development], The Center for Education Initiatives [Extending and Improving Educational Opportunities], Continental Program Marketing [Acquiring and Placing Quality Programming], Higher Education Telecommunication Consortium [Building on the Distinctive Resources of Colleges and Universities], and the Hartford Gunn Institute [Planning for a Productive and Effective Second Generation of Public Broadcasting]. *Membership* in the CEN component of ATG is available to public television and telecommunications organizations and agencies.

Children's Television International (CTI)/GLAD Productions, Inc. Planting Field Drive, South Riding, VA 20152. (800)CTI-GLAD (284-4523). Fax (703)327-6470. Ray Gladfelter, Pres. and Dir. of Customer Services. An educational organization that develops, produces, and distributes a wide variety of color television and video programming and related publications as a resource to aid the social, cultural, and intellectual development of children and young adults. Programs cover language arts, science, social studies, history, and art for home, school, and college viewing. *Publications:* Teacher guides for instructional series; *The History Game: A Teacher's Guide*; complimentary catalog for educational videos.

Close Up Foundation. 44 Canal Center Plaza, Alexandria, VA 22314. (703)706-3300. Fax (703)706-0000. E-mail alumni@closeup.org. Website http://www.closeup.org. Stephen A. Janger, CEO. A nonprofit, nonpartisan civic education organization promoting informed citizen participation in public policy and community service. Programs reach more than a million participants each year. Close Up brings 25,000 secondary and middle school students and teachers and older Americans each year to Washington for week-long government studies programs and produces television programs on the C-SPAN cable network for secondary school and home audiences. *Meetings* are scheduled most weeks during the academic year in Washington, DC, all with a government, history, or current issues focus. *Membership:* 25,000 participants. *Publications: Current Issues*; *The Bill of Rights: A User's Guide*; *Perspectives*; *International Relations*; *The American Economy*; documentary videotapes on domestic and foreign policy issues.

Community College Association for Instruction and Technology (CCAIT). New Mexico Military Institute, 101 W. College Blvd., Roswell, NM, 88201-5173. (505)624-8382. Fax (505)624-8390. E-mail klopfer@yogi.nmmi.cc.nm.us. Jerry Klopfer, Pres. A national association of community and junior college educators interested in the discovery and dissemination of information relevant to instruction and media technology in the community environment. Facilitates member exchange of data, reports, proceedings, and other information pertinent to instructional technology and the teaching-learning process; sponsors AECT convention sessions, an annual video competition, and social activities. *Membership:* 250. *Dues:* $20. *Meetings:* 1998, AECT National Convention, St. Louis, Feb 18-22. *Publications:* Regular newsletter; irregular topical papers.

(AACC) Community College Satellite Network (CCSN). One Dupont Cir.. NW, Suite 410, Washington, DC 20036. (202)728-0200. Fax (202)833-2467. E-mail CCSN@AACC.NCHE.EDU. Website http://www.aacc.nche.edu. Monica W. Pilkey, Dir. An office of the American Association of Community Colleges (AACC), CCSN provides leadership and facilitates distance education, teleconferencing, and satellite training to the nation's community colleges. CCSN offers satellite training, discounted teleconferences, free program resources, and general informational assistance in telecommunications to the nation's community colleges. CCSN meets with its members at various industry trade shows and is very active in the AACC annual convention held each spring. CCSN produces a directory of community college satellite downlink and videoconference facilities. *Membership:* 150. *Dues:* $400 for AACC members; $800 for non-AACC members. *Publications: Schedule of Programming* (2/yr.; contains listings of live and taped teleconferences for training and staff development); *CCSN Fall & Spring Program Schedule* (listing of live and taped teleconferences for training, community and staff development, business and industry training, and more); *Teleconferencing at U.S. Community Colleges* (directory of contacts for community college satellite downlink facilities and videoconference capabilities). A free catalog is available.

Computer Assisted Language Instruction Consortium (CALICO). 317 Liberal Arts Building, Southwest Texas State University, 601 University Dr., San Marcos, TX 78666. (512)245-2360. Fax (512)245-8298. E-mail execdir@calico.org. Website http://www.calico .org. Robert Fischer, Exec. Dir.. CALICO is devoted to the dissemination of information on the application of technology to language teaching and language learning. *Membership:* 1,000 members from United States and 20 foreign countries. *Dues:* $50, indiv. *Meetings:* 1999,

June, Miami University, Oxford, Ohio. *Publications: CALICO Journal* (q.), *CALICO Monograph Series.*

Computer Learning Foundation. P.O. Box 60007, Palo Alto, CA 94306-0007. (650)327-3347. Fax (650)327-3349. Website http://www.ComputerLearning.org. Sally Bowman Alden, Exec. Dir. The Computer Learning Foundation is in international non-profit educational foundation dedicated to the improvement of education and preparation of youth for the workplace through the use of technology. Foundation programs provide parents and educators with the information, resources, and assistance they need to use technology effectively with children. The Computer Learning Foundation is the official host each October of Computer Learning Month, a month-long focus on the important role technology plays in our lives and a major national grassroots educational effort. During Computer Learning Month, the Computer Learning Foundation announces new materials and projects and hosts North American annual competitions for children, adults, community groups, and schools. Thousands of dollars in technology products are awarded to winners and their schools. The Computer Learning Foundation is endorsed by and collaborates with 56 U.S. state departments and Canadian ministries of education and 26 national nonprofit organizations; however, the Foundation is funded by corporate and individual donations. *Publication: Computer Learning,* annual publication.

Computer-Using Educators, Inc. (CUE). 1210 Marina Village Parkway, Suite 100, Alameda, CA 94501. (510)814-6630. Fax (510)814-0195. E-mail cueinc@cue.org. Website http://www.cue.org. Bob Walczak, Exec, Dir. CUE, a California nonprofit corporation, was founded in 1976 by a group of teachers interested in exploring the use of technology to improve learning in their classrooms. The organization has never lost sight of this mission. Today, CUE has an active membership of 11,000 professionals worldwide in schools, community colleges, and universities. CUE's 23 affiliates in California provide members with local year-round support through meetings, grants, events, and mini-conferences. Special Interest Groups (SIGs) support members interested in a variety of special topics. CUE's annual conferences, newsletter, advocacy, Website, and other programs help the technology-using educator connect with other professionals. *Membership:* 11,000 individual, corporate, and institutional members. *Dues:* $30. *Meetings:* 1999 Spring CUE Conference, May 6-8, Palm Springs, CA; Fall CUE Conference, Oct. 28-30, Sacramento; 2000, May 11-13, Palm Springs, Nov 9-11, Sacramento. *Publication: CUE NewsLetter.*

Consortium of College and University Media Centers. 121 Pearson Hall-ITC, Iowa State University, Ames, IA 50011-2203. (515)294-1811. Fax (515)294-8089. E-mail donrieck @iastate.edu; ccumc@ccumc.org. Website www.ccumc.org. Don Rieck, Exec. Dir. CCUMC is a professional group of higher education media personnel whose purpose is to improve education and training through the effective use of educational media. Assists educational and training users in making films, video, and educational media more accessible. Fosters cooperative planning among university media centers. Gathers and disseminates information on improved procedures and new developments in instructional technology and media center management. *Membership:* 400. *Dues:* $175 institutional; $175, corporate; $25, student; $175, associate. *Meetings:* 1999, Oct 21-26, Burlington, VT; 2000, Oct 20-25, Denton, TX. *Publication: Media Review* (journal).

*Continuing Library Education Network and Exchange Round Table (CLENERT). 50 E. Huron St., Chicago, IL 60611. (800)545-2433. Website http://www.ala.org. An affiliate of the American Library Association, CLENERT seeks to provide access to quality continuing education opportunities for librarians and information scientists and to create an awareness of the need for such education in helping individuals in the field to respond to societal and technological changes. *Membership:* 350. *Dues:* open to all ALA members; $15, indiv.; $50, organization. *Publication: CLENExchange* (q.), available to nonmembers by subscription at $20.

Copyright Clearance Center, Inc. (CCC). 222 Rosewood Dr., Danvers, MA 01923. (978)750-8400. Fax (978)750-4470. E-mail ihinds@copyright.com. Website http://www .copyright.com/. Joseph S. Alen, Pres. CCC, the largest licenser of photocopy reproduction rights in the world, was formed in 1978 to facilitate compliance with U.S. copyright law. CCC provides licensing systems involving the reproduction and distribution of copyrighted materials throughout the world. CCC currently manages rights relating to over 1.75 million works and represents more than 9,600 publishers and hundreds of thousands of authors and other creators, directly or through their representatives. CCC licensed customers in the United States number over 9,000 corporations and subsidiaries (including 90 of the Fortune 100 companies), as well as thousands of government agencies, law firms, document suppliers, libraries, academic institutions, copy shops, and bookstores in the United States. CCC is a member of the International Federation Rights Organizations (IFRRO) and has bilateral agreements with RROs in 11 countries worldwide, under which it repatriates fees for overseas use of U.S. works.

Corporation for Public Broadcasting (CPB). 901 E Street, NW, Washington, DC 20004-2037. (202)879-9600. Fax (202)783-1039. E-mail info@cpb.org. Website http://www .cpb.org. Robert T. Coonrod, Pres. and CEO. A private, nonprofit corporation created by Congress in 1967 to develop noncommercial television, radio, and online services for the American people. CPB created the Public Broadcasting Service (PBS) in 1969 and National Public Radio (NPR) in 1970. CPB distributes grants to over 1,000 local public television and radio stations that reach virtually every household in the country. The Corporation is the industry's largest single source of funds for national public television and radio program development and production. In addition to quality educational and informational programming, CPB and local public stations make important contributions in the areas of education, training, community service, and application of emerging technologies. *Publications: Annual Report; CPB Public Broadcasting Directory* ($15).

Council for Basic Education. 1319 F St. NW, Suite 900, Washington, DC 20004-1152. (202)347-4171. Email info@c-b-e.org. Website http://www.c-b-e.org. Christopher T. Cross, Pres. Maxine P. Frost, Chair of Board of Directors. CBE's mission is to strengthen teaching and learning of the core subjects (mathematics, English, language arts, history, government, geography, the sciences, foreign languages, and the arts) in order to develop the capacity for lifelong learning and foster responsible citizenship. As an independent, critical voice for education reform, CBE champions the philosophy that all children can learn, and that the job of schools is to achieve this goal. CBE advocates this goal by publishing analytical periodicals and administering practical programs as examples to strengthen content in curriculum and teaching. CBE is completing a kit of Standards for Excellence in Education, which includes a CD-ROM; guides for teachers, parents, and principals, and a book of standards in the core subjects. *Membership:* 3,000.

Council for Exceptional Children (CEC). 1920 Association Dr., Reston, VA 20191-1589. (703)620-3660. TTY: (703)264-9446. Fax (703)264-9494. E-mail cec@cec.sped.org. Website http://www.cec.sped.org. Nancy Safer, Exec. Dir. CEC is the largest international professional organization dedicated to improving educational outcomes for individuals with exceptionalities (students with disabilities and the gifted). CEC advocates appropriate governmental policies, sets professional standards, provides professional development, advocates for newly and historically underserved individuals with exceptionalities, and helps professionals obtain conditions and resources necessary for effective professional practice. Services include professional development opportunities and resources, 17 divisions for specialized information, public policy advocacy and information, conferences, and standards for the preparation and certification of special educators and professional practice. CEC has expanded its professional development activities to include distance learning activities such as satellite broadcasts and Internet-based study groups. The CEC annual convention features the most current educational technology as well as adaptive and assistive technology in formats ranging from full-day workshops to hands-on demonstrations. In collaboration with another agency, CEC is involved in a research project that examines teachers' use of technology to promote literacy in children with exceptionalities. *Membership:* teachers, administrators, students, parents, related support service providers. *Publications:* Journals and newsletters with information on new research findings, classroom practices that work, and special education publications. (*See also* the ERIC Clearinghouse on Disabilities and Gifted Education.)

(CEC) Technology and Media Division (TAM). Council for Exceptional Children. The Technology and Media Division (TAM) of The Council for Exceptional Children (CEC) encourages the development of new applications, technologies, and media for use as daily living tools by special populations. This information is disseminated through professional meetings, training programs, and publications. TAM members receive four issues annually of the *Journal of Special Education Technology* containing articles on specific technology programs and applications, and five issues of the TAM newsletter, providing news of current research, developments, products, conferences, and special programs information. *Membership:* 1,700. *Dues:* $10 in addition to CEC membership.

Council on International Non-Theatrical Events (CINE). 1001 Connecticut Ave. NW, Suite 625, Washington, DC 20036. (202)785-1136. Fax (202)785-4114. Website http://www.cine.org. Donna Tschiffely, Exec. Dir. Coordinates the selection and placement of U.S. documentary, television, short subject, and didactic films in more than 100 overseas film festivals annually. A Golden Eagle Certificate is awarded to each professional film considered most suitable to represent the United States in international competition and to winning films made by adults, amateurs, youths, and university students. Prizes and certificates won at overseas festivals are presented at an annual awards ceremony. CINE receives approximately 1300 entries annually for the competition. Deadlines for receipt of entry forms are Feb 1 and Aug 1. *Meeting:* CINE Showcase and Awards held annually in Washington, DC. *Publications: CINE Annual Yearbook of Film and Video Awards; Worldwide Directory of Film and Video Festivals and Events.*

*East-West Center. 1601 East-West Rd., Honolulu, HI 96848-1601. (808)944-7111. Fax (808)944-7376. E-mail ewcinfo@ewc.hawaii.edu. Website http://www.ewc.hawaii.edu. Dr. Charles E. Morrison, Pres. The U.S. Congress established the East-West Center in 1960 with a mandate to foster mutual understanding and cooperation among the governments and peoples of Asia, the Pacific, and the United States. Officially known as the Center for Cultural and Technical Interchange Between East and West, it is a public, nonprofit institution with an international board of governors. Funding for the center comes from the U.S. government, with additional support provided by private agencies, individuals, and corporations, and several Asian and Pacific governments, private agencies, individuals, and corporations. The center, through research, education, dialog, and outreach, provides a neutral meeting ground where people with a wide range of perspectives exchange views on topics of regional concern. Scholars, government and business leaders, educators, journalists, and other professionals from throughout the region annually work with Center staff to address issues of contemporary significance in such areas as international economics and politics, the environment, population, energy, the media, and Pacific islands development.

ECT Foundation. c/o AECT, 1025 Vermont Ave. NW, Suite 820, Washington, DC 20005. Hans-Erik Wennberg, Pres. The ECT Foundation is a nonprofit organization whose purposes are charitable and educational in nature. Its operation is based on the conviction that improvement of instruction can be accomplished, in part, by the continued investigation and application of new systems for learning and by periodic assessment of current techniques for the communication of information. In addition to awarding scholarships, internships, and fellowships, the foundation develops and conducts leadership training programs for emerging professional leaders. Its operations are closely allied to AECT program goals, and the two organizations operate in close conjunction with each other.

*Education Development Center, Inc. 55 Chapel St., Newton, MA 02158-1060. (617)969-7100. Fax (617)969-5979. Website http://www.edc.org. Janet Whitla, Pres. Seeks to improve education at all levels, in the United States and abroad, through curriculum development, institutional development, and services to the school and the community. Produces video-cassettes, primarily in connection with curriculum development and teacher training. *Publication: Annual Report.*

Educational Communications. P.O. Box 351419, Los Angeles, CA 90035. (310)559-9160. Fax (310)559-9160. E-mail ECNP@aol.com. Website http://home.earthlink.net/~dragonflight /ecoprojects.htm. Nancy Pearlman, CEO. Educational Communications is dedicated to enhancing the quality of life on this planet and provides radio and television programs about the environment. Serves as a clearinghouse on ecological issues. Programming is available on 100 stations in 25 states. *Publications: Compendium Newsletter* (bi-monthly)*; Directory of Environmental Organizations.*

Educational Products Information Exchange (EPIE Institute). 103 W. Montauk Highway, Hampton Bays, NY 11946. (516)728-9100. Fax (516)728-9228. E-mail kowoski@aurora .lionet.edu. Website http://www.epie.org. P. Kenneth Komoski, Exec. Dir. Assesses educational materials and provides consumer information, product descriptions, and citations for virtually all educational software and curriculum-related Websites. All of EPIE's services are available to schools and state agencies as well as parents and individuals. Online access is restricted to states with membership in the States Consortium for Improving Software Selection (SCISS). *Publication: The Educational Software Selector Database (TESS),* available to anyone. All publication material now available on CD-ROM.

Educational Resources Information Center (ERIC). National Library of Education (NLE), Office of Educational Research and Improvement (OERI), 555 New Jersey Ave. NW, Washington, DC 20208-5720. (202)219-2289. Fax (202)219-1817. E-mail eric@inet.ed.gov. Keith Stubbs, Dir. ERIC is a federally funded, nationwide information network that provides access to the English-language education literature. The ERIC system consists of clearing-houses, adjunct clearinghouses, and system support components, including ACCESS ERIC, the ERIC Document Reproduction Service (EDRS), and the ERIC Processing and Reference Facility. ERIC actively solicits papers, conference proceedings, literature reviews, and cur-riculum materials from researchers, practitioners, educational associations and institutions, and federal, state, and local agencies. These materials, along with articles from nearly 800 different journals, are indexed and abstracted for entry into the ERIC database. The ERIC database (the largest education database in the world) now contains more than 850,000 records of documents and journal articles. Users can access the ERIC database online, on CD-ROM, or through print and microfiche indexes. ERIC microfiche collections, which contain the full text of most ERIC documents, are available for public use at more than 1,000 locations worldwide. Reprints of ERIC documents, on microfiche or in paper copy, can also be ordered from EDRS. Copies of journal articles can be found in library periodical collections, through interlibrary loan, or from article reprint services. A list of the ERIC Clearinghouses, together with addresses, telephone numbers, and brief domain descriptions, follows here. *Publications: Resources in Education* (U.S. Government Printing Office); *Current Index to Journals in Education* (Oryx Press).

    ACCESS ERIC. Aspen Systems Corp., 2277 Research Blvd., Mailstop 6L, Rockville, MD 20850. 1-800-LET-ERIC [538-3742]. Fax (301)519-6760. E-mail accesseric@accessiceric.org. ACCESS ERIC coordinates ERIC's outreach and system-wide dissemination activities, develops new ERIC publications, and provides general reference and referral services. Its publications include several reference directories designed to help the public understand and use ERIC as well as provide information about current education-related issues, research, and practice. *Publications: A Pocket*

Guide to ERIC; *All About ERIC*; *The ERIC Review*; the Parent Brochure series; *Catalog of ERIC Clearinghouse Publications*; *ERIC Calendar of Education-Related Conferences*; *ERIC Directory of Education-Related Information Centers*; *ERIC User's Interchange*; *Directory of ERIC Resource Collections.* Databases: ERIC Digests Online (EDO); Education-Related Information Centers; ERIC Resource Collections; ERIC Calendar of Education-Related Conferences. (The databases are available through the Internet: http://www.accesseric.org.)

ERIC Clearinghouse for Community Colleges (JC) (formerly Junior Colleges). University of California at Los Angeles (UCLA), 3051 Moore Hall, P.O. Box 951521, Los Angeles, CA 90025-1521. (310)825-3931, (800)832-8256. Fax (310)206-8095. E-mail ericcc@ucla.edu. Website http://www.gseis.ucla.edu/ERIC/eric.html. Arthur M. Cohen, Dir. Selects, synthesizes, and distributes reports and other documents about two-year public and private community and junior colleges, technical institutes, and two-year branch university programs, and outcomes of these institutions; linkages between two-year colleges and business, industrial, and community organizations; and articulation between two-year colleges and secondary and four-year postsecondary institutions.

ERIC Clearinghouse for Social Studies/Social Science Education (SO). Indiana University, Social Studies Development Center, 2805 East 10th St., Suite 120, Bloomington, IN 47408-2698. (812)855-3838, (800)266-3815. Fax (812)855-0455. E-mail ericso@indiana.edu. Website http://www.indiana.edu/~ssdc.eric_chess.htm. All levels of social studies and social science education; the contributions of history, geography, and other social science disciplines; applications of theory and research to social science education; education as a social science; comparative education (K–12); content and curriculum materials on social topics such as law-related education, ethnic studies, bias and discrimination, aging, and women's equity. Music and art education are also covered. Includes input from the Adjunct ERIC Clearinghouses for Law-Related Education, for U.S.-Japan Studies, for Service Learning, and for International Civics.

> **Adjunct ERIC Clearinghouse for Art Education.** Indiana University, Social Studies Development Center, 2805 East 10th St., Suite 120, Bloomington, IN 47408-2698. (812)855-3838, (800)266-3815. Fax (812)855-0455. E-mail clarkgil @indiana.edu; zimmerm@ucs.indiana.edu. Enid Zimmerman, Director. Adjunct to the ERIC Clearinghouse on Social Studies/Social Science Education.

> **Adjunct ERIC Clearinghouse for Law-Related Education (ADJ/LR).** Indiana University, Social Studies Development Center, 2805 East 10th St., Suite 120, Bloomington, IN 47408-2698. (812)855-3838, (800)266-3815. Fax (812)855-0455. E-mail patrick@indiana.edu, tvontz@indiana.edu. Website http://www.indiana .edu/~ssdc/iplre.html. John Patrick and Robert Leming, Co-Directors. Adjunct to the ERIC Clearinghouse on Social Studies/Social Sciences Education.

> **Adjunct ERIC Clearinghouse for United States-Japan Studies (ADJ/JS).** 2805 E. 10th St., Suite 120, Bloomington, IN 47408-2698. (812)855-3838, (800)266-3815. Fax (812)855-0455. E-mail japan@indiana.edu. Website http://www.indiana.edu/~japan. Marcia Johnson, Assoc. Dir. Provides information on topics concerning Japan and U.S.-Japan relations. Adjunct to the ERIC Clearinghouse for Social Studies/Social Science Education. *Publications: Guide to Teaching Materials on Japan; Teaching About Japan: Lessons and Resources; The Constitution and Individual Rights in Japan: Lessons for Middle and High School Students; Internationalizing the U.S. Classroom: Japan as a Model; Tora no Maki II: Lessons for Teaching About Contemporary Japan;*

The Japan Digest Series (complimentary, concise discussions of various Japan-related topics): *Fiction About Japan in the Elementary Curriculum; Daily Life in Japanese High Schools; Rice: It's More Than Food in Japan; Ideas for Integrating Japan into the Curriculum; Japanese Education; Japanese-US Economic Relations; Japan's Economy: 21st Century Challenges; Shinbun* (bi-annual project newsletter).

ERIC Clearinghouse on Adult, Career, and Vocational Education (ERIC/ACVE). The Ohio State University, Center on Education and Training for Employment, 1900 Kenny Rd., Columbus, OH 43210-1090. (614)292-7069, (800)848-4815, ext. 2-7069. Fax (614)292-1260. E-mail ericacve@postbox.acs.ohio-state.edu. Website http://www.ericacve.org. Susan Imel, Dir. Judy Wagner, Assoc. Dir. All levels and settings of adult and continuing, career, and vocational/technical education. Adult education, from basic literacy training through professional skill upgrading. Career awareness, career decision making, career development, career change, and experience-based education. Vocational and technical education, including new subprofessional fields, industrial arts, corrections education, employment and training programs, youth employment, work experience programs, education and business partnerships, entrepreneurship, adult retraining, and vocational rehabilitation for individuals with disabilities. Includes input from the Adjunct ERIC Clearinghouse on Consumer Education.

> **Adjunct ERIC Clearinghouse for Consumer Education (ADJ/CN).** National Institute for Consumer Education, 207 Rackham Bldg., Eastern Michigan University, Ypsilanti, MI 48197-2237. (313)487-2292. Fax (313)487-7153. E-mail nice@emuvax.emich.edu. E-mail NICE@online.emich.edu. Website http://www.emich.edu/public/coe/nice. Rosella Bannister, Dir. Adjunct to the ERIC Clearinghouse on Adult, Career, and Vocational Education.

ERIC Clearinghouse on Assessment and Evaluation (formerly Tests, Measurement, and Evaluation). The University of Maryland, 1129 Shriver Lab, College Park, Maryland 20742-5701 (301)405-7449, (800)464-3742, Fax: (301)405-8134. E-mail ericae@.net. Website http://ericae.net. Lawrence M. Rudner, Dir. Tests and other measurement devices; methodology of measurement and evaluation; application of tests, measurement, or evaluation in educational projects and programs; research design and methodology in the area of assessment and evaluation; and learning theory. Includes input from the Adjunct Test Collection Clearinghouse.

ERIC Clearinghouse on Counseling and Student Services (formerly Counseling and Personnel Services). University of North Carolina at Greensboro, School of Education, 201 Ferguson Building, P.O. Box 26171, Greensboro, NC 27402-6171. (336)334-4114, (336)334-4116, (800)414-9769. E-mail ericcass@uncg.edu. Website http://www.uncg.edu/~ericcass2. Garry R. Walz, Dir. Preparation, practice, and supervision of counselors and therapists at all educational levels and in all settings; theoretical development of counseling and student services; assessment and diagnosis procedures such as testing and interviewing and the analysis and dissemination of the resultant information; outcomes analysis of counseling interventions; groups and case work; nature of pupil, student, and adult characteristics; identification and implementation of strategies that foster student learning and achievement; personnel workers and their relation to career planning, family consultations, and student services activities; identification of effective strategies for enhancing parental effectiveness; and continuing preparation of counselors and therapists in the use of new technologies for professional renewal and the implications of such technologies for service provision. *Meeting:* Annual Assessment Conference. *Publications: Career Transitions in Turbulent Times; Exemplary Career Development Programs & Practices; Career Development; Counseling Employment Bound Youth; Internationalizing Career*

Planning; Saving the Native Son; Cultural and Diversity Issues in Counseling; Safe Schools, Safe Students; many others. Call for catalog.

ERIC Clearinghouse on Disabilities and Gifted Education (EC). 1920 Association Dr., Reston, VA 20191-1589. (703)264-9474, (800)328-0272. TTY: (703)264-9449. E-mail ericec@cec.sped.org. Website http://ericec.org. ERIC EC is part of the U.S. Department of Education's information network. ERIC EC collects the professional literature on disabilities and gifted education for inclusion in the ERIC database. ERIC EC also responds to requests for information on disabilities and gifted education; serves as a resource and referral center for the general public; conducts general information searches; and publishes and disseminates free or low-cost materials on disability and gifted education research, programs, and practices.

ERIC Clearinghouse on Educational Management (EA). University of Oregon (Dept. 5207), 1787 Agate St., Eugene, OR 97403-5207. (541)346-5043, (800)438-8841. Fax (541)346-2334. E-mail ppiele@oregon.uoregon.edu. Philip K. Piele, Dir. The governance, leadership, management, and structure of K–12 public and private education organizations; local, state, and federal education law and policy-making; practice and theory of administration; preservice and inservice preparation of administrators; tasks and processes of administration; methods and varieties of organization and organizational change; and the social context of education organizations.

ERIC Clearinghouse on Elementary and Early Childhood Education (PS) and the **National Parent Information Network (NPIN)**. University of Illinois, Children's Research Center, 51 Gerty Dr., Champaign, IL 61820. (217)333-1386, (800)583-4135. Fax (217)333-3767. E-mail ericeece@uiuc.edu. Website http://ericps.crc.uiuc.edu /ericeece.html. Lilian G. Katz, Dir. (l-katz@uiuc.edu). The physical, cognitive, social, educational, and cultural development of children from birth through early adolescence; prenatal factors; parents, parenting, and family relationships that impinge on education; learning theory research and practice related to the development of young children, including the preparation of teachers for this educational level; interdisciplinary curriculum and mixed-age teaching and learning; educational, social, and cultural programs and services for children; the child in the context of the family and the family in the context of society; theoretical and philosophical issues pertaining to children's development and education. Includes input from the Adjunct ERIC Clearinghouse for Child Care.

> **Adjunct ERIC Clearinghouse for Child Care (ADJ/CC)**. Adjunct ERIC Clearinghouse for Child Care (ADJ/CC). National Child Care Information Center, 301 Maple Ave., Suite 602, Vienna, VA 22180. (703)938-6555, (800)516-2242. Fax (800)716-2242. E-mail agoldstein@acf.dhhs.gov. Website http://ericps.crc.uiuc.edu/nccic/nccichome.html. Anne Goldstein, Proj. Dir. Adjunct to the ERIC Clearinghouse on Elementary and Early Childhood Education. Works with Bureau, Administration for Children and Families (ACF) of DHHS, to complement, enhance, and promote child care linkages and to serve as a mechanism for supporting quality, comprehensive services for children and families. NCCIS's activities include: dissemination of child care information in response to requests from States, Territories and Tribe, other policymakers, child care organizations, providers, business communities, parents, and the general public; outreach to ACF child care grantees and the boarder child care community; publication of the child care *Bulletin* and development and dissemination of other publications on key child care issues; and coordination of National Leadership Forums, which provide an opportunity for experts from across the country to participate in one-day conferences on critical issues affecting children and families. Working closely with ACF

Regional offices, the NCCIC also provides technical assistance to states through a network of state technical assistance specialists. Many materials produced and distributed by NCCIC are available in Spanish. NCCIC is the Adjunct ERIC Clearinghouse for Child Care.

ERIC Clearinghouse on Higher Education (HE). George Washington University, One Dupont Cir. NW, Suite 630, Washington, DC 20036-1183. (202)296-2597, (800)773-3742. Fax (202)452-1844. E-mail eric@eric-he.edu. Website http://www .eriche.org. Adrianna Kezar, Dir. Topics relating to college and university conditions, problems, programs, and students. Curricular and instructional programs, and institutional research at the college or university level. Federal programs, professional education (medicine, law, etc.), professional continuing education, collegiate computer-assisted learning and management, graduate education, university extension programs, teaching and learning, legal issues and legislation, planning, governance, finance, evaluation, interinstitutional arrangements, management of institutions of higher education, and business or industry educational programs leading to a degree. *Publications: Higher Education Leadership: Analyzing the Gender Gap; The Virtual Campus: Technology and Reform in Higher Education; Early Intervention Programs: Opening the Door to Higher Education; Enriching College with Constructive Controversy; A Culture for Academic Excellence: Implementing the Quality Principles in Higher Education; From Discipline to Development: Rethinking Student Conduct in Higher Education; Proclaiming and Sustaining Excellence: Assessment as a Faculty Role; The Application of Customer Satisfaction Principles to Universities; Saving the Other Two-Thirds: Practices and Strategies for Improving the Retention and Graduation of African American Students in Predominately White Institutions; Enrollment Management: Change for the 21st Century; Faculty Workload: States' Perspectives.*

ERIC Clearinghouse on Information & Technology (IR) (formerly Information Resources). Syracuse University, 4-194 Center for Science and Technology, Syracuse, NY 13244-4100. (315)443-3640, (800)464-9107. Fax (315)443-5448. E-mail eric @ericir.syr.edu. AskERIC (question-answering service via Internet) askeric@ericir .syr.edu. R. David Lankes, Dir. Educational technology and library and information science at all levels. Instructional design, development, and evaluation within educational technology, along with the media of educational communication: computers and microcomputers, telecommunications, audio and video recordings, film, and other audiovisual materials as they pertain to teaching and learning. The focus is on the operation and management of information services for education-related organizations. Includes all aspects of information technology related to education.

ERIC Clearinghouse on Languages and Linguistics (FL). Center for Applied Linguistics, 4646-403 St., NW, Washington, DC 20016-1859.(202)362-0700, Ext. 200 Fax (202)362-3740. Fax (202)659-5641. E-mail eric@cal.org. Website http://www .cal.org/ericcll. Joy Peyton, Dir. Dr. Craig Packard, User Services Coordinator, contact person. Languages and language sciences. All aspects of second language instruction and learning in all commonly and uncommonly taught languages, including English as a second language. Bilingualism and bilingual education. Cultural education in the context of second language learning, including intercultural communication, study abroad, and international education exchange. All areas of linguistics, including theoretical and applied linguistics, socio-linguistics, and psycholinguistics. Includes input from the National Clearinghouse for ESL Literacy Education (NCLE).

Adjunct ERIC Clearinghouse for ESL Literacy Education (ADJ/LE). National Clearinghouse for ESL Literacy Education, Center for Applied Linguistics (CAL),4646-403 St., NW, Washington, DC 20016-1859.(202)362-0700, Ext. 200. Fax (202)362-3740. E-mail ncle@cal.org. Website http://www.cal.org

/ncle/. Joy Kreeft Peyton, Dir. Adjunct to the ERIC Clearinghouse on Languages and Linguistics. NCLE is the national clearinghouse focusing on the education of adults learning English as a second or additional language. NCLE collects, analyzes, synthesizes, and disseminates information on literacy education for adults and out-of-school youth. NCLE publishes books (available from Delta Systems in McHenry, IL), free ERIC digests and annotated bibliographies on a wide range of topics, and *NCLE Notes,* a newsletter. *Publication: Literacy and Language Diversity in the United States,* by Terrence Wiley (1996; McHenry, IL: Delta Systems).

ERIC Clearinghouse on Reading, English, and Communication (CS) (formerly Reading and Communication Skills). Indiana University, Smith Research Center, Suite 150, 2805 E. 10th St., Bloomington, IN 47408-2698. (812)855-5847, (800)759-4723. Fax (812)855-4220. E-mail ericcs@indiana.edu. Website http://www.indiana.edu/~eric_rec. Carl B. Smith, Dir. Reading, English, and communication (verbal and nonverbal), preschool through college; research and instructional development in reading, writing, speaking, and listening; identification, diagnosis, and remediation of reading problems; speech communication (including forensics), mass communication; interpersonal and small group interaction; interpretation; rhetorical and communication theory; speech sciences; and theater. Preparation of instructional staff and related personnel. All aspects of reading behavior with emphasis on physiology, psychology, sociology, and teaching; instructional materials, curricula, tests and measurement, and methodology at all levels of reading; the role of libraries and other agencies in fostering and guiding reading; diagnostics and remedial reading services in schools and clinical settings. Preparation of reading teachers and specialists. The Website makes available a wealth of information pertaining to the full gamut of language arts topics enumerated above.

ERIC Clearinghouse on Rural Education and Small Schools (RC). Appalachia Educational Laboratory (AEL), 1031 Quarrier St., P.O. Box 1348, Charleston, WV 25325-1348. (304)347-0465; (800)624-9120. Fax (304)347-0487. E-mail lanhamb @ael.org. Web page http://www.ael.org/erichp.htm. Hobart Harmon, Acting Dir. Economic, cultural, social, or other factors related to educational programs and practices for rural residents; American Indians and Alaska Natives, Mexican Americans, and migrants; educational practices and programs in all small schools; and outdoor education. Check Website to subscribe to print newsletter, or call toll-free.

ERIC Clearinghouse on Science, Mathematics, and Environmental Education (SE). The Ohio State University, 1929 Kenny Road, Columbus, OH 43210-1080. (614)292-6717, (800)276-0462. Fax (614)292-0263. E-mail ericse@osu.edu. Website http://www.ericse.org. Science, mathematics, and environmental education at all levels, and within these three broad subject areas, the following topics: development of curriculum and instructional materials; teachers and teacher education; learning theory and outcomes (including the impact of parameters such as interest level, intelligence, values, and concept development upon learning in these fields); educational programs; research and evaluative studies; media applications; computer applications.

ERIC Clearinghouse on Teaching and Teacher Education (SP) (formerly Teacher Education). American Association of Colleges for Teacher Education (AACTE), 1307 New York Avenue, N.W., Suite 300, Washington, DC 2005. (202)293-2450, (800)822-9229. Fax (202)457-8095. E-mail query@aacte.org. Website http://www.ericsp.org. Mary E. Dilworth, Dir. School personnel at all levels. Teacher recruitment, selection, licensing, certification, training, preservice and inservice preparation, evaluation, retention, and retirement. The theory, philosophy, and practice of teaching. Curricula and general education not specifically covered by other clearing-houses. Organization, administration, finance, and legal issues relating to teacher education programs and institutions. All aspects of health, physical, recreation, and dance education. Includes input from the Adjunct ERIC Clearinghouse on Clinical Schools.

> **Adjunct ERIC Clearinghouse on Clinical Schools (ADJ/CL)**. American Association of Colleges for Teacher Education, One Dupont Cir. NW, Suite 610, Washington, DC 20036-1186. (202)293-2450, (800)822-9229. Fax (202)457-8095. E-mail iabdalha@inet.ed.gov. Website http://www.aacte.org/menu2.html. Ismat Abdal-Haqq, Coord. Adjunct to the ERIC Clearinghouse on Teaching and Teacher Education.

ERIC Clearinghouse on Urban Education. Teachers College, Columbia University, Institute for Urban and Minority Education, Main Hall, Rm. 303, Box 40, 525 W. 120th St., New York, NY 10027-6696. (212)678-3433, (800)601-4868. Fax (212)678-4012. E-mail eric-cue@columbia.edu. Website http://eric-web.tc.columbia .edu. Erwin Flaxman, Dir. Programs and practices in public, parochial, and private schools in urban areas and the education of particular ethnic minority children and youth in various settings; the theory and practice of educational equity; urban and minority experiences; and urban and minority social institutions and services.

ERIC Document Reproduction Service (EDRS). 7420 Fullerton Rd., Suite 110, Springfield, VA 22153-2852. (703)440-1400, (800)443-ERIC (3742). Fax (703)440-1408. E-mail service@edrs.com. Website http://edrs.com. Peter M. Dagutis, Dir. Provides subscription services for ERIC document collections in electronic format (from 1996 forward) and on microfiche (from 1966 forward). On- demand delivery of ERIC documents is also available in formats including paper, electronic PDF image, fax, and microfiche. Delivery methods include shipment of hardcopy documents and microfiche, document fax-back, and online delivery. Back collections of ERIC documents, annual subscriptions, cumulative indexes, and other ERIC-related materials are also available. ERIC documents can be ordered by toll-free phone call, fax, mail, or online through the EDRS Website. Document ordering also available from DIALOG and OCLC.

ERIC Processing and Reference Facility. 1100 West Street, 2nd Floor, Laurel, MD 20707-3598. (301)497-4080, (800)799-ERIC (3742). Fax (301)953-0263. E-mail ericfac@inet.ed.gov. Web page http://ericfac.piccard.csc.com. Ted Brandhorst, Dir. A central editorial and computer processing agency that coordinates document processing and database building activities for ERIC; performs acquisition, lexicographic, and reference functions; and maintains systemwide quality control standards. The ERIC Facility also prepares *Resources in Education (RIE); ERIC Processing Manual; Thesaurus of ERIC Descriptors; Identifier Authority List (IAL);* ERIC Ready References; and other products.

Educational Videos and CD-ROM (originally the PCR Collection). Penn State Media Sales, 118 Wagner Building, University Park, PA 16802. Purchasing info (800)770-2111, (814)863-3102. Fax (814)865-3172. Rental information (800)826-0132. Fax (814)863-2574. Special Services Building, Penn State University, University Park, PA 16802. E-mail mediasales @cde.psu.edu. Website http://www.cde.psu.edu/MediaSales. Sue Oram, Media Sales Coordinator. Makes available to professionals videos in the behavioral sciences judged to be useful for university teaching and research. Also distributes training videos to business and industry. A catalog of the videos in the collection is available online. Special topics and individual brochures available. The online catalog now contains videos in the behavioral sciences (psychology, psychiatry, anthropology), animal behavior, sociology, teaching and learning, folklife and agriculture, business, education, biological sciences, and Pennsylvania topics. Videos and CD-ROMs may be submitted for international distribution. Stock footage available also.

Eisenhower National Clearinghouse for Mathematics and Science Education. 1929 Kenny Road, Columbus, OH 43210-1079. (800)621-5785, (614)292-7784. Fax (614)292-2066. E-mail info@enc.org. Website http://www.enc.org. Dr. Len Simutis, Dir. The Eisenhower National Clearinghouse for Mathematics and Science Education (ENC) is located at The Ohio State University and funded by the U.S. Department of Education's Office of Educational Research and Improvement (OERI). ENC provides K–12 teachers and other educators with a central source of information on mathematics and science curriculum materials, particularly those that support education reform. Among ENC's products and services are ENC Online, which is available through a toll-free number and the Internet; 12 demonstration sites located throughout the nation; and a variety of publications, including the *Guidebook of Federal Resources for K–12 Mathematics and Science*, which lists federal resources in mathematics and science education. In 1998 ENC produced CD-ROMs on topics such as equity and professional development, including curriculum resources and the ENC Resource Finder, which is the same searchable catalog of curriculum resources as the ENC Online. STET users include K–12 teachers, other educators, policymakers, and parents. *Publications: ENC Update* (newsletter); *ENC Focus* (a magazine on selected topics); *Ideas that Work: Mathematics Professional Development* and *Ideas that Work: Science Professional Development* (two booklets on professional development); *Guidebook of Federal Resources for K–12 Mathematics and Science* (federal programs in mathematics and science education). ENC Online is available online (http://www.enc.org) or toll-free at (800)362-4448.

Far West Laboratory for Educational Research and Development (FWL). See listing for WestEd.

Federal Communications Commission (FCC). 445-12th St. S.W., Washington, DC 20554. (202)418-0190. Website http://www.fcc.gov. William Kennard, Chairman. The FCC regulates the telecommunications industry in the United States.

Federal Educational Technology Association (FETA). FETA Membership, Sara Shick, P.O. Box 3412, McLean, VA 22103-3412. (703)406-3040. Fax (703)406-4318 (Clear Spring Inc.). E-mail feta@clearspringinc.com. Website http://www.feta.org. Beth Borko, Board Chair. An affiliate of AECT, FETA is dedicated to the improvement of education and training through research, communication, and practice. It encourages and welcomes members from all government agencies, federal, state, and local; from business and industry; and from all educational institutions and organizations. FETA encourages interaction among members to improve the quality of education and training in any arena, but with specific emphasis on government-related applications. *Membership:* 150. *Dues:* $20. *Meetings:* meets in conjunction with AECT InCITE, concurrently with SALT's Washington meeting in August, and periodically throughout the year in Washington, DC. *Publication:* Newsletter (occasional).

Film Arts Foundation (FAF). 346 9th St., 2nd Floor, San Francisco, CA 94103. (415)552-8760. Fax (415)552-0882. E-mail info@filmarts.org. Website http://www.filmarts .org. Innbo Shim, Admin. Dir. Service organization that supports and promotes independent film and video production. Services include low-cost 16mm, Super-8, S-VHS, and AVID equipment rental; resource library; group legal and health plans; monthly magazine; seminars; grants program; annual film and video festival; nonprofit sponsorship; exhibition program; and advocacy and significant discounts on film- and video-related products and services. *Membership:* 3,300 plus. *Dues:* $45. *Meetings:* Annual Festival. *Publications: Release Print*; *AEIOU (Alternative Exhibition Information of the Universe)*; *Media Catalog* (over 200 titles of independent media projects completed with FAF's nonprofit fiscal sponsorship).

*Film/Video Arts (F/VA). 817 Broadway, 2nd Floor, New York, NY 10003. (212)673-9361. Fax (212)475-3467. Frank Millspaugh, Exec. Dir. Film/Video Arts is the largest nonprofit media arts center in the New York region. Dedicated to the advancement of emerging and established media artists of diverse backgrounds, F/VA is unique in providing a fertile environment where aspiring producers can obtain training, rent equipment, and edit their projects all under one roof. Every year more than 2,500 individuals participate in F/VA's programs. More than 50 courses are offered each semester, covering topics such as rudimentary technical training in 16mm filmmaking and video production, advanced editing courses in online systems, history, cultural analysis, installation art, fundraising, grant writing, and distribution. F/VA is supported by the New York State Council on the Arts, the National Endowment for the Arts, and numerous foundations and corporations, and is therefore able to offer courses and production services at the lowest possible rates. Artists who got their start at F/VA include Jim Jarmusch, Mira Nair, Leslie Harris, Kevin Smith, and Cheryl Dunye. F/VA takes pride in meeting the needs of a broad range of filmmakers, working on features, documentaries, shorts, experimental pieces, industrials, cable shows, music videos, and more by offering affordable services essential to the creation of their work and development of their careers. *Membership:* $40, indiv., $70, organization.

Freedom of Information Center. 127 Neff Annex, University of Missouri, Columbia, MO 65211. (573)882-4856. Fax (573)884-4963. E-mail Kathleen_Edwards@jmail.missouri.edu. Website http://www.missouri.edu/~foiwww. Kathleen Edwards, Manager. The Freedom of Information Center is a research library that maintains files documenting actions by governments, media, and society affecting the movement and content of information. Open 8:00 A.M. to 5:00 P.M., Monday through Friday, except holidays. Located at Missouri's School of Journalism. *Membership:* Research and referral services are available to all. *Publication: Access to Public Information: A Resource Guide to Government in Columbia and Boone County, Missouri.* Updated periodically at Website.

George Eastman House (formerly International Museum of Photography at George Eastman House). 900 East Ave., Rochester, NY 14607. (716)271-3361. Fax (716)271-3970. Website http://www.eastman.org. Anthony Bannon, Dir. World-renowned museum of photography and cinematography established to preserve, collect, and exhibit photographic art and technology, film materials, and related literature, and to serve as a memorial to George Eastman. Services include archives, traveling exhibitions, research library, school of film preservation, center for the conservation of photographic materials, and photographic print service. Educational programs, exhibitions, films, symposia, music events, tours, and internship stipends offered. Eastman's turn-of-the-century mansion and gardens have been restored to their original grandeur. *Dues:* $40, library; $50, family; $40, indiv.; $36, student; $30, senior citizen; $75, Contributor; $125, Sustainer; $250, Patron; $500, Benefactor; $1,000, George Eastman Society. *Membership:* 4,000.*Publications: IMAGE*; *Microfiche Index to Collections*; *Newsletter*; *Annual Report: The George Eastman House and Gardens*; *Masterpieces of Photography from the George Eastman House Collections*; and exhibition catalogs.

The George Lucas Educational Foundation. P.O. Box 3494, San Rafael, CA 94912. (415)662-1600. Fax (415)662-1605. E-mail edutopia@glef.org. Website http://glef.org. Dr. Milton Chen, Exec. Dir. The Foundation promotes innovative efforts to improve education, especially those that integrate technology with teaching and learning, so all students will be prepared to learn and live in an increasingly complex world. Projects include a documentary film and resource book, a Website, and bi-annual newsletter, all of which feature compelling education programs from around the country. The target audience is community and opinion leaders, parents, educators, media, corporate executives, and elected officials. The Foundation works to give these stakeholders useful tools to develop, make, and sustain changes in teaching and learning. The George Lucas Educational Foundation is a private operating foundation, not a grantmaking organization. *Publication: EDUTOPIA* (bi-annual newsletter).

Graphic Arts Technical Foundation (GATF). 200 Deer Run Road, Sewickley, PA 15143-2600. (412)741-6860. Fax (412)741-2311. E-mail info@gatf.org. Website http://www .gatf.org. George Ryan, Pres. GATF is a member-supported, nonprofit, scientific, technical, and educational organization dedicated to the advancement of graphic communications industries worldwide. For 73 years GATF has developed leading-edge technologies and practices for printing, and each year the Foundation develops new products, services, and training programs to meet the evolving needs of the industry. *Membership:* 1,600 corporate members, 520 teachers, 100 students. *Dues:* $40, teachers; $30, students; corporate dues based on percentage of sales (range $350-$4,000). *Meetings:* Annual GATF/PIA Joint Fall Conference. *Publications: Professional Print Buying; Computer-to-Plate: Automating the Printing Industry; Understanding Electronic Communications: Printing in the Information Age; On-Demand Printing: The Revolution in Digital and Customized Printing.*

Great Plains National ITV Library (GPN). P.O. Box 80669, Lincoln, NE 68501-0669. (402)472-2007, (800)228-4630. Fax (800)306-2330. E-mail gpn@unl.edu. Web page http://gpn.unl.edu. Steven Lenzen, Dir. Produces and distributes educational media, video, laserdiscs, and CD-ROMs, prints and Internet courses. Available for purchase or lease for broadcast use. *Publications: GPN Educational Video Catalogs* by curriculum areas; periodic brochures. Complete listing of GPN's product line is available via the Internet along with online purchasing. Free previews available.

Health Sciences Communications Association (HeSCA). One Wedgewood Dr., Suite 27, Jewett City, CT 06351-2428. (203)376-5915. Fax (203)376-6621. E-mail HeSCAOne@aol.com. Website http://www.hesca.washington.edu. Ronald Sokolowski, Exec. Dir. An affiliate of AECT, HeSCA is a nonprofit organization dedicated to the sharing of ideas, skills, resources, and techniques to enhance communications and educational technology in the health sciences. It seeks to nurture the professional growth of its members; serve as a professional focal point for those engaged in health sciences communications; and convey the concerns, issues, and concepts of health sciences communications to other organizations which influence and are affected by the profession. International in scope and diverse in membership, HeSCA is supported by medical and veterinary schools, hospitals, medical associations, and businesses where media are used to create and disseminate health information. *Membership:* 150. *Dues:* $150, indiv.; $195, institutional ($150 additional institutional dues); $60, retiree; $75, student; $1,000, sustaining. All include subscriptions to the journal and newsletter. *Meetings:* Annual meetings, May-June. *Publications: Journal of Biocommunications; Feedback* (newsletter); *Patient Education Sourcebook Vol. II.*

Hollywood Film Archive. 8391 Beverly Blvd., #321, Hollywood, CA 90048. (213)933-3345. D. Richard Baer, Dir. Archival organization for information about feature films produced worldwide, from the early silents to the present. *Publications:* Comprehensive movie reference works for sale, including *Variety Film Reviews* (1907–1996) and the *American Film Institute Catalogs* (1893–1910,1911–20, 1921–30, 1931–40, 1941–50, 1961–70), as well as the *Film Superlist* (1894–1939, 1940–1949, 1950–1959) volumes, which provide information both on copyrights and on motion pictures in the public domain; *Harrison's Reports and Film Reviews* (1919–1962).

HOPE Reports, Inc. 58 Carverdale Dr., Rochester, NY 14618-4004. (716)442-1310. Fax (716)442-1725. E-mail hopereport@aol.com. Thomas W. Hope, Chairman and CEO; Mabeth S. Hope, Vice Pres. Supplies statistics, marketing information, trends, forecasts, and salary and media studies to the visual communications industries through printed reports, custom studies, consulting, and by telephone. Clients and users in the United States and abroad include manufacturers, dealers, producers, and media users in business, government, health sciences, religion, education, and community agencies. *Publications: Hope Reports Presentation Media Events Calendar* (annual); *Video Post-Production; Media Market Trends; Educational Media Trends through the 1990's; LCD Panels and Projectors; Overhead Projection System; Presentation Slides; Producer & Video Post Wages & Salaries;*

Noncommercial AV Wages & Salaries; Corporate Media Salaries; Digital Photography: Pictures of Tomorrow; Hope Reports Top 100 Contract Producers; Contract Production II; Executive Compensation; Media Production; Outsource or Insource.

Institute for Development of Educational Activities, Inc. (|I|D|E|A|). 259 Regency Ridge, Dayton, OH 45459. (937)434-6969. Fax (937)434-5203. E-mail IDEADayton@aol.com. Website http://www.idea.org. Dr. Steven R. Thompson, Pres. |I|D|E|A| is an action-oriented research and development organization originating from the Charles F. Kettering Foundation. It was established in 1965 to assist the educational community in bridging the gap that separates research and innovation from actual practice in the schools. Its goal is to design and test new responses to improve education and to create arrangements that support local application. Activities include developing new and improved processes, systems, and materials; training local facilitators to use the change processes; and providing information and services about improved methods and materials. |I|D|E|A| sponsors an annual fellowship program for administrators and conducts seminars for school administrators and teachers.

Institute for the Future (IFTF). 2744 Sand Hill Rd., Menlo Park, CA 94025-7020. (650)854-6322. Fax (650)854-7850. Website http://www.iftf.org. Robert Johansen, Pres. The cross-disciplinary professionals at IFTF have been providing global and domestic businesses and organizations with research-based forecasts and action-oriented tools for strategic decision making since 1968. IFTF is a nonprofit, applied research and consulting firm dedicated to understanding technological, economic, and societal changes and their long-range domestic and global consequences. Its work falls into four main areas: Strategic Planning, Emerging Technologies, Health Care Horizons, and Public Sector Initiatives. IFTF works with clients to think systematically about the future, identify socioeconomic trends and evaluate their long-term implications, identify potential leading-edge markets around the world, understand the global marketplace, track the implications of emerging technologies for business and society, leverage expert judgment and data resources, offer an independent view of the big picture, and facilitate strategic planning processes.

Institute for the Transfer of Technology to Education (ITTE). See National School Boards Association.

Instructional Telecommunications Council (ITC). One Dupont Cir., NW, Suite 410, Washington, DC, 20036-1176. (202)293-3110. Fax (202)833-2467. E-mail cdalziel@aacc.nche .edu. Website http://www.sinclair.edu/communit/itc. Christine Dalziel, contact person. ITC represents over 500 educational institutions from the United States and Canada that are involved in higher educational instructional telecommunications and distance learning. ITC holds annual professional development meetings, tracks national legislation, supports research, and provides members with a forum to share expertise and materials. *Membership:* 504. *Dues:* $1,500, Regional Consortia; $525, Institutional; $452, Associate; $550, Corporate; $125, Indiv. *Meetings:* 1999 Telelearning Conference. *Publications: New Connections: A Guide to Distance Education* (2nd ed.); *New Connections: A College President's Guide to Distance Education; Federal Disability Law and Distance Learning; ITC News* (monthly publication/newsletter); ITC Listserv.

International Association for Language Learning Technology (IALL). IALL Business Manager, Malacester College, 1600 Grand Ave., St. Paul, MN 55105-1899. (612)696-6336. E-mail browne@macalstr.edu. Website http://polyglot.lss.wisc.edu/IALL/. Nina Garrett, Pres. Thomas Browne, Bus. Mgr. An affiliate of AECT, IALL is a professional organization working for the improvement of second language learning through technology in learning centers and classrooms. *Members:* 700. *Dues:* $40, regular; $15, student; $40, library; $55 commercial. *Meetings:* Biennial IALL conferences treat the entire range of topics related to technology in language learning as well as management and planning. IALL also sponsors sessions at conferences of organizations with related interests, including AECT. *Publications:*

IALL Journal of Language Learning Technologies (3 times annually); materials for labs, teaching, and technology.

International Association of Business Communicators (IABC). One Hallidie Plaza, Suite 600, San Francisco, CA 94102. (415)544-4700. Fax (415)544-4747. E-mail service _centre@iabc.com. Website http://www.iabc.com. Elizabeth Allan, Pres. and CEO. IABC is the worldwide association for the communication and public relations profession. It is founded on the principle that the better an organization communicates with all its audiences, the more successful and effective it will be in meeting its objectives. IABC is dedicated to fostering communication excellence, contributing more effectively to organizations' goals worldwide, and being a model of communication effectiveness. *Membership:* 13,500 plus. *Dues:* $175 in addition to local and regional dues. *Meetings:* 1999, June 20-23, Washington, DC; 2000, June 25-28, Vancouver. *Publication: Communication World.*

International Association of School Librarianship (IASL). Box 34069, Dept. 300, Seattle, WA 98124-1069. (604)925-0266. Fax: (604)925-0566. E-mail iasl@rockland.com. Website http://www.rhi.hi.is/~anne/iasl.html. Dr. Ken Haycock, Exec. Dir. Seeks to encourage development of school libraries and library programs throughout the world; promote professional preparation and continuing education of school librarians; achieve collaboration among school libraries of the world; foster relationships between school librarians and other professionals connected with children and youth and to coordinate activities, conferences, and other projects in the field of school librarianship. *Membership:* 900 plus. *Dues:* $50, personal and institution for North America, Western Europe, Japan, and Australia; $15 for all other countries. *Meetings:* 1999, Birmingham, AL, November. *Publications: IASL Newsletter* (q.); *School Libraries Worldwide* (semi-annual); *Conference Professionals and Research Papers* (annual); *Connections: School Library Associations and Contact People Worldwide; Sustaining the Vision: A Collection of Articles and Papers on Research in School Librarianship; School Librarianship: International Issues and Perspectives; Information Rich but Knowledge Poor? Issues for Schools and Libraries Worldwide: Selected Papers from the 26th Annual Conferences of the IASL.*

International Center of Photography (ICP). 1130 Fifth Ave., New York, NY 10128. (212)860-1777. Fax (212)360-6490. ICP Midtown, 1133 Avenue of the Americas, New York, NY 10036. (212)768-4680. Fax (212)768-4688. Website http://www.icp.org. Willis Hartshorn, Dir.; Phyllis Levine, Dir. of Public Information. A comprehensive photographic institution whose exhibitions, publications, collections, and educational programs embrace all aspects of photography from aesthetics to technique; from the 19th century to the present; from master photographers to newly emerging talents; from photojournalism to the avant garde. Changing exhibitions, lectures, seminars, workshops, museum shops, and screening rooms make ICP a complete photographic resource. ICP offers a two-year NYU-ICP Master of Arts in Studio Art with Studies in Photography and one-year certificate programs in Documentary Photography and Photojournalism and General Studies in Photography. *Membership:* 6,500. *Dues:* $50, indiv.; $60, double; $125, Supporting Patron; $250, Photography Circle; $500, Silver Card Patron; $1,000, Gold Card Patron;$2,500 Benefactor; corporate memberships available. *Meetings:* ICP Infinity Awards. *Publications: Reflections in a Glass Eye; Images from the Machine Age: Selections from the Daniel Cowin Collection; Library of Photography; A Singular Elegance: The Photographs of Baron Adolph de Meyer; Talking Pictures: People Speak about the Photographs That Speak to Them; Encyclopedia of Photography: Master Photographs from PFA Collection; Man Ray in Fashion; Quarterly Program Guide; Quarterly Exhibition Schedule.*

International Council for Educational Media (ICEM). ICEM, Robert LeFranc, ICEM Secretariat, 29 rue d'Ulm, 25230 Oaris, Cedex 05, France. 33-1-46. Fax 33-1-46-35-78-89. Ms. Jackie Hall, General Secretariat, FUS, Grup de Fundacions, Provenca 324,3r -E08037 Barcelona, Spain; 34 3 458 30 04, fax 34 3 458 87 10. E-mail icem-cime@bcn.servicom.es. Website http://www.cndp.fr/icem icem-cime@bcn.servicom.es and http://www.cndp.fr/icem.

Richard Cornell, Pres. and U.S. member, University of Central Florida, Education Room 310, Orlando, FL, 32816-0992. (407)823-2053, fax (407)823-5135. E-mail cornell@pegasus .cc.ucf.edu. Website http://pegasus.cc.ucf.edu/~cornell/icem-usa. Deputy Member from the United States: Marina McIsaac, College of Education, Box 870111, Arizona State University, Tempe, AZ 85287-0111, (602)965-4961, fax (602)965-7193. E-mail mmcisaac@asu.edu. The objectives of ICEM are to provide a channel for the international exchange of information and experience in the field of educational technology, with particular reference to preschool, primary, and secondary education, technical and vocational training, and teacher and continuing education; encourage organizations with a professional responsibility for the design, production, promotion, distribution, and use of educational media in member countries; promote an understanding of the concept of educational technology on the part of both educators and those involved in their training; contribute to the pool of countries by the sponsorship of practical projects involving international cooperation and co-production; advise manufacturers of hardware and software on the needs of an information service on developments in educational technology; provide consultancy for the benefit of member countries; and cooperate with other international organizations in promoting the concept of educational technology. ICEM has established official relations with UNESCO.

International Graphics Arts Education Association (IGAEA). 200 Deer Run Road, Sewickley, PA 15143-2328. (412)741-6860. Fax (412)741-2311. Website http://www .igaea.org. 1998-99 Pres. Wanda Murphy, e-mail wmurphy184@aol.com. (704)922-8891. Fax (704)922-8891. IGAEA is an association of educators in partnership with industry, dedicated to sharing theories, principles, techniques, and processes relating to graphic communications and imaging technology. Teachers network to share and improve teaching and learning opportunities in fields related to graphic arts, imaging technology, graphic design, graphic communications, journalism, photography, and other areas related to the large and rapidly changing fields in the printing, publishing, packaging, and allied industries. *Membership:* approx. 600. *Dues:* $20, regular; $12, associate (retired); $5, student; $10, library; $50-$200, sustaining membership based on number of employees. *Meetings:* 1999, Ferris State University, Big Rapids, MI, Aug 1-6. *Publications: The Communicator; Visual Communications Journal* (annual); *Research and Resources Reports.*

*International Information Management Congress (IMC). 1650 38th St., #205W, Boulder, CO 80301. (303)440-7085. Fax (303)440-7234. Website http://www.iimc.org. John A. Lacy, CEO. IMC's mission is to facilitate the successful adoption of imaging, document management, and workflow technologies. IMC's primary activities include conferences, exhibitions, publications, and membership functions. *Dues:* $85, affiliate (any individual with an interest in the document-based information systems field); $200, associate (any association or society with common goals within the industry); $350-$5100, sustaining (any corporate organization with a common interest in the industry). *Meeting:* Future exhibitions planned for Dubai, UAE, and Singapore (please contact IMC for more information). *Publication: Document World Magazine* (bi-monthly).

International Society for Technology in Education (ISTE) (formerly International Council for Computers in Education [ICCE]). 1787 Agate St., Eugene, OR 97403-1923. (541)346-4414. Fax (541)346-5890. E-mail iste@oregon.uoregon.edu. Website http://www .iste.org. David Moursund, CEO; Maia S. Howes, Exec. Sec. ISTE is the largest nonprofit professional organization dedicated to the improvement of all levels of education through the use of computer-based technology. Technology-using educators from all over the world rely on ISTE for information, inspiration, ideas, and updates on the latest electronic information systems available to the educational community. ISTE is a prominent information center and source of leadership to communicate and collaborate with educational professionals, policymakers, and other organizations worldwide. 10, 000*Membership:* 12,000 individuals, 75 organizational affiliates, 25 Private Sector Council members. *Dues:* $58, indiv.; $220, all-inclusive (U.S.); $420, Technology Leadership *Membership*; $1,500 - $5,000, Private Sector Council. *Meetings:* Tel-Ed and NECC. *Publications: The Update Newsletter* (7/yr.);

Learning and Leading with Technology (formerly *The Computing Teacher*) (8/yr.); *The Journal of Research on Computing in Education* (q.); guides to instructional uses of computers at the precollege level and in teacher training, about 80 books, and a range of distance education courses that carry graduate-level credit.

International Society for Performance Improvement (ISPI). 1300 L St. NW, Suite 1250, Washington, DC 20005. (202)408-7969. Fax (202)408-7972. E-mail info@ispi.org. Website http://www.ispi.org. Richard D. Battaglia, Exec. Dir. ISPI is an international association dedicated to increasing productivity in the workplace through the application of performance and instructional technologies. Founded in 1962, its members are located throughout the United States, Canada, and 45 other countries. The society offers an awards program recognizing excellence in the field. *Membership:* 5,500. *Dues:* $125, active members; $40, students and retirees. *Meetings:* Annual Conference and Expo, spring; Human Performance Technology Institute (HPTI), late spring and fall. (HPTI is an educational institute providing knowledge, skills and resources necessary to make a successful transition from a training department to a human performance improvement organization.) Annual Conference & Expo will be held in Cincinnati OH, April 10-14, 2000. *Publications: Performance Improvement Journal* (10/yr.); *Performance Improvement Quarterly*; *News & Notes* (newsletter, 10/yr.); *Annual Membership Directory*; *ISPI Book Program and Catalog.*

International Telecommunications Satellite Organization (INTELSAT). 3400 International Dr. NW, Washington, DC 20008. (202)944-7500. Fax (202)944-7890. Website http://www.intelsat.int. Conng L. Kullman, Dir. Gen. and CEO; Tony A. Trujillo, Dir., Corporate Communications. INTELSAT owns and operates a global communications satellite system providing capacity for voice, video, corporate/private networks, and Internet in more than 200 countries and territories. In addition, the INTELSAT system provides educational and medical programming via satellite for selected participants around the world.

International Teleconferencing Association (ITCA). 100 Four Falls Corporate Center, Suite 105, West Conshohocken, PA 19428. (610)941-2015. Fax (610)941-2015. E-mail staff@itca.org and president@itca.org. Website http://www.itca.org. Henry S. Grove III, Pres.; Eileen Hering, Manager, Member Services; Rosalie DiStasio, Asst. Manager, Member Services. ITCA, an international nonprofit association, is dedicated to the growth and development of teleconferencing as a profession and an industry. ITCA provides programs and services that foster the professional development of its members, champions teleconferencing and related technology as communications tools, recognizes and promotes broader applications and the development of teleconferencing and related technologies, and serves as the authoritative resource for information and research on teleconferencing and related technologies. *Membership:* ITCA represents over 1,000 teleconferencing professionals throughout the world. ITCA members use teleconferencing services to advise customers and vendors, conduct research, teach courses via teleconference, and teach about teleconferencing. They represent such diverse industry segments as health care, aerospace, government, pharmaceutical, education, insurance, finance and banking, telecommunications, and manufacturing. *Dues:* $6,250, Platinum Sustaining, $2,500, Gold Sustaining; $1,250, Sustaining; $625, Organizational; $325, small business; $125, indiv.; and $35, student. *Meetings:* spring and fall MultimediaCom Shows; spring show in San Jose, fall show in Boston, August 30-September 2. *Publications: Forum* newsletter; *Member Directories; White Paper; Teleconferencing Success Stories.*

ITVA (International Television Association). 6311 N. O'Connor Rd., Suite 230, Irving, TX 75039. (972)869-1112. Fax (972)869-2980. E-mail itvahq@worldnet.att.net. Website http://www.itva.org. Fred M. Wehrli, Exec. Dir. Founded in 1968, ITVA's mission is to advance the video profession, serve the needs and interests of its members, and promote the growth and quality of video and related media. Association members are video, multimedia, and film professionals working in or serving the corporate, governmental, institutional, or educational markets. ITVA provides professional development opportunities through local, regional, and national workshops, video festivals, networking, and publications. ITVA welcomes anyone who is interested in professional video and who is seeking to widen horizons either through career development or networking. ITVA offers its members discounts on major medical, production, and liability insurance; hotel, car rental, and long distance telephone discounts; and a MasterCard program. The association is also a member of the Small Business Legislative Council. *Membership:* 9,000; 77 commercial member companies. *Dues:* $150, indiv.; $425, organizational; $1,750, Commercial Silver; $750, Commercial Bronze. *Meetings:* Annual International Conference, early summer. *Publications: ITVA News* (6/yr.); *Membership Directory* (annual); *Handbook of Treatments*; *It's a Business First . . . and a Creative Outlet Second*; *Handbook of Forms*; *Copyright Basics for Video Producers; How to Survive Being Laid Off; The Effectiveness of Video in Organizations: An Annotated Bibliography; Management Matters; A Report on the IRS Guidelines Classifying Workers in the Video Industry.*

International Visual Literacy Association, Inc. (IVLA). Gonzaga University, E. 502 Boone AD 25, Spokane, WA 99258-0001. (509)328-4220 ext. 3478, fax (509)324-5812. E-mail bclark@soe.gonzaga.edu. Richard Couch, Pres. Dr. Barbara I. Clark, Exec. Treas. IVLA provides a multidisciplinary forum for the exploration, presentation, and discussion of all aspects of visual learning, thinking, communication, and expression. It also serves as a communication link bonding professionals from many disciplines who are creating and sustaining the study of the nature of visual experiences and literacy. It promotes and evaluates research, programs, and projects intended to increase effective use of visual communication in education, business, the arts, and commerce. IVLA was founded in 1968 to promote the concept of visual literacy and is an affiliate of AECT. *Dues:* $40, regular; $20, student and retired; $45 outside United States. *Meeting:* Meets in conjunction with annual AECT Convention. *Publications: Journal of Visual Literacy; Readings from Annual Conferences.*

ITA, The International Recording Media Association. 182 Nassau St., Princeton, NJ 08542-7005. (609)279-1700. Fax (609)279-1999. E-mail info@recordingmedia.org. Website http://www.recordingmedia.org. Charles Van Horn, Exec. V.P.; Phil Russo, Dir. of Operations. IRMA is the advocate for the growth and development of all reading media and is the industry forum for the exchange of information regarding global trends and innovations. Members include recording media manufacturers, rights holders to video programs, recording and playback equipment manufacturers, and audio and video replicators. For more than 29 years, the Association has provided vital information and educational services throughout the magnetic and optical recording media industries. By promoting a greater awareness of marketing, merchandising, and technical developments, the association serves all areas of the entertainment, information, and delivery systems industries. *Membership:* 450 corporations. *Dues:* Corporate membership dues based on sales volume. *Meetings:* 30th Annual Conference (IRMA Executive Forum) LaQuita Resort, LaQuita, CA. March 15-19, 2000. Mar 10-14, 1999, Amelia Island, FL; REPLItech North America, June 8-10 1999, San Francisco. *Publications: Membership Newsletter; Seminar Proceedings; 1999 International Source Directory.*

Library Administration and Management Association (LAMA). 50 E. Huron St., Chicago, IL 60611. (312)280-5038. Fax (312)280-5033. E-mail lama@ala.org. Website http://www .ala.org/lama. Karen Muller, Exec. Dir.; Thomas L. Wilding, Pres. July 1998-July 1999. Carol L. Anderson, Pres. Elect. A division of the American Library Association, LAMA provides an organizational framework for encouraging the study of administrative theory, improving the practice of administration in libraries, and identifying and fostering administrative skills. Toward these ends, the association is responsible for all elements of general administration that are common to more than one type of library. Sections include Buildings and Equipment Section (BES); Fundraising & Financial Development Section (FRFDS); Library Organization & Management Section (LOMS); Personnel Administration Section (PAS); Public Relation Section (PRS); Systems & Services Section (SASS); and Statistics Section (SS). *Membership:* 4,996. *Dues:* $45 (in addition to ALA membership);

$15, library school students. *Meetings:* 1999 ALA Annual Conference, New Orleans, Jun 24-Jun 30; 2000, Chicago, Jul 6-12; ALA Midwinter Meeting, 1999; 2000, San Antonio, Jan 14-19; 2001, Washington, DC, Jan 12-17. *Publications: Library Administration & Management* (q); *LEADS from LAMA* (electronic newsletter, irregular).

Library and Information Technology Association (LITA). 50 E. Huron St., Chicago, IL 60611. (312)280-4270, (800)545-2433, ext. 4270. Fax (312)280-3257. E-mail lita@ala.org. Website http://www.lita.org. Jacqueline Mundell, Exec. Dir. An affiliate of the American Library Association, LITA is concerned with library automation; the information sciences; and the design, development, and implementation of automated systems in those fields, including systems development, electronic data processing, mechanized information retrieval, operations research, standards development, telecommunications, video communications, networks and collaborative efforts, management techniques, information technology, optical technology, artificial intelligence and expert systems, and other related aspects of audiovisual activities and hardware applications. *Membership:* 5,400. *Dues:* $45 plus membership in ALA; $25, library school students; $35, first year. *Meetings:* National Forum, fall. *Publications: Information Technology and Libraries; LITA Newsletter* (electronic only; see Website).

Library of Congress. James Madison Bldg., 101 Independence Ave. SE, Washington, DC 20540. (202)707-5000. Fax (202)707-1389. National Reference Service, (202)707-5522. Website http://www.loc.gov. The Library of Congress is the major source of research and information for the Congress. In its role as the national library, it catalogs and classifies library materials in some 460 languages, distributes the data in both printed and electronic form, and makes its vast collections availabl᷏ through interlibrary loan and on-site to anyone over high school age. The Library is the largest library in the world, with more than 115 million items on 532 miles of bookshelves. The collections include more than 17 million cataloged books, 2 million recordings, 12 million photographs, 4 million maps, and 49 million manuscripts. It contains the world's largest television and film archive, acquiring materials through gift, purchase, and copyright deposit. In 1998, the materials produced by the Library in Braille and recorded formats for persons who are blind or physically challenged were circulated to a readership of 769,000. The collections of the Motion Picture, Broadcasting and Recorded Sound Division include more than 770,000 moving images. The Library's public catalog, as well as other files containing copyright and legislative information, are available over the Internet.

Lister Hill National Center for Biomedical Communications. National Library of Medicine, 8600 Rockville Pike, Bethesda, MD 20894. (301)496-4441. Fax (301)402-0118. Website http://www.nlm.nih.gov. Alexa McCray, Ph.D., Dir. The center conducts research and development programs in three major categories: Computer and Information Science; Biomedical Image and Communications Engineering; and Educational Technology Development. Major efforts of the center include its involvement with the Unified Medical Language System (UMLS) project; research and development in the use of expert systems to embody the factual and procedural knowledge of human experts; research in the use of electronic technologies to distribute biomedical information not represented in text and in the storage and transmission of x-ray images over the Internet; and the development and demonstration of new educational technologies, including the use of microcomputer technology with videodisc-based images, for training health care professionals. A Learning Center for Interactive Technology serves as a focus for displaying new and effective applications of educational technologies to faculties and staff of health sciences, educational institutions, and other visitors, and health professions educators are assisted in the use of such technologies through training, demonstrations, and consultations.

Magazine Publishers of America (MPA). 919 Third Ave., 22nd Floor, New York, NY 10022. (212)872-3700. Fax (212)888-4217. E-mail infocenter@magazine.org. Website http://www.magazine.org. Donald D. Kummerfeld, Pres. MPA is the trade association of the consumer magazine industry. MPA promotes the greater and more effective use of magazine advertising, with ad campaigns in the trade press and in member magazines, presentations to advertisers and their ad agencies, and magazine days in cities around the United States. MPA runs educational seminars, conducts surveys of its members on a variety of topics, represents the magazine industry in Washington, DC, and maintains an extensive library on magazine publishing. *Membership:* 230 publishers representing more than 1,200 magazines. *Meetings:* 1999 American Magazine Conference, Boca Resort & Country Club, Boca Raton, FL, Oct 28–31; 2000, Southampton Princess, Bermuda, Oct 22–25. *Publications: Newsletter of Consumer Marketing*; *Newsletter of Research*; *Newsletter of International Publishing*; *Magazine*; *Washington Newsletter.*

Medical Library Association (MLA). 6 N. Michigan Ave., Suite 300, Chicago, IL 60602-4805. (312)419-9094. Fax (312)419-9094. E-mail info@mlahq.org. Website http://www.mlanet.org. Rachael K. Anderson, Pres.; Carla J. Funk, Exec. Dir., Kimberly Pierceall, Dir. of Communications. MLA is a professional organization of 5,000 individuals and institutions in the health sciences information field, dedicated to fostering medical and allied scientific libraries, promoting professional excellence and leadership of its members, and exchanging medical literature among its members. *Membership:* 5,000 individual and institutional. *Dues:* $110, regular; $25, students; $75, introductory; $65, affiliate; $2100, life. Institutional dues depend on number of periodical subscriptions. *Meeting:* 1999, Chicago, May 14-20. *Publications: MLA News* (newsletter, 10/yr.); *Bulletin of the Medical Library Association* (q.); *Dockit* series; monographs.

Mid-continent Regional Educational Laboratory (McREL). 2550 S. Parker Rd., Suite 500, Aurora, CO 80014. (303)337-0990. Fax (303)337-3005. E-mail info@mcrel.org. Website http://www.mcrel.org. J. Timothy Waters, Exec. Dir. One of 10 Office of Educational Research and Improvement (OERI) regional educational laboratories designed to help educators and policymakers work toward excellence in education for all students. Using the best available information and the experience and expertise of professionals, McREL seeks to identify solutions to education problems, tries new approaches, furnishes research results, conducts evaluation and policy studies, and provides training to teachers and administrators. McREL serves Colorado, Kansas, Missouri, Nebraska, North Dakota, South Dakota, and Wyoming. Its specialty areas are curriculum, learning, and instruction. *Publications: Changing Schools* (q. newsletter); *Noteworthy* (annual monograph on topics of current interest in education reform). Check Website for catalog listing many other publications.

Minorities in Media (MIM). Wayne State University, College of Education, Instructional Technology, Detroit, Michigan 48202. (313)577-5139. Fax (313)577-1693. E-mail GPOWELL @CMS.CC.WAYNE.EDU. Dr. Gary C. Powell, Pres. MIM is a special interest group of AECT that responds to the challenge of preparing students of color for an ever-changing international marketplace and recognizes the unique educational needs of today's diverse learners. It promotes the effective use of educational communications and technology in the learning process. MIM seeks to facilitate changes in instructional design and development, traditional pedagogy, and instructional delivery systems by responding to and meeting the significant challenge of educating diverse individuals to take their place in an ever-changing international marketplace. MIM encourages all of AECT's body of members to creatively develop curricula, instructional treatments, instructional strategies, and instructional materials that promote an acceptance and appreciation of racial and cultural diversity. Doing so will make learning for all more effective, relevant, meaningful, motivating, and enjoyable. MIM actively supports the Wes McJulien Minority Scholarship, and selects the winner. *Membership:* contact MIM president. *Dues:* $20, student; $30, nonstudent. *Publications:* Newsletter is forthcoming online. The MIM listserv is a membership benefit.

Museum Computer Network (MCN). 8720 Georgia Ave., Suite 501, Silver Spring, MD 20910. (301)585-4413. Fax (301)495-0810. E-mail mcn@athena.mit.edu; membership office: mdevine@asis.org. Website http://world.std.com/nmcn/index.html. Michele Devine, Admin. Guy Herman, Pres. As a nonprofit professional association, membership in MCN provides access to professionals committed to using computer technology to achieve the cultural aims of museums. Members include novices and experts, museum professionals, and vendors and consultants, working in application areas from collections management to administrative computing. Activities include advisory services and special projects. *Dues:* $300, sponsor; $150, vendor; $150, institution; $60, indiv. *Meeting:* Annual Conference, held in the fall; educational workshops. *Publications: Spectra* (newsletter); *CMI.* Subscription to *Spectra* is available to libraries only for $75 plus $10 surcharge for delivery.

Museum of Modern Art, Circulating Film and Video Library. 11 W. 53rd St., New York, NY 10019. (212)708-9530. Fax (212)708-9531. E-mail circfilm@moma.org. Website http://www.moma.org. William Sloan, Libr. Provides film and video rentals and sales of over 1,300 titles covering the history of film from the 1890s to the present. It also incorporates the Circulating Video Library, an important collection of work by leading video artists. The Circulating Library continues to add to its holdings of early silents, contemporary documentaries, animation, avant-garde, and independents and to make these available to viewers who otherwise would not have the opportunity to see them. The Circulating Film Library has 16mm prints available for rental, sale, and lease. A few of the 16mm titles are available on videocassette. The classic film collection is not. The video collection is available in all formats for rental and sale. *Publications:* Information on titles may be found in the free *Price List,* available from the Library. *Circulating Film and Video Catalog Vols. 1 and 2,* a major source book on film and history, is available from the Museum's Publications, Sales, and Service Dept. (For mail order, a form is included in the *Price List.*)

National Aeronautics and Space Administration (NASA). NASA Headquarters, Code FE, Washington, DC 20546. (202)358-1110. Fax (202)358-3048. E-mail malcom.phelps@hq .nasa.gov. Website http://www.nasa.gov. Dr. Malcom V. Phelps, Asst. Dir.; Frank C. Owens, Dir., Education Division. From elementary through postgraduate school, NASA's educational programs are designed to capture students' interest in science, mathematics, and technology at an early age; to channel more students into science, engineering, and technology career paths; and to enhance the knowledge, skills, and experiences of teachers and university faculty. NASA's educational programs include NASA Spacelink (an electronic information system); videoconferences (60-minute interactive staff development videoconferences to be delivered to schools via satellite); and NASA Television (informational and educational television programming). Additional information is available from the Education Division at NASA Headquarters and counterpart offices at the nine NASA field centers. Over 200,000 educators make copies of Teacher Resource Center Network materials each year, and thousands of teachers participate in interactive video teleconferencing, use Spacelink, and watch NASA Television. Additional information may be obtained from Spacelink (spacelink.msfc.nasa.gov or http://spacelink.msfc.nasa.gov).

National Alliance for Media Arts and Culture (NAMAC). 346 9th St., San Francisco, CA 94103. (415)431-1391. Fax (415)431-1392. E-mail namac@namac.org. Website http://www.namac.org. Helen DeMichel, National Dir. NAMAC is a nonprofit organization dedicated to increasing public understanding of and support for the field of media arts in the United States. Members include media centers, cable access centers, universities, and media artists, as well as other individuals and organizations providing services for production, education, exhibition, distribution, and preservation of video, film, audio, and intermedia. NAMAC's information services are available to the general public, arts and non-arts organizations, businesses, corporations, foundations, government agencies, schools, and universities. *Membership:* 200 organizations, 150 individuals. *Dues:* $50-$250, institutional (depending on annual budget); $50, indiv. *Publications: Media Arts Information Network*; *The National Media Education Directory.*

National Association for the Education of Young Children (NAEYC). 1509 16th St. NW, Washington, DC 20036-1426. (202)232-8777, (800)424-2460. Fax (202)328-1846. E-mail naeyc@naeyc.org. Website http://www.naeyc.org. Marilyn M. Smith, Exec. Dir.; Pat Spahr, contact person. Dedicated to improving the quality of care and education provided to young children (birth-8 years). *Membership:* over 100,000. *Dues:* $25. *Meeting:* 1999 Annual Conference, Nov 10-13, New Orleans. *Publications: Young Children* (journal); more than 60 books, posters, videos, and brochures.

National Association for Visually Handicapped (NAVH). 22 W. 21st St., 6th Floor, New York, NY 10010. (212)889-3141. Fax (212)727-2931. E-mail staff@navh.org. Website http://www.navn.org. Lorraine H. Marchi, Founder/CEO. Dir.; Eva Cohen, Asst. to CEO. Dir., 3201 Balboa St., San Francisco, CA 94121. (415)221-3201. Serves the partially sighted (not totally blind). Offers informational literature for the layperson and the professional, most in large print. Maintains a loan library of large-print books. Provides counseling and guidance for the visually impaired and their families and the professionals and paraprofessionals who work with them. *Membership:* 12,000. *Dues:* $40 indiv.; free for those unable to afford membership. *Publications:* Newsletter updated quarterly, distributed free throughout the English-speaking world; *NAVH Update* (quarterly); *Visual Aids and Informational Material Catalog; Large Print Loan Library;* informational pamphlets on topics ranging from *Diseases of the Macula* to knitting and crochet instructions.

National Association of Regional Media Centers (NARMC). NARMC, Education Service Center, Region 20, 1314 Hines Ave., San Antonio, TX 78208. (210)270-9256. Fax (210)224-3130. E-mail jtaylor@tenet.edu. Website http://esu3.k12.ne.us/prof/narmc. Larry Vice, Pres.; James H. Taylor, Treasurer. An affiliate of AECT, NARMC is committed to promoting leadership among its membership through networking, advocacy, and support activities that will enhance the equitable access to media, technology, and information services to educational communities. The purpose of NARMC is to foster the exchange of ideas and information among educational communications specialists whose responsibilities relate to the administration of regional media centers and large district media centers. *Membership:* 285 regional centers (institutions), 70 corporations. *Dues:* $55, institutions; $250, corporations. *Meetings:* held annually with AECT/Incite. Regional meetings are held throughout the United States annually. *Publication:* Membership newsletter is *'ETIN.* NARMC Press was established in 1996 to provide members with publications related to the field of media and technology. These publications are available for purchase through this publication outlet. Publications are solicited and submitted from the NARMC membership. Current publications include *An Anthology of Internet Acceptable Use Policies* and *Basic MAC/Windows Internet.* In addition, there is the *Annual Membership Report* and the *Bi-annual Survey Report of Regional Media Centers.*

*National Association of State Textbook Administrators (NASTA). E-mail president @nasta.org. Website http://www.nasta.org. William Lohman, Pres. NASTA's purposes are to (1) foster a spirit of mutual helpfulness in adoption, purchase, and distribution of instructional materials; (2) arrange for study and review of textbook specifications; (3) authorize special surveys, tests, and studies; and (4) initiate action leading to better quality instructional materials. Services provided include a working knowledge of text construction, monitoring lowest prices, sharing adoption information, identifying trouble spots, and discussions in the industry. The members of NASTA meet to discuss the textbook adoption process and to improve the quality of the instructional materials used in the elementary, middle, and high schools. NASTA is not affiliated with any parent organization and has no permanent address. *Membership:* Textbook administrators from each of the 23 states that adopt textbooks at the state level. *Dues:* $25, indiv. *Meetings:* conducted with the American Association of Publishers and the Book Manufacturers' Institute.

The National Cable Television Institute (NCTI). 801 W. Mineral Ave., Littleton CO 80120. (303)797-9393. Fax (303)797-9394. Email info@ncti.com. Website http://www.ncti.com. Byron Leech, Pres.; Julie Pushefski, Dir. Student Services. The National Cable Television Institute is the largest independent provider of broadband technology training in the world. More than 120,000 students have graduated from these courses since 1968. NCTI partners with companies by providing self-paced study manuals to be complemented by company hands-on experiences. NCTI administers lessons and final examinations and issues the Certificate of Graduation, which is recognized throughout the industry as a symbol of competence and technical achievement.

The National Center for Improving Science Education. 1726 M Street, NW, #704, Washington, DC 20036. (202)467-0652. Fax (202)467-0659. E-mail info@ncise.org. Website www.wested.org. Senta A. Raizen, Dir. A division of WestEd (see separate listing) that works to promote changes in state and local policies and practices in science curriculum, teaching, and assessment through research and development, evaluation, technical assistance, and dissemination. *Publications: Science and Technology Education for the Elementary Years: Frameworks for Curriculum and Instruction; Developing and Supporting Teachers for Elementary School Science Education; Assessment in Elementary School Science Education; Getting Started in Science: A Blueprint for Elementary School Science Education; Elementary School Science for the 90s; Building Scientific Literacy: Blueprint for the Middle Years; Science and Technology Education for the Middle Years: Frameworks for Curriculum and Instruction; Assessment in Science Education: The Middle Years; Developing and Supporting Teachers for Science Education in the Middle Years; The High Stakes of High School Science; Future of Science in Elementary Schools: Educating Prospective Teachers; Technology Education in the Classroom: Understanding the Designed World; What College-Bound Students Abroad Are Expected to Know About Biology* (with AFT); *Examining the Examinations: A Comparison of Science and Mathematics Examinations for College-Bound Students in Seven Countries. Bold Ventures series: Vol. 1: Patterns of U.S. Innovations in Science and Mathematics Education; Vol. 2: Case Studies of U.S. Innovations in Science Education; Vol. 3: Case Studies of U.S. Innovations in Mathematics.* A publications catalog and project summaries are available on request.

National Center to Improve Practice (NCIP). Education Development Center, Inc., 55 Chapel St., Newton, MA 02158-1060. (617)969-7100 ext. 2387. TTY (617)969-4529. Fax (617)969-3440. E-mail ncip@edc.org. Website http://www.edc.org/FSC/NCIP. Judith Zorfass, Project Dir.; Lucy Lorin, information. NCIP, a project funded by the U.S. Department of Education's Office for Special Education Programs (OSEP), promotes the effective use of technology to enhance educational outcomes for students (preschool to grade 12) with sensory, cognitive, physical, social, and emotional disabilities. NCIP's award-winning Website offers users online discussions (topical discussions and special events) about technology and students with disabilities, an expansive library of resources (text, pictures, and video clips), online workshops, "guided tours" of exemplary classrooms, "spotlights" on new technology, and links to more than 100 sites dealing with technology and/or students with disabilities. NCIP also produces a series of videos illustrating how students with disabilities use a range of assistive and instructional technologies to improve their learning. *Dues:* Membership and dues are not required. *Meetings:* NCIP presents sessions at various educational conferences around the country. *Publications:* Video Profile Series: *Multimedia and More: Help for Students with Learning Disabilities; Jeff with Expression: Writing in the Word Prediction Software; "Write" Tools for Angie: Technology for Students Who Are Visually Impaired; Telling Tales in ASL and English: Reading, Writing and Videotapes; Welcome to My Preschool: Communicating with Technology.* Excellent for use in training, workshops, and courses, videos may be purchased individually or as a set of five by calling (800)793-5076. A new video to be released this year focuses on standards, curriculum, and assessment in science.

National Clearinghouse for Bilingual Education (NCBE). The George Washington University, 2011 "I" Street NW, Suite 200, Washington, DC 20006. (202)467-0867. Fax (800)531-9347, (202)467-4283. E-mail askncbe@ncbe.gwu.edu. Website http://www.ncbe.gwu.edu. Dr. Minerva Gorena, Interim Dir. NCBE is funded by the U.S. Department of Education's Office of Bilingual Education and Minority Languages Affairs (OBEMLA) to collect, analyze, synthesize, and disseminate information relating to the education of linguistically and culturally diverse students in the United States. NCBE is operated by The George Washington

University Graduate School of Education and Human Development, Center for the Study of Language and Education in Washington, DC. Online services include the NCBE Website containing an online library of hundreds of cover-to-cover documents, resources for teachers and administrators, and library of links to related Internet sites; an e-mail-based, bi-weekly news bulletin, *Newsline;* an electronic discussion group, *NCBE Roundtable;* and an e-mail-based question answering service, *AskNCBE. Publications:* short monographs, syntheses, and reports. Request a publications catalog for prices. The catalog and some publications are available at no cost from the NCBE and other Websites.

National Commission on Libraries and Information Science (NCLIS). 1110 Vermont Ave. NW, Suite 820, Washington, DC 20005-3552. (202)606-9200. Fax (202)606-9203. E-mail info@nclis.gov. Website http://www.nclis.gov. Robert S. Willard, Acting Exec. Dir. A permanent independent agency of the U.S. government charged with advising the executive and legislative branches on national library and information policies and plans. The Commission reports directly to the president and Congress on the implementation of national policy; conducts studies, surveys, and analyses of the nation's library and information needs; appraises the inadequacies of current resources and services; promotes research and development activities; conducts hearings and issues publications as appropriate; and develops overall plans for meeting national library and information needs and for the coordination of activities at the federal, state, and local levels. The Commission provides general policy advice to the Institute of Museum and Library Services (IMLS) director relating to library services included in the Library Services and Technology Act (LSTA). *Membership:* 16 commissioners (14 appointed by the president and confirmed by the Senate, the Librarian of Congress, and the Director of the IMLS). *Publication: Annual Report.*

National Communication Association (NCA) (formerly Speech Communication Association), 5105 Backlick Rd., Bldg. E, Annandale, VA 22003. (703)750-0533. Fax (703)914-9471. Web page http://www.natcom.org. James L. Gaudino, Exec. Dir. A voluntary society organized to promote study, criticism, research, teaching, and application of principles of communication, particularly of speech communication. *Membership:* 7,000. *Meetings:* 1999 Annual Meeting, Nov 4-7, Chicago. *Publications: Spectra Newsletter* (mo.); *Quarterly Journal of Speech*; *Communication Monographs*; *Communication Education*; *Critical Studies in Mass Communication*; *Journal of Applied Communication Research*; *Text and Performance Quarterly*; *Communication Teacher*; *Index to Journals in Communication Studies through 1995*; *National Communication Directory of NCA and the Regional Speech Communication Organizations* (CSSA, ECA, SSCA, WSCA). For additional publications, request brochure.

National Council for Accreditation of Teacher Education (NCATE). 2010 Massachusetts Ave. NW, Suite 500, Washington, DC 20036. (202)466-7496. Fax (202)296-6620. E-mail ncate@ncate.org. Website http://www.ncate.org. Arthur E. Wise, Pres. NCATE is a consortium of professional organizations that establishes standards of quality and accredits professional education units in schools, colleges, and departments of education, and is interested in the self-regulation and improvement of standards in the field of teacher education. *Membership:* Over 500 colleges and universities, over 30 educational organizations. *Publications: Standards, Procedures and Policies for the Accreditation of Professional Education Units*; *A Guide to College programs in Teacher Preparation Quality Teaching* (newsletter, 2/yr.).

National Council of Teachers of English (NCTE), Commission on Media. 1111 W. Kenyon Rd., Urbana, IL 61801-1096. (217)328-3870. Fax (217)328-0977. Andrew Garrison, Commission Dir. Rebecca Rickly, Committee Chair. The functions of the Commission are to study emerging technologies and their integration into English and language arts curricula and teacher education programs; identify the effects of such technologies on teachers, students, and educational settings, with attention to people of color, handicapped, and other students who are not well served in current programs; explore means of disseminating information about such technologies to the NCTE membership; serve as liaison between NCTE and other groups interested in computer-based education in English and language arts; and maintain liaison with the NCTE Commission on Media and other Council groups concerned with instructional technology.

National Council of the Churches of Christ in the USA. Communication Commission, 475 Riverside Dr., New York, NY 10115. (212)870-2574. Fax (212)870-2030. Website http://www.ncccusa.org. Randy Naylor, Dir. Ecumenical arena for cooperative work of Protestant and Orthodox denominations and agencies in broadcasting, film, cable, and print media. Offers advocacy to government and industry structures on media services. Services provided include liaison to network television and radio programming; film sales and rentals; distribution of information about syndicated religious programming; syndication of some programming; cable television and emerging technologies information services; and news and information regarding work of the National Council of Churches, related denominations, and agencies. Works closely with other faith groups in the Interfaith Broadcasting Commission. Online communication via Ecunet/NCCLink. *Membership:* 35 denominations. *Publication: EcuLink.*

National Education Knowledge Industry Association (NEKIA) (formerly Council for Educational Development and Research). 1200 19th St., NW, Suite 300, Washington, DC 20036. (202)429-5101. Fax (202)785-3849. Website http://www.nekia.org. C. Todd Jones, Pres. The National Education Knowledge Industry Association (NEKIA) is the only national trade association for organizations dedicated to educational research and development. The mission of NEKIA is to serve the nation's common schools by making cost-effective education innovation and expertise available to all communities. Members of NEKIA include the nations' foremost research and development institutions devoted to using research-based products and services to enhance the quality of education for the common good. NEKIA serves as a national voice for its members, making sure knowledge from research, development, and practical experience is part of the national discussion on education. NEKIA also ensures that educational research and development institutions are able to maintain neutrality and objectivity in reporting findings, and ensures a field-based, decentralized system of setting priorities. *Membership:* 15. *Publications: Checking Up on Early Childhood Care and Education; What We Know About Reading Teaching and Learning; Plugging In: Choosing and Using Educational Technology; Probe: Designing School Facilities for Learning; Education Productivity; Technology Infrastructure in Schools.*

National Education Telecommunications Organization & EDSAT Institute (NETO/ EDSAT). 1899 "L" Street NW, Suite 600, Washington, DC 20036. (202)293-4211. Fax (202)293-4210. E-mail neto-edsat@mindspring.com. Website http://www.netoedsat.org. Shelly Weinstein, Pres. and CEO. NETO/EDSAT is a nonprofit organization bringing together U.S. and non-U.S. users and providers of telecommunications to deliver education, instruction, health care, and training in classrooms, colleges, workplaces, health centers, and other distance education centers. NETO/EDSAT facilitates and collaborates with key stakeholders in the education and telecommunications fields. Programs and services include research and education, outreach, seminars and conferences, and newsletters. The NETO/ EDSAT mission is to help create an integrated multitechnology infrastructure, a dedicated satellite that links space and existing secondary access roads (telephone and cable) over which teaching and education resources are delivered and shared in a user-friendly format with students, teachers, workers, and individuals. NETO/EDSAT seeks to create a modern-day "learning place" for rural, urban, migrant, suburban, disadvantaged, and at-risk students that provides equal and affordable access to and utilization of educational resources. *Membership:* Members include more than 60 U.S. and non-U.S. school districts, colleges, universities, state agencies, public and private educational consortia, libraries, and other distance education providers. *Publications: NETO/EDSAT "UPDATE"* (newsletter, q.); *Analysis of a Proposal for an Education Satellite, EDSAT Institute,* 1991; *Global Summit on Distance Education Final Report,* Oct 1996; *International Report of the NETO/EDSAT Working*

Group on the Education and Health Care Requirements for Global/Regional Dedicated Networks, June 1998.

National Endowment for the Humanities (NEH). Division of Public Programs, Media Program, 1100 Pennsylvania Ave., NW, Room 426, Washington, DC 20506. (202)606-8269. E-mail info@neh.gov. Website http://www.neh.gov. Fax (202)606-8557. Jim Vore, Mgr. of Media/Special Projects. The NEH is an independent federal grant-making agency that supports research, educational, and public programs grounded in the disciplines of the humanities. The Media Program supports film and radio programs in the humanities for public audiences, including children and adults. *Publications: Overview of Endowment Programs; Humanities Projects in Media* (for application forms and guidelines).

National Federation of Community Broadcasters (NFCB). Ft. Mason Center, Bldg. D, San Francisco, CA 94123. (415)771-1160. E-mail nfcb@aol.com. Website http://www.nfcb.org. Lynn Chadwick, Pres. NFCB represents non-commercial, community-based radio stations in public policy development at the national level and provides a wide range of practical services, including technical assistance. *Membership:* 200. *Dues:* range from $150 to $2500 for participant and associate members. *Meetings:* 1999, San Francisco. *Publications: Legal Handbook; Audio Craft; Community Radio News.*

National Film Board of Canada (NFBC). 350 Fifth Ave., Suite 4820, New York, NY 10118. (212)629-8890. Fax (212)629-8502. E-mail j.sirabella@nfb.ca. John Sirabella, U.S. Marketing Mgr./Nontheatrical Rep. Established in 1939, the NFBC's main objective is to produce and distribute high-quality audiovisual materials for educational, cultural, and social purposes.

National Film Information Service (offered by the Margaret Herrick Library of the Academy of Motion Picture Arts and Sciences). Center for Motion Picture Study, 333 So. La Cienega Blvd., Beverly Hills, CA 90211. (310)247-3000. The purpose of this service is to provide information on film. The service is fee-based and all inquiries must be accompanied by a #10 self-addressed stamped envelope. NFIS does not reply to e-mail queries.

National Gallery of Art (NGA). Department of Education Resources: Art Information and Extension Programs, Washington, DC 20565. (202)842-6273. Fax (202)842-6935. Website http://www.hga.gov. Ruth R. Perlin, Head. This department of NGA is responsible for the production and distribution of educational audiovisual programs, including interactive technologies. Materials available (all loaned free to schools, community organizations, and individuals) range from films, videocassettes, and color slide programs to videodiscs and CD-ROMs. A free catalog of programs is available upon request. Two videodiscs on the gallery's collection are available for long-term loan. *Publication: Extension Programs Catalogue.*

National Information Center for Educational Media (NICEM). P.O. Box 8640, Albuquerque, NM 87198-8640. (505)265-3591, (800)926-8328. Fax (505)256-1080. E-mail nicem @nicem.com. Web page http://www.nicem.com. Roy Morgan, Exec. Dir.; Marjorie M. K. Hlava, Pres., Access Innovations, Inc. The National Information Center for Educational Media maintains an international database of information about educational nonprint materials for all age levels and subject areas in all media types. NICEM editors collect, catalog, and index information about media that is provided by producers and distributors. This information is entered into an electronic masterfile. Anyone who is looking for information about educational media materials can search the database by a wide variety of criteria to locate existing and archival materials. Producer and distributor information in each record then leads the searcher to the source of the educational media materials needed. NICEM makes the information from the database available in several forms and through several vendors. CD-ROM editions are available from NICEM, SilverPlatter, and BiblioFile. Online access to the database is available through NICEM, EBSCO, SilverPlatter, and The Library

Corporation. NICEM also conducts custom searches and prepares custom catalogs. NICEM is used by college and university media centers, public school libraries and media centers, public libraries, corporate training centers, students, media producers and distributors, and researchers. *Membership:* NICEM is a nonmembership organization. There is no charge for submitting information to be entered into the database. Corporate member of AECT, AIME, NAMTC, CCUMC. *Publications: A-V Online on SilverPlatter; NICEM A-V MARC by BiblioFile; NICEM Reference CD-ROM; NICEM MARC CD-ROM; NICEM Producer & CD-ROM.*

National ITFS Association (NIA). 2330 Swan Blvd., Milwaukee, WI 53226. (414)229-5470. Fax (414)229-4777. Website http://www.itfs.org. Patrick Gossman, Chair, Bd. of Dirs.; Don MacCullough, Exec. Dir. Established in 1978, NIA/ITFS is a nonprofit, professional organization of Instructional Television Fixed Service (ITFS) licensees, applicants, and others interested in ITFS broadcasting. The goals of the association are to gather and exchange information about ITFS, gather data on utilization of ITFS, and act as a conduit for those seeking ITFS information or assistance. The NIA represents ITFS interests to the FCC, technical consultants, and equipment manufacturers. The association provides its members with a quarterly newsletter and an FCC regulation update as well as information on excess capacity leasing and license and application data. *Meetings:* With AECT and InCITE. *Publications: National ITFS Association Newsletter* (q.); FCC regulation update.

National PTA. 330 N. Wabash, Suite 2100, Chicago, IL 60611. (312)670-6782. Fax (312)670-6783. Website http://www.pta.com. Ginny Markell, Pres.; Patty Yoxall, Public Relations Dir. Advocates the education, health, safety, and well-being of children and teens. Provides parenting education and leadership training to PTA volunteers. The National PTA continues to be very active in presenting Family and Television Critical TV Viewing workshops across the country in cooperation with the National Cable Television Association. The workshops teach parents and educators how to evaluate programming so they can make informed decisions about what to allow their children to see. The National PTA in 1997 convinced the television industry to add content information to the TV rating system. *Membership:* 6.8 million. *Dues:* vary by local unit. *Meeting:* National convention, held annually in June in different regions of the country, is open to PTA members; convention information available on the Website. *Publications: Our Children* (magazine); *What's Happening in Washington* (legislative newsletters). In addition, information can be downloaded from the Website. Catalog available.

National Press Photographers Association, Inc. (NPPA). 3200 Croasdaile Dr., Suite 306, Durham, NC 27705. (919)383-7246. Fax (919)383-7261. E-mail nppa@mindspring.com. Website http://www.nppa.org. Bradley Wilson, Dir. An organization of professional news photographers who participate in and promote photojournalism in publications and through television and film. Sponsors workshops, seminars, and contests; maintains an audiovisual library of subjects of media interest. *Membership:* 9,000. *Dues:* $75, domestic; $105, international; $40, student. *Meetings:* Annual convention and education days. An extensive array of other conferences, seminars, and workshops are held throughout the year. *Publications: News Photographer* (magazine, mo.); *The Best of Photojournalism* (annual book).

National Public Broadcasting Archives (NPBA). Hornbake Library, University of Maryland, College Park, MD 20742. (301)405-9255. Fax (301)314-2634. E-mail tc65@umail.umd.edu. Website http://www.library.umd.edu/UMCP/NPBA/npba.ntml. Thomas Connors, Archivist. NPBA brings together the archival record of the major entities of noncommercial broadcasting in the United States. NPBA's collections include the archives of the Corporation for Public Broadcasting (CPB), the Public Broadcasting Service (PBS), and National Public Radio (NPR). Other organizations represented include the Midwest Program for Airborne Television Instruction (MPATI), the Public Service Satellite Consortium (PSSC), America's Public Television Stations (APTS), Children's Television Workshop (CTW), and the Joint Council for Educational Telecommunications (JCET). NPBA also makes available the personal papers of many individuals who have made significant contributions to public broadcasting, and its reference library contains basic studies of the broadcasting industry, rare pamphlets, and journals on relevant topics. NPBA also collects and maintains a selected audio and video program record of public broadcasting's national production and support centers and of local stations. Oral history tapes and transcripts from the NPR Oral History Project and the Televisionaries Nal History Project are also available at the archives. The archives are open to the public from 9 A.M. to 5 P.M., Monday through Friday. Research in NPBA collections should be arranged by prior appointment. For further information, call (301)405-9988.

*National Religious Broadcasters (NRB). 7839 Ashton Ave., Manassas, VA 20109. (703)330-7000. Fax (703)330-7100. E-mail ssmith@nrb.organization. Website http://www.nrb .org. E. Brandt Gustavson, Pres. NRB essentially has two goals: (1) to ensure that religious broadcasters have access to the radio and television airwaves and (2) to encourage broadcasters to observe a high standard of excellence in their programming and station management for the clear presentation of the gospel. Holds national and regional conventions. *Membership:* 1,000 organizational stations, program producers, agencies, and individuals. *Dues:* based on income. *Meetings:*55th Annual NRB Convention and Exhibition, Jan 31-Feb 3, 1998, Washington, DC. *Publications: Religious Broadcasting Magazine* (mo.); *Annual Directory of Religious Media*; *Religious Broadcasting Resources Library Brochure*; *Religious Broadcasting Cassette Catalog.*

National School Boards Association (NSBA) Institute for the Transfer of Technology to Education (ITTE). 1680 Duke St., Alexandria, VA 22314. (800)838-6722. Fax (703)683-7590. E-mail itte@nsba.org. Website http://www.nsba.org/itte. Cheryl S. Williams, Dir. ITTE was created to help advance the wise uses of technology in public education. ITTE renders several services to state school boards associations, sponsors conferences, publishes, and engages in special projects. The Technology Leadership Network, the membership component of ITTE, is designed to engage school districts nationwide in a dialogue about technology in education. This dialogue is carried out via newsletters, meetings, special reports, projects, and online communications. The experience of the Network is shared more broadly through the state associations' communications with all school districts. *Membership:* Over 400 school districts in 44 states, Canada, and the United Kingdom. *Dues:* Based upon the school district's student enrollment. *Meetings:* 1999, Technology & Learning Conference, Nov 10-12, Dallas; Oct 28-30; Nov 15-17, Denver. *Publications: Investing in School Technology: Strategies to Meet the Funding Challenge/School Leader's Version; Technology for Students with Disabilities: A Decision Maker's Resource Guide; Leadership and Technology: What School Board Members Need to Know; Plans and Policies for Technology in Education: A Compendium; Telecommunications and Education: Surfing and the Art of Change; Multimedia and Learning: A School Leader's Guide; Electronic School: Technology Leadership News: Legal Issues* and *Education Technology: A School Leader's Guide; Models of Success: Case Study of Technology in Schools; Technology & School Design: Creating Spaces for Learning; Leader's Guide to Education Technology; Teachers and Technology: Staff Development for Tomorrow's Schools; Education Leadership Toolkit: A Desktop Companion* (q.).

National School Supply and Equipment Association (NSSEA). 8300 Colesville Rd., Suite 250, Silver Spring, MD 20910. (301)495-0240. Fax (301)495-3330. E-mail nssea @aol.com. Website http://www.nssea.org. Tim Holt, Pres. A service organization of more than 1,600 manufacturers, distributors, retailers, and independent manufacturers' representatives of school supplies, equipment, and instructional materials. Seeks to maintain open communications between manufacturers and dealers in the school market and to encourage the development of new ideas and products for educational progress. *Meetings:* 2000, School Equipment Show, Tampa, FL, March 2-4; 2000, Ed Expo '00, Dallas, TX, March 9-11; Fall Trade Show & Education Conference, Kansas City, MO, Oct 26-28. *Publications: Tidings*; *Annual Membership Directory.*

National Science Foundation (NSF). 4201 Wilson Blvd., Arlington, VA 22230. (703)306-1070. Mary Hanson, Chief, Media Relations and Public Affairs. Linda Boutchyard, Contact Person, lboutchy@nsf.gov. NSF is an independent federal agency responsible for fundamental research in all fields of science and engineering, with an annual budget of about $3 billion. NSF funds reach all 50 states, through grants to more than 2,000 universities and institutions nationwide. NSF receives more than 50,000 requests for funding annually, including at least 30,000 new proposals. Applicants should refer to the NSF Guide to Programs. Scientific material and media reviews are available to help the public learn about NSF-supported programs. NSF news releases and tipsheets are available electronically via *NSFnews*. To subscribe, send an e-mail message to listmanager@nsf.gov; in the body of the message, type "subscribe nsfnews" and then type your name. Also see NSF news products at http://www.nsf.gov/od/lpa/news/start.htm, http://www.eurekalert.org/, and http://www.ari .net/newswise. In addition, NSF has developed a Website that offers information about NSF directorates, offices, programs, and publications at http://nsf.gov.

National Telemedia Council Inc. (NTC). 120 E. Wilson St., Madison, WI 53703. (608)257-7712. Fax (608)257-7714. E-mail NTelemedia@aol.com. Website http://danenet .wicip.org/NTC. Rev. Stephen Umhoefer, Interim Pres.; Marieli Rowe, Exec. Dir. The NTC is a national, nonprofit professional organization dedicated to promoting media literacy, or critical media viewing skills. This is done primarily through work with teachers, parents, and caregivers. NTC activities include publishing *Telemedium: The Journal of Media Literacy,* the Teacher Idea Exchange (T.I.E.), the Jessie McCanse Award for individual contribution to media literacy, assistance to media literacy educators and professionals. *Dues:* $30, basic; $50, contributing; $100, patron. *Publications: Telemedium; The Journal of Media Literacy* (q. newsletter).

Native American Public Telecommunications (NAPT). 1800 North 33rd St., P.O. Box 83111, Lincoln, NE 68501-3111. (402)472-3522. Fax (402)472-8675. Website http://nativetelecomn.org. Frank Blythe, Exec. Dir. The mission of NAPT is to inform, educate, and encourage the awareness of tribal histories, cultures, languages, opportunities, and aspirations through the fullest participation of America Indians and Alaska Natives in creating and employing all forms of educational and public telecommunications programs and services, thereby support-ing tribal sovereignty. *Publication: The Vision Maker* (newsletter).

*Network for Continuing Medical Education (NCME). One Harmon Plaza, 6th Floor, Secaucus, NJ 07094. (201)867-3550. Produces and distributes videocassettes, CD-ROMs & Web Based Programs to hospitals for physicians' continuing education. Programs are developed for physicians in the practice of General Medicine, Anesthesiology, Emergency Medicine, Gastroenterology, and Surgery. Physicians who view all the programs can earn up to 25 hours of Category 1 (AMA) credit and up to 10 hours of Prescribed (AAFP) credit each year. *Membership:* More than 1,000 hospitals provide NCME programs to their physicians. *Dues:* subscription fees: VHS-$2,160/yr. Sixty-minute videocassettes & CD-ROMs are distributed to hospital subscribers every 18 days.

The NETWORK, Inc. 136 Fenno Drive, Rowley, MA 01969. (978)948-7764. Fax (978)948-7836. E-mail davidc@network.org. David Crandall, contact person. A nonprofit research and service organization providing training, research and evaluation, technical assis-tance, and materials for a fee to schools, educational organizations, and private sector firms with educational interests. The NETORK has been helping professionals manage and learn about change since 1969. A Facilitator's Institute is held at least annually for trainers and staff developers who use the simulations. *Publications: An Action Guide for School Improve-ment*; *Making Change for School Improvement: A Simulation Game*; *Systems Thinking/ Systems Changing: A Simulation Game; People, Policies, and Practices: Examining the Chain of School Improvement; Systemic Thinking: Solving Complex Problems; Benchmarking: A Guide for Educators.*

New England Educational Media Association (NEEMA). c/o Jean Keilly, 58 South Mammoth Road, Manchester, NH 03109. (603)622-9626. Fax (603)424-6229. An affiliate of AECT, NEEMA is a regional professional association dedicated to the improvement of instruction through the effective utilization of school library media services, media, and technology applications. For over 75 years, it has represented school library media professionals through activities and networking efforts to develop and polish the leadership skills, professional representation, and informational awareness of the membership. The Board of Directors consists of departments of education as well as professional leaders of the region. An annual conference program and a Leadership Program are offered in conjunction with the various regional state association conferences.

The New York Festivals (formerly the International Film and TV Festival of New York). 780 King St., Chappaqua, NY 10514. (914)238-4481. Fax (914)236-5040. E-mail info @nyfests.com. Website http://www.nyfests.com. Bilha Goldberg, Vice Pres. The New York Festivals sponsors the International Non-Broadcast Awards, which are annual competitive festivals for industrial and educational film and video productions, filmstrips and slide programs, multi-image business theater and interactive multimedia presentations, and television programs. Entry fees begin at $125. First entry deadline is Aug 3 for U.S. entrants and Sept 15 for overseas entrants. The Non-Broadcast competition honors a wide variety of categories, including Education Media. As one of the largest competitions in the world, achieving finalist status is a notable credit to any company's awards roster. Winners are announced each year at a gala awards show in New York City and published on the World Wide Web.

North Central Regional Educational Laboratory (NCREL). 1900 Spring Rd., Suite 300, Oak Brook, IL 60523-1480. (630)571-4700, (800)356-2735. Fax (630)571-4716. E-mail info @ncrel.org. Website http://www.ncrel.org/. Jan Bakker, Resource Center Dir. NCREL's work is guided by a focus on comprehensive and systemic school restructuring that is research-based and learner-centered. One of 10 Office of Educational Research and Improvement (OERI) regional educational laboratories, NCREL disseminates information about effective programs, develops educational products, holds conferences, provides technical assistance, and conducts research and evaluation. A special focus is on technology and learning. In addition to conventional print publications, NCREL uses computer networks, videoconferencing via satellite, and video and audio formats to reach its diverse audiences. NCREL's Website includes the acclaimed *Pathways to School Improvement.* NCREL operates the Midwest Consortium for Mathematics and Science Education, which works to advance systemic change in mathematics and science education. Persons living in Illinois, Indiana, Iowa, Michigan, Minnesota, Ohio, and Wisconsin are encouraged to call NCREL Resource Center with any education-related questions. NCREL also hosts the North Central Regional Technology in Education Consortium which helps states and local educational agencies successfully integrate advanced technologies into K–12 classrooms, library media centers, and other educational settings. *Publication: Learning Point* (q).

Northwest College and University Council for the Management of Educational Technology (NW/MET). c/o WITS, Willamette University, 900 State St., Salem, OR 97301. (503)370-6650. Fax (503)375-5456. E-mail mmorandi@willamette.edu. Listserv NW-MET @willamette.edu. Judi Ross, Pres.; Marti Morandi, Membership Chair. NW/MET was the first regional group representing institutions of higher education in Alberta, Alaska, British Columbia, Idaho, Montana, Oregon, Saskatchewan, and Washington to receive affiliate status in AECT. *Membership* is restricted to Information Technology managers with campus-wide responsibilities for Information technology services in the membership region. Corresponding membership is available to those who work outside the membership region. Current issues under consideration include managing emerging technologies, reorganization, copyright, and management/administration issues. Organizational goals include identifying the unique status problems of media managers in higher education. *Membership:* approx. 75. *Dues:* $35. *Meetings:* An annual conference and business meeting are held each year, rotating through the region. *Publications:* An annual newsletter and *NW/MET Journal.*

Northwest Regional Educational Laboratory (NWREL). 101 SW Main St., Suite 500, Portland, OR 97204. (503)275-9500. Fax (503)275-0448. E-mail info@nwrel.org. Website http://www.nwrel.org. Dr. Ethel Simon-McWilliams, Exec. Dir. One of 10 Office of Educational Research and Improvement (OERI) regional educational laboratories, NWREL works with schools and communities to improve educational outcomes for children, youth, and adults. NWREL provides leadership, expertise, and services based on the results of research and development. The specialty area of NWREL is school change processes. It serves Alaska, Idaho, Oregon, Montana, and Washington. *Membership:* 817. *Dues:* None. *Publication: Northwest Report* (newsletter).

On-line Audiovisual Catalogers (OLAC). Formed as an outgrowth of the ALA conference, OLAC seeks to permit members to exchange ideas and information, and to interact with other agencies that influence audiovisual cataloging practices. *Membership:* 700. *Dues:* available for single or multiple years; $10-$27, indiv.; $16-$45, institution. *Meetings:* bi-annual. *Publication: OLAC Newsletter.*

Online Computer Library Center, Inc. (OCLC). 6565 Frantz Rd., Dublin, OH 43017-3395. (614)764-6000. Fax (614)764-6096. E-mail oclc@oclc.org. Website http://www.oclc.org. 1Jay Jordan, Pres. and CEO. Nita Dean, Mgr., Public Relations. A nonprofit membership organization that engages in computer library service and research and makes available computer-based processes, products, and services for libraries, other educational organizations, and library users. From its facility in Dublin, Ohio, OCLC operates an international computer network that libraries use to catalog books, order custom-printed catalog cards and machine-readable records for local catalogs, arrange interlibrary loans, and maintain location information on library materials. OCLC also provides online reference products and services for the electronic delivery of information. More than 34,000 libraries contribute to and/or use information in WorldCat (the OCLC Online Union Catalog). OCLC FOREST PRESS, a division of OCLC since 1988, publishes the Dewey Decimal Classification. Reservation Resources, a division of OCLC since 1994, provides preservation reformatting services worldwide. *Publications: OCLC Newsletter* (6/yr.); *OCLC Reference News* (4/yr.); *Annual Report.*

Pacific Film Archive (PFA). University of California, Berkeley Art Museum, 2625 Durant Ave., Berkeley, CA 94720-2250. (510)642-1437 (library); (510)642-1412 (general). Fax (510)642-4889. E-mail pfalibrary@uclink.berkeley.edu. Website http://www.bampfa.berkeley .edu. Edith Kramer, Dir. and Curator of Film; Nancy Goldman, Head, PFA Library and Film Study Center. Sponsors the exhibition, study, and preservation of classic, international, documentary, animated, and avant-garde films. Provides on-site research screenings of films in its collection of over 7,000 titles. Provides access to its collections of books, periodicals, stills, and posters (all materials are noncirculating). Offers BAM/PFA members and University of California, Berkeley, affiliates reference and research services to locate film and video distributors, credits, stock footage, etc. Library hours are 1 P.M.-5 P.M. Mon.-Thurs. *Membership:* through parent organization, the Berkeley Art Museum. *Dues:* $40 indiv. and nonprofit departments of institutions. *Publication: BAM/PFA Calendar* (6/yr.).

Pacific Resources for Education and Learning (PREL). 828 Fort Street Mall Suite 500, Honolulu, HI 96813-4321. (808)533-6000. Fax (808)533-7599. E-mail askprel@prel.hawaii .edu. Website http://prel.hawaii.edu. John W. Kofel, Exec. Dir. One of 10 regional educational laboratories designed to help educators and policymakers solve educational problems in their schools. Using the best available information and the expertise of professionals, PREL furnishes research results, provides training to teachers and administrators, and helps to implement new approaches in education. The PREL Star program, funded by a U.S. Department of Education Star Schools Grant, utilizes telecommunications technology to provide distance learning opportunities to the Pacific region. PREL serves American Samoa, Commonwealth of the Northern Mariana Islands, Federated States of Micronesia, Guam, Hawaii, Republic of the Marshall Islands, and Republic of Palau.

Photographic Society of America (PSA). 3000 United Founders Blvd., Suite 103, Oklahoma City, OK 73112. (405)843-1437. Fax (405)843-1438. E-mail 74521,2414@compuserve.com. Website http://www.psa-photo.org. Jacque Noel, Operations Mgr. A nonprofit organization for the development of the arts and sciences of photography and for the furtherance of public appreciation of photographic skills. Its members, largely advanced amateurs, consist of individuals, camera clubs, and other photographic organizations. Divisions include electronic imaging, color slide, video motion picture, nature, photojournalism, travel, pictorial print, stereo, and techniques. Sponsors national, regional, and local meetings, clinics, and contests. *Membership:* 7,000. *Dues:* $40, North America; $45 elsewhere. *Meetings:* 1999 International Conference of Photography, Aug 30-Sep 4, Toronto, Delta Meadowvale Hotel. *Publication: PSA Journal.*

Professors of Instructional Design and Technology (PIDT). Instructional Technology Dept., 220 War Memorial Hall, Virginia Tech, Blacksburg, VA 24061-0341. (540)231-5587. Fax (540)231-9075. E-mail moorem@VT.EDU. Dr. Mike Moore, contact person. An informal organization designed to encourage and facilitate the exchange of information among members of the instructional design and technology academic and corporate communities. Also serves to promote excellence in academic programs in instructional design and technology and to encourage research and inquiry that will benefit the field while providing leadership in the public and private sectors in its application and practice. *Membership:* 300 faculty employed in higher education institutions whose primary responsibilities are teaching and research in this area, their corporate counterparts, and other persons interested in the goals and activities of the PIDT. *Dues:* none. *Meetings:* Annual conference; see above e-mail address for information and registration.

*Public Broadcasting Service (PBS). 1320 Braddock Pl., Alexandria, VA 22314. Website http://www.pbs.org. Ervin S. Duggan, CEO and Pres. National distributor of public television programming, obtaining all programs from member stations, independent producers, and sources around the world. PBS services include program acquisition, distribution, and scheduling; development and fundraising support; engineering and technical development; and educational resources and services. Through the PBS National Program Service, PBS uses the power of noncommercial television, the Internet, and other media to enrich the lives of all Americans through quality programs and education services that inform and inspire. Subsidiaries of PBS include PBS Adult Learning Service, and PBS Video, which are described below. PBS is owned and operated by local public television organizations through annual membership fees and governed by a board of directors elected by PBS members for three-year terms.

PBS Adult Learning Service (ALS). 1320 Braddock Pl., Alexandria, VA 22314-1698. (800)257-2578. Fax (703)739-8471. E-mail als@pbs.org. Website http://www.pbs .org/als/college. Will Philipp, Senior Dir. The mission of ALS is to help colleges, universities, and public television stations increase learning opportunities for distance learners; enrich classroom instruction; update faculty; train administrators, management, and staff; and provide other educational services for local communities. A pioneer in the widespread use of video and print packages incorporated into curricula and offered for credit by local colleges, ALS began broadcasting telecourses in 1981. Since that time, over 3 million students have earned college credit through telecourses offered in partnership with more than two-thirds of the nation's colleges and universities. In 1988, ALS established the Adult Learning Satellite Service (ALSS) to provide colleges, universities, and other organizations with a broad range of educational programming via direct satellite. Since 1994, ALS has facilitated the capability for colleges nationwide to offer full two-year degrees at a distance through the popular Going the Distance® project. Over 170 colleges are currently participating in 37 states. In 1998, ALS launched the first teleWEBcourse[SM], *Internet Literacy*, an online credit offering available through the PBS Website. *Membership:* 700-plus colleges, universities, hospitals, and government agencies are now ALSS Associates. Organizations that are not Associates can still acquire ALS programming, but at higher fees. *Dues:* $1,500; multisite and consortia rates are available. *Publications: ALSS Programming Line-Up* (catalog of available programming, 3/yr.); *The Agenda* (news magazine about issues of interest to distance learning and adult learning administrators); *Changing the Face of Higher Education* (an overview of ALS services); *Teaching Telecourses: Opportunities and Options; Ideas for Increasing Telecourse Enrollment; Going the Distance® Handbook* (case studies for offering distance learning degrees).

PBS VIDEO. 1320 Braddock Pl., Alexandria, VA 22314. (703)739-5380; (800)344-3337. Fax (703)739-5269. Jon Cecil, Dir., PBS VIDEO Marketing. Markets and distributes PBS television programs for sale on videocassette or videodisc to colleges, public libraries, schools, governments, and other organizations and institutions. *Publications: PBS VIDEO Catalogs of New and Popular Video* (6/yrs). *Website: PBS VIDEO Online Catalog* at http://shop2.org/pbsvideo/.

Public Library Association (PLA). 50 E. Huron St., Chicago, IL 60611. (312)280-5PLA. Fax (312)280-5029. E-mail pla@ala.org. Greta Southard, Exec. Dir. An affiliate of the American Library Association, PLA is concerned with the development, effectiveness, and financial support of public libraries. It speaks for the profession and seeks to enrich the professional competence and opportunities of public librarians. Sections include Adult Lifelong Learning, Community Information, Metropolitan Libraries, Public Library Systems, Small and Medium-sized Libraries, Public Policy for Public Libraries, Planning, Measurement and Evaluation, and Marketing of Public Library Services. *Membership:* 8,500. *Dues:* $50, open to all ALA members. *Meetings:* 1999 PLA Spring Symposium, Mar 25-28; 2000 PLA National Conference, Mar 28-Apr 1, "Public Libraries: Vital, Valuable, Virtual." *Publication: Public Libraries* (bi-monthly). Two PLA Committees of particular interest to the Educational Technology field are listed below.

Audiovisual Committee (of the Public Library Association). 50 E. Huron St., Chicago, IL 60611. (312)280-5752. James E. Massey, Chair. Promotes use of audiovisual materials in public libraries.

Technology in Public Libraries Committee (of the Public Library Association). 50 E. Huron St., Chicago, IL 60611. (312)280-5752. William Ptacek, Chair. Collects and disseminates information on technology applications in public libraries.

*Puppeteers of America, Inc. (POA). #5 Cricklewood Path, Pasadena, CA 91107-1002. (818)797-5748. Gayle Schluter, Membership Officer. Website http://www.puppeteers.org. Formed in 1937, POA holds festivals for puppetry across the country, sponsors local guilds, presents awards, sponsors innovative puppetry works, provides consulting, and provides materials through the Audio-Visual Library. *Membership:* over 2,000. *Dues:* $40, regular; $50, couple; $20, junior; $60, family; $30, journal subscription. *Meetings:* National Festival, Aug 1-7, 1999, Seattle. *Publication: The Puppetry Journal* (q).

Recording for the Blind and Dyslexic (RFB&D). 20 Roszel Road, Princeton, NJ 08540. Main phone (609)452-0606. Customer Service (800)221-4792. Fax (609)987-8116. E-mail information@rfbd.org. Website http://www.rfbd.org. Richard Scribner, Pres. RFB&D is a national nonprofit organization that provides educational and professional books in accessible format to people with visual impairments, learning disabilities, or other physical disabilities that prevent them from reading normal printed material. This includes students from kindergarten to graduate school and people who no longer attend school but who use educational books to pursue careers or personal interests. RFB&D's 78,000-volume collection of audio titles is the largest educational resource of its kind in the world. RFB&D provides a wide range of library services as well as "E-Text" books on computer disk, including dictionaries, computer manuals, and other reference books. For an additional fee, a custom recording service is also available, to make other publications accessible. Potential individual members must complete an application form, which contains a "disability verification" section. *Membership:* 39,139 individuals, 275 institutions. *Dues:* for qualified individuals, $50 registration, $25 annual. Institutional Memberships also available (contact Customer Service).

Recording Industry Association of America, Inc. (RIAA). 1330 Connecticut Ave. NW #300, Washington DC, 20036; (202)775-0101. Fax (202)775-7253. Website http://www.riaa.com/. Hilary Rosen, Pres. and CEO. Founded in 1952, RIAA's mission is to promote the mutual interests of recording companies, as well as the betterment of the industry overall through successful government relations (both federal and state), intellectual property protection, and international activities; evaluating all aspects of emerging technologies and technology-related issues; and promoting an innovative and secure online marketplace. RIAA represents the recording industry, whose members create and/or distribute approximately 90 percent of all legitimate sound recordings produced and sold in the United States. RIAA is the official certification agency for gold, platinum, and multi-platinum record awards. *Membership:* Over 250 recording companies. *Publications: Annual Report; Fact Book.*

Reference and User Services Association (RUSA). 50 E. Huron St., Chicago, IL 60611. (800)545-2433, ext. 4398. Fax (312)944-8085. Cathleen Bourdon, Exec. Dir. A division of the American Library Association, RUSA is responsible for stimulating and supporting in every type of library the delivery of reference information services to all groups and of general library services and materials to adults. *Membership:* 5,500. *Dues:* $45 plus membership in ALA. *Publications: RUSQ* (q.); *RUSA Update.*

*Research for Better Schools, Inc. (RBS). 444 North Third St., Philadelphia, PA 19123-4107. (215)574-9300. Fax (215)574-0133. Website http://www.rbs.org/. John Connolly, Exec. Dir. RBS is a private, nonprofit corporation that currently operates the Mid-Atlantic Eisenhower Consortium for Mathematics and Science Education, and the Mid-Atlantic Telecommunications Alliance. In its 30 years of service to the education community, RBS has also offered educational technology, development, evaluation, technical assistance, and training services with client funding. RBS also operates an educational publications division.

Smithsonian Institution. 1000 Jefferson Drive SW, Washington, DC 20560. (202)357-2700. Fax (202)786-2515. Website http://www.si.edu. I. Michael Heyman, Sec. An independent trust instrumentality of the United States that conducts scientific, cultural, and scholarly research; administers the national collections; and performs other educational public service functions, all supported by Congress, trusts, gifts, and grants. Includes 16 museums, including the National Museum of Natural History, the National Museum of American History, the National Air and Space Museum, and the National Zoological Park. Museums are free and open daily except December 25. The Smithsonian Institution Traveling Exhibition Service (SITES) organizes exhibitions on art, history, and science and circulates them across the country and abroad. *Membership:* Smithsonian Associates. *Dues:* $24-$45. *Publications: Smithsonian; Air & Space/Smithsonian; The Torch* (staff newsletter, mo.); *Research Reports* (semi-technical, q.); Smithsonian Institution Press Publications, 470 L'Enfant Plaza, Suite 7100, Washington, DC 20560.

Society for Applied Learning Technology (SALT). 50 Culpeper St., Warrenton, VA 20186. (540)347-0055. Fax (540)349-3169. E-mail info@lti.org. Website http://www.salt.org. Raymond G. Fox, Pres. The society is a nonprofit, professional membership organization that was founded in 1972. Membership in the society is oriented to professionals whose work requires knowledge and communication in the field of instructional technology. The society provides members with a means to enhance their knowledge and job performance by participation in society-sponsored meetings, subscription to society-sponsored publications, association with other professionals at conferences sponsored by the society, and membership in special interest groups and special society-sponsored initiatives. In addition, the society offers member discounts on society-sponsored journals, conferences, and publications. *Membership:* 1,000. *Dues:* $45. *Meetings:* Orlando Multimedia. '99, Kissimmee, FL; Interactive Multimedia '99, Arlington, VA. *Publications: Journal of Educational Technology Systems; Journal of Instruction Delivery Systems; Journal of Interactive Instruction Development.* Send for list of books.

Society for Computer Simulation (SCS). P.O. Box 17900, San Diego, CA 92177-7900. (619)277-3888. Fax (619)277-3930. E-mail info@scs.org. Website http://www.scs.org. Bill Gallagher, Exec. Dir. Founded in 1952, SCS is a professional-level technical society devoted to the art and science of modeling and simulation. Its purpose is to advance the understanding, appreciation, and use of all types of computer models for studying the behavior of actual or hypothesized systems of all kinds and to sponsor standards. Additional office in Ghent, Belgium. *Membership:* 1,900. *Dues:* $75 (includes journal subscription). *Meetings:* Local, regional, and national technical meetings and conferences, such as the Western Simulation Multiconference Jan 17-21, 1999, San Francisco; Summer and Winter Computer Simulation Conferences, Applied Simulation Technologies Conference, Apr 12-15, 1999, San Diego; and National Educational Computing Conference (NECC). *Publications: Simulation* (mo.); *Simulation* series (q.); *Transactions of SCS* (q.).

Society for Photographic Education (SPE). P.O. Box 2811, Daytona Beach, FL 32120-2811. (904)255-8131, ext. 3944. Fax (904)255-3044. E-mail SocPhotoEd@aol.com or SPENews @aol.com. Website http://www.spenational.org. James J. Murphy, Exec. Dir. An association of college and university teachers of photography, museum photographic curators, writers, and publishers. Promotes discourse in photography education, culture, and art. *Membership:* 1,700. *Dues:* $55. *Meetings:* 1999, Mar 11-14, Tucson; 2000, Mar 16-19, Cleveland. *Publication: Exposure* (newsletter).

Society of Cable Telecommunications Engineers (SCTE). 140 Philips Rd., Exton, PA 19341-1319. (610)363-6888. Fax (610)363-5898. E-mail info@scte.org. Website http://www .scte.org. John Clark, Pres. SCTE is dedicated to the technical training and further education of members. A nonprofit membership organization for persons engaged in engineering, construction, installation, technical direction, management, or administration of cable television and broadband communications technologies. Also eligible for membership are students in communications, educators, government and regulatory agency employees, and affiliated trade associations. SCTE provides technical training and certification, and is an American National Standards Institute (ANSI)-approved Standards Development Organization for the cable telecommunications industry. *Membership:* 15,500 U.S. and International. *Dues:* $40. *Meetings:* 2000, Conference on Emerging Technologies, Jan. 11-13, Anaheim, CA; Cable-Tec Expo, May 25-27, Orlando (hardware exhibits and engineering conference); 2000 Cable-Tec Expo, June 5-8; 2000 Las Vegas (hardware exhibits and engineering conference). *Publications: The Interval;* technical documents, standards, training materials, and videotapes (some available in Spanish).

Society of Photo Technologists (SPT). 11112 S. Spotted Rd., Cheney, WA 99004. (888)662-7678 or (509)624-9621. Fax (509)323-4811 or (509)624-5320. E-mail ccspt@ concentric.net. An organization of photographic equipment repair technicians, which improves and maintains communications between manufacturers and independent repair technicians. *Membership:* 1,000. *Dues:* $80-$360. *Publications: SPT Journal; SPT Parts and Services Directory; SPT Newsletter; SPT Manuals—Training and Manufacturer's Tours.*

Southeastern Regional Media Leadership Council (SRMLC). Dr. Vykuntapathi Thota, Director, Virginia State University, P.O. Box 9198, Petersburg, VA 23806. (804)524-5937. Fax (804)524-5757. An affiliate of AECT, the purpose of the SRMLC is to strengthen the role of the individual state AECT affiliates within the Southeastern region; to seek positive change in the nature and status of instructional technology as it exists within the Southeast; to provide opportunities for the training and development of leadership for both the region and the individual affiliates; and to provide opportunities for the exchange of information and experience among those who attend the annual conference.

SouthEastern Regional Vision for Education (SERVE). SERVE Tallahassee Office, 1203 Governor's Square Blvd., Suite 400, Tallahassee, FL 32301. (800)352-6001, (904)671-6000. Fax (904)671-6020. E-mail bfry@SERVE.org. Mr. Don Holznagel, Exec. Dir. Betty Fry, Contact Person. SERVE is a regional educational research and development laboratory funded by the U.S .Department of Education to help educators, policymakers, and communities improve schools so that all students achieve their full potential. The laboratory offers the following services: field-based models and strategies for comprehensive school improvement; publications on hot topics in education, successful implementation efforts, applied research projects, and policy issues; database searches and information search training; a regional bulletin board service that provides educators electronic communication and Internet access; information and assistance for state and local policy development; and services to support the coordination and improvement of assistance for young children and their families. The Eisenhower Mathematics and Science Consortium at SERVE promotes improvement of education in these targeted areas by coordinating regional resources, disseminating exemplary instructional materials, and offering technical assistance for implementation of effective teaching methods and assessment tools. *Meetings:* For dates and topics of conferences and workshops, contact Betty Fry, (800)352-6001. *Publications: Reengineering High Schools for Student Success*; *Schools for the 21st Century: New Roles for Teachers and Principals* (rev. ed.); *Designing Teacher Evaluation Systems That Promote Professional Growth*; *Learning by Serving: 2,000 Ideas for Service-Learning Projects*; *Sharing Success: Promising Service-Learning Programs*; *Future Plans* (videotape, discussion guide, and pamphlet); *Future Plans Planning Guides*.

Southwest Educational Development Laboratory (SEDL). 211 East Seventh St., Austin, TX 78701. (512)476-6861. Fax (512)476-2286. E-mail info@sedl.org. Website http://www .sedl.org/. Dr. Wesley A. Hoover, Pres. and CEO; Dr. Joyce Pollard, Dir., Institutional Communications & Policy Services. One of 10 Office of Educational Research and Improvement (OERI) regional educational laboratories designed to help educators and policymakers solve educational problems in their schools. Using the best available information and the experience and expertise of professionals, SEDL seeks to identify solutions to education problems, tries new approaches, furnishes research results, and provides training to teachers and administrators. SEDL serves Arkansas, Louisiana, New Mexico, Oklahoma, and Texas. *Publications: SEDLETTER* for free general distribution; a range of topic-specific publications related to educational change, education policy, mathematics, language arts, science, and disability research.

Special Libraries Association. 1700 Eighteenth St., NW, Washington, DC, 20009-2514. (202)234-4700. Fax (202)265-9317. Email sla@sla.org. Website http://www.sla.org. Dr. David R. Bender, Exec. Dir. The Special Libraries Association is an international association representing the interests of nearly 15,000 information professionals in 60 countries. Special librarians are information and resource experts who collect, analyze, evaluate, package, and disseminate information to facilitate accurate decision making in corporate, academic, and government settings. The association offers myriad programs and services designed to help its members serve their customers more effectively and succeed in an increasingly challenging environment of information management and technology. These services include career and employment services, and professional development opportunities. *Membership:* 14,500. *Dues:* $105, indiv.; $25, student. *Meetings:* 1999, Jan 21-23, San Francisco; Jun 5-10, Minneapolis; 2000, Jan 20-22, St. Louis, Jun 10-15, Philadelphia, Oct 16-19, Brighton, United Kingdom. *Publication: Information Outlook* (monthly glossy magazine that accepts advertising). Special Libraries Association also has an active book publishing program.

Teachers and Writers Collaborative (T&W). 5 Union Square W., New York, NY 10003-3306. (212)691-6590. Toll-free (888)266-5789. Fax (212)675-0171. E-mail info@twc.org. Website http://www.twc.org. Nancy Larson Shapiro, Dir. Sends writers and other artists into New York public schools to work with teachers and students on writing and art projects. Hosts seminars for creative work from across the United States and beyond. Recent projects include the creation of WriteNet, a series of online forums and information for people interested in teaching creative writing. Also, in conjunction with NBC TV, T&W set up a series of residencies around the country focused on teaching creative writing using "classic" literature. See Website for updated schedule of events. *Membership:* over 1,000; for people interested in the teaching of writing. *Dues:* $35, basic personal membership. *Publications: Teachers & Writers* (magazine, 5/yr); *The Story in History; The T&W Handbook of Poetic Forms; Personal Fiction Writing; Luna, Luna, Creative Writing from Spanish and Latino Literature; The Nearness of You: Students and Teachers Writing On-Line.* Request free publications catalog for list of titles.

Theatre Library Association (TLA). 149 W. 45th St., New York, NY 10036. (212)944-3895. Fax (212)944-4139. Website http://www.brown.edu/Facilities/University_Library/beyond /TLA/TLA.html. Maryann Chach, Exec. Sec. Seeks to further the interests of collecting, preserving, and using theater, cinema, and performing arts materials in libraries, museums, and private collections. *Membership:* 500. *Dues:* $30, indiv.; $30, institutional; $20, students and retirees. *Publication: Performing Arts Resources* (membership annual, Vol. 20, Denishawn Collections).

USA Toy Library Association (USA-TLA). 2530 Crawford Ave., Suite 111, Evanston, IL 60201. (847)864-3330. Fax (847)864-3331. E-mail foliog@aol.com. Judith Q. Iacuzzi, Exec. Dir. The mission of the USA-TLA is to provide a networking system answering to all those interested in play and play materials to provide a national resource to toy libraries, family centers, resource and referrals, public libraries, schools, institutions serving families of special need, and other groups and individuals involved with children; to support and expand the number of toy libraries; and to advocate for children and the importance of their play in healthy development. Individuals can find closest toy libraries by sending an e-mail or written inquiry in a self-addressed stamped envelope. *Membership:* 60 institutions, 150 individuals. *Dues:* $165, comprehensive; $55, basic; $15, student. *Meetings:* National meetings in the spring and fall. *Publications: Child's Play* (q. newsletter); *How to Start and Operate a Toy Library; Play Is a Child's Work* (videotapes); other books on quality toys and play.

University Continuing Education Association (UCEA). One Dupont Cir. NW, Suite 615, Washington, DC 20036. (202)659-3130. Fax (202)785-0374. Website http://www.nucea.edu. E-mail postmaster@nucea.edu. Tom Kowalik, Pres. 1999-2000. Kay J. Kohl, Exec. Dir.; Susan Goewey, Dir. of Pubs; Philip Robinson, Dir. of Govt. Relations & Public Affairs, Joelle Brink, Dir. of Information Services. UCEA is an association of public and private higher education institutions concerned with making continuing education available to all population segments and to promoting excellence in continuing higher education. Many institutional members offer university and college courses via electronic instruction. *Membership:* 425 institutions, 2,000 professionals. *Dues:* vary according to membership category. *Meetings:* UCEA has an annual national conference and several professional development seminars throughout the year. *Publications:* monthly newsletter; quarterly; occasional papers; scholarly journal, *Continuing Higher Education Review; Independent Study Catalog.* With Peterson's, *The Guide to Distance Learning; Guide to Certificate Programs at American Colleges and Universities*; UCEA-ACE/Oryx Continuing Higher Education book series; *Lifelong Learning Trends* (a statistical factbook on continuing higher education); organizational issues series; membership directory.

WestEd. 730 Harrison St., San Francisco, CA 94107-1242. (415)565-3000. Fax (415)565-3012. E-mail tross@wested.org. Website http://www.WestEd.org. Glen Harvey, CEO. WestEd is a nonprofit research, development, and service agency dedicated to improving education and other opportunities for children, youth, and adults. Drawing on the best from research and practice, WestEd works with practitioners and policymakers to address critical issues in education and other related areas, including early childhood intervention; curriculum, instruction and assessment; the use of technology; career and technical preparation; teacher and administrator professional development; science and mathematics education; and safe schools and communities. WestEd was created in 1995 to unite and enhance the capacity of Far West Laboratory and Southwest Regional Laboratory, two of the nation's original education laboratories. In addition to its work across the nation, WestEd serves as the regional education laboratory for Arizona, California, Nevada, and Utah. A publications catalog is available.

Western Public Radio (WPR). Ft. Mason Center, Bldg. D, San Francisco, CA 94123. (415)771-1160. Fax (415)771-4343. E-mail wprsf@aol.com. Karolyn van Putten, Ph.D., Pres./ CEO; Lynn Chadwick, Vice Pres./COO. WPR provides analog and digital audio production training, public radio program proposal consultation, and studio facilities for rent. WPR also sponsors a continuing education resource for audio producers, www.radiocollege.org.

World Future Society (WFS). 7910 Woodmont Ave., Suite 450, Bethesda, MD 20814. (301)656-8274, fax (301)951-0394. E-mail wfsinfo@wfs.org. Website http://www.wfs.org. Edward Cornish, Pres. Organization of individuals interested in the study of future trends and possibilities. Its purpose is to provide information on trends and scenarios so that individuals and organizations can better plan their future. *Membership:* 30,000. *Dues:* $39, general; $95, professional; call Society for details on all membership levels and benefits. *Meeting:* 1999, Ninth General Assembly, July 29-Aug 1, Washington; 2000, Annual Conference, July 23-25, Houston. *Publications: The Futurist: A Journal of Forecasts, Trends and Ideas About the Future; Futures Research Quarterly; Future Survey.* The society's bookstore offers audio- and videotapes, books, and other items.

Young Adult Library Services Association (YALSA). 50 E. Huron St., Chicago, IL 60611. (312)280-4390. Fax (312)664-7459. E-mail yalsa@ala.org. Website http://www .ala.organization/yalsa. Julie A. Walker, Exec. Dir.; Linda Waddle, Deputy Exec. Dir.; Joel Shoemaker, Pres. An affiliate of the American Library Association, YALSA seeks to advocate, promote, and strengthen service to young adults as part of the continuum of total library services, and assumes responsibility within the ALA to evaluate and select books and non-book media and to interpret and make recommendations regarding their use with young adults. Committees include Best Books for Young Adults, Popular Paperbacks, Recommended Books for the Reluctant Young Adult Reader, Media Selection and Usage, Publishers' Liaison, and Selected Films for Young Adults. *Membership:* 2,223. *Dues:* $40 (in addition to ALA membership); $15, students. *Publication: Journal of Youth Services in Libraries* (q.).

Canada

This section includes information on nine Canadian organizations whose principal interests lie in the general fields of educational media, instructional technology, and library and information science.

*ACCESS NETWORK. 3720—76 Ave., Edmonton, AB T6B 2N9, Canada. (403)440-7777. Fax (403)440-8899. E-mail promo@ccinet.ab.ca. Dr. Ronald Keast, Pres.; John Verburgt, Creative Services Manager. The ACCESS Network (Alberta Educational Communications Corporation) was purchased by Learning and Skills Television of Alberta in 1995. The newly privatized network works with Alberta's educators to provide all Albertans with a progressive and diverse television-based educational and training resource to support their learning and skills development needs using cost-effective methods and innovative techniques, and to introduce a new private sector model for financing and efficient operation of educational television in the province.

Association for Media and Technology in Education in Canada (AMTEC). 3-1750 The Queensway, Suite 1318, Etobicoke, ON M9C 5H5, Canada. (604)323-5627. Fax (604)323-5577. E-mail maepp@langara.bc.ca. Website http://www.amtec.ca. Dr. Geneviev Gallant, Pres.; Dr. .Len Proctor, Pres. Elect; Mary Anne Epp, Sec./Treas. AMTEC is Canada's national association for educational media and technology professionals. The organization provides national leadership through annual conferences, publications, workshops, media festivals, and awards. It responds to media and technology issues at the international, national, provincial, and local levels, and maintains linkages with other organizations with similar interests. *Membership:* AMTEC members represent all sectors of the educational media and technology fields. *Dues:* $101.65, Canadian regular; $53.50, student and retiree. *Meeting:* Annual Conferences take place in late May or early June. 1999, Ottawa; 2000, Vancouver. *Publications: Canadian Journal of Educational Communication* (q.); *Media News* (3/yr.); *Membership Directory* (with membership).

*Canadian Broadcasting Corporation (CBC)/Société Radio-Canada (SRC). P.O. Box 500, Station A, Toronto, Ontario, Canada. Website http://www.cbc.ca. The CBC is a publicly owned corporation established in 1936 by an Act of the Canadian Parliament to provide a national broadcasting service in Canada in the two official languages. CBC services include English and French television networks; English and French AM mono and FM stereo radio networks virtually free of commercial advertising; CBC North, which serves Canada's North by providing radio and television programs in English, French, and eight native languages; Newsworld and its French counterpart, Le Réseau de l'information (RDI), 24-hour national satellites to cable English-language and French-language news and information service respectively, both funded entirely by cable subscription and commercial advertising revenues; and Radio Canada International, a shortwave radio service that broadcasts in seven languages and is managed by CBC and financed by External Affairs. The CBC is financed mainly by public funds voted annually by Parliament.

Canadian Education Association/Association canadienne d'éducation (CEA). 252 Bloor St. W., Suite 8-200, Toronto, ON M5S 1V5, Canada. (416)924-7721. Fax (416)924-3188. E-mail cea-ace@acea.ca. Website http://www.acea.ca. Penny Milton, Exec. Dir.; Suzanne Tanguay, Dir. of Communication Services. The Canadian equivalent of the U.S. National Education Association, CEA has one central objective: to promote the improvement of education. It is the only national, bilingual organization whose function is to inform, assist, and bring together all sectors of the educational community. *Membership:* all 12 provincial and territorial departments of education, the federal government, 400 individuals, 120 organizations, 100 school boards. *Dues:* $120, indiv.; $320, organization; $500, businesses; 10 cents per pupil, school boards. *Meetings:* Annual CEA Convention. *Publications: Promoting*

Achievement in School: What Works; CEA Handbook; Education Canada (q.); *CEA News-letter* (8/yr.); *Education in Canada: An Overview; Class Size, Academic Achievement and Public Policy; Disruptive Behaviour in Today's Classroom; Financing Canadian Education; Secondary Schools in Canada: The National Report of the Exemplary Schools Project; Making Sense of the Canadian Charter of Rights and Freedom: A Handbook for Administrators and Teachers; The School Calendar.*

Canadian Library Association. 200 Elgin St., Suite 602, Ottawa, ON K2P IL5, Canada. (613)232-9625. Fax (613)563-9895. E-mail ai075@freenet.carleton.ca. Website http://www.cla.amlibs.ca. Vicki Whitmell, Exec. Dir. The mission of the Canadian Library Association is to provide leadership in the promotion, development, and support of library and information services in Canada for the benefit of Association members, the profession, and Canadian society. In the spirit of this mission, CLA aims to engage the active, creative participation of library staff, trustees, and governing bodies in the development and management of high quality Canadian library service; to assert and support the right of all Canadians to the freedom to read and to free universal access to a wide variety of library materials and services; to promote librarianship and to enlighten all levels of government as to the significant role that libraries play in educating and socializing the Canadian people; and to link libraries, librarians, trustees, and others across the country for the purpose of providing a unified nationwide voice in matters of critical concern. *Membership:* 2,300 individuals, 700 institutions, 100 Associates and Trustees. *Dues:* $50-$300. *Meetings:* 1999 Annual Conference, Jun 18-22, Toronto; 2000, Edmonton, June. *Publication: Feliciter* (membership magazine, 10/yr.).

Canadian Museums Association/Association des musées canadiens (CMA/AMC). 280 Metcalfe St., Suite 400, Ottawa, ON K2P 1R7, Canada. (613)567-0099. Fax (613)233-5438. E-mail info@museums.ca. Website http://www.museums.ca. John G. McAvity, Exec. Dir. The Canadian Museums Association is a nonprofit corporation and registered charity dedicated to advancing public museums and museum works in Canada, promoting the welfare and better administration of museums, and fostering a continuing improvement in the qualifications and practices of museum professionals. *Membership:* 2,000. *Meeting:* CMA Annual Conference, spring. *Publications: Museogramme* (bi-mo. newsletter); *Muse* (q. journal, Canada's only national, bilingual, scholarly magazine devoted to museums, it contains museum-based photography, feature articles, commentary, and practical information); *The Official Directory of Canadian Museums and Related Institutions* (1997-99 edition) lists all museums in Canada plus information on government departments, agencies, and provincial and regional museum associations.

Canadian Publishers' Council (CPC). 250 Merton St., Suite 203, Toronto, ON M4S 1B1 Canada. (416)322-7011. Fax (416)322-6999. Website http://www.pubcouncil.ca. Jacqueline Hushion, Exec. Dir. CPC members publish and distribute an extensive list of Canadian and imported learning materials in a complete range of formats from traditional textbook and ancillary materials to CDs and interactive video. The primary markets for CPC members are schools, universities and colleges, bookstores, and libraries. CPC also provides exhibits throughout the year and works through a number of subcommittees and groups within the organization to promote effective book publishing. CPC was founded in 1910. *Membership:* 27 companies, educational institutions, or government agencies that publish books as an important facet of their work.

National Film Board of Canada (NFBC). 350 Fifth Ave., Suite 4820, New York, NY 10118. (212)629-8890. Fax (212)629-8502. E-mail gsem78a@prodigy.com. John Sirabella, U.S. Marketing Mgr./Nontheatrical Rep. Established in 1939, the NFBC's main objective is to produce and distribute high-quality audiovisual materials for educational, cultural, and social purposes.

Ontario Film Association, Inc. (also known as the Association for the Advancement of Visual Media/L'association pour l'avancement des médias visuels). 100 Lombard St. 303, Toronto, ON M5C 1M3 Canada (416)363-3388; Fax:1-800-387-1181, E-mail info @accessola.com. Website www.accessola.org. Lawrence A. Moore, Exec. Dir. A membership organization of buyers, and users of media whose objectives are to promote the sharing of ideas and information about visual media through education, publications, and advocacy. *Membership:* 112. *Dues:* $120, personal membership; $215, associate membership. *Meeting:* OFA Media Showcase, spring.

Part Four
Graduate Programs

Introduction

This directory describes graduate programs in Instructional Technology, Educational Media and Communications, School Library Media, and closely allied programs in the United States. This year's list includes four new programs. One institution indicated that its program had been discontinued, so it has been deleted from the listings. Master's, Specialist, and doctoral degrees are combined into one unified list.

Information in this section can be considered current as of late 1999 for most programs. In the majority of cases, department chairs or their representatives responded to a questionnaire mailed or e-mailed to them during November 1999. Programs for which we received no updated information are indicated by an asterisk (*).

Entries provide as much of the following information as was furnished by respondents: (1) name and address of the institution; (2) chairperson or other individual in charge of the program; (3) types of degrees offered and specializations, emphases, or tracks, including information on careers for which candidates are prepared; (4) special features of the degree program; (5) admission requirements; (6) degree requirements; (7) number of full-time and part-time faculty; (8) number of full-time and part-time students; (9) types of financial assistance available; and (10) the number of degrees awarded by type in 1998. All grade point averages (GPAs), test scores, and degree requirements are minimums unless stated otherwise. The Graduate Record Examination, Miller Analogies Test, National Teacher's Examination, and other standardized tests are referred to by their acronyms. The Test of English as a Foreign Language (TOEFL) appears in many of the *Admission Requirements,* and in most cases this test is required only for international students. Although some entries explicitly state application fees, most do not. Prospective students should assume that most institutions require a completed application, transcripts of all previous collegiate work, and a nonrefundable application fee.

Directors of advanced professional programs for instructional technology or media specialists should find this degree program information useful as a means of comparing their own offerings and requirements with those of institutions offering comparable programs. The Alphabetical Listing, along with the Classified List, should also assist individuals in locating institutions that best suit their interests and requirements. In addition, a comparison of degree programs across several years may help scholars with historical interests trace trends and issues in the field over time.

Additional information on the programs listed, including admission procedure instructions, may be obtained by contacting individual program coordinators. General or graduate catalogs and specific program information usually are furnished for a minimal charge. In addition, most graduate programs now have e-mail contact addresses and Websites that provide a wealth of descriptive information.

We are greatly indebted to those individuals who responded to our requests for information. Although the editors expended considerable effort to ensure currency and completeness of the listings, there may be institutions within the United States that now have programs of which we are unaware. Readers are encouraged to furnish new information to the publisher who, in turn, will contact the program for inclusion in the next edition of *EMTY*.

Oratile Maribe Branch

Section Editor

Graduate Programs in Instructional Technology [IT]

CLASSIFIED LIST

Computer Applications

California State University-San Bernardino [M.A.]
State University of New York at Stony Brook [Master's: Technological Systems Management/Educational Computing]
University of Iowa [M.A.]
Valdosta State University [M.Ed. in IT/Technology Applications]

Computer Education

Appalachian State University [M.A.: Educational Media and Technology/Computers]
Arizona State University, Dept. of Educational Media and Computers [M.A., Ph.D.: Educational Media and Computers]
Arkansas Tech University [Master's]
Buffalo State College [M.S.: Education/Educational Computing]
California State University-Dominguez Hills [M.A., Certificate: Computer-Based Education]
California State University-Los Angeles [M.A. in Education/Computer Education]
California State University-San Bernardino [Advanced Certificate Program: Educational Computing]
Central Connecticut State University [M.S.: Educational Technology/Computer Technologies]
Concordia University [M.A.: Computer Science Education]
East Carolina University [M.A.: Education/IT Computers]
Eastern Washington University [M.Ed.: Computer Education]
Fairfield University [M.A.: Media/Educational Technology with Computers in Education]
Florida Institute of Technology [Master's, Ph.D.: Computer Education]
Fontbonne College [M.S.]
George Mason University [M.Ed.: Special Education Technology, Computer Science Educator]
Iowa State University [M.S., M.Ed., Ph.D.: Curriculum and IT/Instructional Computing]
Jacksonville University [Master's: Computer Education]
Kansas State University [M.S. in Secondary Education/Educational Computing; Ed.D., Ph.D.: Curriculum and Instruction/Educational Computing]

Kent State University [M.A., M.Ed.: Instructional Computing]
Minot State University [M.Ed., M.S.: Math and Computer Science]
New York Institute of Technology [Specialist Certificate: Computers in Education]
North Carolina State University [M.S., M.Ed.: IT-Computers]
Northern Illinois University [M.S.Ed., Ed.D.: IT/Educational Computing]
Northwest Missouri State University [M.S.: School Computer Studies; M.S.Ed.: Educational Uses of Computers]
Nova Southeastern University [M.S., Ed.S.: Computer Science Education]
Ohio University [M.Ed.: Computer Education and Technology]
Pace University [M.S.E.: Curriculum and Instruction/Computers]
San Diego State University [Master's in Educational Technology/Computers in Education]
San Francisco State University [Master's: Instructional Computing]
San Jose State University [Master's: Computers and Interactive Technologies]
State University of New York at Stony Brook [Master's: Technological Systems Management/Educational Computing]
State University College of Arts and Sciences at Potsdam [M.S.Ed.: IT and Media Management/Educational Computing]
Syracuse University [M.S., Ed.D., Ph.D., Advanced Certificate: Media Production]
Texas A&M University-Commerce [Master's: Learning Technology and Information Systems/Educational Micro Computing]
Texas Tech University [M.Ed.: IT/Educational Computing]
University of Georgia [M.Ed., Ed.S.: Computer-Based Education]
University of Illinois at Urbana-Champaign [M.A., M.S., Ed.M.: Educational Computing; Ph.D.: Education Psychology/Educational Computing]
University of North Texas [M.S.: Computer Education and Instructional Systems]
The University of Oklahoma [Master's: Computer Applications]
University of Toledo [Master's, Ed.S., D.Ed.: Instructional Computing]

University of Washington [Master's, Ed.D., Ph.D.]
Virginia Polytechnic Institute and State University [M.A., Ed.D., Ph.D.: IT]
Wright State University [M.Ed.: Computer Education; M.A.: Computer Education]

Distance Education
Fairfield University [M.A.: Media/Educational Technology with Satellite Communications]
Iowa State University [M.S., M.Ed., Ph.D.: Curriculum and IT]
New York Institute of Technology [Specialist certificate]
Nova Southeastern University [M.S., Ed.D.: IT]
San Jose State University [Master's: Telecommunications & online courses via Internet]
Texas A&M University [Ph.D.: EDCI]
Texas Tech University [M.Ed.: IT]
University of Northern Colorado [Ph.D.: Educational Technology]
Western Illinois University [Master's]

Educational Leadership
Auburn University [Ed.D.]
Barry University [Ph.D.: Educational Technology Leadership]
George Washington University [M.A.: Education and Human Development/Educational Technology Leadership]
United States International University [Master's, Ed.D.: Technology Leadership for Learning]
University of Colorado at Denver [Ph.D.: Educational Leadership and Innovation/Curriculum, Learning, and Technology]
Valdosta State University [M.Ed., Ed.S.: IT/Technology Leadership]

Human Performance
Boise State University [M.S.: IT and Performance Technology]
Governors State University [M.A.: Communication with Human Performance and Technology]
University of Southern California [Ed.D.: Human Performance Technology]
University of Toledo [Master's, Ed.S., Ed.D.: Human Resources Development]

Information Studies
Drexel University [M.S., M.S.I.S.]
Emporia State University [Ph.D.: Library and Information Management]
Rutgers [M.L.S.: Information Retrieval; Ph.D.: Communication (Information Systems)]
Simmons College [M.S.: Information Science/Systems]
Southern Connecticut State University [Sixth Year Professional Diploma: Library-Information Studies/IT]

St. Cloud State University [Master's, Ed.S.: Information Technologies]
Texas A&M-Commerce [Master's: Learning Technology and Information Systems/Library and Information Science]
University of Alabama [Ph.D.]
University of Arizona [M.A.: Information Resources and Library Science]
University of Central Arkansas [M.S.: Information Science/Media Information Studies]
University of Maryland [Doctorate: Library and Information Services]
University of Missouri-Columbia [Ph.D.: Information and Learning Technologies]
The University of Oklahoma [Dual Master's: Educational Technology and Library and Information Systems]
The University of Rhode Island [M.L.I.S.]
University of Washington [Master's, Ed.D., Ph.D.]
Western Oregon State College [MS: Information Technology]

Innovation
Pennsylvania State University [M.Ed., M.S., Ed.D., Ph.D.: Instructional Systems/Emerging Technologies]
University of Colorado at Denver [Ph.D.: Educational Leadership and Innovation]
Walden University [M.S., Ph.D.: Educational Change and Technology Innovation]

Instructional Design and Development
Auburn University [M.Ed., M.S.]
Bloomsburg University [M.S.: IT]
Brigham Young University [M.S., Ph.D.]
Clarion University of Pennsylvania [M.S.: Communication/Training and Development]
Fairfield University [Certificate of Advanced Studies: Media/Educational Technology: Instructional Development]
George Mason University [M.Ed.: IT/Instructional Design and Development]
Governors State University [M.A.: Communication with Human Performance and Training/Instructional Design]
Indiana University [Ph.D., Ed.D.: Instructional Analysis, Design, and Development]
Iowa State University [M.S., M.Ed., Ph.D.: Curriculum and IT/Instruction Design]
Ithaca College [M.S.: Corporate Communications]
Lehigh University [Master's]
Michigan State University [M.A.: Educational Technology and Instructional Design]
North Carolina Central University [M.S.: Instructional Development/Design]
Northern Illinois University [M.S.Ed., Ed.D.: IT/Instructional Design]

Pennsylvania State University [M.Ed., M.S., D.Ed., Ph.D.: Instructional Systems/Systems Design]

Purdue University [Master's, Specialist, Ph.D.: Instructional Development]

San Francisco State University [Master's/Training and Designing Development]

San Jose State University [M.S.: Instructional Design and Development]

Southern Illinois University at Carbondale [M.S.: Education/Instructional Design]

State University of New York at Albany [M.Ed., Ph.D.: Curriculum and Instruction/Instructional Design and Technology]

State University of New York at Stony Brook [Master's: Technological Systems Management/Educational Computing]

Syracuse University [M.S., Ed.D., Ph.D., Advanced Certificate: Instructional Design; Educational Evaluation; Instructional Development]

Towson State University [M.S.: Instructional Development]

University of Cincinnati [M.A., Ed.D.: Curriculum and Instruction/Instructional Design and Technology]

University of Colorado at Denver [Master's, Ph.D.: Instructional Design]

University of Houston at Clear Lake [Instructional Design]

University of Illinois at Urbana-Champaign [M.A., M.S., Ed.M.; Ph.D. in Educational Psychology/Instructional Design]

University of Iowa [M.A., Ph.D.: Training and Human Resources Development]

University of Massachusetts-Boston [M.Ed.]

University of Northern Colorado [Ph.D. in Educational Technology/Instructional Development and Design]

The University of Oklahoma [Master's]

University of Toledo [Master's, Specialist, doctorate: Instructional Development]

University of Washington [Master's, Ed.D., Ph.D.]

Utah State University [M.S., Ed.S.: Instructional Development]

Virginia Polytechnic Institute and State University [Master's, Ed.D., Ph.D.: IT]

Instructional Technology [IT]

Appalachian State University [M.A.: Educational Media and Technology]

Arizona State University, Learning and IT Dept. [M.Ed., Ph.D.]

Azusa Pacific University [M.Ed.]

Barry University [M.S., Ed.S.: Educational Technology]

Bloomsburg University [M.S.: IT]

Boise State University [M.S.]

Boston University [Ed.M., Certificate of Advanced Graduate Study: Educational Media & Technology; Ed.D.: Curriculum and Teaching/Educational Media and Technology]

California State University-Los Angeles [M.A.: Education/IT]

California State University-San Bernardino [Advanced Certificate in Educational Technology]

Central Connecticut State University [M.S.: Educational Technology]

Clarke College [M.A.: Technology and Education]

East Carolina University [M.A.: Education/IT Computers]

East Tennessee State [M.Ed.]

Eastern Michigan University [M.A.: Educational Psychology/Educational Technology]

Edgewood College [M.A.: Education/IT]

Fairfield University [M.A., Certificate of Advanced Study: Media/Educational Technology]

Fitchburg State College [M.S.: Communications Media/IT]

Florida Institute of Technology [Master's, Ph.D.]

George Mason University [M.Ed., Ph.D.]

George Washington University [M.A.: Education and Human Development/Educational Technology Leadership]

Georgia Southern University [M.Ed., Ed.S.: IT; Ed.D.: Curriculum Studies/IT]

Georgia State University [M.S., Ph.D.]

Harvard University [M.Ed.: Technology in Education]

Indiana State University [Master's, Ed.S.]

Indiana University [M.S., Ed.S., Ed.D., Ph.D.]

Iowa State University [M.S., M.Ed., Ph.D.: Curriculum and IT]

Jacksonville University [Master's: Educational Technology and Integrated Learning]

Johns Hopkins University [M.S. in Educational Technology for Educators]

Kent State University [M.Ed., M.A; Ph.D.: Educational Psychology/IT]

Lehigh University [Master's; Ed.D.: Educational Technology]

Lesley College [M.Ed., Certificate of Advanced Graduate Study: Technology Education; Ph.D.: Education/Technology Education]

Mankato State University [M.S.: Educational Technology]

Michigan State University [M.A.: Educational Technology]

Montclair State College [certification]

New York Institute of Technology [Master's]

New York University [M.A., Certificate of Advanced Study in Education, Ed.D., Ph.D.]

North Carolina Central University [M.A.: Educational Technology]

North Carolina State University [M.Ed., M.S.: It— Computers; Ph.D.: Curriculum and Instruction/IT]

Northern Illinois University [M.S.Ed., Ed.D.]

Nova Southeastern University [Ed.S., M.S.: Educational Technology; M.S., Ed.D.: IT]

Ohio University [M.Ed.: Computer Education and Technology]

Purdue University [Master's, Specialist, Ph.D.: Educational Technology]

Radford University [M.S.: Education/Educational Media/Technology]

Rosemont College [M.Ed.: Technology in Education; Certificate in Professional Study in Technology in Education]

San Diego State University [Master's: Educational Technology]

Southern Connecticut State University [M.S.]

Southern Illinois University at Carbondale [M.S.: Education; Ph.D.: Education/IT]

State University College of Arts and Sciences at Potsdam [M.S.: Education/IT]

State University of New York at Albany [M.Ed., Ph.D.: Curriculum and Instruction/Instructional Theory, Design, and Technology]

State University of West Georgia [M.Ed., Ed.S.]

Texas A&M University [M.Ed.: Educational Technology; Ph.D.: EDCI/Educational Technology; Ph.D.: Educational Psychology Foundations/Learning and Technology]

Texas Tech University [M.Ed.; Ed.D.]

Texas A&M University-Commerce [Master's: Learning Technology and Information Systems/Educational Media and Technology]

United States International University [Ed.D.: Technology and Learning]

University of Central Florida [M.A.: IT/Instructional Systems, IT/Educational Media; doctorate: Curriculum and Instruction/IT]

University of Cincinnati [M.A., Ed.D.: Curriculum and Instruction/Instructional Design and Technology]

University of Colorado at Denver [Master's, Ph.D.: Learning Technologies]

University of Connecticut [Master's, Ph.D.: Educational Technology]

University of Georgia [M.Ed., Ed.S., Ph.D.]

University of Hawaii-Manoa [M.Ed.: Educational Technology]

University of Louisville [M.Ed.: Occupational Education/IT]

University of Maryland [Ph.D.: Library Science and Educational Technology/Instructional Communication]

University of Massachusetts-Lowell [M.Ed., Ed.D., Certificate of Advanced Graduate Study: Educational Technology]

University of Michigan [Master's, Ph.D.: IT]

University of Missouri-Columbia [Master's, Ed.S., Ph.D.]

University of Nebraska at Kearney [M.S.]

University of Nevada [M.S., Ph.D.]

University of Northern Colorado [M.A., Ph.D.: Educational Technology]

University of Northern Iowa [M.A.: Educational Technology]

The University of Oklahoma [Master's: Educational Technology Generalist; Educational Technology; Teaching with Technology; dual Master's: Educational Technology and Library and Information Systems; doctorate: Instructional Psychology and Technology]

University of South Alabama [M.S., Ph.D.]

University of South Carolina [Master's]

University of Southern California [M.A., Ed.D., Ph.D.]

University of Tennessee-Knoxville [M.S.: Education, Ed.S., Ed.D., Ph.D.]

The University of Texas [Master's, Ph.D.]

University of Toledo [Master's, Specialist, doctorate]

University of Virginia [M.Ed., Ed.S., Ed.D., Ph.D.]

University of Washington [Master's, Ed.D., Ph.D.]

University of Wisconsin-Madison [M.S., Ph.D.]

Utah State University [M.S., Ed.S., Ph.D.]

Virginia Polytechnic Institute and State University [M.A., Ed.D., Ph.D.: IT]

Virginia State University [M.S., M.Ed.: Educational Technology]

Wayne State University [Master's, Ed.D., Ph.D., Ed.S.]

Webster University [Master's]

Western Illinois University [Master's]

Western Washington University [M.Ed.: IT in Adult Education; Elementary Education; IT in Secondary Education]

Wright State University [Specialist: Curriculum and Instruction/Educational Technology; Higher Education/Educational Technology]

Integration

Bloomsburg University [M.S.: IT]

George Mason University [M.Ed.: IT/Integration of Technology in Schools]

Jacksonville University [Master's: Educational Technology and Integrated Learning]

University of Northern Colorado [Ph.D.: Educational Technology/Technology Integration]

Management

Bloomsburg University [M.S.: IT]

Central Connecticut State University [M.S.: Educational Technology/Media Management]

Drexel University [M.S., M.S.I.S.]

Emporia State University [Ph.D.: Library and Information Management]

Fairfield University [Certificate of Advanced Studies: Media/Educational Technology with Media Management]

Fitchburg State College [M.S.: Communications Media/Management]

Indiana University [Ed.D., Ph.D.: Implementation and Management]

Minot State University [M.S.: Management]

Northern Illinois University [M.S.Ed., Ed.D.: IT/Media Administration]

Rutgers [M.L.S.: Management and Policy Issues]

Simmons College [M.L.S.: History (Archives Management); Doctor of Arts: Administration; Media Management]

State University College of Arts and Science [M.S.: Education/IT and Media Management]

State University of New York at Stony Brook [Master's: Technological Systems Management]

Syracuse University [M.S., Ed.D., Ph.D., Advanced Certificate]

University of Tennessee-Knoxville [Certification: Instructional Media Supervisor]

Virginia Polytechnic Institute and State University [M.A., Ed.D., Ph.D.: IT]

Wright State University [M.Ed.: Media Supervisor; Computer Coord.]

Media

Appalachian State University [M.A.: Educational Media and Technology/Media Management]

Arizona State University, Dept. of Educational Media and Computers [M.A., Ph.D.: Educational Media and Computers]

Boston University [Ed.M., Certificate of Advanced Graduate Study: Educational Media and Technology; Ed.D.: Curriculum and Teaching/Educational Media and Technology]

Central Connecticut State University [M.S.: Educational Technology/Materials Production]

Fitchburg State College [M.S.: Communications Media]

Indiana State University [Ph.D.: Curriculum and Instruction/Media Technology]

Indiana University [Ed.D., Ph.D.: Instructional Development and Production]

Jacksonville State University [M.S.: Education/Instructional Media]

Montclair State College [certification]

Radford University [M.S.: Education/Educational Media/Technology]

San Jose State University [Master's.: Media Design and Development/Media Services Management]

Simmons College [Master's: Media Management]

St. Cloud State University [Master's, Ed.S.: Educational Media]

State University College of Arts and Science at Potsdam [M.S.: Education/IT and Media Management]

Syracuse University [M.S., Ed.D., Ph.D., Advanced Certificate: Media Production]

Texas A&M University-Commerce [Master's: Learning Technology and Information Systems/Educational Media and Technology]

University of Central Florida [M.Ed.: IT/Educational Media]

University of Iowa [M.A.: Media Design and Production]

University of Nebraska at Kearney [M.S., Ed.S.: Educational Media]

University of Nebraska-Omaha [M.S.: Education/Educational Media; M.A.: Education/Educational Media]

University of South Alabama [M.A., Ed.S.]

University of Tennessee-Knoxville [Ph.D.: Instructional Media and Technology; Ed.D.: Curriculum and Instruction/Instructional Media and Technology]

University of Virginia [M.Ed., Ed.S., Ed.D., Ph.D.: Media Production]

Virginia Polytechnic Institute and State University [M.A., Ed.D., Ph.D.: IT]

Wright State University [M.Ed.: Educational Media; Media Supervision; M.A.: Educational Media]

Multimedia

Bloomsburg University [M.S.: IT]

Brigham Young University [M.S.: Multimedia Production]

Fairfield University [M.A.: Media/Educational Technology with Multimedia]

Ithaca College [M.S.: Corporate Communications]

Jacksonville University [Master's: Educational Technology and Integration Learning]

Johns Hopkins University [Graduate Certificate]

Lehigh University [Master's]

New York Institute of Technology [Specialist Certificate]

San Francisco State University [Master's: Instructional Multimedia Design]

State University of New York at Stony Brook [Master's: Technological Systems Management/Educational Computing]

Syracuse University [M.S., Ed.D., Ph.D., Advanced Certificate: Media Production]

Texas A&M University [M.Ed.: Educational Technology]

University of Northern Colorado [Ph.D.: Educational Technology/Interactive Technology]

University of Virginia [M.Ed., Ed.S., Ed.D., Ph.D.: Interactive Multimedia]

University of Washington [Master's, Ed.D., Ph.D.]

Utah State University [M.S., Ed.S.]
Wayne State University [Master's: Interactive Technologies]
Western Illinois University [Master's: Interactive Technologies]

Research
Brigham Young University [M.S., Ph.D.: Research and Evaluation]
Drexel University [M.S., M.S.I.S.]
Iowa State University [Ph.D.: Educational/ Technology Research]
Syracuse University [M.S., Ed.D., Ph.D., Advanced Certificate: Educational Research and Theory]
University of Washington [Master's, Ed.D., Ph.D.]

School Library Media
Alabama State University [Master's, Ed.S., Ph.D.]
Arkansas Tech University [Master's]
Auburn University [M.ED., Ed.S.]
Bloomsburg University [M.S.]
Boston University [Massachusetts certification]
Bridgewater State College [M.Ed.]
Central Connecticut State University [M.S.: Educational Technology/Librarianship]
Chicago State University [Master's]
East Carolina University [M.L.S., Certificate of Advanced Study]
East Tennessee State [M.Ed.: Instructional Media]
Emporia State University [Ph.D.: Library and Information Management; M.L.S.; School Library certification]
Kent State University
Louisiana State University [M.L.I.S., C.L.I.S. (post-Master's certificate), Louisiana School Library certification]
Mankato State University [M.S.]
Northern Illinois University [M.S.Ed. Instructional Technology with Illinois state certification]
Nova Southeastern University [Ed.S, M.S.: Educational Media]
Radford University [M.S.: Education/Educational Media; licensure]
Rutgers [M.L.S., Ed.S.]
Simmons College [M.L.S.: Education]
Southern Illinois University at Edwardsville [M.S. in Education: Library/Media]
Southwestern Oklahoma State University [M.Ed.: Library/Media Education]
St. Cloud State University [Master's, Ed.S.]
St. John's University [M.L.S.]
State University of West Georgia [M.Ed., Ed.S.: Media]
Towson State University [M.S.]
University of Alabama [Master's, Ed.S.]
University of Central Arkansas [M.S.]
University of Georgia [M.Ed., Ed.S]
University of Maryland [M.L.S.]

University of Montana [Master's, Ed.S.]
University of North Carolina [M.S.]
University of Northern Colorado [M.A.: Educational Media]
University of South Florida [Master's]
University of Toledo
University of Wisconsin-La Crosse [M.S.: Professional Development/Initial Instructional Library Specialist; Instructional Library Media Specialist]
Utah State University [M.S., Ed.S.]
Valdosta State University [M.Ed., Ed.S.: Instructional Technology/Library/Media]
Webster University
Western Maryland College [M.S.]
William Paterson College [M.Ed., Ed.S., Associate]

Special Education
George Mason University [M.Ed.: IT/Assistive/ Special Education Technology; M.Ed.: Special Education Technology; Ph.D.: Special Education Technology]
Johns Hopkins University [M.S. in Special Education/Technology in Special Education]
Minot State University [M.S.: Early Childhood Special Education; Severe Multiple Handicaps; Communication Disorders]
Western Washington University [M.Ed.: IT in Special Education]

Systems
Bloomsburg University [M.S.: IT]
Drexel University [M.S., M.S.I.S.]
Florida State University [M.S., Ed.S., Ph.D.: Instructional Systems]
Pennsylvania State University [M.Ed., M.S., D.Ed., Ph.D.: Instructional Systems]
Simmons College [Master's: Information Science/Systems]
Southern Illinois University at Edwardsville [M.S.: Education/Instructional Systems Design]
State University of New York at Stony Brook [Master's: Technological Systems Management]
Texas A&M University-Commerce [Master's: Learning Technology and Information Systems]
University of Central Florida [M.A.: IT/Instructional Systems]
University of Maryland, Baltimore County [Master's: School Instructional Systems]
University of North Texas [M.S.: Computer Education and Instructional Systems]
The University of Oklahoma [Dual Master's: Educational Technology and Library and Information Systems]

Technology Design
Governors State University [M.A.: Design Logistics]
Kansas State University [Ed.D., Ph.D.: Curriculum and Instruction/Educational Computing, Design, and Telecommunications]
United States International University [Master's, Ed.D.: Designing Technology for Learning]
University of Colorado at Denver [Master's, Ph.D.: Design of Learning Technologies]

Telecommunications
Appalachian State University [M.A.: Educational Media and Technology/Telecommunications]
Johns Hopkins University [Graduate Certificate]
Kansas State University [Ed.D., Ph.D.: Curriculum and Instruction/Educational Computing, Design, and Telecommunications]
San Jose State University [Telecommunications and Distance Learning]
Western Illinois University [Masters: Telecommunications]

Training
Clarion University of Pennsylvania [M.S.: Communication/Training and Development]

Pennsylvania State University [M.Ed., M.S., D.Ed., Ph.D.: Instructional Systems/Corporate Training]
St. Cloud State University [Master's, Ed.S.: Human Resources Development/Training]
Syracuse University [M.S., Ed.D., Ph.D., Advanced Certificate]
University of Maryland, Baltimore County [Master's: Training in Business and Industry]
University of Northern Iowa [M.A.: Communications and Training Technology]
Wayne State University [Master's: Business and Human Services Training]

Video Production
California State University-San Bernardino [M.A.]
Fairfield University [Certificate of Advanced Study: Media/Educational Technology with TV Production]

ALPHABETICAL LIST

Institutions in this section are listed alphabetically by state.

ALABAMA

Alabama State University. P.O. Box 271, Montgomery, AL 36101-0271. (334)229-4462. Fax (334)229-4961. Website http://www.alasu.edu. Dr. Deborah Little, Coord. Instructional Technology and Media. *Specializations:* School media specialist preparation (K–12) only; Master's and Specialist degrees. *Admission Requirements:* Master's: undergraduate degree with teacher certification, two years' classroom experience. Specialist: Master's degree in library/media education. *Degree Requirements:* Master's: 33 semester hours with 300 clock-hour internship. Specialist: 33 semester hours in 600-level courses. *Faculty:* 3 full-time, 2 part-time. *Students:* Master's, 27 part-time; Specialist, 6 part-time. *Financial Assistance:* assistantships, student loans, and scholarships. *Degrees Awarded 1997:* Master's, 9; Specialist, 1.

Auburn University. Educational Foundations, Leadership, and Technology, 3402 Haley Center, Auburn, AL 36849-5216. (334)844-4291. Fax (334)844-4292. E-mail bannosh@mail.auburn.edu. Susan H. Bannon, Coord., Educational Media and Technology. *Specializations:* M.Ed. (non-thesis) and Ed.S. for Library Media certification; M.Ed. (non-thesis) for instructional design specialists who want to work in business, industry, and the military. Ed.D. in Educational Leadership with emphasis on curriculum and new instructional technologies. *Features:* All programs emphasize interactive technologies and computers. *Admission Requirements:* All programs: recent GRE test scores, 3 letters of recommendation, bachelor's degree from accredited institution, teacher certification (for library media program only). *Degree Requirements:* Library Media Master's: 52 qtr. hours. Instructional Design: 48 qtr. hours. Specialist: 48 qtr. hours. Ed.D.: 120 qtr. hours beyond B.S. degree. *Faculty:* 3 full-time, *Students:* 2 full-time, 15 part-time. *Financial Assistance:* graduate assistantships.

Jacksonville State University. Instructional Media Div., Jacksonville, AL 36265. (256)782-5011. E-mail mmerrill@jsucc.jsu.edu. Martha Merrill, Coord., Dept. of Educational Resources. *Specializations:* M.S. in Education with emphasis on Library Media. *Admission Requirements:* Bachelor's degree in Education. *Degree Requirements:* 36-39 semester hours including 24 in library media. *Faculty:* 2 full-time. *Students:* 20 full- and part-time. *Degrees Awarded 1997:* approx. 10.

University of Alabama. School of Library and Information Studies, Box 870252, Tuscaloosa, AL 35487-0252. (205)348-4610. Fax (205)348-3746. E-mail GCOLEMAN@UA1VM.UA.EDU. Website http://www.slism.slis.ua.edu. J. Gordon Coleman, Jr., Chair. Marion Paris, Ph.D., contact person. *Specializations:* M.L.I.S., Ed.S., and Ph.D. degrees in a varied program including school, public, academic, and special libraries. Ph.D. specializations in Historical Studies, Information Studies, Management, and Youth Studies; considerable flexibility in creating individual programs of study. *Admission Requirements:* M.L.I.S., Ed.S.: 3.0 GPA; 50 MAT or 1500 GRE. Doctoral: 3.0 GPA; 60 MAT or 1650 GRE. *Degree Requirements:* Master's: 36 semester hours. Specialist: 33 semester hours. Doctoral: 48 semester hours plus 24 hours dissertation research. *Faculty:* 10 full-time. *Students:* Master's, 55 full-time, 20 part-time; Specialist, 2 full-time; doctoral, 6 full-time, 6 part-time. *Financial Assistance:* assistantships, grants, student loans, scholarships, work assistance, campus work. *Degrees Awarded 1997:* Master's, 69; Ph.D., 1.

University of South Alabama. Dept. of Behavioral Studies and Educational Technology, College of Education, University Commons 3100, Mobile, AL 36688. (334)380-2861. Fax (334)380-2758. John Lane, Dept. Chair; Gayle Davidson-Shivers, Program Dir. *Specializations:* M.A. and Ed.S. in Educational Media, M.S. in Instructional Technology, Ph.D. in Instructional Technology. *Features:* The program emphasizes an extensive training sequence in the instructional systems design process, as well as multimedia-based training. *Admissions Requirements:* Master's: undergraduate degree in appropriate academic field; admission to Graduate School; 40 MAT or 800 GRE (any two areas). Ph.D.: Master's degree, transcripts, three recommendations, goal statement, GRE score. *Degree Requirements:* Master's: 3.0 GPA, 61 qtr. hours. Ph.D.: 120 qtr. hours, dissertation. *Faculty:* 20 full-time in department. *Students:* Master's, 30; Ph.D., 65. *Financial Assistance:* 10 graduate assistantships. *Degrees Awarded 1997:* 10.

ARIZONA

Arizona State University, Dept. of Learning and Instructional Technology. Box 870611, Tempe, AZ 85287-0611. (602)965-3384. Fax (602)965-0300. Website http://seamonkey.ed.asu.edu/~gail/programs/lnt.htm. James D. Klein, Prof. (james.klein@asu.edu); Nancy Archer, Admissions Secretary (icnla@asuvm.inre.asu.edu). *Specializations:* M.Ed. and Ph.D. with focus on the design, development, and evaluation of learning systems. *Features:* Research and publication prior to candidacy. *Admission Requirements:* M.Ed.: 3.0 undergraduate GPA, 500 GRE (verbal) or 50 MAT, 550 TOEFL. Ph.D.: 3.2 undergraduate GPA, 1200 GRE (V+Q), 600 TOEFL. *Degree Requirements:* M.Ed.: 30 semester hours, internship, comprehensive exam. Ph.D.: 84 semester hours beyond bachelor's degree, comprehensive exam, research/publication, dissertation. *Faculty:* 6 full-time. *Students:* M.Ed., 15 full-time, 20 part-time; Ph.D., 10 full-time, 10 part-time. *Financial Assistance:* assistantships, tuition waivers, and student loans for qualified applicants. *Degrees Awarded 1997:* M.Ed., 11; Ph.D., 2.

Arizona State University, Dept. of Educational Media and Computers. Box 870111, Tempe, AZ 85287-0111. (602)965-7192. Fax (602)965-7193. E-mail bitter@asu.edu. Dr. Gary G. Bitter, Coord. *Specializations:* M.A. and Ph.D. in Educational Media and Computers. *Features:* A three semester-hour course in Instructional Media Design is offered via CD-ROM or World Wide Web. *Admission Requirements:* M.A.: Bachelor's degree, 550 TOEFL, 500 GRE, 45 MAT. *Degree Requirements:* M.A.: 36 semester hours (24 hours in educational media and computers, 9 hours education, 3 hours outside education); internship; comprehensive exam; practicum; thesis not required. Ph.D.: 93 semester hours (24 hours in educational media and computers, 57 hours in education, 12 hours outside education); thesis; internship; practicum. *Faculty:* 5 full-time, 1 part-time. *Financial Assistance:* assistantships, grants, student loans, and scholarships.

University of Arizona. School of Information Resources and Library Science, 1515 E. First St., Tucson, AZ 85719. (520)621-3565. Fax (520)621-3279. E-mail sirls@u.arizona.edu. Website http://www.sir.arizona.edu. The School of Information Resources and Library Science offers courses focusing on the study of information and its impact as a social phenomenon. The School offers a M.A. degree with a major in Information Resources and Library Science, which is heavily weighted in technology and emphasizes theoretical constructs. Competence and adaptability in managing information and in utilizing advancing technologies are key aims of the curriculum. The program is fully accredited by the American Library Association. The School offers coursework that leads toward the Ph.D. degree with a major in Library Science. *Features:* The School offers a virtual education program via the Internet. Between two and three courses are offered per semester. *Admission Requirements:* Very competitive for both degrees. Minimum criteria include: undergraduate GPA of 3.0 or better; competitive GRE scores; two letters of recommendation reflecting the writer's opinion of the applicant's potential as a graduate student; resume of work and educational experience; written statement of intent. The School receives a large number of applications and accepts the best qualified students. Admission to the doctoral program may require a personal interview and a faculty member must indicate willingness to work with the student. *Degree Requirements:* M.A.: Minimum of 36 units of graduate credit. Students may elect the thesis option replacing 6 units of coursework. Ph.D.: At least 48 hours of coursework in the major, a substantial number of hours in a minor subject supporting the major, dissertation. The University has a

12-unit residency requirement, which may be completed in the summer or in a regular semester. More detailed descriptions of the program are available at the School's Website. *Faculty:* 5 full-time. *Students:* 220 total; M.A.: 51 full-time; Ph.D.: 12 full-time. *Degrees Awarded 1999:* M.A.: 75.

ARKANSAS

Arkansas Tech University. Russellville, AR 72801-2222. (501)968-0434. Fax (501)964-0811. E-mail SECZ@atuvm.atu.edu, czimmer@cswnet.com. Website http://www.atu.edu, http://www.angelfire.com/ar/librarymedia. Connie Zimmer, Asst. Prof. of Secondary Education, Coord. *Specializations:* Master's degrees in Education in Instructional Technology with specializations in library media education, computer education, general program of study, and training education. NCATE accredited institution. *Admission Requirements:* GRE, 2.5 undergraduate GPA, Bachelor's degree. *Degree Requirements:* 36 semester hours, B average in major hours, action research project. *Faculty:* 1 full-time, 5 part-time. *Students:* 22 full-time, 57 part-time. *Financial Assistance:* graduate assistantships, grants, student loans. *Degrees Awarded 1997:* 50.

University of Central Arkansas. Educational Media/Library Science, Campus Box 4918, Conway, AR 72035. (501)450-5463. Fax (501)450-5680. E-mail selvinr@mail.uca.edu. Website http://www.coe.uca.edu/aboutaat.htm. Selvin W. Royal, Prof., Chair, Academic Technologies and Educational Leadership. *Specializations:* M.S. in Educational Media/Library Science and Information Science. Tracks: School Library Media, Public Information Agencies, Media Information Studies. *Admission Requirements:* Transcripts, GRE scores, 2 letters of recommendation, personal interview, written rationale for entering the profession. *Degree Requirements:* 36 semester hours, optional thesis, practicum (for School Library Media), professional research paper. *Faculty:* 5 full-time, 2 part-time. *Students:* 6 full-time, 42 part-time. *Financial Assistance:* 3 to 4 graduate assistantships each year. *Degrees Awarded 1997:* 28.

CALIFORNIA

Azusa Pacific University. 901 E. Alosta, Azusa, CA, 91702. (626)815-5376, fax (626)815-5416. E-mail arnold@apu.edu. Brian Arnold, contact person. *Specializations:* M.Ed. with emphasis in Technology. *Admission Requirements:* Undergraduate degree from accredited institution, 3.0 GPA, ownership of a designated laptop computer and software. *Faculty:* 2 full-time, 16 part-time. *Students:* 180 part-time. *Financial Assistance:* student loans. *Degrees Awarded 1997:* 20.

California State University-Dominguez Hills. 1000 E. Victoria St., Carson, CA 90747. (310)243-3524. Fax (310)243-3518. E-mail pdesberg@dhvx20.csudh.edu. Website http://www .csudh.soe.edu. Peter Desberg, Prof., Coord., Computer-Based Education Program. *Specializations:* M.A. and Certificate in Computer-Based Education. *Admission Requirements:* 2.75 GPA. *Degree Requirements:* M.A.: 30 semester hours including project. Certificate: 15 hours. *Faculty:* 2 full-time, 2 part-time. *Students:* 50 full-time, 40 part-time. *Degrees Awarded 1997:* M.A., 20.

California State University-Los Angeles. Div. of Educational Foundations and Interdivisional Studies, Charter School of Education, 5151 State University Drive, Los Angeles, CA 90032. (323)343-4330. Fax (323)343-5336. E-mail efis@calstatela.edu. Website http://web .calstatela.edu/academic/found/efis/index.html. Dr. Fernando A. Hernandez, Div. Chair. *Specializations:* M.A. degree in Education, option in New Media Design and Production; Computer Education and Leadership. *Degree Requirements:* 2.75 GPA in last 90 qtr. units, 45 qtr. units, comprehensive written exam or thesis or project. Must also pass Writing Proficiency Examination (WPE), a California State University-Los Angeles requirement. *Faculty:* 7 full-time. *Degrees Awarded 1998:* 20.

*California State University-San Bernardino. 5500 University Parkway, San Bernardino, CA 92407. (909)880-5600, (909)880-5610. Fax (909)880-7010. E-mail monaghan @wiley.csusb.edu. Website http://soe.csusb.edu/soe/programs/eyec/. Dr. Jim Monaghan, Program Coord. *Specializations:* M.A. with two emphases: Video Production and Computer Applications. These emphases allow students to choose courses related to the design and creation of video products or courses involving lab and network operation of advanced microcomputer applications. The program does not require teaching credential certification. Advanced certificate programs in Educational Computing and Educational Technology are available. *Admission Requirements:* Bachelor's degree, appropriate work experience, 3.0 GPA, completion of introductory computer course and expository writing course. *Degree Requirements:* 48 units including a master's project (33 units completed in residence); 3.0 GPA; grades of "C" or better in all courses. *Faculty:* 5 full-time, 1 part-time. *Students:* 106. *Financial Assistance:* Contact Office of Graduate Studies. *Degrees Awarded 1996:* 12.

San Diego State University. Educational Technology, San Diego, CA 92182-1182. (619)594-6718. Fax (619)594-6376. E-mail patrick.harrison@sdsu.edu. Website http://edweb .sdsu.edu. Dr. Patrick Harrison, Prof., Chair. *Specialization:* Master's degree in Educational Technology with specializations in Computers in Education, Workforce Education, and Lifelong Learning. The Educational Technology Dept. participates in a College of Education joint doctoral program with The Claremont Graduate School. *Degree Requirements:* 36 semester hours (including 6 prerequisite hours), 950 GRE (verbal & quantitative). *Faculty:* 8 full-time, 5 part-time. *Students:* 120. *Financial Assistance:* graduate assistantships. *Degrees Awarded 1996:* Master's, 40.

San Francisco State University. College of Education, Dept. of Instructional Technology, 1600 Holloway Ave., San Francisco, CA 94132. (415)338-1509. Fax (415)338-0510. E-mail michaels@sfsu.edu. Dr. Eugene Michaels, Chair; Mimi Kasner, Office Coord. *Specializations:* Master's degree with emphasis on Instructional Multimedia Design, Training and Designing Development, and Instructional Computing. The school also offers an 18-unit Graduate Certificate in Training Systems Development, which can be incorporated into the master's degree. *Features:* This program emphasizes the instructional systems approach, cognitivist principles of learning design, practical design experience, and project-based courses. *Admission Requirements:* Bachelor's degree, appropriate work experience, 2.5 GPA, interview with the department chair. *Degree Requirements:* 30 semester hours, field study project, or thesis. *Faculty:* 1 full-time, 16 part-time. *Students:* 250-300. *Financial Assistance:* Contact Office of Financial Aid. *Degrees Awarded 1998:* 50.

San Jose State University. One Washington Square, San Jose, CA 95192-0076 (408)924-3618 (Office), Fax (408)3713. Website http://www.sjsu.edu.depts/it/Home.html. Dr. Roberta Barba, Program Chair. *Degrees:* Master's degree. *Special Features:* Has six areas of specialization: Instructional Design and Development, Media Design and Development, Media Services and Management, Computers and Interactive Technologies, Telecommunications and Distance Learning, and Teaching and Technology. We offer many courses that can be taken online via the Internet. Three certificate programs are offered: Multimedia, training methods for business and industry, and computer concepts and applications. *Admission Requirements:* Baccalaureate degree from approved university, appropriate work experience, minimum GPA of 2.5, and minimum score of 550 on TOEFL (Test of English as a Foreign Language). 36 semester hours (which includes 6 prerequisite hours). *Faculty:* 4 full-time, 12 part-time. *Students:* 10 full-time, 260 part-time. *Financial Assistance:* assistantships, grants, student loans and scholarships are available. *Degrees Awarded 1998:* 52.

*United States International University. School of Education, 10455 Pomerado Rd., San Diego, CA 92131-1799. (619)635-4715. Fax (619)635-4714. E-mail feifer@sanac.usiu.edu. Richard Feifer, contact person. *Specializations:* Master's in Designing Technology for Learning, Planning Technology for Learning, and Technology Leadership for Learning.

Ed.D. in Technology and Learning offers three specializations: Designing Technology for Learning, Planning Technology for Learning, and Technology Leadership for Learning. *Features:* Interactive multimedia, cognitive approach to integrating technology and learning. *Admission Requirements:* Master's: English proficiency, interview, 3.0 GPA with 1900 GRE or 2.0 GPA with satisfactory MAT score. *Degree Requirements:* Ed.D.: 88 graduate qtr. units, dissertation. *Faculty:* 2 full-time, 4 part-time. *Students:* Master's, 32 full-time, 12 part-time; doctoral, 6 full-time, 1 part-time. *Financial Assistance:* internships, graduate assistantships, grants, student loans, scholarships. *Degrees Awarded 1996:* Master's, 40; Ed.D., 2.

University of Southern California. 702C W.P.H., School of Education, Los Angeles, CA 90089-0031. (213)740-3288. Fax (213)740-3889. Instructional Technology, Dept. of Educational Psychology and Technology. E-mail kazlausk@mizar.usc.edu. Website http://www .usc.edu/department/itp/; also http://www.usc.edu/department/education/sed.index.htm. Dr. Richard Clark, Prof., Doctoral programs; Dr. Edward J. Kazlauskas, Prof., Program Chair, Master's programs in Instructional Technology. *Specializations:* M.A., Ed.D., Ph.D. to prepare individuals to teach instructional technology; manage educational media and training programs in business, industry, research and development organizations, schools, and higher educational institutions; perform research in instructional technology and media; and deal with computer-driven technology. A new Ed.D. program in Human Performance Technology was implemented in 1996 with satellite programs in Silicon Valley and Orange County. *Features:* Special emphasis on instructional design, systems analysis, and computer-based training. *Admission Requirements:* Bachelor's degree, 1000 GRE. *Degree Requirements:* M.A.: 28 semester hours, thesis optional. Doctoral: 67 units, 20 of which can be transferred from a previous master's degree. Requirements for degree completion vary according to type of degree and individual interest. Ph.D. requires coursework in an outside field in addition to coursework in instructional technology and education and more methodology and statistics work. *Faculty:* 5 full-time, 1 part-time. *Students:* M.A., 5 full-time, 15 part-time; doctoral, 50 full-time, 15 part-time. *Financial Assistance:* part-time, instructional technology-related work available in the Los Angeles area and on campus.

COLORADO

University of Colorado at Denver. School of Education, Campus Box 106, P.O. Box 173364, Denver CO 80217-3364. (303)556-6022. Fax (303)556-4479. E-mail brent.wilson @cudenver.edu. Website http://www.cudenver.edu/public/education/ilt/ILThome.html. Brent Wilson, Program Chair, Information and Learning Technologies, Div. of Technology and Special Services. *Specializations:* M.A.; Ph.D. in Educational Leadership and Innovation with emphasis in Curriculum, Learning, and Technology. *Features:* Design and use of learning technologies; instructional design. Ph.D. students complete 10 semester hours of doctoral labs (small groups collaborating with faculty on difficult problems of practice). Throughout the program, students complete a product portfolio of research, design, teaching, and applied projects. The program is cross-disciplinary, drawing on expertise in technology, adult learning, systemic change, research methods, reflective practice, and cultural studies. *Admission Requirements:* M.A. and Ph.D.: satisfactory GPA, GRE, writing sample, letters of recommendation, transcripts. *Degree Requirements:* M.A.: 36 semester hours including 19 hours of core coursework and portfolio; practicum and additional requirements for state certification in library media; internship required for careers in corporate settings. Ph.D.: 40 semester hours of coursework and labs, plus 30 dissertation hours; portfolio; dissertation. *Faculty:* 5 full-time, 3 part-time. *Students:* M.A., 25 full-time, 120 part-time; Ph.D., 6 full-time, 20 part-time. *Financial Assistance:* assistantships, internships. *Degrees Awarded 1998:* M.A.: 33; Ph.D: 3.

University of Northern Colorado. Div. of Educational Psychology, Statistics, and Technology, College of Education, Greeley, CO 80639. (970)351-2368. Fax (970)351-1622. E-mail bauer@edtech.unco.edu. Website http://www.edtech.unco.edu/COE/EDTECH/EDTECH.html.

Jeffrey Bauer, Assoc. Prof., Chair, Educational Technology. *Specializations:* M.A. in Educational Technology; M.A. in Educational Media; Ph.D. in Educational Technology with emphases in Distance Education, Instructional Development/Design, Interactive Technology, and Technology Integration. *Features:* Graduates are prepared for careers as instructional technologists, course designers, trainers, instructional developers, media specialists, and human resource managers. *Admission Requirements:* M.A.: Bachelor's degree, 3.0 undergraduate GPA, 1500 GRE. Ph.D.: 3.2 GPA, three letters of recommendation, congruency between applicant's statement of career goals and program goals, 1650 GRE, interview with faculty. *Faculty:* 5 full-time, 2 part-time. *Students:* M.A., 5 full-time, 60 part-time; Ph.D., 12 full-time, 22 part-time. *Financial Assistance:* assistantships, grants, student loans, scholarships. *Degrees Awarded 1997:* M.A., 25; Ph.D., 5.

CONNECTICUT

Central Connecticut State University. 1615 Stanley St., New Britain, CT 06050. (860)832-2130. Fax (860)832-2109. E-mail abedf@ccsu.ctstateu.edu. Website http://www .ccsu.edu. Farough Abed, Coord., Educational Technology Program. *Specializations:* M.S. in Educational Technology. Curriculum emphases include instructional technology, instructional design, message design, and computer technologies. *Features:* The program supports the Center for Innovation in Teaching and Technology to link students with client-based projects. *Admission Requirements:* Bachelor's degree, 2.7 undergraduate GPA. *Degree Requirements:* 33 semester hours, optional thesis or master's final project (3 credits). *Faculty:* 2 full-time, 4 part-time. *Students:* 45. *Financial Assistance:* graduate assistant position. *Degrees Awarded 1997:* 14.

Fairfield University. N. Benson Road, Fairfield, CT 06430. (203)254-4000. Fax (203)254-4047. E-mail imhefzallah@fair1.fairfield.edu. Dr. Ibrahim M. Hefzallah, Prof., Dir., Educational Technology Dept.; Dr. Justin Ahnn, Asst. Prof. of Educational Technology, E-mail jahnn@fair.fairfield.edu. *Specializations:* M.A. and a certificate of Advanced Studies in Educational Technology in one of four areas of concentrations: Computers-in-Education, Instructional Development, School Media Specialist, and Television Production; customized course of study also available. *Features:* Emphasis on theory, practice, and new instructional developments in computers in education, multimedia, and satellite communications. *Admission Requirements:* Bachelor's degree from accredited institution with 2.67 GPA. *Degree Requirements:* 33 credits. *Faculty:* 2 full-time, 8 part-time. *Students:* 4 full-time, 110 part-time. *Financial Assistance:* assistantships, student loans. *Degrees Awarded 1999:* 18.

Southern Connecticut State University. Dept. of Library Science and Instructional Technology, 501 Crescent St., New Haven, CT 06515. (203)392-5781. Fax (203)392-5780. E-mail libscienceit@scsu.ctstateu.edu. Website http://scsu.ctstateu.edu. Nancy Disbrow, Chair. *Specializations:* M.S. in Instructional Technology; Sixth-Year Professional Diploma Library-Information Studies (student may select area of specialization in Instructional Technology). *Degree Requirements:* For Instructional Technology only, 36 semester hours. For sixth-year degree: 30 credit hours with 6 credit hours of core requirements, 9-15 credit hours in specialization. *Faculty:* 1 full-time. *Students:* 3 full-time and 38 part-time in M.S./IT program. *Financial Assistance:* graduate assistantship (salary $1,800 per semester; assistants pay tuition and a general university fee sufficient to defray cost of student accident insurance). *Degrees Awarded 1997:* M.S., 2.

University of Connecticut. U-64, Storrs, CT 06269-2064. (860)486-0181. Fax (860)486-0180. E-mail sbrown@UConnvm.UConn.edu, or myoung@UConnvm.UConn.edu. Website http://www.ucc.uconn.edu/~wwwepsy/. Scott W. Brown, Chair; Michael Young, contact person. *Specializations:* M.A. and Ph.D. degrees with an emphasis in Educational Technology as a specialization within the Program of Cognition and Instruction, in the Dept. of Educational Psychology. *Features:* The emphasis in Educational Technology is a unique program at UConn. It is co-sponsored by the Department of Educational Psychology in the School of Education and the Psychology Department in the College of Liberal Arts and Sciences. The emphasis in Educational Technology within the Cognition and Instruction Program seeks to provide students with knowledge of theory and applications regarding the use of advanced technology to enhance learning and thinking. This program provides suggested courses and opportunities for internships and independent study experiences that are directed toward an understanding of both the effects of technology on cognition and instruction, and the enhancement of thinking and learning with technology. Facilities include the UCEML computer lab, featuring Mac and IBM networks upgraded for 1998, and a multimedia development center. The School of Education also features a multimedia classroom and auditorium. Faculty research interests include interactive videodisc for anchored instruction and situated learning, telecommunications for cognitive apprenticeship, technology-mediated interactivity for generative learning, and in cooperation with the National Research Center for Gifted and Talented, research on the use of technology to enhance cooperative learning and the development of gifted performance in all students. *Admission Requirements:* Admission to the graduate school at UConn, GRE scores (or other evidence of success at the graduate level). Previous experience in a related area of technology, education, or training is a plus. *Faculty:* The program in Cognition and Instruction has 7 full-time faculty; 3 full-time faculty administer the emphasis in Educational Technology. *Students:* M.A. 4, Ph.D., 18. *Financial Assistance:* graduate assistantships, research fellowships, teaching assistantships, and federal and minority scholarships are available competitively. *Degrees Awarded 1998:* Ph.D., 4 and M.A., 2.

DISTRICT OF COLUMBIA

George Washington University. School of Education and Human Development, Washington, DC 20052. (202)994-1701. Fax (202)994-2145. Website http://www.gwu.edu/~etl. Dr. William Lynch, Educational Technology Leadership Program. Program is offered through Jones Education Company (JEC). Contact student advisors at (800)777-MIND. *Specialization:* M.A. in Education and Human Development with a major in Educational Technology Leadership. *Features:* 36-hour degree program available via cable television, satellite, Internet, and/or videotape to students across North America and in other locations. The degree is awarded by George Washington University (GWU). Students may work directly with JEC or GWU to enroll. Student advisors at JEC handle inquiries about the program, send out enrollment forms and applications, process book orders, and set up students on an electronic listserv or Web forum. *Admission Requirements:* Application fee, transcripts, GRE or MAT scores (50th percentile), two letters of recommendation from academic professionals, computer access, undergraduate degree with 2.75 GPA. *Degree Requirements:* 36 credit hours (including 24 required hours). Required courses include computer application management, media and technology application, software implementation and design, public education policy, and quantitative research methods. *Faculty:* Courses are taught by GWU faculty. *Financial Assistance:* For information, contact the Office of Student Financial Assistance, GWU. Some cable systems that carry JEC offer local scholarships.

FLORIDA

Barry University. Dept. of Educational Computing and Technology, School of Education, 11300 N.E. Second Ave., Miami Shores, FL 33161. (305)899-3608. Fax (305)899-3718. E-mail jlevine@bu4090.barry.edu. Joel S. Levine, Dir. *Specializations:* M.S. and Ed.S. in Educational Technology, Ph.D. degree in Educational Technology Leadership. *Features:* Majority of the courses (30/36) in M.S. and Ed.S. programs are in the field of Educational Technology. *Admission Requirements:* GRE scores, letters of recommendation, GPA, interview, achievements. *Degree Requirements:* M.S. or Ed.S.: 36 semester credit hours. Ph.D.: 54 credits beyond the master's including dissertation credits. *Faculty:* 7 full-time, 10 part-time. *Students:* M.S., 8 full-time, 181 part-time; Ed.S., 5 full-time, 44 part-time; Ph.D., 3 full-time, 15 part-time. *Financial Assistance:* assistantships, student loans. *Degrees Awarded 1999:* M.S., 37; Ed.S., 6; Ph.D., 2.

Florida Institute of Technology. Science Education Dept., 150 University Blvd., Melbourne, FL 32901-6988. (407)674-8126. Fax (407)674-7598. E-mail fronk@fit.edu. Dr. Robert Fronk, Dept. Head. Website http://www.fit.edu/AcadRes/sci-ed/degree.html#comp-tech-ed. *Specializations:* Master's degree options in Computer Education and Instructional Technology; Ph.D. degree options in Computer Education and Instructional Technology. *Admission Requirements:* 3.0 GPA for regular admission; 2.75 for provisional admission. *Degree Requirements:* Master's: 33 semester hours (15 in computer and technology education, 9 in education, 9 electives); practicum; no thesis or internship required. Ph.D.: 48 semester hours (12 in computer and technology education, 12 in education, 24 dissertation and research). *Faculty:* 5 full-time. *Students:* 11 full-time, 10 part-time. *Financial Assistance:* graduate student assistantships (full tuition plus stipend) available. *Degrees Awarded 1997:* Master's, 7; Ph.D., 3.

Florida State University. Instructional Systems Program, Dept. of Educational Research, College of Education, 305 Stone Bldg., Tallahassee, FL 32306. (904)644-4592. Fax (904)644-8776. Website http://www.fsu.edu/~edres/. *Specializations:* M.S., Ed.S, Ph.D. in Instructional Systems with specializations for persons planning to work in academia, business, industry, government, or military. *Features:* Core courses include systems and materials development, development of multimedia, project management, psychological foundations, current trends in instructional design, and research and statistics. Internships are recommended. *Admission Requirements:* M.S.: 3.2 GPA in last two years of undergraduate program, 1000 GRE (verbal plus quantitative), 550 TOEFL (for international applicants). Ph.D.: 1100 GRE (V+Q), 3.5 GPA in last two years; international students, 550 TOEFL. *Degree Requirements:* M.S.: 36 semester hours, 2-4 hour internship, written comprehensive exam. *Faculty:* 5 full-time, 5 part-time. *Students:* M.S., 55; Ph.D., 50. *Financial Assistance:* some graduate research assistantships on faculty grants and contracts, university fellowships. *Degrees Awarded 1997:* M.S., 38; Ph.D., 14 (approximate).

Jacksonville University. Div. of Education, 2800 University Boulevard North, Jacksonville, FL 32211. (904)745-7132. Fax (904)745-7159. E-mail mjanz@mail.ju.edu. Dr. Margaret Janz, Interim Dir., School of Education, or Dr. June Main, Coord. of MAT in Integrated Learning with Educational Technology (jmain@junix.ju.edu). *Specializations:* The Master's in Educational Technology and Integrated Learning is an innovative program designed to guide certified teachers in the use and application of educational technologies in the classroom. It is based on emerging views of how we learn, our growing understanding of multiple intelligences, and the many ways to incorporate technology in teaching and learning. Activity-based classes emphasize instructional design for a multimedia environment to reach all students. M.A.T. degrees in Computer Education and in Integrated Learning with Educational Technology. *Features:* The M.A.T. in Computer Education is for teachers who are already certified in an area of education, for those who wish to be certified in Computer Education, kindergarten through community college level. *Degree Requirements:* M.A.T. in Computer Education and in Integrated Learning with Educational Technology: 36 semester hours, including 9-12 hours in core education graduate courses and the rest in computer education with comprehensive exam in last semester of program. Master's in Educational Technology and Integrated Learning: 36 semester hours, including 9 in core graduate education courses, 6 in integrated learning, and the rest in educational technology. Comprehensive exam is to develop a practical group of multimedia applications. *Financial Assistance:* student loans and discounts to graduate education students. *Students:* Computer Education, 8; Integrated Learning with Educational Technology, 20. *Degrees Awarded 1996-97:* Computer Education, 12; Integrated Learning with Educational Technology, 24.

Nova Southeastern University. Fischler Center for the Advancement of Education, 3301 College Ave., Fort Lauderdale, FL 33314. (954)475-7440. (800)986-3223, ext. 8563. Fax (954)262-3905. E-mail simsmich@fcae.nova.edu. Michael Simonson, Program Prof., Instructional Technology and Distance Education. *Specializations:* M.S. and Ed.D. in Instructional Technology and distance Education. *Features:* Program courses delivered via distance education and face-to-face instruction on weekends and during week-long summer institutes. Emphasis on developing leaders in distance education and instructional technology. Instructional design, systems design, distance education, and media and technology are stressed. Computer-based learning at a distance is emphasized and used as an integral component of course delivery. Courses geared to the working professional. M.S. Practicum is job-related, as is the practical dissertation. *Admission Requirements:* M.S.: three letters of recommendation, completed application and transcripts. Ed.D.: Three letters of recommendation, completed application, transcripts, and completed master's degree in Instructional Technology or distance Education, or related area. *Degree Requirements:* M.S.: 21 months and 30 semester credits. Ed.D.: 3 years and 66 semester credits. *Faculty:* 6 full-time and 20 adjuncts. *Students:* 250 full time. *Degrees Awarded 1998:* 40 M.S. and 20 Ed.D.

University of Central Florida. College of Education, ED Room 318, UCF, Orlando, FL 32816-1250. (407)823-2153. Fax (407)823-5622. Websites http://pegasus.cc.ucf.edu/~edmedia and http://pegasus.cc.ucf.edu/~edtech. Richard Cornell, Instructional Systems (cornell@pegasus .cc.ucf.edu); Judy Lee, Educational Media (jlee@pegasus.cc.ucf.edu); Glenda Gunter, Educational Technology (ggunter@pegasus.cc.ucf.edu). *Specializations:* M.A. in Instructional Technology/Instructional Systems; M.Ed. in Instructional Technology/Educational Media; M.A. in Instructional Technology/Educational Technology. A doctorate in Curriculum and Instruction with an emphasis on Instructional Technology is offered. *Admission Requirements:* Interviews for Educational Media and Educational Technology programs. *Degree Requirements:* M.A. in Instructional Technology/Instructional Systems, 39-42 semester hours. M.Ed. in Instructional Technology/Educational Media, 39-45 semester hours. M.A. in Instructional Technology/Educational Technology, 36-45 semester hours. Practicum required in all three programs; thesis, research project, or substitute additional coursework. *Students:* Instructional Systems, 70; Educational Media, 35; Educational Technology, 50. Full-time, 120; part-time, 35. *Faculty:* 4 full-time, 6 part-time. *Financial Assistance:* competitive graduate assistantships in department and college, numerous paid internships, limited number of doctoral fellowships. *Degrees Awarded 1997:* 40.

University of South Florida. Instructional Technology Program, Secondary Education Dept., College of Education. 4202 Fowler Ave. East, EDU 208B, Tampa, FL 33620. (813)974-1632 (M.Ed.); (813)974-1629 (doctoral). Fax (813)974-3837. E-mail breit@tempest.coedu.usf.edu (M.Ed.), jwhite@typhoon.coedu.usf.edu (doctoral). Website http://www.coedu.usf.edu /institute_tech/. Dr. Frank Breit, master's program, Dr. James A. White, doctoral program. *Specialization:* M.Ed. in Curriculum and Instruction with emphasis in Instructional Technology; Ph.D. in Curriculum and Instruction with emphasis in Instructional Technology. *Features:* Students gain practical experience in the Florida Center for Instructional Technology (FCIT), which provides services to the Dept. of Education and other grants and contracts, and the Virtual Instructional Team for the Advancement of Learning (VITAL), which provides USF faculty with course development services. The College of Education is one of the largest in the United States in terms of enrollment and facilities. As of Fall 1997, a new, state-of-the-art building was put into service. *Admission Requirements:* M.Ed.: 3.0 undergraduate GPA, at least half of undergraduate degree earned from accredited institution, and 800 GRE (V+Q), or 2.5 undergraduate GPA in last half of undergraduate degree from accredited institution and 1000 GRE, or a prior graduate degree from an accredited institution and 800 GRE. Applicants must also have a minimum of two years of relevant educational or professional experience as judged by the program faculty. Ph.D.: contact Dr. White for full details; include 3.0 undergraduate GPA in last half of coursework or 3.5 GPA at master's level and 1000 GRE, a master's degree from an accredited institution, three letters of recommendation, and favorable recommendations from program faculty. *Degree Requirements:*

M.Ed.: 36-38 semester hours, comprehensive exam. Ph.D.: 77-79 hours, two research tools, two semesters of residency, qualifying examination, and dissertation. *Faculty:* 3 full-time, 2 part-time. *Students:* M.Ed.: 100 full-time, 100 part-time (approx.); Ph.D.: 2 full-time, 14 part-time. *Financial Assistance:* assistantships, grants, loans, scholarships, and fellowships. *Degrees Awarded 1997:* M.Ed.: 40; Ph.D., 2.

GEORGIA

Georgia Southern University. College of Education, Statesboro, GA 30460-8131. (912)681-5307. Fax (912)681-5093. Kenneth F. Clark, Assoc. Prof., Dept. of Leadership, Technology, and Human Development. *Specialization:* M.Ed. The school also offers a six-year specialist degree program (Ed.S.), and an Instructional Technology strand is available in the Ed.D. program in Curriculum Studies. *Features:* Strong emphasis on technology. *Degree Requirements:* 36 semester hours, including a varying number of hours of media for individual students. *Financial Assistance:* See graduate catalog for general financial aid information. *Faculty:* 4 full-time.

Georgia State University. Middle-Secondary Education and Instructional Technology, University Plaza, Atlanta, GA 30303. (404)651-2510. Fax (404)651-2546. E-mail swharmon @gsu.edu. Website http://www.gsu.edu/~wwwmst/. Dr. Stephen W. Harmon, contact person. *Specializations:* M.S., Ed.S., and Ph.D. in Instructional Technology or Library Media. *Features:* Focus on research and practical application of instructional technology in educational and corporate settings. *Admission Requirements:* M.S.: Bachelor's degree, 2.5 undergraduate GPA, 44 MAT or 800 GRE, 550 TOEFL. Ed.S.: Master's degree, teaching certificate, 3.25 graduate GPA, 48 MAT or 900 GRE. Ph.D.: Master's degree, 3.30 graduate GPA, 53 MAT or 500 verbal plus 500 quantitative GRE or 500 analytical GRE. *Degree Requirements:* M.S.: 36 sem. hours, internship, portfolio, comprehensive examination. Ed.S.: 30 sem. hours, internship, and scholarly project. Ph.D.: 66 sem. hours, internship, dissertation. *Faculty:* 6 full-time, 3 part-time. *Students:* 200 M.S., 30 Ph.D. *Financial Assistance:* assistantships, grants, student loans. *Degrees Awarded 1997:* Ph.D., 5; M.S., 30.

State University of West Georgia (formerly West Georgia College). Dept. of Research, Media, and Technology, 137 Education Annex, Carrollton, GA 30118. (770)836-6558. Fax (770)836-6729. E-mail bmckenzi@westga.edu. Website http://www.westga.edu/soe/rmt/. Dr. Barbara K. McKenzie, Assoc. Prof., Chair. *Specializations:* M.Ed. with specializations in Media and Instructional Technology and add-on certification for students with master's degrees in other disciplines. The school also offers an Ed.S. program in Media with two options, Media Specialist or Instructional Technology. The program strongly emphasizes technology in the schools. *Admission Requirements:* M.Ed.: 800 GRE, 44 MAT, 550 NTE Core, 2.5 undergraduate GPA. Ed.S.: 900 GRE, 48 MAT, or 575 NTE and 3.25 graduate GPA. *Degree Requirements:* Minimum of 60 qtr. hours. *Faculty:* 5 full-time in Media/Technology and 3 in Research; 3 part-time in Media/Technology. *Students:* 6 full-time, 130 part-time. *Financial Assistance:* two graduate assistantships and three graduate research assistantships for the department. *Degrees Awarded 1998:* M.Ed., 20; Ed.S., 20.

University of Georgia. Dept. of Instructional Technology, College of Education, 604 Aderhold Hall, Athens, GA 30602-7144. (706)542-3810. Fax (706)542-4032. E-mail kgustafs @coe.uga.edu. Website http://itech1.coe.uga.edu. Kent L. Gustafson, Prof. and Chair. *Specializations:* M.Ed. and Ed.S. in Instructional Technology; Ph.D. for leadership positions as specialists in instructional design and development and college faculty. The program offers advanced study for individuals with previous preparation in instructional media and technology, as well as a preparation for personnel in other professional fields requiring a specialty in instructional systems or instructional technology. Representative career fields for graduates include designing new courses, tutorial programs, and instructional materials in the military, industry, medical professional schools, allied health agencies, teacher education, staff development, state and local school systems, higher education, research, and instructional products development. *Features:* Minor areas of study available in a variety of other departments. Personalized programs are planned around a common core of courses and include practica, internships, or clinical experiences. Research activities include special assignments, applied projects, and task forces, as well as thesis and dissertation studies. *Admission Requirements:* All degrees: application to graduate school, satisfactory GRE score, other criteria as outlined in Graduate School Bulletin. *Degree Requirements:* M.Ed.: 36 semester hours with 3.0 GPA, portfolio with oral exam. Ed.S.: 30 semester hours with 3.0 GPA and portfolio exam. Ph.D.: three full years of study beyond the master's degree, two consecutive semesters full-time residency, comprehensive exam with oral defense, internship, dissertation with oral defense. *Faculty:* 10 full-time, 3 part-time. *Students:* M.Ed and Ed.S., 18 full-time, 53 part-time; Ph.D., 24 full-time, 10 part-time. *Financial Assistance:* graduate assistantships available. *Degrees Awarded 1998:* M.Ed. and Ed.S., 31; Ph.D., 0.

Valdosta State University. College of Education, 1500 N. Patterson St., Valdosta, GA 31698. (912)333-5927. Fax (912)333-7167. E-mail cprice@valdosta.edu. Catherine B. Price, Prof., Head, Dept. of Instructional Technology. *Specializations:* M.Ed. in Instructional Technology with three tracks: Library/Media, Technology Leadership, or Technology Applications; Ed.S. in Instructional Technology; Ed.D. in Curriculum and Instruction. *Features:* The program has a strong emphasis on technology in M.Ed., Ed.S., and Ed.D.; strong emphasis on applied research in Ed.S and Ed.D. *Admission Requirements:* M.Ed.: 2.5 GPA, 750 GRE. Ed.S.: Master's in Instructional Technology or related area, 3.0 GPA, 850 GRE. Ed.D.: Master's degree, 3 years of experience, 3.50 GPA, 1000 GRE. *Degree Requirements:* M.Ed.: 33 semester hours. Ed.S.: 27 semester hours. *Faculty:* 7 full-time, 3 part-time. *Students:* 15 full-time, 90 part-time. *Financial Assistance:* graduate assistantships, student loans, scholarships. *Degrees Awarded 1998:* M.Ed., 16; Ed.S., 2; and Ed.D., 14 (new programs).

HAWAII

University of Hawaii-Manoa. Dept. of Educational Technology, 1776 University Ave., Honolulu, HI 96822. (808) 956-7671. Fax (808) (956-3905). E-mail edtech-dept@hawaii.edu. Website http://www2.hawaii.edu/edtech. Geoffrey Z. Kucera, Prof., Chair. *Specialization:* M.Ed. in Educational Technology. *Degree Requirements:* Minimum 39 semester hours, including 3 in practicum, 3 in internship; thesis and non-thesis available. *Faculty:* 5 full-time, 2 part-time. *Financial Assistance:* Consideration given to meritorious second-year students for tuition waivers and scholarship applications. *Degrees warded July 1997-June 1998:* 9. *Degrees Awarded July 1998-June 1999:* 9.

IDAHO

Boise State University. IPT, 1910 University Drive, Boise, ID 83725. (208)385-4457, (800)824-7017 ext. 4457. Fax (208)342-7203. E-mail bsu-ipt@micron.net. Website http://www .cot.idbsu.edu/~ipt/. Dr. David Cox, IPT Program Dir.; Jo Ann Fenner, IPT Program Developer and distance program contact person. *Specialization:* M.S. in Instructional & Performance Technology available in a traditional campus setting or via computer conferencing to students located anywhere on the North American continent. The program is fully accredited by the Northwest Association of Schools and Colleges and is the recipient of an NUCEA award for Outstanding Credit Program offered by distance education methods. *Features:* Leading experts in learning styles, evaluation, and leadership principles serve as adjunct faculty in the program via computer and modem from their various remote locations. *Admission Requirements:* Undergraduate degree with 3.0 GPA, one-to-two page essay describing why you want to pursue this program and how it will contribute to your personal and professional development, and a resume of personal qualifications and work experience. *Degree Requirements:* 36 semester hours in instructional and performance technology and related coursework; project or thesis available for on-campus program, and an oral comprehensive exam required for distance program (included in 36 credit hours). *Faculty:* 3 full-time, 7 part-time. *Students:* 140 part-time. *Financial Assistance:* DANTES funding for some military personnel, low-interest loans to eligible students, graduate assistantships for on-campus enrollees. *Degrees Awarded 1997:* 12.

ILLINOIS

Chicago State University. Dept. of Library Science and Communications Media, Chicago, IL 60628. (312)995-2278, (312)995-2503. Fax (312)995-2473. Janice Bolt, Prof., Chair, Dept. of Library Science and Communications Media. *Specialization:* Master's degree in School Media. Program has been approved by NCATE; AECT/AASL through accreditation of University College of Education; State of Illinois Entitlement Program. *Admission Requirements:* Teacher's certification or Bachelor's in Education; any B.A. or B.S. *Degree Requirements:* 36 semester hours; thesis optional. *Faculty:* 2 full-time, 5 part-time. *Students:* 88 part-time. *Financial Assistance:* assistantships, grants, student loans. *Degrees Awarded 1997:* 15.

Concordia University. 7400 Augusta St., River Forest, IL 60305-1499. (708)209-3088. Fax (708)209-3176. E-mail boosmb@crf.cuis.edu. Website http://www.curf.edu. Dr. Manfred Boos, Chair, Mathematics/Computer Science Education Dept. *Specialization:* M.A. in Computer Science Education. *Admission Requirements:* 2.85 GPA (2.25 to 2.85 for provisional status); bachelor's degree from regionally accredited institution; two letters of recommendation. *Degree Requirements:* 33 semester hours of coursework. *Faculty:* 7 full-time, 5 part-time. *Students:* 3 full-time, 18 part-time. *Financial Assistance:* number of graduate assistantships, Stafford student loans, Supplement Loan for Students. *Degrees Awarded 1998:* 5.

Governors State University. College of Arts and Sciences, University Park, IL 60466. (708)534-4082. Fax (708)534-7895. E-mail m-stelni@govst.edu. Michael Stelnicki, Prof., Human Performance and Training. *Specializations:* M.A. in Communication with HP&T major. *Features:* Emphasizes three professional areas: Instructional Design, Performance Analysis, and Design Logistics. *Admission Requirements:* Undergraduate degree in any field. *Degree Requirements:* 36 credit hours (trimester), all in instructional and performance technology; internship or advanced field project required. Metropolitan Chicago area based. *Faculty:* 2 full-time. *Students:* 32 part-time. *Degrees Awarded 1998:* 8.

Northern Illinois University. Leadership and Educational Policy Studies Dept., College of Education, DeKalb, IL 60115-2896. (815)753-0464. Fax (815)753-9371. E-mail LSTOTT @NIU.EDU. Website http://coe.cedu.niu.edu. Dr. Peggy Bailey, Chair, Instructional Technology. *Specializations:* M.S.Ed. in Instructional Technology with concentrations in Instructional Design, Distance Education, Educational Computing, and Media Administration; Ed.D. in Instructional Technology, emphasizing instructional design and development, computer education, media administration, and preparation for careers in business, industry, and higher education. In addition, Illinois state certification in school library media is offered in conjunction either with degree or alone. *Features:* considerable flexibility in course selection, including advanced seminars, numerous practicum and internship opportunities, individual study, and research. Program is highly individualized. More than 60 courses offered by several departments or faculties, including communications, radio/television/film, art, journalism, educational psychology, computer science, and research and evaluation. Facilities include well-equipped computer labs. Students are encouraged to create individualized Web pages. Master's program started in 1968, doctorate in 1970. *Admission Requirements:* M.S.: 2.75 undergraduate GPA, GRE verbal and quantitative scores, two references. Ed.D.: 3.5 M.S. GPA, GRE verbal and quantitative scores (waiver possible), writing sample, three references. *Degree Requirements:* M.S.: 39 hours, including 30 in instructional technology; no thesis. Ed.D.: 63 hours beyond master's, including 15 hours for dissertation. *Faculty:* 8 full-time, 12 part-time. *Students:* M.S., 135 part-time; Ed.D., 115 part-time. *Financial Assistance:* assistantships available at times in various departments, scholarships, minority assistance. *Degrees Awarded 1997:* M.S., 26; Ed.D., 6.

Southern Illinois University at Carbondale. Dept. of Curriculum and Instruction, Carbondale, IL 62901-4610. (618)536-2441. Fax (618)453-4244. E-mail sashrock@siu.edu. Website http://www.siu.edu/~currinst/index.html. Sharon Shrock, Coord., Instructional Technology/ Development. *Specializations:* M.S. in Education with specializations in Instructional Development and Instructional Technology; Ph.D. in Education including specialization in Instructional Technology. *Features:* All specializations are oriented to multiple education settings. The ID program emphasizes nonschool (primarily corporate) learning environments. *Admission Requirements:* M.S.: Bachelor's degree, 2.7 undergraduate GPA, transcripts. Ph.D.: Master's degree, 3.25 GPA, MAT or GRE scores, letters of recommendation, transcripts, writing sample. *Degree Requirements:* M.S., 32 credit hours with thesis; 36 credit hours without thesis; Ph.D. , 40 credit hours beyond the master's degree in courses, 24 credit hours for the dissertation. *Faculty:* 5 full-time, 2 part-time. *Students:* M.S., 35 full-time, 45 part-time; Ph.D., 8 full-time, 19 part-time. *Financial Assistance:* some graduate assistantships and scholarships available to qualified students. *Degrees Awarded 1997:* Master's, 16; Ph.D., 4.

Southern Illinois University at Edwardsville. Instructional Technology Program, School of Education, Edwardsville, IL 62026-1125. (618)692-3277. Fax (618)692-3359. E-mail cnelson@siue.edu. Website http://www.siue.edu. Dr. Charles E. Nelson, Dir., Dept. of Educational Leadership. *Specialization:* M.S. in Education with concentrations in (1) Instructional Design and (2) Teaching, Learning, and Technology. *Features:* evening classes only. *Degree Requirements:* 36 semester hours; thesis optional. *Faculty:* 6 part-time. *Students:* 125. *Degrees Awarded 1997:* 30.

University of Illinois at Urbana-Champaign. Dept. of Educational Psychology, 210 Education Bldg., 1310 S. 6th St., Champaign, IL 61820. (217)333-2245. Fax (217)244-7620. E-mail c-west@uiuc.edu. Charles K. West, Prof., Div. of Learning and Instruction, Dept. of Educational Psychology. *Specializations:* M.A., M.S., and Ed.M. with emphasis in Instructional Design and Educational Computing. Ph.D. in Educational Psychology with emphasis in Instructional Design and Educational Computing. *Features:* Ph.D. program is individually tailored and strongly research-oriented, with emphasis on applications of cognitive science to instruction. *Admission Requirements:* Excellent academic record, high GRE scores, and strong letters of recommendation. *Degree Requirements:* 8 units for Ed.M., 6 units and thesis for M.A. or M.S. Ph.D.: 8 units coursework, approx. 4 units of research methods courses, minimum 8 hours of written qualifying exams, 8 units thesis credits. *Faculty:* 8 full-time, 5 part-time. *Students:* 31 full-time, 7 part-time. *Financial Assistance:* scholarships, research assistantships, and teaching assistantships available; fellowships for very highly academically talented; some tuition waivers. *Degrees Awarded 1997:* Ph.D., 5.

Western Illinois University. Instructional Technology and Telecommunications, 37 Harrabin Hall, Macomb, IL 61455. (309)298-1952. Fax (309)298-2978. E-mail mh-hassan@wiu.edu. Website http://www.wiu.edu/users/miitt/. M.H. Hassan, Chair. *Specialization:* Master's degree. *Features:* New program approved by Illinois Board of Higher Education in January 1996 with emphases in Instructional Technology, Telecommunications, Interactive Technologies, and Distance Education. Selected courses delivered via satellite TV and compressed video. *Admission Requirements:* Bachelor's degree 3.0/4.0 GRE score. *Degree Requirements:* 32 semester hours, thesis or applied project, or 35 semester hours with portfolio. *Certificate Program in Instructional Technology Specialization:* Graphic applications, training development, video production. Each track option is made of 5 courses or a total of 15 semester hours. *Admission Requirements:* Bachelor's degree. Must be completed within three years. *Faculty:* 8 full-time. *Students:* 35 full-time, 150 part-time. *Financial Assistance:* graduate and research assistantships, internships, residence hall assistants, veterans' benefits, loans, and part-time employment.

INDIANA

Indiana State University. Dept. of Curriculum, Instruction, and Media Technology, Terre Haute, IN 47809. (812)237-2937. Fax (812)237-4348. E-mail efthomp@befac.indstate.edu. Dr. James E. Thompson, Program Coord. *Specializations:* Master's degree in Instructional Technology with education focus or with non-education focus; Specialist Degree program in Instructional Technology; Ph.D. in Curriculum, Instruction with specialization in Media Technology. *Degree Requirements:* Master's: 32 semester hours, including 18 in media; thesis optional; Ed.S.: 60 semester hours beyond bachelor's degree; Ph.D., approximately 100 hours beyond bachelor's degree. *Faculty:* 5 full-time. *Students:* 17 full-time, 13 part-time. *Financial Assistance:* 7 assistantships. *Degrees Awarded 1997:* Master's, 2; Ph.D., 1.

*Indiana University. School of Education, W. W. Wright Education Bldg., Rm. 2276, 201 N. Rose Ave., Bloomington, IN 47405-1006. (812)856-8451 (information), (812)856-8239 (admissions). Fax (812)856-8239. Thomas Schwen, Chair, Dept. of Instructional Systems Technology. *Specializations:* M.S. and Ed.S. degrees designed for individuals seeking to be practitioners in the field of Instructional Technology. Offers Ph.D. and Ed.D. degrees with four program focus areas: Foundations; Instructional Analysis, Design, and Development; Instructional Development and Production; and Implementation and Management. *Features:* Requires computer skills as a prerequisite and makes technology utilization an integral part of the curriculum; eliminates separation of various media formats; and establishes a series of courses of increasing complexity integrating production and development. The latest in technical capabilities have been incorporated in the new Center for Excellence in Education, including teaching, photographic, computer, and science laboratories, a 14-station multimedia laboratory, and television studios. *Admission Requirements:* M.S.: Bachelor's degree from an accredited institution, 1350 GRE (3 tests required), 2.65 undergraduate GPA. Ed.D. and Ph.D.: 1550 GRE (3 tests required), 3.5 graduate GPA. *Degree Requirements:* M.S.: 40 credit hours (including 16 credits in required courses); colloquia; an instructional product or master's thesis; and 12 credits in outside electives. Ed.D.: 60 hours in addition to previous master's degree, thesis. Ph.D.: 90 hours, thesis. *Faculty:* 6 full-time, 5 part-time. *Financial Assistance:* assistantships, scholarships. *Degrees Awarded 1996:* M.S., 59; Ed.S., 1; Ed.D., 1; Ph.D., 5.

Purdue University. School of Education, Dept. of Curriculum and Instruction, W. Lafayette, IN 47907-1442. (765)494-5669. Fax (765)496-1622. E-mail edtech@soe.purdue.edu. Website http://www.soe.purdue.edu/edci/et/. Dr. James D. Lehman, Prof. of Educational Technology. *Specializations:* Master's degree, Educational Specialist, and Ph.D. in Educational Technology. Master's program started in 1982, Specialist and Ph.D. in 1985. *Admission Requirements:* Master's and Ed.S.: 3.0 GPA, three letters of recommendation, statement of personal goals. Ph.D.: 3.0 GPA, three letters of recommendation, statement of personal goals, 1000 GRE (V+Q). *Degree Requirements:* Master's: 33 semester hours (15 in educational technology, 9 in education, 12 unspecified); thesis optional. Specialist: 60-65 semester hours (15-18 in educational technology, 30-35 in education), thesis, internship, practicum. Ph.D.: 90 semester hours (15-18 in educational technology, 42-45 in education), thesis, internship, practicum. *Faculty:* 6 full-time. *Students:* M.S., 51; Ed.S, 1; Ph.D., 55. *Financial Assistance:* assistantships and fellowships. *Degrees Awarded 1998:* Master's, 10; Ph.D., 3.

IOWA

Clarke College. Graduate Studies, 1550 Clarke Drive, Dubuque, IA 52001. (319)588-6331. Fax (319)588-6789. E-mail RADAMS@KELLER.CLARKE.EDU. Website http://www.clarke.edu. Robert Adams, Clarke College, (319)588-6416. *Specializations:* M.A. in Technology and Education. *Admission Requirements:* 2.5 GPA, GRE (verbal & quantitative) or MAT, $25 application fee, two letters of recommendation. *Degree Requirements:* 25 semester hours in computer courses, 12 hours in education. *Faculty:* 1 full-time,

1-2 part-time. *Students:* 20 part-time. *Financial Assistance:* scholarships, student loans. *Degrees Awarded 1997:* 8.

Iowa State University. College of Education, Ames, IA 50011. (515)294-6840. Fax (515)294-9284. Gary Downs, Prof. and Dept. Head. *Specializations:* M.S., M.Ed., and Ph.D. in Curriculum and Instructional Technology with specializations in Instructional Computing, Ph.D. in Education with emphasis in Instructional Computing, Technology Research. *Features:* Practicum experiences related to professional objectives, supervised study and research projects tied to long-term studies within the program, development and implementation of new techniques, teaching strategies, and operational procedures in instructional resources centers and computer labs, program emphasis on technologies for teachers. *Admission Requirements:* M.S. and M.Ed.: Three letters, top half of undergraduate class, autobiography. Ph.D.: Three letters, top half of undergraduate class, autobiography, GRE scores. *Degree Requirements:* Master's: 30 semester hours, thesis, no internship or practicum. Ph.D.: 78 semester hours, thesis, no internship or practicum. *Faculty:* 4 full-time, 6 part-time. *Students:* Master's, 40 full-time, 40 part-time; Ph.D., 30 full-time, 20 part-time. *Financial Assistance:* 10 assistantships. *Degrees Awarded 1998:* Master's, 2; Ph.D., 2.

University of Iowa. Div. of Psychological and Quantitative Foundations, College of Education, Iowa City, IA 52242. (319)335-5519. Fax (319)335-5386. Website http://www.uiowa .edu/~coe2/facstaff/salessi.htm. Stephen Alessi, 361 Lindquist Center, Iowa City, IA 52242. *Specializations:* M.A. and Ph.D. with specializations in Training and Human Resources Development, Computer Applications, and Media Design and Production (MA only). *Features:* Flexibility in planning to fit individual needs, backgrounds, and career goals. The program is interdisciplinary, involving courses within divisions of the College of Education, as well as in the schools of Business, Library Science, Radio and Television, Linguistics, and Psychology. *Admission Requirements:* MA: 2.8 undergraduate GPA, 500 GRE (V+Q), personal letter of interest. Ph.D.: Master's degree, 1000 GRE (V+Q), 3.2 GPA on all previous graduate work for regular admission. Conditional admission may be granted. Teaching or relevant experience may be helpful. *Degree Requirements:* MA: 35 semester hours, 3.0 GPA, final project or thesis, comprehensive exam. Ph.D.: 90 semester hours, comprehensive exams, dissertation. *Faculty:* 4 full-time, 3 part-time. *Financial Assistance:* assistantships, grants, student loans, and scholarships.

University of Northern Iowa. Educational Technology Program, Cedar Falls, IA 50614-0606. (319)273-3250. Fax (319)273-5886. E-mail SmaldinoS@UNI.edu. Website www.uni.edu /edtech. Sharon E. Smaldino, contact person. *Specialization:* M.A. in Educational Technology, M.A. in Communications and Training Technology. *Admission Requirements:* Bachelor's degree, 3.0 undergraduate GPA, 500 TOEFL. *Degree Requirements:* 38 semester credits, optional thesis worth 6 credits or alternative research paper of project, comprehensive exam. *Faculty:* 3 full-time, 6 part-time. *Students:* 120. *Financial Assistance:* assistantships, grants, student loans, scholarships, student employment. *Degrees Awarded 1997:* 20.

KANSAS

Emporia State University. School of Library and Information Management, 1200 Commercial, P.O. Box 4025, Emporia, KS 66801. (316)341-5203. Fax (316)341-5233. E-mail vowellfa@esumail.emporia.edu. Website http://www.emporia.edu/slim/slim.htm. Faye N. Vowell, Dean. *Specializations:* Master's of Library Science (ALA accredited program); School Library Certification program, which includes 27 hours of the M.L.S. program; Ph.D. in Library and Information Management. *Features:* The M.L.S. program is also available in Colorado, Oregon, Utah, and Nebraska. Internet courses are under development. *Admission Requirements:* Selective admissions process for M.L.S. and Ph.D. based on a combination of admission criteria, including (but not limited to) GRE or TOEFL score, personal interview, GPA, statement of goals and references. Request admission packet for specific criteria. *Degree Requirements:* M.L.S.: 42 semester hours, comprehensive exam.

Ph.D.: total of 83-97 semester hours depending on the number of hours received for an M.L.S. *Faculty:* 12 full-time, 35 part-time. *Students:* M.L.S.: 64 full-time, 305 part-time; Ph.D.: 23 part-time. *Financial Assistance:* assistantships, grants, student loans, scholarships. *Degrees Awarded 1997:* 156.

Kansas State University. Educational Computing, Design, and Telecommunications, 363 Bluemont Hall, Manhattan, KS 66506. (913)532-7686. Fax (913)532-7304. E-mail dmcgrath@coe.educ.ksu.edu. Website http://www2.educ.ksu.edu/Faculty/McGrathD/ECDT /ECDTProg.htm. Dr. Diane McGrath, contact person. *Specializations:* M.S. in Secondary Education with an emphasis in Educational Computing, Design, and Telecommunications; Ph.D. and Ed.D. in Curriculum & Instruction with an emphasis in Educational Computing, Design, and Telecommunications. Master's program started in 1982; doctoral in 1987. *Admissions Requirements:* M.S.: B average in undergraduate work, one programming language, 590 TOEFL. Ed.D. and Ph.D.: B average in undergraduate and graduate work, one programming language, GRE or MAT, three letters of recommendation, experience or course in educational computing. *Degree Requirements:* M.S.: 30 semester hours (minimum of 12 in Educational Computing); thesis, internship, or practicum not required, but all three are possible. Ed.D.: 94 semester hours (minimum of 18 hours in Educational Computing or related area approved by committee, 16 hours dissertation research, 12 hours internship); thesis. Ph.D.: 90 semester hours (minimum of 21 hours in Educational Computing, Design, and Telecommunications or related area approved by committee, 30 hours for dissertation research); thesis; internship or practicum not required but available. *Faculty:* 2 full-time, 1 part-time. *Students:* M.S., 10 full-time, 27 part-time; doctoral, 16 full-time, 14 part-time. *Financial Assistance:* currently four assistantships directly associated with the program; other assistantships sometimes available in other departments depending on skills and funds available. *Degrees Awarded 1997:* M.S., 7.

KENTUCKY

University of Louisville. School of Education, Louisville, KY 40292. (502)852-0609. Fax (502)852-4563. E-mail cparkins@louisville.edu. Website http://www.louisville.edu/edu. Carolyn Rude-Parkins, Dir., Education Resource & Technology Center. *Specialization:* M.Ed. in Early Childhood, Middle School, Secondary Education, Training and Development with Instructional Technology focus. *Features:* Technology courses appropriate for business or school audiences. Program is based on ISTE standards as well as ASTD standards. *Admission Requirements:* 2.75 GPA, 800 GRE, 2 letters of recommendation, application fee. *Degree Requirements:* 30 semester hours, thesis optional. *Faculty:* 2 full-time, 3 part-time. *Students:* 4 full-time, 30 part-time. *Financial Assistance:* graduate assistantships. *Degrees Awarded 1997:* 10.

LOUISIANA

Louisiana State University. School of Library and Information Science, Baton Rouge, LA 70803.(225)388-3158. Fax (225)388-4581, Website http://adam.slis.lsu.edu. Bert R. Boyce, Dean, Prof., School of Library and Information Science. *Specializations:* M.L.I.S., C.L.I.S. (post-master's certificate), Louisiana School Library Certification. An advanced certificate program is available. *Degree Requirements:* M.L.I.S.: 40 hours, comprehensive exam, one semester full-time residence, completion of degree program in five years. *Faculty:* 10 full-time. *Students:* 84 full-time, 86 part-time. *Financial Assistance:* A large number of graduate assistantships are available to qualified students. *Degrees Awarded 1997:* 91.

MARYLAND

The Johns Hopkins University. Graduate Div. of Education, Technology for Educators Program, Columbia Gateway Park, 6740 Alexander Bell Drive, Columbia, MD 21046. (410)309-9537. Fax (410)290-0467. Website http://www.jhu.edu. Dr. Jacqueline A. Nunn, Dept. Chair; Dr. Linda Tsantis, Program Coord. (tsantis@jhu.edu). *Specialization:* The Dept. of Technology for Education offers programs leading to the M.S. degree in Education, the M.S. in Special Education, and three specialized advanced Graduate Certificates: Technology for Multimedia and Internet-Based Instruction; Teaching with Technology for School to Career Transition; and Assistive Technology for Communication and Social Interaction. *Features:* Focuses on training educators to become decision makers and leaders in the use of technology, with competencies in the design, development, and application of emerging technologies for teaching and learning. Incorporates basic elements that take into account the needs of adult learners, the constantly changing nature of technology, and the need for schools and universities to work together for schoolwide change. The Center for Technology in Education is a partnership project linking research and teaching of the University with the leadership and policy direction of the Maryland State Dept. of Education. The Center is directed by Dr. Nunn (2500 E. Northern Parkway, Baltimore, MD 21214-1113, 254-8466, jnunn@jhuniz.hcf.jhu.edu). *Admission Requirements:* Bachelor's degree with strong background in teaching, curriculum and instruction, special education, or a related service field. *Degree Requirements:* M.S. in Education, Technology for Educators: 36 semester hours (including 9 credits technical courses, 18 credits instructional courses, 9 credits research and school improvement courses). M.S. in Special Education, Technology in Special Education: 36 semester hours (including 9 credits technical courses, 15 credits instructional courses, 12 credits research and school improvement courses). *Faculty:* 2 full-time, 30 part-time. *Students:* 201 part-time. *Financial Assistance:* grants, student loans, scholarships. *Degrees Awarded 1997:* 38.

Towson State University. College of Education, Hawkins Hall, Rm. 103B, Towson, MD 21252. (410)830-6268. Fax (410)830-2733. E-mail wiser@toe.towson.edu. Website http://www.towson.edu/~coe/istc.html. Dr. David R. Wiser, Asst. Prof.. Dept.: Reading, Special Education, & Instructional Development, School Library Media and Education Technology. Prof., General Education Dept. *Specializations:* M.S. degrees in Instructional Development and School Library Media. *Admission Requirements:* Bachelor's degree from accredited institution with 3.0 GPA. (Conditional admission granted for many applicants with a GPA over 2.75). *Prerequisites:* For School Library Media & Education Technology specializations include teacher certification or completion of specific coursework. *Degree Requirements:* 36 graduate semester hours without thesis. *Faculty:* 7 full-time, 5 adjunct. *Students:* 150. *Financial Assistance:* graduate assistantships, work study, scholarships. *Degrees Awarded 1998:* 18.

University of Maryland. College of Library and Information Services, 4105 Hornbake Library Bldg., South Wing, College Park, MD 20742-4345. (301)405-2038. Fax (301)314-9145. Ann Prentice, Dean and Program Chair. *Specializations:* Master's of Library Science, including specialization in School Library Media; doctorate in Library and Information Services including specialization in Educational Technology/Instructional Communication. *Features:* Program is broadly conceived and interdisciplinary in nature, using the resources of the entire campus. The student and the advisor design a program of study and research to fit the student's background, interests, and professional objectives. Students prepare for careers in teaching and research in information science and librarianship and elect concentrations including Educational Technology and Instructional Communication. *Admission Requirements:* Doctoral: Bachelor's degree (the majority of doctoral students enter with master's degrees in Library Science, Educational Technology, or other relevant disciplines), GRE general tests, three letters of recommendation, statement of purpose. Interviews required when feasible for doctoral applicants. *Degree Requirements:* M.L.S.: 36 semester hours; thesis optional. *Faculty:* 15 full-time, 8 part-time. *Students:* Master's, 106 full-time, 149 part-time; doctoral, 5 full-time, 11 part-time. *Financial Assistance:* assistantships, grants, student loans, scholarships, fellowships.

University of Maryland, Baltimore County (UMBC). Dept. of Education, 1000 Hilltop Circle, Baltimore, MD 21250. (410)455-2310. Fax (410)455-3986. Email gist@umbc.edu. Website http://www.research.umbc.edu/~eholly/ceduc/isd/. Dr. William R. Johnson, Dir., Graduate Programs in Education. *Specializations:* M.A. degrees in School Instructional Systems, Post-Baccalaureate Teacher Certification, Training in Business and Industry. *Admissions Requirements:* 3.0 undergraduate GPA, GRE scores. *Degree Requirements:* 36 semester hours (including 18 in systems development for each program); internship. *Faculty:* 18 full-time, 25 part-time. *Students:* 59 full-time, 254 part-time. *Financial Assistance:* assistantships, scholarships. *Degrees Awarded 1997:* 68.

Western Maryland College. Dept. of Education, Main St., Westminster, MD 21157. (410)857-2507. Fax (410)857-2515. E-mail rkerby@wmdc.edu. Dr. Ramona N. Kerby, Coord., School Library Media Program, Dept. of Education. *Specializations:* M.S. in School Library Media. *Degree Requirements:* 33 credit hours (including 19 in media and 6 in education), comprehensive exam. *Faculty:* 1 full-time, 7 part-time. *Students:* 140, most part-time.

MASSACHUSETTS

Boston University. School of Education, 605 Commonwealth Ave., Boston, MA 02215-1605. (617)353-3181. Fax (617)353-3924. E-mail whittier@bu.edu. Website http://web.bu.edu /EDUCATION. David B. Whittier, Asst. Prof. and Coord., Program in Educational Media and Technology. *Specializations:* Ed.M., C.A.G.S. (Certificate of Advanced Graduate Study) in Educational Media and Technology; Ed.D. in Curriculum and Teaching, Specializing in Educational Media and Technology; preparation for Massachusetts public school certificates as Library Media Specialist and Instructional Technologist. *Features:* The Master's Program prepares graduates for professional careers as educators, instructional designers, developers of educational materials, and managers of the human and technology-based resources necessary to support education and training with technology. Graduates are employed in settings such as K–12 schools, higher education, industry, medicine, government, and publishing. Students come to the program from many different backgrounds and with a wide range of professional goals. The doctoral program sets the study of Educational Media & Technology within the context of education and educational research in general, and curriculum and teaching in particular. In addition to advanced work in the field of Educational Media and Technology, students examine and conduct research and study the history of educational thought and practice relating to teaching and learning. Graduates make careers in education as professors and researchers, technology directors and managers, and as developers of technology-based materials and systems. Graduates also make careers in medicine, government, business, and industry as instructional designers, program developers, project managers, and training directors. Graduates who work in both educational and non-educational organizations are often responsible for managing the human and technological resources required to create learning experiences that include the development and delivery of technology-based materials and distance education. *Admission Requirements:* Ed.M.: good recommendations, solid graduate test scores, 2.7 undergraduate GPA, GRE or MAT must be completed within past five years. C.A.G.S.: Ed.M., good recommendations, solid graduate test scores, 2.7 undergraduate GPA, GRE or MAT must be completed within past five years. Ed.D.: 3 letters of recommendation, 50 MAT or GRE scores, transcripts, writing samples, statement of goals and qualifications, analytical essay, 2.7 GPA. *Degree Requirements:* Ed.M.: 36 credit hours (including 22 hours from required core curriculum, 14 from electives). C.A.G.S.: 32 credits beyond Ed.M., one of which must be a curriculum and teaching course and a mini-comprehensive exam. Ed.D.: 60 credit hours of courses in Educational Media and Technology, curriculum and teaching, and educational thought and practice with comprehensive exams;

coursework and apprenticeship in research; 60 credit hours; dissertation. *Faculty:* 1 full-time, 1 half-time, 10 part-time. *Students:* 2 full-time, 12 part-time. *Financial Assistance:* U.S. Government sponsored work study, assistantships, grants, student loans, scholarships. *Degrees Awarded 1997:* Ed.M., 11; Ed.D., 1.

Bridgewater State College. Library Media Program, Hart Hall, Rm. 219, Bridgewater, MA 02325. (508)697-1320. Fax (508)697-1771. E-mail fzilonis@bridgew.edu. Website http://www.bridgew.edu. Mary Frances Zilonis, Coord., Library Media Program. *Specialization:* M.Ed. in Library Media Studies. *Features:* This program heavily emphasizes teaching and technology. *Degree Requirements:* 39 semester hours; comprehensive exam. *Faculty:* 2 full-time, 6 part-time. *Students:* 58 in degree program, 30 non-degree. *Financial Assistance:* Graduate assistantships, graduate internships. *Degrees Awarded 1997:* 5.

Fitchburg State College. Div. of Graduate and Continuing Education, 160 Pearl St., Fitchburg, MA 01420. (978)665-3181. Fax (978)665-3658. E-mail dgce@fsc.edu. Website http://www.fsc.edu. Dr. Lee DeNike, Chair. *Specialization:* M.S. in Communications Media with specializations in Management, Technical and Professional Writing, Instructional Technology, and Library Media. *Features:* Collaborating with professionals working in the field both for organizations and as independent producers, Fitchburg offers a unique M.S. program. The objective of the Master of Science in Communications/Media Degree Programs is to develop in candidates the knowledge and skills for the effective implementation of communication within business, industry, government, not-for-profit agencies, health services, and education. *Admission Requirements:* MAT or GRE scores, official transcript(s) of a baccalaureate degree, two or more years of experience in communications or media, department interview and portfolio presentation, three letters of recommendation. *Degree Requirements:* 36 semester credit hours. *Faculty:* 1 full-time, 7 part-time. *Students:* 84 part-time. *Financial assistance:* assistantships, student loans, scholarships. *Degrees Awarded 1998:* 40.

Harvard University. Appian Way, Cambridge, MA 02138. (617)495-3541. Fax (617)495-3626. E-mail Admit@hugse2.harvard.edu. Website http://GSEWeb.harvard.edu /TIEHome.html. David Perkins, Interim Dir. of Technology in Education Program. *Specialization:* M.Ed. in Technology in Education; an advanced certificate program is available. *Admission Requirements:* Bachelor's degree, MAT or GRE scores, 600 TOEFL, 3 recommendations. Students interested in print information about the TIE Program should e-mail a request to the address above. *Degree Requirements:* 32 semester credits. *Faculty:* 1 full-time, 9 part-time. *Students:* approx. 50: 39 full-time, 11 part-time. *Financial Assistance:* within the school's policy. *Degrees Awarded 1997:* 50.

Lesley College. 29 Everett St., Cambridge, MA 02138-2790. (617)349-8419. Fax (617)349-8169. E-mail nroberts@mail.lesley.edu. Website http://www.lesley.edu/soe/tech-in-ed/techined.html. Dr. Nancy Roberts, Prof. of Education. *Specializations:* M.Ed. in Technology Education; C.A.G.S. (Certificate of Advanced Graduate Study) in Technology Education; Ph.D. in Education with a Technology Education major. *Features:* M.Ed. program is offered off-campus at 65 sites in 16 states; contact Professional Outreach Associates [(800)843-4808] for information. The degree is also offered completely online. Contact Maureen Yoder, myoder@mail.lesley.edu, or (617)348-8421 for information. *Degree Requirements:* M.Ed.: 33 semester hours in technology, integrative final project in lieu of thesis, no internship or practicum. C.A.G.S.: 36 semester hours. Ph.D. requirements available on request. *Faculty:* 9 full-time, 122 part-time on the master's and C.A.G.S. levels. *Students:* 1200 part-time. *Degrees Awarded 1997:* 575.

Simmons College. Graduate School of Library and Information Science, 300 The Fenway, Boston, MA 02115-5898. (617)521-2800. Fax (617)521-3192. E-mail jbaughman@simmons.edu. Website http://www.simmons.edu/gslis/. Dr. James C. Baughman, Prof. *Specializations:* M.S. Dual degrees: M.L.S./M.A. in Education (for School Library Media Specialists);

M.L.S./M.A. in History (Archives Management Program). A Doctor of Arts in Administration is also offered. *Features:* The program prepares individuals for a variety of careers, media technology emphasis being only one. There are special programs for School Library Media Specialist and Archives Management with strengths in Information Science/Systems, Media Management. *Admission Requirements:* B.A. or B.S. degree with 3.0 GPA, statement, three letters of reference. *Degree Requirements:* 36 semester hours. *Faculty:* 14 full-time. *Students:* 75 full-time, 415 part-time. *Financial Assistance:* assistantships, grants, student loans, scholarships. *Degrees Awarded 1997:* Master's, 185.

University of Massachusetts-Boston. Graduate College of Education, 100 Morrissey Blvd., Boston, MA 02125. (617)287-5980. Fax (617)287-7664. E-mail babcock@umbsky.cc .umb.edu. Website http://www.umb.edu. Donald D. Babcock, Graduate Program Dir. *Specialization:* M.Ed. in Instructional Design. *Admission Requirements:* MAT or previous master's degree, goal statement, three letters of recommendation, resume, interview. *Degree Requirements:* 36 semester hours, thesis or project. *Faculty:* 1 full-time, 9 part-time. *Students:* 8 full-time, 102 part-time. *Financial Assistance:* graduate assistantships providing tuition plus stipend. *Degrees Awarded 1997:* 24.

University of Massachusetts-Lowell. College of Education, One University Ave., Lowell, MA 01854-2881. (508)934-4621. Fax (508)934-3005. E-mail John_Lebaron@uml.edu. Website http://www.uml.edu/College/Education/. John LeBaron, Faculty Chair. *Specializations:* M.Ed and Ed.D. Educational Technology may be pursued in the context of any degree program area. The Certificate of Advanced Graduate Study (C.A.G.S.), equivalent to 30 credits beyond a M.Ed., is also offered. *Admission Requirements:* Bachelor's degree in cognate area, GRE or MAT scores, statement of purpose, three recommendations. *Degree Requirements:* M.Ed.: 30 credits beyond bachelor's. Ed.D.: 60 credits beyond master's. *Faculty:* 1 full-time for technology courses. *Students:* 454. *Financial Assistance:* assistantships, student loans, limited scholarships. *Degrees Awarded 1997:* M.Ed., 120; Ed.D., 14; C.A.G.S., 5.

MICHIGAN

Eastern Michigan University. 234 Boone Hall, Ypsilanti, MI 48197. (734)487-3260. Fax (734)484-6471. Anne Bednar, Prof., Coord., Dept. of Teacher Education. *Specialization:* M.A. in Educational Psychology with concentration in Educational Technology. *Admission Requirements:* Bachelor's degree, 2.75 undergraduate GPA or MAT score, 500 TOEFL. *Degree Requirements:* 30 semester hours, optional thesis worth 6 credits. *Faculty:* 3 full-time. *Students:* 15. *Financial Assistance:* graduate assistantship. *Degrees Awarded 1997:* 12.

Michigan State University. College of Education, 431 Erickson, East Lansing, MI 48824. (517)355-6684. Fax (517)353-6393. E-mail yelons@pilot.msu.edu. Dr. Stephen Yelon. *Specialization:* M.A. in Educational Technology and Instructional Design. *Admission Requirements:* Bachelor's degree, 800 TOEFL, recommendations, goal statement. *Degree Requirements:* 30 semester hours, certification exam, field experience. *Faculty:* 5 full-time. *Students:* approx. 45. *Financial Assistance:* some assistantships for highly qualified students. *Degrees Awarded 1997:* approx. 12.

University of Michigan. Dept. of Educational Studies, 610 East University, Ann Arbor MI 48109-1259. (313)763-4668. Fax (313)763-4663. E-mail carl.berger@umich.edu. Website http://www.soe.umich.edu. Carl F. Berger, Chair. *Specializations:* M.Ed.; Ph.D. in Instructional Technology with concentrations in Science, Math, or Literacy. *Features:* Programs are individually designed. *Admission Requirements:* GRE, B.A. for M.Ed., master's for Ph.D. *Degree Requirements:* M.Ed.: 30 hours beyond B.A. Ph.D.: 60 hours beyond B.A. or 30 hours beyond master's plus comprehensive exams and dissertation. *Faculty:* 3 full-time, 6 part-time. *Students:* 35 full-time, 7 part-time. *Financial Assistance:* assistantships, grants, student loans, scholarships, internships. *Degrees Awarded 1997:* M.Ed., 15; Ph.D., 3.

Wayne State University. 381 Education, Detroit, MI 48202. (313)577-1728. Fax (313)577-1693. Website http://www.coe.wayne.edu/InstructionalTechnology. E-mail rrichey@coe.wayne .edu. Rita C. Richey, Prof., Program Coord., Instructional Technology Programs, Div. of Administrative and Organizational Studies, College of Education. *Specializations:* M.Ed. degrees in Performance Improvement and Training, K–12 Educational Technology, and Interactive Technologies. Ed.D. and Ph.D. programs to prepare individuals for leadership in business, industry, health care, and the K–12 school setting as instructional design and development specialists; media or learning resources managers or consultants; specialists in instructional video; and computer-assisted instruction and multimedia specialists. The school also offers a six-year specialist degree program in Instructional Technology. *Features:* Guided experiences in instructional design and development activities in business and industry are available. *Admission Requirements:* Ph.D.: Master's degree, 3.5 GPA, GRE, MAT, strong professional recommendations, interview. *Degree Requirements:* M.Ed.: 36 semester hours, including required project; internship recommended. *Faculty:* 6 full-time, 5 part-time. *Students:* M.Ed., 525; doctoral, 95, most part-time. *Financial Assistance:* student loans, scholarships, and paid internships. *Degrees Awarded 1997-1998:* M.Ed., 57; doctoral, 16.

MINNESOTA

Mankato State University. MSU Box 20, P.O. Box 8400, Mankato, MN 56001-8400. (507)389-1965. Fax (507)389-5751. E-mail pengelly@mankato.msus.edu. Website http://lme .mankato.msus.edu. Frank R. Birmingham Ph.D., Dept. of Library Media Education. *Specialization:* M.S. in Educational Technology with three tracks. *Admission Requirements:* Bachelor's degree, 2.75/4.0 for last 2 years of undergraduate work. *Degree Requirements:* 32 semester hour credits, comprehensive exam. *Faculty:* 4 full-time. *Degrees Awarded 1997:* 12.

St. Cloud State University. College of Education, St. Cloud, MN 56301-4498. (612)255-2022. Fax (612)255-4778. E-mail jberling@tigger.stcloud.msus.edu. John G. Berling, Prof., Dir., Center for Information Media. *Specializations:* Master's degrees in Information Technologies, Educational Media, and Human Resources Development/Training. A Specialist degree is also offered. *Admission Requirements:* Acceptance to Graduate School, written preliminary examination, interview. *Degree Requirements:* Master's: 51 qtr. hours with thesis; 54 qtr. hours, Plan B; 57 qtr. hours, portfolio; 200-hour practicum is required for media generalist licensure. Coursework applies to Educational Media Master's program. *Faculty:* 7 full-time. *Students:* 15 full-time, 150 part-time. *Financial Assistance:* assistantships, scholarships. *Degrees Awarded 1997:* Master's, 12.

Walden University. 155 5th Avenue South, Minneapolis, MN 55401. (800)444-6795. E-mail www@waldenu.edu or info@waldenu.edu. Websites http://www.waldenu.edu; http://www .waldenu.edu/ecti/ecti.html. Dr. Gwen Hillesheim, Chair. *Specializations:* M.S. in Educational Change and Technology Innovation. Ph.D. in Education in Learning and Teaching with specialization in Educational Technology. In 1998 a specialization in Distance Learning will be added. In addition, there is a generalist Ph.D. in Education in which students may choose and design their own areas of specialization. *Features:* Delivered primarily online. *Admission Requirements:* Accredited bachelor's. Ph.D.: accredited master's, goal statement, letters of recommendation. *Degree Requirements:* Master's: 45 credit curriculum, 2 brief residencies, master's project. *Faculty:* 18 part-time. *Students:* 50 full-time, 53 part-time in master's program. *Financial Assistance:* student loans, 3 fellowships with annual review. *Degrees Awarded 1997:* 4 (program instituted in 1996).

MISSOURI

Fontbonne College. 6800 Wydown Blvd., St. Louis, MO 63105. (314)889-1497. Fax (314)889-1451. E-mail mabkemei@fontbonne.edu. Dr. Mary K. Abkemeier, Chair. *Specialization:* M.S. in Computer Education. *Features:* Small classes and coursework immediately applicable to the classroom. *Admission Requirements:* 2.5 undergraduate GPA, 3 letters of recommendation. *Degree Requirements:* 33 semester hours, 3.0 GPA. *Faculty:* 2 full-time, 12 part-time. *Students:* 4 full-time, 90 part-time. *Financial Assistance:* grants. *Degrees Awarded 1998:* 32.

Northwest Missouri State University. Dept. of Computer Science/Information Systems, 800 University Ave., Maryville MO 64468. (660)562-1600. E-mail pheeler@mail.nwmissouri .edu. Website http://www.nwmissouri.edu/~csis. Dr. Phillip Heeler, Chair. *Specializations:* M.S. in School Computer Studies; M.S.Ed. in Educational Uses of Computers. *Features:* These degrees are designed for computer educators at the elementary, middle school, high school, and junior college level. *Admission Requirements:* 3.0 undergraduate GPA, 700 GRE (V+Q). *Degree Requirements:* 32 semester hours of graduate courses in computer science and/or educational computing courses. *Faculty:* 12 full-time, 4 part-time. *Students:* 5 full-time, 20 part-time. *Financial Assistance:* assistantships, grants, student loans, and scholarships. *Degrees Awarded 1998:* 10.

University of Missouri-Columbia. College of Education, 217 Townsend Hall, Columbia, MO 65211. (573)882-4546. Fax (573)884-4944. Jim Laffey, Assoc. Prof. (Cilaffey@showme .missouri.edu). Website http://www.coe.missouri.edu/sisInformation Science and Learning Technologies Program, School of Information Science & Learning Technologies. *Specializations:* Master's degree program prepares professionals to design, develop, and implement technology in educational settings. Ph.D. in Information Science & Learning Technologies prepares professionals to understand and influence learning, information organization and retrieval, and performance in diverse learning environments, especially through the design, development, and use of interactive technologies. An Education Specialist degree program is also available. *Features:* Master's program is competency-based. Graduates leave with the ability to plan, implement, and evaluate educational technology innovations, and to design, develop, and evaluate technology-based learning and performance support products. Ph.D. program includes a major in Information Science and Learning Technologies with research tools, and R&D apprenticeship experiences. In addition to the competency-based objectives of the master's program, doctoral graduates will be able to conduct systematic research which contributes to the knowledge base of learning, information organization and retrieval, performance, and technology. *Admission Requirements:* Master's: Bachelor's degree, GRE score. Ph.D.: 3.2 graduate GPA, 1500 GRE, letter of recommendation, statement of purpose. *Faculty:* Master's, 8 full-time, 10 part-time; Ph.D., 13 full-time, 18 part-time, plus selected faculty in related fields. *Students:* Master's, 18 full-time, 52 part-time; Ph.D., 13 full-time, 12 part-time. *Financial Assistance:* master's: assistantships, grants, student loans, scholarships. Ph.D.: graduate assistantships with tuition waivers; numerous academic scholarships ranging from $200 to $18,000. *Degrees Awarded 1998:* Master's, 7 Ph.D., 5.

Webster University. Instructional Technology, St. Louis, MO 63119. (314)968-7490. Fax (314)968-7118. E-mail steinmpe@websteruniv.edu. Website http://www.websteruniv.edu. Paul Steinmann, Assoc. Dean and Dir., Graduate Studies and Instructional Technology. *Specialization:* Master's degree (M.A.T.); State Certification in Media Technology is a program option. *Admission Requirements:* Bachelor's degree with 2.5 GPA. *Degree Requirements:* 33 semester hours (including 24 in media); internship required. *Faculty:* 5. *Students:* 7 full-time, 28 part-time. *Financial Assistance:* partial scholarships, minority scholarships, government loans, and limited state aid. *Degrees Awarded 1997:* 6.

MONTANA

University of Montana. School of Education, Missoula, MT 59812. (406)243-5785. Fax (406)243-4908. E-mail cjlott@selway.umt.edu. Dr. Carolyn Lott, Assoc. Prof. of Library/ Media. *Specializations:* M.Ed. and Specialist degrees; K–12 School Library Media specialization with School Library Media Certification endorsement. *Admission Requirements:* (both degrees): GRE, letters of recommendation, 2.5 GPA. *Degree Requirements:* M.Ed.: 37 semester credit hours (18 overlap with library media endorsement). Specialist: 28 semester hours (18 overlap). *Faculty:* 2 full-time. *Students:* 5 full-time, 20 part-time. *Financial Assistance:* assistantships; contact the University of Montana Financial Aid Office. *Degrees Awarded 1998:* 5.

NEBRASKA

University of Nebraska at Kearney. Kearney, NE 68849-1260. (308)865-8833. Fax (308)865-8097. E-mail fredrickson@unk.edu. Dr. Scott Fredrickson, Dir. of Instructional Technology. Website http://www.unk.edu/departments/pte. *Specializations:* M.S. in Instructional Technology, M.S. in Educational Media, Specialist in Educational Media. *Admission Requirements:* M.S. and Specialist: GRE, acceptance into graduate school, approval of Instructional Technology Committee. *Degree Requirements:* M.S.: 36 credit hours, master's comprehensive exam or field study. Specialist: 39 credit hours, field study. *Faculty:* 5 full-time, 10 part-time. *Students:* 62 full-time. *Financial Assistance:* assistantships, grants, student loans. *Degrees Awarded 1997:* M.S., 12; Ed.S., 0.

University of Nebraska-Omaha. Dept. of Teacher Education, College of Education, Kayser Hall 208D, Omaha, NE 68182. (402)5543790. Fax (402)554-3491. E-mail langan@unomaha .edu. John Langan, Teacher Education. *Specializations:* M.S. in Education, M.A. in Education, both with Educational Media concentration. *Degree Requirements:* 36 semester hours (including 24 in media), practicum; thesis optional. *Faculty:* 2 full-time, 4 part-time. *Students:* 10 full-time, 62 part-time. *Financial Assistance:* Contact Financial Aid Office. *Degrees Awarded 1997:* 45.

NEVADA

University of Nevada. Counseling and Educational Psychology Dept., College of Education, Reno, NV 89557. (702)784-6327. Fax (702)784-1990. E-mail ljohnson@unr.edu. Website http://www.unr.edu/unr/colleges/educ/cep/cepindex.html. Dr. LaMont Johnson, Program Coord., Information Technology in Education. Marlowe Smaby, Dept. Chair. *Specializations:* M.S. and Ph.D. *Admission Requirements:* Bachelor's degree, 2.75 undergraduate GPA, 750 GRE (V+Q). *Degree Requirements:* 36 semester credits, optional thesis worth 6 credits, comprehensive exam. *Faculty:* 2 full-time, 1 part-time. *Students:* M.S., 15; Ph.D., 10. *Degrees Awarded 1997:* M.S., 4; Ph.D., 1.

NEW JERSEY

Montclair State University. Dept. of Reading and Educational Media, Upper Montclair, NJ 07043. (973)655-7040. Fax (973)655-5310. Website http://www.monclair.edu. Robert R. Ruezinsky, Dir. of Academic Technology. *Specializations:* No degree program exists. Two certification programs, A.M.S. and E.M.S, exist on the graduate level. *Certification Requirements:* 18-21 semester hours of media and technology are required for the A.M.S. program and 30-33 hours for the E.M.S. program. *Faculty:* 7 part-time. *Students:* 32 part-time.

Rutgers-The State University of New Jersey. Ph.D. Program in Communication, Information, and Library Studies, The Graduate School, New Brunswick, NJ 08901-1071. (732)932-7447. Fax (732)932-6916. Dr. Lea P. Stewart, Dir. Master's Program, Dept. of Library and Information Studies, School of Communication, Information and Library Studies. (732)932-9717. Fax (732)932-2644. Dr. Carol Kuhlthan, Chair. *Specializations:* M.L.S. degree with specializations in Information Retrieval, Technical and Automated Services, Reference, School Media Services, Youth Services, Management and Policy Issues, and Generalist Studies. Ph.D. programs in Communication; Media Studies; Information Systems, Structures, and Users; Information and Communication Policy and Technology; and Library and Information Services. The school also offers a six-year specialist certificate program. *Features:* Ph.D. Program provides doctoral-level coursework for students seeking theoretical and research skills for scholarly and professional leadership in the information and communication fields. A course on multimedia structure, organization, access, and production is offered. *Admission Requirements:* Ph.D.: Master's degree in Information Studies, Communication, Library Science, or related field; 3.0 undergraduate GPA; GRE scores; TOEFL (for applicants whose native language is not English). *Degree Requirements:* M.L.S.: 36 semester hours, in which the hours for media vary for individual students; practicum of 150 hours. *Faculty:* M.L.S., 15 full-time, 12 adjunct; Ph.D., 43. *Students:* M.L.S., 97 full-time, 199 part-time; Ph.D., 104. *Financial Assistance:* M.L.S.: scholarships, fellowships, and graduate assistantships. Ph.D.: assistantships. *Degrees Awarded 1998:* Master's, 169; Ph.D., 8.

William Paterson University. College of Education, 300 Pompton Rd., Wayne, NJ 07470. (973)720-2140. Fax (973)720-2585. Website http://pwcweb.wilpaterson.edu/wpcpages/library /default.htp. Dr. Amy G. Job, Librarian, Assoc. Prof., Coord., Program in Library/Media, Curriculum and Instruction Dept. *Specializations:* M.Ed. for Educational Media Specialist, Associate Media Specialist, Ed.S. *Admission Requirements:* Teaching certificate, 2.75 GPA, MAT or GRE scores, 1 year teaching experience. Ed.S.: certificate, 2.75 GPA. *Degree Requirements:* M.Ed.: 33 semester hours, including research projects and practicum. Ed.S.: 18 sem. hours. *Faculty:* 6 full-time, 2 part-time. *Students:* 30 part-time. *Financial Assistance:* limited. *Degrees Awarded 1998:* M.Ed., 4; Ed.S., 2.

NEW YORK

Buffalo State College. 1300 Elmwood Ave., Buffalo, NY 14222-1095. (716)878-4923. Fax (716)878-6677. E-mail nowakoaj@buffalostate.edu. Dr. Anthony J. Nowakowski, Program Coord. *Specializations:* M.S. in Education in Educational Computing. *Admission Requirements:* Bachelor's degree from accredited institution, 3.0 GPA in last 60 hours, 3 letters of recommendation. *Degree Requirements:* 33 semester hours (15 hours in computers, 12-15 hours in education, 3-6 electives); thesis or project (see: www.buffalostate.edu/edc). *Faculty:* 5 part-time. *Students:* 3 full-time, 98 part-time. *Degrees Awarded 1997:* 16.

Fordham University. Rose Hill Campus, 441 E. Fordham Rd., Bronx, NY. 10458. (718)817-4860. Fax (718)817-4868. E-mail pcom@murray.fordham.edu. Website http://www .fordham.edu. Robin Andersen, Dept. Chair, James Capo, Dir. of Graduate Studies. *Specializations:* M.A. in Public Communications. *Features:* Internship or thesis option; full-time students can complete program in twelve months. *Admission Requirements:* 3.0 undergraduate GPA. *Degree Requirements:* 10 courses plus internship or thesis. *Faculty:* 8 full-time, 2 part-time. *Students:* 8 full-time, 22 part-time. *Financial Assistance:* assistantships, student loans, scholarships. *Degrees Awarded 1997:* 12.

Ithaca College. School of Communications, Ithaca, NY 14850. (607)274-1025. Fax (607)274-1664. E-mail Herndon@Ithaca.edu. Website http://www.ithaca.edu/rhp/corpcomm /corpcomm1/. Sandra L. Herndon, Prof., Chair, Graduate Communications; Roy H. Park, School of Communications. *Specialization:* M.S. in Communications. Students in this program find employment in such areas as instructional design, multimedia, public relations and marketing, and employee communication. The program can be tailored to individual career goals. *Admission Requirements:* 3.0 GPA, TOEFL 550 (where applicable). *Degree Requirements:* 36 semester hours, seminar. *Faculty:* 8 full-time. *Students:* approx. 25 full-time, 10 part-time. *Financial Assistance:* graduate assistantships. *Degrees Awarded 1998:* 18.

New York Institute of Technology. Dept. of Instructional Technology, Tower House, Old Westbury, NY 11568. (516)686-7777. Fax (516)686-7655. E-mail dplumer460@aol.com. Website http://www.nyit.edu. Davenport Plumer, Chair, Depts. of Instructional Technology and Elementary Education - pre. Service & in-service. *Specializations:* M.S. in Instructional Technology; M.S. in Elementary Education; Specialist Certificates in Computers in Education, Distance Learning, and Multimedia (not degrees, but are earned after the first 18 credits of the master's degree). *Features:* Computer integration in virtually all courses; online courses; evening, weekend, and summer courses. *Admission Requirements:* Bachelor's degree from accredited college with 3.0 cumulative average. *Degree Requirements:* 36 credits with 3.0 GPA for M.S., 18 credits with 3.0 GPA for certificates. *Faculty:* 11 full-time, 42 part-time. *Students:* 112 full-time, 720 part-time. *Financial Assistance:* graduate assistantships, institutional and alumni scholarships, student loans. *Degrees Awarded 1998:* M.S., 51; Specialist, 41.

New York University. Educational Communication and Technology Program, School of Education, 239 Greene St., Suite 300, New York, NY 10003. (212)998-5520. Fax (212)995-4041. Website http://www.nyu.edu. Francine Shuchat Shaw, Assoc. Prof., Dir.; Donald T. Payne, Assoc. Prof., Doctoral Advisor. *Specializations:* M.A., Ed.D., and Ph.D. in Education for the preparation of individuals to perform as instructional media designers, developers, producers, and researchers in education, business and industry, health and medicine, community services, government, museums, and other cultural institutions; and to teach in educational communications and instructional technology programs in higher education, including instructional television, microcomputers, multimedia, and telecommunications. The school also offers a post-M.A. 30-point Certificate of Advanced Study in Education. *Features:* Emphasizes theoretical foundations, especially a cognitive perspective of learning and instruction, and their implications for designing media-based learning environments. All efforts focus on multimedia, instructional television, and telecommunications; participation in special research and production projects and field internships. *Admission Requirements:* M.A.: 3.0 undergraduate GPA, responses to essay questions, interview related to academic and professional goals. Ph.D.: 3.0 GPA, 1000 GRE, responses to essay questions, interview related to academic or professional preparation and career goals. For international students, 600 TOEFL and TWE. *Degree Requirements:* M.A.: 36 semester hours including specialization, elective courses, thesis, English Essay Examination. Ph.D.: 57 semester hours including specialization, foundations, research, content seminar, and elective coursework; candidacy papers; dissertation; English Essay Examination. *Faculty:* 2 full-time, 10 part-time. *Students:* M.A.: 40 full-time, 35 part-time. Ph.D.: 14 full-time, 20 part-time. *Financial Assistance:* graduate and research assistantships, student loans, scholarships, and work assistance programs. *Degrees Awarded 1997:* M.A., 12; Ph.D., 2.

Pace University. Westchester Dept., School of Education, Bedford Road, Pleasantville, NY 10570. (914)773-3829, (914)773-3979. Fax (914)773-3521. Website http://www.pace.edu. E-mail keyes@pacevm.dac.pace.edu. Dr. Carol Keyes, Chair. *Specialization:* M.S.E. in Curriculum and Instruction with a concentration in Computers. Computer courses are related to evaluating program packages, instructional applications of computer technology in educational software, and the Internet, multimedia in the classroom, and cognitive processing with computers. *Admission Requirements:* GPA 3.0, interview. *Degree Requirements:* 33-34 semester hours (15 in computers, 18 in educational administration). *Faculty:* 8 full-time, 50 part-time. *Students:* 60-70 part-time. *Financial Assistance:* assistantships, scholarships.

St. John's University. Div. of Library and Information Science, 8000 Utopia Parkway, Jamaica, NY 11439. (718)990-6200. Fax (718)990-2071. E-mail libis@stjohns.edu. Website http://www .stjohns.edu/gsas/dlis/. James Benson, Dir. *Specializations:* M.L.S. with specialization in School Media. The school also offers a 24-credit Advanced Certificate program. *Admission Requirements:* 3.0 GPA, 2 letters of reference, statement of professional goals. *Degree Requirements:* 36 semester hours, comprehensive exam, practicum. *Faculty:* 7 full-time, 12 part-time. *Students:* 19 full-time, 78 part-time. *Financial Assistance:* 8 assistantships. *Degrees Awarded 1997:* Master's, 48.

State University College of Arts and Science at Potsdam. School of Education, 116 Satterlee Hall, Potsdam, NY 13676. (315)267-2535. Fax (315)267-4895. E-mail mlynarhc@potsdam.edu, Dr. Charles Mlynarczyk, Chair, Teacher Education. *Specializations:* M.S. in Education in Instructional Technology and Media Management with concentrations in General K–12,

Educational Communications Specialist, and Training and Development. *Degree Requirements:* 33 semester hours, including internship or practicum; culminating project required. *Faculty:* 3 full-time, 2 part-time. *Students:* 26 full-time, 45 part-time. *Financial Assistance:* student loans, student assistantships. *Degrees Awarded 1998:* 41.

State University of New York at Albany. School of Education, 1400 Washington Ave., Albany, NY 12222. (518)442-5032. Fax (518)442-5008. E-mail swan@cnsunix.albany.edu. Karen Swan (ED114A), contact person. *Specialization:* M.Ed. and Ph.D. in Curriculum and Instruction with specializations in Instructional Theory, Design, and Technology. Med offered entirely online over the WWW. *Admission Requirements:* Bachelor's degree, GPA close to 3.0; transcript, three letters of recommendation. Students desiring New York State permanent teaching certification should possess preliminary certification. *Degree Requirements:* M.Ed.: 30 semester hours with 15-18 credits in specialization. Ph.D.: 78 semester hours, internship, portfolio certification, thesis. *Faculty:* 13 full-time, 7 part-time. *Students:* 100 full-time, 350 part-time. *Financial Assistance:* fellowships, assistantships, grant, student loans, minority fellowships. *Degrees Awarded 1997:* M.Ed., 165; Ph.D., 7.

State University of New York at Stony Brook. Technology & Society, College of Engineering & Applied Sciences, SUNY at Stony Brook, Stony Brook, NY 11794-2250. (516)632-8763. (516)632-7809. E-mail dferguson@dts.tns.sunysb.edu. Website http://www.ceas .sunysb.edu/DTS/. Prof. David L. Ferguson, Contact Person. *Specializations:* Master's Degree in Technological Systems Management with concentration in Educational Computing. *Features:* Emphasis on courseware design, multimedia and modeling, applications, and problem-solving. *Admission Requirements:* Bachelor's degree in engineering, natural sciences, social sciences, mathematics, or closely related area; 3.0 undergraduate GPA, experience with computer applications or computer applications or use of computers in teaching. *Degree Requirements:* 30 semester credits, including two general technology core courses, 5 required educational computing courses, and 3 eligible electives. *Faculty:* 5 full-time, 3 part-time. *Students:* 10 full-time, 15 part-time. *Financial Assistance:* assistantships, grants, student loans. *Degrees Awarded 1997:* 5.

Syracuse University. Instructional Design, Development, and Evaluation Program, School of Education, 330 Huntington Hall, Syracuse, NY 13244-2340. (315)443-3703. Fax (315)443-9218. E-mail lltucker@sued.syr.edu. Website http://www.idde.syr.edu. Philip L. Doughty, Prof., Chair. *Specializations:* M.S., Ed.D., and Ph.D. degree programs for Instructional Design of programs and materials, Educational Evaluation, Human Issues in Instructional Development, Media Production (including computers and multimedia), and Educational Research and Theory (learning theory, application of theory, and educational media research). Graduates are prepared to serve as curriculum developers, instructional developers, program and product evaluators, researchers, resource center administrators, communications coordinators, trainers in human resource development, and higher education instructors. The school also offers an advanced certificate program. *Features:* Field work and internships, special topics and special issues seminar, student- and faculty-initiated minicourses, seminars and guest lecturers, faculty-student formulation of department policies, and multiple international perspectives. *Admission Requirements:* M.S.: undergraduate transcripts, recommendations, personal statement, interview recommended; TOEFL for international applicants; GRE recommended. Doctoral: Relevant master's degree from accredited institution, GRE (3 tests required) scores, recommendations, personal statement, TOEFL for international applicants; interview recommended. *Faculty:* 2 full-time, 4 part-time. *Degree Requirements:* M.S.: 36 semester hours, comprehensive exam and portfolio required. *Students:* M.S., 22 full-time, 23 part-time; doctoral, 25 full-time, 30 part-time. *Financial Assistance:* fellowships, scholarships, and graduate assistantships entailing either research or administrative duties in instructional technology. *Degrees Awarded 1998:* M.S., 8; doctorate, 7.

NORTH CAROLINA

Appalachian State University. Dept. of Leadership and Educational Studies, Boone, NC 28608. (704)262-2243. Fax (704)262-2128. E-mail Webbbh@appstate.edu. Website http://www.ced.appstate.edu/ltl.html. John H. Tashner, Prof., Coord. *Specialization:* M.A. in Educational Media and Technology with three areas of concentration: Computers, Tele-communications, and Media Production. *Features:* IMPACT NC (business, university, and public school) partnership offers unusual opportunities. *Degree Requirements:* 36 semester hours (including 15 in Computer Education), internship; thesis optional. *Faculty:* 2 full-time, 1 part-time. *Students:* 10 full-time, 60 part-time. *Financial Assistance:* assistantships, grants, student loans. *Degrees Awarded 1997:* 15.

East Carolina University. Dept. of Library Studies and Educational Technology, Green-ville, NC 27858-4353. (919)328-6621. Fax (919)328-4368. E-mail kesterd@mail.ecu.edu. Website eastnet.educ.ecu.edu/schofed/lset. Dr. Diane D. Kester, Assoc. Prof., Chair. *Speciali-zations:* Master of Library Science; Certificate of Advanced Study (Library Science); Master of Arts in Education (Instructional Technology Computers). *Features:* M.L.S. graduates are eligible for North Carolina School Media Coord. certification; C.A.S. graduates are eligible for North Carolina School Media Supervisor certification; M.A.Ed. graduates are eligible for North Carolina Instructional Technology-Computers certification. *Admission Requirements:* Master's: Bachelor's degree; C.A.S.: M.L.S. or equivalent degree. *Degree Requirements:* M.L.S.: 38 semester hours; M.A.Ed.: 36 semester hours; C.A.S.: 30 semester hours. *Faculty:* 9 full-time. *Students:* 7 full-time, 150 part-time. *Financial Assistance:* assistantships. *Degrees Awarded 1997:* M.L.S., 21; M.A.Ed., 19; C.A.S., 3.

North Carolina Central University. School of Education, 1801 Fayetteville St., Durham, NC 27707. (919)560-6692. Fax (919)560-5279. Dr. James N. Colt, Assoc. Prof., Coord., Graduate Program in Educational Technology. *Specialization:* M.A. with special emphasis on Instructional Development/Design. *Features:* Graduates are prepared to implement and utilize a variety of technologies applicable to many professional ventures, including institu-tions of higher education (college resource centers), business, industry, and professional schools such as medicine, law, dentistry, and nursing. *Admission Requirements:* Undergraduate degree, GRE. *Degree Requirements:* 33 semester hours (including thesis). *Faculty:* 2 full-time, 2 part-time. *Students:* 19 full-time, 18 part-time. *Financial Assistance:* assistantships, grants, student loans. *Degrees Awarded 1998:* 15.

North Carolina State University. Dept. of Curriculum and Instruction, P.O. Box 7801, Raleigh, NC 27695-7801. (919)515-1779. Fax (919)515-6978. E-mail esvasu@unity.ncsu.edu. Dr. Ellen Vasu, Assoc. Prof. *Specializations:* M.Ed. and M.S. in Instructional Technology-Computers (program track within one Master's in Curriculum and Instruc-tion). Ph.D. in Curriculum and Instruction with focus on Instructional Technology as well as other areas. *Admission Requirements:* Master's: Undergraduate degree from an accredited institution, 3.0 GPA in major or in latest graduate degree program; transcripts; GRE or MAT scores; 3 references; goal statement, interview (see http://www2.ncsu.edu/ncsu/cep /ci/it/mitmain.html). Ph.D.: Undergraduate degree from accredited institution, 3.0 GPA in major or latest graduate program; transcripts; recent GRE scores, writing sample, interview, three references, vita, goal statement (see http://www2.acs.ncsu.edu/grad/admision.htm). *Degree Requirements:* Master's: 36 semester hours, practicum, thesis optional; Ph.D.: 60 hours beyond master's (minimum 33 in Curriculum and Instruction core, 27 in Research); other information available upon request. *Faculty:* 2 full-time. *Students:* Master's, 32 part-time; Ph.D., 6 part-time. *Degrees Awarded 1997:* Master's, 1; Ph.D., 2.

University of North Carolina. School of Information and Library Science (CB#3360), Chapel Hill, NC 27599. (919)962-8062, 962-8366. Fax (919)962-8071. E-mail daniel @ils.unc.edu. Website http://www.ils.unc.edu/. Evelyn H. Daniel, Prof., Coord., School Media Program. *Specialization:* Master of Science Degree in Library Science (M.S.L.S.)

with specialization in school library media work. *Features:* Rigorous academic program plus teaching practicum requirement; excellent placement record. *Admission Requirements:* Competitive admission based on all three GRE components, undergraduate GPA, letters of recommendation, and student statement of career interest. *Degree Requirements:* 48 semester hours, comprehensive exam, master's paper. *Faculty:* 18 full-time, 10 part-time. *Students:* 30 full-time, 20 part-time. *Financial Assistance:* grants, assistantships, student loans. *Degrees Awarded 1997* (School Media Certification): 30.

NORTH DAKOTA

Minot State University. 500 University Ave. W., Minot, ND 58707. (701)858-3250. Fax (701)839-6933. Dr. Jack L. Rasmussen, Dean of the Graduate School. *Specializations:* M.S. in Elementary Education (including work in educational computing); M.S. in Special Education with Specialization in Severe Multiple-Handicaps, Early Childhood Special Education, Education of the Deaf, and Learning Disabilities; M.S. in Communication Disorders, Specializations in Audiology and Speech Language Pathology. *Features:* All programs include involvement in computer applications appropriate to the area of study, including assistive technologies for persons with disabilities. Computer laboratories are available for student use in the library and various departments. Some courses are offered through the Interactive Video Network, which connects all universities in North Dakota. All programs have a rural focus and are designed to offer a multitude of practical experiences. *Admission Requirements:* $25 fee, three letters of recommendation, 300-word autobiography, transcripts, GRE in Communication Disorders or GMAT for M.S. in Management. *Degree Requirements:* 30 semester hours (hours in computers, education, and outside education vary according to program); written comprehensive exams; oral exams; thesis or project. *Faculty:* 10 full-time. *Students:* 61 full-time, 63 part-time. *Financial Assistance:* loans, assistantships, scholarships. *Degrees Awarded 1997:* M.S.: Elementary Education, 15; S.P.Ed., Severe Multiple Handicaps, 4; S.P.Ed. Early Childhood Special Education, 4; Communication Disorders, 35; S.P.Ed. Learning Disabilities, 13.

OHIO

*Kent State University. 405 White Hall, Kent, OH 44242. (330)672-2294. Fax (330)672-2512. E-mail tchandler@emerald.edu.kent.edu. Website http://amethyst.educ.kent./edu/itec/. Dr. Theodore Chandler, Coord., Instructional Technology Program. *Specializations:* M.Ed. or M.A. in Instructional Technology, Instructional Computing, and Library/Media Specialist; Ph.D. in Educational Psychology with emphasis in Instructional Technology. *Features:* Programs are planned individually to prepare students for careers in elementary, secondary, or higher education, business, industry, government agencies, or health facilities. Students may take advantage of independent research, individual study, practica, and internships. *Admission Requirements:* Master's: Bachelor's degree with 2.75 undergraduate GPA. *Degree Requirements:* Master's: 34 semester hours; thesis required for M.A. *Faculty:* 5 full-time, 7 part-time. *Students:* 39. *Financial Assistance:* 6 graduate assistantships, John Mitchell and Marie McMahan Awards, 4 teaching fellowships. *Degrees Awarded 1996:* Master's: 14.

Ohio University. School of Curriculum and Instruction, 248 McCracken Hall, Athens, OH 45701-2979. (740)593-9826. Fax (740)593-0177. Sandra Turner, Chair. *Specialization:* M.Ed. in Computer Education and Technology. Ph.D. in Curriculum and Instruction with emphasis in Technology also available; call for details. *Admission Requirements:* Bachelor's degree, 2.5 undergraduate GPA, 35 MAT, 420 GRE (verbal), 400 GRE (quantitative), 550 TOEFL, three letters of recommendation. *Degree Requirements:* 54 qtr. credits, optional thesis worth 2-10 credits or alternative seminar and paper. Students may earn two graduate degrees simultaneously in education and in any other field. *Faculty:* 2 full-time, 1 part-time. *Students:* M.Ed.: 60. *Financial Assistance:* assistantships. *Degrees to Awarded 1998:* 25.

*University of Cincinnati. College of Education, 401 Teachers College, ML002, Cincinnati, OH 45221-0002. (513)556-3577. Fax (513)556-2483. Website http://uc.edu/. Randall Nichols and Janet Bohren, Div. of Teacher Education. *Specialization:* M.A. or Ed.D. in Curriculum and Instruction with an emphasis on Instructional Design and Technology; Educational Technology degree programs for current professional, technical, critical, and personal knowledge. *Admission Requirements:* Bachelor's degree from accredited institution, 2.8 undergraduate GPA; conditional admission for candidates not meeting first two criteria possible. *Degree Requirements:* 54 qtr. hours, written exam, thesis or research project. *Faculty:* 3 full-time. *Students:* 20 full-time. *Financial Assistance:* scholarships, assistantships, grants. *Degrees Awarded 1996:* M.A., 12.

University of Toledo. Area of Education, 2801 West Bancroft, Toledo, OH 43606. (419)530-6176. Fax (419)530-7719. E-mail APATTER@UTNET.UTOLEDO.EDU. Website http://carver.carver.utoledo. Dr. Lester J. Elsie, Dir. *Specializations:* Master's (M.Ed. and M.S.Ed.), Ed.S, doctorate (Ed.D., Ph.D.) degrees in Instructional Development, Library/Media Education, Instructional Computing, and Human Resources Development. *Admission Requirements:* Master's: 3.0 undergraduate GPA, GRE, recommendations; Ed.S.: Master's: GRE, recommendations; Doctorate: Master's degree, GRE, TOEFL, recommendations, entrance writing sample, and interview. *Degree Requirements:* Master's: 36 semester hours, master's project; Ed.S.: 32 semester hours, internship; doctorate: 84 semester hours, dissertation. *Faculty:* 5 full-time, 1 part-time. *Students:* Master's, 10 full-time, 72 part-time; Ed.S., 2 full-time, 21 part-time; doctoral, 9 full-time, 56 part-time. *Financial Assistance:* assistantships, student loans, scholarships, work assistance program. *Degrees Awarded 1997:* Master's, 26; Ed.S., 3; doctoral, 3.

Wright State University. College of Education and Human Services, Dept. of Educational Leadership, 228 Millett Hall, Dayton, OH 45435. (937)775-2509 or (937)775-2182. Fax (937)775-4485. Website http://www.ed.wright.edu. Dr. Bonnie K. Mathies, Asst. Dean Communication and Technology. E-mail bonnie.mathies@wright.edu. *Specializations:* M.Ed. in or for Media Supervisor or Computer Coord.; M.A. in Educational Media or Computer Education; Specialist degree in Curriculum and Instruction with a focus on Educational Technology; Specialist degree in Higher Education with a focus on Educational Technology. *Admission Requirements:* Completed application with nonrefundable application fee, bachelor's degree from accredited institution, official transcripts, 2.7 overall GPA for regular status (conditional acceptance possible), statement of purpose, satisfactory scores on MAT or GRE. *Degree Requirements:* M.Ed. requires a comprehensive exam that includes a portfolio with videotaped presentation to the faculty. M.A. requires a 6-hour thesis. *Faculty:* 2 full-time, 12 part-time, including other university full-time faculty and staff. *Students:* approx. 3 full-time, approx. 200 part-time. *Financial Assistance:* 3 graduate assistantships in the College's Educational Resource Center; plus graduate fellowship for full-time students available limited number of small graduate scholarships. *Degree Awarded 1998:* 11.

OKLAHOMA

Southwestern Oklahoma State University. School of Education, 100 Campus Drive, Weatherford, OK 73096. (405)774-3140. Fax (405)774-7043. E-mail mossg@swosu.edu. Website http://www.swosu.edu. Gregory Moss, Asst. Prof., Chair, Dept. of School Service Programs. *Specialization:* M.Ed. in Library/Media Education. *Admission Requirements:* 2.5 GPA, GRE or GMAT scores, letter of recommendation, GPA x 150 + GRE = 1100. *Degree Requirements:* 32 semester hours (including 24 in library media). *Faculty:* 1 full-time, 4 part-time. *Students:* 17 part-time. *Degrees Awarded 1997:* 11.

*The University of Oklahoma. Instructional Psychology and Technology, Dept. of Educational Psychology, 321 Collings Hall, Norman, OK 73019. (405)325-2882. Fax (405)325-6655. E-mail psmith@ou.edu. Website http://www.uoknor.edu/education/iptwww/. Dr. Patricia L. Smith, Chair. *Specializations:* Master's degree with emphases in Educational Technology

Generalist, Educational Technology, Computer Application, Instructional Design, Teaching with Technology; Dual Master's Educational Technology and Library and Information Systems. Doctoral degree in Instructional Psychology and Technology. *Features:* Strong interweaving of principles of instructional psychology with design and development of Instructional Technology. Application of IP&T in K–12, vocational education, higher education, business and industry, and governmental agencies. *Admission Requirements:* Master's: acceptance by IPT program and Graduate College based on minimum 3.00 GPA for last 60 hours of undergraduate work or last 12 hours of graduate work; written statement that indicates goals and interests compatible with program goals. Doctoral: 3.0 in last 60 hours undergraduate, 3.25 GPA, GRE scores, written statement of background and goals. *Degree Requirements:* Master's: approx. 39 hours coursework (specific number of hours dependent upon Emphasis) with 3.0 GPA; successful completion of thesis or comprehensive exam. Doctorate: see program description from institution or http://www.ou.education.iptwww. *Faculty:* 10 full-time. *Students:* Master's: 10 full-time, 200 part-time; doctoral: 10 full-time, 50 part-time. *Financial Assistance:* assistantships, grants, student loans, scholarships. *Degrees Awarded 1996:* Master's, 35; doctoral, 4.

OREGON

*Western Oregon State College. 345 N. Monmouth Ave., Monmouth, OR 97361. (503)838-8471. Fax (503)838-8228. E-mail engler@fsa.wosc.osshe.edu. Dr. Randall Engle, Chair. *Specialization:* M.S. in Information Technology. *Features:* Offers advanced courses in library management, instructional development, multimedia, and computer technology. Additional course offerings in distance delivery of instruction and computer-interactive video instruction. *Admission Requirements:* 3.0 GPA, GRE or MAT. *Degree Requirements:* 45 qtr. hours; thesis optional. *Faculty:* 3 full-time, 6 part-time. *Students:* 6 full-time, 131 part-time. *Financial Assistance:* assistantships, grants, student loans, scholarship, work assistance. *Degrees Awarded 1996:* 12.

PENNSYLVANIA

Bloomsburg University. Institute for Interactive Technologies, 1210 McCormick Bldg., Bloomsburg, PA 17815. (717)389-4506. Fax (717)389-4943. E-mail tphillip@bloomu.edu. Website http://iit.bloomu.edu. Dr. Timothy L. Phillips, contact person. *Specialization:* M.S. in Instructional Technology with emphasis on preparing for careers as interactive media specialists. The program is closely associated with the Institute for Interactive Technologies. *Features:* Instructional design, authoring languages and systems, media integration, managing multimedia projects. *Admission Requirements:* Bachelor's degree. *Degree Requirements:* 33 semester credits (27 credits & 6 credit thesis, or 30 credits & three credit internship). *Faculty:* 4 full-time. *Students:* 53 full-time, 50 part-time. *Financial Assistance:* assistantships, grants, student loans. *Degrees Awarded 1997:* 50.

Clarion University of Pennsylvania. Becker Hall, Clarion, PA 16214. (814)226-2245. Fax (814)226-2186. Carmen S. Felicetti, Chair, Dept. of Communications. *Specialization:* M.S. in Communication with specialization in Training and Development. The curriculum is process and application oriented with basic courses in television and computer applications, Internet, Web, and html authoring. Major projects are team and client oriented with an emphasis on multimedia presentations. *Admission Requirements:* Bachelor's degree; 2.75 undergraduate GPA, MAT score. *Degree Requirements:* 36 semester credits (including 27 specific to Training and Development) with 3.0 GPA, optional thesis worth 6 credits. *Faculty:* 9 full-time. *Financial Assistance:* ten 1/4 time or five 20-hour graduate assistantships. *Degrees awarded 1997:* 5.

Drexel University. College of Information Science and Technology, Philadelphia, PA 19104. (215)895-2474. Fax (215)895-2494. Richard H. Lytle, Prof. and Dean. Website http://www.cis.drexel.edu. *Specializations:* M.S. in Library and Information Science;

M.S.I.S. in Information Systems. *Admission Requirements:* GRE scores; applicants with a minimum 3.2 GPA in last half of undergraduate credits may be eligible for admission without GRE scores. *Degree Requirements:* 60 credits. *Faculty:* 16 full-time, 47 adjunct. *Students:* M.S., 29 full-time, 174 part-time; M.S.I.S., 23 full-time, 275 part-time. *Degrees Awarded 1997:* M.S., 69; M.S.I.S, 57.

Lehigh University. College of Education, Bethlehem, PA 18015. (610)758-3231. Fax (610)758-6223. E-mail WMC0@LEHIGH.EDU. Website http://www.lehigh.edu. Leroy Tuscher, Coord., Educational Technology Program. *Specializations:* M.S. degree with emphasis on design and development of interactive multimedia (both stand-alone and on the Web) for teaching and learning; Ed.D. in Educational Technology. *Admission Requirements:* M.S.: competitive; 2.75 undergraduate GPA or 3.0 graduate GPA, GRE recommended, transcripts, at least 2 letters of recommendation, statement of personal and professional goals, application fee. Ed.D.: 3.5 graduate GPA, GRE required. Deadlines are Jul 15 for fall admission, Dec 1 for spring admission, Apr 30 for summer admission. *Degree Requirements:* M.S.: 33 semester hours (including 8 in media); thesis option. Ed.D.: 48 hours past the master's plus dissertation. *Faculty:* 3 full-time, 2 part-time. *Students:* M.S.: 13 full-time, 34 part-time; Ed.D.: 6 full-time, 32 part-time. *Financial Assistance:* university graduate and research assistantships, graduate student support as participants in R&D projects, employment opportunities in local businesses and schools doing design and development. *Degrees Awarded 1997:* M.S., 16; Ed.D., 3.

Pennsylvania State University. 314 Keller Bldg., University Park, PA 16802. (814)865-0473. Fax (814)865-0128. E-mail bgrabowski@psu.edu. B. Grabowski, Prof. in Charge. *Specializations:* M.Ed., M.S., D.Ed, and Ph.D. in Instructional Systems. Current teaching emphases are on Corporate Training, Interactive Learning Technologies, and Educational Systems Design. Research interests include multimedia, visual learning, educational reform, emerging technologies, and constructivist learning. *Features:* A common thread throughout all programs is that candidates have basic competencies in the understanding of human learning; instructional design, development, and evaluation; and research procedures. Practical experience is available in mediated independent learning, research, instructional development, computer-based education, and dissemination projects. *Admission Requirements:* D.Ed., Ph.D.: GRE, TOEFL, transcript, three letters of recommendation, writing sample, vita or resume, and letter of application detailing rationale for interest in the degree. *Degree Requirements:* M.Ed.: 33 semester hours; M.S.: 36 hours, including either a thesis or project paper; doctoral: candidacy exam, courses, residency, comprehensives, dissertation. *Faculty:* 10 full-time, 5 affiliate and 1 adjunct. *Students:* Master's: approx. 46; doctoral: 103. *Financial Assistance:* assistantships, graduate fellowships, student aid loans, internships; assistantships on grants, contracts, and projects. *Degrees Awarded 1998:* master's, 43; doctoral, 6.

Rosemont College. Graduate Studies in Education, 1400 Montgomery Ave., Rosemont, PA 19010-1699. (610)526-2982; (800)531-9431 outside 610 area code. Fax (610)526-2964. E-mail roscolgrad@rosemont.edu. Website http://techined.rosemont.edu/CSTE/info.html. Dr. Richard Donagher, Dir. *Specializations:* M.Ed. in Technology in Education, Certificate in Professional Study in Technology in Education. *Admission Requirements:* GRE or MAT scores. *Degree Requirements:* Completion of 12 units (36 credits) and comprehensive exam. *Faculty:* 7 full-time, 10 part-time. *Students:* 110 full- and part-time. *Financial Assistance:* graduate student grants, assistantships, Federal Stafford Loan Program. *Degrees Awarded 1997:* 13.

RHODE ISLAND

The University of Rhode Island. Graduate School of Library and Information Studies, Rodman Hall, Kingston, RI 02881-0815. (401)874-2947. Fax (401)874-4964. Website http://www.uri.edu/artsci/lsc. W. Michael Novener, Assoc. Prof. and Dir. *Specializations:* M.L.I.S. degree with specialties in Archives, Law, Health Sciences, Rare Books, and Youth

Services Librarianship. *Degree Requirements:* 42 semester-credit program offered in Rhode Island and regionally in Boston and Amherst, MA, and Durham, NH. *Faculty:* 7 full-time, 24 part-time. *Students:* 48 full-time, 196 part-time. *Financial Assistance:* graduate assistantships, some scholarship aid, student loans. *Degrees Awarded 1997:* 73.

SOUTH CAROLINA

University of South Carolina. Educational Psychology Dept., Columbia, SC 29208. (803)777-6609. Dr. Margaret Gredler, Prof., Chair. *Specialization:* Master's degree. *Degree Requirements:* 33 semester hours, including instructional theory, computer design, and integrated media. *Faculty:* 3. *Students:* 10.

TENNESSEE

East Tennessee State University. College of Education, Dept. of Curriculum and Instruction., Box 70684, Johnson City, TN 37614-0684. (423)439-4186. Fax (423)439-8362. *Specializations:* M.Ed. in Instructional Media (Library), M.Ed. in Instructional Technology. *Admission Requirements:* Bachelor's degree from accredited institution, transcripts, personal essay; in some cases, GRE and/or interview. *Degree Requirements:* 39 semester hours, including 18 hours in instructional technology. *Faculty:* 2 full-time, 4 part-time. *Students:* 9 full-time, 40 part-time. *Financial Assistance:* Scholarships, assistantships, aid for disabled. *Degrees Awarded 1997:* 12.

*University of Tennessee-Knoxville. College of Education, Education in the Sciences, Mathematics, Research, and Technology Unit, 319 Claxton Addition, Knoxville, TN 37996-3400. (423)974-4222 or (423)974-3103. Dr. Al Grant, Coord., Instructional Media and Technology Program. *Specializations:* M.S. in Ed., Ed.S., and Ed.D. under Education in Sciences, Mathematics, Research, and Technology; Ed.D. in Curriculum and Instruction, concentration in Instructional Media and Technology; Ph.D. under the College of Education, concentration in Instructional Media and Technology. *Features:* Coursework in media management, advanced software production, utilization, research, theory, psychology, instructional computing, television, and instructional development. Coursework will also meet the requirements for state certification as Instructional Materials Supervisor in the public schools of Tennessee. *Admission Requirements:* Send for Graduate Catalog, The University of Tennessee. *Degree Requirements:* M.S.: 33 semester hours; thesis optional. *Faculty:* 1 full-time, with additional assistance from Ed SMRT Unit, College of Ed. and university faculty. *Students:* M.S., 2 part-time; Ed.S., 2 part-time.

TEXAS

Texas A&M University. Educational Technology Program, Dept. of Curriculum & Instruction, College of Education, College Station, TX 77843. (409)845-7276. Fax (409)845-9663. E-mail zellner@tamu.edu. Website http://educ.coe.tamu.edu/~edtc/edtc/prog/edtcintro.html. Ronald D. Zellner, Assoc. Prof., Coord. *Specializations:* M.Ed. in Educational Technology; EDCI Ph.D. program with specializations in Educational Technology and in Distance Education; Ph.D. in Educational Psychology Foundations: Learning & Technology. The purpose of the Educational Technology Program is to prepare educators with the competencies required to improve the quality and effectiveness of instructional programs at all levels. A major emphasis is placed on multimedia instructional materials development and techniques for effective distance education and communication. Teacher preparation with a focus on field-based instruction and school to university collaboration is also a major component. The program goal is to prepare graduates with a wide range of skills to work as professionals and leaders in a variety of settings, including education, business, industry, and the military. *Features:* Program facilities include laboratories for teaching, resource development, and production. Computer, video, and multimedia development are supported in a number of facilities. The college and university also maintain facilities for distance education materials development and fully equipped classrooms for course delivery to nearby collaborative school districts and sites throughout the state. *Admission Requirements:* M.Ed.: Bachelor's degree, 800 GRE, 550 TOEFL; Ph.D.: 3.0 GPA, 800 GRE. *Degree Requirements:* M.Ed.: 39 semester credits, oral exam; Ph.D.: coursework varies with student goals. *Faculty:* 4 full-time. *Students:* M.Ed., 25 full-time, 15 part-time; Ph.D., 2 full-time, 6 part-time. *Financial Assistance:* several graduate and teaching assistantships. *Degrees Awarded 1997:* M.Ed., 18.

Texas A&M University-Commerce. Dept. of Secondary and Higher Education, East Texas Station, Commerce, TX 75429-3011. (903)886-5607. Fax (903)886-5603. E-mail bob_mundayb@tamu-commerce.edu. Dr. Robert Munday, Prof., Head. *Specialization:* M.S. or M.Ed. degree in Learning Technology and Information Systems with emphases on Educational Computing, Educational Media and Technology, and Library and Information Science. *Admission Requirements:* 700 GRE (combined). *Degree Requirements:* 36 hours (Educational Computing): 30 hours in Educational Technology. M.S. (Educational Media and Technology): 21 hours in Educational Technology. M.S. (Library and Information Science): 15 hours in Library/Information Science, 12 hours in Educational Technology. *Faculty:* 3 full-time, 5 part-time. *Students:* 30 full-time, 150 part-time. *Financial Assistance:* graduate assistantships in teaching and research, scholarships, federal aid program.

Texas Tech University. College of Education, Box 41071, TTU, Lubbock, TX 79409. (806)742-1997, ext. 299. Fax (806)742-2179. Website http://www.educ.ttu.edu. Dr. Robert Price, Dir., Instructional Technology. *Specializations:* M.Ed. in Instructional Technology (Educational Computing and Distance Education emphasis); Ed.D. in Instructional Technology. *Features:* Program is NCATE accredited and follows ISTE and AECT guidelines. *Admission Requirements:* Holistic evaluation based on GRE scores, GPA, student goals and writing samples. *Degree Requirements:* M.Ed.: 39 hours (24 hours in educational technology, 15 hours in education or outside education); practicum. Ed.D.: 87 hours (45 hours in educational technology, 18 hours in education, 15 hours in resource area or minor); practicum. *Faculty:* 5 full-time. *Students:* M.Ed., 10 full-time, 20 part-time; Ed.D., 15 full-time, 15 part-time. *Financial Assistance:* teaching and research assistantships available ($8,500 for 9 months); small scholarships. *Degrees Awarded 1998:* Ed.D., 5; M.Ed., 6.

University of North Texas. College of Education, Box 311337, Denton, TX 76203-1337. (940)565-2057. Fax (940)565-2185. Website http://www.cecs.unt.edu. Dr. Terry Holcomb, Program Coord., Computer Education and Cognitive Systems. Dr. Jon Young, Chair, Dept. of Technology and Cognition. *Specializations:* M.S. in Computer Education and Instructional Systems. *Admission Requirements:* 1000 GRE (400 verbal and 400 quantitative minimums). *Degree Requirements:* 36 semester hours (including 27 in Instructional Technology and Computer Education), comprehensive exam. *Faculty:* 7 full-time, 1 part-time. *Students:* 90+ 500 service/ minor students, approx. half full-time. *Degrees Awarded 1997:* 30.

The University of Texas. College of Education, Austin, TX 78712. (512)471-5211. Fax (512)471-4607. Website http://www.edb.utexas./coe/depts/ci/c&i.html. Paul Resta, Prof., Dept. of Curriculum and Instruction, College of Education, The University of Texas, Austin, Texas 78753. E-mail resta@mail.utexas.edu. *Specializations:* Master's degree (MA and MEd). Ph.D. program emphasizes research, design, and development of instructional systems and communications technology. *Features:* The program is interdisciplinary in nature, although certain competencies are required of all students. Programs of study and dissertation research are based on individual needs and career goals. Learning resources include a model Learning Technology Center, computer labs and classrooms, a television studio, and interactive multimedia lab. Many courses are offered cooperatively by other departments, including Radio-TV Film, Computer Science, and Educational Psychology. *Admission Requirements:* Both degrees: 3.5 GPA, 1150 GRE. *Degree Requirements:* Master's: 30-36 semester hours depending on selection of program (21 in Instructional Technology plus research course); thesis option. A 6-hour minor is required outside the department. Ph.D.: written comprehensive and specialization exam with oral defense, dissertation with oral defense. *Faculty:* 3 full-time, 4 part-time. *Students:* approx. 45 master's, 55 doctoral. *Financial Assistance:* Assistantships may be available to develop instructional materials, teach undergraduate computer tools, and assist with research projects. There are also some paid internships. *Degrees Awarded 1997:* Master's, 13; doctorate, 9.

UTAH

Brigham Young University. Dept. of Instructional Psychology and Technology, 201 MCKB, BYU, Provo, UT 84602. (801)378-5097. Fax (801)378-8672. E-mail paul_merrill @byu.edu. Website http://www.byu.edu/acd1/ed/InSci/InSci.html. Paul F. Merrill, Prof., Chair. *Specializations:* M.S. degrees in Instructional Design, Research and Evaluation, and Multimedia Production. Ph.D. degrees in Instructional Design, and Research and Evaluation. *Features:* Course offerings include principles of learning, instructional design, assessing learning outcomes, evaluation in education, empirical inquiry in education, project management, quantitative reasoning, microcomputer materials production, multimedia production, naturalistic inquiry, and more. Students participate in internships and projects related to development, evaluation, measurement, and research. *Admission Requirements:* Both degrees: Transcript, three letters of recommendation, letter of intent, GRE scores. Apply by Feb 1. Students agree to live by the BYU Honor Code as a condition for admission. *Degree Requirements:* Master's: 38 semester hours, including prerequisite (3 hours), core courses (14 hours), specialization (12 hours), internship (3 hours), thesis or project (6 hours) with oral defense. Ph.D.: 94 semester hours beyond the bachelor's degree, including: prerequisite and skill requirements (21 hours), core course (16 hours), specialization (18 hours), internship (12 hours), projects (9 hours), and dissertation (18 hours). The dissertation must be orally defended. Also, at least two consecutive 6-hour semesters must be completed in residence. *Faculty:* 9 full-time, 2 half-time. *Students:* Master's, 25 full-time, 2 part-time; Ph.D., 47 full-time, 3 part-time. *Financial Assistance:* internships, tuition scholarships, loans, and travel to present papers. *Degrees Awarded 1997:* Master's, 7; Ph.D., 3.

Utah State University. Dept. of Instructional Technology, College of Education, Logan, UT 84322-2830. (435)797-2694. Fax (435)797-2693. E-mail dsmellie@cc.usu.edu. Website http://www.coe.usu:edu/it/. Dr. Don C. Smellie, Prof., Chair. *Specializations:* M.S. and Ed.S. with concentrations in the areas of Instructional Development, Multimedia, Educational Technology, and Information Technology/School Library Media Administration. Ph.D. in Instructional Technology is offered for individuals seeking to become professionally involved in instructional development in corporate education, public schools, community colleges, and universities. Teaching and research in higher education is another career avenue for graduates of the program. *Features:* M.S. and Ed.S. programs in Information Technology/School Library Media Administration and Educational Technology are also delivered via an electronic distance education system. The doctoral program is built on a strong master's and Specialist's program in Instructional Technology. All doctoral students complete a core with the remainder of the course selection individualized, based upon career goals. *Admission Requirements:* M.S. and Ed.S.: 3.0 GPA, a verbal and quantitative score at the 40th percentile on the GRE or 43 MAT, three written recommendations. Ph.D.: Master's degree in Instructional Technology, 3.0 GPA, verbal and quantitative score at the 40th percentile on the GRE, three written recommendations. *Degree Requirements:* M.S.: 39 sem. hours; thesis or project option. Ed.S.: 30 sem. hours if M.S. is in the field, 40 hours if not. Ph.D.: 62 total hours, dissertation, 3-sem. residency, and comprehensive examination. *Faculty:* 9 full-time, 7 part-time. *Students:* M.S., 70 full-time, 85 part-time; Ed.S., 6 full-time, 9 part-time; Ph.D., 15 full-time, 14 part-time. *Financial Assistance:* approx. 18 to 26 assistantships (apply by April 1). *Degrees Awarded 1997:* M.S., 42; Ed.S., 3; Ph.D., 3.

VIRGINIA

George Mason University. Instructional Technology Programs, Mail Stop 4B3, 4400 University Dr., Fairfax, VA 22030-4444. (703)993-2051. Fax (703)993-2013. E-mail mbehrman@wpgate.gmu.edu. Website http://gse.gmu.edu/programs/it/index.htm. Dr. Michael Behrmann, Coord. of Instructional Technology Academic Programs. *Specializations:* M.Ed. in Curriculum and Instruction with tracks in Instructional Design and Development, Integration of Technology in Schools, and Assistive/Special Education Technology; M.Ed. in Special Education; Ph.D. with specialization in Instructional Technology or Special Education Technology. Certificate Programs (12-15cr) in: Integration of Technology in Schools; Multimedia Development; Assistive Technology. *Features:* Master's program started in 1983 and doctoral in 1984. Integration of Technology in Schools is a cohort program in which students are admitted in the Spring semester only. ID & D full time immersion admits students in summer. All other tracks admit throughout the year. *Admission Requirements:* Teaching or training experience, introductory programming course or equivalent; introductory course in educational technology or equivalent. *Degree Requirements:* M.Ed. in Curriculum and Instruction: 36 hours; practicum, internship, or project. M.Ed. in Special Education: 36-42 hours. Ph.D.: 56-62 hours beyond master's degree for either specialization. Certificate programs: 12-15 hours. *Faculty:* 6 full-time, 5 part-time. *Students:* M.Ed. in Curriculum and Instruction: 5 part-time, 125 part-time. M.Ed. in Special Education: 10 full-time, 8 part-time. Ph.D.: 19 part-time, 10 full time. ITS certificate, 250; MM Certificate, 30; At Certificate, 45. *Financial Assistance:* Assistantships and tuition waivers available for full-time graduate students. *Degrees Awarded 1997:* M.Ed. in Curriculum and Instruction, 17; M.Ed. in Special Education Technology, 6.

Radford University. Educational Studies Dept., College of Education and Human Development, P.O. Box 6959, Radford, VA 24142. (540)831-5302. Fax (540)831-5059. E-mail ljwilson@runet.edu. Website http://www.radford.edu. Dr. Linda J. Wilson. *Specialization:* M.S. in Education with Educational Media/Technology emphasis. *Features:* School Library Media Specialist licensure. *Admission Requirements:* Bachelor's degree, 2.7 undergraduate GPA. *Degree Requirements:* 33 semester hours, practicum; thesis optional. *Faculty:* 2 full-time, 3 part-time. *Students:* 2 full-time, 23 part-time. *Financial Assistance:* assistantships, grants, student loans, scholarships. *Degrees Awarded 1998:* 6.

University of Virginia. Dept. of Leadership, Foundations, and Policy, Curry School of Education, Ruffner Hall, Charlottesville, VA 22903. (804)924-7471. Fax (804)924-0747. E-mail jbbunch@virginia.edu. Website http://curry.edschool.virginia.edu/curry/dept/edlf/instrtech/. John B. Bunch, Assoc. Prof., Coord., Instructional Technology Program, Dept. of Leadership, Foundations and Policy Studies. *Specializations:* M.Ed., Ed.S., Ed.D, and Ph.D. degrees with focal areas in Media Production, Interactive Multimedia, and K–12 Educational Technologies. *Admission Requirements:* Undergraduate degree from accredited institution in any field, undergraduate GPA 3.0,1000 GRE (V+Q), 600 TOEFL. Admission application deadline is March 1st of each year for the fall semester for both master's and doctoral degrees. *Degree Requirements:* M.Ed.: 36 semester hours, comprehensive examination. Ed.S.: 60 semester hours beyond undergraduate degree. Ed.D.: 54 semester hours, dissertation, at least one conference presentation or juried publication, comprehensive examination, residency; Ph.D.: same as Ed.S. with the addition of 18 semester hours. For specific degree requirements, see Website, write to the address above, or refer to the UVA *Graduate Record. Faculty:* 4 full-time, 1 part-time. *Students:* M.Ed. 24; Ed.D, 3; Ph.D., 15. *Financial Assistance:* Some graduate assistantships and scholarships are available on a competitive basis. *Degrees Awarded 1996:* Master's, 4; doctorate, 2.

Virginia Polytechnic Institute and State University (Virginia Tech). College of Human Resources and Education, 220 War Memorial Hall, Blacksburg, VA 24061-0341. (540)231-5587. Fax (540)231-9075. Website http://www.chre.vt.edu/Admin/IT/. E-mail moorem@vt.edu David M. (Mike) Moore, Program Area Leader, Instructional Technology,

Dept. of Teaching and Learning. *Specializations:* M.A., Ed.D., and Ph.D. in Instructional Technology. Preparation for education, higher education, faculty development, business, and industry. *Features:* Areas of emphasis are Instructional Design, Educational Computing, Evaluation, and Media Management and Development. Facilities include two computer labs (70 IBM and Macintosh computers), plus interactive video, speech synthesis, telecommunication labs, distance education classroom, and computer graphics production areas. *Admission Requirements:* Ed.D. and Ph.D.: 3.3 GPA from master's degree, GRE scores, interview, writing samples, three letters of recommendation, transcripts. MA.: 3.0 GPA Undergraduate. *Degree Requirements:* Ph.D.: 96 hrs. above B.S., 2 year residency, 12 hrs. research classes, 30 hrs. dissertation; Ed.D.: 90 hrs. above B.S., 1 year residency, 12 hrs. research classes; MA.: 30 hrs. above B.S. *Faculty:* 7 full-time, 5 part-time. *Students:* 35 full-time and 10 part-time at the doctoral level. 10 full-time and 15 part-time at the masters level. *Financial Assistance:* 10 assistantships, limited tuition scholarships. *Degrees Awarded 1998:* doctoral, 6; masters, 3.

Virginia State University. School of Liberal Arts & Education, Petersburg, VA 23806. (804)524-6886. Vykuntapathi Thota, Chair, Dept. of Education. *Specializations:* M.S., M.Ed. in Educational Technology. *Features:* Video Conferencing Center and PLATO Laboratory, internship in ABC and NBC channels. *Degree Requirements:* 30 semester hours plus thesis for M.S.; 33 semester hours plus project for M.Ed.; comprehensive exam. *Faculty:* 1 full-time, 2 part-time. *Students:* 8 full-time, 50 part-time. *Financial Assistance:* scholarships through the School of Graduate Studies.

WASHINGTON

Eastern Washington University. Dept. of Computer Science, Cheney, WA 99004-2431. (509)359-7093. Fax (509)359-2215. E-mail LKieffer@ewu.edu. Dr. Linda M. Kieffer, Assoc. Prof. of Computer Science. *Specializations:* M.Ed. in Computer and Technology Supported Education; M.S. in Computer Education (Interdisciplinary). Master's program started in 1983. *Features:* Many projects involve the use of high-level authoring systems to develop educational products, technology driven curriculum, and Web projects. *Admission Requirements:* 3.0 GPA for last 90 qtr. credits. *Degree Requirements:* M.S.: 52 qtr. hours (30 hours in computers, 15 hours outside education; the hours do not total to 52 because of freedom to choose where Methods of Research is taken, where 12 credits of supporting courses are taken, and where additional electives are taken); research project with formal report. M.Ed.: 52 qtr. hours (28 hours in computer education, 16 hours in education, 8 hours outside education). *Faculty:* 3 full-time. *Students:* approx. 35. *Financial Assistance:* some research and teaching fellowships. *Degrees Awarded 1997:* 3.

University of Washington. College of Education, 115 Miller Hall, Box 353600 Seattle, WA 98195-3600. (206)543-1847. Fax (206)543-8439. E-mail stkerr@u.washington.edu. Website http://www.educ.washington.edu/COE/c-and-i/c_and_i_med_ed_tech.htm. Stephen T. Kerr, Prof. of Education. *Specializations:* M.Ed., Ed.D, and Ph.D. for individuals in business, industry, higher education, public schools, and organizations concerned with education or communication (broadly defined). *Features:* Emphasis on instructional design as a process of making decisions about the shape of instruction; additional focus on research and development in such areas as message design (especially graphics and diagrams); electronic information systems; interactive instruction via videodisc, multimedia, and computers. *Admission Requirements:* M.Ed.: goal statement (2-3pp.), writing sample, 1000 GRE (verbal plus quantitative), undergraduate GPA indicating potential to successfully accomplish graduate work. Doctoral: GRE scores, letters of reference, transcripts, personal statement, master's degree or equivalent in field appropriate to the specialization with 3.5 GPA, two years of successful professional experience and/or experience related to program goals. *Degree Requirements:* M.Ed.: 45 qtr. hours (including 24 in media); thesis or project optional. Ed.D.: see www.educ.washington.edu/COE/admissions/DoctorOfEducationProgram.htm. Ph.D.: see www.educ.washington.edu/COE/admissions/DoctorOfPhilosophyDegree.htm.

Faculty: 2 full-time, 3 part-time. *Students:* 12 full-time, 32 part-time; 26 M.Ed., 18 doctoral. *Financial Assistance:* assistantships awarded competitively and on basis of program needs; other assistantships available depending on grant activity in any given year. *Degrees Awarded 1997:* M.Ed., 10; doctorate, 4.

Western Washington University. Woodring College of Education, Instructional Technology, MS 9087, Bellingham, WA 98225-9087. (360)650-3387. Fax (360)650-6526. E-mail Les.Blackwell@wwu.edu. Website http://www.wce.wwu.edu/depts/IT/. Dr. Les Blackwell, Prof., Department Chair. *Specializations:* M.Ed. with emphasis in Instructional Technology in Adult Education, Special Education, Elementary Education, and Secondary Education. *Admission Requirements:* 3.0 GPA in last 45 qtr. credit hours, GRE or MAT scores, 3 letters of recommendation, and, in some cases, 3 years of teaching experience. *Degree Requirements:* 48-52 qtr. hours (24-28 hours in instructional technology; 24 hours in education-related courses, thesis required; internship and practicum possible). *Faculty:* 6 full-time, 8 part-time. *Students:* 5 full-time, 10 part-time. *Financial Assistance:* assistantships, student loans, scholarships. *Master's Degrees Awarded 1998:* 4.

WISCONSIN

Edgewood College. Dept. of Education, 855 Woodrow St., Madison, WI 53711-1997. (608)257-4861, ext. 2293. Fax (608)259-6727. E-mail schmied@edgewood.edu. Website http://www.edgewood.edu. Dr. Joseph E. Schmiedicke, Chair, Dept. of Education. *Specializations:* M.A. in Education with emphasis on Instructional Technology. Master's program started in 1987. *Features:* Classes conducted in laboratory setting with emphasis on applications and software. *Admission Requirements:* 2.75 GPA. *Degree Requirements:* 36 semester hours. *Faculty:* 2 full-time, 3 part-time. *Students:* 5 full-time, 135 part-time. *Financial Assistance:* grants, student loans. *Degrees Awarded 1997:* 12.

University of Wisconsin-La Crosse. Educational Media Program, Rm. 235C, Morris Hall, La Crosse, WI 54601. (608)785-8121. Fax (608)785-8128. E-mail Phill.rm@mail.uwlax.edu. Dr. Russell Phillips, Dir. *Specializations:* M.S. in Professional Development with specializations in Initial Instructional Library Specialist, License 901; Instructional Library Media Specialist, License 902 (39 credits). *Degree Requirements:* 30 semester hours, including 15 in media; no thesis. *Faculty:* 2 full-time, 4 part-time. *Students:* 21. *Financial Assistance:* guaranteed student loans, graduate assistantships.

University of Wisconsin-Madison. Dept. of Curriculum and Instruction, School of Education, 225 N. Mills St., Madison, WI 53706. (608)263-4672. Fax (608)263-9992. E-mail adevaney@facstaff.wisc.edu. Ann De Vaney, Prof. *Specializations:* M.S. degree and State Instructional Technology License; Ph.D. programs to prepare college and university faculty. *Features:* The program is coordinated with media operations of the university. Traditional instructional technology courses are processed through a social, cultural, and historical frame of reference. Current curriculum emphasizes communication and cognitive theories, critical cultural studies, and theories of textual analysis and instructional development. Course offered in the evening. *Admission Requirements:* Master's and Ph.D.: Previous experience in Instructional Technology preferred, previous teaching experience, 3.0 GPA on last 60 undergraduate credits, acceptable scores on GRE, 3.0 GPA on all graduate work. *Degree Requirements:* M.S.: 24 credits plus thesis and exam; Ph.D.: 3 years of residency beyond the bachelor's (master's degree counts for one year; one year must be full-time), major, minor, and research requirements, preliminary exam, dissertation, and oral exam. *Faculty:* 3 full-time, 1 part-time. *Students:* M.S., 33; Ph.D., 21. Most master's candidates are part-time; half of Ph.D. students are full-time. *Financial Assistance:* several stipends of approx. $1000 per month for 20 hours of work per week; other media jobs are also available. *Degrees Awarded 1997:* M.S., 16; Ph.D., 3.

Part Five
Mediagraphy

Print and Nonprint Resources

Introduction

CONTENTS

This resource lists media-related journals, books, ERIC documents, journal articles, and nonprint media resources of interest to practitioners, researchers, students, and others concerned with educational technology and educational media. The primary goal of this section is to list current publications in the field. The majority of materials cited here were published in 1999 or early 2000. Media-related journals include those listed in past issues of *EMTY* and new entries in the field.

It is not the intention of the authors for this chapter to serve as a specific resource location tool, although it may be used for that purpose in the absence of database access. Rather, readers may peruse the categories of interest in this chapter to gain an idea of recent developments within the field. For archival purposes, this chapter serves as a snapshot of the field in 2001. Readers must bear in mind that technological developments occur well in advance of publication and should take that fact into consideration when judging the timeliness of resources listed in this chapter.

SELECTION

Items were selected for the Mediagraphy in several ways. The ERIC (Educational Resources Information Center) Database was the source for most ERIC document and journal article citations. Others were reviewed directly by the editors. Items were chosen for this list when they met one or more of the following criteria: reputable publisher, broad circulation, coverage by indexing services, peer review, and coverage of a gap in the literature. The editors chose items on subjects that seem to reflect the Instructional Technology field as it is today. Due to the increasing tendency for media producers to package their products in more than one format and for single titles to contain mixed media, titles are no longer separated by media type. The editors make no claims as to the comprehensiveness of this list. It is, instead, intended to be representative.

OBTAINING RESOURCES

Media-Related Periodicals and Books. Publisher, price, and ordering/subscription address are listed wherever available.

ERIC Documents. ERIC documents can be read and often copied from their microfiche form at any library holding an ERIC microfiche collection. The identification number beginning with ED (for example, ED 332 677) locates the document in the collection. Copies of most ERIC documents can also be ordered from the ERIC Document Reproduction Service. Prices charged depend on format chosen (microfiche or paper copy), length of the document, and method of shipping. Online orders, fax orders, and expedited delivery are available.

To find the closest library with an ERIC microfiche collection, contact:

ACCESS ERIC
1600 Research Blvd.
Rockville, MD 20850-3172
1-800-LET-ERIC (538-3742)
E-mail: acceric@inet.ed.gov

To order ERIC documents, contact:

ERIC Document Reproduction Service (EDRS)
7420 Fullerton Rd., Suite 110
Springfield, VA 22153-2852
voice: 1-800-443-ERIC (443-3742), 703-440-1400
fax: 703-440-1408
E-mail: service@edrs.com.

Journal Articles. Photocopies of journal articles can be obtained in one of the following ways: (1) from a library subscribing to the title, (2) through interlibrary loan, (3) through the purchase of a back issue from the journal publisher, or (4) from an article reprint service such as UMI.

UMI Information Store
500 Sansome Street, Suite 400
San Francisco, CA 94111
1-800-248-0360 (toll-free in U.S. and Canada)
(415) 433-5500 (outside U.S. and Canada)
E-mail: orders@infostore.com

Journal articles can also be obtained through the Institute for Scientific Information (ISI):

ISI Document Solution
P.O. Box 7649
Philadelphia, PA 19104-3389
(215)386-4399
Fax (215)222-0840 or (215)386-4343
E-mail: ids@isinet.com

ARRANGEMENT

Mediagraphy entries are classified according to major subject emphasis under the following headings:

- Artificial Intelligence, Robotics, and Electronic Performance Support Systems
- Computer-Assisted Instruction
- Distance Education
- Educational Research
- Educational Technology
- Information Science and Technology
- Innovation
- Instructional Design and Development
- Interactive Multimedia
- Libraries and Media Centers

- Media Technologies
- Professional Development
- Simulation, Gaming, and Virtual Reality
- Special Education and Disabilities
- Telecommunications and Networking

Brooke Price

Section Editor

Mediagraphy

ARTIFICIAL INTELLIGENCE, ROBOTICS, AND ELECTRONIC PERFORMANCE SUPPORT SYSTEMS

Artificial Intelligence Review. Kluwer Academic Publishers, 101 Philip Drive, Norwell, MA 02061. [6 issues/yr., $182 indiv., $364 inst.]. Serves as a forum for the work of researchers and application developers from Artificial Intelligence, Cognitive Science, and related disciplines.

Baylor, Amy. (1999). Intelligent agents as cognitive tools for education. **Educational Technology, 39** (2), 36–40. Examines the educational potential for intelligent agents as cognitive tools. Discusses the role of intelligent agents: managing large amounts of information (information overload), serving as a pedagogical expert, and creating programming environments for the learner.

Berners-Lee, Tim. (1999). Realizing the full potential of the Web. **Technical Communication: Journal for the Society of Technical Communication, 46** (1), 79–82. Argues that the first phase of the Web is communication through shared knowledge. Predicts that the second side to the Web, yet to emerge, is that of machine-understandable information, with humans providing the inspiration and the intuition.

Chun, Tham Yoke. (1999). World Wide Web robots: An overview. **Online &CD-ROM Review, 23** (3), 135–142. Traces the development of World Wide Web Robots and provides an overview of their main functions and workings. The focus is on search robots.

Cook, Albert M., & Cavalier, Albert R. (1999). Young children using assistive robotics for discovery and control. **Teaching Exceptional Children, 31** (5), 72–78. Discusses the use of robotics with children with severe disabilities. Spotlights a toddler with developmental delays and quadriplegic athetoid cerebral palsy who is able to use a robotic arm and computer control systems to reach and manipulate objects. Provides guidelines for selecting and using assistive robotics.

Doty, Keith L. (1999). Neural network-based landmark recognition and navigation with IAMRs. Understanding the principles of thought and behavior. **Tech Directions, 58** (9), 28–30. Research on neural networks and hippocampal function demonstrating how mammals construct mental maps and develop navigation strategies is being used to create Intelligent Autonomous Mobile Robots (IAMRs).

Hamzei, G. H. Shah, Mulvaney, D. J., & Sillitoe, I. P. (1999). Multi-layer hierarchical rule learning in reactive robot control using incremental decision trees. **Journal of Robotic and Intelligent Systems, 24** (2), 99–124.

Harbeck, Julia D., & Sherman, Thomas M. (1999). Seven principles for designing developmentally appropriate Web sites for young children. **Educational Technology, 39** (4), 39–44. Illustrates how each of these principles may guide decisions about Web-based design for young children consistent with developmentally appropriate practice: (1) simple, clean and concrete design; (2) adult guidance; (3) progressive and individualized; (4) relevant to children; (5) integrated activities; (6) active and enjoyable; and (7) exploratory with multiple options.

International Journal of Robotics Research. Sage Science, (805) 499-0721. [Mo., $122 indiv., $686 inst.]. Interdisciplinary approach to the study of robotics for researchers, scientists, and students.

Jain, L. C., & Fanelli, A. M. (2000). **Recent advances in artificial neural networks: Design and applications**. [Book, 376p., $89.95]. CRC Press LLC, 2000 NW Corporate Blvd., Boca Raton, FL 33431, (800) 272–7737, www.crcpress.com. Collects the latest neural network paradigms and reports on their promising new applications with contributions from world-renowned experts; offers valuable information for real-world application.

Johns, T. F., & Lixun, Wang. (1999). Four versions of a sentence-shuffling program. **System**, **27** (3), 329–338. Traces the origin and development of a text-based computer-assisted language-learning activity, namely the shuffling of sentences of a text and the reconstruction on screen of that text. Emphasizes the elements of continuity between the first version, implemented on a mainframe computer, and the latest version.

Journal of Robotic and Intelligent Systems. Kluwer Academic Publishers, 101 Philip Drive, Norwell, MA 02061. [Mo., $850]. The main objective is to provide a forum for the fruitful interaction of ideas and techniques that combine systems and control science with artificial intelligence—and other related computer science—concepts.

Keramus, J. (1999). **Robot technology fundamentals.** [Book, 448p., $63.85]. Delmar Publishers, (800)347-7707, www.delmar.com. Addresses practical issues and latest developments of industrial robotics, written in lay terminology.

Knowledge-Based Systems. Elsevier Science Inc., 655 Avenue of the Americas, New York, NY 10010-5107. [Q., $730]. Interdisciplinary applications-oriented journal on fifth-generation computing, expert systems, and knowledge-based methods in system design.

Miglino, Orazio, Lund, Henrik Hautop, & Cardaci, Maurizio. (1999). Robotics as an educational tool. **Journal of Interactive Learning Research**, **10** (1), 25–47. Explores a new educational application of Piaget's theories of cognitive development: the use, as a teaching tool, of physical robots conceived as artificial organisms.

Minds and Machines. Kluwer Academic Publishers, 101 Philip Drive, Norwell, MA 02061. [Q., $379, American inst.]. Discusses issues concerning machines and mentality, artificial intelligence, epistemology, simulation, and modeling.

Motes, Michael A., & Wiegmann, Douglas A. (1999). Computerized Cognition Laboratory. **Teaching of Psychology**, **26** (1), 62–65. Describes a software package entitled the "Computerized Cognition Laboratory" that helps integrate the teaching of cognitive psychology and research methods. Allows students to explore short-term memory, long-term memory, and decision making. Can also be used to teach the application of several statistical procedures.

Sandler, B. Z. (1999). **Robotics: Designing the mechanisms for automated machinery** (2nd ed.). [Book, 464p., $69]. Academic Press, ap@acad.com, www.apnet.com. Describes the design process for building machines. Includes plans for using *Mathematica* as a design tool.

Waddell, Steve, & Doty, Keith L. (1999). Robotics. **Tech Directions**, **58** (7), 34–35, 36–40. "Why Teach Robotics?" (Waddell) suggests that the United States lags behind Europe and Japan in use of robotics in industry and teaching. "Creating a Course in Mobile Robotics" (Doty) outlines course elements of the Intelligent Machines Design Lab.

Wagman, M. (2000). **Scientific discovery processes in humans and computers: Theory and research in psychology and artificial intelligence.** [Book, 216p., $65]. Greenwood, 88 Post Road West, Westport, CT 06881, (203)226-3571, www.auburnhouse.com/praeger.htm. Analyzes current theory and research in the psychological and computational sciences, directed toward the elucidation of scientific discovery processes and structures. Also looks at and offers a comparative evaluation of human scientific discovery processes and computer scientific discovery processes.

Wagman, M. (1999). **The human mind according to artificial intelligence: Theory, research and implications.** [Book, 184p., $59]. Greenwood, 88 Post Road West, Westport, CT 06881, (203)226-3571, www.auburnhouse.com/praeger.htm. Discusses and evaluates the strengths and weaknesses of artificial intelligence in several application domains. Also assesses its roles as a collaborative partner, a competitive foe, and a theoretical model.

Weiss, G. (1999). **Multiagent systems: A modern approach to distributed artificial intelligence.** [Book, 640p., $62]. MIT Press, Five Cambridge Center, Cambridge, MA 02142-1493, (617)253-5646, mitpress-orders@mit.edu, www-mitpress.mit.edu. Covers basic and advanced topics regarding multiagent systems and contemporary distributed artificial intelligence; suitable as textbook.

COMPUTER-ASSISTED INSTRUCTION

Abeles, Tom, & Pita, Doroteia. (1999). Technology and the future of higher education. **Educational Technology & Society, 2** (3). Focuses on technology and the future of higher education. Discusses how technology is forcing change on the roles and models of education, content versus the learner, the role of faculty, and accreditation and value of courses.

Agapova, Olga I., & Ushakov, Alex S. (1999). How technology changes education. **TECHNOS, 8** (1), 27–31. To understand how technology changes today's classrooms, two Russian educators working in the United States examine instruction through their technology-based course in high school chemistry.

Bennett, Linda. (1999). In response—Designing an online journal. **T.H.E. Journal, 26** (7), 52–55. Describes the development of an online journal for preservice elementary school teachers in response to current trends for the integration of technology into the curriculum.

BYTE.com. Box 550, Hightstown, NJ 08520-9886, www.byte.com. [Mo., $29.95, $34.95 Canada and Mexico, $50 elsewhere]. Current articles on microcomputers provide technical information as well as information on applications and products for business and professional users.

Calderon-Young, Estelita. (1999). Technology for teaching foreign languages among community college students. **Community College Journal of Research and Practice, 23** (2), 161–169. Examines the use of new technology in foreign-language classrooms, specifically language labs equipped with interactive computers, interactive software packages, CD-ROMs, e-mail, and the Internet.

CALICO Journal. Computer Assisted Language Instruction Consortium, Southwest Texas State University, 116 Centennial Hall, San Marcos, TX 78666, info@calico.org, www.calico.org. [Q.; $50 indiv., $90 inst., $140 corporations]. Provides information on the applications of technology in teaching and learning languages.

Catenazzi, Nadia, & Sommaruga, Lorenzo. (1999). The evaluation of the Hyper Apuntes interactive learning environment. **Computers & Education, 32** (1), 35–49. Describes Hyper Apuntes, an interactive learning environment developed at the University Carlos III of Madrid, which teaches students the basic concepts of computer programming. Discusses results of an evaluation of the courseware that assessed its usability and utility and collected suggestions for improving the system.

Chen, Ai Yen, Mashhadi, Azam, Ang, Daniel, & Harkrider, Nancy. (1999). Cultural issues in the design of technology-enhanced learning systems. **British Journal of Educational Technology, 30** (3), 217–230. Focuses on the cultural and pedagogical considerations in the design of student-centered learning systems, with particular reference to three cases in Singapore.

Children's Software Review. Active Learning Associates, Inc., 44 Main St., Flemington, NJ 08822, www.childrenssoftware.com. [6/yr., $24]. Provides reviews and other information about software to help parents and educators more effectively use computers with children.

Collis, Betty. (1999). Designing for differences: Cultural issues in the design of WWW-based course-support sites. **British Journal of Educational Technology**, **30** (3), 201–215. Examines factors affecting the cultural appropriateness of Web-based course-support sites. Identifies a strategy for accommodating different values of these factors in Web-based course-support systems, based on a set of 10 design guidelines. Describes and evaluates the TeleTOP Method from the University of Twente (The Netherlands) to illustrate the design guidelines.

Computer Book Review. Bookwire, P.O. Box 61067, Honolulu, HI 96839, www.bookwire .com/cbr. [Q., $20 ($30 outside North America)]. Provides critical reviews of books on computers and computer-related subjects.

Computers and Composition. Ablex Publishing Corp., 100 Prospect Street, P.O. Box 811, Stamford, CT 06904-0811, (203)323-9606, fax (203)357-8446, www.jaipress.com. [3/yr., $55 indiv.]. International journal for teachers of writing focuses on the use of computers in writing instruction and related research and dialogue.

Computers & Education. Elsevier Science Inc., 655 Avenue of the Americas, New York, NY 10010-5107. [8/yr., $1,078]. Presents technical papers covering a broad range of subjects for users of analog, digital, and hybrid computers in all aspects of higher education.

Computers and the Humanities. Kluwer Academic Publishers, 101 Philip Drive, Norwell, MA 02061. [Q., $317 US inst.]. Contains papers on computer-aided studies, applications, automation, and computer-assisted instruction.

Computers in Human Behavior. Pergamon Press, 660 White Plains Rd., Tarrytown, NY 10591-5153. [6/yr., $845]. Addresses the psychological impact of computer use on individuals, groups, and society.

Computers in the Schools. Haworth Press, 10 Alice Street, Binghamton, NY 13904-1580, (800)HAWORTH, fax (800)895-0582, getinfo@haworthpressinc.com, www.haworthpress.com. [Q., $60 indiv., $90 inst., $300 libraries]. Features articles that combine theory and practical applications of small computers in schools for educators and school administrators.

Cooper, Linda. (1999). Anatomy of an online course. **T.H.E. Journal**, **26** (7), 49–51. Describes how to plan an online course based on experiences with a college computer science course. Topics include course layout, HTML conversion, uploading files to the server and editing, online testing, the initial class meeting, student course evaluations, a summary of student perceptions, and course revisions.

Cornell, Richard. (1999). The onrush of technology in education: The professor's new dilemma. **Educational Technology**, **39** (3), 60–64. Compares the negative attitudes of professors toward pressure to integrate information technology to similar reactions to audiovisual materials 30 years ago.

Cronje, J. C., & Clarke, P. A. (1999). Teaching "teaching on the Internet" on the Internet. **South African Journal of Higher Education**, **13** (1), 213–226. Describes a University of Pretoria (South Africa) computer-mediated course in distance education, designed to determine how the World Wide Web could be used as a virtual classroom with an e-mail listserv as a parallel discussion forum. A virtual classroom was created with virtual posters, virtual desks, and virtual portfolios. Student e-mail communications were analyzed to assess instructional effectiveness.

Dalby, Jonathan, & Kewley-Port, Diane. (1999). Explicit pronunciation training using automatic speech recognition technology. **CALICO Journal**, **16** (3), 425–445. Describes a system, provisionally named Pronto, that uses automatic speech recognition for training pronunciation of second languages in adult learners. Methods are included for developing training in Pronto, and results are presented from evaluating classes of speech recognizers for use in different aspects of pronunciation training.

Daniel, Joseph I. (1999). Computer-aided instruction on the World Wide Web: The third generation. **Journal of Economic Education**, 30 (2), 163–174. Reviews the development of computer-aided instruction (CAI) and provides criteria for effective CAI on the World Wide Web. Presents an experimental CAI package called "oo_Micro!" intended to satisfy those criteria. Describes the package contents and procedures and provides an Internet address where a demonstration can be found.

Dede, Chris. (1999). The multiple-media difference. **TECHNOS, 8** (1), 16–18. Describes a graduate course on distance learning that uses seven kinds of asynchronous and synchronous interactive media. All students were able to find their voices in one of the media, and many achieved profound learning experiences at a distance. One of the disadvantages of using multiple media is the problem of measuring the outcomes of "distributed learning."

Donnelly, Roisin C. A. L., & Gorman, Michael P. (1999). Planning and developing an interactive computerised tutorial for learning in higher education. **Teaching in Higher Education**, 4 (3), 397–410. Describes one college teacher's efforts to make the information technology segment of a graduate course more accessible and appealing to students. The approach centered on development of a tutorial program. The process of developing and refining the tutorial is discussed.

Dr. Dobb's Journal. Miller Freeman Inc., 600 Harrison Street, San Francisco, CA 94107, 1(800)456-1215. www.djj.com/djj. [Mo., $25 US, $45 Mexico and Canada, $70 elsewhere]. Articles on the latest in operating systems, programming languages, algorithms, hardware design and architecture, data structures, and telecommunications; in-depth hardware and software reviews.

Enomoto, Ernestine, Nolet, Victor, & Marchionini, Gary. (1999). The Baltimore Learning Community Project: Creating a networked community across middle schools. **Journal of Educational Multimedia and Hypermedia, 8** (1), 99–115. Discusses the Baltimore Learning Community Project, a collaborative effort that includes the Baltimore City Public Schools, the University of Maryland (UM), and Johns Hopkins University. Focuses on the UM component that involves the development of telecommunications software applications for middle school science and social studies teachers.

Erwin, T. Dary, & Rieppi, Ricardo. (1999). Comparing multimedia and traditional approaches in undergraduate psychology classes. **Teaching of Psychology, 26** (1), 58–61. Compares the effectiveness of multimedia and traditional classes. Results show that (1) students in both classes did not differ on abilities before enrollment, (2) students in the multimedia class averaged higher examination scores, and (3) there are no consistent patterns between learning preferences and final examination scores in either case.

Forcier, R. C. (1999). **The computer as an educational tool: Productivity and problem solving** (2nd ed.). [Book, 383p., $55]. Prentice Hall Merrill, www.prenticehall.com. Examines the computer's role in education, problem solving, and as a cognitive tool. Integrates theory and current issues.

Fraser, Catherine C. (1999). Goethe gossips with grass: Using computer chatting software in an introductory literature course. **Unterrichtspraxis/Teaching German, 32** (1), 66–74. Students in a third-year introduction to German literature course chatted over networked computers, using "FirstClass" software.

Guernsey, Lisa. (1999). Textbooks and tests that talk back. **Chronicle of Higher Education, 45** (23), A21–A22. New computer software for physics, mathematics, computer science, and statistics courses at North Carolina State University and in some high schools allows students to solve problems on the computer, recording every answer submitted to provide faculty with a record of student performance and providing immediate feedback to students.

Gunn, Cathy. (1999). They love it, but do they learn from it? Evaluating the educational impact of innovations. **Higher Education Research and Development, 18** (2), 185–199. Describes a case-specific method for assessing the impact of innovations in computer-assisted college instruction that uses objectives and subjective data to assess instructional effects on learning and outcomes. A case study illustrating its practical application is included.

Hall, Valerie G., & Martin, Linda E. (1999). Making decisions about software for classroom use. **Reading Research and Instruction, 38** (3), 187–196. Discusses the challenge for teachers having limited instruction when choosing appropriate software packages for classroom instruction. Discusses generating a review form that can guide teachers in the selection of educational software. Presents a list of criteria for evaluating software.

Hanson-Smith, Elizabeth. (1999). CALL for grammar: Audio, visuals and variety. **ESL Magazine, 2** (4), 20–21. Highlights methods of teaching grammar that have been adapted for computer-assisted language learning.

Herrneckar, Adam D. (1999). Instructional design for Web-based, post-secondary distance education. **Journal of Instruction Delivery Systems, 13** (2), 6–9. Discusses Web-based distance education opportunities in post-secondary education, reviews traditional models for instructional design along with available educational technology, and suggests a derivative framework based on environmental factors and circumstance. Examines constructivism, computer-mediated communication, communication mechanisms, assessment, and virtual access.

Higher Education Technology News. Business Publishers, Inc., 8737 Colesville Road, Suite 1100, Silver Spring, MD 20910-3928. 1(800)274-6737. [Bi-w., $297]. For teachers and those interested in educational uses of computers in the classroom. Features articles on applications and educational software.

Home Office Computing. Box 51344, Boulder, CO 80321-1344. [Mo., $19.97, foreign $27.97]. For professionals who use computers and conduct business at home.

InfoWorld. InfoWorld Publishing, 155 Bovet Road, Suite 800, San Mateo, CA 94402, (650)572-7341. [W., $155]. News and reviews of PC hardware, software, peripherals, and networking.

Instructor. Scholastic Inc., 555 Broadway, New York, NY 10012, (212)505-4900. [8/yr., $19.95; 2 yrs. $29.90]. Features articles on applications and advances of technology in education for K–12 and college educators and administrators.

Joo, Jae-Eun. (1999). Cultural issues of the Internet in the classroom. **British Journal of Educational Technology, 30** (3), 245–250. Investigates cultural issues that the Internet has introduced into classrooms, with illustrations of good practice to stimulate critical discussions among educators on ethical and cultural aspects of Internet use, including equality of access and participation for all people and mutual respect for, and promotion of, underrepresented languages and cultures.

Journal of Computer Assisted Learning. Blackwell Scientific Ltd., Journal Subscriptions, journals.cs@blacksci.co.uk, www.blackwell-science.com. [Q., $98.50 indiv., $424.50 inst.]. Articles and research on the use of computer-assisted learning.

Journal of Educational Computing Research. Baywood Publishing Co., 26 Austin Avenue, P.O. Box 337, Amityville, NY 11701. [8/yr., $104 indiv., $250 inst.]. Presents original research papers, critical analyses, reports on research in progress, design and development studies, article reviews, and grant award listings.

Journal of Research on Computing in Education. ISTE, University of Oregon, 1787 Agate Street, Eugene, OR 97403-1923, (800)336-5191, cust_svc@ccmail.uoregon.edu, www.iste.org. [Q., $38 1 yr., $73 2 yrs., $108 3 yrs.]. Contains articles reporting on the latest research findings related to classroom and administrative uses of technology, including system and project evaluations.

Katz, Arnold. (1999). A computer-aided exercise for checking novices' understanding of market equilibrium changes. **Journal of Economic Education, 30** (2), 148–162. Describes a computer-aided supplement to the introductory microeconomics course, using simulation-based tools for reviewing what they have learned from lectures and conventional textbooks, that enhances students' understanding of comparing market equilibria.

Lambacher, Stephen. (1999). A CALL tool for improving second language acquisition of English consonants by Japanese learners. **Computer Assisted Language Learning, 12** (2), 137–156. Explains the use of a computer-assisted language-learning tool that utilizes acoustic data in real time to help Japanese second-language learners improve their perception and production of English consonants. The basic features of the speech-learning software, which runs on a networked workstation and is used for pronunciation training, are described.

Lan, Jiang, & Dagley, Dave. (1999). Teaching via the Internet: A brief review of copyright law and legal issues. **Educational Technology Review.** (11), 25–30. Focuses on legal problems related to copyright that might arise from teaching via the Internet. Discusses the basics of copyright law, owners' rights, subject matter of copyright, copyright requirements, infringement action and remedies,; the fair use doctrine, guidelines for classroom copying, two views about controls on the Internet, the White Paper, and copyright law outside of the United States.

Learning and Leading with Technology: Serving Teachers in the Classroom. ISTE, University of Oregon, 1787 Agate Street, Eugene, OR 97403-1923, (800)336-5191, cust_svc @ccmail.uoregon.edu, www.iste.org. [8/yr, $38 1 yr., $73 2 yrs., $108 3 yrs.]. Focuses on the use of technology, coordination, and leadership; written by educators for educators. Appropriate for classroom teachers, lab teachers, technology coordinators, and teacher educators.

Lee, June. (1999). Effectiveness of computer-based instructional simulation: A meta analysis. **International Journal of Instructional Media, 26** (1), 71–85. Discusses computer simulation and analyzes evidence concerning the effectiveness of simulation by examining the relationship between two forms of simulations, pure and hybrid; and two modes of instruction, presentation and practice. Presents results of a meta-analysis of 19 studies on simulation effects, including effect size for academic achievement and for attitude.

Leu, Donald J., Jr., Leu, Deborah Diadiun, & Leu, Katherine R. (1999). **Teaching with the Internet: Lessons from the classroom**. [Book, 336p., $28.95]. Christopher-Gordon, 1520 Providence Highway, Suite #12, Norwood, MA 02062, (800)934-8322. This book shows teachers how to effectively integrate the Internet into the classroom and illustrates how teachers are developing classroom communities filled with the excitement of learning and discovery. Each chapter begins with a story of how a talented teacher uses the Internet in the classroom and then discusses the lessons that can be learned from this experience.

Logo Exchange. ISTE, University of Oregon, 1787 Agate Street, Eugene, OR 97403-1923, (800)336-5191, cust_svc@ccmail.uoregon.edu, www.iste.org. [Q., $29, $44 intl., $34 intl. air]. Brings ideas from Logo educators throughout the world, with current information on Logo research, resources, and methods.

MacArthur, Charles A. (1999). Word prediction for students with severe spelling problems. **Learning Disability Quarterly, 22** (3), 158–172. Two studies compared handwriting, word processing, and word prediction with speech-synthesis software (PR) among three intermediate-grade students with severe spelling problems.

MacDonald, Lucy, & Caverly, David C. (1999). Techtalk: Technology and developmental math. **Journal of Developmental Education, 22** (3), 32–33. Reviews the evolution of math software from the 1980s to the present. Discusses how current notions of learning styles have changed software applications and how critical thinking and problem solving have affected software development. Addresses the overall effect of technology on math anxiety and explores what new technology tools are available for the delivery of math assistance.

MacWorld. MacWorld Communications, Box 54529, Boulder, CO 80322-4529. [Mo., $19.97]. Describes hardware, software, tutorials, and applications for users of the Macintosh microcomputer.

McCarthy-Tucker, Sherri N. (1999). Student preferences for electronically assisted options in a community college introductory psychology course. **Community College Journal of Research and Practice**, **23** (5), 499–510. Investigates which students most benefit from electronically assisted instruction by looking at how students choose to learn when given a variety of traditional and electronic options in an Introductory Psychology course.

McLoughlin, Catherine. (1999). Culturally responsive technology use: Developing an on-line community of learners. **British Journal of Educational Technology**, **30** (3), 231–243. Traces the development of an online unit for Indigenous Australian learners and accounts for cultural issues that had an impact on the design of learning tasks and the associated avenues for communication provided to learners. In this context, culturally responsive design was ensured by the adoption of Lave's (1991) community of practice model.

McQueen, Tena F., & Fleck, Robert A., Jr. (1999). An evaluation of alternative technology-based instructional formats. **T.H.E. Journal**, **26** (11), 108–115. Describes three technology-based alternative approaches to traditional classroom instruction that have been tried at Columbus State University (Georgia) to meet the needs of nontraditional part-time students: vendor-developed courses delivered via the Internet, vendor-developed tutorials and tests on CD-ROM, and instructor-developed and vendor-assisted Web-based instruction.

Microcomputer Abstracts. Information Today, 143 Old Marlton Pike, Medford, NJ 08055, (800)300-9868. [4/yr., $199 US, $208 Canada/Mexico, $214 elsewhere]. Abstracts literature on the use of microcomputers in business, education, and the home, covering more than 175 publications.

Morse, Timothy E. (1999). An overview of technology applications in special education. **School Business Affairs**, **65** (2), 11–15. Special education uses three types of computer-based instruction software: drill and practice, tutorials, and computer simulation. Assistive technology applications (electronic communication devices, voice-activated software, and print readers) are available for students whose disabilities do not allow them to perform functional tasks independently. Medical assistive and administrative technologies are described.

Mudge, Stephen M. (1999). Delivering multimedia teaching modules via the Internet. **Innovations in Education and Training International**, **36** (1), 11–16. Discusses advantages and disadvantages of using the Internet for delivering teaching modules and makes recommendations for successful use of the Internet. Highlights include the availability of information at all times and from remote locations, multimedia capabilities, infrastructure needed, security issues, updating, needed skills, and difficulties in finding valid information.

PC Magazine: The Independent Guide to IBM-Standard Personal Computing. Ziff-Davis Publishing Co., Box 54093, Boulder, CO 80322. [22 issues, $22.97]. Comparative reviews of computer hardware and general business software programs.

PC Week. Ziff-Davis Publishing Co., 1 Park Avenue, New York, 10016. [W., $195, Canada and Mexico $250, free to qualified personnel]. Provides current information on the IBM PC, including hardware, software, industry news, business strategies, and reviews of hardware and software.

PC World. PC World Communications, Inc., Box 55029, Boulder, CO 80322-5029. [Mo., $19.97 US, $34.97 Mexico, $65.97 elsewhere]. Presents articles on applications and columns containing news, systems information, product announcements, and hardware updates.

Peterson, Mark. (1999). Piloting and the creation of a CALL centre: The case of the Japan Advanced Institute of Science and Technology. **Computer Assisted Language Learning**, **12** (2), 163–170. Recent interest in computer-assisted language learning (CALL) has been accompanied by an expansion in the demand for CALL centers. The planning and creation of these facilities present educators and administrators with a unique set of challenges. This article highlights these factors and illustrates how a CALL center can be successfully implemented through piloting.

Powell, Jack V. (1999). Interrelationships between importance, knowledge and attitude of the inexperienced. **Computers & Education, 32** (2), 127–136. Reports on the use of a computerized simulation integrated within a preservice methods course for early-childhood majors. Compares the difference in response to importance, knowledge, and attitude related to computer utilization in the course between the computer simulation group and a control group taught by traditional means.

Price, Charlotte, Bunt, Andrea, & McCalla, Gordon. (1999). L2tutor: A mixed-initiative dialogue system for improving fluency. **Computer Assisted Language Learning, 12** (2), 83–112. Introduces a computer-assisted language-learning system called L2tutor that is designed to provide an immersion experience for travelers before they leave on a trip to a country where a different language is spoken. The learner takes part in a fully mixed-initiative dialog with the system to gain fluency and hone vocabulary and grammatical skills.

Reinhardt, Linda. (1999). Confessions of a "techno-teacher." **College Teaching, 47** (2), 48–50. A college psychology teacher enamored of instructional technology examines what techniques and applications have worked, which ones have not worked well, and what might work with some modification. Topics include various audiovisual aids, strategies for designing instructional materials, and creation of new forms for computer-enhanced classroom presentation.

Salmon, Gilly. (1999). Computer mediated conferencing in large scale management education. **Open Learning, 14**, (2). 34–43. Discusses the history, principles, culture, and teaching approaches of the United Kingdom Open University and its Business School (OUBS). Focuses on management students and the OUBS's position in a dynamic and competitive MBA market place

Social Science Computer Review. Sage Publications Inc., 2455 Teller Road, Thousand Oaks, CA 91320, order@sagepub.com, www.sagepub.com. [Q., $63 indiv., $274 inst.]. Features include software reviews, new product announcements, and tutorials for beginners.

Software Magazine. Sentry Publishing Co., Inc., 1 Research Drive, Suite 400B, Westborough, MA 01581-3907. [6 issues/yr., $42 US, $58 Canada, $140 elsewhere, free to qualified personnel]. Provides information on software and industry developments for business and professional users and announces new software packages.

Squires, David. (1999). Educational software for constructivist learning environments: Subversive use and volatile design. **Educational Technology, 39** (3), 48–54. Discusses designers' need to design educational software for subversive use, recognizing that users fit the use of technology-based environments into contextually tuned "situated" learning environments. In this sense, good design is volatile design, or design that changes with contextual use. These ideas are illustrated with reference to a range of technology-based learning environments.

Thoms, Karen Jarrett. (1999). Teaching via ITV: Taking instructional design to the next level. **T.H.E. Journal, 26** (9), 60–66. Addresses visual literacy and instructional-design issues as they relate to teaching courses via two-way interactive television (ITV).

Wachowicz, Krystyna A., & Scott, Brian. (1999). Software that listens: It's not a question of whether, it's a question of how. **CALICO Journal, 16** (3), 253–276. Reviews speech-interactive learning activities in selected commercial products: activities for vocabulary development, conversational practice, and pronunciation. Suggests that the effectiveness of speech-interactive computer-assisted language learning is determined less by capabilities of the speech recognizer than by (a) design of language-learning activity and feedback and (b) inclusion of repair strategies to safeguard against recognizer error.

DISTANCE EDUCATION

Adelskold, Goran, Aleklett, Kjell, Axelsson, Rune, & Blomgren, Jan. (1999). Problem-based distance learning of energy issues via computer network. **Distance Education, 20** (1), 129–143. Reports experiences with problem-based learning that was modified for distance education and used for teaching energy issues at Uppsala University (Sweden).

Albrecht, Robert C. (1999). Western Governors University: University of the future. **Mid-Western Educational Researcher, 12** (1), 7–8. Western Governors University (WGU) was initiated by 15 western governors in response to perceived needs in the marketplace and as a supplement to traditional institutions. WGU features competency-based credentials (certificates and degrees) rather than course-based programs; distance learning; focus on nontraditional, working students; third-party assessment of student competencies; and "unbundled" faculty functions.

Ambler, Marjane. (1999). Editor's essay: Educating the native student at distance. **Tribal College, 10** (3), 6–9. Previews the issue's articles on distance education, stating that tribal colleges are committed to increasing access to education. Cautions against proceeding rashly into new technology, but also denotes the danger in delaying technology implementation, because only those colleges that adapt and provide such services will survive.

American Journal of Distance Education. American Center for the Study of Distance Education, Pennsylvania State University, 110 Rackley Building, University Park, PA 16802-3202, www.cde.psu.edu/ACSDE/. [3/yr., $45 indiv., $75 inst.]. Created to disseminate information and act as a forum for criticism and debate about research in and practice of politics, as well as administration of distance education.

Balch, David E., & Patino, I. F. (1999). Learning online at Rio Hondo Community College. **Catalyst, 28** (1), 17–20. Recounts Rio Hondo Community College's decision to "go online" in anticipation of reduced funding, needed expansion, increased inservice training, changing student demographics, and the movement into computer technology.

Bhalalusesa, Eustella. (1999). The distance mode of learning in higher education: The Tanzanian experience. **Open Learning, 14** (2), 14–23. Describes the distance mode of delivery in higher education practiced at the Open University of Tanzania (OUT).

Blumenstyk, Goldie. (1999). A company pays top universities to use their names and their professors. **Chronicle of Higher Education, 45** (41), A39, A41. A new company is offering selected universities a chance to profit directly from the scholarly materials produced by its faculty, particularly in the areas of corporate training, continuing education, distance learning, and the international-student market.

Bowman, Connie, & Ward, Patricia. (1999). Extending the vision: Mentoring through university-school partnerships. **Mid-Western Educational Researcher, 12** (4), 33–37. Describes the development of an award-winning university/school partnership whose core is teacher development through mentoring.

Bruce, Bertram. (1999). Education online: Learning anywhere, any time. **Journal of Adolescent & Adult Literacy, 42** (8), 662–665. Looks at the frames (of time, space, roles, and knowledge) that define learning and examines how such frames would be radically altered by online learning.

Cini, Marie A., & Vilic, Boris. (1999). Online teaching: Moving from risk to challenge. **Syllabus, 12** (10), 38–40. Describes a minicourse used at Duquesne University that teaches faculty effective online instruction skills and helps them adapt to the cultural change of the new online environment.

Cohen, Arthur M. (1999). The hopeful marriage of community colleges and distance education: True love at last? **Catalyst, 28** (1), 3–7. Discusses the marriage between higher education and interactive media, which holds the promise of education beyond the boundaries of the traditional classroom.

Davis, Thomas, & McLeod, Martha. (1999). Designing the tribal virtual college of tomorrow. **Tribal College, 10** (3), 10–13. Discusses the steps taken by Bay Mills (Michigan) and Salish Kootenai (Montana) Colleges in developing online educational opportunities for tribal virtual colleges.

Distance Education Report. Magna Publications, Inc., 2718 Dryden Drive, Madison, WI 53704. [Mo., $399]. Digests periodical, Internet, and conference information into monthly reports.

DuBois, Glenn. (1999). State University of New York: Fulfilling the promise. **Community College Journal of Research and Practice, 23** (3), 255–268. Addresses the historical origins of the State University of New York and its system of community colleges, particularly its contemporary structure and nature in the areas of funding, governance, faculty, students, and programs. Discusses current issues such as (1) statewide budget problems, (2) the under-prepared student, (3) distance learning, and (4) instructional technology.

Eaton, Judith S. (1999). Distance education is on your doorstep. **Trusteeship, 7** (1), 23–27. As distance learning brings changes to traditional higher-education institutions and creates new educational providers, the college or university governing board must reexamine issues of institutional purpose, quality, and finance.

Feyten, C. M., & Nutta, J. (1999). **Virtual instruction: Issues and insights from an international perspective.** [Book, 278p., $45]. Libraries Unlimited, (800)237-6124, lu-books@lu.com, www.lu.com. Includes essays about the theoretical issues raised by recent developments in distance, online, and virtual learning.

Garrison, D. Randy, & Anderson, Terry D. (1999). Avoiding the industrialization of research universities: Big and little distance education. **American Journal of Distance Education, 13** (2), 48–63. In contrast to the big industrial mode of distance education, an approach to distance education called "little distance education" is described that is consistent with the traditional goals and values of creating knowledge through a critical community of learners.

Geissinger, Helen. (1999). Girls' access to education in a developing country. **International Review of Education/Internationale Zeitschrift fuer Erziehungswissenschaft/Revue Internationale de l'Education, 43** (5–6), 423–438. Describes the number of barriers that prevent girls from accessing education at every level in Papua New Guinea, from physical and geographical factors to psychosocial and economic factors. Proposes distance education as one of the few "second chances" for these girls.

Hackmann, Donald G., & Berry, James E. (1999). Distance learning in educational administration doctoral programs: The wave of the future? **Journal of School Leadership, 9** (4), 349–367. A survey of 109 doctoral-granting educational-administration institutions indicated that about half use some form of distance learning (off-campus courses, interactive video, or Internet courses) and 60 percent are planning to do so.

Hickman, Clark J. (1999). Public policy implications associated with technology assisted distance learning. **Adult Learning, 10** (3), 17–20. Discusses six major themes related to public policy and distance learning: (1) quality/evaluation and accreditation, (2) credentialing, (3) enhanced public access, (4) organization and governance, (5) partnerships, and (6) financial support.

Jarvis, Peter. (1999). Global trends in lifelong learning and the response of the universities. **Comparative Education, 35** (2), 249–257. Argues that globalization is standardizing the way in which higher education responds to the pressures of the international division of labor, but because Western countries have more knowledge workers, they will point the way for the development of higher education in developing nations.

Journal of Distance Education. Canadian Association for Distance Education, Secretariat, One Stewart Street, Suite 205, Ottawa, ON K1N 6H7, Canada. (Text in English and French). [2/yr., $40, add $5 outside Canada]. Aims to promote and encourage scholarly work of empirical and theoretical nature relating to distance education in Canada and throughout the world.

Kessler, David, & Keefe, Barbara. (1999). Going the distance. **American School & University, 71** (11), 44, 46, 48. Examines the planning process behind successfully providing full access to distance-learning programs for all students.

Kintzer, Frederick C. (1999). Articulation and transfer: A symbiotic relationship with life-long learning. **International Journal of Lifelong Education, 18** (3), 147–154. Outlines three possible futures for higher education: "nonuniversities" that modify courses and offer distance learning to adult reentry students, increasing involvement of business/industry in post-secondary education delivery, and technologically delivered nontraditional and non-sponsored education.

Lever-Duffy, Judy. (1999). The evolution of distance education. **Catalyst, 28** (1), 8–13. Provides an overview of distance education technologies. Discusses synchronous and asynchronous distance delivery approaches and the extent to which they offer students the opportunity to interact with other students and faculty.

Li, Yawan, & Chen, Jikun. (1999). Comparative research into Chinese conventional and television-based higher education. **Open Learning, 14** (2), 3–13. Reports on findings of a joint Sino-Japanese study comparing conventional and television-based higher education in China, examining student satisfaction and student expectation of higher education, relative to the resourcing of conventional and radio and television universities ("universities without walls") in China.

Loeding, Barbara L., & Wynn, Marjorie. (1999). Distance learning planning, preparation, and presentation: Instructors' perspectives. **International Journal of Instructional Media, 26** (2), 181–192. Describes experiences and concerns of instructors using the Instructional Television Fixed Signal (ITFS) program, a low-cost television system in which classes originating on the University of South Florida Lakeland campus are simultaneously broadcast live to various ITFS sites. Presents guidelines for distance learning regarding planning, preparation, and presentation.

Mangan, Katherine S. (1999). Top business schools seek to ride a bull market in on-line M.B.A.'s. **Chronicle of Higher Education, 45** (19), A27–A28. Internet-based master's programs in business administration (M.B.A.s) serve a market that could bring significant revenues to business schools, providing new access to mid- to upper-level managers who want degrees to advance their careers but who cannot take time off from work, or to young executives whose bosses offer to pay for the degree but not for time off.

McKinney, Kristen J., & Schuyler, Gwyer. (1999). At the crossroads of distance and continuing education in the community college. **Catalyst, 28** (1), 21–24. Explores how community colleges have incorporated distance education technology into both traditional continuing-education programs and for-credit curricula.

Meyen, Edward L., Tangen, Paul, & Lian, Cindy H. T. (1999). Developing online instruction: Partnership between instructors and technical developers. **Journal of Special Education Technology, 14** (1), 18–31. Discusses the design, development, and teaching of two graduate-level special-education courses online using audio streaming technology.

Miller, Lawrence G., Hyatt, Sue Y., Brennan, Joyce, Bertani, Raymond, & Trevor, Thomas. (1999). Overcoming barriers for "niche" learners through distance education. **Catalyst, 28** (1), 14–16. Focuses on students who fit into "niches," and discusses how the Chattanooga State Technical Community College's distance learning program accommodates these learners.

Ndahi, Hassan B. (1999). Utilization of distance learning technology among industrial and technical teacher education faculty. **Journal of Industrial Teacher Education, 36** (4), 21–37. Responses from 84 of 179 industrial and technical teacher educators indicated that 63 percent used distance learning technologies; 84.8 percent had equipment problems; 88.6 percent lacked information on technology uses; and 96 percent thought poor teaching skills were an obstacle to effective use.

Neal, Ed. (1999). Distance education: Prospects and problems. **National Forum, 79** (1), 40–43. Discusses the history of distance education and reminds educators of its benefits and pitfalls.

Offer, B., & Lev, Y. (1999). Teacher-learner interaction in the process of operating DL (distance learning) systems. **Educational Media International, 36** (2), 132–136. Discusses the use of distance learning systems, teacher/learner interactions in the classroom as well as in distance learning, student achievement, training teachers to use interactions, the model of decision making to operate distance learning, and an example of a distance learning system in Israel between universities and secondary schools.

Okula, Susan. (1999). Going the distance: A new avenue for learning. **Business Education Forum, 53** (3), 7–10. Explores uses of distance education in secondary, higher, and corporate education, appropriateness for types of learners, and uses of distance learning in business education.

Olsen, Florence. (1999). "Virtual" institutions challenge accreditors to devise new ways of measuring quality. **Chronicle of Higher Education, 45** (48), A29–A30. Technology-intensive changes in higher education have convinced some administrators and accreditors that new models for college and university accreditation are needed.

Open Learning. Pitman Professional, Subscriptions Dept., P.O. Box 77, Harlow, Essex CM19 5BQ, England. [3/yr., £68 UK, £73 Europe, $78 elsewhere]. Academic, scholarly publication on aspects of open and distance learning anywhere in the world. Includes issues for debate and research notes.

Open Praxis. International Centre for Distance Education, National Extension College, 18 Brooklands Avenue, Cambridge CB2 2HN, England. [2/yr., $70 indiv., $55 libraries]. Reports on activities and programs of the ICDE.

Peraya, Daniel, & Levrat, Bernard. (1999). The Swiss Virtual Campus: History and perspectives. **Educational Media International, 36** (2), 97–109. Discussion of the development of distance education in Switzerland focuses on a history of the Swiss Virtual Campus and an explanation of the role of the Educational Technologies Unit of the University of Geneva (TECFA).

Phillips, Melodie R., & Peters, Mary Jane. (1999). Targeting rural students with distance learning courses: A comparative study of determinant attributes and satisfaction levels. **Journal of Education for Business, 74** (6), 351–356. A marketing course attended by 65 on-campus students and 30 accessing it via interactive video resulted in no differences in student satisfaction. On-site students had more problems with instructor accessibility than did off-site students, possibly because instructors overcompensated to avoid isolation of the distant learners.

Phillips, V., & Yager, C. (1999). **The best distance learning graduate schools 1999: Earning your degree without leaving home.** [Book, 336p., $16]. Princeton Review, www.review.com/index.cfm. Provides comprehensive information about 170 graduate distance learning programs.

Pollock, Kent. (1999). Open U: A new era in higher ed. **Converge, 2** (3), 16–18, 20. Discusses the team approach to instructional design, delivery, and evaluation; educational quality; emphasis on independent learning; cost effectiveness; and partnerships with U.S. universities.

Powers, Kris. (1999). **A self-fulfilling prophecy: Online distance learning for introductory computing**. [Paper, 11p.]. (Presented at the 20th National Educational Computing Conference Proceedings, Atlantic City, NJ, June 22–24, 1999). Describes novel approaches for adapting an introductory computing course for online distance learning, including discussions of the underlying pedagogy and objectives as well as the implementation and results of the online course.

Riedling, Ann M. (1999). Distance education: The technology—What you need to know to succeed, an overview. **Educational Technology Review**, (11), 8–13. Explores distance education evolution and research concerning distance learning formats.

Roach, Ronald. (1999). The higher education technology revolution. **Black Issues in Higher Education, 16** (13), 92–96. Fifteen developments in technology that have laid the foundation for the current information-technology environment on college and university campuses are listed.

Ryan, Cathy. (1999). Forum: Revisiting the writing requirement. **Business Communication Quarterly, 62** (1), 64–68. Considers four changes being introduced into the educational marketplace by corporate and virtual instruction. Argues that business communication programs need to develop their own knowledge infrastructure so that content can be delivered on demand and so that students have choice in how the material is delivered (real-time, online, and virtual delivery).

Saba, Farhad, Ed. (1999). Hardware systems in distance education: What the policy makers and managers must know. **Distance Education Report, 3** (6), 1, 4. Discusses the distinctions made between hardware and technology as applied to distance education.

Saba, Farhad. (1999). Toward a systems theory of distance education. **American Journal of Distance Education, 13** (2), 24–31. Discusses limitations of "Comparing Distance Learning and Classroom Learning: Conceptual Considerations," Smith and Dillon's physical science view of educational technology.

Simerly, Robert G. (1999). Providing leadership for technology enhanced education: The challenge of institutional macro change. **Journal of Continuing Higher Education, 47** (1), 40–48. Describes paradigm shifts that have led to the macro change of technology-enhanced education.

Smith, Patricia L., & Dillon, Connie L. (1999). Toward a systems theory of distance education: A reaction. **American Journal of Distance Education, 13** (2), 32–36. Contends that comparison studies offer one important view from which to frame questions about the study of distance education. Responds to Farhad Saba's ("Toward a Systems Theory of Distance Education") major premises about distance-education research.

Smith, Patricia L., & Dillon, Connie L. (1999). Comparing distance learning and classroom learning: Conceptual considerations. **American Journal of Distance Education, 13** (2), 6–23. Proposes a schema system based on media-attribute theory that can be used to classify both media and delivery systems based on research related to learning and motivation in distance education.

Spooner, F., Jordan, L., Algozzine, B., & Spooner, M. (1999). Student ratings of instruction in distance learning and on-campus classes. **Journal of Educational Research, 92**, 132–140. Evaluates implementations of distance learning technology in two situations, both involving students with physical disabilities. Includes a summary of relevant studies and a set of implementation guidelines.

Tait, Alan, Ed., & Mills, Roger, Ed. (1999). **The convergence of distance and conventional education: Patterns of flexibility for the individual learner.** [Book, 193p., $29.99]. Routledge Studies in Distance Education. Routledge, 29 West 35th Street, New York, NY 10001, (800)634–7064, info@routledge.com. These 14 essays address convergence, the breaking down of barriers between open and distance learning and conventional education and the creation of more multimodal institutions.

Walter, L. James, Liu, Daonian, & Brooks, David W. (1999). An Internet-based course: Leadership issues. **Journal of Science Education and Technology, 8** (2), 151–154. Discusses leadership issues that arose during the creation and offering of an Internet-based course for high school chemistry teachers, including course organization, recruiting students, and technological support available to participating students.

Wetsit, Deborah. (1999). Emphasizing the human being in distance education. **Tribal College, 10** (3), 14–18. Contends that new distance learning technology creates a danger of dehumanizing students and instructors. Discusses the need for teachers to focus on culture and relevancy and to build relationships with their students.

White, Ken W., Ed., & Weight, Bob H., Ed. (2000). **The online teaching guide: A handbook of attitudes, strategies, and techniques for the virtual classroom**. [Book, 192p., $29]. Allyn & Bacon, 160 Gould Street, Needham Heights, MA 02494-2310. Presents 14 papers that offer guidance to college teachers venturing into online instruction. It is based on the experiences and ideas of faculty at the University of Phoenix (Arizona) online campus, which has been offering online courses since 1989.

Williams, Marcia L., Paprock, Kenneth, & Covington, Barbara. (1999). **Distance learning: The essential guide**. [Book, 166p., $29.95]. Sage Publications Inc., 2455 Teller Road, Thousand Oaks, CA 91320, order@sagepub.com, www.sagepub.com. Intended for individuals engaged in open and distance learning activities, this guide is designed with an applications focus that provides a "quick start" for immediate work needs. Built on an intuitive set of "How do I" questions, the book presents the foundation needed to teach from a distance.

Winston, Gordon C. (1999). For-profit higher education: Godzilla or Chicken Little? **Change, 31** (1), 12–19. Examines the economics of the growing sector of for-profit higher education institutions compared to the cost-price-subsidy structure of traditional institutions.

Winters, R. Oakley. (1999). Technology and the future of Appalachian education. **Appalachian Heritage, 28** (2), 12–14. Proposes that Appalachia pursue an economic development strategy based on exporting knowledge and training.

EDUCATIONAL RESEARCH

American Educational Research Journal. American Educational Research Association, 1230 17th Street, NW, Washington, DC 20036-3078. [Q., $41 indiv., $56 inst.]. Reports original research, both empirical and theoretical, and brief synopses of research.

Collins, Timothy. (1999). Research: The region's educational needs. **Appalachian Heritage, 28** (2), 50–59. Discusses common themes in the limited research on Appalachian institutions of higher education: interinstitutional links, and links between institutions and the broader community. Reviews trends that offer research opportunities (the impact of K–12 reforms on higher education, effects of information technology on higher education, student leadership training, service learning, resource sharing, Appalachian Studies) and suggests information sources.

Cross, K. Patricia. (1999). What do we know about students' learning, and how do we know it? **Innovative Higher Education, 23** (4), 255–270. Although research has a great deal to tell educators about how college students learn, the educational community is becoming dependent on research and ignoring what can be learned from the principles of good practice in the classroom. Research should be the beginning, not the conclusion, of the investigation into student learning processes.

Current Index to Journals in Education (CIJE). Oryx Press, 4041 N. Central at Indian School Road, Phoenix, AZ 85012-3397, [Mo., $245, $280 outside North America; semi-ann. cumulations $250, $285 foreign; combination $475]. A guide to articles published in some 830 education and education-related journals. Includes complete bibliographic information, annotations, and indexes. Semi-annual cumulations available. Contents are produced by the ERIC (Educational Resources Information Center) system, Office of Educational Research and Improvement, and the U.S. Department of Education.

Education Index. H. W. Wilson, 950 University Avenue, Bronx, NY 10452. [Mo., except July and August, $1,295 for CD-ROM, including accumulations]. Author-subject index to educational publications in the English language. Cumulated quarterly and annually.

Educational Research. Routledge, 11 Fetter Lane, London EC4P 4EE, England. [3/yr., £40 indiv., $68 US and Canada]. Reports on current educational research, evaluation, and applications.

Educational Researcher. American Educational Research Association, 1230 17th Street, NW, Washington, DC 20036-3078. [9/yr., $44 indiv., $61 inst.]. Contains news and features of general significance in educational research.

Elam, Jimmy H. (1999). Use of optometric education. **Optometric Education, 24** (2), 47–51. To enhance the information technology literacy of optometry students, the Southern College of Optometry (Tennessee) developed an academic assignment, the Electronic Media Paper, in which second-year students had to search two different electronic media for information. Results suggest Internet use for searching may be a useful tool for specific academic assignments and for searching for other optometric information.

Gay, L. H., & Airasian, Peter. (1999). **Educational research: Competencies for analysis and applications** (6th ed.). [Book, 661p., $71.75]. Prentice Hall, www.prenticehall.com. This market-leading text offers all the skills and procedures students need to become competent consumers and producers of educational research. It uses a direct, step-by-step approach to the topic, placing a strong emphasis on evaluation of student performance.

Hines, Edward R. (1999). Policy research in higher education: Data, decisions, dilemmas, and disconnect. **Mid-Western Educational Researcher, 12** (1), 2–6. Dichotomizes academic research and educational policy making as distinct and often conflicting cultures. Examines legislative support of higher education as an illustration of the research-policy disconnection. Summarizes recent criticisms of higher education research. Discusses differing "mind frames" of researchers and policymakers, their mutual need for each other, and ways to improve communication.

Lagemann, Ellen Condliffe. (2000). **An elusive science: The troubling history of education research**. [Book, 264p., $25.00]. University of Chicago Press, 5801 South Ellis, Chicago, IL 60637, (773)702–7700, www.press.uchicago.edu. Takes a comprehensive look at the field of Educational Research as well as the difficulties plaguing the field.

Lagemann, Ellen Condliffe, & Shulman, Lee S., Ed. (1999). **Issues in education research: Problems and possibilities**. [Book, 424p., $39.95]. Jossey-Bass Inc., 350 Sansome Street, San Francisco, CA 94104, (888)378-2537, fax (800)605-2665. This volume provides an overview of the tensions, dilemmas, issues, and possibilities that characterize educational research. The contributions of more than 20 researchers examine the state of educational research, its future directions, and some of the major trends that have affected the field.

Leitner, Erich. (1999). Academic oligarchy and higher education research: Implications for the reform of institutions of higher education in Austria. **Higher Education Policy, 12** (1), 27–40. Describes the higher education reform discussion in Austria, which led to major system reorganization in 1993. It is noted that a previous academic oligarchy played a central role because a high proportion of university faculty also served in the parliament. Research on higher education played little part in reform because few studies were available.

LeTendre, Gerald K. (1999). The problem of Japan: Qualitative studies and international educational comparisons. **Educational Researcher, 28** (2), 38–46. Reviews qualitative (historical and ethnographic) studies of education in Japan that advance a general understanding of educational theory and practice. Japan, which is neither an educational paradise nor an examination hell, is the source of much data of value to educational research in the United States.

Liu, Leping, Ed. (1999). **Information technology in educational research and statistics**. [Book, 241p., $59.95]. Haworth Press, 10 Alice Street, Binghamton, NY 13904-1580, (800)HAWORTH, www.haworthpressinc.com. This important book focuses on creating new ideas for using educational technologies such as the Internet, the World Wide Web, and various software packages to further research and statistics. Explores ongoing debates relating to the theory of research, research methodology, and successful practices. It also covers the debate on what statistical procedures are appropriate for what kinds of research designs.

Miller, D. W. (1999). The black hole of education research. **Chronicle of Higher Education, 45** (48), A17–A18. Critics feel education scholarship lacks rigor and a practical focus on achievement, wasting substantial resources. Research on effectiveness of educational reforms is often weak, inconclusive, or simply inadequate, and good scholarship may have little influence on classroom practice. Popular policies often persist despite strong research evidence of their harm. Some critics fault teacher education for poor use of research.

Nisbet, John. (1999). How it all began: Educational research 1880–1930. **Scottish Educational Review, 31** (1), 3–9. Traces the history of experimental educational research, based on application of the scientific method to pedagogy. Highlights the beginnings of educational research in German studies of psychology and child development, U.S. development of standardized tests and research-based administration, and European experimental studies. Discusses the rivalry in Scotland between school-based and more formal research styles.

Paulsen, Michael B. (1999). How college students learn: Linking traditional educational research and contextual classroom research. **Journal of Staff, Program & Organizational Development, 16** (2), 63–71. Introduces the topic of the journal issue—how college students learn— linking traditional educational research and contextual classroom research. The cognitive-mediation model of college student learning is briefly described in combination with some research that supports it. The article presents some implications for faculty development within this context.

Pautler, Albert J., Jr., Ed. (1999). **Workforce education: Issues for the new century**. [Book, 299p., $21.95, school price $17.56]. Prakken Publications, P.O. Box 8623, Ann Arbor, MI 48107-8623, (800)530-9673. This book contains 22 papers on workforce education issues for the new century:

Quigley, B. Allen. (1999). Lions at the gate: Adult education research, research-in-practice, and speculative audacity. **PAACE Journal of Lifelong Learning, 8**, 1–19. Presents a rationale for change in adult education research. Suggests that graduate adult education programs teach relevant research methods based on practitioner problems and encourage action and participatory methods in theses and dissertations.

Research in Science & Technological Education. Taylor & Francis Group, 11 New Fetter Lane, London EC4P 4EE, www.tandf.co.uk. [2/yr., $104 indiv., $578 inst.]. Publication of original research in the science and technological fields. Includes articles on psychological, sociological, economic, and organizational aspects of technological education.

Resources in Education (RIE). Superintendent of Documents, US Government Printing Office, P.O. Box 371954, Pittsburgh, PA 15250-7954, www.access.gpo.gov. [Mo., $78 US, $97.50 elsewhere]. Announcement of research reports and other documents in education, including abstracts and indexes by subject, author, and institution. Contents produced by the ERIC (Educational Resources Information Center) system, Office of Educational Research and Improvement, and the U.S. Department of Education.

Ronis, Diane. (2000). **Brain compatible assessments. K–College**. [Book, 162p., $38.95]. Skylight Professional Development, 2626 S. Clearbrook Drive, Arlington Heights, IL 60005-5310, (800)348-4474. This guide uses current brain research to show that some traditional instructional and assessment methods may actually work against the brain's natural way of learning. The guide shows how to enhance traditional methods of assessment using techniques derived from recent research on the brain. Practical approaches to assessment are illustrated with lesson plans that include opportunities for assessment.

Tobin, Kenneth. (1999). The value to science education of teachers researching their own praxis. **Research in Science Education, 29** (2), 159–169. Introduces a special issue that focuses on teachers and other practitioners undertaking research on their professional praxis. Discusses some experiences as a teacher-researcher, outlines the studies presented in the special issue, and considers questions of voice in the presentation of teacher-researcher studies.

Wraga, William G. (1999). "Extracting sun-beams out of cucumbers": The retreat from practice in reconceptualized curriculum studies. **Educational Researcher, 28** (1), 4–13. Documents and explains three manifestations of the split between theory and practice in reconceptualized curriculum studies. Evaluates this split against the educational theory of John Dewey, considers the obligations of professional schools and land-grant universities, and suggests implications of the curriculum theory-practice split for curriculum development and schooling.

EDUCATIONAL TECHNOLOGY

Abramovich, Sergei. (1999). Revisiting an ancient problem through contemporary discourse. **School Science and Mathematics, 99** (3), 148–155. Presents a computer-mediated discourse on the Pythagorean equation in a university classroom of preservice and inservice teachers.

Agron, Joe, Ed. (1999). Poised for the millennium. **American School & University, 71** (5), 18–22, 24, 26, 28. Presents advice from five school administrators on how schools are meeting facility and business challenges in the new millennium. Issues discussed concern power needs, the Y2K computer problem, the explosion of new educational technology, school security, educational finance, and building deterioration.

Almeida d'Eca, Teresa. (1999). **New information and communication technologies in portuguese schools: Paving the way for the next millennium**. [Paper, 9p.]. (Presented at the Joint National Conference of the Popular Culture and American Culture Associations, San Diego, CA, March 31–April 3, 1999). This paper describes three government-funded technology programs in Portugal and the changes they brought about in Portuguese schools.

Anderson, M. Brownell. (1999). In progress: Reports of new approaches in medical education. **Academic Medicine, 74** (5), 561–618. The annual, peer-reviewed collection of reports on innovative approaches to medical education includes 72 brief reports of teaching techniques and approaches, categorized by their emphasis on students, technology use, development of professional skills/attitudes, teaching and assessment strategies, graduate medical education, and continuing medical education.

Appropriate Technology. Intermediate Technology Publications, Ltd., 103–105 Southampton Row, London, WC1B 4HH, England, journals.edit@itpubs.org.uk. [Q., $28 indiv., $37 inst.]. Articles on less technologically advanced, but more environmentally sustainable, solutions to problems in developing countries.

Austin, Terri, & Rogers, Jody. (1999). Harnessing the power of technology and partnerships to build capacity. **TECHNOS, 8** (2), 28–33. Describes school reform efforts in Anderson Community Schools (Anderson, Indiana) that are partnering schools, parents, and the community so students have the education and training to perform jobs needed in the future.

Barnes, Susan B. (1999). Education and technology: A cultural Faustian bargain. **Bulletin of Science, Technology & Society, 19** (1), 11–16. Explores the advantages and disadvantages of integrating computers into education and describes the cultural implications for educational policy.

Beaudin, James A., & Sells, Jeffrey A. (1999). Computing the real costs of school technology. **School Business Affairs, 65** (7), 34–40, 42. Computers and other new technologies are changing how school buildings must be designed. Introduces full range of building designs that high-tech learning necessitates.

Bingham, Margaret. (1999). Stories with data and data with stories. **T.H.E. Journal, 26** (9), 20, 22, 24. Discusses the need for tools and instruments to measure and document the impact of technology, particularly microcomputers, on teaching and learning.

Bowman, Joel P., & Klopping, Inge. (1999). Bandstands, bandwidth, and business communication: Technology and the sanctity of writing. **Business Communication Quarterly, 62** (1), 82–90. Offers an overview of the history of human communication and communication technology. Notes that, as information technology has changed, perceptions of written communication have also changed.

British Journal of Educational Technology. National Council for Educational Technology, Millburn Hill Road, Science Park, Coventry CV4 7JJ, England. [Q., $101 indiv., $230 inst.]. Published by the National Council for Educational Technology, this journal includes articles on education and training, especially theory, applications, and development of educational technology and communications.

Bruce, Bertram. (1999). Challenges for the evaluation of new information and communication technologies. **Journal of Adolescent & Adult Literacy, 42** (6), 450–455. Explores some reasons why information and communication technologies are difficult to evaluate.

CÆLL Journal. ISTE, University of Oregon, 1787 Agate Street, Eugene, OR 97403-1923, (800)336-5191, cust_svc@ccmail.uoregon.edu, www.iste.org. [Q., $29; $39 intl., $42 intl. air]. Focuses on current issues facing computer-using language teachers; covers trends, products, applications, research, and program evaluation.

Canadian Journal of Educational Communication. Association for Media and Technology in Education in Canada, 3-1750 The Queensway, Suite 1318, Etobicoke, ON M9C 5H5, Canada. [3/yr., $75]. Concerned with all aspects of educational systems and technology.

Daniels, Lisa. (1999). Introducing technology in the classroom: PowerPoint as a first step. **Journal of Computing in Higher Education, 10** (2), 42–56. With minimal costs, desktop presentation programs such as PowerPoint can be a first step in introducing computer technology into the college classroom.

Dewert, Marjorie Helsel. (1999). The times they are a-changin': A look at technology-related requirements for teacher licensure and certification. **Journal of Computing in Teacher Education, 15** (2), 4–6. Discusses technology-related requirements for teacher licensure and certification, describing the Milken Exchange State-by-State Education Technology Policy Survey.

Dickson, Gary W., & Segars, Albert. (1999). Redefining the high-technology classroom. **Journal of Education for Business, 74** (3), 152–156. Defines the physical and virtual space of high-tech classrooms in terms of one-to-many, many-to-one, one-to-one, and many-to-many communications modes.

Easterbrooks, Susan. (1999). Improving practices for students with hearing impairments. **Exceptional Children, 65** (4), 537–554. This review of educational practices for students with hearing impairments summarizes federal efforts to address these students' needs; offers current statistics on this population; and reviews communication options and current challenges in the areas of new technologies, approaches, and options. Promising practices and recommendations are highlighted.

Educational Technology. Educational Technology Publications, Inc., 700 Palisade Avenue, Englewood Cliffs, NJ 07632-0564, (800)952-BOOK. [Bi-mo., $119 US, $139 elsewhere]. Covers telecommunications, computer-aided instruction, information retrieval, educational television, and electronic media in the classroom.

Educational Technology Abstracts. Taylor & Francis Group, 11 New Fetter Lane, London EC4P 4EE, www.tandf.co.uk. [6/yr., $292 indiv., $791 inst.]. An international publication of abstracts of recently published material in the field of educational and training technology.

Education Technology News. Business Publishers, Inc. 951 Pershing Drive, Silver Spring, MD 20910-9973, (800)274-6737, fax (301)589-8493, bpinews@bpinews.com, www.bpinews.com. [Bi-w., $337]. Newsletter containing news, product reviews, funding sources, useful Internet sites, and case studies for technology coordinators, administrators, and teachers.

Educational Technology Research and Development. AECT, ETR&D Subscription Dept., 1800 N. Stonelake Drive, Suite 2, Bloomington, IN 47404, www.aect.org. [Q., $55 US, $63 foreign]. Focuses on research, instructional development, and applied theory in the field of educational technology; peer-reviewed.

Eisenberg, Mike, & Lowe, Carrie. (1999). Call to action: Getting serious about libraries and information in education. **MultiMedia Schools**, 6 (2), 18–21. Discusses the importance of a team of technology teachers, library and information professionals, and administrators working together to achieve technology's potential in schools.

Electronic School. NSBA Distribution Center, P.O. Box 161, Annapolis Jct., MD 20701-0161, (800)706-6722, fax (301)604-0158, www.nsba.org/itte. [Q., $5 per issue]. Provides resource for all school personnel covering school technology trends, staff development, funding, telecommunications, and restructuring.

Frayer, Dorothy A. (1999). Creating a campus culture to support a teaching and learning revolution. **CAUSE/EFFECT**, 22 (2), 10-17, 50. Details four strategies that have helped create a campus culture at Duquesne University (Pennsylvania) that embraces technological tools for pedagogical change.

Green, Kenneth C. (1999). A high-tech convergence. **Trusteeship**, 7 (1), 18–22. Despite much debate and discussion, many in higher education understand little of the consequences of trends in technology.

Guiney, Susan. (1999). Technology funding in schools: Politics, pedagogy, and values. **School Business Affairs**, 65 (8), 32–37. Although schools are planning and implementing local area networks and Internet access, acquiring and maintaining technology can be exceptionally costly.

Hannafin, Robert D. (1999). Can teacher attitudes about learning be changed? **Journal of Computing in Teacher Education**, 15 (2), 7–13. Examined 12 public school teachers' attitudes, beliefs, and expectancies about learning environments to see whether they could be affected by a series of three graduate technology courses.

Heinich, R., & Molenda, M., Russell, J. D., & Smaldino, S. E. (1999). **Instructional media and technologies for learning** (6th ed.). [Book, 428p., $44.25]. Prentice Hall, www.prenhall.com. Updates classic practitioner's guide to instructional media and technology.

Higher Education Technology News. Business Publishers, Inc. 951 Pershing Drive, Silver Spring, MD 20910-9973, (800)274-6737, fax (301) 589-8493, bpinews@bpinews.com, www.bpinews.com. [25/yr., $297]. Presents short news items concerning higher education and technology in a newsletter format.

Hull, Darrell. (1999). The power and peril in technology. **Community College Journal, 70** (1), 38–44. States that community colleges should evaluate the intent of the technology being implemented and determine how it serves their mission and delivery of education.

International Journal of Technology and Design Education. Kluwer Academic Publishers, 101 Philip Drive, Norwell, MA 02061, (617)871-6600, fax (617)871-6528, kluwer@wkap.com. [3/yr., $104 indiv., $172 inst.]. Publishes research reports and scholarly writing about aspects of technology and design education.

Jonassen, D. H., Peck, K. L., & Wilson, B. G. (1999). **Learning with technology: A constructivist perspective.** [Book, 234p.]. Columbus, OH: Merrill/Prentice Hall, www.merrilleducation .com. Pursues constructivist learning theory through technology, capitalizing on the themes of meaning making, exploration, visualization, constructing reality, community, critical thinking, and immersion.

Journal of Science Education and Technology. Kluwer Academic/Plenum Publishers, 233 Spring Street, New York, NY 10013-1578, (781)871-6600, info@plenum.com, www.plenum .com. [Q., $68 indiv., $325 inst.]. Publishes studies aimed at improving science education at all levels in the United States.

Knott, Ron. (1999). What does the WWW offer mathematics students and teachers? **Teaching Mathematics and Its Applications, 18** (1), 2–9. Presents a brief history of the World Wide Web and explains what a WWW browser is and what it can do for math teachers and students. Compares information on the Web with book-based information and gives examples of useful Web sites for mathematics teaching and learning.

Kubarek, Diane. (1999). Introducing and supporting a Web course management tool. **Syllabus, 12** (10), 52–55. Explores Cornell's use of CourseInfo, one of the new course-management tools that provides the support infrastructure to help faculty create and maintain course Web sites.

Lamb, A. (1999). **Building treehouses for learning: Technology in today's classroom** (2nd ed.). [Book, 613p., $34.95]. ISTE, University of Oregon, 1787 Agate Street, Eugene, OR 97403-1923, (800)336-5191, cust_svc@ccmail.uoregon.edu, www.iste.org. Discusses the design and development of effective informational and instructional materials and techniques for managing a technology-rich K–12 classroom; for beginning teachers.

Lauzon, Allan C. (1999). Situating cognition and crossing borders: Resisting the hegemony of mediated education. **British Journal of Educational Technology, 30** (3), 261–276. Explores situated cognition, arguing that the construct of "community of practice" is useful as an analytical lens through which to examine the domain of educational technology.

Maiden, Jeffrey A., & Beckham, James. (1999). Educational technology funding trends and issues. **School Business Affairs, 65** (1), 17–19. Technology is a funding priority among federal education programs, which provide schools with networking capabilities and students with Internet access.

Manoucherhri, Azita. (1999). Computers and school mathematics reform: Implications for mathematics teacher education. **Journal of Computers in Mathematics and Science Teaching, 18** (1), 31–48. Investigates the extent to which computers were being used by middle and high school mathematics teachers in Missouri.

McCollum, Kelly. (1999). Colleges struggle to manage technology's rising costs. **Chronicle of Higher Education, 45** (24), A27–A30. Colleges and universities are discovering that planning is the most effective way to make decisions about spending for new technology.

Merbler, John B., Hadadian, Azar, & Ulman, Jean. (1999). Using assistive technology in the inclusive classroom. **Preventing School Failure, 43** (3), 113–117. Provides an overview of assistive technology for students with disabilities in inclusive settings and legal considerations regarding assistive technology.

Merisotis, Jamie P., & Phipps, Ronald A. (1999). What's the difference? Outcomes of distance vs. traditional classroom-based learning. **Change, 31** (3), 12–17. Examination of research comparing outcomes of technology-based distance education and traditional classroom-based learning found shortcomings and gaps.

Moll, Marita. (1999). Calling for time out: Education in the fast lane of technological change. **Education Canada, 39** (2), 30-33. Challenges the assumption that new technologies in the classroom are superior to traditional ones. Argues that new technologies serve business-related goals of education, which currently overshadow social and individual-development purposes of learning.

Monke, Lowell. (1999). Infusing technology into a school: Tracking the unintended consequences. **Bulletin of Science, Technology & Society, 19** (1), 5–10. Examines the technological transformation of Des Moines Public Schools.

Nicaise, Molly, & Crane, Michael. (1999). Knowledge constructing through hypermedia authoring. **Educational Technology Research and Development, 47** (1), 29–50. Examines how educational theory translates into classroom practice. Students in a graduate course learned about educational theory by creating a hypermedia chapter for a Web-based book.

Privateer, Paul Michael. (1999). Academic technology and the future of higher education: Strategic paths taken and not taken. **Journal of Higher Education, 70** (1), 60-79. If American colleges and universities are to become contemporary and effective organizations, their strategic academic-technology agenda should be focused on production of intelligence rather than on storage and recall of random and quickly outmoded information.

Rickard, Wendy. (1999). Framing the issues: What's next on the NLII's agenda? **Educom Review, 34** (4), 34–37. Discusses four issues identified by EDUCAUSE's National Learning Infrastructure Initiative (NLII) as being key to its mission to create new collegiate learning environments that harness the power of information technology.

Rickard, Wendy. (1999). Technology, education, and the changing nature of resistance. **Educom Review, 34** (1), 42–45. Discusses information technology in higher education.

Schwartz, Daniel L., Brophy, Sean, & Lin, Xiaodong. (1999). Software for managing complex learning: Examples from an educational psychology course. **Educational Technology Research and Development, 47** (2), 39–59. Describes a software shell, STAR.Legacy, designed to guide attempts to help students learn from case- , problem- , and project-based learning.

Science Communication (formerly **Knowledge: Creation, Diffusion, Utilization**). Sage Publications Inc., 2455 Teller Road, Thousand Oaks, CA 91320, order@sagepub.com, www.sagepub.com. [Q., $85 indiv., $363 inst.]. An international, interdisciplinary journal examining the nature of expertise and the translation of knowledge into practice and policy.

Selfe, Cynthia L. (1999). Technology and literacy: A story about the perils of not paying attention. **College Composition and Communication, 50** (3), 411–436. Asserts that composition specialists must pay attention to technology issues.

Sherman, Sharon, & Weber, Robert. (1999). Using technology to strengthen mathematics and science instruction in elementary and middle schools. **Journal of Women and Minorities in Science and Engineering, 5** (1), 67–78. Investigates whether the study of technology could strengthen instruction in mathematics and science in the elementary and middle schools, especially for women and underrepresented groups.

SIGTC Connections. ISTE, University of Oregon, 1787 Agate Street, Eugene, OR 97403-1923, (800)336-5191, cust_svc@ccmail.uoregon.edu, www.iste.org. [Q., $29, $39 intl., $42 intl. air]. Provides forum to identify problems and solutions and to share information on issues facing technology coordinators.

Simerly, Robert G. (1999). Practical guidelines and suggestions for designing and implementing technology-enhanced education. **Journal of Continuing Higher Education, 47** (2), 39–48. Offers guidelines for integrating technology-enhanced education into the curricula.

Smith, Burck. (1999). Buying technology in higher education. **Converge, 2** (5), 48–50. Discusses academic procurement of technology, composed of smaller purchases for individual departments, versus administrative procurement, composed of larger investments with organizational impact.

Strauss, Howard. (1999). The future of the Web, intelligent devices, and education. **Educom Review, 34** (4), 16–19, 52–54. Examines past trends in hardware, software, networking, and education, in an attempt to determine where they are going and what their broad implications might be.

Technology Leadership News. NSBA Distribution Center, P.O. Box 161, Annapolis Jct., MD 20701-0161, (800)706-6722, fax (301)604-0158, www.nsba.org/itte. [9/yr., $75]. Official newsletter of the National School Boards Association Institute for the Transfer of Technology to Education. Updates issues, trends, products, programs, applications, district profiles, case studies, government initiatives, funding, and video conferences in lay terms.

TECHNOS. Agency for Instructional Technology, Box A, 1800 North Stonelake Drive, Bloomington, IN 47402-0120. [Q., $26 indiv., $24 libr., $30 foreign]. A forum for discussion of ideas about the use of technology in education, with a focus on reform.

TechTrends. AECT, 1800 N Stonelake Drive, Suite 2, Bloomington, IN 47404, www.aect.org. [6/yr., $40 US, $44 elsewhere, $6 single copy]. Targeted at leaders in education and training; features authoritative, practical articles about technology and its integration into the learning environment.

T.H.E. Journal (Technological Horizons in Education). T.H.E., 150 El Camino Real, Suite 112, Tustin, CA 92680-3670. [11/yr., $29 US, $95 elsewhere]. For educators of all levels. Focuses on a specific topic for each issue, as well as on technological innovations as they apply to education.

Useem, Andrea. (1999). Wiring African universities proves a formidable challenge. **Chronicle of Higher Education, 45** (30), A51–A53. Lack of funds and competition for scarce resources have made it impossible for many African universities to gain access to technology. Internet use is extremely limited, and the infrastructure is inadequate to support rapid expansion.

Victor, David. (1999). Electronic classrooms and virtual publishing: A look beyond the writing requirement. **Business Communication Quarterly, 62** (1), 74–81. Argues that the new information technologies are opening a doorway to a new form of institution for higher education.

Waks, Leonard. (1999). The global network society and STS education. **Bulletin of Science, Technology & Society, 19** (1), 46–48. Anticipates the impact of the globalization of markets and expanding communication technology on education in science, technology, and society (STS).

Wilson, Brent G. (1999). Evolution of learning technologies: From instructional design to performance support to network systems. **Educational Technology, 39** (2), 32–35. Discusses three evolving paradigms for supporting learning and work performance: instructional design, performance support, and network systems. Describes an overall trend toward greater flexibility and empowerment, and shows how each paradigm reflects the technologies available at the time of its initial development.

Young, Jeffrey R. (1999). Are wireless networks the wave of the future? **Chronicle of Higher Education, 45** (22), A25–A26. Some college administrators feel the next major trend in educational technology will be wireless networks that let students and professors connect to the Internet with radio waves rather than cumbersome cables.

Young, Jeffrey R. (1999). Black colleges band together to get a jump on technology. **Chronicle of Higher Education, 45** (29), A31–A32. Many historically black colleges and universities have developed several projects to improve technology on campus and promote its use.

INFORMATION SCIENCE AND TECHNOLOGY

Anderson, Mary Alice. (1999). *Information Power:* Because student achievement is the bottom line. **MultiMedia Schools, 6** (2), 22–23. Describes the *Information Power: Partnerships for Student Learning* (1998) guidelines and their significance for school library media specialists. Discusses standards in three broad areas (information literacy, independent learning, and social responsibility), roles and responsibilities of media specialists in technology integration, collaboration, leadership, and advocacy.

Balas, Janet L. (1999). Online resources for adaptive information technologies. **Computers in Libraries, 19** (6), 38–40. Describes several online resources devoted to the issue of information access by the disabled; librarians serving disabled users and seeking to employ adaptive technology will find a great deal of information on these sites.

Beagle, Donald. (1999). Conceptualizing an information commons. **Journal of Academic Librarianship, 25** (2), 82–89. Concepts from Strategic Alignment, a technology-management theory, are used to discuss the Information Commons as a new service-delivery model in academic libraries. The Information Commons, as a conceptual, physical, and instructional space, involves an organizational realignment from print to the digital environment.

Bearman, David, & Trant, Jennifer. (1999). Museums and the Web '99. **Bulletin of the American Society for Information Science, 25** (5), 23–26. Discusses issues addressed at the Museums and the Web '99 conference (New Orleans, Louisiana, March 11–14, 1999). Highlights include how interaction with the virtual conditions views of the world; shared experiences of being online; virtual objects; new metaphors for seeking, finding, and using information; evaluating creations; reconstructing; and building an engaging virtual social space for culture.

Bernbom, Gerald. (1999). Institution-wide information management and its assessment. **New Directions for Institutional Research, 26** (2), 71–83. Discusses issues and practices in information management (IM) in a number of fields, with emphasis on the role of IM for institutional research and assessment, particularly in colleges and universities.

Breaks, Michael. (1999). **Management of electronic information**. [Paper, 18p.]. (Presented at the [International Association of Technological University Libraries] IATUL Conference, Chania, Greece, May 17–21, 1999). Discusses the management of library collections of electronic information resources within the classical theoretical framework of collection development and management.

Burns, Taodhg, & Rashid, Shahida. (1999). The new world of information professionalism. **Information Outlook, 3** (7), 25–29. Suggests that in an era of increasingly universal computer literacy and quickly developing technologies, information professionals must be able to determine current needs and learn new skills and applications to supply them.

Canadian Journal of Information and Library Science/Revue canadienne des sciences de l'information et de bibliothèconomie. CAIS, University of Toronto Press, Journals Dept., 5201 Dufferin Street, Downsview, ON M3H 5T8, Canada. [Q., $65 indiv., $95 inst., orders outside Canada add $15]. Published by the Canadian Association for Information Science to contribute to the advancement of library and information science in Canada.

CD-ROM Databases. Worldwide Videotex, Box 3273, Boynton Beach, FL 33424-3273. [Mo., $150 US, $190 elsewhere]. Descriptive listing of all databases being marketed on CD-ROM, with vendor and system information.

Christian, Eliot. (1999). Experiences with information locator services. **Journal of Government Information, 26** (3), 271–285. Relates experiences in developing and promoting services interoperable with the Global Information Locator Service (GILS) standard. Describes sample implementations and touches on the strategic choices made in public policy, standards, and technology.

Current issues for higher education information resources management. (1999). **CAUSE/EFFECT, 22** (1), 6–12. Discusses some emerging issues for information resources and use in higher education, including challenges in advanced networking; distributed-information technology (IT); authentication, authorization, and access management; distance learning; intellectual property in a networked environment; and campus-business continuity planning. Funding, staffing, student, and planning issues identified at a recent conference of campus IT professionals are also summarized.

Driscoll, Marcy P., & Dick, Walter. (1999). New research paradigms in instructional technology: An inquiry. **Educational Technology Research and Development, 47** (2), 7–18. Reviews the current state of research paradigms in the field of instructional technology from the perspective of research standards and paradigms recommended by Leslie J. Briggs in the early 1980s.

Duberman, Josh. (1999). Reflections in a funhouse mirror: Web trends and evolving roles for information specialists. **Searcher, 7** (2), 30-33. Considers how the role of information specialists is changing and evolving due to the use of the Internet and the World Wide Web.

Econtent (formerly **Database**). Online, Inc. 462 Danbury Road, Wilton, CT 06897. [Bi-mo., $55 US, $65 Canada, $90 intl. airmail.]. Features articles on topics of interest to online database users; includes database search aids.

Ferguson, B. (1999). **Cataloging nonprint materials** (a Blitz Cataloging Workbook). [Book, 180p., $21]. Libraries Unlimited, (800)237-6124, lu-books@lu.com, www.lu.com. Provides basic instruction for cataloging nonprint materials, as a supplement to primary cataloging texts.

Gale Directory of Databases (in 2 vols: Vol. 1, **Online Databases**; Vol 2, **CD-ROM, Diskette, Magnetic Tape Batch Access, and Handheld Database Products**). Gale Group, P.O. Box 9187, Farmington Hills, MI 48333-9187. [Ann. plus semi-ann. update $280; Vol. 1, $199; Vol. 2, $119]. Contains information on database selection and database descriptions, including producers and their addresses.

Hancock, Joelie, Ed. (1999). **Teaching literacy using information technology: A collection of articles from the Australian Literacy Educators' Association**. [Book, 141p, $19.95]. International Reading Association, 800 Barksdale Road, P.O. Box 8139, Newark, DE 19714-8139, www.reading.org. Offers practical information for classroom teachers and teacher-educators on effectively incorporating computer technology in the classroom. The book focuses on the change associated with the growing presence in educational institutions of the new communication and information processing technologies, which is most significant for language and literacy educators.

Haycock, Ken, & Jopson, Geoff. (1999). Propositions for information technology: Planning for success. **Teacher Librarian, 26** (3), 15–20. Describes the West Vancouver (British Columbia) School Board's goals related to the appropriate and effective use of information technology as both a school and a community resource. Highlights include social issues, learning issues, professional and personal competencies for teacher-librarians, integration of information delivery systems, and a community-based information infrastructure.

Hazzan, Orit. (1999). Information technologies and objects to learn with. **Educational Technology, 39** (3), 55–59. Presents an explanation for the increase in the number of computer users. Suggests that, in addition to providing electronic communication services, information technologies may also support thinking and learning processes.

Henderson, Albert. (1999). Information science and information policy: The use of constant dollars and other indicators to manage research investments. **Journal of the American Society for Information Science, 50** (4), 366–379. Compares constant dollar spending on research with constant dollar spending on libraries between 1960 and 1995. Evaluation of the indirect cost policy by which library costs are reimbursed as a function of science grant management suggests it has failed to promote cost-effective research. Evaluation of the impact of various information technologies finds enhancements to dissemination but misconceptions about savings potential.

Hundley, Stephen P. (1999). Selling schools to information technology professionals. **CUPA Journal, 49** (3–4), 13–15. Most higher-education institutions cannot compete with business/industry for information technology (IT) workers, but they can level the playing field by capitalizing on workers' desire for professional development opportunities. Strategies include using the appeal of the institution's mission as a training ground for future IT workers, redesigning computer-support positions, access to professional development activities, professional recognition, and intercollegiate cooperation.

Information Processing and Management. Pergamon Press, 660 White Plains Road, Tarrytown, NY 10591-5153. [Bi-mo., $152 indiv. whose inst. subscribes, $811 inst.]. International journal covering data processing, database building, and retrieval.

Information Retrieval and Library Automation. Lomond Publications, Inc., Box 88, Mt. Airy, MD 21771. [Mo., $66 US, foreign $79.50]. News, articles, and announcements on new techniques, equipment, and software in information services.

Information Services & Use. I.O.S. Press, Box 10558, Burke, VA 22009-0558. [4/yr., $254]. An international journal for those in the information management field. Includes online and offline systems, library automation, micrographics, videotex, and telecommunications.

The Information Society. Taylor & Francis Group, 11 New Fetter Lane, London EC4P 4EE, www.tandf.co.uk Taylor and Francis, 47 Runway Road, Suite G, Levittown, PA 19057, tisj@indiana.edu. [Q., $82 indiv.; $178 inst.]. Provides a forum for discussion of the world of information, including transborder data flow, regulatory issues, and the impact of the information industry.

Information Technology and Libraries. American Library Association, ALA Editions, 50 East Huron Street, Chicago, IL 60611-2795, (800)545-2433, fax (312) 836-9958. [Q., $50 US, $55 Canada, Mexico, $60 elsewhere]. Articles on library automation, communication technology, cable systems, computerized information processing, and video technologies.

Information Today. Information Today, 143 Old Marlton Pike, Medford, NJ 08055, (800)300-9868. [11/yr., $59.95, Canada and Mexico $78, outside North America $85]. Newspaper for users and producers of electronic information services. Articles and news about the industry, calendar of events, and product information.

Innovative use of information technology by colleges. (1999). [Case study, 93p., $20]. Council on Library and Information Resources, 1775 Massachusetts Avenue, NW, Suite 500, Washington, DC 20036, www.clir.org. A study of the innovative uses of technology on college campuses in the spring of 1998. A letter was sent to heads of libraries of colleges and mid-sized universities in the United States encouraging librarians who felt their institutions had used technology in a way that significantly enhanced teaching and learning and who were willing to host a study team for a site visit to apply to the project.

Journal of the American Society for Information Science. American Society for Information Science, 8720 Georgia Avenue, Suite 501, Silver Spring, MD 20910-3602, (301)495-0900, www.asis.org. [14/yr., inst. rate $1259 US, $1399 Canada/Mexico, $1518 outside N. America]. Provides an overall forum for new research in information transfer and communication processes, with particular attention paid to the context of recorded knowledge.

Journal of Database Management. Idea Group Publishing, 4811 Jonestown Road, Suite 230, Harrisburg, PA 17109-1751. [Q., $85 indiv., $195 inst.]. Provides state-of-the-art research to those who design, develop, and administer DBMS-based information systems.

Journal of Documentation. Aslib, The Association for Information Management, Staple Hall, Stone House Court, London EC3A 7PB, +44 (0) 20 7903 0000, aslib@aslib.com. [6/yr., £176 ($275) members, £220 ($345) nonmembers]. Describes how technical, scientific, and other specialized knowledge is recorded, organized, and disseminated.

Kent, Kai Iok Tong, & Sousa, Antonio C. M. (1999). The IT Observatory. **Educational Media International, 36** (1), 46–48. Describes the IT Observatory, a service of the Macau Productivity and Technology Center (CPTTM), that provides information on demand. The CPTTM is a nonprofit organization funded by the Macau government and private businesses to enhance the productivity of Macau businesses by introducing new technologies and new management practices.

Kobulnicky, Paul J. (1999). Critical factors in information technology planning for the academy. **CAUSE/EFFECT, 22** (2), 19–26. Information technology planning at higher-education institutions should be derived from academic planning at the institutional, school, and department levels, and must respond to associated issues of leadership, sustainable funding, productivity, and faculty motivation.

Library & Information Science Research. Ablex Publishing Corp., 100 Prospect Street, P.O. Box 811, Stamford, CT 06904-0811, (203)323-9606, fax (203)357-8446, www.jaipress.com. [Q., $95 indiv., $242 inst.]. Reports library-related research to practicing librarians, emphasizing planning and application.

Moquin, Bert, & Travis, Jon E. (1999). Community colleges in the highway: Major issues for technology planning. **Community College Journal of Research and Practice, 23** (2), 147–159. Rates the importance of planning topics, as identified by technology personnel at Texas community colleges, related to the information superhighway (ISH). Finds, through a Delphi study, that significant issues that should be considered in strategic technology planning include training, cost, planning, security/legal, uses and innovations, technical, faculty/staff, and government involvement. Asserts that these areas provide technology planners with a basis for implementing ISH initiatives.

Moursand, D. (1999). **Project-based learning using information technology.** [Book, 160p., $24.95]. ISTE, University of Oregon, 1787 Agate Street, Eugene, OR 97403-1923, (800)336-5191, cust_svc@ccmail.uoregon.edu, www.iste.org. Offers a methodological approach to implementing technology-assisted project-based learning projects. Designed for inservice and preservice teachers.

Novek, Eleanor M. (1999). **Do professors dream of electronic students? Faculty anxiety and the new information technologies**. [Paper, 22p.]. (Presented at the 90th Eastern Communication Association Annual Meeting, Charleston, WV, April 29–May 2, 1999). This survey of faculty attitudes toward technology calls for more critical dialogue on the uses, effects, and hidden costs of information technology in the classroom and the national political economy.

Nowicki, Stacy. (1999). Information literacy and critical thinking in the electronic environment. **Journal of Instruction Delivery Systems, 13** (1), 25–28. Information literacy is especially important to users of virtual libraries and online learners because they primarily conduct research outside the library and beyond the reach of information professionals.

Overton, Stephanie D. (1999). Setting standards in technology education. **TECHNOS, 8** (1), 32–35. Describes the Technology for All Americans Project (TfAAP) of the International Technology Education Association (ITEA). The project's goal was to articulate a vision of what it means to be technologically literate, how this can be achieved at the national level, and why it is important.

Pappas, M. L., Geitget, G. A., & Jefferson, C. A. (1999). **Searching electronic resources** (2nd ed.). [Book, 105p., $34.95]. Linworth, (800)786-5017, fax (614)436-9490, linworth.com. Provides a revised information search process model, including a four-step search process. Includes individual search strategy forms for popular CD-ROMS and online databases.

Pernal, Michael. (1999). Six strategies for beating the competition for information technology workers. **CUPA Journal, 49** (3–4), 17–19. Connecticut State University has achieved success in recruiting and retaining information technology (IT) workers through six strategies: modifying the administrative structure to make positions and salaries more attractive, grooming students for IT positions, promoting benefits of university employment, transferring state civil-service employees, acquainting potential employees with university missions, and recruiting non-IT professionals with IT skills.

Pittinsky, Matthew. (1999). Studying today to envision tomorrow: The future of enterprise academic computing systems. **Educom Review, 34** (3), 38–41. Defines the six key pressures that have given rise to the emerging enterprise academic computing imperative.

Preston, Cecilia M. (1999). Internet 2 and the next generation Internet: A realistic assessment. **Searcher, 7** (1), 66–70. Describes new developments, such as Internet 2 and the Next Generation Internet (NGI) initiative, as well as other potential advances in high-performance applications that these new electronic resources will create. Relates these developments to the evolution of the Internet and looks ahead to their likely impact beyond the higher-education and research communities.

Resource Sharing & Information Networks. Haworth Press, 10 Alice Street, Binghamton, NY 13904-1580, (800)HAWORTH, fax (800)895-0582, getinfo@haworth.com, www .haworthpress.com. [2/yr., $42 indiv., $200 inst. and libraries]. A forum for ideas on the basic theoretical and practical problems faced by planners, practitioners, and users of network services.

Rosenblatt, Susan. (1999). Information technology investments in research libraries. **Educom Review, 34** (4), 28–32, 44–46. Examines investments that will ensure that library information technology (IT) meets future academic needs. Looks back on the introduction of IT to research libraries. Assesses outcomes of IT investments in terms of cost and service benefits, then focuses on developing new service models.

Saunders, Laverna M. (1999). The human element in the virtual library. **Library Trends, 47** (4), 771–787. Introduces the concept of the virtual library and explores how the increasing reliance on computers and digital information has affected library users and staff. Discusses users' expectations, democratization of access, human issues, organizational change, technostress, ergonomics, assessment, and strategies for success and survival.

Smith, Diane. (1999). New technologies and old-fashioned economics: Creating a brave new world for U.S. government information distribution and use. **Journal of Government Information, 26** (1), 21–24. Asserts that the U.S. government information's five stakeholders— federal agencies, Government Printing Office (GPO), depository libraries, commercial sector, and the public—will need to change drastically in reaction to improved technologies. Notes that the concept of the Federal Depository Library Program (FDLP) network may have outlived its relevance and that new ways to assist users in cost-effectively and efficiently locating government information should be explored.

Smith, Steven D. (1999). Building access for digital images: Databases, meta-data, interfaces. **Microform and Imaging Review, 28** (2), 51–55. When providing access to digital images, there are three elements to consider: structure, location, and appearance. These considerations are illustrated with two examples, a book and a photograph collection. Each of the elements is then described in detail.

Stielow, F. (1999). **Creating a virtual library: A how-to-do-it manual.** [Book, 200p., $55]. Neal-Schuman, fax (800)584-2414, orders@neal-schuman.com, www.neal-schuman.com. Guides the creation and maintenance of single-interface, Web-based catalogs; written by MCI's Cybrarian of the Year.

Tearle, Penni, Dillon, Patrick, & Davis, Niki. (1999). Use of information technology by English university teachers: Development and trends at the time of the national inquiry into higher education. **Journal of Further and Higher Education, 23** (1), 5–15. Reports findings of a British study of information technology-assisted teaching and learning (ITATL) in six higher-education institutions, focusing on five major themes: emerging educational markets for information technology use, implications for networking, contexts of educational and communications-technology use, learning benefits, and issues in cost/benefit measurement and accountability.

Technology and its ramifications for data systems. (1999). **CAUSE/EFFECT, 22** (2), 3–5. Examines the impact of technology on post-secondary education stemming from data definitions and analytical conventions in (1) configuring new institutions and programs, (2) understanding new faculty roles and work patterns, (3) measuring and analyzing student participation, (4) assessing student progress and learning gains, and (5) analyzing revenue and expenditure flows.

Trilling, Bernie, & Hood, Paul. (1999). Learning, technology, and education reform in the knowledge age or "we're wired, Webbed, and Windowed, now what?" **Educational Technology, 39** (3), 5–18. Focuses on questions about the Knowledge Age; surveys needed skills, theoretical supports, and main features of this new learning landscape. Examines three current models of reform and discusses a fourth alternative that arises out of new demands of the Knowledge Age. Discusses critical work to be done in bringing educational technology to the service of an emerging alternative-education model.

Trow, Martin. (1999). Lifelong learning through the new information technologies. **Higher Education Policy, 12** (2), 201–217. A discussion of the role of information technology in lifelong learning looks at such issues as the speed of technological and educational change and its relationship to policy formation and the use of policy to support experimentation.

Van Epps, Sharyn. (1999). Vision to reality: Transforming the school library into the information technology hub of the school. **MultiMedia Schools, 6** (2), 32–35. Discusses the technology plan of the Department of Defense Dependents Schools (DoDDS). Highlights include articulating the role of the information specialist; defining the competencies of the information specialist as teacher, instructional partner, and program administrator; establishing an instructional technology support team; and making the transition from vision to reality.

Van Wingen, Rachel Senner, Hathorn, Fred, & Sprehe, J. Timothy. (1999). Principles for information technology investment in U.S. federal electronic records management. **Journal of Government Information, 26** (1), 33–42. The United States Environmental Protection Agency (EPA) underwent a business process reengineering (BPR) exercise with respect to future co-location of previously separate regulatory docket facilities. Their experience suggests that future mandatory electronic records management (ERM) requirements will cause federal agencies to take a more thorough account of the full information life cycle when planning an information technology system's life cycle.

Walker, G., & Janes, J. (1999). **Online retrieval: A dialogue of theory and practice** (2nd ed.) [Book, 325p., $55]. Libraries Unlimited, (800)237-6124, lu-books@lu.com, www.lu.com. Designed for beginning searchers at all levels. Includes a description of the Dialog and Lexis-Nexis databases.

Web Feet. Rock Hill Press, 14 Rock Hill Road, Bala Cynwyd, PA 19004, (888) ROCK HILL, fax (610)667-2291, www.rockhillpress.com. [12/yr., $165]. Indexes Websites for general interest, classroom use, and research; reviews Websites for quality, curricular relevance, timeliness, and interest.

West, Ann. (1999). The information technology staff crisis: Plan for it! **CUPA Journal, 49** (3–4), 3–7. The challenge of recruiting, retaining, and retraining college and university information technology (IT) staff affects the entire institution. Some issues in the impending IT staff crisis are outlined, particularly trends in demand for technology workers, and steps are suggested for campus IT leaders to take to minimize the effect of staff turnover on implementation of critical technology directions.

Williams, Brian K., Sawyer, Stacey C., & Hutchinson, Sarah E. (1999). **Using information technology: A practical introduction to computers & communications** (3rd ed.). [Book, 610p., $56.72]. McGraw-Hill Companies, P.O. Box 182604, Columbus, OH 43272, (800)262-4729, customer.service@mcgraw-hill.com, www.mhhe.com. Intended for use as a concepts textbook to accompany a one-semester or one-quarter introductory course on computers or microcomputers.

Zeidberg, David S. (1999). The archival view of technology: Resources for the scholar of the future. **Library Trends, 47** (4), 796–805. Archivists need to apply traditional principles of records management to electronic documents if these records are to survive for research by future scholars. Additionally, archivists must ensure that the electronic records preserved remain accessible as hardware and software change over time.

INNOVATION

Barker, Philip. (1999). Electronic course delivery, virtual universities and lifelong learning. **Educational Technology Review, 11**, 14–18. Discusses how new computer-based approaches to teaching and learning—electronic course delivery (ECD) and a virtual-university paradigm—might be applied to the problems of supporting lifelong learning within the context of post-compulsory education. Describes a case study that involved applying ECD techniques within a conventional university framework.

Feldberg, Ross S. (1999). Increasing student involvement in lectures: (Very) low tech innovations in a biochemistry lecture class. **Biochemical Education, 27** (2), 71–73. Argues that the traditional lecture format is a poor mode for learning. Outlines a simple but effective approach for eliciting student participation in an intermediate-size lecture course (50–100).

Gergen, Mary, Chrisler, Joan C., & LoCicero, Alice. (1999). Innovative methods: Resources for research, publishing, and teaching. **Psychology of Women Quarterly, 23** (2), 431–456. Reviews a selection of innovative methods congenial to research in feminist psychology and describes undergraduate and graduate courses that emphasize these methods in their curricula.

Innovative use of information technology by colleges. (1999). [Paper, 93p., $20]. Council on Library and Information Resources, 1775 Massachusetts Avenue, NW, Suite 500, Washington, DC 20036, www.clir.org. The Council on Library and Information Resources' (CLIR's) College Libraries Committee began its study of the innovative uses of technology on college campuses in the spring of 1998. A letter was sent to heads of libraries of colleges and mid-sized universities in the United States encouraging librarians who felt their institutions had used technology in a way that significantly enhanced teaching and learning, and who were willing to host a study team for a site visit, to apply to the project.

Katsirikou, Anthi. (1999). **The innovation in every day life of libraries**. [Paper, 8p.]. http://educate.lib.chalmers.se/IATUL/proceedcontents/chanpap/katsirik.html. This paper examines the role of innovation in library operations, with the aim to incorporate innovative procedures that achieve convenience in practice and efficiency and effectiveness in a simultaneous economic reduction. The methodology outlined in this paper is that of best practices.

Kotiw, Michael, Learmonth, Robert P., & Sutherland, Mark W. (1999). Biological methods: A novel course in undergraduate biology. **Biochemical Education, 27** (3), 131–134. Describes a novel course in first-year undergraduate practical biology that introduces students to the principles and practices of a variety of biological techniques.

Larrance, Anneke J. (1999). What small colleges can do together. **New Directions for Higher Education, 27** (2), 109–115. Small colleges can be effective in consortial arrangements because they are more independent and often less fiercely competitive than larger institutions, making better personal relations possible. The Associated Colleges of the St. Lawrence Valley in northern New York, with four member institutions, has expanded student opportunities, shared resources, avoided duplication, used faculty talents well, and provided innovative programs.

Laughlin, Janet, & Fleming, Phyllis. (1999). Innovations and motivators from the Virginia Master Teacher Seminar. **Inquiry, 4** (1), 16–25. Presents 13 "best practice" motivators and innovations shared by teachers from across the country at the July 1998 Virginia Master Teacher Seminar. Teachers who attended the seminar not only wanted to master the teaching craft but also sought more knowledge as students on their way to mastery. Encourages readers to borrow ideas presented.

Laurillard, Diana. (1999). Investing in information technology pays big dividends. **Planning for Higher Education, 27** (4), 1–8. A college or university's investment in information technology (IT) makes possible more effective teaching methods using both traditional and IT-based techniques, as well as making both student learning and faculty use of time more productive. A possible plan for making the transition from traditional to mixed teaching methods is presented.

Maehl, William H. (2000). **Lifelong learning at its best: Innovative practices in adult credit programs.** [Book, 357p., $34.95]. Jossey-Bass Higher and Adult Education Series. Jossey-Bass Inc., Publishers, 350 Sansome Street, San Francisco, CA 94104, (888)378-2537, fax (800)605-2665. This book describes a wide range of lifelong learning program models and educational strategies that have proved successful with adult learners across the nation.

Parrilla, Angeles. (1999). Educational innovations as a school answer to diversity. **International Journal of Inclusive Education, 3** (2), 93–110. Reports ongoing research analyzing types of educational innovation created by schools in Seville, Spain, to address diversity issues. So far, schools are not fully integrated, and teaching practices have not changed very much. The schools most experienced with integration are more innovative. Classroom organization and management have become more inclusive.

Robson, Maggie, & Hunt, Kathy. (1999). An innovative approach to involving parents in the education of their early years children. **International Journal of Early Years Education, 7** (2), 185–193. Evaluated a multimedia project to increase self-esteem of parents of inner-city primary school children in Hartlepool, England, to increase their understanding of the preschool curriculum, and to involve them in their children's school life.

Rodd, Jillian. (1999). Encouraging young children's critical and creative thinking skills: An approach in one English elementary school. **Childhood Education, 75** (6), 350–354. Describes the Talents Unlimited Program, implemented in an elementary school in southwest England, which provides a framework for developing creative and critical thinking skills. Describes an evaluation that found that five-year-olds taught with this approach performed better on specific critical and creative thinking skills tasks than did peers. Discusses factors contributing to Talents Unlimited's success and implications for teachers.

Roffe, Ian. (1999). Innovation and creativity in organizations: A review of the implications of training and development. **Journal of European Industrial Training, 23** (4–5), 224–237. A literature review identified principles for supporting innovation and creativity in organizations: an integrated approach, the right climate, and appropriate incentives. Staff development should focus on such skills as teamwork, communication, vision, change management, and leadership. Internet and intranet communications are beginning to be applied.

Shayer, Michael. (1999). Cognitive Acceleration through Science Education II: Its effects and scope. **International Journal of Science Education**, 21 (8), 883–902. Addresses some criticisms of the Cognitive Acceleration through Science Education (CASE) project. Offers a different description of the CASE teaching method and presents evidence from the program.

Sherwood, Donna W., & Kovac, Jeffrey. (1999). Writing in chemistry: An effective learning tool. **Journal of Chemical Education, 76** (10), 1399–1403. Presents some general strategies for using writing in chemistry courses based on experiences in developing a systematic approach to using writing as an effective learning tool in chemistry courses, and testing this approach in high-enrollment general chemistry courses at the University of Tennessee-Knoxville.

Wallner, Anton S., & Latosi-Sawin, Elizabeth. (1999). Technical writing and communication in a senior-level chemistry seminar. **Journal of Chemical Education, 76** (10), 1404–1406. Describes a senior-level capstone experience that integrates various communication and research skills to prepare chemistry majors for entry into graduate school and professional life.

Walshok, Mary Lindenstein. (1999). Dialogue and collaboration as keys to building innovative educational initiatives in a knowledge-based economy. **New Directions for Adult and Continuing Education**, (81), 77–86. CONNECT is an "incubator without walls" formed by the University of California-San Diego and area businesses to spur economic development through creative educational initiatives and partnerships. It focuses on problem solving using multidisciplinary and cross-professional approaches.

Walter, L. James, Liu, Daonian, & Brooks, David W. (1999). An Internet-based course: Leadership issues. **Journal of Science Education and Technology, 8** (2), 151–154. Discusses leadership issues that arose during the creation and offering of an Internet-based course for high school chemistry teachers, including course organization, recruiting students, and technological support available to participating students.

Williamson, Vicki. (1999). **Innovation and change in professional practice: Meaning to change and changing the meaning**. [Paper, 9p.]. Http://educate.lib.chalmers.se/IATUL /proceedcontents/chanpap/williams.html. This paper focuses on innovation and the change triggered by the introduction of new approaches to planned change in professional practice. It presents a range of ideas and theories about innovation and change and speculates about how new approaches get introduced and become accepted into professional practice.

INSTRUCTIONAL DESIGN AND DEVELOPMENT

Budd, John M., & Miller, Lisa K. (1999). Teaching for technology: Current practice and future direction. **Information Technology and Libraries**, 18 (2), 78–83. Highlights some professional associations' statements regarding education and the place of technology in educational programs. Examines the content of core curricula of a set of library and information science programs. Suggests content elements of an ideal core, designed to meet the intellectual and practical needs of information professionals of the future.

Carlson, R. D. (1998–1999). Portfolio assessment of instructional technology. **Journal of Educational Technology Systems, 27** (1), 81–92. Analyzes the current trend toward authentic assessment methods, including portfolios. Describes the results of two case studies.

Considine, D. M., & Haley, G. E. (1999). **Visual messages: Integrating imagery into instruction** (2nd ed.). [Book, 394p., $45]. Libraries Unlimited, (800)237-6124, lu-books@lu.com, www.lu.com. Promotes bridging the curriculum of the classroom to home learning. Defines visual literacy and traces the history of the media literacy movement. Focuses on helping students think critically about the way the media use images to influence attitudes and behavior.

Dagley, Dave, & Lan, Jiang. (1999). An analysis of copyright-related legal cases and decisions: Implications to designing Internet-based learning activities. **Educational Technology Review, 11**, 19–24. To provide information about potential legal problems that might arise from using and distributing instructional materials and designing activities for Internet-based instruction, this article analyzes court cases and decisions relating to course packets; illustrations and figures; learning activities; video, sound, and graphic images; and hyperlinks.

Educational Technology & Society. Online journal of International Forum of Educational Technology & Society and the IEEE Learning Technology Task Force; available at http://ifets .ieee.org/periodical/. Publishes academic articles on the issues affecting the developers of educational systems and educators who implement and manage such systems, discussing the perspectives of both communities and their relation to each other.

Evaluation Practice. Elsevier Science/Regional Sales Office, Customer Support Department— JAI Books, P.O. Box 945, New York, NY 10159-0945. [Tri-annual, $80 indiv., $180 inst]. Interdisciplinary journal aimed at helping evaluators improve practice in their disciplines, develop skills, and foster dialogue.

Fitzgerald, Gail E., Allen, Bryce L., & Reeves, Thomas C. (1999). A scholarly review process for interactive learning and information system products. **Journal of Interactive Learning Research, 10** (1), 59–65. Describes a new scholarly review process for courseware and other interactive learning and information system products. The purpose is to provide a mechanism to support faculty in the creative scholarship of designing and developing interactive products, evaluating their quality, disseminating results, and providing opportunities for the professional community to view and discuss their work.

French, Deanie, Hale, Charles, Johnson, Charles, & Farr, Gerald, Ed. (1999). **Internet based learning: An introduction and framework for higher education and business**. [Book, 214p., $25]. Stylus Publishing, Inc., 22883 Quicksilver Drive, Sterling, VA 20166-2012, styluspub@aol.com. This contributed volume is designed for junior college faculty, senior college faculty, and business trainers who wish to integrate new Internet technology for learning.

Goldsworthy, Richard. (1999). Lenses on learning and technology: Roles and opportunities for design and development. **Educational Technology, 39** (4), 59–62. Presents a model of differing ways to view technology in its relationship with learning. Discusses these five overlapping categories (or lenses) that capture key areas in which technology may facilitate learning: (1) from technology, (2) with technology, (3) around technology, (4) through technology, and (5) through technology-supported assessment and management.

Griffith, William. (1999). The reflecting team as an alternative case teaching model: A narrative, conversational approach. **Management Learning, 30** (3), 343–362. Presents a reflecting team case model that is a conversational, student-centered, narrative-based alternative to the traditional hierarchical, instructor-centered, analytical model.

Hannaford, Marion. (1999). **Developing innovative information technology projects**. [Paper, 13p.]. (Presented at the Annual Meeting of the American Educational Research Association, Montreal, Quebec, Canada, April 19–23, 1999). As several initiatives relating to integrating the use of information technologies (IT) were started in Prince Edward Island, the Faculty of Education at the University of Prince Edward Island saw a unique opportunity where the merging of some of the initiatives and collaboration among the participants might be more productive and advance the initiatives with a research basis.

Harbeck, Julia D., & Sherman, Thomas M. (1999). Seven principles for designing developmentally appropriate Web sites for young children. **Educational Technology, 39** (4), 39–44. Illustrates how each of these principles may guide decisions about Web-based design for young children consistent with developmentally appropriate practice.

Human-Computer Interaction. Lawrence Erlbaum Associates, 365 Broadway, Hillsdale, NJ 07642. [Q., $50 indiv. US and Canada, $80 elsewhere, $320 inst., $350 elsewhere]. A journal of theoretical, empirical, and methodological issues of user science and of system design.

Instructional Science. Kluwer Academic Publishers, 101 Philip Drive, Norwell, MA 02061, (617)871-6600, fax (617)871-6528, kluwer@wkap.com. [Bi-mo., $374 inst.]. Promotes a deeper understanding of the nature, theory, and practice of the instructional process and the learning resulting from this process.

Journal of Educational Technology Systems. Baywood Publishing Co., 26 Austin Avenue, Box 337, Amityville, NY 11701. [Q., $175]. In-depth articles on completed and ongoing research in all phases of educational technology and its application and future within the teaching profession, enhancing instruction and facilitation of learning in the typical class-room, design and implementation of telecommunication networks and Web sites, contributions of librarians to Web-based teaching.

Journal of Interactive Instruction Development. Learning Technology Institute, Society for Applied Learning Technology, 50 Culpeper Street, Warrenton, VA 22186. [Q., $40 member, $60 non-member; add $18 postage outside N. America]. A showcase of success-ful programs that will heighten awareness of innovative, creative, and effective approaches to courseware development for interactive technology.

Journal of Technical Writing and Communication. Baywood Publishing Co., 26 Austin Avenue, Box 337, Amityville, NY 11701. [Q., $48 indiv., $170 inst.]. Essays on oral and written communication, for purposes ranging from pure research to needs of business and industry.

Journal of Visual Literacy. International Visual Literacy Association, c/o John C. Belland, 122 Ramseyer Hall, 29 West Woodruff Avenue, Ohio State University, Columbus, OH 43210. [Bi-ann., $40]. Interdisciplinary forum on all aspects of visual/verbal languaging.

Kammerdiener, Troy, & Smith, Lon. (1999). **Supporting a Web-based curriculum with a diverse mix of authoring competency**. [Paper, 9p.]. (Presented at the Society for Infor-mation Technology & Teacher Education 10th International Conference, San Antonio, TX, February 28–March 4, 1999). Presents an academic World Wide Web authoring tool called AutoHTML. This tool, a work in progress, is designed to allow the novice user to construct high-level Web pages with a consistent look and feel. The system works with a standard Web browser without the addition of component plug-ins.

Montgomery, Paula K., Ed. & Thomas, Nancy Pickering. (1999). **Information literacy and information skills instruction: Applying research to practice in the school library media center.** [Book, 190p., $30]. Library and Information Problem-Solving Skills Series. Libraries Unlimited, (800)237-6124, lu-books@lu.com, www.lu.com. Brings together the literature on information skills instruction with particular reference to models related to infor-mation seeking and the information search process, including representational, instructional/ teaching, and facilitation models.

Performance Improvement. International Society for Performance Improvement, 1300 L Street NW, Suite 1250, Washington, DC 20005. [10/yr., $69]. Journal of ISPI; promotes performance science and technology. Contains articles, research, and case studies relating to improving human performance.

Performance Improvement Quarterly. International Society for Performance Improve-ment, 1300 L Street NW, Suite 1250, Washington, DC 20005. [Q., $50]. Presents the cut-ting edge in research and theory in performance technology.

Ritchie, Donn, & Earnest, John. (1999). The future of instructional design: Results of a Delphi study. **Educational Technology, 39** (1), 35–42. Discusses results of a Delphi study of academic professors and practitioners that identified trends that may influence the field of instructional design in the near future. Trends identified include diverse cultural perspectives, growth of online access to information, distance training and information networks, and customized instructional materials for users.

Saba, Farhad. (1999). Software systems in distance teaching and learning. **Distance Education Report, 3** (7), 1–2. Focuses on software for distance education. Discusses the cost of course development and highlights three classes of distance education tools: communication tools, course development tools, and digital imaging and video production software.

Schnackenberg, Heidi L. (1999). **Teacher in-service training and the incorporation of technology into teaching**. [Paper, 8p.]. (Presented at the Annual Convention of the Association for Educational Communications and Technology, Houston, TX, February 10-14, 1999). Describes the teacher "inservice" training that was developed as the result of a technology needs assessment at two elementary schools in Quebec. The workshop was developed as an initial vehicle for enabling teachers to incorporate technology into their teaching.

Shellnut, Bonnie, Knowlton, Allie, & Savage, Tim. (1999). Applying the ARCS model to the design and development of computer-based modules for manufacturing engineering courses. **Educational Technology Research and Development, 47** (2), 100–110. Describes how a multimedia design team at Wayne State University (Michigan), working on an engineering-education project, incorporated Kellers's ARCS (attention, relevance, confidence, and satisfaction) model into the design and development of a computer-based instructional module for a college engineering course in economics.

Solloway, Sharon G., & Harris, Edward L. (1999). Creating community online: Negotiating students' desires and needs in cyberspace. **Educom Review, 34** (2), 8–9, 12–13. Describes the adaptation of a traditional graduate education course to an online format. Compares this course with an undergraduate model. Discusses course requirements of the graduate online course, creation of the online community, student attitudes, and problems. Offers advice for course planning and development, course orientation, and instruction and management.

Spector, J. Michael. (1999). **Teachers as designers of collaborative distance learning**. [Paper, 8p.]. (Presented at the 10th Society for Information Technology & Teacher Education International Conference, San Antonio, TX, February 28–March 4, 1999). There is an obvious growth in the use of distributed and online learning environments. There is some evidence to believe that collaborative learning environments can be effective, especially when using advanced technology to support learning in and about complex domains.

Training. Lakewood Publications, Inc., 50 S. Ninth, Minneapolis, MN 55402. [Mo., $78 US, $88 Canada, $99 elsewhere]. Covers all aspects of training, management, and organizational development, motivation, and performance improvement.

Welsh, Thomas M. (1999). Implications of distributed learning for instructional designers: How will the future affect the practice? **Educational Technology, 39** (2), 41–45. Defines a distributed course as one in which instructional events that have traditionally occurred in the classroom are made available to either distant or local learners. Discusses the challenges for distributed course designers and presents a taxonomy for distributed course design. Addresses design, development, and evaluation processes and related issues.

INTERACTIVE MULTIMEDIA

ChanLin, Lih-Juan. (1999). Gender differences and the need for visual control. **International Journal of Instructional Media, 26** (3), 329–335. Describes a study that investigated the effects of visual control (self-controlled versus system-controlled) and gender difference on learning with scientific multimedia instruction, observed how boys and girls differed in navigating and processing visual information in a hypermedia environment, and examined how visual control influenced learning.

Dinchak, Marla. (1999). **Using the World Wide Web to create a learner-centered classroom**. [Paper, 6p.]. (Presented at the NISOD International Conference on Teaching and Leadership Excellence, 1999). This presentation aims to explain the practical application of the World Wide Web as a primary tool for creating a learner-centered classroom. Based on Terry O'Banion's book, *A Learning College for the 21st Century,* a model that places learning and the learner first is proposed. Six key principles are explained and are utilized as the guiding assumptions in Maricopa Community Colleges' learner-centered paradigm.

Donlevy, James G., & Donlevy, Tia Rice, Ed. (1999). What's up in technology? A multimedia curriculum for exploring high-technology careers. **International Journal of Instructional Media, 26** (3), 249–251. Reviews a multimedia curriculum called "What's Up in Technology?" that was developed by the educational television channel Thirteen/WNET to introduce secondary school students to high-technology careers.

Donlevy, James G., & Donlevy, Tia Rice. (1999). wNetSchool. **International Journal of Instructional Media, 26** (1), 9–10. Describes wNetSchool, a professional Web service developed by television station WNET (New York City) that is available without charge to elementary and secondary school teachers. It includes standards-based lesson plans and classroom activities, a multimedia primer, online mentors, and links to model schools where the Internet is used effectively to support the curriculum.

England, Elaine, & Finney, Andy. (1999). **Managing multimedia: Project management for interactive media** (2nd ed.). [Book, 423p., $41.95]. Addison-Wesley, www.awlonline.com. This book covers the spectrum of managing an interactive multimedia project by covering such subjects as scoping the project, selecting the team, and designing the interface.

Gavin, Tim. (1999). Going beyond limits: Integrating multimedia distribution systems into the curriculum. **Book Report, 18** (1), 37, 39–41. A multimedia distribution system affords many opportunities for teachers and students. The systematic use of e-mail, Internet access, and live video presentations provides sound pedagogical applications that enhance student/teacher discourse and liberate learning from the confines of the classroom.

Goos, G., Hartmanis, J., & van Leeuwen, J. (1999). **Interactive multimedia documents: Modeling, authoring, and implementation experiences**. [Book, 161p., $35]. Springer-Verlag New York, Inc., 175 Fifth Avenue, New York, NY 10010. Presents an integrated approach to interactive multimedia documents.

Journal of Educational Multimedia and Hypermedia. Association for the Advancement of Computing in Education, Box 2966, Charlottesville, VA 22902-2966, aace@virginia.edu, www.aace.org. [Q., $40 indiv., $50 foreign]. A multidisciplinary information source presenting research about and applications for multimedia and hypermedia tools.

Journal of Hypermedia and Multimedia Studies. ISTE, University of Oregon, 1787 Agate Street, Eugene, OR 97403-1923, (800)336-5191, cust_svc@ccmail.uoregon.edu, www.iste.org. [Q., $29, $39 intl., $42 intl. air]. Features articles on projects, lesson plans, and theoretical issues, as well as reviews of products, software, and books.

Journal of Interactive Learning Research. Association for Advancement of Computing in Education, Box 2966, Charlottesville, VA 22902-2966, aace@virginia.edu, www.aace.org. [Q., $40 indiv., $50 foreign]. International journal publishes articles on how intelligent computer technologies can be used in education to enhance learning and teaching. Reports on research and developments, integration, and applications of artificial intelligence in education.

Kenny, R. (2001). **Teaching TV production in a digital world: Integrating media literacy.** [Book, 410p., $37.50]. Libraries Unlimited, (800)237-6124, lu-books@lu.com, www.lu.com. Presents an alternative approach to teaching television production to high school students.

Includes thematic mapping, media and visual literacy, broadcast history, video production skills, and multimedia animation.

Klinger, S. (1999). Coding categories to record student talk at a multimedia interface. **Journal of Computer Assisted Learning, 15** (2), 109–117. Using case study methodology, this paper examines how pairs of first-time high school student users navigated through a multimedia geography CD-ROM together. Discusses coding methods for student activity, student interaction, dialog analysis, multimedia literacy, and further research needs.

Larrabee, Marva J., & Blanton, Bonnie L. (1999). Innovations for enhancing education of career counselors using technology. **Journal of Employment Counseling, 36** (1), 13–23. Discusses a Career Development Training Institute (CDTI) project, which developed a multimedia CD-ROM for a basic first course in career development. Data collected support the conclusion that the multimedia presentation approach is compatible with adapting the traditional lecture styles of teaching used by many career development educators.

Lee, Sung Heum, & Boling, Elizabeth. (1999). Screen design guidelines for motivation in interactive multimedia instruction: A survey and framework for designers. **Educational Technology, 39** (3), 19–26. Identifies guidelines from the literature relating to screen design and design of interactive instructional materials. Describes two types of guidelines—those aimed at enhancing motivation and those aimed at preventing loss of motivation—for typography, graphics, color, and animation and audio. Proposes a framework for considering motivation in the design of interactive multimedia instruction.

Lu, Gang, Wan, Hongwen, & Liu, Shouying. (1999). Hypermedia and its application in education. **Educational Media International, 36** (1), 41–45. Discusses the main features of hypermedia and its significance in the application to education. Highlights include multimedia teaching materials, interaction, convenience in storing and using information, problem solving and critical thinking, individuality in study, and the design of nodes and links in hypermedia.

Oh, Paul. (1999). E-Classroom: Add a little spice . . . **Instructor, 108** (8), 75–76. Presents multimedia tools to enhance language arts and social studies lessons.

Phelps, Julia, & Reynolds, Ross. (1999). Formative evaluation of a Web-based course in meteorology. **Computers & Education, 32** (2), 181–193. Describes the formative-evaluation process for the EuroMET (European Meteorological Education and Training) project, Web-based university courses in meteorology that were created to address the education and training needs of professional meteorologists and students throughout Europe. Usability and interactive and multimedia elements are discussed.

Robson, Maggie, & Hunt, Kathy. (1999). An innovative approach to involving parents in the education of their early years children. **International Journal of Early Years Education, 7** (2), 185–193. Evaluated a multimedia project to increase self-esteem of parents of inner-city primary school children in Hartlepool, England, to increase their understanding of the preschool curriculum and to involve them in their children's school life.

Rowley, James B., & Hart, Patricia M. (2000). **High-performance mentoring: A multimedia program for training mentor teachers. Facilitator's guide.** [Book, 224p., $39.95]. Corwin Press, Inc., A Sage Publications Company, 2455 Teller Road, Thousand Oaks, CA 91320, order@corwinpress.com. Designed to be used with a training workshop that helps veteran teachers be effective mentors to beginning teachers and provides instructions on how to facilitate a successful workshop. The book offers six chapters that include strategies and materials to help readers learn how to plan and promote a workshop; facilitate a successful workshop; select, match, and support mentor teachers; and assess the mentor teacher program.

Shabajee, Paul. (1999). Making values and beliefs explicit as a tool for the effective development of educational multimedia software—A prototype. **British Journal of Educational Technology, 30** (2), 101–113. Describes a prototype process for the development of educational multimedia materials, based on the ARKive project in the United Kingdom, which can help educational multimedia software developers produce more coherent and effective learning resources by making explicit the value/belief system on which the project is founded.

Simanowitz, Dylan, & Horsburgh, David. (1999). Using CD ROM and learning materials to structure learning experiences for students with basic skills need in literacy. **RaPAL Bulletin, 39,** 22–36. A European project developed guidelines for use of multimedia in adult basic education, reviewed existing multimedia resources, and developed strategies for teaching literacy using multimedia. Individual learning styles and processes can be accommodated with the media, but teachers need new skills to plan and monitor individually based multimedia learning.

Smithey, Margaret W., & Hough, Bradley W. (1999). Connecting preservice teachers with technology. **T.H.E. Journal, 26** (8), 78–79. Discusses the importance of introducing preservice teachers to the use of technology and how to integrate it into their classrooms. Describes one teacher's development of multimedia programs and emphasizes availability of and access to computers in schools, careful planning, the use of appropriate technology, and student motivation.

Timm, Joan Thrower. (1999). Selecting computer programs and interactive multimedia for culturally diverse students: Promising practices. **Multicultural Education, 6** (4), 30-31. Discusses issues in selecting computer programs and interactive multimedia for culturally diverse students, including the necessity of including diverse cultural referents and acknowledging the cognitive style of students who will be using the programs.

Wilson, Melvin (Skip). (1999). Student-generated multimedia presentations: Tools to help build and communicate mathematical understanding. **Journal of Computers in Mathematics and Science Teaching, 18** (2), 145–156. Describes computer activities that offer middle school students opportunities to cooperatively explore problem situations and connect mathematical understandings to each other, to their experiences, and to other disciplines.

Zahn, Susan Brown, Zahn, Christopher J., Rajkumar, T. M., & Duricy, Dan. (1999). Using multimedia as a communication tool. **International Journal of Instructional Media, 26** (2), 221–230. Describes a team-taught, interdisciplinary multimedia development course for undergraduate students that was created to address issues concerning students' needs to learn how to evaluate and develop applications for new communication technology. Topics include a collaborative learning model, course objectives, and student assessment.

LIBRARIES AND MEDIA CENTERS

Baule, S. M. (1999). **Facilities planning for your school library media center.** [Book, 100p., $36.95]. Linworth, (800)786-5017, fax (614)436-9490, linworth.com. Updates facilities planning to include new technological requirements. Emphasizes flexibility, planning, expandability, and security.

Benefiel, Candace R., Gass, Elaine, & Arant, Wendi. (1999). A new dialogue: A student advisory committee in an academic library. **Journal of Academic Librarianship, 25** (2), 111–113. To give students a direct voice in library user policy and the library a point of contact with the student body, the Evans Libraries at Texas A&M University formed a Student Advisory Committee.

Bielefield, A., & Cheeseman, L. (1999). **Interpreting and negotiating licensing agreements: A guidebook for the library, research, and teaching professions.** [Book, 150p., $55]. Neal-Schuman, fax(800) 584-2414, orders@neal-schuman.com, www.neal-schuman.com. Presents in non-legal language information about copyright licenses, including useful wording for licenses, model clauses, and a glossary.

Book Report. Linworth Publishing, 480 E. Wilson Bridge Road, Suite L., Worthington, OH 43085-2372, (800)786-5017, fax (614)436-9490, orders@linworth.com, linworth.com. [5/school yr., $44 US, $9 single copy]. Journal for junior and senior high school librarians provides articles, tips, and ideas for day-to-day school library management, as well as reviews of audiovisuals and software, all written by school librarians.

Chesbro, Melinda. (1999). The catalog takes to the highway. **School Library Journal, 45** (5), 33–35. Discusses new developments in online library catalogs, including Web-based catalogs, interconnectivity within the library, interconnectivity between libraries, graphical user interfaces, pricing models, and a checklist of questions to ask when purchasing a new online catalog.

Clyde, L. A. (2000). **Managing infotech in school library media centers.** [Book, 304p., $35]. Libraries Unlimited, (800)237-6124, lu-books@lu.com, www.lu.com. Presents a method for developing information technology plans and managing technology within the framework of the learning mission of the individual school. Offers an overview of many educational technologies, with recommendations.

Coffman, Steve. (1999). Building Earth's largest library: Driving into the future. **Searcher, 7** (3), 34–37, 40-47. Examines the Amazon.com online bookstore as a blueprint for designing the world's largest library.

Collection Building. M.C.B. University Press Ltd., 60-62 Toller Lane, Bradford, W. Yorks. BD8 9BY, England, www.mcb.co.uk. [Q., $599]. Focuses on all aspects of collection building, ranging from microcomputers to business collections, to popular topics and censorship.

Computers in Libraries. Information Today, 143 Old Marlton Pike, Medford, NJ 08055, (800)300-9868. [10/yr., $89.95 US, $99.95 Canada and Mexico, $59.95 outside N. America]. Covers practical applications of microcomputers to library situations, as well as recent news items.

Crawford, Gregory A. (1999). Issues for the digital library. **Computers in Libraries, 19** (5), 62–64. Discusses issues facing libraries using digital information resources, based on experiences at the Pennsylvania State University at Harrisburg library.

Crotts, Joe. (1999). Subject usage and funding of library monographs. **College & Research Libraries, 60** (3), 261–273. This investigation at California State University, Chico seeks to identify those variables that prove indicative of the demand for monographs by subject. Analyzes interrelationships among circulation, expenditure, and enrollment by subject and develops a model for allocating subject funding based on circulation statistics.

Debowski, Shelda. (1999). The evolution of the school library collection: Implications for effective management. **Orana, 35** (1), 41–48. Explores some of the collection and service-related issues that should be considered by those developing an electronic collection in a school library.

DiMattia, Susan S., & Blumenstein, Lynn C. (1999). Virtual libraries: Meeting the corporate challenge. **Library Journal, 124** (4), 42–44. Discusses virtual libraries in corporate settings from the viewpoint of five special librarians.

Dobb, Linda S. (1999). Four retreats and a forum: A meditation on retreats as a response to change. **Library Trends, 47** (4), 699–710. Describes four library retreats held by the Bowling Green State University library staff from 1995 to 1998. The retreats reflect changes in library work and management theory that have occurred. The importance of technology to library work is recognized, but there is also a growing realization of the importance of developing a flexible staff capable of learning new skills.

Dogget, Sandra L. (2000). **Beyond the book: Technology integration into the secondary school library media curriculum.** [Book, 177p., $29.50]. Libraries Unlimited, (800)237-6124, lu-books@lu.com, www.lu.com. Provides a wealth of information on what the secondary school library media specialist needs to know regarding technology in the coming century.

Dugdale, Christine. (1999). The role of electronic reserves in serving and shaping new teaching and learning environments in UK universities. **Journal of Information Science,** **25** (3), 183–192. Describes the ResIDe Electronic Reserve at the University of the West of England (UWE), Bristol, an example of an electronic reserve that has been addressing many access problems and supporting different teaching/learning initiatives. Discusses new roles for the ResIDe electronic library, electronic information management, new librarian roles, and management of ResIDe.

The Electronic Library. Information Today, 143 Old Marlton Pike, Medford, NJ 08055, (800)300-9868. [Bi-mo, $127 US, $137 Canada and Mexico]. International journal for minicomputer, microcomputer, and software applications in libraries; independently assesses current and forthcoming information technologies.

Farmer, L. S., & Fowler, W. (1999). **More than information: The role of the library media center in the multimedia classroom.** [Book, 150p., $34.95]. Linworth, (800)786-5017, fax (614)436-9490, linworth.com. Uses multimedia as a focus to discuss the media specialists' role in the shift toward using technology in education. Covers several multimedia-related issues, including assessment, authorship, resources and projects, modernized classrooms, and broadening the learning community.

Goodrich, Jeanne. (1999). The technology vendor's conference: An information technology planning success story. **Journal of Library Administration, 26** (3–4), 75–90. This case study describes the use of an information technology vendor conference to assure the smooth opening of a public library in Portland, Oregon. Vendors of hardware, telecommunications, integrated library systems, and networks met with library administration and staff to troubleshoot problems and share information and to ensure a timely opening.

Gorman, Audrey J. (1999). Start making sense: Libraries don't have to be confusing places for kids with reading disabilities. **School Library Journal, 45** (7), 22–25. Defines dyslexia, the most common reading disability. Discusses the multisensory approach to working with learning disabled children. Discusses how public libraries can develop services and collections to address the needs of learning disabled populations.

Gorman, Michael. (1999). New libraries, old values. **Australian Library Journal, 48** (1), 43–52. Lists values that should underpin librarians' work: stewardship, service, intellectual freedom, privacy, rationalism, commitment to literacy and learning, unfettered access to recorded knowledge and information, and democracy.

Government Information Quarterly. Elsevier Science/Regional Sales Office, Customer Support Department—JAI Books, P.O. Box 945, New York, NY 10159-0945. [Q., $113 indiv., $269 inst.]. International journal of resources, services, policies, and practices.

Hannesdottir, Sigrun Klara. (1999). Library Power: An international perspective. **School Libraries Worldwide, 5** (2), 111–120. This evaluation of Library Power for the international community is based on two questions: (1) What lessons can be learned from countries with different educational systems and can the international school library community utilize any part of the outcome of the Library Power project?; and (2) Are the questions that Library Power addressed universal questions related to school librarianship?

Helfer, Doris Small. (1999). The changing academic library and what the University of California is attempting to do. **Searcher, 7** (3), 10, 12, 14, 16. Describes work at the University of California libraries to accommodate change and plans for digital technology.

Himmelfarb, Gertrude. (1999). Revolution in the library. **Library Trends, 47** (4), 612–619. There is an electronic revolution in the library that may prove to be a revolution in the humanities and in the nature of learning and education. The humanities are an essentially human enterprise of which the record reposes in books in libraries. The central role of libraries in preserving these ideas must survive the electronic revolution.

Hopkins, Dianne McAfee, & Zweizig, Douglas L. (1999). Student learning opportunities summarize Library Power. **School Libraries Worldwide, 5** (2), 97–110. Examines the Library Power program from the standpoint of student learning opportunities. Summarizes, from a student perspective, the findings of earlier studies and focuses on the areas of staffing, the facility, professional development, curriculum, instruction, and school reform.

Hopwood, Susan H. (1999). Long-range planning and funding for Innovation. **Computers in Libraries, 19** (1), 22–24, 26–27. Describes strategic planning at Marquette University libraries. Highlights include technology-planning efforts for a Web-based online catalog; goals of improving user independence and speed of access to information; staff participation; funding issues, including support of the Parents Association; and software selection.

Houghton, J. M., & Houghton, R. S. (1999). **Decision points: Boolean logic for computer users and beginning online searchers.** [Book, 163p., $25]. Libraries Unlimited, (800)237-6124, lu-books@lu.com, www.lu.com. For educators working with grades 5–12; suggests strategies to help students retrieve information, build information literacy, and make considered decisions.

Iannuzzi, P., Mangrum, C. T., & Strichart, S. S. (1999). **Teaching information literacy skills.** [Book and disk, $24.95]. Prentice Hall, www.prenhall.com. Describes information literacy instruction and provides computerized applications.

Information Outlook (formerly **Special Libraries**). Special Libraries Association, 1700 18th Street, NW, Washington, DC 20009-2508, www.sla.com. [Mo., $80 US, $95 elsewhere]. Discusses administration, organization, and operations. Includes reports on research, technology, and professional standards.

Information Services and Use. Elsevier Science Publishers, Box 10558, Burke, VA 22009-0558. [4/yr., $254]. Contains data on international developments in information management and its applications. Articles cover online systems, library automation, word processing, micrographics, videotex, and telecommunications.

Janes, Joseph, & McClure, Charles R. (1999). The Web as a reference tool: Comparisons with traditional sources. **Public Libraries, 38** (1), 30-33, 36–39. This preliminary study suggests that the same level of timeliness and accuracy can be obtained for answers to reference questions using resources in freely available World Wide Web sites as using traditional print-based resources. Discusses implications for library collection development, new models of consortia, training needs, and costing and budget issues.

Journal of Academic Librarianship. Elsevier Science/Regional Sales Office, Customer Support Department - JAI Books, P.O. Box 945, New York, NY 10159-0945. [6/yr., $81 indiv., $195 inst.]. Results of significant research, issues and problems facing academic libraries, book reviews, and innovations in academic libraries.

Journal of Government Information (formerly **Government Publications Review**). Elsevier Science Ltd., Journals Division, 660 White Plains Road, Tarrytown, NY 10591-5153. [6/yr., $534]. An international journal covering production, distribution, bibliographic control, accessibility, and use of government information in all formats and at all levels.

Journal of Librarianship and Information Science. Worldwide Subscription Service Ltd., Unit 4, Gibbs Reed Farm, Ticehurst, E. Sussex TN5 7HE, England. [Q., $155]. Deals with all aspects of library and information work in the United Kingdom and reviews literature from international sources.

Journal of Library Administration. Haworth Press, 10 Alice Street, Binghamton, NY 13904-1580, (800)HAWORTH, fax (800)895-0582, getinfo@haworth.com, www.haworthpress .com. [8/yr., $45 indiv., $125 inst.] Provides information on all aspects of effective library management, with emphasis on practical applications.

Kemp, Roger L. (1999). A city manager looks at trends affecting public libraries. **Public Libraries, 38** (2), 116–119. Highlights some important conditions, both present and future, that will have an impact on public libraries.

King, Monica. (1999). Protecting public-access computers in libraries. **Public Libraries, 38** (3), 166–167, 170–173. Describes one public library's development of a computer-security plan, along with helpful products used.

Kur, Sally. (1999). From tablets to keyboards: The "new" library. **Community College Journal, 70** (1), 45–48. Discusses the changing face of libraries as a result of the penetration of technology into the home, school, and workplace. Charts the evolution of libraries from the perspectives of strategic planning, role, service delivery, organization and staffing, the librarian's role, budgeting and finance, assessment and accountability, and alliances.

Kurzeja, Karen, & Charbeneau, Brett. (1999). Remote but not alone. **Computers in Libraries, 19** (4), 20–22, 24–26. Describes the experiences at the Williamsburg (Virginia) Regional Library when the children's department closed for two months for renovations and temporary quarters were created in a bookmobile in a nearby parking lot. Discusses technology challenges involved in hooking up computers, selecting an appropriate collection that would fit, and equipment used.

Library Computing (formerly **Library Software Review**). Sage Publications Inc., 2455 Teller Road, Thousand Oaks, CA 91320, order@sagepub.com, www.sagepub.com. [Q., $59 indiv., $252 US inst..]. Emphasizes practical aspects of library computing for libraries of all types, including reviews of automated systems ranging from large-scale mainframe-based systems to microcomputer-based systems, and both library-specific and general-purpose software used in libraries.

Library and Information Science Research. Ablex Publishing Corp., 100 Prospect Street, P.O. Box 811, Stamford, CT 06904-0811, (203)323-9606, fax (203)357-8446. Www.jaipress .com. [Q., $95 indiv., $245 inst.]. Research articles, dissertation reviews, and book reviews on issues concerning information resources management.

Library Hi Tech. Pierian Press, Box 1808, Ann Arbor, MI 48106, (800)678-2435, www .pierianpress.com. [Q., $169]. Concentrates on reporting on the selection, installation, maintenance, and integration of systems and hardware.

Library Hi Tech News. Pierian Press, Box 1808, Ann Arbor, MI 48106, (800)678-2435, www.pierianpress.com. [10/yr., $199]. Supplements *Library Hi Tech,* updating many of the issues addressed in-depth in the journal and keeping readers fully informed about the latest developments in library automation, new products, network news, new software and hardware, and people in technology.

Library Journal. 245 West 17th Street, New York, NY 10011, (212)463-6819. [20/yr., $109 US, $138.50 Canada, $188.50 elsewhere]. A professional periodical for librarians, with current issues and news, professional reading, a lengthy book review section, and classified advertisements.

Library Quarterly. University of Chicago Press, 5720 S. Woodlawn Avenue, Chicago, IL 60637. [Q., $35 indiv., $73 inst.]. Scholarly articles of interest to librarians.

Library Resources and Technical Services. Association for Library Collections and Technical Services, 50 E. Huron Street, Chicago, IL 60611-2795. [Q., $55 nonmembers]. Scholarly papers on bibliographic access and control, preservation, conservation, and reproduction of library materials.

Library Trends. University of Illinois Press, Journals Dept., 1325 S. Oak Street, Champaign, IL 61820. [Q., $60 indiv., $85 inst., add $7 elsewhere]. Each issue is concerned with one aspect of library and information science, analyzing current thought and practice and examining ideas that hold the greatest potential for the field.

LISA: Library and Information Science Abstracts. Bowker-Saur Ltd., Maypole House, Maypole Road, E. Grinsted, W. Sussex, RH19 1HH, England, www.bowker-saur.com. [Mo., $960 US, £545 elsewhere]. More than 500 abstracts per issue from more than 500 periodicals, reports, books, and conference proceedings.

Lugo, Mark-Elliot. (1999). Art for libraries' sake. **American Libraries, 30** (6), 90–94. Illustrates the benefits of an aggressive library program of regularly scheduled and professionally curated art exhibitions and related events. Describes the Visual Arts Program at the Pacific Beach branch library (San Diego).

Ma, Jin-Chuan. (1999). Fund allocations for information resources in China's key universities. **College & Research Libraries, 60** (2), 174–178. Examines funding problems, and suggests proposals for change: Establish a deducting-percentage system; enhance integrated resources development; revise existing provisions.

Machovec, George S., Ed. (1999). Electronic frontiers: Management challenges for the new millennium. **Online Libraries and Microcomputers, 17** (5), 1–3. Discusses the following management challenges libraries must cope with in the paradigm shift from print to electronic access to information: becoming involved in network issues; leveraging resources; duplicating efforts; partnering; dealing with legal, political, or economic issues; maintaining standards; serving remote users; and acquiring, selecting and organizing electronic resources.

Morris, Dilys E., & Wool, Gregory. (1999). Cataloging: Librarianship's best bargain. **Library Journal, 124** (11), 44–46. Iowa State University's cost study proves academic librarians can keep cataloging in-house and save staff costs. Several factors play a role in the productivity surge at ISU: increasing use of shared cataloging, growth of online authoring files, expanding role of support staff, increasing automation of catalogers' work, and structural flattening of the organization.

Olson, Renee. (1999). The rescuers. **School Library Journal, 45** (1), 24–29. Describes programs developed by the Chicago School District to renovate and revitalize its school libraries. Topics include funding, other educational reforms in the district, updating library collections, updating librarians' skills, increasing budgets through grants, flexible scheduling, corporate support, relations with the Chicago Public Library, and traveling regional library media specialists.

Prostano, E. T., & Prostano, J. S. (1999). **The school library media center** (5th ed.). [Book, 184p., $47.50]. Libraries Unlimited, (800)237-6124, lu-books@lu.com, www.lu.com. Focusing on the operation of school library media centers as systems, this newest edition integrates trends and developments of the preceding decade. Issues include the impact of global forces and school districts, programming and goals, guidance and consultation, and curriculum development and improvement.

The Public-Access Computer Systems Review. University Libraries, University of Houston, Houston, TX 77204-2091, LThompson@uh.edu. [Irreg., free to libraries]. An electronic journal that contains articles about all types of computer systems that libraries make available to their patrons and technologies to implement these systems.

Public Libraries. Public Library Association, American Library Association, ALA Editions, 50 East Huron Street, Chicago, IL 60611-2795, (800)545-2433, fax (312)836-9958. [Bi-mo., $50 US nonmembers, $60 elsewhere, $10 single copy]. News and articles of interest to public librarians.

Public Library Quarterly. Haworth Press, 10 Alice Street, Binghamton, NY 13904-1580, (800)HAWORTH, fax (800)895-0582, getinfo@haworth.com, www.haworthpress.com. [Q., $50 indiv., $165 inst.]. Addresses the major administrative challenges and opportunities that face the nation's public libraries.

Rankin, V. (1999). **The thoughtful researcher: Teaching the research process to middle school students.** [Book, 227p., $29]. Libraries Unlimited, (800)237-6124, lu-books@lu.com, www.lu.com. Guides the research of middle schoolers, focusing on thinking skills, critical thinking, and quality outcomes; includes time management and visual information displays as helpful tools.

The Reference Librarian. Haworth Press, 10 Alice Street, Binghamton, NY 13904-1580, (800)HAWORTH, fax (800)895-0582, getinfo@haworth.com, www.haworthpress.com. [2/yr., $60 indiv., $225 inst.]. Each issue focuses on a topic of current concern, interest, or practical value to reference librarians.

Reference Services Review. Pierian Press, Box 1808, Ann Arbor, MI 48106, (800)678-2435, www.pierianpress.com. [Q., $169]. Dedicated to the enrichment of reference knowledge and the advancement of reference services. It prepares its readers to understand and embrace current and emerging technologies affecting reference functions and information needs of library users

RQ. Reference and Adult Services Association, American Library Association, ALA Editions, 50 East Huron Street, Chicago, IL 60611-2795, (800)545-2433, fax (312)836-9958. [Q., $50 nonmembers, $55 nonmembers Canada and Mexico, $60 elsewhere, $15 single copy]. Disseminates information of interest to reference librarians, bibliographers, adult services librarians, those in collection development and selection, and others interested in public services; double-blind refereed.

Sager, Don, Dewey, Patrick R., Dowlin, Kenneth, & Hogan, Patricia M. (1999). John Henry versus the computer: The impact of the Internet on reference service. **Public Libraries, 38** (1), 21–25. Highlights include the reliability of Internet information sources, its timeliness as a tool for information access and dissemination, the Internet as change agent for libraries, reference publishing, helping the searcher refine requests, and an administrator's perspective.

Scally, Patricia H. (1999). Digital technology projects: Already thriving in public libraries. **Public Libraries, 38** (1), 48–50. Describes the results of a survey of public libraries that was conducted to identify digital technology projects. Highlights include kinds of collections being digitized (primarily photographs); costs; hardware and software used; experience levels of personnel; reasons for digitizing, including providing access to fragile materials; and technology in the participating libraries.

Schafer, Jay, & Thornton, Glenda A. (1999). From ownership to access: Re-engineering library services. **Reference Librarian**, (63), 25–40. Describes the restructuring of a traditional Interlibrary Loan Department at the Auraria Library, University of Colorado at Denver, into Information Delivery/Interlibrary Loan (ID/ILL) and its move to Collection Development Services. Discusses cost-effectiveness of ownership versus access, the collection philosophy, and components of the ID/ILL Department.

School Library Journal. Box 57559, Boulder, CO 80322-7559, (800)456-9409, fax (800)824-4746. [Mo., $97.50 US, $139 Canada, $149 elsewhere]. For school and youth service librarians. Reviews approximately 4,000 children's books and 1,000 educational media titles annually.

School Library Media Activities Monthly. LMS Associates LLC, 17 E. Henrietta Street, Baltimore, MD 21230-3190. [10/yr., $49 US, $54 elsewhere]. A vehicle for distributing ideas for teaching library media skills and for the development and implementation of library media skills programs.

School Library Media Research. American Association of School Librarians, American Library Association. Available online, www.ala.org/aasl/SLMR/ index.html]. For library media specialists, district supervisors, and others concerned with the selection and purchase of print and nonprint media and with the development of programs and services for preschool through high school libraries.

Schuyler, Michael. (1999). Adapting for impaired patrons. **Computers in Libraries, 19** (6), 24, 26, 28–29. Describes how a library, with an MCI Corporation grant, approached the process of setting up computers for the visually impaired. Discusses preparations, which included hiring a visually impaired user as a consultant and contacting the VIP (Visually Impaired Persons) group; equipment; problems with the graphical user interface; and training.

Share and share alike? (1999). **American Libraries, 30** (2), 40, 42, 44. Presents an interview with two librarians who are participating in joint-use projects, one between a public library and a school library, and one between a public library and an academic library. Personnel, commingling collections, changing library roles, and governance boards are considered.

Simpson, Carol. (1999). Migration—Not just for ducks. **Book Report, 17** (5), 34–36. Discusses the planning process for migrating to a new library media center automation system, including identification of the need to migrate, solicitation of stakeholder support, enumeration of required attributes of a new system, writing the request for proposal (RFP), and maximizing vendor demonstrations.

Simpson, Carol. (1999). Migration, a moving experience. **Book Report, 18** (1), 49–51. Discusses the processes involved in migrating a library's automation system. Highlights include getting information from vendor demonstrations, setting up an evaluation database to analyze RFPs (requests for proposals), making a spreadsheet that compares costs of packages, making recommendations once the data are analyzed, and implementation decisions to make

St. Lifer, Evan. (1999). Libraries succeed at funding books and bytes. **Library Journal, 124** (1), 50–52. Presents the annual budget report for public libraries for 1999, including budget projections; local taxes; rise of technology budgets; materials, salary, and operating budgets; per capita funding; fundraising; net costs; and the role of the Gates Library Foundation.

Stackpole, Laurie E., & King, Richard James. (1999). Electronic journals as a component of the digital library. **Issues in Science & Technology Librarianship, 22.** Describes services of the Naval Research Laboratory Library, which provides users in four geographical locations with digital library services, including over 500 electronic journals.

Sutter, L., & Sutter, H. (1999). **Where to go and what to do: Pathfinder and research approaches for the elementary age child.** [Book, 125p., $36.95]. Linworth, (800)786-5017, fax (614)436-9490, linworth.com. Groups sets of materials in a variety of media formats together for in-depth research on a broad collection of subjects, applying the pathfinder approach.

Includes information about specific research process models, library skills, Websites, and children's magazines.

Teacher Librarian. Box 34069, Dept. 284, Seattle, WA 98124-1069, TL@rockland.com. [Bi-mo. except July-August, $49]. "The journal for school library professionals"; previously known as *Emergency Librarian.* Articles, review columns, and critical analyses of management and programming issues for children's and young adult librarians.

Thomas, N. P. (1999). **Information literacy and information skills instruction: Applying research to practice in the school library media center.** [Book, 190p., $30]. Libraries Unlimited, (800)237-6124, lu-books@lu.com, www.lu.com. Synthesizes material from research, scholarly writings, and prescriptive literature into a review on information skills instruction, with a meta-analysis of research in bibliographic instruction, literacy skills, instruction, and learning styles. Designed for use in information skills instruction classes for school media specialists.

Thompson, Bruce, & Cook, Colleen. (2000). **Reliability and validity of SERVQUAL scores used to evaluate perceptions of library service quality.** [Paper, 37p.]. (Presented at the Annual Meeting of the Southwest Educational Research Association, Dallas, TX, January 27–29, 2000). Research libraries are increasingly supplementing collection counts with perceptions of service quality as indices of status and productivity. The present study was undertaken to explore the reliability and validity of scores from the SERVQUAL measurement protocol (A. Parasuraman et al., 1991), which has previously been used in this type of application in libraries.

Thompson, H. M., & Henley, S. A. (2000). **Fostering information literacy: Connecting national standards, goals 2000, and the SCANS report.** [Book, 275p., $37.50]. Libraries Unlimited, (800)237-6124, lu-books@lu.com, www.lu.com. Presents a plan for the strategic implementation of information literacy in all K–12 levels. Sketches the relationships between the Information Literacy Standards for Student Learning (AASL/AECT) and national subject area curriculum standards.

The Unabashed Librarian. Box 2631, New York, NY 10116. [Q., $40 US, $48 elsewhere]. Down-to-earth library items: procedures, forms, programs, cataloging, booklists, software reviews.

Van Vliet, L. W. (1999). **Media skills for middle schools: Strategies for library media specialists and teachers.** [Book, 231p., $28]. Libraries Unlimited, (800)237-6124, lu-books @lu.com, www.lu.com. Provides lesson plans for teaching information and computer skills as an integral part of the middle school curriculum. Emphasizes the role shared by media specialists, teachers, and administrators in connecting students to electronic information sources.

Wadham, T. (1999). **Programming with Latino children's material: A how-to-do-it manual for librarians.** [Book, 225p., $39.95]. Neal-Schuman, fax (800)584–2414, orders @neal-schuman.com, www.neal-schuman.com. Provides background about Latino culture and literature; describes useful media center materials.

White, Herbert S. (1999). Public library reference service—Expectations and reality. **Library Journal, 124** (11), 56, 58. Discusses expectations of public library reference service and the reality of what librarians can provide amid declining resources. Suggests reference librarians should define the gap between potential and reality in reference service and inform the customers about how little money it would take to provide better service. Argues that librarians betray the profession by performing clerical work regularly.

Wood, Joan. (1999). Stone soup: A recipe for successful coalitions. **Illinois Libraries, 81** (1), 25–28. Considers the implications of community connections by examining a coalition developed by the Pekin Public Library (Illinois): the Pekin Intergenerational Network (PIN). Highlights include recognizing the need for coalitions, developing a team, and evaluating the coalition's progress.

Woolls, B. (1999). **The school library media manager** (2nd ed.). [Book, 354p., $50]. Libraries Unlimited, (800)237-6124, lu-books@lu.com, www.lu.com. Places the school library media program in the context of recent changes in guidelines and technology. Provides an overview of the profession, covering available education programs, guidelines for selecting a position, and all aspects of media center management.

Yucht, Alice. (1999). Strategy: VOCAL-izing for library support. **Teacher Librarian, 25** (6), 30–31. Suggests that to reach those responsible for funding, librarians need to be more assertive in making the school library's role and services understood.

Zuidema, Karen Huwald. (1999). Reengineering technical services processes. **Library Resources & Technical Services, 43** (1), 37–52. Describes the framework in which the research library at the University of Illinois at Chicago (UIC) reengineered its technical services operations.

MEDIA TECHNOLOGIES

AV market place 1999: The complete business directory of audio, audio visual, computer systems, film, video, programming, with industry yellow pages. (1999). [Book, $195]. R. R. Bowker, 121 Chanlon Road, New Providence, NJ 07974, (888)269-5372, info@bowker.com, www.bowker.com. Comprehensive directory of vendors, manufacturers, producers, distributors, services, media techniques, and applications.

Broadcasting and Cable. Box 6399, Torrence, CA 90504, www.broadcastingcable.com. [W., $149 US, $219 Canada, $350 elsewhere]. All-inclusive newsweekly for radio, television, cable, and allied business.

Cablevision. Cahners Business Information, 245 West 17th Street, New York, NY 10011-5300, (212)645-0067, www.cvmag.com. [Semi-mo.; $75 US, $165 elsewhere]. A newsmagazine for the cable television industry. Covers programming, marketing, advertising, business, and other topics.

Caldwell, John Thornton, Ed. (2000). **Electronic media and technoculture.** [Book, 278p., $21]. Rutgers University Press, 100 Joyce Kilmer Avenue, Piscataway, NJ 08854, (800)446-9323. Maps the intellectual terrain that has greeted the arrival of what is variously termed "new media," "digital media," and "electronic culture."

Cartwright, Steven R., & Cartwright, G. Phillip. (1999). **Training with media: Designing and producing video, multimedia and videoconferencing training programs with CDROM**. [Book, 232p., $44.95]. Butterworth-Heinemann, www.bh.com. Examines why, how, and when technology can be used for training and describes successful approaches to creating effective technology-based training.

Communication Abstracts. Sage Publications Inc., 2455 Teller Road, Thousand Oaks, CA 91320, order@sagepub.com, www.sagepub.com. [Bi-mo., $175 indiv., $700 inst.]. Abstracts communication-related articles, reports, and books. Cumulated annually.

Educational Media International. Routledge, 11 New Fetter Lane, London EC49.4EE, UK. [Q., $64 indiv., $248 inst.]. The official journal of the International Council for Educational Media.

Ekhaml, L. (1999). Ask an expert with style. **School Library Media Activities Monthly, 15** (6), 27–30. Discusses e-mail use in elementary/secondary education, focusing on a comparison/ review of award-winning, Internet-based Virtual Reference Desk Exemplary Services (Ask Dr. Math, Ask A Volcanologist, How Things Work, AskERIC, Mad Scientist, Shamu, and

American Art) that provide ask-an-expert question-and-answer services. Home pages, delivery format, response time, and language are examined, and six additional sites are reviewed.

Federal Communications Commission Reports. Superintendent of Documents, Government Printing Office, Box 371954, Pittsburgh, PA 15250-7954. [Irreg., price varies]. Decisions, public notices, and other documents pertaining to FCC activities.

Historical Journal of Film, Radio, and Television. Carfax Publishing Limited in association with the International Association for Media and History, 875–81 Massachusetts Avenue, Cambridge, MA 02139. [Q., $185 indiv., $532 inst.]. Articles by international experts in the field, news and notices, and book reviews concerning the impact of mass communications on political and social history of the 20th century.

International Journal of Instructional Media. Westwood Press, Inc., 116E 16th Street, New York 10003. [Q., $135 per vol., $30 single issue]. Focuses on quality research; ongoing programs in instructional media for education, distance learning, computer technology, instructional media and technology, telecommunications, interactive video, management, media research and evaluation, and utilization.

Journal of Broadcasting and Electronic Media. Broadcast Education Association, 1771 N Street, NW, Washington, DC 20036-2891. [Q., $40 US, $25 student, $50 elsewhere]. Includes articles, book reviews, research reports, and analyses. Provides a forum for research relating to telecommunications and related fields.

Journal of Educational Media (formerly **Journal of Educational Television**). Carfax Publishing Co., 875–81 Massachusetts Avenue, Cambridge, MA 02139. [3/yr., $146 indiv., $544 inst.]. This journal of the Educational Television Association serves as an international forum for discussions and reports on developments in the field of television and related media in teaching, learning, and training.

Journal of Popular Film and Television. Heldref Publications, 1319 Eighteenth Street, NW, Washington, DC 20036-1802, (800)365-9753. [Q., $36 indiv., $70 inst.]. Articles on film and television, book reviews, and theory. Dedicated to popular film and television in the broadest sense. Concentrates on commercial cinema and television, film and television theory or criticism, filmographies, and bibliographies. Edited at the College of Arts and Sciences of Northern Michigan University and the Department of Popular Culture, Bowling Green State University.

Library Talk (formerly **Technology Connection**). Linworth Publishing, 480 E. Wilson Bridge Road, Suite L., Worthington, OH 43085-2372, (800)786-5017, fax (614)436-9490, orders@linworth.com, linworth.com. [6/yr., $43 US, $7 single copy]. The only magazine published for the elementary school library media and technology specialist. A forum for K–12 educators who use technology as an educational resource, this journal includes information on what works and what does not, new product reviews, tips and pointers, and emerging technology.

Lunenfeld, Peter. (2000). **The digital dialectic: New essays on new media**. [Book, 401p., $17.95]. MIT Press, Five Cambridge Center, Cambridge, MA 02142-1493, (617)253-5646, mitpress-orders@mit.edu, www-mitpress.mit.edu. Maps out the trajectories that digital technologies have traced upon our cultural imagery.

Media International. Reed Business Information, Publisher. Oakfield House, Perrymount Road, W. Sussex RH16 3DH, UK. [Mo., £42 Europe, £76 elsewhere]. Contains features on the major media developments and regional news reports from the international media scene and global intelligence on media and advertising.

Multimedia Monitor (formerly **Multimedia and Videodisc Monitor**). Phillips Business Information, Inc., 1201 Seven Locks Road, Potomac, MD 20854, (301)424-3338, fax (301)309-3847, pbi@phillips.com. [Mo., $395 indiv., $425 foreign]. Describes current events in the worldwide interactive multimedia marketplace and in training and development, including regulatory and legal issues.

Multimedia Schools. Information Today, 143 Old Marlton Pike, Medford, NJ 08055, (800)300-9868. [6/yr., $39.95 US, $54 Canada and Mexico, $63 elsewhere]. Reviews new titles, evaluates hardware and software, offers technical advice and troubleshooting tips, and profiles high-tech installations.

Multimedia Systems. Springer-Verlag New York Inc., Secaucus, NJ 07096-2485, (800)SPRINGER, custserv@springer-ny.com. [6/yr., $415 US]. Publishes original research articles and serves as a forum for stimulating and disseminating innovative research ideas, emerging technologies, state-of-the-art methods, and tools in all aspects of multimedia computing, communication, storage, and applications among researchers, engineers, and practitioners.

NICEM (National Information Center for Educational Media) EZ. NICEM, P.O. Box 8640, Albuquerque, NM 87198-8640, (505)265-3591, (800)926-8328, fax (505)256-1080, nicem@nicem.com. A custom search service to help those without access to the existing NICEM products. Taps the resources of this specialized database. Fees are $50 per hour search time plus $.20 for each unit identified.

NICEM (National Information Center for Educational Media) NlightN. Contact NlightN, The Library Corp, 1807 Michael Faraday Ct., Reston, VA 20190, (800)654-4486, fax (703)904-8238, help@nlightn.com, www.nlightn.com. [Subscription service]. NlightN, an Internet online service, widens the accessibility of information in the NICEM database to users of the Internet. The NICEM database of 425,000 records, updated quarterly, provides information on nonprint media for all levels of education and instruction in all academic areas.

Purcell, Lee. (2000). **CD-R/DVD: Digital recording to optical media with CDROM**. [Book, 500p., $49.95]. McGraw-Hill, 1221 Avenue of the Americas, New York, NY 10020, (800)352-3566. Packed with advice for selecting the right equipment and putting it to work, *CD-R/DVD* offers a wealth of practical tips and techniques, as well as insights from industry insiders.

Reed, Maxine K., Reed, Robert M., & Phenner, Lee, Ed. (1999). **In television, cable, video and multimedia: A comprehensive guide to 100 exciting careers in television, video, and new media**. [Book, 288p., $18.95]. Facts-on-File, Inc., 11 Penn Plaza, 15th Floor, New York, NY 10001-2006, (800)322-8755. Helps job seekers discover the position they want in these dynamic and competitive fields.

Schmidt, W. D., & Rieck, D. A. (2000). **Managing media services: Theory and practice** (2nd ed.). [Book, 440p., $49]. Libraries Unlimited, (800)237-6124, lu-books@lu.com, www.lu.com. Covers all aspects of the media manager's role: supervision, budgeting, public relations, evaluation, and management. Intended for graduate-level media management classes; also includes a section on managing innovations.

Telematics and Informatics. Elsevier Science Regional Sales Office, Customer Support Department, P.O. Box 945, New York, NY 10159-0945, (888)4ES-INFO, usinfo-f@elsevier .com. [3/yr., $49 indiv., $668 inst.]. Publishes research and review articles in applied telecommunications and information sciences in business, industry, government, and educational establishments. Focuses on important current technologies, including microelectronics, computer graphics, speech synthesis and voice recognition, database management, data encryption, satellite television, artificial intelligence, and the ongoing computer revolution. Contributors and readers include professionals in business and industry, as well as in government and academia, who need to keep abreast of current technologies and their diverse applications.

Video Systems. Intertec Publishing Corp., 9800 Metcalf, Overland Park, KS 66212-2215. [Mo., $45, free to qualified professionals]. For video professionals. Contains state-of-the-art audio and video technology reports. Official publication of the International Television Association.

Videography. Miller Freeman, PSN Publications, 2 Park Avenue, 18th Floor, New York, NY 10016. [Mo., $30]. For the video professional; covers techniques, applications, equipment, technology, and video art.

PROFESSIONAL DEVELOPMENT

Anglin, G. J. (1999). **Critical issues in instructional technology.** [Book, 275p., $47]. Libraries Unlimited, (800)237-6124, lu-books@lu.com, www.lu.com. Addresses critical issues in the field, including communications; learning and instructional technology; instructional technology in schools, higher education, and industry; and research, theory, and instructional design.

Baden, Clifford. (1999). The Harvard Management for Lifelong Education Program: Creative approaches to designing a professional development program. **New Directions for Adult and Continuing Education, 81,** 47–55. The Harvard Institute for the Management of Lifelong Education is a professional development program for leaders in post-secondary lifelong education. It exemplifies creative design and delivery; ideas come from multiple sources and the program is continuously reinvented.

Bascia, Nina. (1999). **The other side of the equation: Professional development and the organizational capacity of teacher unions**. [Paper, 23p.]. (Presented at the Annual Meeting of the American Educational Research Association, Montreal, Quebec, Canada, April 19–23, 1999). This paper describes the three types of nonformal and informal professional development provided by teachers' organizations. The first type is a minimal approach, the second focuses on contextual variation and teacher diversity, and the third consists of informal learning opportunities developed by teachers themselves. The article identifies strategies for improving the "fit" between available professional development and teachers' occupational needs.

Bossers, Ann, Kernaghan, Jan, Hodgins, Lisa, Merla, Leann, O'Connor, Charlene, & Van Kessel, Monique. (1999). Defining and developing professionalism. **Canadian Journal of Occupational Therapy, 66** (3), 116–121. Presents a schematic representation of professionalism and information about two self-study courses on becoming a professional. Describes a professional portfolio guide for students in occupational therapy and discusses implications and directions for fostering professionalism.

Byrd, David M., & McIntyre, D. John, Ed. (1999). **Research on professional development schools. Teacher education yearbook VII.** [Book, 289p., $26.95]. Corwin Press, Inc., A Sage Publications Company, 2455 Teller Road, Thousand Oaks, CA 91320, (805)499-9774, fax (805)499-5323, order@corwinpress.com. This book examines the current standard practice of confining teacher preparation to four years of coursework, examining the growing interest in career-spanning teacher education.

Clark, Richard W. (1999) **Effective professional development schools.** [Book, 294p., $27.95]. Agenda for Education in a Democracy Series, vol. 3. Jossey-Bass Inc., Publishers, 350 Sansome Street, San Francisco, CA 94104, (888)378-2537, fax (800)605-2665. This book presents a theoretical basis for professional development schools (PDSs) as well as practical guidance for establishing, funding, and evaluating them. It offers a comprehensive view of the role that PDSs play in today's educational renewal efforts and insights about the potential that a quality PDS can bring to learning at many levels.

Clark, W. Bruce. (1999). **Professional development for teaching technology across the curriculum: Best practices for Alberta school jurisdictions.** [Report, 77p.]. Learning Resources Distributing Centre, 12360-142 Street, Edmonton, Alberta, Canada T5L 4X9, ednet.edc.gov.ab.ca/technology/. This report focuses on promising practices in professional development as they relate to implementation of Alberta Education's 1998 "Information and Communication Technology, Interim Program of Studies."

Duquette, Cheryll, & Cook, Sharon Anne. (1999). Professional development schools: Preservice candidates' learning and sources of knowledge. **Alberta Journal of Educational Research**, **45** (2), 198–207. A survey of 23 Canadian student teachers in conventional placements or professional-development schools (PDS) found that their practica had taught them about curriculum, pupils and pupil-teacher interactions, discipline and classroom management, and the teaching profession. Compared to others, PDS student teachers relied more on weekly seminars and peer discussions to support their learning.

Guskey, Thomas R. (1999). **New perspectives on evaluating professional development.** [Paper, 25p.]. (Presented at the Annual Meeting of the American Educational Research Association, Montreal, Quebec, Canada, April 19–23, 1999). Basic questions about the evaluation of professional development efforts are explored, including the nature and purposes of evaluation, the critical levels of professional development evaluation, and the difference between evidence and proof in evaluation. Evaluation, which is defined as the systematic investigation of merit or worth, can be characterized as planning, formative, or summative.

Heaton, Lisa A., & Washington, Lisa A. (1999). **Developing technology training for principals.** [Paper, 37p.]. (Presented at the Annual Meeting of the American Educational Research Association, Montreal, Quebec, Canada, April 19–23, 1999). New standards in the state of Virginia are being instituted to require that professional development programs for preservice principals include experience with technology. This study was designed to identify relevant topics that should be part of that experience.

Hopkins, Dianne McAfee, & Zweizig, Douglas L. (1999). Power to the media center (and to the people, too). **School Library Journal**, **45** (5), 24–27. Considers characteristics of successful school library media programs based on information from surveys of schools that participated in the national Library Power initiative. Discusses the importance of shared vision, professional development, planning opportunities, leadership from the principal, support staff, complementary school reforms, and community and district advocacy.

Johnson, D. (1999). **The indispensable teacher's guide to computer skills.** [Book, 119p., $39.95]. Linworth, (800)786-5017, fax (614)436-9490, linworth.com. Provides practical guidelines for teachers, librarians, and technology coordinators for conducting staff development. Contains rubrics for specific computer competencies appropriate for teachers.

Journal of Technology and Teacher Education. Association for the Advancement of Computing in Education (AACE), P.O. Box 2966, Charlottesville, VA 22902, AACE@virginia .edu, www.aace.org. [Q., $40 US, $50 intl.]. Serves as an international forum to report research and applications of technology in preservice, inservice, and graduate teacher education.

Journal of Computing in Teacher Education. ISTE, University of Oregon, 1787 Agate Street, Eugene, OR 97403-1923, (800) 336-5191, cust_svc@ccmail.uoregon.edu, www.iste.org. [Q., $29, $39 intl., $42 intl. air]. Contains refereed articles on preservice and inservice training, research in computer education and certification issues, and reviews of training materials and texts.

Kennedy, Deborah. (1999). The importance of association for ESL professionals. **ESL Magazine, 2** (3), 14–18. Discusses the importance of associations for English-as-a-Second-Language (ESL) professionals. Focuses on professional associations, professional development, networking opportunities, professional standards, representation and advocacy, and services for members. A list of associations for ESL professionals is included.

Koch, Richard, & Schwartz-Petterson, Jean. (2000). **The portfolio guidebook: Implementing quality in an age of standards.** [Book, 141p., $15.95]. Bill Harp Professional Teachers Library. Christopher-Gordon Publishers, Inc., 1502 Providence Highway, Suite 12, Norwood, MA 02062. This portfolio book provides an actual step-by-step complete system of writing assessment from the ground up and across all grade levels. The book suggests that teachers purposefully gather student portfolios, reflect meaningfully on them, and then validly and reliably rate them with statistical success that will also feed meaningfully back into the classroom. The system presented in the book was developed based on lessons learned during a three-year portfolio research project.

Law, Sue. (1999). Leadership for learning: The changing culture of professional development in schools. **Journal of Educational Administration, 37** (1), 66–79. Explores school leadership in Britain's newly privatized and marketized professional development environment. Considers a model to identify key elements in a "professional development culture." Examines the development coordinator's role as a "delegated leader." Suggests a model for exploring the relationship between continuing professional-development leadership and staff commitment.

Livneh, Cheryl, & Livneh, Hanoch. (1999). Continuing professional education among educators: Predictors of participation in learning activities. **Adult Education Quarterly, 49** (2), 91–106. Scores on the Characteristics of Lifelong Learners in the Professions scale for 256 teachers and administrators identified self-motivation as the greatest predictor of participation in learning activities, followed by external motivation. Participants with lower levels of educational attainment spent more time on learning activities.

London, Harold, & Sinicki, Carole. (1999). Peer coaching: A hands-on form of administrative staff development. **NCA Quarterly, 73** (3), 392–395. Asserts that high turnover in educational administrative personnel, especially principals, necessitates that attention and resources be allocated to administrative staff development. Recommends peer coaching as a way for principals to help each other, and presents a model for implementing a staff development program.

Miller, Susan. (1999). Professional development for the library media specialist. **Book Report, 17** (5), 20–21. Discusses the importance of professional development for library media specialists and presents suggestions for staying current in the field, including participation in conferences, taking advantage of continuing-education opportunities, reading professional journals, and using Internet resources.

Norman, Michele M. (1999). Beyond hardware. **American School Board Journal, 186** (7), 16–20. The Department of Education recommends that schools allocate at least 30 percent of technology funding to professional development. Programs generally begin with strategic planning and a realistic budget, are designed to improve student achievement, emphasize people over technology, and have widespread stakeholder support.

Novick, Rebecca, & Grimstad, Jane. (1999). **Actual schools, possible practices: New directions in professional development.** [Publication, 45p.]. Northwest Regional Educational Laboratory, Child and Family Program, 101 SW Main Street, Suite 500, Portland, OR 97204-3297. Examines the literature on promising practices in professional development, focusing on the role of effective inservice professional development in successful elementary school reform, promising practices, and results of a survey of educators from the northwest United States.

Page, Dan. (1999). Second chance to get things right the first time. **Converge, 2** (3), 50–52, 54. Describes the planning and successful integration of technology into the Oswego School District (New York). Highlights include creating a sustainable effort, building barriers against obsolescence, steady focus on professional development, inservice professional development, and looking to a bright future.

Paterson, Alasdair. (1999). **Ahead of the game: Developing academic library staff for the 21st century**. [Paper, 6p.]. (Presented at the [International Association of Technological University Libraries] IATUL Conference, Chania, Greece, May 17–21, 1999). Available at http://educate.lib.chalmers.se/IATUL/proceedcontents/chanpap/paterso n.html. This paper focuses on issues related to library personnel in the British academic library. A background discussion on staff salaries, decreases in funding and increases in availability of information in more electronic formats, and the print culture and the electronic library leads to a statement of the need for increased information technology skills and training.

Professional staff development: A key to school improvement. (1999). **NCA Quarterly, 73** (3), 387–391. Asserts that an essential element in the school improvement process is the creation of a professional staff development program. Outlines recent literature that offers guidelines for implementing these programs and addresses program and participant evaluation. Contains 19 references.

Spangler, Mary S. (1999). The Practitioner's guide to midlevel management development. **New Directions for Community Colleges, 27** (105), 21–28. Describes how the Administrative Leadership Institute (ALI) was conceptualized, developed, and implemented over a three-year period in the Los Angeles Community College District to fulfill the need for a systematic mid-level management training program. The program's mission is to provide a supportive environment characterized by respect, collegiality, and trust among and for its managers.

Thacker, Jerry. (1999). Using teacher evaluation for professional growth. **ERS Spectrum, 17** (1), 24–27. During the 1995–1996 school year, administrators in Lawrence Township School District in Indianapolis, Indiana, worked with teachers to develop an evaluation system that would encourage teachers to engage in positive self-assessment and grow professionally throughout their careers. Teachers like the new system better than the previous one.

Vukelich, Carol, & Wrenn, Lisa C. (1999). Quality professional development: What do we think we know? **Childhood Education, 75** (3), 153–160. Explains tenets of quality professional development using a beginning teacher's experiences for illustration. Suggests that professional development should focus on a single subject; focus on participants' needs; be ongoing and sustained; engage participants in pursuit of answers to genuine questions, problems, and curiosities; provide participants with meaningful engagement; help participants develop collegial relationships; and encourage participants to reflect on their teaching.

Walker, Elaine M., Mitchel, Charles P., & Turner, Wayne. (1999). **Professional development and urban leadership: A study of urban administrators' perceptions of what matters most in their professional development**. [Paper, 32p.]. (Presented at the Annual Meeting of the American Educational Research Association, Montreal, Quebec, Canada, April 19–23, 1999). The study finds that urban administrators have a wide variety of needs that they seek to have met through professional development opportunities. Educational administration programs at the college level cannot prepare administrators adequately for their complex roles, so the need for continuous professional development becomes paramount.

SIMULATION, GAMING, AND VIRTUAL REALITY

Alford, Randall J. (1999). Going virtual, getting real. **Training and Development, 53** (1), 34–44. Presents an account of how one company went completely virtual—no office at all—and reaped the eventual rewards. Describes implementation processes, communication challenges, and customer reactions.

Andrews, Dee H., Dineen, Toni, & Bell, Herbert H. (1999). The use of constructive modeling and virtual simulation in large-scale team training: A military case study. **Educational Technology, 39** (1), 24–28. Discusses the use of constructive modeling and virtual simulation in team training; describes a military application of constructive modeling, including technology issues and communication protocols; considers possible improvements; and discusses applications in team-learning environments other than military, including industry and education.

Brougere, Gilles. (1999). Some elements relating to children's play and adult simulation/gaming. **Simulation & Gaming, 30** (2), 134–146. This introduction to a special issue on play and simulation/gaming examines the distinction often made between children's play and adult gaming. It illustrates the diversity of play activities and the pedagogical uses of gaming and demonstrates that these two fields of reflection have everything to gain through mutual enrichment.

Carlson, J. Matthew. (1999). Cooperative games: A pathway to improving health. **Professional School Counseling, 2** (3), 230–236. Cooperative games program was conducted with second graders who had a previous problem with low cooperative skills and excluding children. These games are a viable intervention for counselors to promote cooperation, fun, good health, and positive social interaction. A shift in attitude was observed during the program, as well as an improvement in group cohesion and cooperation.

De Jean, Jillian, Upitis, Rena, Koch, Corina, & Young, Jonathan. (1999). The story of "Phoenix Quest": How girls respond to a prototype language and mathematics computer game. **Gender and Education, 11** (2), 207–223. Presents a case study of the experiences of six girls with the "Phoenix Quest" (PQ) computer game and compares the responses of 41 boys and 57 girls to the same game. PQ was designed to explore language and mathematics in ways appealing to girls. Celebrating and challenging a female protagonist was important to girls.

Fister, Sarah. (1999). CBT fun and games. **Training, 36** (5), 68–70, 72, 74–76, 78. Use of games in computer-based training (CBT) can enliven material, encourage discovery and experiential learning, and make visceral connections for learners. However, humor can offend or wear thin, and games can be perceived as playing rather than as learning.

Higgins, J. J., Lawrie, A. M., & White, A. Goodith. (1999). Recognizing coherence: The use of a text game to measure and reinforce awareness of coherence in text. **System, 27** (3), 339–349. Describes three pilot projects carried out with a special version of a computer-assisted language-learning activity, known as SEQUITUR, that seeks to develop awareness of cohesive devices and coherence features by displaying the start of a text and offering possible continuations.

Jarrell, Andrea. (1999). Virtual campus tours. **Currents, 25** (3), 48–51. College campus "tours" offered online have evolved to include 360-degree views; live video; animation; talking tour guides; interactive maps with photographic links; and detailed information about buildings, departments, and programs. Proponents feel they should enhance, not replace, real tours. The synergy between the virtual tour and other prospective student communications is a critical factor in successful use.

Katz, Yaacov J. (1999). Kindergarten teacher training through virtual reality: Three-dimensional simulation methodology. **Educational Media International, 36** (2), 151–156. This study examined the effectiveness and efficiency of a three-dimensional virtual reality simulation model designed to train kindergarten teachers in the understanding of kindergarten children's needs and perceptions. Results of statistical analysis indicated that the virtual reality simulation was more effective than a workshop method.

Kumar, David, & Bristor, Valerie J. (1999). Integrating science and language arts through technology-based macrocontexts. **Educational Review, 51** (1), 41–53. Videos, virtual reality, and the World Wide Web create effective macrocontexts for integrating science and language arts. Contexts must be readily available, appropriate for the level, and interesting to students.

McDonough, Jerome P. (1999). Designer selves: Construction of technologically mediated identity within graphical, multiuser virtual environments. **Journal of the American Society for Information Science, 50** (10), 855–869. Describes software designers' actions affecting identity performance in computer-mediated communications, particularly within graphical multi-user virtual environments, based on ethnographic research.

Millians, David. (1999). Simulations and young people: Developmental issues and game development. **Simulation & Gaming, 30** (2), 199–226. Describes the age-related developmental issues that typically confront teachers and writers in developing and implementing educational simulation/games. Examines physical, personal and social, language, and cognitive factors.

Murray, Garold L. (1999). Autonomy and language learning in a simulated environment. **System, 27** (3), 295–308. Computer-assisted language-learning literature points to a need for experimentation with innovative learning structures to realize the full potential of recent technological developments.

Reid, Robert D., & Sykes, Wylmarie. (1999). Virtual reality in schools: The ultimate educational technology. **T.H.E. Journal, 26** (7), 61–63. Discusses the use of virtual reality as an educational tool. Highlights include examples of virtual reality in public schools that lead to a more active learning process, simulated environments, integrating virtual reality into any curriculum, benefits to teachers and students, and overcoming barriers to implementation.

Shaffer, David Williamson, & Kaput, James J. (1999). Mathematics and virtual culture: An evolutionary perspective on technology and mathematics education. **Educational Studies in Mathematics, 37** (2), 97–119. Argues that mathematics education in virtual culture should strive to give students generative fluency to learn varieties of representational systems, provide opportunities to create and modify representational forms, develop skill in making and exploring virtual environments, and emphasize mathematics as a fundamental way of making sense of the world, reserving most exact computation and formal proof.

Simulation and Gaming. Sage Publications, Inc., 2455 Teller Road, Thousand Oaks, CA 91320, order@sagepub.com, www.sagepub.com. [Q., $70 indiv., $317 inst., $19 single issue]. An international journal of theory, design, and research focusing on issues in simulation, gaming, modeling, role-play, and experiential learning.

Small, Henry. (1999). Visualizing science by citation mapping. **Journal of the American Society for Information Science, 50** (9), 799–813. Discusses science mapping in the general context of information visualization and reviews attempts to construct maps of science using citation data, focusing on the use of co-citation clusters.

Wheatley, Walter J. (1999). Enhancing the effectiveness and excitement of management education: A collection of experiential exercises derived from children's games. **Simulation & Gaming, 30** (2), 181–198. Discusses the significance of play in culture; quotes an old proverb "a lesson taught with an entertaining facet is a lesson retained." Presents 13 children's games that are currently being used in management training and development programs. Describes the purpose, activity, preparation, and debriefing involved for each game.

Williamson, David M., Bejar, Isaac I., & Hone, Anne S. (1999). "Mental model" comparison of automated and human scoring. **Journal of Educational Measurement, 36** (2), 158–184. Contrasts "mental models" used by automated scoring for the simulation division of the computerized Architect Registration Examination with those used by experienced human graders for 3,613 candidate solutions. Discusses differences in the models used and the potential of automated scoring to enhance the validity evidence of scores.

Winn, William, & Jackson, Randy. (1999). Fourteen propositions about educational uses of virtual reality. **Educational Technology**, **39** (4), 5–14. Offers propositions about virtual reality in education. Some of the propositions arise from empirical studies of performance and cognition in virtual environments (VEs); others come from behavioral, cognitive, and human-factors research.

SPECIAL EDUCATION AND DISABILITIES

Abdulezer, Susan. (1999). IndTech: The gift. **Converge, 2** (3), 44–47. IndTech, "Independence through Technology," is a program in the New York City Public Schools (District 75) in which special needs students mass produce adaptive devices for special needs students of that district. Discussion includes research and development, the production sites, and empowerment of all participants.

Baumgartner, Lisa, Ed., & Merriam, Sharan B., Ed. (2000). **Adult learning and development: Multicultural stories**. [Book, 292p., $28.50]. Krieger Publishing, P.O. Box 9542, Melbourne, FL 32902, (800)724–0025, info@krieger-pub.com, www.web4u.com/krieger-publishing. This book contains 28 personal stories and poems about growth and development in adulthood that were written by individuals who were purposely chosen to reflect the diversity of U.S. culture and sociocultural factors, such as race and ethnicity, gender, class, sexual orientation, and able-bodiedness, that affect development in adulthood.

Castellani, John. (1999). **Teaching and learning with the Internet: Issues for training special education teachers**. [Paper, 9p.]. (Presented at the 10th Society for Information Technology & Teacher Education International Conference, San Antonio, TX, February 28–March 4, 1999). This paper is a report on the findings of a study conducted in a graduate-level course for teaching and learning with the Internet for high school teachers working with students having severe learning and emotional disabilities. Qualitative interview data were used to explore issues throughout the course as teachers used information in their classrooms.

Cole, Karen B., & Leyser, Yona. (1999). Curricular and instructional adaptations: Views of special and general education student teachers and their cooperating teachers. **Teacher Educator, 34** (3), 157–172. Examined general and special education student teachers' and cooperating teachers' perceptions of the importance, and use of, various instructional strategies needed in diverse and inclusive classrooms. Surveys ranked 45 instructional strategies on actual use and from most to least important.

Donlevy, Jim. (1999). Reaching higher standards: Special education, real-world certifications in technology and the community college connection. **International Journal of Instructional Media, 26** (3), 241–248. Discussion of educational reforms being implemented in New York state focuses on concerns of special education professionals concerning the impact of the reforms on students with special needs. Discusses strategies for increasing student success and recommends programs in technology with real-world certification as well as connections to community college curriculums.

Foegen, Anne, & Hargrave, Constance P. (1999). Group response technology in lecture-based instruction: Exploring student engagement and instructor perceptions. **Journal of Special Education Technology, 14** (1), 3–17. This study examined use of group-response technology (GRT) to gather responses of 26 students during instruction in a college course. Classroom observation data indicated no differences in engagement between those who used GRT and those using journals; however, GRT use provided the instructor with real-time data about student learning.

Gallagher, Peggy A., & McCormick, Katherine. (1999). Student satisfaction with two-way interactive distance learning for delivery of early childhood special education coursework. **Journal of Special Education Technology, 14** (1), 32–47. Two preservice master's-level courses in early childhood special education were taught twice across two academic years through distance learning using two-way interactive television (ITV). Results indicated the 103 student participants generally rated ITV as acceptable, but most would choose traditional course delivery.

Jordan, Dale R. (2000). **Understanding and managing learning disabilities in adults.** [Book, 137p., $22.50]. Professional Practices in Adult Education and Human Resource Development Series. Krieger Publishing, P.O. Box 9542, Melbourne, FL 32902, (800)724-0025, info@krieger-pub.com, www.web4u.com/krieger-publishing. This book reviews learning disabilities (LD) in adults and makes suggestions for helping adults cope with these disabilities. Each chapter covers a type of learning disability or related syndrome or explains characteristics of the brain.

Journal of Special Education Technology. Peabody College of Vanderbilt University, Box 328, Nashville, TN 37203, (615)322-8150. [Q., $30]. The *Journal of Special Education Technology* provides "information, research, and reports of innovative practices regarding the application of educational technology toward the education of exceptional children."

Ludlow, Barbara L., Foshay, John B., & Duff, Michael C. (1999). **Digital audio/video for computer- and Web-based instruction for training rural special education personnel.** [Paper, 10p.]. (Presented at the 19th Rural Special Education for the New Millennium Conference, Proceedings of the American Council on Rural Special Education (ACRES), Albuquerque, New Mexico, March 25–27, 1999). Video presentations of teaching episodes in home, school, and community settings and audio recordings of parents' and professionals' views can be important adjuncts to personnel preparation in special education. This paper describes instructional applications of digital media and outlines steps in producing audio and video segments.

Mates, B. T., Wakefield, Doug, & Dixon, Judith M. (2000). **Adaptive technology for the Internet: Making electronic resources accessible.** [Book, 224p., $36]. ALA Editions, (800)545-2433, www.ala.org/editions. Provides advice for purchasing and managing adaptive technologies such as screen readers, Braille screens, voice recognition systems, hearing assistance devices, and HTML coding for accessibility for library settings.

Meyen, Edward L., Tangen, Paul, & Lian, Cindy H. T. (1999). Developing online instruction: Partnership between instructors and technical developers. **Journal of Special Education Technology, 14** (1), 18–31. Discusses the design, development, and teaching of two graduate-level special-education courses online using audio streaming technology. The teamwork involved in developing the system is described and suggestions are offered on how to engage instructional and technical developers in the creation of online instruction.

Morse, Timothy E. (1999). An overview of technology applications in special education. **School Business Affairs, 65** (2), 11–15. Special education uses three types of computer-based instruction software: drill and practice, tutorials, and computer simulation. Assistive technology applications (electronic communication devices, voice-activated software, and print readers) are available for students whose disabilities do not allow them to perform functional tasks independently. Medical assistive and administrative technologies are described.

Ryndak, Diane Lea, Morrison, Andrea P., & Sommerstein, Lynne. (1999). Literacy before and after inclusion in general education settings: A case study. **Journal of the Association for Persons with Severe Handicaps, 24** (1), 5–22. This seven-year case study describes a young woman with moderate to severe disabilities and her use of literacy during various stages of her educational career, after receiving special education in a self-contained special education class and after receiving services in a general education setting.

Smith, Sean Joseph, Jordan, LuAnn, Corbett, Nancy L., & Dillon, Ann S. (1999). Teachers learn about ADHD on the Web: An online graduate special education course. **Teaching Exceptional Children**, **31** (6), 20–27. Describes a Web-based graduate course about attention-deficit hyperactivity disorder (ADHD) offered by the Department of Special Education at the University of Florida.

Spooner, F., Jordan, L., Algozzine, B., & Spooner, M. (1999). Student ratings of instruction in distance learning and on-campus classes. **Journal of Educational Research**, **92** (3), 132–140. Evaluates implementations of distance learning technology in two situations, both involving students with physical disabilities. Includes a summary of relevant studies and a set of implementation guidelines.

Tobin, Tary, & Sprague, Jeffrey. (1999). Alternative education programs for at-risk youth: Issues, best practice, and recommendations. **Oregon School Study Council Bulletin, 42** (4). This publication discusses definitions of alternative education, outlines common program features, and lists challenges to providing quality services. The paper focuses on alternatives for students who are at risk for school failure, dropout, or delinquency. Few studies on the effectiveness of alternative programs have been conducted and results of studies that have been performed are difficult to generalize beyond their specific settings; therefore, the report provides an outline of research on the common features found in alternative-education programs and describes a model alternative program.

Vannatta, Rachel A., & Reinhart, Paul M. (1999). **Integrating, infusing, modeling: Preparing technology using educators**. [Paper, 7p.]. (Presented at the 10th Society for Information Technology & Teacher Education International Conference, San Antonio, TX, February 28–March 4, 1999). This paper presents the results of a 1997–1998 Goals 2000 Preservice Teacher Education Grant that created a partnership between the State University of New York at Oswego and two local elementary schools. The program was designed to provide preservice teachers in elementary education and special education methods classes the opportunity to observe expert teachers integrate technology in the elementary classroom through a video conferencing system and to experience the infusion of technology in their education courses.

Weiss, Tim, & Nieto, Faye. (1999). **Using the Internet to connect parents and professionals: The challenges**. [Paper, 9p.]. (Presented at the 19th Rural Special Education for the New Millennium Conference, Proceedings of the American Council on Rural Special Education (ACRES), Albuquerque, New Mexico, March 25–27, 1999). Alaska has been forced by geography and weather to look at numerous innovative solutions to improving communication between families and schools. The Internet is showing more impact than any other technique that has been tried. This has been especially helpful to parents of children with disabilities, due to a severe shortage of special education professionals. Although not every family has a computer, public Internet access is available at 90 percent of the public school libraries and at native corporation or tribal council offices.

Wilson, Barbara A. (1999). Inclusion: Empirical guidelines and unanswered questions. **Education and Training in Mental Retardation and Developmental Disabilities**, 34 (2), 119–133. Guidelines for the inclusion of students with severe disabilities in general education programs include (1) respecting parent and student preferences regarding programming; (2) fostering the general-education teacher's sense of empowerment, control, and support; (3) facilitating friendships among children; and (4) structuring classrooms to maximize learning for all students.

TELECOMMUNICATIONS AND NETWORKING

Adams, Helen. (1999). Telementoring: Providing authentic learning opportunities for students. **Book Report, 17** (4), 27–29. Describes the Hewlett Packard (HP) E-Mail Mentoring Program. Lists the program's four main components (teacher contacts, student participants, HP employee members, HP itself) and the application process. Relates how a library media specialist at Rosholt (Wisconsin) High School experienced the program. Concludes with the benefits of "telemontoring."

Bailey, Gerald D., & Lumley, Dan. (1999). Virtual teaming. **American School Board Journal, 186** (7), 21–24. Technology is allowing people with differing venues and schedules to meet and form powerful teams. To succeed, virtual teams must hold some synchronous, real-time meetings, follow a five-step continuous-improvement model, provide coaching and support, encourage face-to-face contact, and expect trial and experimentation.

Baines, Susan. (1999). Servicing the media: Freelancing, teleworking and "enterprising" careers. **New Technology, Work and Employment, 14** (1), 18–31. Although freelancers who offer services to the media almost all work from home, they are not isolated in "electronic cottages." They heavily use electronic communications.

Bajjaly, Stephen T. (1999). **The community networking handbook**. [Book, 204p., $32]. American Library Association, ALA Editions, 50 East Huron Street, Chicago, IL 60611-2795, (800)545-2433, fax (312)836-9958. Outlines the complete community networking process: planning, developing partnerships, funding, marketing, content, public access, and evaluation, and discusses the variety of roles that the local public library can play in this process.

Boardwatch. Penton Media, P.O. Box 901979, Cleveland, OH 44190-1979. [M., $72 US]. The Internet access industry's handbook. Each issue features the leading online editorial covering the Internet, World Wide Web, and the communications industry

Brandt, D. Scott. (1999). Outreach, or, how far do you reach? **Computers in Libraries, 19** (4), 31–33. Considers what library outreach means in the age of networked information and suggests that outreach should focus more on libraries and librarians as resources for advice on how to search in general, rather than where to find familiar information.

Buzzeo, T., & Kurtz, J. (1999). **Terrific connections with authors, illustrators, and storytellers: Real space and virtual links**. [Book, 185p., $26.50]. Libraries Unlimited, (800)237-6124, lu-books@lu.com, www.lu.com. Describes a method for creating encounters between students and authors using telecommunications.

Canadian Journal of Educational Communication. Association for Media and Technology in Education in Canada, 3-1750 The Queensway, Suite 1318, Etobicoke, ON M9C 5H5, Canada. [3/yr., $75]. Concerned with all aspects of educational systems and technology.

Chaptal, Alain. (1999). Savoirs College: A global initiative targeted to the curriculum. **Educational Media International, 36** (2), 137–140. Examines the current state of information and communications technology in France, and describes Savoirs College, a global initiative that integrates television, the Web, and CD-ROM to offer secondary school teachers educational resources, products, and services that will help them integrate technology into the curriculum.

Chen, Chaomei. (1999). Visualizing semantic spaces and author co-citation networks in digital libraries. **Information Processing & Management, 35** (3), 401–420. Describes the development and application of visualization techniques for users to access and explore information in digital libraries effectively and intuitively.

Chou, Chien. (1999). Developing CLUE: A formative evaluation system for computer network learning courseware. **Journal of Interactive Learning Research, 10** (2), 179–193. Describes the design and development of the Computer Logging of User Entries (CLUE)

system for evaluating computer network-based learning courseware, or Web-based distance-education courseware.

Classroom Connect. Classroom Connect, 1241 East Hillsdale Blvd., Suite 100, Foster City, CA 94404, (800)638-1639, fax (888)801-8299, orders@classroom.com. [9/yr., $45]. Provides pointers to sources of lesson plans for K–12 educators as well as descriptions of new Web sites, addresses for online "keypals," Internet basics for new users, classroom management tips for using the Internet, and online global projects. Each issue offers Internet adventures for every grade and subject.

Computer Communications. Elsevier Science, Inc., P.O. Box 882, Madison Square Station, New York, NY 10159-0882. [18/yr., $1,181]. Focuses on networking and distributed computing techniques, communications hardware and software, and standardization.

Computer network security: Best practices for Alberta school jurisdictions. (1999). [Paper, 130p.]. Learning Resources Distributing Centre, 12360-142 St., Edmonton, Alberta, Canada T5L 4X9, 780-427-5775, ednet.edc.gov.ab.ca/technology. Provides a snapshot of the computer network security industry and addresses specific issues related to network security in public education.

Cooper, G., & Cooper, G. (1999). **More virtual field trips.** [Book, 200p., $25.50]. Libraries Unlimited, (800)237-6124, lu-books@lu.com, www.lu.com. Organized by subject area; provides "trips" and topics reflecting current curricular requirements and goals.

Demetriadis, Stavros, Karoulis, Athanasios, & Pombortsis, Andreas. (1999). "Graphical" Jogthrough: Expert based methodology for user interface evaluation, applied in the case of an educational simulation interface. **Computers & Education, 32** (4), 285–299. Describes the use of the "Graphical" Jogthrough method for evaluating the user-interface design of the Network Simulator, an educational simulation program that enables users to virtually build a computer network, install hardware and software components, make necessary settings, and test the functionality of the network. Presents evaluation results and illustrates the usefulness of the method for designers.

EDUCAUSE Review. EDUCAUSE, 1112 Sixteenth Street, NW, Suite 600, Washington, DC 20036-4823, (800)254-4770, info@educause.edu. [Bi-mo., $24 US/Canada and Mexico, $48 elsewhere]. Features articles on current issues and applications of computing and communications technology in higher education. Reports of EDUCAUSE consortium activities.

Eisenman, Gordon, & Thornton, Holly. (1999). Telementoring: Helping new teachers through the first year. **T.H.E. Journal, 26** (9), 79–82. Describes a mentoring program developed at Augusta State University that used e-mail and a list server to link experienced teachers with new teachers who needed advice about classroom management, administrative demands, overcoming a sense of isolation, and the need for support.

EMMS (Electronic Mail & Micro Systems). Telecommunications Reports, 1333 H Street NW, 11th Floor-W., Washington, DC 20005, brp.com. [Semi-mo., $765 US]. Covers technology, user, product, and legislative trends in graphic, record, and microcomputer applications.

Enomoto, Ernestine, Nolet, Victor, & Marchionini, Gary. (1999). The Baltimore Learning Community Project: Creating a networked community across middle schools. **Journal of Educational Multimedia and Hypermedia, 8** (1), 99–115. Discusses the Baltimore Learning Community Project, a collaborative effort that includes the Baltimore City Public Schools, the University of Maryland (UM), and Johns Hopkins University. Focuses on the UM component that involves the development of telecommunications software applications for middle school science and social studies teachers.

Entman, Robert M. (1999). **Residential access to bandwidth: Exploring new paradigms.** [Paper, 42p., $12]. (A Report of the 13th Annual Aspen Institute Conference on Telecommunications Policy, Aspen, Colorado, August 9–13, 1998). Aspen Institute, Publications Office, P.O. Box 222, 109 Houghton Lab Lane, Queenstown, MD 21658, (410)820-5326, publications@aspeninst.org. 1998 Aspen Systems Conference on Telecommunications Policy met to consider ways of speeding the deployment of telecommunication systems that allow for robust, reliable, and innovative communications services to the home.

Ewing, J. M., Dowling, J. D., & Coutts, N. (1999). Learning using the World Wide Web: A collaborative learning event. **Journal of Educational Multimedia and Hypermedia, 8** (1), 3–22. Discusses the place of learning theory in the planning, design, and implementation of learning tasks using information and communications technology.

Falk, Howard. (1999). Computer intrusions and attacks. **Electronic Library, 17** (2), 115–119. Examines some frequently encountered unsolicited computer intrusions, including computer viruses, worms, Java applications, trojan horses or vandals, e-mail spamming, hoaxes, and cookies. Also discusses virus-protection software, both for networks and for individual users.

Falk, Howard. (1999). Network kits. **Electronic Library, 17** (3), 181–186. Describes interconnection methods, speed, and comparative equipment costs of networking starter kits.

Fox, Jordan. (1999). Technology in residence. **American School & University, 71** (12), 111–115. Discusses the necessity for incorporating current technology in today's college residence halls to meet the more diverse and continued activities of its students. Technology addressed covers data networking and telecommunications, heating and cooling systems, and fire-safety systems.

Fuhr, Norbert. (1999). Towards data abstraction in networked information retrieval systems. **Information Processing & Management, 35** (2), 101–119. Discussion of networked information retrieval and the interoperability of heterogeneous information-retrieval systems shows how differences concerning search operators and database schemas can be handled by applying data-abstraction concepts in combination with uncertain inference.

Galbreath, Jeremy. (1999). The network computer: Is it right for education? **Educational Technology, 39** (1), 57–61. Examines the network computer, originally conceived as an alternative device to personal computers to access the Internet and World Wide Web, from a technology perspective and looks at potential uses in education.

Gauch, John M., Gauch, Susan, Bouix, Sylvain, & Zhu, Xiaolan. (1999). Real time video scene detection and classification. **Information Processing & Management, 35** (3), 381–400. Describes the VISION (video indexing for searching over networks) digital video library system that was developed at the University of Kansas as a test-bed for evaluating automatic and comprehensive mechanisms for library creation and content-based search and retrieval of video over local and wide area networks.

Gregory, V. L., Stauffer, M. H., & Keene, T. W. (1999). **Multicultural resources on the Internet: The United States and Canada.** [Book, 375p., $30]. Libraries Unlimited, (800)237-6124, lu-books@lu.com, www.lu.com. Gathers and organizes information about Internet sources addressing multicultural issues, selected for permanence and quality.

Gundling, Ernest. (1999). How to communicate globally. **Training and Development, 53** (6), 28–31. Discusses factors that must be considered before selecting a technology to use for global communication such as availability, user skills, cultural variables, level of rapport, importance of the message, and language modification.

Hahn, Saul. (1999). Studies on developments of the Internet in Latin America: Unexpected results. **Bulletin of the American Society for Information Science, 25** (5), 15–17. Several technology projects, originally intended to extend the Internet to major universities in Latin America, have grown into major developments for other sectors, especially the commercial one.

Hawkes, Mark. (1999). Exploring network-based communication in teacher professional development. **Educational Technology**, 39 (4), 45–52. Presents and applies a teacher professional-development-oriented analytical framework to provide clarity to the discussion of what role network-based communication may play in teacher professional-development experiences.

Hawkes, Mark, Cambre, Marjorie, & Lewis, Morgan. (1999). **The Ohio SchoolNet Telecommunity evaluation. Year three evaluation results: Examining interactive video adoption and resource needs.** [Paper, 60p.]. North Central Regional Educational Laboratory, 1900 Spring Road, Suite 300, Oak Brook, IL 60523-1480, (630)571-4700. Evaluation of the Ohio SchoolNet Telecommunity program focused on key Telecommunity objectives of technology deployment, teacher professional development, and student impact.

Heide, A., & Stilborne, L. (1999). **The teacher's complete and easy guide to the Internet.** [Book, 336p., $29.95]. Teachers College Press. Shares Internet experiences of teachers and their classes and provides a directory of resources.

Howard, Tharon, Benson, Chris, Gooch, Rocky, & Goswami, Dixie, Ed. (1999). **Electronic networks: Crossing boundaries/creating communities.** [Book, 242p., $20]. Heinemann, 361 Hanover St., Portsmouth, NH 03801-3912, (603)431-7894, www.heinemann.com. Provides information teachers need to integrate instructional technologies into their classrooms.

Hughes, David, III. (1999). Wizard Works: A traveling tech academy. **MultiMedia Schools**, 6 (1), 38–42. Describes a project that offered customized training in Internet access and networking to enable participants to implement specific technology-related projects in their communities.

Huws, Ursula, Jagger, Nick, & O'Regan, Siobhan. (1999). **Teleworking and globalisation. Towards a methodology for mapping and measuring the emerging global division of labour in the information economy.** [Book, 117p., £30]. Grantham Book Services, Ltd., Isaac Newton Way, Alma Park Industrial Estate, Grantham NG31 9SD, England. Discusses a cluster analysis that was performed involving more than 50 variables and 206 countries to group countries and identify their position in the emerging global division of labor in information-processing work because no tools have yet been developed to investigate the new spatial employment patterns.

International Journal of Educational Telecommunications. Association for the Advancement of Computing in Education, P.O. Box 2966, Charlottesville, VA 22901, (804)973-3987, fax (804)978-7449, AACE@virginia.edu, www.aace.org. [Q., $75 indiv., $95 inst., $20 single copy]. Reports on current theory, research, development, and practice of telecommunications in education at all levels.

The Internet and Higher Education. Elsevier Science/Regional Sales Office, Customer Support Department—JAI Books, P.O. Box 945, New York, NY 10159-0945. [Q., $70 indiv., $210 inst.]. Designed to reach faculty, staff, and administrators responsible for enhancing instructional practices and productivity via the use of information technology and the Internet in their institutions.

Internet Reference Services Quarterly. Haworth Press, 10 Alice St., Binghamton, NY 13904-1580, (800)-HAWORTH, fax (800)895-0582, getinfo@haworth.com, www.haworthpress .com. [Q., $36 indiv., $48 institutions, $48 libraries]. Describes innovative information practice, technologies, and practice. For librarians of all kinds.

Internet Research (formerly **Electronic Networking: Research, Applications, and Policy**). MCB University Press Ltd., 60-62 Toller Lane, Bradford, W. Yorks. BD8 9BY, England. [Q., $869 US paper & electronic, $369 electronic only]. A cross-disciplinary journal presenting research findings related to electronic networks, analyses of policy issues related to networking, and descriptions of current and potential applications of electronic networking for communication, computation, and provision of information services.

Internet World. Penton Media. Internet World, P.O. Box 901979, Cleveland, OH 44190-1979, www.iw.com. [M., $160 US, $200 Canada, $295 elsewhere]. Analyzes developments of the Internet, electronic networking, publishing, and scholarly communication, as well as other network issues of interest to a wide range of network users.

Irvin, L. Lennie. (1999). The shared discourse of the networked computer classroom. **Teaching English in the Two-Year College, 26** (4), 372–379. Argues that networked classrooms offer a number of opportunities for effective writing instruction.

Johnson, Denise. (1999). Nothing ventured, nothing gained: The story of a collaborative telecommunications project. **Childhood Education, 75** (3), 161–166. Describes a classroom e-mail project conducted during the 1996–1997 school year in a southern suburban school.

Journal of Online Learning. ISTE, University of Oregon, 1787 Agate Street, Eugene, OR 97403-1923, (800)336-5191, cust_svc@ccmail.uoregon.edu, www.iste.org. [Q., $29, $39 intl., $42 intl. air]. Reports activities in the areas of communications, projects, research, publications, international connections, and training.

Keenan, Thomas P., & Trotter, David Mitchell. (1999). The changing role of community networks in providing citizen access to the Internet. **Internet Research, 9** (2), 100–108. Examines the changing role of community network associations or freenets in providing Internet access and discusses the withdrawal of states from the telecommunications field.

Kirkup, Gill. (1999). A computer of one's own (with an Internet connection). **Adults Learning (England), 10** (8), 23–25. Responses from 2,340 Open University students (52 percent women) showed that more men than women had access to computers at home and work; only 32 percent of women used networked communications; men were more likely to use e-mail and the Web at home; and gender differences were less significant at work.

Koehler, Wallace. (1999). Unraveling the issues, actors, & alphabet soup of the great domain name debates. **Searcher, 7** (5), 16, 18, 20–26. Examines the interconnected issues surrounding domain naming.

Kouki, R., & Wright, D. (1999). **Telelearning via the Internet.** [Book, 208p., $45.95]. IGP Books, (800)345-4332, fax (717)533-8661, www.idea-group.com. Discusses online learning from an organizational and managerial perspective. Topics include copyright, security, accreditation, and cost effectiveness, as well as planning and design.

Link-Up. Information Today, 143 Old Marlton Pike, Medford, NJ 08055, (800)300-9868. [Bi-mo., $32.95 US, $40 Canada/Mexico; $60 elsewhere]. Newsmagazine for individuals interested in small computer communications; covers hardware, software, communications services, and search methods.

Lippincott, Joan K. (1999). Assessing the academic networked environment. **New Directions for Institutional Research, 102**/26 (2), 21–35. Describes a project of the Coalition for Networked Information, founded in 1990 to advance scholarship interest in the networked-computer environment.

Loew, Robert, Stengel, Ingo, Bleimann, Udo, & McDonald, Aidan. (1999). Security aspects of an enterprise-wide network architecture. **Internet Research, 9** (1), 8–15. Presents an overview of two projects that concern local area networks and the common point between networks as they relate to network security.

Lowery, Catherine, & Franklin, Kathy K. (1999). **Utilizing networked computer workstations to conduct electronic focus groups**. [Paper, 22p.]. (Presented at the Annual Meeting of the Mid-South Educational Research Association, Point Clear, AL, November 16–19, 1999). Researchers at the University of Arkansas at Little Rock conducted a study of faculty attitudes about the use of technology in the college classroom using electronic focus group sessions. This paper examines the electronic focus group data collection procedure.

Manning, Sherry. (1999). Dialing for dollars: Telecommunication pays. **Business Officer**, **32** (10), 31–35. Advances in telecommunications and provision of telecommunications services to college students can increase institutional revenue, improve campus and educational services, and aid in student retention.

Maxwell, Marsha. (1999). Connecting 500 students in one week! **CAUSE/EFFECT**, **22** (1), 59–60. Describes a Bryant College (Rhode Island) program to expedite computer connections for students at the beginning of the school semester.

McDavitt, Tish. (1999). How technology influences interior design. **College Planning & Management**, **2** (8), 37–39. Examines telecommunication technology's influences on interior school design and effective learning, and discusses how to implement this technology into the school.

Moberg, Thomas. (1999). Campus network strategies: A small college perspective. **CAUSE/EFFECT**, **22** (1), 25–31, 35. Offers advice to administrators and faculty in small colleges on planning, building, and managing campus computer networks.

Mower, Pat, & LaLonde, Donna E. (1999). Hexiety: An interclass experiment. **Mathematics and Computer Education**, **33** (1), 6–15. Describes a cooperative effort using telecommunications. Utilizes a potential e-mail dialog between the authors and a secondary mathematics teacher from a rural Kansas community who had heard about the interclass Hexiety project, which allows students to develop a context for their mathematical knowledge, to present ideas about the project.

Network Magazine. CMP Media INC, 600 Harrison Street, San Francisco, CA 94107, www.networkmagazine.com. [Mo., $125]. Provides users with news and analysis of changing technology for the networking of computers.

Online. Online, Inc., 213 Danbury Rd., Wilton, CT 06897, www.onlineinc.com/onlinemag/. [6/yr., $55 US half-off special]. For online information system users. Articles cover a variety of online applications for general and business use.

Online-Offline. Rock Hill Press, 14 Rock Hill Road, Bala Cynwyd, PA 19004, (888)ROCK-HILL, fax (610)667-2291, www.rockhillpress.com. [9/yr., $66.50]. Examines classroom resources, linking curricular themes with Web sites and other media.

Palloff, Rena M., & Pratt, Keith. (1999). **Building learning communities in cyberspace: Effective strategies for the online classroom.** [Book, 206p., $29.95]. Jossey-Bass Higher and Adult Education Series. Jossey-Bass Publishers, 350 Sansome Street, San Francisco, CA 94104, (888)378-2537, www.josseybass.com. Offers suggestions for developing well-planned and effective computer-mediated distance learning. Part 1 lays the foundation for a distance education framework.

Pearson, John. (1999). Electronic networking in initial teacher education: Is a virtual faculty of education possible? **Computers & Education**, **32** (3), 221–238. Reports on the use of an electronic network in a school-based initial teacher education course to facilitate discussion between participants. Discusses computer conferencing; the presence of a public audience on the network; collaboration; and issues regarding participation in a virtual community.

Polo, James E., Rotchford, Louise M., & Setteducati, Paula M. (1999). Creating innovative partnerships. **New Directions for Adult and Continuing Education**, (81), 67–76. Bell Atlantic Corporation offers an associate degree in applied science (telecommunications) to its employees through a consortium of community colleges. The NEXT STEP program has become a creative partnership of education, labor, and industry.

The promise of global networks. 1999 annual review. (1999). [Collected Papers, 210p., $12]. The Aspen Institute, Publications Office, 109 Houghton Lab Lane, P.O. Box 222, Queenstown, MD 21658, (410)820-5326. This collection of commissioned papers provides a variety of perspectives on the impact of global information networks.

Reese, J. (1999). **Internet books for educators, parents, and children.** [Book, 299p., $35.50]. Libraries Unlimited, (800)237-6124, lu-books@lu.com, www.lu.com. Lists and annotates recommended books about the Internet, covering more than 250 English-language materials published since 1995.

Richardson, Laura A. (1999). **Optimizing a middle school's network capabilities for accessing information, improving school communications and interacting with the global community through network training.** [Practicum, 120p.]. Nova Southeastern University, Ed.D. Practicum. The problem addressed in this practicum was that most teachers at the author's middle school were not fully using the school's network resources in their day-to-day classroom activities, in spite of district technology initiatives.

Rose, Janet. (1999). Signing across the miles: Two-way video comes to school. **Perspectives in Education and Deafness, 17** (3), 14–15. Describes use of two-way video with deaf middle and high school students at the Colorado School for the Deaf and the Blind to communicate with other students using sign language.

Saba, Farhad. (1999). The death of distance and the rise of the network society. **Distance Education Report, 3** (1), 1–2. Discusses the rise of computer networks, telecommuting possibilities, the growing global economy, and possible resulting trends in the population of cities.

Saba, Farhad, & Mahon, J. Michael. (1999). An introduction for distance educators [and] five essential factors every administrator needs to know about integrated telecommunications infrastructures. **Distance Education Report,** (April), 1–8 [special report]. Discusses telecommunications developments that are affecting distance educators.

Schienbein, Ralph. (1999). **Network design: Best practices for Alberta school jurisdictions.** [Report, 110p.]. Learning Resources Distributing Centre, 12360-142 Street, Edmonton, Alberta, Canada T5L 4X9, (780)427-5775, ednet.edc.gov.ab.ca/technology. Examines subsections of the computer network topology that relate to end-to-end performance and capacity planning in schools. Active star topology, Category 5 wiring, Ethernet, and intelligent devices are assumed.

Sturgeon, Julie. (1999). Smart networking decisions: A case study. **School Planning and Management, 38** (8), 39–42. Describes one decision-making approach for quickly implementing a communications network into a school district.

Tamburini, Fabio. (1999). A multimedia framework for second language teaching in self-access environments. **Computers & Education, 32** (2), 137–149. Presents an account of a self-access language-teaching scheme operated at the University of Bologna (Italy) that was developed to teach English to university students by building a self-access environment available over a computer network.

Telecommunications. (North American Edition.) Horizon House Publications, Inc., 685 Canton St., Norwood, MA 02062. [Mo., $130 US, $210 elsewhere, free to qualified individuals]. Feature articles and news for the field of telecommunications.

Trentin, Guglielmo. (1999). Network-based collaborative education. **International Journal of Instructional Media, 26** (2), 145–157. Discusses telematics and the use of computer networks to support collaborative education, both among teachers for training and planning and among students in their learning process.

Williams, Elizabeth A., & Anderson, Cary M. (1999). Applications of technology to assist student affairs researchers. **New Directions for Student Services**, (85), 61–71. Technologies that may be used to search for, gather, analyze, and disseminate information during the research process are explored.

Wodarz, Nan. (1999). The next generation Internet. **School Business Affairs, 65** (2), 43–44. Internet2 will take three to five years to develop, will be 1,000 times faster than Internet, and will cost at least $500 million. Key developers are universities, several federal agencies, and leading computer and telecommunications firms. Internet2 will support face-to-face communications technology to facilitate "real-time" networking.

Young, Jeffrey R. (1999). In global contest to build networks, does the race go to the swiftest? **Chronicle of Higher Education, 45** (47), A21, A24. Canadian universities now have the fastest research network backbone in the world, CA*Net 3, claiming it can transmit the contents of the Library of Congress in one second. In the United States, network officials feel that their competing Internet2 project supports more research into new network applications than the Canadian project.

Young, Jeffrey R. (1999). Internet2 spurs equipment upgrades, but use in research remains limited. **Chronicle of Higher Education, 45** (49), A27–A28. Reports on the progress of the Internet2 project and the impact it is having at the institutions currently utilizing it.